PERSPECTIVES
ON ARGUMENT

PERSPECTIVES ON ARGUMENT

THIRD EDITION

Nancy V. Wood

University of Texas at Arlington

Prentice Hall

Upper Saddle River, New Jersey 07458

Library of Congress Cataloging-in-Publication Data

Wood, Nancy V.
  Perspectives on argument / Nancy V. Wood.—3rd ed.
    p. cm.
  Includes index.
    1. English language—Rhetoric. 2. Persuasion (Rhetoric). 3. College readers.
4. Report writing. I. Title.

PE1431 .W66 2000
808'.042—dc21   00-033997
                                                  CIP

Editor in Chief: Leah Jewell
Acquisitions Editor: Corey Good
Editorial Assistant: Jennifer M. Collins
Assistant Editor: Vivian Garcia
VP, Director of Production and Manufacturing: Barbara Kittle
Senior Managing Editor: Mary Rottino
Senior Production Editor: Shelly Kupperman
Prepress and Manufacturing Manager: Nick Sklitsis
Prepress and Manufacturing Buyer: Mary Ann Gloriande
Marketing Director: Beth Gillette Mejia
Marketing Manager: Brandy Dawson
Art Director: Leslie Osher
Interior Designer: Anne Bonanno Nieglos
Cover Designer: Bruce Kenselaar

Credits

Excerpt from "Sports Only Exercise Our Eyes" from *The Best of Sydney J. Harris*. Copyright © by
    Sydney J. Harris. Reprinted by permission of Houghton Mifflin Company: All rights reserved.

Excerpt from "Safe Lifting Technique" by John Warde, *The New York Times*, March 11, 1990.
    Copyright © by The New York Times Company. Reprinted by permission.

Credits continue on page 669, which constitutes an extension of the copyright page.

This book was set in 10/12 Palatino by The Clarinda Co. and
printed and bound by Hamilton Printing Co.
The cover was printed by Phoenix Color Corp.

© 2001, 1998, 1995 Prentice-Hall, Inc.
A Division of Pearson Education
Upper Saddle River, New Jersey 07458

Printed in the United States of America
10 9 8 7 6 5 4 3 2 1

ISBN 0-13-022564-9

Prentice-Hall International (UK) Limited, *London*
Prentice-Hall of Australia Pty. Limited, *Sydney*
Prentice-Hall Canada Inc., *Toronto*
Prentice-Hall Hispanoamerica, S.A., *Mexico*
Prentice-Hall of India Private Limited, *New Delhi*
Prentice-Hall of Japan, Inc., *Tokyo*
Pearson Education Asia Pte. Ltd., *Singapore*
Editora Prentice-Hall do Brasil, Ltda., *Rio de Janeiro*

Contents

3   A Process for Reading Argument   60

4   A Process for Writing Argument   88

▲ PART TWO   Understanding the Nature of Argument for Reading and Writing   121

5   The Essential Parts of an Argument: The Toulmin Model   122

6 Types of Claims 158

▲ PART FOUR   Further Applications: Rogerian Argument/Argument and Literature   343

11   Rogerian Argument and Common Ground   344

Questions to Help You Read Creatively and Move from Reading to Writing 434

Alternate Table of Contents

ALPHABETICAL LISTING OF ISSUES IN THE ESSAYS

MAJOR WRITING ASSIGNMENTS

(Other writing assignments, in addition to those listed here, appear in the Exercises and Activities sections at the ends of the chapters.)

Issue Proposal, 25
    Provides initial information about an issue and shows how to test it to see if it is arguable. Student example, 27.

Argument Style Paper, 46
    Describes student's usual style of argument and analyzes the outside influences on this style.

Analyze the Rhetorical Situation, 81
    Analyzes the elements of the rhetorical situation in a written essay.

Summary-Response Paper, 87
    Summarizes an essay and provides the writer's response to its ideas.

Exploratory Paper, 116, 119
    Describes three or more perspectives on an issue and helps writers identify their own perspective. Student example, 116.

Toulmin Analysis, 148
    Analyzes the claim, support, and warrants in student-provided essays, cartoons, advertisements, or letters to the editor. Student example, 148.

CLASS PROJECTS

Class Debate, 242
Students select an issue and divide into three groups of affirmative, negative, and critics/respondents to conduct a debate.

Class Symposium, 318
Students organize into small symposium groups to read abstracts and answer questions.

Critical Reading: Reading the Letters and Reporting to the Class, 369
Students divide into groups to analyze and evaluate argumentative strategies in a written argument.

Class Literary Debate, 401
Students divide into three groups of prosecution, defense, and jury to conduct a debate about a character in a play.

EXAMPLES OF ARGUMENT STRATEGIES IN "READER" ARTICLES

1. **Argument Papers.** Exploratory: Cose, 583; Gillis, 614. Rogerian: Gardner, 474 (see paragraph 14); Negroponte, 536; Feder, 609. Position: Figueroa, 598; Gingrich, 648.
2. **Claims.** Fact: Wolf, 438; Cohen, 511; *The New Wired World*, 534; Faludi, 645. Definition: Newman, 509; Kennedy, 594; Kolata, 611. Cause: Vitz, 486; Males and Docuyanan, 512; Miller, 551; Weiss, 606. Value: Scott, 495; Dickerson, 517; Pollan, 603; Barash, 633. Policy: Coltrane, 444; Canada, 520; hooks, 567. Inferred claim (Irony): Scott, 495. Qualified claim: Cose, 583; Faludi, 645.
3. **Language and Style.** Language that appeals to logic: Hirsch, 475; Sollod, 478. Language that appeals to emotion: Glaser, 463; Grann, 481; Goldberg, 589. Language that develops *ethos:* Gardner, 472; Garcia, 491.
4. **Organizational Patterns.** Claim plus reasons: Will, 505. Cause and effect: Leland, 524; Dvorak, 528. Chronological or narrative: Dickerson, 517; Ehrenreich, 659. Comparison and contrast: Carvajal, 529; Kurzweil, 538. Problem-solution: Newman, 509; Dertouzos, 556; Stolberg, 618; Hochschild, 636; Gingrich, 648.
5. **Proofs: *Ethos.*** Self as authority: Adler, 445; Edy, 456; Turkle, 545. Quoted authorities: Coontz, 451; Males and Docuyanan, 512; Kennedy, 594.
6. **Proofs: *Logos.*** Sign: hooks, 567. Induction: Doloff, 436; Wiesenfeld, 489. Cause: Zack, 562. Deduction: Wolf, 438; Sollod, 478. Analogy: Adler, 445; Grann, 481; Carvajal, 529, Kurzweil, 538. Definition: Sullivan, 465; Bennett, 467; Dyer, 570. Statistics: Adler, 445; Coontz, 451; Vobejda, 641; Conniff, 643.
7. **Proofs: *Pathos.*** Motives: Pan and Keene-Osborn, 582; Goldberg, 589; Specter, 607. Values: Adler, 458; FitzPatrick, 507; Stulman, 561.
8. **Refutation.** Sullivan, 465; Bennett, 467; Joyce, 622; Silver, 628.
9. **Adaptation to Rhetorical Situation.** Doloff, 436; Edy 456; Grann, 481.
10. **Support.** Examples: Adler, 458; Fein, 468; Koch, 503; Maas, 553; Arenson, 558. Facts: Cohen, 511; Conniff, 643; De Parle, 656. Narration: Dickerson, 517; Hamer and Copeland, 624; Silver, 628. Personal examples: Edy, 456; Glaser, 463; Wiesenfeld, 489; Gómez-Peña, 574; Kondo, 577; Ehrenreich, 659.
11. **Warrants.** Henry, 441; Gilligan, 499; Carvajal, 529; Kondo, 577; Barash, 633; Faludi, 645.

PREFACE

PURPOSE

The most important purpose of *Argument* is to teach students strategies for critical reading, critical thinking, research, and writing that will help them participate in all types of argument both inside and outside of the classroom. A basic assumption is that argument exists everywhere and that students need to learn to participate productively in all forms of argument, including those they encounter in school, at home, on the job, and in the national and international spheres. Such participation is critical not only in a democratic society but also in a global society, in which issues become more and more complex each year. Students who use this book will learn to identify controversial topics that are "at issue," to read and form reactions and opinions of their own, and to write argument papers that express their individual views and perspectives.

A central idea of this text is that modern argument is not always polarized as right or wrong, but that instead it often invites a variety of perspectives on an issue. Another idea, equally important, is that not all argument results in the declaration of winners. The development of common ground and either consensus or compromise are sometimes as acceptable as declaring winners in argument. Students will learn to take a variety of approaches to argument, including taking a position and defending it, seeking common ground at times, withholding opinion at other times, negotiating when necessary, and even changing their original beliefs when they can no longer make a case for them. The perspectives and abilities taught here are those that an educated populace in a world community needs to coexist cooperatively and without constant destructive conflict.

SPECIAL FEATURES

Both instructors and students who pick up *Argument* have the right to ask how it differs from some of the other argument texts that are presently available. They deserve to know why they might want to use this book instead of another. This text, which is targeted for first-year and second-year students enrolled in argument or argument and literature classes in two-year and four-year colleges, is both a reader and a rhetoric. Within this reader and rhetoric format are a number of special features that, when taken together, make the book unique.

- **Reading, critical thinking, and writing** are taught as integrated and interdependent processes. Comprehensive chapters on the reading and writing processes show how they can be adapted to argument. Extensive instruction in critical reading and critical thinking appear throughout. Assignments and questions that invite critical reading, critical thinking, and original argumentative writing appear at the end of every chapter in "The Rhetoric" and at the end of every section of "The Reader."
- **Cross-gender and cross-cultural communication styles** are presented in a unique chapter that provides for a classroom in which every student can find a voice. Students learn to identify and develop their own unique styles of argument and to recognize how their styles may have been influenced by family background, gender, ethnic background, or country of origin. Also included are international students' perspectives on the argument styles of their countries. Many readings in the book are by authors of varied cultural and ethnic backgrounds.
- **Explanations of the elements and structure of argument** include the **Toulmin model of argument,** the **classical modes of appeal,** the **traditional categories of claims** derived from classical stasis theory, and the **rhetorical situation.** Theory is integrated and translated into language that students can easily understand and apply. For example, students learn to apply theory to recognize and analyze the parts of an argument while reading and to develop and structure their own ideas while writing.
- **Audience analysis** includes the concepts of the familiar and the unfamiliar audience as well as Chaim Perelman's concept of the universal audience.
- **Productive invention strategies** help students develop ideas for papers.
- **Library and online research is presented as a creative activity** that students are invited to enjoy. Workable strategies for research and note taking are provided. Students are taught to document researched argument papers according to both **MLA** and **APA style.**
- **Exercises, class projects, and writing assignments at the ends of the chapters invite individual, small group, and whole class participation.** Collaborative exercises encourage small groups of students to engage in critical thinking, and whole class projects invite students to participate in activities that require an understanding of argument. Classroom-tested **writing assignments** include the **exploratory paper,** which teaches students to explore an issue from several different perspectives; the **position paper based on "The Reader,"** which teaches students to incorporate readily available source material from "The Reader" in their first position paper; the **researched position paper,** which teaches students to locate outside research, evaluate it, and use it to develop an issue of their own choosing; and the **Rogerian argument paper,** which teaches students an alternative strategy that relies on establishing common ground with the audience. **Examples of student papers** are provided for each major type of paper. The writing assignments in this book are models for assignments that students are likely to encounter in their other classes.

- **Summary charts at the end of the rhetoric section present the main points of argument** in a handy format. They also integrate the reading and writing processes for argument by placing strategies for both side by side and showing the interconnections.
- **A total of 124 different readings** in the rhetoric section and "The Reader" provide students with multiple perspectives on the many issues presented throughout the book. Twelve of these readings are argument papers written by students.
- **The readings in "The Reader" are clustered under eighteen subissues** that are related to the seven major general issue areas that organize "The Reader." This helps students focus and narrow broad issues. Furthermore, the readings in each subissue group "talk" to each other, and questions invite students to join the conversation.

NEW TO THIS EDITION

- **New five-part organization** creates **clearer assignment sequences,** more **immediate application of theory,** and more **flexibility for instructors.** The three chapters on the research paper now follow the three chapters on argument theory, which encourages the use of theory in writing the research paper. The stand-alone chapters on Rogerian argument and argument and literature appear in Part Four and can be taught at any point in the course.
- **Improved explanations, clearer assignments,** and **new examples of the exploratory argument paper and the Rogerian argument paper** appear in Chapters 4 and 11.
- **Revised and improved assignments and assignment sequences** that have been classroom-tested repeatedly appear at the end of every chapter. Less productive assignments have been deleted.
- **Earlier and more complete information** on **incorporating and documenting sources,** and **using electronic sources** in particular, appear in Chapters 4 and 11.
- Information on **how to evaluate online sources** has been added to the research section of Chapter 9.
- **More than half (65) of the 124 essays in the book are new. Three-fourths (57) of the 75 essays in "The Reader" are new.**
- **Four new issue areas** explore issues associated with the **family, computers, race and culture,** and **genetic engineering.**
- **Thirteen new issue questions,** each **accompanied by sets of three to seven essays** that provide different perspectives on the questions, appear in "The Reader." These questions include, "How Do Men's and Women's Ideas about Themselves Influence the Roles They Play in Their Families?" "What Are Some Variations on the Traditional Family? How Effective Are These Variations?" "What Can Be Done to Improve Schools?" "How Should We Treat Convicted Criminals?" "Do Violent Video Games and Books Cause Young

People to Commit Crime?" "How Are Computers Changing the Culture?" "How Are Computers Changing Their Users?" "How Are Computers Changing Education?" "How Do Race and Culture Contribute to an Individual's Sense of Identity?" "How Close Has America Come to Achieving Racial Equality?" "To What Extent Should Genetic Engineering Be Applied to Agriculture?" "To What Extent Should Genetic Engineering Be Applied to Animals?" and "To What Extent Should Genetic Engineering Be Applied to Humans?"

- **Four new examples of student writing** provide models for an **issue proposal** and **three new Rogerian argument papers,** including a **Rogerian response paper.**
- **New essays for analysis** have been added to Chapters 1, 4, 5, 6, and 7.
- **New examples of summary and response** appear in Chapter 3.
- **More immediate connections between theory and practice** are now included in Chapters 5, 6, and 7; in them, **new assignments teach students to use the Toulmin model, the claim questions, and the proofs to generate material for argument** papers.
- **Streamlined Chapters 8, 9, 10** now function as one long assignment that culminates in the **researched position paper.**

ORGANIZATION

The book is organized into five parts and, as much as possible, chapters have been written so that they stand alone. Instructors may thus assign them either in sequence or in a more preferred order to supplement their own course organization.

Part One: Engaging with Argument for Reading and Writing. This part introduces students to issues and the characteristics of argument in Chapter 1, helps them begin to develop a personal style of argument in Chapter 2, and provides them with processes for reading and writing argument in Chapters 3 and 4. Writing assignments include the issue proposal, the argument style paper, the analysis of the rhetorical situation paper, the summary-response paper, and the exploratory paper.

Part Two: Understanding the Nature of Argument for Reading and Writing. This part identifies and explains the parts of an argument according to Stephen Toulmin's model of argument in Chapter 5, explains the types of claims and purposes for argument in Chapter 6, and presents the types of proofs along with clear examples and tests for validity in Chapter 7. Writing assignments include the Toulmin analysis and the position paper based on "The Reader."

Part Three: Writing a Research Paper That Presents an Argument. This part teaches students to write a claim, clarify purpose, and analyze the audience in Chapter 8, to use various creative strategies for inventing ideas and gathering research materials in Chapter 9, and to organize, write, revise, and prepare the final manuscript for a researched position paper in Chapter 10. Methods for locating and using resource materials in the library and online are presented in Chapters 9 and 10. An Appendix to Chapter 10 provides full instruction for documenting sources using both MLA and APA styles.

Part Four: Further Applications: Rogerian Argument/Argument and Literature. This part explains Rogerian argument in Chapter 11 as an alternative to traditional argument and as an effective method for building common ground and resolving differences. Chapter 12 suggests ways to apply argument theory to reading and writing about literature. Writing assignments include Rogerian argument papers and papers about argument and literature. A summary exercise in the Appendix to Chapter 11 invites students to review and synthesize argument theory as they analyze and respond to a well-known classic argument.

Part Five: The Reader. This part is organized around the broad issues concerning families, education, crime and the treatment of criminals, computers, race and culture in America, genetic engineering, and social responsibility. Strategies and questions to help students explore issues and move from reading and discussion to writing are also included.

THE INSTRUCTOR'S MANUAL AND COMPANION WEBSITE

In preparing the *Instructor's Manual,* my co-contributors and I have included chapter-by-chapter suggestions for using the book in both the traditional and the computer classroom. We have also included sample syllabi. Three instructors have written day-by-day teaching journals, in which they detail how they worked with this book in class and how the students responded. Also included in the manual are strategies for teaching students to use electronic databases, the Internet, and other resources for conducting online and library research. Another chapter suggests how student argument papers can be developed with the help of tutors in a writing center and by online MOOs and chat groups. A set of class handouts ready for photocopying is also provided. Copies of this manual may be obtained from your Prentice Hall representative.

A Companion Website for *Perspectives on Argument* can be accessed at <http://www.prenhall.com/wood>. Beth Break is the author of this site.

ACKNOWLEDGMENTS

My greatest debt is to my husband, James A. Wood, who has also taught and written about argument. He helped me work out my approach to argument by listening to me, by discussing my ideas, and by contributing ideas of his own. The process renewed my faith in peer groups and writing conferences. Most writers, I am convinced, profit from talking through their ideas with someone else. I was lucky to find someone so knowledgeable and generous with his time and insights.

I also owe a debt to the first-year English program at The University of Texas at Arlington. When I joined the department a few years ago, I found myself caught up in the ideas and controversies of this program. It provided me with much of the interest and motivation to write this book.

For the past several years, I have trained the graduate teaching assistants in our department who teach argument. An exceptionally alert group of these students volunteered to meet with me and recommend revisions for this third edition. They include Nicole Siek, Christine Flynn Cavanaugh, Vera Csorvasi, Martha Villagomez, Barbara Saurer, Sara Latham, Vannetta Causey, Donna Brown, Kody Lightfoot, Beth Brunk, and Chris Murray. Graduate students, many of whom are now faculty members elsewhere, who have contributed recommendations for revisions in earlier editions and that remain a part of the third edition include Leslie Snow, Samantha Masterton, Lynn Atkinson, J. T. Martin, Kimberly Ellison, Corri Wells, Steve Harding, Barbara Chiarello, Collin G. Brooke, Tracy Bessire, Cheryl Brown, Matthew Levy, Alan Taylor, and Deborah Reese. I hope they will be pleased when they see that I have followed many of their suggestions for improvement. Many other graduate teaching assistants in our program have also taught with this book and have made useful recommendations and suggestions. I am grateful to them for their insight and enthusiasm.

I am also indebted to other colleagues and friends who have helped me with this book. The late James Kinneavy is the originator of the exploratory paper as it is taught in this book. Audrey Wick, Director of First Year English at our university and a seasoned teacher of argument, has provided me with much counsel and advice, including one of her favorite class projects, the literary debate that appears at the end of Chapter 12 on argument and literature. My colleague Tim Morris helped me think through some of the ideas in Chapter 12, and he provided me with many excellent examples of poems and other literary works that make arguments. I owe a special debt of gratitude to Nicole Siek and Sara Latham, who joined me in reading and voting on all of the new essays in the third edition. I have only included those that survived our joint scrutiny. Christine Flynn Cavanaugh helped locate examples of online research and made recommendations for evaluating such material. Beth Brunk, Corri Wells, Steve Newton, Deborah Reese, Brad McAdon, Samantha Masterton, and Leslie Snow have all either provided chapters or have co-authored chapters in the *Instructor's Manual*. Beth Brunk formatted and typed it. It has been a constant pleasure to work with these bright, energetic, and creative colleagues, and I am grateful to all of them for the contributions they have made to this third edition.

I wish I had the space to acknowledge by name the many students from argument classes, including my own, who read the first and second editions and made recommendations for this third edition. Some of them also contributed their own essays to be used as examples, and their names appear on their work. I paid particularly close attention to these student's comments, and I know their suggestions and contributions have made this a better book for other argument students throughout the country.

At Prentice Hall, my greatest debt is to Phil Miller, President, Humanities and Social Sciences, who got me started with this project. I also thank Vivian Garcia, Assistant Development Editor, who was immensely helpful throughout the project, and Leah Jewell, editor in chief. These individuals provided excellent help with all of the various stages of writing and final editing. Thanks also to Brandy Dawson, Marketing Manager, who has always encouraged me along the way. Shelly Kupperman, Senior Production Editor, did her usual impressive and conscientious job of seeing the book through all phases of production. Bruce Emmer and Diane Garvey Nesin provided outstanding editorial suggestions. Fred Courtright obtained the permissions for this edition. I have felt fortunate to work with such conscientious, reliable, and capable professionals.

I am also indebted to John Schaeffer and the faculty of Blinn College who volunteered suggestions for revisions—and I was able to incorporate all of them. Bob Esch at the University of Texas at El Paso has been generous with his comments and observations, and he has also sent me suggestions for essays for this third edition. I also want to acknowledge the many instructors and students around the country who have e-mailed observations and suggestions for improvement. It a special treat to receive e-mail from people who are using the book and have ideas for improving it.

Other colleagues around the country provided additional ideas and recommended changes that have helped improve the first, second, and third editions. They include Margaret W. Batschelet, University of Texas at San Antonio; Linda D. Bensel-Meyers, University of Tennessee; Gregory Clark, Brigham Young University; Dan Damesville, Tallahassee Community College; Alexander Friedlander, Drexel University; William S. Hockman, University of Southern Colorado; James Kinneavy, University of Texas at Austin; Elizabeth Metzger, University of South Florida; Margaret Dietz Meyer, Ithaca College; Susan Padgett, North Lake College; Randall L. Popken, Tarleton State University; William E. Sheidley, United States Air Force Academy; Diane M. Thiel, Florida International University; Jennifer Welsh, University of Southern California; Shannon Martin, Elizabethtown Community College; Keith Rhodes, Northwest Missouri State University; Kim Donehower, University of Maryland; Lynce Lewis Gaillet, Georgia State University; Carol David, Iowa State University; and Sue Preslar, University of North Carolina, Charlotte. I am grateful to them for the time and care they took reviewing the manuscript.

Finally, I thank all of you who use this book. I would like to hear about your experiences with it, and I am especially interested in your ideas for improving the chapters and readings. My e-mail address is <woodnv@uta.edu>.

This book has been a genuinely collaborative effort, and I expect that it will continue to be. I hope students will profit from the example and learn to draw on the expertise of their instructors and classmates to help them write their papers. Most writing is more fun and more successful when it is, at least partly, a social process.

N. V. W.

PART ONE

Engaging with Argument for Reading and Writing

The strategy in Part One is to introduce you to issues and the special characteristics of argument, in Chapter 1; to help you begin to develop a personal style of argument, in Chapter 2; and to help you develop your processes for reading and writing argument, in Chapters 3 and 4. The focus in these chapters is on you and how you will engage with argument both as a reader and as a writer. When you finish reading Part One:

- You will understand what argument is and why it is important in a democratic society.
- You will have found some issues (topics) to read and write about.
- You will have analyzed your present style of argument and considered ways to adapt it for special contexts.
- You will have new strategies and ideas to help you read argument critically.
- You will have adapted your present writing process to help you think critically and write argument papers.
- You will have experience with writing an issue proposal, a summary-response paper, and an exploratory argument paper.

CHAPTER ONE

A Perspective on Argument

You engage in argument, whether you realize it or not, nearly every day. Argument deals with *issues*, topics that have not yet been settled, invite two or more differing opinions, and are consequently subject to question, debate, or negotiation. Pick up today's newspaper and read the headlines to find some current examples. Here are some issues raised by headlines of the past: Should the Internet be censored? Has the quality of health care declined? Should same-sex marriages be legal? What can be done about the teacher shortage? How can population growth best be controlled in third-world countries? Should politicians be held to higher ethical standards than everyone else? Do we need better gun laws? Or think of examples of issues that may be closer to your daily experience: Why are you going to college? What close relationships should you form, and how will they affect your life? Which is the more important consideration in selecting a major: finding a job or enjoying the subject? How can one minimize the frustrations caused by limited campus parking? Is it good or bad policy to go to school and work at the same time?

All of these issues, whether they seem remote or close to you, are related to the big issues that have engaged human thought for centuries. In fact, all of the really important issues—those dealing with life and death, the quality of life, ways and means, war and peace, the individual and society, the environment—these and others like them are discussed, debated, and negotiated everywhere in the world on a regular basis. There are usually no simple or obvious positions to take on such important issues. Still, the positions we do take on them and ultimately the decisions and actions we take in regard to them can affect our lives in significant ways. In democratic societies, individuals are expected to engage in effective argument on issues of broad concern. They are also expected to make moral judgments and to evaluate the decisions and ideas that emerge from argument.

The purpose of this book is to help you participate in two types of activities: evaluating other people's arguments and formulating arguments of your own. The book is organized in parts, and each part will help you become a more effective participant in the arguments that affect your life. Part One will help you engage with argument personally as you begin to identify the issues, the argument styles, and the processes for reading and writing that will work best for you; Part Two will help you understand the nature of argument as you learn more about its essential parts and how they operate in argument to convince an audience; Part Three will provide you with a process for thinking critically and writing an argument paper that requires both critical thought and research; Part Four will teach you an alternative approach to traditional argument and alert you to uses of argument in literature; and Part Five will provide you with many good examples of effective argument to analyze and draw on as you create original arguments of your own.

WHAT IS YOUR CURRENT PERSPECTIVE ON ARGUMENT?

You may never have been in an argument class before. If that is the case, as it is with most students, you will have a few ideas about argument, but you will not have a totally clear idea about what you will be studying in this class. It is best to begin the study of any new subject by thinking about what you already know. Then you can use what you know to learn more, which is the way all of us acquire new knowledge.

What does the word *argument* make you think about? The following list contains some common student responses to that question. Place a check next to those that match your own. If other ideas come to your mind, add them to the list.

_____ 1. It is important to include both sides in argument.

_____ 2. Argument is angry people yelling at each other.

_____ 3. Argument is a debate in front of a judge; one side wins.

_____ 4. Argument takes place in courtrooms before judges and juries.

_____ 5. Argument is what I'd like to be able to do better at home, at work, with my friends so that I'd get my way more often.

_____ 6. Argument is standing up for your ideas, defending them, and minimizing the opposition by being persuasive.

_____ 7. Argument requires one to keep an open mind.

_____ 8. Argument papers are difficult to write because they require more than a collection of personal feelings and opinions about a subject.

_____ 9. Argument, to me, is like beating a dead horse. I have done papers in high school about subjects I'm supposed to care about, like abortion, homosexuality, drugs, capital punishment. They're old news. They no longer spark my imagination.

_____ 10. Argument is something I like to avoid. I see no reason for it. It makes things unpleasant and difficult. And nothing gets settled anyway.

Whether your present views of argument are positive, negative, or just vague, it's best to acknowledge them so that you can now begin expanding on them or even modifying some of them in order to develop a broad perspective on argument.

A definition of argument at this point should help clarify the broad perspective we are seeking. There are many approaches and views of argument, and consequently various definitions have been suggested. Some focus on identifying opposing views, providing evidence, and declaring winners. Others emphasize reasoning, understanding, agreement, and consensus. Both types of definition are useful, depending on the context and the purpose of the argument. Chaim Perelman and L. Olbrechts-Tyteca, respected modern argument theorists, provide the definition that we will use in this book. They suggest that the goal of argument "is to create or increase the adherence of minds to the theses presented for [the audience's] assent."[1] In other words, the goal of argument is at times to reach agreement on controversial issues among participants and at other times merely to increase the possibility of agreement. This definition is broad enough to include both argument that focuses on opposing views and the declaration of winners and argument that emphasizes understanding and results in consensus. Both approaches to argument are taught in this book. This definition further invites argument participants either to agree to the best position on a matter of dispute or to carve out a new position that all participants can agree on. Using this definition as a starting point, we can now add to it and consider argument in its broadest sense.

DEVELOPING A BROAD PERSPECTIVE ON ARGUMENT

Think about the implications of this idea: *Argument is everywhere.*[2] It is not only found in obvious places such as courts of law, legislative assemblies, or organized debates. Indeed, it is a part of all human enterprise, whether at home, at school, at work, or on the national or international scene. Home argument, for example, might center on spending money, dividing the household work, raising the children, and planning for the future. School argument might include such issues as increasing student fees, finding parking, understanding grades, or selecting classes and professors. Work argument might focus on making hiring decisions, delegating responsibility, or establishing long-term goals. National argument might deal with providing health care, abolishing crime, or electing leaders. International argument might deal with protecting human rights, abolishing hunger, or negotiating international trade agreements. Thus argument appears in virtually any context in which human beings interact and hold divergent views about topics that are at issue. Furthermore, argument is a perspective, a point of view that

---

[1]Chaim Perelman and L. Olbrechts-Tyteca, *The New Rhetoric: A Treatise on Argumentation* (Notre Dame, Ind.: University of Notre Dame Press, 1969), p. 45.

[2]I am indebted to Wayne Brockriede for this observation and for some of the other ideas in this chapter. See his article "Where Is Argument?" *Journal of the American Forensic Association,* 11 (1975): 179–182.

people adopt to identify, interpret, analyze, communicate, and try to reach settlements or conclusions about subjects that are at issue.

If we accept the idea that argument can indeed be found anywhere, we discover that it can also appear in different guises and involve varying numbers of people. In fact, argument can take eight forms, as in the following list. Some, like organized debate and courts of law, will not surprise you. Others may.

FORMS OF ARGUMENT

Argument, in its most basic form, can be described as a **claim** (the arguer's position on a controversial issue) which is **supported by reasons and evidence** to make the claim convincing to an audience. All of the forms of argument described below include these components.

1. *Debate, with participants on both sides trying to win.* In a debate, people take sides on a controversial issue that is usually stated as a proposition. For example, the proposition "Resolved that health care be affordable for all Americans" might be debated by an affirmative debater arguing in favor of this idea and a negative debater arguing against it. A judge, who listens to the debate, usually selects one of the debaters as the winner. The debaters do not try to convince one another but instead try to convince the judge, who is supposed to be impartial. Debates are useful for exploring and sometimes resolving issues that have distinct pro and con sides. Debates on television often feature people who hold conflicting views. The judge for these programs is the viewing public, who may or may not pick a winner.

2. *Courtroom argument, with lawyers pleading before a judge and jury.* As in a debate, lawyers take opposing sides and argue to convince a judge and jury of the guilt or innocence of a defendant. Lawyers do not try to convince one another. Also as in debate, someone is designated the winner. Television provides opportunities to witness courtroom argument, particularly on cable channels devoted exclusively to televising real trials. You can also visit court, since trials are open to the public.

3. *Dialectic, with people taking opposing views and finally resolving the conflict.* In dialectic, two or more people argue as equals to try to discover what seems to be the best position. A questioning strategy is often used to test the validity of each opposing view. The ancient philosopher Plato used this form of argument in his *Dialogues* to examine such questions as What is truth? What is the ideal type of government? and What is more important: honesty and justice or political power? Dialectic is used by some professors to help students think about and finally arrive at positions that can be generally accepted, by most of the class. For example, dialectic might be used to ascertain students' views on the roles men and women might assume in a family or whether religion should or should not be taught in school. Participants explain and justify their own positions and test others' positions. The object is to discover a common bedrock of ideas that everyone can agree on. There are no winners. There is instead a consensual discovery of a new position on the issue that is agreeable to everyone.

4. *Single-perspective argument, with one person arguing to convince a mass audience.* We encounter argument in single-perspective form constantly on television and in newspapers, journals, books, and public speeches. It is usually clear what the issue is and what position is being taken. Opposing views, if referred to at all, are usually refuted. Specific examples of such argument range from a politician trying to influence voters to change their ideas about taxes to an environmentalist trying to influence management to eliminate toxic waste to an advertiser trying to sell sportswear. The arguer does not usually know what immediate effect the message has had on the audience unless a poll or vote is taken, unless there is an opportunity for the readers to write letters to the editor, or unless there is a publicized change in policy or behavior. It is not clear, in other words, whether anyone "wins."

5. *One-on-one, everyday argument, with one person trying to convince another.* Convincing another person, one on one, is very different from convincing an impartial outside judge or a large unspecified audience. In the one-on-one situation, one person has to focus on and identify with the other person, think about what he or she wants and values, and be conciliatory if necessary. Each person either wins, loses, or succeeds in part. Example of this form of argument might include convincing a partner to sell the business, convincing an employment officer to hire a favored candidate, or convincing a potential customer to buy a car.

6. *Academic inquiry, with one or more people examining a complicated issue.* The purpose of academic argument is to discover new views, new knowledge, and new truths about a complex issue. For example, physicists engage in academic inquiry about the nature of gravity, historians about the causes of major wars, and political scientists about the benefits of a strong state government. There are no clear-cut pro and con positions, no judges, and no emphasis on winning. Anyone can participate, and there are potentially as many views as there are participants. Inquiry is a common form of argument that you will encounter in many of your college classes, where you will also be assigned to write inquiry papers. Virtually every discipline includes matters that are still open to inquiry, matters that people are still thinking and arguing about. Many professors expect their students to be able to identify the issues for inquiry in an academic discipline and also to participate in the ongoing search for answers. Imagine, for example, people reasoning together in a sociology class about whether war is ever justified or in a psychology class about whether discrimination can ever be eliminated from society. These are not simple questions with yes or no answers. Inquiry can, however, produce insight into very difficult questions, with each new participant contributing a new reason, a new example, or a new angle that the others may not have considered. As the conversation progresses, participants achieve better understanding through mutual feedback, and some may even change their minds in order to bring their ideas in line with those of other participants. The inquiry form of argument is appropriate for the complex issues that one can find in every area of study and in every field of human endeavor. Like other forms of argument, it focuses on an issue and examines evidence. It is conducted through a cooperative search for

knowledge, however, rather than focusing on finding a winning position at the expense of others. Its result, ideally, is a consensus theory of truth that may take some time to emerge.

7. *Negotiation, with two or more people working to reach consensus.* This is an important form of argument that is used to formulate plans of action that solve problems. Both the Palestinians and the Israelis, for example, could not claim ownership of the same land, so a joint plan for separate states had to be negotiated. One country could not kill sea life that another country depended on, so rights to the sea had to be negotiated. Closer to home, people negotiated who gets the car, who picks up the check, or who takes out the newspapers. Negotiation most often takes place between two people, one on one, or in group meetings. It involves both competition and cooperation, and for it to be successful, everyone must state his or her favored position and support it. Everyone must also be willing to listen to alternative views and reasons and modify original views in order to reach consensus.

8. *Internal argument, or working to convince yourself.* We all use internal argument for individual decision making and to increase motivation. New Year's resolutions are one example of internal argument and decision making. As in other forms of argument, different possibilities are identified, reasons both for and against are considered, and conclusions are finally reached.

Now reconsider some of the student perspectives on argument listed at the beginning of this chapter. Most of those ideas fit into one of the eight forms of argument just described. The exception is item 2, argument with angry people yelling at each other. No argument can be effective if people stop listening and stop thinking and engage in vocal fighting, so "having an argument" of this sort is not part of the broad perspective on argument defined in this chapter. Look back also at item 8 (argument is difficult to write because it requires more than opinion), item 9 (I'm tired of some of the topics for argument), and item 10 (argument makes me uncomfortable). If you found yourself initially in sympathy with those responses, you may now have discovered forms of argument that could be acceptable vehicles for your ideas. Here is the list again: debate, courtroom argument, dialectic, single-perspective argument, one-on-one argument, academic inquiry, negotiation, and internal argument. Which have been successful forms for you in the past? Which others are you drawn to? Why?

These examples and explanations of forms of argument demonstrate that effective argument does not take place automatically. Special conditions are necessary if argument is to be effective. Let's look at some of those conditions to expand our perspective on argument even further.

UNDER WHAT CONDITIONS DOES ARGUMENT WORK BEST?

To work best, argument requires (1) an arguable issue, (2) a person who will argue, (3) an audience that will listen, (4) some common ground between the arguer and the audience, (5) a forum in which the argument can take place, and (6) some changes in the audience. Let's look at some optimal requirements for each of these important elements.

1. *An issue.* An argument needs to have as its central focus an issue that has not yet been settled. Furthermore, there must be the potential for at least two or more views on that issue. For example, some people seem to think that the handgun issue has only two sides—everyone should, by constitutional right, be allowed to own handguns, or no one should be allowed to own them. Between these two extreme views, however, people can and do take a variety of positions, including the view that owning and using handguns may be acceptable under certain conditions but not others or that handguns themselves can be modified to limit their use.

2. *An arguer.* Every argument requires an arguer who is motivated to take a position on an issue, get information and think about it, and communicate it to others. This person needs to develop expertise on an issue and be willing to take the risk to express his or her own ideas about it. Furthermore, the arguer should seek to go beyond the "current wisdom" about an issue and find fresh perspectives and approaches that will suggest original insights to the audience. For example, an individual arguing for tougher handgun laws needs to present fresh reasons and evidence to get people's attention and agreement.

3. *An audience.* Every argument needs an audience that is willing to listen or read and consider new views or perspectives. The audience should also be capable of understanding, thinking, questioning, discussing, and answering. It may be composed of one or more people who are personally known to the arguer, or it may be unknown, in which case the arguer must imagine and invoke its background, motives, and values. The arguer should want to communicate with this audience. It should not be composed of people who are usually ignored or who are not respected by the arguer. It is a compliment to draw someone into discussion on an issue, so the audience should be valued, and to be effective, the arguer must show that he or she cares about the audience, its interests, and its state of mind. This approach will ensure an audience that listens and does not shut the arguer out or otherwise try to escape. Receptive audiences are potentially willing to change their minds, a desirable outcome of argument.[3] Consider, for example, an audience member who favors handgun ownership, who is a parent of schoolchildren, and who is willing to listen to an opposing view because a respectful fellow parent has described the number of children who own handguns in their children's school.

4. *Common ground.* Effective argument requires a community of minds that is achieved through common language and the establishment of some common ground that is relevant to the issue. People from different countries obviously need a common language, but they also need an understanding and respect for one another's cultural differences in order to argue effectively. People from different

---

[3]Some of the observations in this chapter about the special conditions for argument, especially for the audience, are derived from Perelman and Olbrechts-Tyteca, *The New Rhetoric*, pt. 1.

disciplines must be able to understand and respect one another's technical jargon and other words and concepts central to the understanding of a particular field of study. In addition, they need to share some background, values, and views to make communication possible. Three situations are possible when one works to establish common ground in argument. First, if two parties agree totally, they do not argue. For example, two parents who agree that their child should go to college do not argue about that part of the child's future. Second, if two parties are too far apart, they usually do not understand one another well enough to argue. The United States did not have enough common ground with Iraq in 1991 to work out differences, and the two countries went to war. There were several causes for this war. Iraq had invaded Kuwait, and the United States was committed to help this country maintain its independence. Kuwait's independence was important to the United States because Kuwait was a major source of U.S. oil. Finally, Iraq was developing a powerful military with nuclear potential, so it seemed important to the United States to stop that military growth. Common ground in this situation virtually did not exist, and as a result, reasoned argument gave way to "an argument," and many people were killed. The third possible situation for establishing common ground creates more effective conditions for argument than the first two. Common ground may be established through the discovery of common interests—common ideas, motives, or values—or even through recognizing common friends or enemies. As soon as two parties realize they have something in common, they can more easily achieve identification, even if it is minimal, and engage in constructive argument. Imagine, once again, two parties who disagree on handgun ownership. One party believes handgun ownership should be forbidden to stop random killing. The other party believes people should own handguns to protect themselves from random killers. Both agree that random killing is bad and must be stopped, and this basic agreement provides the common ground they need to begin to engage in constructive argument about handgun ownership. Figure 1.1 provides a diagram of these three possible situations for establishing common ground in argument.

5. *A forum.* People need safe forums for argument where they can feel creative and know they will be heard. Such widely available forums include magazines and journals, newspapers, books, letters and reports, television programs of all sorts, courtrooms, legislative assemblies, motion pictures, art, drama, fiction, poetry, advertisements, and music. College is another safe forum for arguments. Professors and students argue in class, at meals, and in dorms and apartments. Outside speakers present argument. The argument class, with its discussions, papers, and other assignments, can be a safe forum for practicing argument, particularly if both the students and the instructor work to create an environment in which all students participate and are respected.

6. *Audience outcomes.* Successful arguments should produce changes in the audience. These changes will vary with the audience and situation. At times the audience becomes convinced and decides to change its mind. Or a successful negotiation is achieved, people find themselves in consensus, a decision is reached, and a plan of action is proposed. Other arguments may not have such clear-cut results.

THE ISSUE: WAS HUMAN LIFE CREATED, OR DID IT EVOLVE?

Possibility 1: Complete agreement and no argument. Two creationists believe the biblical language about the six days of creation literally, agree totally, and share the same common ground. They have nothing to argue about.

Possibility 2: Total disagreement, no common ground, and no argument. A creationist literally believes the biblical six days of creation, and an evolutionist believes that human life evolved from a single cell over eons of time. They disagree totally, and there is no common ground. Productive argument is nearly impossible.

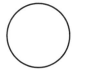

Possibility 3: Two parties discover something in common, and there is a possibility of argument. Another creationist allows that biblical language may be metaphorical and therefore that creation may have occurred over eons of time. An evolutionist also believes humans took eons to evolve. They share common ground on that point but disagree on other points. The common ground creates the possibility for productive argument.

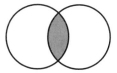

Figure 1.1   Establishing Common Ground

A hostile audience may be brought to a neutral point of view. A neutral audience may decide to take a stand. Sometimes it is a significant accomplishment to get the audience's attention and to raise its level of consciousness. This success can lay the groundwork for a possible future change of mind.

At times an event can create a massive change in the way that people view issues. The Million Man March held in Washington, D.C., in the fall of 1995 changed many peoples' perceptions about the size, commitment, and solidarity of the black male community. The Stand for Children demonstration held in Washington the following summer also changed public perceptions about the issues that are of major concern to women. As private American citizens and public organizations prepared to assemble at the Stand for Children demonstration, Betty Friedan wrote in the *New Yorker* that the probable outcome of the Stand for Children rally would be "to bring out some new thinking." The demonstration, she predicted, would help identify the "most urgent concerns of women today." These would not be the "gender issues" (abortion, date rape, sexual harassment, pornography, and the like) that engaged women in the past but rather issues associated with "jobs and families." Women will not abandon their concern for gender issues, she contended, but the Stand for Children demonstration would largely refocus their attention on a concern for children and their future. Friedan concluded that a major shift in thinking would come about as a result of the demonstration.[4] And indeed, in the months that followed this gathering of some 200,000 people, in the writing and discussion about women's issues that appeared in the press, there did seem to be a new interest and concern for children, including adequate family and public resources for their care and their future. The event seemed to cause the change in focus that Friedan predicted.

More recently, an e-mail blitz on Washington in 1999 created new interest in the resolve to settle the problems associated with Social Security. The heightened awareness generated by what was known as the Internet March for Social Security made that issue a major theme in the president's State of the Union Address that year, and the issue later became a focus for political debate by politicians.

How much can you expect to change people's thinking as you discuss and write about the issues that are important to you? Some students in argument class wonder if they must convince their teachers along with their classmates of their point of view in every paper they write if they are to get good grades. This demand may be too great, since audiences and the outcomes of argument vary so much. Convincing the teacher and your fellow students that the argument paper is effective with a particular audience is probably the best possible outcome in argument class. As one professor put it, "My ambition is to return a paper and say that I disagreed with it completely—but the writing was excellent—A!"[5]

UNDER WHAT CONDITIONS DOES ARGUMENT FAIL?

We have just examined the optimal conditions for argument. Now let's look at the conditions that can cause it to flounder or fail. No argument, we have seen, can take place when there is no real disagreement, no uncertainty, or no possibility for two or more views. Also, neutral people who do not have enough interest in an issue to form an opinion do not argue. For example, some young people do not want to argue about possible retirement plans because they are neutral on this issue. Argument also cannot take place unless people perceive an issue as a subject for argument. An example might be a college orientation session where various department representatives argue in favor of their areas as majors. This is not an issue for students who have already decided, and thus they will not identify issues or perceive this session as a forum for argument.

Big problems or risky problems that may require radical change are difficult for some people to argue about. Finding a new career or dissolving a longtime re-

---

[4]Betty Friedan, "Children's Crusade," *New Yorker,* June 3, 1996, pp. 5–6.

[5]Hilton Obenzinger, "The Israeli-Palestinian Conflict: Teaching a Theme-Based Course," *Notes in the Margins,* Winter 1994, p. 12.

lationship may fit into this category, and many people, wisely or not, tend to leave such difficult issues alone rather than argue about them. Religious issues or issues that threaten global disaster are also sometimes too big, too emotional, or too scary for many people to argue about. At the other extreme, some issues may be perceived as low-risk, trivial, boring, or even ridiculous. Some family arguments fall into this category, like what to eat for dinner or who should take out the trash. One person may care, but the rest do not.

Arguments that lack common ground among participants do not work well. It is sometimes difficult to establish common ground and argue constructively with "true believers," for example, who have made up their minds on certain issues and will not listen, budge, or change. Racial bigots fall into this category. It is also difficult to argue with some religious people who take certain issues on faith and do not perceive them as subjects for argument. In fact, argument often fails when one participant perceives a topic as an issue and the other does not. Again, there is no common ground. Finally, argument cannot take place when one party is not motivated to argue. "Don't bring that up again" or "I don't want to discuss that" puts an end to most argument. The cartoon in Figure 1.2 provides a similar example.

We have already described the audience outcomes of effective argument. When argument is not working, as in the situations just described, the outcomes are negative also. Sometimes poor argument results in a standoff: both parties agree to keep their original views and not to cross the line. Or emotions run strong, verbal fighting breaks out, and extreme views are expressed. No one agrees with anyone else. People shake their heads and walk away, or they become hurt and upset. Some individuals may become strident, wanting to debate everyone to demonstrate that they are right. When classroom argument results in such negative outcomes, some students drop the class, others fall silent and refuse to participate, and everyone becomes confused.

One important aim of this book is to provide you with the insight and skill to manage these negative situations so that more constructive argument can take

Figure 1.2   When Argument Fails
Source: Copyright © 1993 by Bill Watterson. Reprinted with permission of Universal Press Syndicate. All Rights Reserved.

place. Students are in an excellent position to overcome some of the fear, resistance, and aversion associated with difficult issues and, by using evidence and good sense, get to work and face some of them. Understanding audience members, especially their attitudes, needs, and values, is an important first step. Another useful idea to keep in mind is that most arguers have more success with some audiences than with others, depending on the amount of common ground. Even in the most difficult situations, some common ground can usually be found among people who seem to disagree on almost everything else. Recent research suggests that one vehicle for establishing common ground is through narratives, with each side relating personal experiences and stories. Even the most hostile adversaries can usually relate to one another's personal experiences and find some unity in the common villains, heroes, or themes in their stories. What sometimes also happens in this process is that the issues themselves change or are transformed in ways that make them easier for both parties to argue.[6]

Arguing effectively in difficult situations requires a conscious effort to avoid both stereotypical reactions and entrenched behavioral patterns. Past habits must be replaced with new strategies that work better. It is sometimes difficult to make such changes because habits can be strong, but it is possible to do so, and the stakes are often high, especially when the choice is constructive argument or verbal fighting and standoffs.

ENGAGING WITH ISSUES

To summarize, the most easily arguable issues are those that invite two or more views, that are perceived by all parties as issues, that are interesting and motivating to all participants, and that inspire research and original thought. They also promise common ground among participants, and they do not appear too big, too risky, too trivial, too confusing, too scary, or too specialized to discuss profitably. But you may also find yourself drawn to some of the more difficult issues that do not meet all of these criteria, and you should not necessarily shun them just because they are difficult. You will need to work with your audience in creative ways and consider the entire context for argument, regardless of the nature of the issues you select. Most important is that you now identify some issues that are arguable and important to you and to your classroom audience. Identifying issues will help you keep a high level of motivation and receive the maximum instructional benefits from argument class. Finding your own arguable issues is much better than accepting assigned issues as writing topics.

So now the search begins. What will help you find your arguable issues? Issues exist in contexts, and the issues most engaging to you will probably emerge from the parts of your life that demand your greatest attention and energy. For

---

[6]Linda Putnam, in the keynote speech at the Texas Speech Communication Association Conference, October 1993, reported these results from her study of negotiations between teachers and labor union leaders.

example, people who are compellingly engaged with their professions think about work issues, new parents think about child-rearing issues, dedicated students think about the issues raised in class, and many teenagers think about peer-group issues. To begin the search for your issues, examine those parts of your life that demand your most concentrated time and attention right now. Also, think about some of the special characteristics of issues in general. Here are a few of them:

▲ **Issues Are Compelling.** People get excited about issues, and they usually identify with a few in particular. In fact, most people can quickly name one or more issues that are so important to them that they think about them often. Some people even build careers or change careers because of issues that are vital to them. James Watson, for example, resigned his post as head of the Human Genome Project because companies were patenting humans genes for future profit, and he believed human genes should not be patented or owned by private parties. People who devote large amounts of time and study to particular issues become the "experts" on those issues. Can you think of some of your own issues that are particularly compelling to you?

▲ **Issues Often Originate in Dramatic Life Situations.** Things happen—a teenager gets shot at school, several major companies decide to downsize and lay off workers, a doctor helps a terminally ill patient die, an oil spill pollutes a beach and kills wildlife. To understand these occurrences better, people react to them intellectually, and issues emerge. Are companies making too much money at the expense of employee morale? Should teenagers (or anyone) be allowed to purchase guns? Should doctors help patients die, or should they be required to let nature take its course? Which is more important, economic growth or environmental protection? Because of their dramatic origins, many issues are intensely interesting to many people. Pay attention to the stories that are newsworthy this week, and identify the issues associated with them. Select the ones that interest you the most.

▲ **Current Issues Are Related to Enduring Issues.** Current issues can be linked to enduring issues, those that have engaged people for ages. For example, recurrent questions about military spending have their roots in age-old issues that are associated with war. Is war ever justified? Should a country be constantly prepared for war? The capital punishment issue has its roots in enduring issues about life. Should life be protected at all costs? Should anyone ever have the right to take the life of another human being? Think about the enduring issues that engage you. They may help you find your arguable issues.

▲ **Issues Go Underground and Then Resurface.** Public concern with particular issues is not constant. Experts may think about their issues continuously, but the public usually thinks about an issue only when something happens that brings it to public attention. How to deal with increasing population is an example of such an issue. Experts on that issue may think about it daily, but the general public may think about it only when new information is released. For example, in

1999 the world population reached six billion people. It had doubled in forty years, a fact that prompted a considerable amount of argument from the media, particularly about future population growth and the ability of the planet to sustain it. As one TV commentator noted, the media often make arguments out of the news. Persistent issues are, of course, always lurking in the background, always important. But we do not think about all of them all of the time. Think back. Are there some issues that used to concern you that you have neither thought about nor read about for a long time? What are they?

▲ **Issues Sometimes Get Solved, but Then New Ones Emerge.** Some issues command so much public attention that the people who can do something about them finally perceive them as problems and pass laws or take other measures to solve them. As soon as an issue is solved, however, other, related issues spring up in its place. For example, for many years, people argued about what to do about health care. As soon as health maintenance organizations (HMOs) became widely accessible, new issues emerged that focused on the quality of care patients received in these organizations and how physicians could profit economically from these changes in the delivery of health care. Are there any new issues of this type that might interest you? Think of problems that now seem solved but probably aren't fully solved.

▲ **Issues Seem to Be Getting More Complex.** Issues seem to become more and more complex as the world becomes more complex. In an interview, the actress Susan Sarandon, who has always been engaged with social issues, stated that in the mid- to late-1960s, when she was in college, the issues seemed simpler, more black and white. The issues at that time, for example, centered on civil rights and the Vietnam War. "We were blessed with clear-cut issues," she says. "We were blessed with clear-cut grievances. Things were not as gray as they are now."[7]

Because issues are now more complex, people need to learn to engage with them in more complex ways. The word *perspectives* as used in this book refers not only to a broader perspective on issues and argument itself but also to the variety of perspectives that individuals can take on particular issues. Few issues are black and white or can be viewed as pro or con anymore. Most invite several different ways of looking at them.

As you develop your own perspectives on the complex issues that engage you, keep in mind that it takes many years to become an expert. You will want to look at what the experts say. But you will not have the background and information to write as comprehensively as they do. When you write your own argument, you will want to research and write on a limited aspect of your issue, one that you can learn enough about. Limiting your topic will permit you to get the information and gain the perspective to be convincing. Suggestions to help you limit your approach to a complex issue will be made in future chapters.

---

[7]Ovid Demaris, "Most of All, the Children Matter," *Parade*, March 1, 1992, pp. 4–5.

EXAMPLES OF ARGUABLE ISSUES

Looking at examples of issues that many people find engaging should help you select ones that will interest you. Computers in education, the future of genetic engineering, the effect of violent video games on their users, the treatment of criminals (particularly young ones), environmental protection, gay rights, men's and women's family roles and responsibilities, Internet censorship, and privacy issues often interest students. In presidential campaigns, a number of public issues emerge that in the past have included welfare reform, taxation policies, gun control, immigration, and drug control. Such issues do not change radically from one election to the next, although certain issues may receive more attention in some years than in others. In Box 1.1, some contemporary public issues have been linked with enduring issues to demonstrate the timeless quality of most of them. See if you can add examples of your own as you read through those in the "current" column.

Box 1.2 illustrates some of the issues you are likely to encounter in your other classes in college. These are examples of issues that your professors argue about, the subjects for academic inquiry. You may be expected to take positions and develop arguments yourself on these or similar issues if you take classes in some of these subjects. As you read, try to add examples from your own classes.

HOW SHOULD YOU ENGAGE WITH ISSUES?

Boxes 1.1 and 1.2 represent only a sampling of issues. When you start focusing on issues, you will identify many more. Here are some final suggestions to help you engage with issues:

- Listen for issues in all of your classes, and identify them with a circled *I* in the margins of your lecture notes. Ask your professors to identify the major issues in their fields.
- Read a newspaper daily, if possible, or at least three or four times a week. If you do not subscribe to a newspaper, read one or more of them in the library or set up a newspaper circulation system in class. You will find stories about issues throughout the paper. The opinion and editorial pages are especially good sources.
- Read a newsmagazine, like *Time* or *Newsweek,* on a regular basis, and look for issues.
- Watch television programs where issues are discussed: newscasts as well as such programs as *The News Hour with Jim Lehrer, To the Contrary, Crossfire, CNN Presents, Nightline, Larry King Live, Meet the Press,* or *60 Minutes.* Some of these programs focus mainly on debate and pro and con argument, and others explore an issue from several perspectives.
- Browse at the newsstand or in the current periodicals in the library and look for issues.

CURRENT ISSUES	ENDURING ISSUES
Ways and Means Issues	
Should everyone pay taxes? In what proportion to their income? Should free trade be limited? How much business profit can be sacrificed to keep the environment clean and safe? Should scholarships and fellowships be taxed? How should we finance health care?	Where should a government get money, and how should it spend it?
Quality of Life Issues	
Should more resources be directed to protecting the environment? Are inner cities or rural areas better places to live? How can we improve the quality of life for children and senior citizens?	What is a minimum quality of life, and how do we achieve it?
Personal Rights versus Social Rights Issues	
Should individuals, the government, or private business be responsible for the unemployed? Health care? Day care? The homeless? Senior citizens? Drug addicts? People with AIDS? Race problems? Minority problems? Dealing with criminals? Worker safety? Deciding who should buy guns?	Can individuals be responsible for their own destinies, or should social institutions be responsible? Can individuals be trusted to do what is best for society?
War and Peace Issues	
How much should the government spend on the military? Should the United States remain prepared for a major world war? Should you, your friends, or your family be required to register for the draft?	Is war justified, and should countries stay prepared for war?

(continued)

BOX 1.1   Examples of Current and Enduring Public Issues

Self-Development Issues

What opportunities for education and training should be available to everyone?

How well are job-training programs helping people get off welfare and find employment?

Should homosexuals be allowed the same opportunities to participate in society as other people?

What opportunities for self-development should societies make available to individuals?

Human Life Issues

Should abortions be permitted?

Should capital punishment be permitted?

Is mercy killing ever justifiable?

Should human life be protected under any conditions?

Foreign Affairs Issues

Which is wiser, to support an American economy or a global economy?

How much foreign aid should we provide, and to which countries?

Should college graduates be encouraged to participate in foreign service like the Peace Corps?

Should the U.S. defend foreign countries from aggressors?

In world politics, how do we balance the rights of smaller countries and different ethnic groups against the needs of larger countries and international organizations?

Law and Order Issues

Is the judicial system effective?

Does the punishment always fit the crime?

Is racial profiling a problem in your community?

What is an appropriate balance between the welfare and protection of society as a whole and the rights of the individual?

BOX 1.1 *(continued)*

- Browse among the new arrivals at the library looking for books that address issues.
- Listen for issues in conversations and discussions with other students. If you get confused, ask, "What is at issue here?" to help focus an argumentative discussion.

Physics	Is there a unifying force in the universe? Is there enough matter in the universe to cause it eventually to stop expanding and then to collapse? What is the nature of this matter?
Astronomy	What elements can be found in interstellar gas? What is the nature of the asteroids?
Biology	What limits, if any, should be placed on genetic engineering?
Chemistry	How can toxic wastes best be managed?
Sociology	Is the cause of crime social or individual? Does television have a significant negative effect on society?
Psychology	Which is the better approach for understanding human behavior, nature or nurture? Can artificial intelligence ever duplicate human thought?
Anthropology	Which is more reliable in dating evolutionary stages, DNA or fossils?
Business	Can small, privately owned businesses still compete with giant conglomerate companies? Are chief executive officers paid too much?
Mathematics	Are boys naturally better than girls at math? Should the use of calculators be encouraged? Should calculators be allowed in testing situations?
Engineering	How important should environmental concerns be in determining engineering processes? To what extent, if any, are engineers responsible for the social use of what they produce? How aggressive should we be in seeking and implementing alternative sources of energy? Should the government fund the development of consumer-oriented technology to the same extent that it funds military-oriented technology?

(continued)

BOX 1.2   Examples of Academic Issues across the Disciplines

History	Have historians been too restrictive in their perspective? Does history need to be retold, and if so, how? Is the course of history influenced more by unusual individuals or by socioeconomic forces?
Political science	Where should ultimate authority to govern reside, with the individual, the church, the state, or social institutions? Is power properly divided among the three branches of government in the United States?
Communication	How can the best balance be struck between the needs of society and freedom of expression in the mass media? How much impact, if any, do mass media have on the behavior of individuals in society?
English	Is the concept of traditional literature too narrowly focused in English departments? If yes, what else should be considered literature?

BOX 1.2 *(continued)*

- Study the table of contents of this book, and sample some of the issues in the various readings at the ends of chapters and in "The Reader." Notice that "The Reader" is organized around broad areas and issues related to them. The articles have been selected to provide various perspectives on many specific current and enduring issues.
- Begin discussing and writing about some of the ideas you get from reading and listening to other people's arguments.

REVIEW QUESTIONS

1. Provide three examples of your own to illustrate the statement, "Argument is everywhere."
2. What are some of the defining characteristics of debate, courtroom argument, academic inquiry, and negotiation?
3. What are some of the conditions necessary for argument to work best?
4. What are some of the conditions that may cause argument to fail?
5. Describe some of the special characteristics of issues.

6. What are some examples of enduring issues?
7. What are some examples of contemporary issues?
8. What are some of the issues you will probably encounter in your other classes this semester?
9. What did you think of when you encountered the word *argument* before you read this chapter? What do you think now?

EXERCISES AND ACTIVITIES

A. CLASS PROJECT: "ARGUMENT IS EVERYWHERE"

Test the idea that argument can be found everywhere. Each member of the class should bring in an example of an argument and explain why it can be defined in this way. Each example should focus on an issue that people are still arguing about and on which there is no general agreement. Each example should also present a position on the issue, and the position should be supported with reasons and evidence. Look for examples in a variety of contexts: newspapers, magazines, the Internet, television, motion pictures, music, sermons, other college classes, conversations, and printed material you find at work, at school, and at home. Bring in actual examples of articles, letters to the editor, bumper stickers, advertisements, or other easily transportable arguments, or bring in clear and complete descriptions and explanations of arguments from sources you cannot bring to class, like lectures, television shows, or billboards. Students should give two- to three-minute oral reports on the arguments they select that include a description of the issue and some of the reasons and evidence. This is most easily achieved by completing the statement, "This arguer wants us to believe . . . , because . . . ." The class should decide if all examples described in this activity are indeed examples of argument.[8]

B. READING, GROUP WORK, AND CLASS DISCUSSION: WHAT MAKES A GOOD ARGUMENT?

Read the following two argumentative essays. Then, in small groups, answer the following questions for each of them:

1. What is the issue?
2. What is the author's position on the issue?
3. What reasons and evidence are given to support the author's position?
4. What makes each of these arguments successful?
5. What are the weaknesses in the arguments, if any?

Then compile a class list of the best argumentative features of each essay, as well as a list of the weaknesses. Keep a copy of this list. It is a starting point. You will add to it as you learn more about what it takes to make a good argument.

---

[8]I am indebted to Cedrick May for the basic idea for this project.

APPLYING TO COLLEGE, MADE EASY*

Nathan Burstein

Essay 1

When Nathan Burstein wrote this essay in September 1999, he was a senior at Mercer Island High School.

Mercer Island, Wash.

Each day, with the arrival of yet more mail from colleges around the country, I get a clearer picture of what the next few months hold for me: late nights spent battling both my parents' moody old typewriter and a pile of applications that now threatens to topple over on innocent civilians standing below. 1

It wasn't always like this. Applying to college used to be fairly simple, with most university-bound students aiming for just a few in-state schools. However, as a greater percentage of 18-year-olds head off to college each year, the admissions process has grown increasingly competitive. No longer is it wise to apply to just one or two schools. Many students now apply to a minimum of four or five colleges to insure acceptance at one. 2

My complaint isn't with the increased competitiveness. What bothers me are the number of forms we must fill out. Why hasn't the college application been standardized? 3

Some will point out that the National Association of Secondary School Principals has created a "common application" form, and nearly 200 colleges accept it and evaluate it as equal to their own. The problem is that this application isn't common enough. Fewer than 20 national universities ranked in the top 50 in this year's *U.S. News & World Report* survey accept it, and almost no public universities accept it. 4

Colleges, instead of spending time and money to create their own forms and mail them out to students, could pool their funds to create one universal application that students could pick up at their schools. Teachers and guidance counselors, who often must write individual recommendations for each school to which a student applies, could conserve their energy and write one excellent recommendation for each student. 5

Saving time, effort and money—if these aren't reasons enough to ease the load on us high school seniors, then colleges should do it for the sake of our collective sanity! ■ 6

FOR DISCUSSION: What were your experiences with applying to college? What is your reaction to Burstein's ideas for making the process easier? Can you think of other suggestions to improve this process?

*New York Times, September 21, 1999, sec. A31.

GIRLS AND COMPUTERS*

This argument from the New York Times *was written by a staff writer.*

1 A new report by the American Association of University Women shows that a troubling gender gap in computer use exists in high schools. Girls make up only a small percentage of students who take high-level computer courses that might lead to technology careers. Yet they are more likely than boys to take data-entry classes, the high-tech equivalent of typing.

2 The report also found that girls tend to use computers in limited ways, such as for word processing, while boys are more likely to use computers to solve problems or to develop their own programs. In one study, girls consistently rated themselves as less competent in computers than boys. This suggests that many girls are starting to see the high-tech world as a masculine domain.

3 Some of the gender gap is created outside the classroom. Computer toys are more heavily marketed to boys, and most computer games and even educational software have more male characters than female characters. But teachers sensitive to these issues could help turn the situation around.

4 In 1992, the association raised the nation's awareness of a gender gap in enrollment in math and science courses in high school. In less than a decade, that gap has been narrowed because educators worked to increase girls' participation. Now educators must insure that girls are not inadvertently left out of the computer revolution. ■

FOR DISCUSSION: Do you agree with the claim that girls are lagging behind boys in computer expertise? Give reasons for your answer. If you believe such problems exist, how could teachers change the situation? What else could be done?

C. BEFORE YOU WRITE: FINDING COMPELLING ISSUES FOR FUTURE ARGUMENT PAPERS

The objective is to make a list of the issues that interest you so that you can draw possible topics from this list for future argument papers. You will need topics for the exploratory paper on page 119, the position paper based on "The Reader" on page 238, the researched position paper on page 318, and the Rogerian argument paper on page 353.

1. *Get acquainted with the issues in "The Reader."* Turn to the table of contents for "The Reader". Eighteen issue questions organize the essays in the seven issue sections. Check all of the issue questions that interest you.

New York Times, October 19, 1998, sec. A20.

2. *Report on the issues in "The Reader."* This exercise will provide all class members with a preview of the issues and articles in "The Reader." Individuals or pairs of students should select from the eighteen issue questions in "The Reader" until they have all been assigned. Then follow these instructions to prepare a report for the class.

   a. Read the description of the issues in the section headed "The Issues" that appears at the beginning of each issue section.
   b. Read "The Rhetorical Situation" for the issue section.
   c. Read the questions at the end of the issue section.
   d. Read the issue question you have selected and the articles that accompany it.
   e. Give a two-minute oral report in which you identify the issue question, briefly describe the articles, and identify at least two issues that these articles have raised for you.

3. *Find "your" issues.* Most students have issues that they really care about. What are yours? Think about what has affected you in the past. Think about your pet peeves. Think about recent news items on television or in the newspaper that have raised issues for you. Make a class list of the issues that concern you and the other students in your class.

4. *Identify campus issues.* What issues on campus concern you? What could be changed at your college to improve student life and learning? Make a class list.

D. BEFORE YOU WRITE: APPLYING THE TWELVE TESTS

Before you write about an issue, apply the "Twelve Tests of an Arguable Issue" that appear in Box 1.3 to make certain that it is an arguable issue. If all of your answers are yes, you will be able to work with your issue productively. If any of your answers are no, you may want to modify your issue or switch to another one.

E. WRITING ASSIGNMENT: WRITING A SHORT ARGUMENT ON A CAMPUS ISSUE

Select the campus issue that interests you the most, apply the twelve tests, and write a 250- to 300-word argument about it. Use the two short arguments on pages 23 and 24 as models. Write a title that identifies your issue. Then make a statement (a claim) that explains your position on the issue, and add reasons and evidence to convince a college official to accept your views and perhaps take action to improve the situation.

F. WRITING ASSIGNMENT: WRITING A ONE-PAGE ISSUE PROPOSAL

Issue proposals help you organize and develop your thoughts for longer argument papers. Once you have selected an issue, test it with the twelve tests, do some background reading as necessary, and write a proposal that follows these principles:

1. Introduce the issue, and then present it in question form.
2. Explain why it is compelling to you.
3. Describe what you already know about it.
4. Explain what more you need to learn.

If you cannot answer yes to all of these questions, change or modify your issue.

Your issue (phrased as a question): _____

Yes _____ No _____   1. Is this an issue that has not been resolved or settled?

Yes _____ No _____   2. Does this issue potentially inspire two or more views?

Yes _____ No _____   3. Are you willing to consider a position different from your own and perhaps even modify your views on this issue?

Yes _____ No _____   4. Are you sufficiently interested and engaged with this issue to inspire your audience to become interested also?

Yes _____ No _____   5. Do other people perceive this as an issue?

Yes _____ No _____   6. Is this issue significant enough to be worth your time?

Yes _____ No _____   7. Is this a safe issue for you? Not too risky? Scary? Will you be willing to express your ideas?

Yes _____ No _____   8. Will you be able to establish common ground with your audience on this issue—common terms, common background and values?

Yes _____ No _____   9. Can you get information and come up with convincing insights on this issue?

Yes _____ No _____   10. Can you eventually get a clear and limited focus on this issue, even if it is a complicated one?

Yes _____ No _____   11. Is it an enduring issue, or can you build perspective by linking it to an enduring issue?

Yes _____ No _____   12. Can you predict some audience outcomes? (Think of your classmates as the audience. Will they be convinced? Hostile? Neutral? Attentive? Remember, any outcomes at all can be regarded as significant in argument.)

BOX 1.3   Twelve Tests of an Arguable Issue

Here is an example of an issue proposal written by a student.

Doran Hayes

Issue Proposal
Professor Gaston
English 1302
3 September 2000

Genetic Engineering

As the science of genetics continues to grow and flourish, soci- 1
ety is faced with moral dilemmas. Americans believe that genetic engineering is a problem of the future, or science fiction, that would
never happen in their lifetimes. In reality, it is a problem of
today. Doctors are already capable of performing procedures that
could, some day soon, allow parents to select the characteristics
they desire in an unborn child. Some people believe that genetic engineering is an attempt to play God. Others believe it could eliminate birth defects, genetic disease, and other imperfections in the
genetic code, making the human gene pool stronger. Should genetic
engineering be restricted, and if so, how and to what extent?

I am interested in this issue because I enjoy the science in- 2
volved. The scientific procedures and abilities are fascinating to
me. But we need to consider the morality of these procedures. Genetic engineering produces issues that could have profound effects
on society. I may just be old-fashioned, but what happened to waiting nine months to know the sex of a baby? What about picking a boy's
and a girl's name because you aren't sure? The idea of one day ordering a baby, like something out of a catalog, is very unsettling.

I know that as genetics progresses, more and more genes are 3
being isolated. The Human Genome Project is currently working to map
the entire human genotype. As more genes are isolated, the characteristics represented can be manipulated. Already, doctors can perform gender selection procedures. Who knows how long before other
characteristics will follow? I know that there are many different
ways to regulate gene expression, including controlled transcrip-
tion of DNA, alternate splicing of RNA, and control of RNA stability. These methods are already being practiced. Debate is already
raging about the morality of such procedures.

I need to learn more about what is actually possible now and in 4
the near future. I would also like to know what kinds of restrictions have already been proposed, who would be responsible for monitoring such restrictions, and what criteria would be used to set
such restrictions. For example, would they be medical or cosmetic
criteria? ■

CHAPTER TWO

Developing Your Personal Argument Style

Some students resist the idea of finding issues and participating in argument because they think they will be required to take an opposing view, to debate, or to be contentious or aggressive in class, and they feel that they do not do these things well. This chapter will develop the important idea that everyone can and should participate in argument but not everyone may participate in the same way. You already have a personal style of argument, developed by several influences in your background. Many of the students who read and commented on this chapter in earlier editions of this book identified family and cultural backgrounds as particularly potent forces in influencing the ways in which they argue. In addition, some researchers think that men tend to argue differently from women, that some Asians argue differently from Europeans and Americans, and that blacks and Hispanics may have distinctive styles that are influenced by their cultures. We will look at some of these causes for differences in this chapter, and you may want to argue about them. They are controversial. This chapter invites differing views on the issues it raises.

The final purpose of this chapter is to encourage you and your classmates to become aware at the outset of how each of you argues best. Thus you will learn to recognize, rely on, and perhaps even improve your existing style of argument. You will also learn from others how to modify or change to another style in certain situations when your preferred style may not be working well. This process will help you learn flexibility. Finally, you will learn to recognize and adapt to other people's styles, and you will therefore become a more sensitive and persuasive arguer, more likely to establish the common ground essential for the give-and-take of argument.

Individual tendencies and preferences in argument are present in many but not all argumentative situations. If you discover, for example, that you prefer reaching consensus over winning the argument in most instances this discovery does not mean that you should always argue for consensus. Furthermore, if you discover that you are reluctant to participate in argument, your reluctance does not mean that you cannot find a way to participate. An awareness of individuals' predominant styles should reduce the dissonance and discomfort experienced by some people in argument classes where a single argument style or perspective may seem to dominate. By acknowledging instead that individualistic and pre-ferred perspectives and styles not only exist but also are valued, everyone in class should feel empowered to join the ongoing conversation about issues with confi-dence and skill. The goal is to create and maintain an inclusive classroom where everyone has a voice and where every approach and style is tolerated and under-stood. This is a worthy real-life goal as well for a world in which cultural, racial, and gender diversity often influence the nature and special characteristics of the ongoing conversations about issues.

THE ADVERSARIAL AND CONSENSUAL STYLES OF ARGUMENT

Most argument classes contain a mix of students who favor either the adversarial or the consensual style of argument. Some students exhibit a combination of these styles. The adversarial approach to argument is the traditional approach. The arguer is intent on changing the other person's mind. Further, the arguer usually tries to re-fute the opponent by showing what is wrong or invalid with the opponent's view. The views of the person doing the arguing are supposed to prevail. You are familiar with this form of argument. You observe it, for example, when political candidates debate public issues to impress voters with their analysis and ability to win.

Some modern authors now amend this view of argument. In *The Argument Culture: Moving from Debate to Dialogue,* sociologist Deborah Tannen states that all topics and all occasions do not call for the same approach to argument.[1] She claims that in our culture, we typically approach issues as though there were only one approach: we present them as a fight between two opposing sides. We look at many issues in an adversarial frame of mind since our assumption is that opposition is the best way to solve problems or to get anything done.

The three groups in our society who are most likely to engage with issues as conflicts are politicians, lawyers, and journalists. When an issue comes to public attention, journalists, for example, often set up a debate between politicians and then jump in themselves to keep the debate going. Journalists look for politicians who are willing to express the most extreme, polarized views on an issue with the ostensible objective of presenting both sides.

---

[1]Deborah Tannen, *The Argument Culture: Moving from Debate to Dialogue* (New York: Random House, 1998).

Our culture also likes to settle issues with litigation that pits one party against the other. We have frequent opportunities to watch trial argument on television and to read about it in the newspaper. The objective is always to declare a winner. The argument culture as exhibited in the media, in the courts, and in the political arena carries over to the classroom, according to Tannen. Often students learn to start essays with opposition, and some students are quick to criticize and attack most of what they read. Sometimes these approaches are necessary, as in courtroom argument or in public and collegiate debate. These forums for argument very often require rebuttal and a declaration of winners. But if this is regarded as the only approach to controversial issues, we often create more problems than we solve.

Tannen claims that as a society, we have to find constructive and creative ways of resolving disputes and differences. It is better, she says, to make an argument for a point of view than to have an argument, as in having a fight. She also notes the value of studying argument in other cultures, because some cultures work for agreement more than others. Her subtitle, *Moving from Debate to Dialogue,* suggests an alternative to the win-lose model of argument. She points out that other ways exist for dealing with issues: negotiating disagreement, mediating conflicts in an effort to find agreement, and resolving differences in order to get things done. The old culture of conflict has the potential at times of becoming destructive to families, workplaces, communities, or even the world. The culture of conflict can be replaced in some situations with other possibilities, including working for consensus.

Which style is more typical of you, the adversarial or the consensual? You probably use both at times, but which are you more likely to turn to first in argument? Which style are you more comfortable with? Box 2.2 on page 47 will help you find out. Now consider the influences in your life that may have caused you to prefer one style over the other.

INDIVIDUAL STYLES OF ARGUMENT

When students are asked to describe their styles of argument—that is, what they do when they have to be convincing—individual differences in style and strategy surface right away. Some of these differences seem to be related to home training and role models, others may be related to gender, and others seem to be attributable to the background and experience provided by different cultures or nationalities. Modern research indicates that men and women describe different approaches to argument often enough to suggest that gender may contribute to differences in argument style. African American, Asian American, Hispanic American, and Native American cultures may also produce recognizably distinct styles and approaches. And students from non-Western cultures sometimes describe approaches to argument that strike Americans as distinctive and even unique.

These differences among styles are usually neither consistent nor strong enough for typecasting. In fact, in some studies, a sizable minority of men indicate they prefer the styles that some researchers have identified as predominantly female.[2] Also, a particular style may be more convincing in some contexts than in others, so that students who have a preferred style find that they vary it at times to meet the demands of particular argumentative situations. Thus no single style emerges as best for all occasions for anyone. For example, one student in the group that test-read this book reported that when he argues with close friends about baseball players, he always wants to be right, he is very contentious and argumentative, and he expects to win. On the job, however, where he has low status in an office of four women, he never argues to win but rather tries to achieve agreement or consensus. Another student said she argues most aggressively when she is secure in her knowledge about the subject. She is tentative or even silent when she is not sure of her facts. Students also point out that there is a difference between home or "kitchen" argument and argument that takes place in school or on the job. Home argument may be more emotional and less controlled, especially in some cultures, than the reasoned discourse that one associates with school or work. Now let us look at some of the factors that may influence the ways in which you prefer to argue.

INFLUENCE OF EXPERIENCE AND ROLE MODELS

Students often identify their early home training as an influence on their style. Some students from military families, for example, say that argument was not encouraged at home. Instead, orders were given in military fashion, and opposing views were not encouraged. Other students, such as those whose parents are teachers, lawyers, or politicians, have reported that arguing about issues occurred frequently in their households. Also, students tend to identify the well-known arguers who are most like themselves as the role models they like to imitate as they develop their own styles. These students watch such individuals on television or in the movies, and when the students find themselves in argumentative situations, they tend to imitate the styles of the people they admire.

INFLUENCE OF GENDER

Some people think there are differences in the ways that men and women argue and that the basis for these differences lies in the power relationships that exist between the sexes in certain situations. Advocates of this view point out that men are often able to dominate an argument, while women tend to remain silent. Men are thus perceived to have more personal power in these situations. In an essay titled "The Classroom Climate: Still a Chilly One for Women," Bernice Sander describes the results of some unequal male-female power relationships.[3] Even though most

---

[2]Carol S. Pearson, "Women as Learners: Diversity and Educational Quality," *Journal of Developmental Education,* 16 (1992): 10.

[3]In *Educating Men and Women Together,* ed. Carol Lasser (Urbana: University of Illinois Press, 1987), pp. 113–123.

people think that women talk more than men in everyday situations, she says, a number of studies show that in formal situations, such as a class, a meeting, or a formal group discussion where argument is conducted, the stereotype of talkative women does not hold up. In these situations, men often talk more than women. Men, Sander claims, talk for longer periods, take more turns, exert more control over what is said, and interrupt more often. Furthermore, their interruptions of women tend to be trivial or personal, and thus they often get women off the track and cause the focus of the discussion to change.

Deborah Tannen, in *You Just Don't Understand: Women and Men in Conversation,* also provides detailed descriptions of some differences between men and women arguing.[4] Tannen asserts that many men make connections with one another primarily through conflict. (She qualifies this assertion because she realizes that she cannot generalize about *all* men.) Tannen quotes Walter Ong, a scholar of cultural linguistics, who claims that men see the world as competitive, and the competition can be either friendly and involved or unfriendly. Men, furthermore, like self-display and achieve it often by reporting what they see and what they know. According to Ong, typical male behavior is centered on "the idea of contest, including combat, struggle, conflict, competition, and contention."[5] Ong further reminds us that many men enjoy ritual combat such as rough play and sports. Friendship among men often takes the form of friendly aggression. Ong also asserts, according to Tannen, that in daily argument, men expect the discussion to stick to the rules of logic. They expect argument to be adversarial, to include clash, to take the form of debate, and to rely primarily on logic.

Here is what one young man in an argument class wrote about his argument style:

> My head is as hard as a rock, and if I choose to disagree with you, I have the capability of tuning you out without you ever knowing it. I see things my way and tend to disagree with most people, even if they're right. Being wrong is a hard pill for me to swallow, and if I can avoid it, I will.[6]

On the questionnaire in Box 2.2 on page 47, this young man marked every item in the adversarial column and no items in the consensual column as being most typical of him.

Tannen says that most women do not like ritualized combat. They do not like conflict, either, and will often try to avoid it at all costs. Women tend to be the peacemakers and to want to work for the general good. They are as interested in making connections with other people as men are in competing. Making connections and keeping the peace are such strong tendencies in women's argument that even when women are being competitive and critical, they often mask their actual intentions with apparent cooperation and affiliation. Women, in fact, are often less

---

[4]Deborah Tannen, *You Just Don't Understand: Women and Men in Conversation* (New York: Ballantine Books, 1990), esp. ch. 6, "Community and Context."

[5]Ibid., p. 150.

[6]From a student paper by Tucker Norris; used with permission.

direct than men in argumentative situations, and their indirect style sometimes causes men to think that women are trying to be devious and to manipulate them.

To summarize Tannen, men's power comes from acting in opposition to others and to natural forces. Women's power comes from their place in a community. For women, in fact, life is often a struggle to keep from being cut off from the group and to stay connected with the community.

Linguistics professor Susan Herring has conducted research on men's and women's styles in electronic argument on the Internet.[7] She identifies some differences in style that she claims are gender-related. Slightly more than two-thirds of the men she studied are much more aggressive than women in their electronic messages. Men write longer posts, are adversarial, and do not seem to mind criticism or ridicule since they say they do not take insults and "flaming" personally. Women, by contrast, say they dislike this type of interaction; they are typically either silent "lurkers" or, when they do participate, typically hedge, apologize, or ask questions rather than making assertions.

Recent studies of the leadership styles of men and women confirm some of the generalizations about gender differences made by Tannen, Herring, and other researchers. Women leaders, for instance, are usually described as more democratic and affiliative, men as more authoritarian and hierarchical. One study, for example, surveyed more than one thousand male and female leaders from a variety of cultures and backgrounds. Women, it was discovered, were most interested in creating a sense of social equality in their groups and in building a consensus of opinion among members of the group. Men were more interested in competing for rank and status in the groups.[8]

Another effort to study some of the possible differences between men and women identifies additional characteristics that could affect their argument styles. Mary Belenky and her associates conducted in-depth interviews of 135 women who were either students in universities or who were clients in social service agencies.[9] Interviewees were asked about preferred types of classrooms for the exchange of ideas. These researchers discovered that debate—the style of argument that has dominated Western education and that is typically associated with the "masculine adversary style of discourse"—was never selected by women as a classroom forum for exchange and discussion. Instead, women students more typically gravitated toward the class in which there was a sense of community as opposed to a sense of hierarchy. In hierarchical groups, some people possess more power and consequently more ability to be heard than others. In groups

[7]Susan Herring, "Gender Differences in Computer-Mediated Communication" (speech to the American Library Association panel titled "Making the Net *Work*: Is There a Z39.50 in Gender Communication?" Miami, June 27, 1994).

[8]William F. Allman, "Political Chemistry," *U.S. News & World Report,* November 2, 1992, p. 65.

[9]Mary Field Belenky, Blythe McVicker Clinchy, Nancy Rule Goldberger, and Jill Mattluck Tarule, *Women's Ways of Knowing: The Development of Self, Voice, and Mind* (New York: Basic Books, 1986), esp. ch. 10, "Connected Teaching."

that favor community, equality is favored, and power relationships become less important.

Critics of this study point out that Belenky and her associates asked only women about their preferences and did not include any men in this study. Men, if provided the chance, might well have expressed the same preferences as the women—that is, they too would have preferred "connected" classrooms with a sense of community to adversarial, doubting classrooms where debate is favored over collaboration.[10]

The requirements of a particular situation may be more influential than gender in determining the argumentative style that an individual or a group prefers at a particular time. In some cases, males find they prefer connection and consensus over contention and winning, and many females like the excitement and energy associated with winning debates. In fact, generalizations about male and female styles of argument do not always hold up. If you feel you are an exception, you will find many other students who are also.

Here is the way one young woman in an argument class characterized her style of argument:

> My parents have played a major role in influencing my argument style. Both of my parents have always been very opinionated and vocal in regard to issues that they feel strongly about. I am also very aware of the lack of respect that females receive while they are speaking. Females are often not taken as seriously [as men], and much of what they have to say is disregarded. I refuse to be ignored. I make it a point to express my feelings on issues that are of importance to me.[11]

This young woman has a distinct style, and she can describe it. She tends toward the adversarial. Her boyfriend, who attended class with her, described himself as a consensual arguer. He was influenced, he said, by his mother, who also favored the consensual approach.

A young male student in an argument class, when asked to describe his style of argument, said that it was important to him to keep the peace, to negotiate, to work things out, and to gain consensus in argument. When he discovered that some of these qualities may be associated with female styles of argument, he quickly changed his description of himself, saying instead that he liked to win at any cost. Apparently, this young man did not want his classmates to question his masculinity, so he switched his description of himself to something less accurate. Actually, however, when questioned, a number of the male students in class admitted they preferred negotiation over winning at any cost. And the women in the class, even those who preferred to think of themselves as winners, still strongly supported the idea of men as negotiators rather than aggressive winners.

---

[10]Richard Fulkerson, "Transcending Our Conception of Argument in Light of Feminist Critique" (paper presented at the Rhetoric Society of America Conference, Tucson, Ariz., May 1996).

[11]From a student paper by Jennifer M. Hart; used with permission.

The tendency to prefer the consensual style of argument, sometimes associated with females, is often evident among real-world groups of men, including those in business and politics. One manager, for example, describes himself in the *Harvard Business Review* as a "soft" manager.[12] He explains that this description does not mean he is a weak manager. As a soft manager, he welcomes argument and criticism from subordinates, is often tentative in making difficult decisions, admits his own human weaknesses, and tries to listen to employees and understand them. In other words, he stresses connection over conflict and negotiation over winning. He believes that these qualities make him more human, more credible, and more open to change than the classic leaders of business with their "towering self-confidence, their tenacity and resolution, their autocratic decision making, and their invulnerable lonely lives at the top."[13]

Other examples of male and female characteristics in argument can be found in the language of politics. Maureen Dowd, writing in the *New York Times Magazine*, analyzes the language used by politicians in a recent election. "Politicians and their strategists," she claims, "have long been entranced by the image of themselves as warriors. Certainly, it is more romantic for a politician to think of himself as a warrior than as a bureaucrat, hack, pencil-pusher, or blowhard."[14] The day after Dowd's article appeared, a male politician was quoted in another newspaper as saying:

> Today it looks as if the Indians are about to overwhelm the wagon train. The wagons are circled and the arrows are flying. . . . We're going to begin a cavalry charge, which is going to bring us into the battle. . . . We've waited to get out on the playing field. The last three weeks has reminded me of a locker room before a big game—everybody nervous, everybody ready—tomorrow, we go charging down the chute.[15]

This quotation, according to Dowd's analysis, would be typical of the language used by many male politicians who gravitate toward male styles of argument. Notice the images associated with battle and sports.

Dowd, in her article, also contrasts the old "blood and guts" politicians with the new "touchy-feely" politicians who exhibit many of the traits some theorists identify as female:

> Bill Clinton and Al Gore, the first baby-boomer ticket, have shared intimacies about their search for the inner man. They have used the sort of feel-better jargon never before heard in the manly arena of politics. They talk about

---

[12]William H. Peace, "The Hard Work of Being a Soft Manager," *Harvard Business Review,* November-December 1991, pp. 40–42, 46–47.

[13]Ibid., p. 40.

[14]Maureen Dowd, "Guns and Poses," *New York Times Magazine,* August 16, 1992, pp. 10, 12.

[15]Karen Potter, "Gramm Gets 'Em Going with a Little Pre-Speechmaking," *Fort Worth Star-Telegram,* August 17, 1992, p. A6.

confronting problems, connecting with people, shattering emotional barriers, embracing the pain and working it out with counseling and self-examination.[16]

Personally, Dowd says, she is thrilled with this new approach and sees it as a "welcome respite from the war talk that usually drives politics."[17] She does not see it as a weakness or as a feminization of style but as a new style that can also be strong and effective.

As you analyze your own argument styles and those of your classmates, you may discover that the people who break the hypothetical male-female stereotypes are some of the most effective arguers in class. In a recent discussion about argument, one woman commented that she disagreed so totally with an anti–gay rights group in her part of the country that she absolutely did not want to cooperate with it in any way or try to reach consensus. Instead, she wanted to argue and win. In another discussion, a businessman made the point that if he didn't work for consensus in his business, he wouldn't get anywhere with his fellow workers, and nothing would ever be accomplished. Deborah Tannen makes a plea for the flexibility that can come from adapting features of both adversarial and consensual styles. Both men and women, she says, could benefit from being flexible enough to borrow one another's best qualities: "Women who avoid conflict at all costs," she suggests, "would be better off if they learned that a little conflict won't kill them. And men who habitually take oppositional stances would be better off if they broke their addiction to conflict."[18] Such flexibility has other advantages as well. It is also useful to realize that what may sometimes seem like an unfair or irrational approach to argument may simply be a manifestation of a particular individual's style. Such a realization makes it less frustrating, usually, to argue with such an individual.

INFLUENCE OF CULTURE

Now consider the possibility that members of different cultural groups in America may exhibit distinct styles of argument and that individuals learn these styles through affiliation with their groups. Here are some differences that may be influenced by cultural identity, as well as by experience.

Some people think that many African Americans tend to focus strongly on issues and that even though they make effective use of logical and ethical appeal, they sometimes also make superior use of emotional appeal. African American students report that much of their experience with argument styles comes from family interactions and also from the broad American cultural backdrop for the African American culture. The many African American magazines and publications on

---

[16]Dowd, "Guns and Poses," p. 10.

[17]Ibid.

[18]Tannen, *You Just Don't Understand*, p. 187.

modern bookstore shelves attest to this group's strong interest in the issues that affect African American culture. Two other distinctly black forums for argument are available to many African Americans: rap music, which is relatively new, and the black church, which is old and traditional. Both provide African Americans with the opportunity to observe and imitate distinctive black styles of argument.

Contemporary issues, presented forcefully and emotionally, form the main content of much rap music, as Sister Souljah, the New York rapper, recognizes. "I think it would be a good idea," she says, "for members of Congress and the Senate and all people who consider themselves policy makers to listen to the call of help that is generated by rap artists."[19] She sees rap music as a deliberate effort to organize black people to think about issues and to engage in social action. She and other rap artists have in fact organized a ten-point program to engage African Americans in such issues as African life, economics, education, spirituality, defense, and how not to support racism. Reviews of rap music also sometimes stress the argumentative slant of some of this music. Rap has been described as "so topical that it'll probably leave newsprint on your ears" and as a "checklist of intractable Big Issues set to a metal soundtrack."[20]

The black church is also regarded as another potent forum for argument. In an article describing a protest against a questionable court decision, the author observes that the African American church was at the forefront of the protest, "stepping into its time-honored role in politics and advocacy for social change."[21] Some of the most influential African American leaders who have addressed black issues have also been preachers in black churches. Included in this group are Martin Luther King Jr., Malcolm X, and Jesse Jackson.

The following description of his argument style was provided by a black student in an argument class. As you can see, he attributes some of his preferences and characteristics as an arguer to the fact that he is young, black, and male.

> What influences my style of argument the most is the fact that I am a young black male. The fact that I am young makes me want to be fair and direct with my opponent. That is, I attempt to be free of vagueness, ambiguity, and fallacies. Also, the fact that I am black affects the way I approach my audience. For instance, I tend to use emotional language, and my language is sometimes racially manipulative. I think that blacks tend to see people's race before they see people's attitudes and feelings. Finally, the fact that I am a male probably influences my argument. I think that males tend to be a bit more harsh in their argument. They tend to want to "rock the boat" and stir some emotions. I think that this is a strong tendency in my argument style. The use of facts, emotions, fairness, and strong language is very typical of black argument.[22]

---

[19]Sheila Rule, "Rappers' Words Foretold Depth of Blacks' Anger," *New York Times,* May 26, 1992, p. B1.

[20]John Austin, "Noize from the 'Hood,'" *Fort Worth Star-Telegram,* March 2, 1993, p. 1.

[21]Gracie Bonds Staples and Anjetta McQueen, "Ministers Lead Prayers in Call for Awakening," *Fort Worth Star-Telegram,* March 27, 1993, p. 1.

[22]From a student paper by Kelvin Jenkins; used with permission.

Some Asian American students, according to recent research, may be more reluctant than other students to participate in argument because of their cultural background. Students who have spent a portion of their school years in Japan, China, or other Far Eastern countries or whose parents or grandparents come from these countries may regard argument class as an odd environment that has little to do with them. This statement may be particularly true if they view these classes as places where pro and con issues are debated and winners are declared. The reason is that argumentation and debate are not traditionally practiced in some of the countries in the Far East. Carl Becker, a professor of Asian curriculum research and development, explains some of the reasons for the lack of argumentation in the Far East. For these Asians, sympathetic understanding and intuition are a more important means of communication than logic and debate. Furthermore, many Asians do not like to take opposite sides in an argument because they do not like becoming personal rivals of those who represent the other side. They value harmony and peace, and argument, as they perceive it, has the potential to disturb the peace.[23] A friend who taught for a brief period in Japan reported that he could not get his Japanese students to take pro and con sides on an issue and debate it. Instead, they all insisted on taking the same side.[24] A book published a few years ago in Japan teaches Japanese how to say no to Americans. Taking an opposing stance and defending it is a skill that must be learned in Japan. It is not part of the traditional culture. Read the short article provided in Exercise E at the end of this chapter for some examples of what Japanese really mean when they say yes to people outside their culture.

Here is the self-reported argument style of a young male Asian American in an argument class. This account was written at the beginning of the semester.

> My style of argument is to avoid argument as much as possible. I think that I argue more with other men than I do with women. I think the reason I don't argue a lot is because I analyze the situation a bit too much, and I can pretty much tell what the outcome is going to be. During argument I usually blank out what the other person is saying and think about when they are going to stop talking.[25]

He was more comfortable and skilled with argument at semester's end. He credited argument class, finally, with teaching him to listen more, argue more, and be less self-centered.

An Asian international student who petitioned to be excused from argument class said that for her, the idea of such a class was very confusing because she could not understand why she or any other student should spend time arguing and trying to convince others to agree with their points of view. She associated

---

[23]Carl B. Becker, "Reasons for the Lack of Argumentation and Debate in the Far East," *International Journal of Intercultural Relations,* 10 (1986): 75–92.

[24]Interview with Clyde Moneyhun.

[25]From a student paper by Jim Lui; used with permission.

such activity with advertising and selling and could not envision it as useful in other contexts. Ironically, this student went on to write a convincing argument about why she should not have to take an argument class. This was an important issue for her, and she wrote a good argument in spite of her reluctance to participate in it.

The Asian students who test-read this book warned that not all Asian cultures are the same and that the reluctance to argue may be stronger in some Asian cultures than others. For example, a Sri Lankan student pointed out that in her country, as well as in India and Bangladesh, argument is encouraged. Students also observed that there is a tradition of lively, contentious, and even combative kitchen arguments among close family members in some Asian cultures. This, they say, is typical of the Korean culture. Amy Tan, in her books about her childhood in a Chinese immigrant household, gives examples of the lively home argument in that culture as well. Outside of the home, however, Asians may tend to be reluctant to enter into argument. For students reluctant to speak out, argument class is a safe place for developing and practicing that special ability.

Since the Hispanic culture promotes strong family ties and group values, many Hispanic students seem to favor connection over contention and negotiation over winning. Female Hispanic students describe their styles of argument variously. One student says she tries to listen and understand others' points of view. Another says she likes the fact that she can express her feelings without hurting other people, while another says she likes a negotiated solution even though she would at times like to be more assertive.

The descriptions of argument style that you have read in this chapter were written by students enrolled in argument classes who responded to an assignment that asked them to describe their current argument styles. These students, along with more than six hundred additional students, also completed a questionnaire about their argument styles and were asked to reveal their gender and their cultural background. The idea was to see if the links between style and gender and background characteristics already discussed in this chapter seemed to have any validity.

The students were questioned in three areas. First, they were asked how they viewed the outcomes of argument. Then they were asked to report on their personal participation in argument. Finally, they were asked about their present style of argument. Several possible answers were provided for each of the three items, and students were asked to identify one item under each question that best described them and then to identify two others that also described them, but perhaps not quite so forcefully. The questions appear in Box 2.1. As you read them, answer them yourself. Under each question, identify the item you agree with most as number 1. Then number as 2 and 3 the additional items that also describe your opinions and practices.

You may now want to compare your own answers to the questions with those reported by other students. The 647 argument class students who completed this questionnaire one week after classes started also identified themselves as male or female and as white, black, Asian, or Hispanic. Sixty-nine percent of them

How would you answer these questions? Check all responses that apply to you.
1. How would you describe the usual outcomes of argument?
_____ Argument helps people understand each other's points of view.
_____ Argument separates and alienates people.
_____ Argument causes conflict and hard feelings.
_____ Argument resolves conflict and solves problems.
_____ Argument can change people's minds.
_____ Argument rarely changes other people's minds.
2. How would you describe your personal participation in argument?
_____ Argument makes me feel energized, and I like to participate.
_____ Argument makes me uncomfortable, and I dislike participating.
_____ I participate a lot.
_____ I participate sometimes.
_____ I never participate.
_____ I think it is fun to argue.
_____ I think it is rude to argue.
3. What is your style of argument at present?
_____ I am contentious and enjoy conflict.
_____ I am a peacekeeper, and I value conflict resolution.
_____ I try to win and show people I am right.
_____ I try to listen, understand, make connections, negotiate solutions.
_____ I tend to use reason and facts more than emotion.
_____ I tend to use emotion more than reason and facts.

BOX 2.1 Student Questionnaire on Attitudes and Style in Argument

were second-semester freshmen, 19 percent were sophomores, and 12 percent were juniors and seniors. Also, 53 percent were male and 47 percent female. Of the males, 69 percent were white, 9 percent were black, 12 percent were Asian, and 10 percent were Hispanic. Of the females, 64 percent were white, 15 percent were black, 13 percent were Asian, and 8 percent were Hispanic. The percentages were weighted to indicate the relative strength of preference for each group in order to make more accurate comparisons.

One of the most interesting results of this study was that no items on the questionnaire were rejected by all students. Every item on the questionnaire was marked by at least a few students as being typical or somewhat typical of themselves. These students' responses suggest the wide diversity of attitudes and preferences among them.

In answer to the first question, about argument outcomes, both male and female students overwhelmingly favored the response that the best outcome of argument is to help them "understand others." Scoring highest in this area, however, were Asian men. "Changing minds" and "resolving conflict" were in second and third places among the preferences of the entire group. Clearly, more students thought argument resolves conflict than thought argument causes it. Only a few students indicated that argument separates and alienates people. There was essentially no difference between male and female responses to this first question.

Male and female students were also very similar in their assessment of their participation in argument. Most students reported that they "participated sometimes" instead of "never" or "a lot." Both women and men reported that they are energized by argument, they like it, and they find it "fun to argue." Asian women were the largest identifiable group among students who said they found argument "uncomfortable" so that they disliked participating. But, not all of them, however, responded in this way. African American men and women ranked themselves slightly higher than the other groups in perceiving argument as energizing and enjoyable. Only a few students, and about the same number of males as females, thought it was "rude to argue" and said they "never participated."

Male and female students differed more in their responses to question 3, "What is your style of argument at present?" than they did in their responses to the other two questions. "Listening and connecting" was the style favored over the others by both men and women of all groups, but more women than men identified themselves with this style. More females than males also reported that they use emotion in argument more than reason, and more males than females favored reason and facts over emotion. White males said they "try to win" more than the other groups. Asian males and females identified themselves as "peace keepers" somewhat more than the other groups, even though a significant number of the students in the other groups saw themselves this way as well. Finally, only a few of the men and even fewer of the women said they were "contentious" and that they "enjoyed conflict."

Although no Native American students participated in this study, research concerning Native American culture and values suggests that Native American students value community and cooperation more than rivalry and competition. Furthermore, in traditional Native American culture, young people are expected to agree with authority figures, especially with those seen as older and wiser. Consequently, Native American students are often reluctant to debate, particularly with the teacher.[26]

We concluded that the differences among these groups of students are certainly not great enough to create stereotypes. College students, in fact, often break stereotypes because of their close association with one another, which often results in greater flexibility, adaptability, and increased tolerance, and because of their common

---

[26]B. C. Howard, *Learning to Persist/Persisting to Learn* (Washington, D. C.: Mid-Atlantic Center for Race Equity, American University, 1987).

goal to become educated. The strongest tendencies among these students that seem to confirm the notion that gender and cultural background may have influence over them as arguers were that Asian students were less enthusiastic about argument than the others, that white males liked to win more than any of the other groups, and that more females than males said they typically try to listen and connect.

Some findings, however, are not typical of some of the tendencies described by recent researchers. For instance, listening, understanding, making connections, and negotiating solutions was a preferred style for nearly as many men as for women, and the contentious, conflictive style was less popular with both groups. Also, it seems clear that these students as a group value knowing the facts; are suspicious of too much emotion, particularly if it results in anger and loss of control; and have positive opinions about the outcomes and uses of argument.

The study mainly emphasizes the many differences in argument style that can be found in argument classrooms. The study confirms the importance of the goals for argument class listed at the beginning of this chapter: students need to learn to value one another's styles, to develop flexibility by extending their own styles and learning to borrow from others, and to adapt to styles other than their own.

INFLUENCE OF NATIONALITY

Argument class can often be thought of as a microcosm of the larger world, particularly when the students in it represent a variety of countries and cultures. Cultural backgrounds outside of the United States can sometimes exert a powerful influence over the way in which individuals view and practice argument. Studying argument across cultures is a complicated field, and most of its findings are tentative because of the vast individual differences in people from culture to culture. Still, even tentative findings are important for the argument classroom. Hypothesizing about how argument differs according to nationality helps students focus on the preferences in argument styles that may be typical of certain groups and cultures. Developing an awareness of these characteristics and preferences and learning to adapt to them not only helps students achieve the goals of the inclusive argument classroom but also helps prepare students for lifelong communicating and negotiating with people from other countries and cultures.

Here are some examples of some possible differences. Deborah Tannen claims that argument in some societies is a way of coming together, a pleasurable sign of intimacy, a kind of game that people play together. This observation is particularly true of Italy, Greece, and Eastern Europe. To outsiders, the argument in these countries may seem to be conflictual rather than a reasoned inquiry into issues. Italian *discussione* strikes outsiders as loud, contentious arguing, but to Italians it is a friendly game. Greeks and Eastern Europeans may appear bossy and overbearing. In their view, however, they are showing friendly caring.[27]

---

[27]Tannen, *You Just Don't Understand,* pp. 160–162.

In the following account, a student from Vietnam describes a different attitude and style of argument in his country:

> The Vietnamese are taught not to argue with their elders. When I was a little child, my parents always told me that it is bad to argue with your parents and elders. Since the first grade, my teachers told us that it is bad to argue, even among friends. That is why I did not like to argue. I did not want to be disrespectful to another person. When I came to the United States and attended school, I learned that in this society you are encouraged to argue for your opinion.[28]

Here is another example of a student, this time from Israel, who attributes his predominant style of argument to his country of origin.

> I am an Arab and a Palestinian, and my argument style is different from other styles used here in the United States. In my country children are taught not to argue with what their elders tell them. This is not only taught at home, but at school too. In school teachers come second to parents when it comes to advice. Parents are considered to be wiser and more experienced in life, and it is considered disrespectful to argue with them. Arguing, in fact, can lead to certain punishment.[29]

International students in your class may be able to provide additional examples that represent predominant styles of argument in their countries and cultures, along with an analysis of what causes them.

Some researchers have speculated about the reasons for the differences in argument styles among different cultures. *Preferred cultural values* and *preferred patterns of thinking* may be the two major factors that differentiate argument styles across cultures.[30] Differences in value systems from culture to culture are often particularly obvious. For example, Americans who relocate to Saudi Arabia are sometimes surprised when they receive copies of newspapers from outside the country. Before the newspapers are delivered, the Saudi censors use wide felt-tipped ink pens to obliterate visual material that is offensive to their cultural values. Pictures of a ballerina's legs and arms may be colored over, as well as other parts of the female anatomy usually kept covered in Arab countries.

You may want to discuss with your classmates, particularly if some of them come from other countries or have lived in another country for a while, what values and patterns of thinking are preferred in their cultures since these are believed to have an effect on the common ground that is established in cross-cultural

---

[28]From a student paper by Lan Mai; used with permission.

[29]From a student paper by Edward Stephan; used with permission.

[30]Gregg B. Walker, "Assessing Multicultural Argument in the Law of the Sea Negotiations: A Rationale and Analytical Framework," in *Spheres of Argument: Proceedings of the Sixth SCA/AFA Conference on Argumentation,* ed. Bruce E. Gronbeck (Annandale, Va.: Speech Communication Association, October 1989), pp. 600–603.

argument.[31] For example, according to some researchers, Americans value individual achievement, hard work, and independence, and in their patterns of thinking, they tend to prefer generalizations backed by examples and experience to pure reasoning unaccompanied by examples. Japanese, like Americans, also value achievement, but they also value serenity and self-confidence. Characteristic of their thinking patterns are the preferences to make suggestions, to give hints, and to communicate indirectly. Researchers who have studied Japanese argument claim that the Japanese like ambiguity, or saying one thing and meaning something else. They often use understatement. Their communication can seem incomplete to outsiders because they often omit logical links, expecting others to infer them. Japanese dislike contention and debate.[32]

You see that understanding the value systems and preferred patterns of reasoning of other cultures can be very important in establishing the common ground necessary for productive argument across cultures. As you read newspaper accounts of intercultural communication and argument, watch for the problems and misunderstandings that can arise from an absence of shared values and shared ways of thinking. Here are two examples.

1. *Japan.* In an article concerning deliberations in Japan about whether or not that country should have a permanent seat on the United Nations Security Council, David Sanger wrote in the *New York Times:*

> The Tokyo Government has not wanted to appear to be openly seeking the Security Council seat, even though countries with far less economic power sit there today. But there is also an underlying fear that Japan, if given a bully pulpit, may have little to say. "We might be ashamed to raise our hand" Seiki Nishihiro, a former Deputy Defense Minister, said during a recent conference.[33]

Nishihiro's comment is puzzling unless one recalls the Japanese reluctance to participate in contentious debate, which is a regular feature of the Security Council.

2. *Russia.* A human interest story about an international student from Russia says she was confident she would do well on her first exam. She studied hard, memorized the material, and wrote it well in the exam booklet. She was surprised, however, when she received a D grade. Her professor had penalized her for writing only what the book said and for not including her own opinions.[34]

---

[31]Ibid. Walker summarizes the results of considerable cross-cultural research into the values and patterns of thought preferred by different cultures. See his article for additional sources and information. Pearson, "Women as Learners," also summarizes some of the cultural values included here.

[32]Michael David Hazen, "The Role of Argument, Reasoning and Logic in Tacit, Incomplete and Indirect Communication: The Case of Japan," in *Spheres of Argument: Proceedings of the Sixth SCA/AFA Conference on Argumentation,* ed. Bruce E. Gronbeck (Annandale, Va.: Speech Communication Association, 1989), pp. 497–503.

[33]David E. Sanger, "Toyko in the New Epoch: Heady Future with Fear," *New York Times,* May 5, 1992, p. A1.

[34]David Wallechinsky, "This Land of Ours," *Parade,* July 5, 1992, p. 4.

This incident can be puzzling unless one realizes that not all countries and cultures encourage critical thinking, evaluative opinion, and argument. Totalitarian governments like the former Soviet Union, in fact, discouraged or even forbade diversity of opinion in public forums.

Argument is fundamental to democracy, and it flourishes in democratic societies. In totalitarian societies, however, if it exists at all, it must usually go underground. Thus argument in such countries may be heard only in the secret meetings of opposition political groups or in private meetings of citizens. Written argument may appear in underground newspapers or in material written by dissidents or political exiles. Forums for argument in such societies are severely limited compared to those in democratic societies. Students from such countries may at first find it difficult to participate in argument.

All participants in argument, whether they come from democratic or totalitarian societies, need to work to establish common ground if argument across cultures and gender boundaries is to be successful. This effort can be difficult and time-consuming. An issue that has historically been argued and debated through the ages is the fishing, navigation, and territorial rights to the oceans of the world. In the 1970s, the United Nations Conference on the Law of the Sea was charged with the task of reaching agreement among nations on access to and use of the seas. This group spent nine years engaged in intercultural argument and negotiation, finally reaching agreement on some, but not all, of the issues.[35]

When Boris Yeltsin was president of Russia, he made an effective attempt to achieve common ground on his visit to Japan in late 1993, when there was considerable tension between the two countries. Unlike some of his predecessors, Yeltsin was accomplished in building common ground. Soon after arriving in Japan, he apologized for Russia's treatment of thousands of Japanese prisoners of war who were sent to Siberia after World War II. More than sixty thousand of them died, and many Japanese believed an apology was long overdue. Later, Yeltsin repeated this apology to the Japanese prime minister and bowed deeply to express his remorse, a gesture that is valued in the Japanese culture.[36] His efforts, according to reports, relieved a considerable amount of tension between the two countries because of the common ground he established. When common ground is not established, the consequences can be devastating. Wars are a frequent alternative to productive argument and negotiation, especially when the differences among the arguing parties are extreme.

The concept of all people knowing how to argue effectively to resolve differences in personal, national, and international relationships is potentially a very powerful idea. Think of a country and a world where major problems are resolved through profitable argument instead of through confrontation, shouting, fighting, or war. You will often fervently disagree with other people; in fact, life would be

---

[35]Walker, "Assessing Multicultural Argument," pp. 599–600.

[36]David E. Sanger, "Yeltsin, in Tokyo, Avoids Islands Issue," *New York Times*, October 14, 1993, p. A5.

boring if you never disagreed. Yet even when you disagree, even when you decide to enter an ongoing argument, you can learn to use a style that is comfortable and natural for you. And that approach is preferable to the alternatives: either remaining silent or becoming involved in destructive arguments that solve nothing and may even cause harm.

REVIEW QUESTIONS

1. What are some of the possible influences on individual styles of argument? Which of these are the most potent for you?
2. What are some of the differences researchers have identified between men's and women's styles of argument? Do you agree or disagree? What in your own experience has influenced your answer to this question?
3. Why might it be important to be aware of different argument styles in international or cross-cultural argument? Give some examples of problems that might arise along with some ideas of how to deal with them.

EXERCISES AND ACTIVITIES

A. SELF-EVALUATION: IS YOUR PREDOMINANT ARGUMENT STYLE CONSENSUAL OR ADVERSARIAL?

Box 2.2 provides a summary of some of the characteristics of consensual and adversarial styles of argument. As you read the lists, check the items that are most typical of you. Does one list describe your style of argument better than the other? Or can your style best be described by items derived from both lists? From this analysis, how would you say you prefer to argue?

B. WRITING ASSIGNMENT: THE ARGUMENT STYLE PAPER

Think about the last time you had to argue convincingly for a certain point of view. Write a 300- to 500-word paper in which you describe your predominant argument style. Include the following information:

1. When you argued, what was the issue, what were you trying to achieve, and what did you do to achieve it?
2. Was that typical of your usual style of argument? If yes, explain why; if no, explain why and describe your usual style.
3. What has influenced your style of argument? Consider home training, role models, gender, culture, nationality, national heritage, or any other life experiences that have influenced you.
4. How would you describe your ideal arguer, and how would you like to be more like this person in your own arguing?
5. What do like best about your current style of argument? What would you like to change? Have you ever tried to change? If so, how? How can you become more flexible in your style?

Which Style Describes You?

CONSENSUAL STYLE	ADVERSARIAL STYLE
_____ I prefer to be indirect.	_____ I am direct and open.
_____ I like to give reasons.	_____ I like to reach conclusions.
_____ I prefer cooperation.	_____ I prefer competition.
_____ I favor group consensus.	_____ I favor individual opinions.
_____ I like affiliation.	_____ I like conflict.
_____ I hate to fight.	_____ I like to fight.
_____ I prefer to avoid confrontation.	_____ I like confrontation.
_____ I dislike contentious argument.	_____ I like contentious argument.
_____ I am nonaggressive.	_____ I am aggressive.
_____ I solicit many views on an issue.	_____ I tend to see issues as two-sided, pro and con, right or wrong.
_____ I am both logical and emotional.	_____ I am primarily logical.
_____ I try to make connections.	_____ I tend to be adversarial.
_____ I prefer negotiating.	_____ I prefer winning.
_____ I favor the personal example, story, or anecdote.	_____ I favor abstract ideas.
_____ I want to keep the community strong.	_____ I want to keep the individual strong.

BOX 2.2 Two Styles of Argument

C. CLASS PROJECT: A CLASSROOM ENVIRONMENT FOR ARGUMENT AND YOUR CLASS AS AN AUDIENCE

1. Read aloud the argument style papers written by class members for Exercise B. Discuss the different styles described in these papers and some of the influences that have helped create them.
2. Discuss creating a classroom environment that can accommodate all of these styles. Jürgen Habermas, a modern European rhetorician, described an ideal environment for argument.[37] Read each item, indicate by raising your hand whether you agree or disagree, and explain why. What would you eliminate? Why? What would you add? Why?

   a. Each person should have the freedom to express ideas and critique other's ideas directly, openly, and honestly.
   b. The use of force and personal power that tend to inhibit some participants are to be eliminated.

---

[37]Habermas's ideas are summarized by James L. Golden, Goodwin F. Berquist, and William E. Coleman in *The Rhetoric of Western Thought*, 4th ed. (Dubuque, Ia.: Kendall Hunt, 1989), p. 438.

    c. Arguments based on an appeal to the past and tradition are to be exposed. These arguments superimpose the past on the present, and everyone does not share the same past.

    d. The aim of argument is to arrive at truth through consensus and an adherence of minds.

What are the implications of accepting or rejecting these statements for your classroom?

3. Characterize your class as an audience as a result of reading the argument style papers. Write for five minutes about the characteristics your class holds in common and also about the types of diversity that are evident in your class. What generalizations can you finally make about your class as an audience? Discuss the results.

D. GROUP WORK AND CLASS DISCUSSION: USING GENDER, NATIONALITY, AND CULTURAL BACKGROUND TO STRENGTHEN ARGUMENT

The following four essays are written by authors who have drawn on their unique experiences as members of a particular culture or gender. When you have read the essays, discuss them in small groups of four or five students each. Appoint a scribe to record your findings and report them to the class. The following questions will help organize your discussion.

1. What experiences associated with their culture or their gender do these authors draw on to strengthen their arguments?
2. What is effective in their arguments as a result? Be specific.
3. What can you conclude about drawing on experiences associated with one's culture, gender, or nationality to strengthen an argument?
4. Would drawing on personal experiences of your own, as these authors have done, be consistent with your personal argument style? If your answer is yes, what experiences associated with your culture, gender, or nationality might you use to develop an issue that is important to you?

Essay 1

WE KNEW WHAT GLORY WAS*

Shirlee Taylor Haizlip

Shirlee Taylor Haizlip is also the author of The Sweeter the Juice: A Family Memoir *in Black and White.*

1   When I was growing up in the 40's and 50's, my father would pack up the car every August and squeeze in my mother, four children, several dolls and a picnic lunch. It was the time before air-conditioning, and the drive was hot, dusty and, after New York, without bathrooms.

*New York Times, June 23, 1996, p. A13.

We left long before dawn, because for a dark-skinned man driving a large 2 shiny sedan holding a white-looking wife, the journey from Connecticut to the South was not without peril. It was essential that each leg of the trip be made before nightfall. We knew that safety lay within the homes and the churches of my father's friends and colleagues, the black ministers we would visit. They were our underground railroad.

My father was a Baptist pastor who ministered to a medium-sized black 3 church in a Connecticut mill town. His father was a minister who had founded a major black Baptist church in Washington. At the beginnings of their careers, both had led small country churches in North Carolina, Virginia and West Virginia. Later, as popular officers of the National Baptist Convention and known for their dramatic oratory, the two were frequent guest preachers at rural churches throughout the South.

Traditionally, my father and his father before him preached a week of revival 4 services at these houses of worship. After my grandfather died, my father continued to return to the South each year. For him, the churches were touchstones of faith, of culture, of triumph over slavery. For him, they were living, breathing links to the past and an indestructible foundation for the future.

There was more than a spiritual connection. When they were in college, my 5 four uncles, all of whom played musical instruments and had glorious voices, would sometimes join my father and present musical programs of spirituals and the light classics to appreciative Southern congregations, all too often deprived of other cultural experiences.

At other times, my dad, resplendent in a white suit, would offer solo recitals. 6 When he crooned "Danny Boy" or "When I Grow Too Old to Dream" in his high tenor vibrato and with exquisite diction, the fans moved a little faster, the backs sat up a little straighter and the shouts of "Sing it, Rev!" were as heartfelt as they were for his renditions of "Amazing Grace" or "His Eye Is on the Sparrow."

I cannot hear the Three Tenors sing without thinking of my father standing 7 in the pulpit of a spare little church, singing like a melancholy angel.

To reach many of the churches, we drove up deserted dirt roads covered by 8 gracefully arching kudzu-fringed trees. Just when we thought we would never get there, a clearing materialized. There at its edge stood the church, often the only building for miles around, plain as a line drawing in a children's coloring book, more often than not in need of a fresh coat of paint. Never lonely looking, it seemed instead a natural part of the landscape, splendid in its simplicity.

Before the service, with admonitions of keeping our "best" clothes clean fad- 9 ing in our ears, my siblings and I would play with other children, running and jumping, catching fireflies, hiding and seeking in the darkening silver twilight. Each night, the revival crowd would get bigger and livelier. By the end of the week, the church was full, the room was hot and the penitents were saved.

During every service, I watched as my father, in high Baptist style, "picture 10 painted" the stories of Moses and Job, Ruth and Esther. I listened as he moaned and hummed and sang the tales of W. E. B. Du Bois and Frederick Douglass, the Scottsboro Boys and Emmett Till. I clapped for joy as he brought the worshipers to their feet with promises of survival now and salvation later. In that place, at that time, we knew what glory was.

11   After the service, in the pitch blackness of a muggy summer night, we would drive back to our host's house, listening to parish gossip and ghost stories, accept offers of freshly made iced tea and every once in a while homemade ice cream. Sweetly, another church night had ended.

12   The best was yet to come. At the close of the week, we celebrated the homecoming, the end of the weeklong revival, behind the church, where picnic benches were felicitously placed among sweet-smelling pines. We ate miles of delicious food and drank lakes of sweet punch.

13   Usually there was a modest graveyard somewhere near the picnic grounds. We did not play there. Our parents had taught us better than that. Mold-covered gravestones barely hinted at the life stories they marked. The bones of slaves lay side by side with the bones of their emancipated children. All of their spirits were free to be free, at last.

14   As I grew older, I would learn about the lives of the church members from the comfort of my mother's side. I would grow to understand that there, in that place, every single church member was *somebody*.

15   In God's house, if nowhere else, they were C.E.O.'s and presidents, directors and chairmen, counselors and managers. In God's house, if nowhere else, they were women of infinite grace and men of profound dignity. Forever, amen.

16   With traditions that began in slavery, the parishioners carried forward, bit by precious bit, the dreams of their forebears. In their roles as deacons, trustees, missionaries and choir members, those domestics, handymen, cotton and tobacco farmers and teachers sang and prayed on hard, scrabbly benches, validating and celebrating themselves and one another, warmly and well, week after week, year after year, generation after generation.

17   Surely their oils and essences seeped into the well-worn pews. Surely the whorls of their fingertips left lovely striations in the wood, at which their grandbabies would stare before they fell off to sleep.

18   Not only did they tend to the church's business, they looked after the elderly and the infirm, encouraged the young to learn, learn, learn and rallied their communities in times of economic stress, natural disaster or social crisis. It did not escape my understanding that the church encompassed all. Seldom were there outcasts.

19   For me as a child, those beautiful little structures were places beyond enchantment. As an adult, I understood that the churches were indeed the collective soul of black folks.

20   I never thought that this particular reality could end. Although I have visited the South as an adult and know that some of those churches have been been abandoned, enlarged or modernized, in my mind's eye all of them remain storybook sanctuaries, testament to my own faith, the faith of my father, his father and the larger black community.

21   Heartsick now, my soul's light has been dimmed. Church after church in the South has been destroyed by fire, torched by arsonists. I watch the televi-

sion images as long as I can. Then I hide my eyes behind my fingers, peeking at the screen as if it were a horror film, while hellish flames consume the heavenly places of my youth.

I ask my father across the void, Who will put out the flames, Dad? Where can 22 we go now to be safe? ■

FOR DISCUSSION: What makes this an effective argument? What do you visualize? How do you participate in this essay and identify with its characters?

A VIEW FROM BERKELEY*

Chang-Lin Tien

▲ *Essay 2*

Chang-Lin Tien was chancellor of the University of California at Berkeley when he wrote this article.

When the debate over affirmative action in higher education started to simmer, 1 the stance I took as the chancellor of the University of California at Berkeley seemed to surprise many people.

To be sure, my view—that we *should* consider race, ethnicity and gender 2 along with many other factors in admissions—has put me at odds with some constituencies, including the majority of the Regents of the University of California. Last July, these officials voted to end affirmative action admission policies.

And with California voters to decide later this year whether to end all state 3 affirmative action programs, silence might seem a more prudent course for the head of a major public university. We already have enough battles to fight, my staff sometimes reminds me: declining public funding, for example.

A few students and friends have hinted that it might make more sense for 4 me, as an Asian-American, to oppose affirmative action.

Asian-Americans, who are not considered underrepresented minorities 5 under affirmative action, have divergent views. Some are disturbed by the "model minority" stereotype; they say it pits them against other minorities and hides the discrimination they still face. Others—including the two Asian-American Regents who voted to end affirmative action—believe the only fair approach is to base admissions on academic qualifications. That also opens the door to more Asians.

So why do I strongly support affirmative action? My belief has been 6 shaped by my role in higher education. And by my experience as a Chinese immigrant. I know first-hand that America can be a land of opportunity. When I came here, I was a penniless 21-year-old with a limited grasp of the language and culture. Yet I was permitted to accomplish a great deal. My research in heat transfer contributed to better nuclear reactor safety and space shuttle design.

*New York Times, March 31, 1996, Special Education Section, p. 30.

My former students are professors and researchers at some of America's best schools and business concerns.

7   But as I struggled to finish my education here, I also encountered the ugly realities of racial discrimination. This, too, is part of America's legacy and it is inextricably connected to the need for affirmative action.

8   When I first arrived in this country in 1956 as a graduate student, for example, I lived in Louisville, Ky. One day I got on a bus and saw that all the black people were in the back, the white people in the front. I didn't know where I belonged, so for a long time I stood near the driver. Finally, he told me to sit down in the front, and I did. I didn't take another bus ride for a whole year. I would walk an hour to avoid that.

9   I served as a teaching fellow at Louisville for a professor who refused to pronounce my name. He addressed me as "Chinaman." One day he directed me to adjust some valves in a large laboratory apparatus. Climbing a ladder, I lost my balance and instinctively grabbed a nearby steam pipe. It was scorchingly hot and produced a jolt of pain that nearly caused me to faint. Yet I did not scream. Instead, I stuffed my throbbing hand into my coat pocket and waited until the class ended. Then I ran to the hospital emergency room, where I was treated for a burn that had singed all the skin off my palm.

10   Outwardly, my response fit the stereotype of the model-minority Asian: I said nothing and went about my business. But my silence had nothing to do with stoicism. I simply did not want to endure the humiliation of having the professor scold me in front of the class.

11   Of course, four decades later, there have been major civil rights advances in America. But serious racial divisions remain. That's why colleges and universities created affirmative admissions programs. The idea was to open the doors to promising minority students who lacked educational and social opportunities.

12   As Berkeley's chancellor, I have seen the promise of affirmative action come true. No racial or ethnic group constitutes a majority among our 21,000 undergraduates. And Berkeley students enter with higher grades and test scores than their predecessors. They graduate at the highest rate in our history.

13   I think that affirmative action should be a temporary measure, but the time has not yet come to eliminate it. Educational opportunities for inner-city minority students, for example, still contrast dramatically with those of affluent students in the suburbs, where many white families live.

14   And as a public institution, the university needs to look at broader societal needs, including greater leadership training of California's African-American and Hispanic population.

15   I try to explain this when, as occasionally happens, Asian-American or white friends complain to me that their child, a straight-A student, didn't get into Berkeley because we give spaces to others. I also say that we use admission criteria other than test scores, grades and ethnicity, including a genius for computers, musical talent, geographical diversity.

16   Besides, a straight-A average wouldn't guarantee admission to Berkeley even if there were no affirmative action. For a freshman class with 3,500 places,

we get about 25,000 applicants. This year, 10,784 of them had a 4.0 high school record.

What's more, helping minority students may not be the most compelling 17 reason for preserving affirmative action.

Every time I walk across campus, I am impressed by the vibrant spirit of this 18 diverse community. In teeming Sproul Plaza, the dozens of student groups who set up tables represent every kind of social, political, ethnic and religious interest. In the dorms, students from barrios, suburbs, farm towns and the inner city come together.

When there are diverse students, staff and faculty (among whom there are 19 still too few minorities) everybody stands to gain.

Of course, interactions between students of different backgrounds can 20 bring misunderstanding. Some white students tell me they feel squeezed out by black and Latino students they believe are less deserving, as well as by over-achieving Asian-American students. Some African-American and Latino students confide they sometimes feel their professors and white classmates consider them academically inferior, a view that's slow to change even when they excel.

Still, the overall message I get time and again from students and recent grad- 21 uates is that they have valued the chance to challenge stereotypes.

So I was stunned by the Regents' decision to end affirmative action admis- 22 sions policies, which goes into effect by 1998. I even debated whether to resign.

In Chinese, however, the character for "crisis" is actually two characters: 23 one stands for danger and the other for opportunity. And I took the Chinese ap-proach. Noting that the Regents had reaffirmed their commitment to diversity when they discarded affirmative action, I decided to stay to try to make a dif-ference.

Recently, I joined the superintendents of the major urban school districts of 24 the San Francisco Bay area to announce a campaign: The Berkeley Pledge.

Under this program, Berkeley is deepening its support for disadvantaged 25 youth trying to qualify for admission. One way will be to provide educational ex-pertise for teachers; another will be to create incentives for pupils at selected school "pipelines" that begin in kindergarten. We also are stepping up our recruit-ment of exceptional minority students.

America has come a long way since the days of Jim Crow segregation. It 26 would be a tragedy if our nation's colleges and universities slipped backward now, denying access to talented but disadvantaged youth and eroding the diver-sity that helps to prepare leaders. ∎

FOR DISCUSSION: What are the major reasons Chancellor Tien provides for retain-ing affirmative action in higher education? Do you share his views? Give reasons for your answer, and use some of your own experiences to support your reasons, just as he does.

Essay 3

GIVING PEOPLE A SECOND CHANCE*

Ernest Martinez

Ernest Martinez writes about his experience as an instructor in inmate vocational education at Wasco State Prison in Wasco, California.

1   I am very proud of being Mexican American and am both privileged and honored to have been blessed with a career as an educator. Yet, I sometimes think that when discussing the many Hispanic issues that we often attribute to a fractured American society, I believe we often do to ourselves what we don't want others to do to us: ostracize ourselves. On the one hand, we rally together as Hispanics to seek out equal opportunity and revel in the triumphs of our unity. But on the other hand, when we hear of our many Hispanic brethren who are ex-convicts who need employment avenues for reentry into society, we close our eyes and ears to their cry for assistance. We blame society for their plight and thrust the burden of our people on the very government we condemn for lack of opportunity.

2   For the past several years, I have been part of the lives of inmates by teaching them vocational studies. These inmates are an example to us all that it is only by the grace of God that we are not in their place. We can all attest to the fact that we have done something for which we have simply not been caught—for example, drinking alcoholic beverages as minors, or driving without a license, or hanging around with the wrong people and being at the wrong place at the wrong time, or telling little "white lies" while filing our taxes. These are all examples of "crimes" that we've gotten away with. And instead of being imprisoned, we are known as law abiding citizens. The inmates of Wasco State Prison have not been so lucky, graced or blessed.

3   I believe many of the inmates with whom I work are persons like you and me. Unfortunately, they took "the road less traveled," and found themselves in a situation that was beyond their ability to handle or solve. This is not only "man as the problem," but the "problems of man." There are many parallels that we can draw between ourselves—those of us in the professional and business communities in need of not only able but willing people—and the backgrounds, personalities, character traits, abilities, needs, and yes, even aspirations, of the many prison inmates wanting and asking for a "Chapter Two" in their lives.

4   The business environment today is not solely based on equipment, products, or services. It's dependent on the skills, talents, and savvy of people. We're not only in an information age today; we are in an Age of Man, whereby sales can only be made and increased through the interpersonal relationships that we create be-

*Hispanic, June 1996, p. 64.

tween provider and consumer, between our companies and our customers. The world-respected organization, business, and management guru Dr. Peter Drucker has said, "Show me an organization or business that does not believe people are their greatest resource and I'll show you an organization with built-in limits to its success, and perhaps one destined for certain failure." Remember the old saying, *"El ojo del amo engorda el caballo."* [The literal meaning is, "The eye of love fattens the horse"; the metaphorical meaning is, that "anything seen through the eyes of love seems better"]. Only if we can secure our fiscally solvent present can we launch into a more expansive tomorrow. And, again, we can only do this if we focus on people as our greatest asset today.

I am of the ardent belief that many prison inmates are highly functional, 5 tremendously skilled, fabulously talented, and often technically gifted. Some are inordinately intelligent, while others are blessed simply with the extraordinary ability to work diligently. I've learned over the years working as educator of vocational studies with inmates that their crime was more a matter of poor judgment rather than of faulty character. And while not so naive as to believe that all inmates are worthy of a "Chapter Two," I can empathize with how hard it is to take a breath when one is in a whirlwind. The momentum of the moment is a tremendous force in this "survival of the fittest" society.

This is not to mean that we are to be guilt-driven, but rather people-motivated. 6 This is not to promote philanthropy, but to be responsible in not overlooking a pool of prospective employees that is often not considered in the equation. This is not to say that every prison inmate is right for our companies, but to instead entertain the financial and accessible feasibility of hiring persons (both men and women) who want to work hard and need the opportunity to do so. And, this is not about hiring the "lessor among us," but to seek the "gold hidden behind and beneath a bushel."

Yes, many among the prison population are the very best of people, both in 7 skill and desire, and in character and spirit. These people represent a select group who did the crime and served their time. They possess abilities, skills, and talents that range from refined artistic propensities, technical adeptness, and computer literacy, to management skills, professional polish, and interpersonal qualities. And, while they may need the power of your push or the compassion of your pull, they are people who can and will show a watching world that it is possible to "turn a large ship in a harbor."

If they can turn their lives around from the dungeons of prison to the epic of 8 hope, they can also be a tremendous testimony to what is possible in the world of Hispanic business and to society at large. ■

FOR DISCUSSION: Do you think this article might persuade businesspersons to hire ex-convicts? Would you be persuaded if you could hire? Why or why not? Give a detailed explanation of your views about hiring individuals who have been through a vocational training program in prison.

Essay 4

WHY I WANT A WIFE*

Judy Brady

Judy Brady's famous essay first appeared in Ms. *in 1971.*

1   I belong to that classification of people known as wives. I am A Wife. And, not altogether incidentally, I am a mother.

2   Not too long ago a male friend of mine appeared on the scene fresh from a recent divorce. He had one child, who is, of course, with his ex-wife. He is looking for another wife. As I thought about him while I was ironing one evening, it suddenly occurred to me that I, too, would like to have a wife. Why do I want a wife?

3   I would like to go back to school so that I can become economically independent, support myself, and, if need be, support those dependent upon me. I want a wife who will work and send me to school. And while I am going to school I want a wife to take care of my children. I want a wife to keep track of the children's doctor and dentist appointments. And to keep track of mine, too. I want a wife to make sure my children eat properly and are kept clean. I want a wife who will wash the children's clothes and keep them mended. I want a wife who is a good nurturant attendant to my children, who arranges for their schooling, makes sure that they have an adequate social life with their peers, takes them to the park, the zoo, etc. I want a wife who takes care of the children when they are sick, a wife who arranges to be around when the children need special care, because, of course, I cannot miss classes at school. My wife must arrange to lose time at work and not lose the job. It may mean a small cut in my wife's income from time to time, but I guess I can tolerate that. Needless to say, my wife will arrange and pay for the care of the children while my wife is working.

4   I want a wife who will take care of *my* physical needs. I want a wife who will keep my house clean. A wife who will pick up after my children, a wife who will pick up after me. I want a wife who will keep my clothes clean, ironed, mended, replaced when need be, and who will see to it that my personal things are kept in their proper place so that I can find what I need the minute I need it. I want a wife who cooks the meals, a wife who is a *good* cook. I want a wife who will plan the menus, do the necessary grocery shopping, prepare the meals, serve them pleasantly, and then do the cleaning up while I do my studying. I want a wife who will care for me when I am sick and sympathize with my pain and loss of time from school. I want a wife to go along when our family takes a vacation so that someone can continue to care for me and my children when I need a rest and change of scene.

5   I want a wife who will not bother me with rambling complaints about a wife's duties. But I want a wife who will listen to me when I feel the need to explain

*Reprinted by permission of the author.

a rather difficult point I have come across in my course of studies. And I want a wife who will type my papers for me when I have written them.

I want a wife who will take care of the details of my social life. When my 6 wife and I are invited out by my friends, I want a wife who will take care of the babysitting arrangements. When I meet people at school that I like and want to entertain, I want a wife who will have the house clean, will prepare a special meal, serve it to me and my friends, and not interrupt when I talk about things that interest me and my friends. I want a wife who will have arranged that the children are fed and ready for bed before my guests arrive so that the children do not bother us. I want a wife who takes care of the needs of my guests so that they feel comfortable, who makes sure that they have an ashtray, that they are passed the hors d'oeuvres, that they are offered a second helping of the food, that their wine glasses are replenished when necessary, that their coffee is served to them as they like it. And I want a wife who knows that sometimes I need a night out by myself.

I want a wife who is sensitive to my sexual needs, a wife who makes love 7 passionately and eagerly when I feel like it, a wife who makes sure that I am satisfied. And, of course, I want a wife who will not demand sexual attention when I am not in the mood for it. I want a wife who assumes the complete responsibility for birth control, because I do not want more children. I want a wife who will remain sexually faithful to me so that I do not have to clutter up my intellectual life with jealousies. And I want a wife who understands that *my* sexual needs may entail more than strict adherence to monogamy. I must, after all, be able to relate to people as fully as possible.

If, by chance, I find another person more suitable as a wife than the wife I 8 already have, I want the liberty to replace my present wife with another one. Naturally, I will expect a fresh, new life; my wife will take the children and be solely responsible for them so that I am left free.

When I am through with school and have a job, I want my wife to quit work- 9 ing and remain at home so that my wife can more fully and completely take care of a wife's duties.

My God, who *wouldn't* want a wife? ■ 10

For Discussion: What is Brady really saying when she says she wants a wife? What solutions would you propose for the problem of who should be responsible for all of the tasks and duties described in this essay?

E. CLASS DISCUSSION AND WRITING ASSIGNMENT: INTERNATIONAL ARGUMENT

Read the following article, in which the author explains what "yes" (*hai*) means in Japanese. Are there other examples of words, gestures, customs, beliefs, or values like this one that could create confusion or distrust among people from different cultures? Draw on the experiences of international students both in and outside of class and on international news reports. Write a paper in which you explain one of the differences you have identified, along with what would be required to achieve common ground and better understanding.

Essay 5

A SIMPLE "HAI" WON'T DO*

Reiko Hatsumi

Reiko Hatsumi writes novels as well as essays.

1   Having spent my life between East and West, I can sympathize with those who find the Japanese yes unfathomable. However, the fact that it sometimes fails to correspond precisely with the Occidental yes does not necessarily signal intended deception. . . . It marks a cultural gap that can have serious repercussions.

2   I once knew an American who worked in Tokyo. He was a very nice man, but he suffered a nervous breakdown and went back to the U.S. tearing his hair and exclaiming, "All Japanese businessmen are liars." I hope this is not true. If it were, all Japanese businessmen would be driving each other mad, which does not seem to be the case. Nevertheless, since tragedies often arise from misunderstandings, an attempt at some explanation might not be amiss.

3   A Japanese yes in its primary context simply means the other has heard you and is contemplating a reply. This is because it would be rude to keep someone waiting for an answer without supplying him with an immediate response.

4   For example: a feudal warlord marries his sister to another warlord. . . . Then he decides to destroy his newly acquired brother-in-law and besieges his castle. Being human, though, the attacking warlord worries about his sister and sends a spy to look around. The spy returns and the lord inquires eagerly, "Well, is she safe?" The spy bows and answers "*Hai,*" which means yes. We sigh with relief thinking, "Ah, the fair lady is still alive!" But then the spy continues, "To my regret she has fallen on her sword together with her husband."

5   *Hai* is also an expression of our willingness to comply with your intent even if your request is worded in the negative. This can cause complications. When I was at school, our English teacher, a British nun, would say, "Now children, you won't forget to do your homework, will you?" And we would all dutifully chorus, "Yes, mother," much to her consternation.

6   A variation of *hai* may mean, "I understand your wish and would like to make you happy but unfortunately . . ." Japanese being a language of implication, the latter part of this estimable thought is often left unsaid.

7   Is there, then, a Japanese *yes* that corresponds to the Western one? I think so, particularly when it is accompanied by phrases such as *sodesu* (It is so) and *soshimasu* (I will do so). A word of caution against the statement, "I will think about it." Though in Tokyo this can mean a willingness to give one's proposal serious

*New York Times, April 15, 1992, p. A12.

thought, in Osaka, another business center, it means a definite no. This attitude probably stems from the belief that a straightforward no would sound too brusque.

When talking to a Japanese person it is perhaps best to remember that al- 8 though he may be speaking English, he is reasoning in Japanese. And if he says "I will think about it," you should inquire as to which district of Japan he hails from before going on with your negotiations. ■

For Discussion: Give some examples of what Japanese persons may really mean when they say yes as described in this article. Do you ever say one thing and mean something else? Give an example. What effect does this have in your communication with others?

CHAPTER THREE

A Process for Reading Argument

This chapter focuses on how to identify an argumentative purpose in a text and also on how to employ active reading strategies to help you read argument. The next chapter focuses on employing active writing strategies to help you write argument. Reading and writing are artificially separated in these two chapters for the sake of instruction. In actual practice, however, they should be integrated activities. To get you started using reading and writing together, the "Write While You Read" box contains a simple idea that can have a huge impact on improving the quality of your reading. Look for other connections between the reading and writing processes while you read this chapter and the next.

You will need a variety of strategies to help you do the reading and writing required by your college courses. These strategies will be most useful to you if you approach them as *processes*. You will usually adapt your reading process to the level of difficulty and to your purpose for reading specific materials. For example, when the reading material is complex and unfamiliar and your purpose is to understand, analyze, evaluate, and perhaps write about it, you will need a well-developed and strategic reading process to help you meet the requirements of these demanding tasks. At other times, you will use a simpler process for simpler reading. Before we look at possible reading processes, however, let us consider how you can recognize an argumentative purpose in the material you read.

Write While You Read

You are probably willing to admit, along with most students, that you sometimes read without thinking. You may begin a reading assignment by counting the pages. Then you go back to stare at the words (or the computer screen) until you reach the end. During this process, your mind is blank or focused elsewhere. The best and quickest way to change this blank reading pattern is to *write while you read*. As soon as you begin reading with a pencil or pen (not a highlighter) in hand—underlining, writing ideas in the margin, summarizing, writing responses—everything changes. *You have to think to write.*

Furthermore, writing while you read helps you with two types of thinking. First, you will *think about* the material you read and perhaps even rephrase it so that it makes better sense to you. Second, you will *think beyond* the material you read and use it to help you generate ideas for your own writing. Your reading, in other words, becomes a springboard for your original thoughts and ideas. So pick up a pencil now and begin to write as you read. This process may take a little more time, but you will end up knowing far more than you would by "just reading," and your book with your annotations and ideas in it will be a valuable addition to your personal library.

RECOGNIZING WRITTEN ARGUMENT

Some texts are obviously intended as argument, and others conceal their argumentative purpose, making it more difficult to recognize. You will recognize an argumentative purpose more easily if you think of a continuum of six types of writing that ranges from obvious argument at one extreme to objective writing at the other. Each of the six types exhibits not only a different authorial intention but also a different relationship between the author and the audience.

1. *Obvious argument.* The author's purpose is clearly and obviously to take a position and to change minds or to convince others. The author's point of view and purpose are clearly expressed along with reasons and supporting details that appeal to a wide audience.

2. *Extremist argument.* Authors who are "true believers" and who write about causes or special projects sometimes use strong values and emotional language to appeal to narrow audiences who already share their views. The aim is to strengthen these views. Imagine a labor union leader, for example, who is writing to workers to convince them to strike. The author's purpose is clearly to persuade.

3. *Hidden argument.* An argumentative purpose is not always obvious. Some ostensibly objective texts, on close examination, actually favor one position over another, but not in an obvious, overt manner. One sign that the text is not

totally objective is selected and stacked supporting material that favors a particular point of view. Also, the presence of emotional language, vivid description, or emotional examples can be another sign that the author has strong opinions and intends not only to inform but also to convince the audience. For example, an author who actually favors reducing student financial aid writes an "objective" report about students who have received aid. However, all the students described in the article either left college early or defaulted on their loans, and they are described as dropouts and parasites on society. No examples of successful students are reported. Even though the author does not state a position or write this article as an obvious argument, it is still clear that the author has a position and that it manifests itself in biased reporting. The intention, even though concealed, is to convince.

4. *Unconscious argument.* Sometimes an author who is trying to write an objective report is influenced unconsciously by strong personal opinions about the subject, and the result is an unconscious intent to change people's minds. Imagine, for example, a strong pro-life newspaper reporter who is sent to write an objective expository article about an abortion clinic. It would be difficult for this individual to describe and explain the clinic without allowing negative perceptions to influence the way the facts are presented. Again, stacked or selected evidence, emotional language, quotes from authorities with well-known positions, or even pictures that establish a point of view may attest to an argumentative purpose while the author is unaware of it.

5. *Exploratory argument.* The author's purpose in exploratory articles, which are commonly found in newspapers and magazines, is to lay out and explain all of the major positions on a controversial issue. The audience is thus invited to view an issue from several perspectives and to understand all of them better. If the author has a position, it may not be revealed.

6. *Objective reporting.* Sometimes authors simply describe, explain, or report facts and ideas that everyone would accept without controversy. The author's own point of view, opinions, or interpretations are deliberately omitted. This is a pure form of expository writing. Examples include almanacs, data lists, weather reports, some news stories, and government, business, science, and technical reports. The audience reads such material to get information.

When you read and analyze argument, you will be studying and interpreting all these types of material with the exception of the last, objective reporting, and sometimes even there opinion creeps in. Now let's examine what you do at present when you read argument.

HOW DO YOU READ NOW?

You already have a reading process, but you may not have consciously adapted it to reading argument. What can you do to improve your present process for reading argument? Consider the following:

What do you do . . .

- Before you read argument?
- While you read argument?
- When the argumentative material is difficult?
- When you finish reading argument?

Many students describe their usual reading process by saying that they do nothing before they read, they then just read, they reread when the material is difficult, and they do nothing when they finish reading. If they add particular strategies for reading argument, these strategies are likely to include trying to identify both sides of the issue, trying to keep an open mind, deciding whether to agree or disagree with the author, or deciding what stand to take. Now consider what else you can do to help you read argument.

PREREADING STRATEGIES

Prereading helps you access what you know about a subject to help you interpret new, incoming material. If you know nothing about a subject, you will need to take special steps to learn more. Otherwise the new material will seem too difficult to read. Here we examine five prereading strategies to help you organize your prior knowledge about a subject, build background when you need it, and begin to analyze the material and make some predictions.

Read the Title and Background the Issue

Read the title and the first paragraph quickly to find out what is at issue. If you do not discover the issue there, read the last paragraph, where it is often stated, or read rapidly through the essay until you discover it. Then access your background on the issue by writing, in phrases only, everything that comes to mind when you think of that issue. This process is called *backgrounding.* Here is an example: Suppose you read the article "Applying to College Made Easy" that appears on page 23. You have applied to college yourself, so you have some background about this subject. Your backgrounding might include the following ideas:

Lots of work and anxiety
Filling out applications
Getting letters of recommendation
Making phone calls and waiting for replies

You can already imagine what this article might be about, and you have created a context for reading it by thinking about what you already know.

Evaluate and Improve Your Background Information

When attempts to background an issue are unsuccessful and it is clear that you lack information, use some special strategies to help you build background. Find and read some other material on the subject that you can easily understand. An encyclopedia or easier books may be good sources of such information, or you can talk with someone who does understand the material, like a professor or a fellow student. Identify words that are used repeatedly and that you do not understand. Look them up in the glossary or dictionary, or figure them out from context.

Survey the Material

Survey a book or an article before you read it to get an introduction to the major ideas and a few of the supporting details.

Books.   To survey a book (not a novel), follow these six steps in this order:

1. Read the *title,* and focus on what it tells you about the contents of the book.
2. Read the *table of contents.* Notice how the content has been divided into chapters and organized.
3. Read the *introduction.* Look for background information about the subject and author and also for information to help you read the book.
4. Examine the special *features* of the book. Are there headings and subheadings in boldface type to highlight major ideas? Is there a glossary? An index? Charts? Other visuals? A bibliography?
5. Read the title and first paragraph of the *first* and *last chapters* to see how the book begins and ends.
6. Read the title and first paragraph of the *other chapters* to get a sense of the flow of ideas.

This procedure should take about half an hour. It will introduce you to the main issue and approaches in a book, and reading will then be much easier.

Articles and Chapters.   To survey an article or a chapter in a book, follow these six steps in this order:

1. Read the *title,* and focus on the information in it.
2. Read the *introduction,* which is usually the first paragraph but can be several paragraphs long. Look for a claim and any forecasts of what is to come.
3. Read the *last paragraph,* and look for the claim.
4. Read the *headings* and *subheadings,* if there are any, to get a sense of the ideas and their sequence. Read the first sentence of each paragraph, if there are no headings, to accomplish the same goal.
5. Study the *visuals:* pictures, charts, graphs. Read their captions. They often illustrate major ideas.
6. Identify the *key words* that represent the main concepts.

Surveying an article or chapter takes ten to fifteen minutes. It introduces you to the issue, the claim, and some of the subclaims and support. Survey before you read to make reading easier; survey when you do research to get a context for the material you quote; and survey when you review to help you focus on the important ideas.

Write Out Your Present Position on the Issue

When you finish backgrounding and surveying, jot down your own current ideas and positions on the issue. This strategy will help guarantee your active interest as you read and will also promote an interaction between your ideas and the author's. Here are examples of such initial position statements, on the article on pages 54–55, "Giving People a Second Chance":

> I favor the idea of a second chance for most people—unless they really do not deserve it because they have committed a particularly horrible crime.

Make Some Predictions, and Write One Big Question

Reading is a constant process of looking back at what you know and looking ahead to predict what you think may come next. Facilitate this natural process by linking what you know with what you predict will be in the text. Write your predictions and one big question to help focus your attention. Change your predictions as you read if they are off target and also stay open to the new ideas you did not predict. Finally, try to answer your big question when you finish reading.

Here is an example of a prediction you might make about the article about giving people a second chance:

> This article will be in favor of giving the people he is writing about a second chance in life.

Here is a big question you might ask before you read:

> Who are these people, and why do they deserve a second chance?

READING STRATEGIES

You have been asked to describe how you read now. Did you indicate that you just read without doing anything in particular to improve your focus and concentration? You can often just read and understand enough, but you will usually need some special reading strategies to help you understand your college reading assignments and other complicated reading materials. Here are some suggestions to help you read such materials.

Use a Pencil to Underline and Annotate Important Ideas

As you begin to read, underline with a pen or pencil and write notes in the margin to help you concentrate and understand. These notes will also help you review and find information later. The key to marking a text is to do it selectively. Do not color an entire paragraph with a yellow highlighter. Instead, underline only the words and phrases that you can later reread and still get a sense of the whole. Then jot the major ideas in the margins, or summarize them at the ends of sections. Write the big ideas along with your personal reactions on the flyleaves of a book or at the ends of chapters or articles. If you do not own the book, write on self-stick notes and attach them to the book pages, or write on separate sheets of paper and keep them organized in a folder or in a section of your notebook.

Here is an example. The essay about girls and computers from Chapter 1 has been underlined and annotated as recommended. A brief summary has been added at the end to capture the main point. Note that this material is now very easy to understand and review.

GIRLS AND COMPUTERS

girls behind

A new report by the American Association of University Women shows that a troubling gender gap in computer use exists in high schools. Girls make up only a small percentage of students who take high-level computer courses that might lead to technology careers. Yet they are more likely than boys to take data-entry classes, the high-tech equivalent of typing.

girls think boys better

The report also found that girls tend to use computers in limited ways, such as for word processing, while boys are more likely to use computers to solve problems or to develop their own programs. In one study, girls consistently rated themselves as less competent in computers than boys. This suggests that many girls are starting to see the high-tech world as a masculine domain.

games for boys

Some of the gender gap is created outside the classroom. Computer toys are more heavily marketed to boys, and most computer games and even educational software have more male characters than female characters. But teachers sensitive to these issues could help turn the situation around.

close gap—math

In 1992, the association raised the nation's awareness of a gender gap in enrollment in math and science courses in high school. In less than a decade, that gap has been narrowed because educators worked to increase girls' participation. Now educators must insure that girls are not inadvertently left out of the computer revolution.

girls behind with computers. Need to bring up to speed like did with math.

Identify and Read the Information in the Introduction, Body, and Conclusion

The organization of ideas in argumentative texts is not very different from other texts. Much of what you read, for example, follows the easily recognizable intro-duction, main body, and conclusion format. The introduction may provide back-ground information about the issue and the author, get attention, state the main point, define important terms, or forecast some of the ideas to be developed in the main body. The main body will explain and develop the author's main point by giving reasons and support to prove it. The end or conclusion either summarizes by restating important points or concludes by stating the most important point, whatever it is that the author wants you to believe. Not all texts follow this pattern exactly, but enough of them do to justify your checking what you read against it.

Look for Claims, Subclaims, Support, and Transitions

All arguments have the structural components you are familiar with from other kinds of reading and writing. The main difference is their names. The special char-acteristics of the components of argument will be described when the Toulmin model is discussed in Chapter 5. We start using Toulmin's terms here, however, to help you get used to them. The thesis of an argument, which shapes the thinking of the entire text and states what the author finally expects you to accept or be-lieve, is called the *claim. Subclaims* are assertions or reasons that develop the claim. They are in themselves almost meaningless without further explanation. *Support* in the form of facts, opinions, evidence, and examples is the most specific material that provides additional information and further explanation. Support makes the claim and subclaims clear, vivid, memorable, and believable. *Transitions* lead the reader from one idea to another and also sometimes state the relationships among ideas. Furthermore, there is a constant movement between general and specific material in all texts, including argumentative texts, and this movement becomes apparent when the ideas are presented in various types of outline form.

Understand the Key Words

Sometimes figuring out the meaning of one word in a difficult passage will sud-denly make the whole passage easier to understand. For example, if you read the title of the article on pages 58–59, "A Simple 'Hai' Won't Do," you may be baffled by it until you learn that *hai* means "yes" in Japanese. Once you have that information, the article makes much more sense.

Unfortunately, many of us simply ignore words we do not know. Our eyes slide over unfamiliar words because there is nothing in our background to help us make sense of them. More thorough readers may stop when they see a strange word, discover they are stumped, and either dismiss the word or make an effort to puzzle it out.

When reading material suddenly seems difficult, go back and look for words you do not understand. Try to identify the key words, those that represent major concepts. In this chapter, *backgrounding* and *rhetorical situation* are examples of key words. First, read the context in which you find the word to help you understand it. A word may be defined in a sentence, a paragraph, or even several paragraphs. Major concepts in argument are often defined at length, and understanding their meaning will be essential to an understanding of the entire argument. If the context does not give you enough information, try the glossary, the dictionary, or another book on the subject. Remember that major concepts require longer explanations than a single synonym. Synonyms are useful for other minor words that are less critical to the understanding of the entire passage.

Analyze the Rhetorical Situation

Rhetorical situation is a term coined by Professor Lloyd Bitzer to describe the elements that combine to constitute a communication situation.[1] To understand these elements as they apply to argument helps us understand what motivates the argument in the first place, who the author is, who the intended audience is, how the audience might react to it, and how we as readers might also respond. By analyzing and understanding the rhetorical situation, we gain critical insight into the entire context as well as the parts of an argument, and this insight ultimately helps us evaluate its final success or failure. Analyzing the rhetorical situation is an important critical reading strategy that can be initiated during the prereading stages but should continue to be used as a tool for analysis throughout the reading process.

According to Bitzer, a rhetorical situation has five elements: the *text,* the *reader* or audience, the *author,* the *constraints,* and the *exigence* or cause. Use the acronym TRACE, from the initial letters of these five words, to help you remember these five elements. Now look at each of them to see how they can help you understand and evaluate argumentative writing.

The *text* is the written argument, which has unique characteristics of its own that can be analyzed. These include such things as format, organization, argumentative strategies, language, and style.

The potential *reader* or audience for the text must care enough to read and pay attention, to change its perceptions as a result, and perhaps to mediate change or act in a new way. A rhetorical situation invites such audience responses and outcomes. Most authors have a targeted or intended reading audience in mind. You may identify with the targeted audience, or you may not, particularly if you belong to a different culture or live in a different time. As you read, compare your reactions to the text with the reactions you imagine the targeted or intended reading audience might have had.

The *author* writes an argument to convince a particular audience. You can analyze the author's position, motives, values, and varying degrees of expertise.

---

[1] Lloyd Bitzer, "The Rhetorical Situation, "*Philosophy and Rhetoric* 1 (January 1968): 1–14.

Constraints include the people, events, values, beliefs, and traditions that constrain or limit the targeted audience and cause it to analyze the situation and react to it in a particular way. They also include the character, background, and style of the author that limit or influence him or her to write in a certain way. Constraints may bring people together or drive them apart. They influence the amount of common ground that will be established between an author and an audience. Here are some examples of constraints: an audience feels constrained to mistrust the media because it thinks reporters exaggerate or lie; reporters believe it is their responsibility to expose character flaws in candidates running for office, so they feel constrained to do so at every opportunity; candidates think voters want to hear rousing platitudes, so they deliver rousing platitudes; voters have lost their faith in public leaders, so they do not want to vote; people are too disturbed by the severity of the environmental crisis to want to listen to information about it, so they shut it out; people are too angry about destroyed property to consider peaceful solutions, so they threaten war; some welfare recipients fear that new changes in the system will deny food and shelter to them and their children, so they do not respond to training opportunities that may benefit them. Or, to continue with closer examples, you parked your car in a no-parking zone because you were late to class, but the police feel constrained by law to give you a ticket; you are angry because your college has made errors with your tuition payments before; you believe everyone should share the household chores, but your partner disagrees; you must transfer credits to graduate on time; without child care, you cannot attend classes; you do not particularly value college athletics, and you do want classes available when you can take them. These constraining circumstances will influence the way you react to the issues in the material you read.

Exigence is the real-life dramatic situation that signals that something controversial has occurred and that people should try to make some sense of it. Exigence is a problem to be solved, a situation that requires some modifying response from an audience. Here are some examples of exigence for argument: people become suspicious of genetically engineered foods because of newspaper reports; several parents report that their children can access pornography on the Internet; a high school student shoots and kills several fellow students; too many homeless people are living in the streets and subways; a third-world country threatens to resume nuclear testing; politicians refuse to sign a nuclear test ban treaty; a football player is badly injured in a game and the fans of the opposing team cheer in delight; human rights are being violated in another country. To bring the idea of exigence closer, here are some examples that might provide you with the exigence to engage in argument: you get a parking ticket; your registration is canceled for lack of payment but you know you paid; you and the person you live with are having trouble deciding who should do the household chores; you try to transfer in some past college credits and your current institution won't accept them; there is no day care provided on your campus for young children; athletics are draining campus resources and there aren't enough classes. In all cases, something is wrong, imperfect, defective, or in conflict. Exigence invites analysis and discussion, and sometimes also a written response to encourage both individual public awareness and discourse about problematic situations.

The following set of questions will help you analyze the rhetorical situation and get insight into its component parts.

1. *Text.* What kind of a text is it? What are its special qualities and features? What is it about?
2. *Reader or audience.* Who is the **targeted audience?** What is the nature of this group? Can it be convinced? What are the anticipated outcomes? How do **you as a reader** compare with the targeted audience? What are your constraints? How much common ground do you share with the author? What is your initial position? Are you motivated to change your mind or modify the situation? How?
3. *Author.* Who is the author? Consider background, experience, education, affiliations, and values. What is motivating the author to write?
4. *Constraints.* What special constraining circumstances will influence the audience's and author's responses to the subject? What beliefs, attitudes, prejudices, people, habits, events, circumstances, or traditions are already in place that will limit or constrain their perceptions?
5. *Exigence.* What happened to cause this argument? Why is it perceived as a defect or problem? Is it new or recurring?

Here is an example of an analysis of the rhetorical situation for the article "We Knew What Glory Was," pages 48–51.

Example

1. *Text.* This is an argumentative essay that uses narrative and description to convince the readers that it is wrong to burn African American churches.
2. *Reader or audience.* The targeted readers are people who have religious values and who enjoy reminiscing about the past. The author expects the readers to identify with her and to be horrified by the burning of the churches.
3. *Author.* The author is an African American woman whose father was the Baptist minister of a traditional black church in Connecticut. Every August he took his family to visit the South and the churches there. The author recalls these trips.
4. *Constraints.* Both the author and most readers are constrained by tradition, which includes the idea that churches should provide safety and sanctuary for their congregations. Churches and their members should automatically be protected from harm.
5. *Exigence.* Arsonists were deliberately burning black churches throughout the South at the time that the author wrote this article.

Read with an Open Mind, and Analyze the Common Ground Between You and the Author

Suppose you now begin to read the article on affirmative action, "A View from Berkeley," by Chang-Lin Tien on pages 51–53. Consider some unfortunately typical responses that readers of argument sometimes make at this point. Suppose you disagree strongly with the article because you believe affirmative action provides unfair and unnecessary advantages for minorities. You may be tempted not to read at all or to read hastily and carelessly, dismissing the author as wrongheaded or mistaken. Or if your initial reaction had been different and you happen to agree with this author's ideas, you might read carefully, marking the best passages and insisting on reading them aloud to someone else. If you are neutral on this issue, with opinions on neither side, you might read with less interest and even permit your mind to wander. These responses, as you can see, will distract you and interfere in negative ways with your understanding of the article. Once you become aware of such unproductive responses, however, you can compensate for them by analyzing the common ground between you and the author and using this information to help you read more receptively and nonjudgmentally. What common ground do you have with Chancellor Tien? When you have established that, try to generate interest, read with an open mind, and suspend major critical judgment until you have finished reading his article. Finally, reassess your original position to determine whether you now have reason to modify or change your perspective on the issue.

As you assess the common ground you think you share with the author, you can use written symbols to indicate how much or how little of it may exist: ○ can mean you and the author are basically alike in your views and share common ground; ◯◯ can mean you are alike on some ideas but not on others and share some common ground; ○○ can mean your ideas are so different from the author's that there is no common ground; and X can mean that you are neutral in regard to the subject, that you consequently have little or no interest in it, and that you are not likely to agree, disagree, or establish common ground with the author. To avoid reading problems, you will now need to compensate for common ground differences that might interfere with comprehension. The symbols ○ ○, for disagreement and no common ground, and X, for neutral and no common ground should signal that you will have to use all of the active strategies for reading that you can muster to give these authors a fair hearing.

STRATEGIES FOR READING DIFFICULT MATERIAL

Read a difficult text all the way through once, to the end, without stopping. You will understand some of it, but not all. Give yourself a comprehension score on a scale of 0 to 10, with 10 high. Now write brief lists of what you do and do not understand. Identify the words that are used repeatedly that you do not understand. Look them up in the glossary or dictionary, and analyze how they are used in context. Next, reread the material, using active reading strategies to help you get meaning. Add more items to the list of material that you can understand, and assess what you still do not understand. Give yourself a new comprehension score. You may want to reread again to gain even better understanding of what you could not understand on the first two readings. As a final step, get together with a fellow classmate or someone else who has read the material, and discuss it until you both understand it better. Consider how you would rate your comprehension now.

POSTREADING STRATEGIES

Postreading strategies help you think about the ideas in your reading and understand them better. They also improve your memory of what you have read. Here are several postreading strategies that will work for you.

Monitor Your Comprehension, Check the Accuracy of Your Predictions, and Answer Your Questions

At this point, insist on understanding. The results of reading are very much a private product that belongs to you and no one else. Only you can monitor and check your understanding of what you have read. One way to check is to look away to see if you can recite from memory the claim and some of the subclaims and support. If you cannot do this right after you have finished reading, you will probably not be able to do it later in discussion or on an exam. Reread, actively using reading strategies, and try again. Comprehension checks of this type help you concentrate and understand. Check your prereading predictions to see if they were accurate. You may need to change them. See if you can now answer the question you posed before you started reading.

Discover the Organization, and Write Summaries or Simplified Outlines

Summaries condense and restate material in a briefer form that will help you understand and remember it. Outlines lay out the ideas in a visual form and show how they are related to each other. To make an outline, write the claim, the most general idea, at the left-hand margin, indent the subclaims under the claim, and indent the support—the specific facts, opinions, examples, illustrations, other data, and statistics—even further. You may not always need to write an outline. Sometimes you can make a simple mental outline and use it to help you remember the claim and some of the ideas that support and develop it.

Two types of summaries can be useful to you. One, written in phrases only, is exemplified on page 66 at the end of the annotated article about girls and computers. This type of summary can help you review main ideas quickly.

A second type of summary, written in paragraph form with complete sentences, helps you understand an article and demonstrate to others that you have understood it. The following is an example of a summary of this second type that has been written in complete sentences. It is a summary of the essay "Why I Want a Wife" on pages 56–57. The summary is followed by an example of a simplified outline of this same essay.

Summary of "Why I Want a Wife." Judy Brady's newly divorced friend wants a wife, which makes Brady reflect on why she, herself, might also like a wife. A wife could take care of the children and run the household while Brady goes back to school. Even though the wife also works, she will be expected to take care of the home as well. A wife could cook, clean, take care of the clothes, never complain, and listen to Brady when she wants to talk. A wife could arrange all of the family's social life and also provide a great sex life. If the wife does not perform adequately, the wife could be replaced with a better one. Brady concludes, "Who *wouldn't* want a wife?"

Simplified Outline of "Why I Want a Wife"

Claim: I would like to have a wife
    Subclaims: I could go back to school.
            My wife would work and run the household.
    Support: She would take care of the children,
    (examples) keep the house clean,
          put my things away,
          fix good meals,
          listen to me,
          take care of my social life, and
          be sensitive to my sexual needs.
Subclaims: My wife could be replaced if she didn't work out
    Support: If so, she gets the children and I start a new life.
Subclaims: When I finish school, my wife quits her job, stays home,
          and becomes a better wife.
          Who wouldn't want a wife?

Make a Map

As an alternative to summaries or outlines, make a map of the ideas in a text. For many students, maps are the preferred way to reduce and reorganize the material they read. To make a map, write the most important idea, the claim, in a circle or on a line, and then attach major subclaims and support to it. Make your map in very brief form. Figures 3.1 and 3.2 are possible maps of the essays "Why I Want a

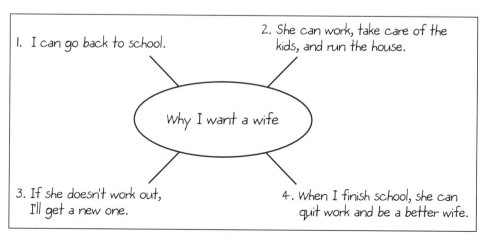

Figure 3.1 Map of Ideas for "Why I Want a Wife"

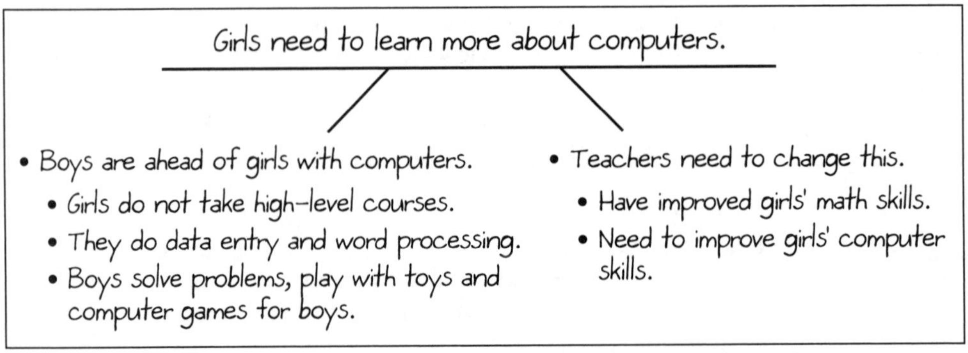

Figure 3.2   **Map of Ideas for "Girls and Computers"**

Wife" and "Girls and Computers." You can be creative with map formats. Use whatever layout will give you a quick picture of the major ideas.

Think Critically and Write a Response

By the time you have written a summary, an outline, or a map to help you understand the ideas in an argumentative essay, you will also have formed some opinions of your own on the issue. Write a response to the essay to help you capture some of your ideas in writing. These ideas can often be starting points for future essays of your own. Here are some ideas and suggestions for what you might include in a response.

- Write your position now.
- Compare it with your initial position before you read the essay.
- Compare the author's position with your own. Do you agree or disagree?
- Add examples, suggestions, or other ideas of your own that the essay made you think about.
- What do you finally think about the essay? Is it convincing or not?

Here is an example of a response to the essay "Why I Want a Wife":

This essay is a condemnation of men who expect their wives to work and take care of the house without any help. This essay has not changed my mind. I agreed with Brady before I read it, and I agree even more strongly now. The essay is humorous, but it is also an angry response to the division of labor issue that exists in many households. Every household needs a housewife to do the chores and keep the family's life running smoothly. Some, but certainly not all, women take on these responsibilities with a reasonable degree of contentment. Others do not, either because of outside work or because they hate this type of work. Families have to solve this problem to avoid constant conflict. A division of labor exists in every other workplace. Why can't a reasonable division of labor also be created at home? I favor an equal division of chores for all members of the household so that everyone gets fair and equal treatment.

ORGANIZING A PROCESS FOR READING ARGUMENT

The reading process for argument explained in this chapter and summarized in Box 3.1 integrates prereading, reading, and postreading strategies and incorpo-

---

Reading Argument

PREREADING STRATEGIES

- **Read the title and first paragraph; background the issue.** Identify the issue. Free-associate and write words and phrases that the issue brings to mind.
- **Evaluate and improve your background.** Do you know enough? If not, read or discuss to get background. Look up a key word or two.
- **Survey the material.** Identify the claim (the main assertion) and some of the subclaims (the ideas that support it); notice how they are organized. Do not slow down and read.
- **Write out your present position on the issue.**
- **Make some predictions, and write one big question.** Jot down two or three ideas that you think the author may discuss, and write one question you would like to have answered.

READING STRATEGIES

- **Use a pencil to underline and annotate** the ideas that seem important. Write a brief summary at the end.
- **Identify** and **read** the information in the **introduction, body,** and **conclusion.**
- **Look for the claim, subclaims, and support.** Box the **transitions** to highlight relationships between ideas and changes of subject.
- **Find the key words** that represent major concepts, and jot down meanings if necessary.
- **Analyze the rhetorical situation.** Remember TRACE: text, reader, author, constraints, exigence.
- **Read with an open mind, and analyze the common ground** between you and the author.

STRATEGIES FOR READING DIFFICULT MATERIAL

- **Read all the way through once** without stopping.
- **Write a list** of what you understand and what you do not understand.

(continued)

BOX 3.1 A Summary of the Reading Process for Argument Explained in This Chapter

- **Identify words and concepts** you do not understand, look them up, and analyze how they are used in context.
- **Reread the material,** and add to your list of what you can and cannot understand.
- **Reread again** if you need to.
- **Discuss the material** with someone who has also read the material and get further clarification and understanding.

POSTREADING STRATEGIES

- **Monitor your comprehension.** Insist on understanding. Check the accuracy of your **predictions,** and answer your **question.**
- **Analyze the organization,** and write either a **simplified outline** or a **summary** to help you understand and remember. Or make a **map.**
- **Write a response** to help you think.
- **Compare your present position** with your position before you read the argument.
- **Evaluate the argument,** and decide whether it is convincing or not.

BOX 3.1 *(continued)*

rates writing at every stage. Before you embark on this process, however, here are three cautionary notes:

1. Read as you usually do, using your own reading process for most reading. Add strategies either when you are not getting enough meaning or when your comprehension is breaking down altogether.
2. Be advised that no one uses all of the reading strategies described in this chapter all of the time. Instead, you should select those that are appropriate to the task, that is, appropriate for a particular type of material and for your reading purpose. You need to practice all of the strategies so that you are familiar with them, and you will be given an opportunity to do so in the exercises and activities. Later, in real-life reading, you will be selective and use only strategies that apply to a particular situation.
3. Even though the strategies will be laid out in an apparent order under the various headings, there is no set order for employing them. You may find yourself stopping to do some prereading in the middle of a difficult text, or you may stop to summarize a section of material, a postreading strategy, before you continue reading. The order of presentation simply makes the strategies easier to explain and use.

The reading strategies described in this chapter—backgrounding, predicting, asking questions, surveying, analyzing the rhetorical situation, summarizing, writing simple outlines, making maps, and writing responses—all work. They help you access what you already know, relate it to new material, see the parts as well as the whole, rephrase the material in your own words, reduce it to a manageable size, and think critically about it. Research studies have demonstrated that these activities help readers understand, analyze, remember, and think about the material they read.

REVIEW QUESTIONS

1. What are some of the signs of a hidden argumentative purpose in an ostensibly objective essay?
2. What are the five elements in the rhetorical situation? Use TRACE to help you remember.
3. What are some prereading strategies that you will now want to use?
4. What are some reading strategies that you will now want to use?
5. What are some postreading strategies that you will now want to use?
6. What can you do when the material is difficult to understand?

EXERCISES AND ACTIVITIES

A. CLASS DISCUSSION: RECOGNIZING WRITTEN ARGUMENT

The following newspaper article was published on the front page of the *New York Times* as an objective story about some people in Los Angeles after riots in 1992 that were a reaction to the acquittal of four police who beat an African American man named Rodney King. First, identify what seems to be the main issue in this article. It is not directly stated. Then read the article carefully to see if you can recognize the author's attitudes, feelings, and opinions toward the subject at issue. What is the author's intention in this article? To explain? To convince? Or both? What does the author hope you will think when you finish reading? Justify your answer with specific examples from the article.

JOBS ILLUMINATE WHAT RIOTS HID: YOUNG IDEALS*   *Essay 1*

Sara Rimer

W hen Disneyland came two weeks ago to the First A.M.E. Church in South- 1
Central Los Angeles to hold interviews for 200 summer jobs, it was a goodwill gesture born of the riots.

When more than 600 young men and women, many in coats and ties or 2
dresses showed up, the Disney officials were taken aback.

America has been bombarded with television images of the youth of South- 3
Central Los Angeles: throwing bricks, looting stores, beating up innocent motorists.

New York Times, June 18, 1992, pp. A1, A12.

The Disneyland staff who interviewed the applicants, ages 17 to 22, found a different neighborhood.

4   "They were wonderful kids, outstanding kids," said Greg Albrecht, a spokesman for Disneyland. "We didn't know they were there." Nor, Mr. Albrecht added, had they known that the young people of South-Central Los Angeles would be so eager to work at Disneyland.

5   Joe Fox, a spokesman for the First A.M.E. Church, said that had there been time to better publicize the Disneyland jobs, thousands would have applied. "People just want to work, period," he said. With hundreds of small businesses destroyed during the riots, jobs are harder to find than ever.

6   One of the 600 who wanted to work at Disneyland was Olivia Miles, at 18 the youngest of seven children of a nurse's aide and a disabled roofer. "My friend Lakesha's mother told us Disneyland was hiring," said Miss Miles, who has worked at McDonald's and Popeye's since she was 15. "I said: 'Disneyland! C'mon, let's go!'"

7   Miss Miles will graduate on June 30 from one of South-Central Los Angeles's public high schools, Washington Preparatory, where she has earned mostly A's and B's and was the co-captain of the drill team. Next fall, she will attend Grambling University in Louisiana.

8   Washington has 2,600 students; 70 percent are black, 30 percent are Hispanic. The principal, Marguerite LaMotte, says that as impressive as Olivia Miles is, she is not exceptional. "I have a lot of Olivia's," she said. Indeed, 118 seniors plan to attend four-year colleges and 131 will go to two-year colleges.

9   The world knows about the gang members; estimates put the number at 100,000 across Los Angeles County, and last year there were 771 gang-related homicides. No one has tried to count the young people like Olivia Miles. They are among the invisible people of South-Central Los Angeles.

10   In some ways, Miss Miles is just another high school senior. One of her favorite shows is *Beverly Hills 90210.* She admires Bill Cosby and Oprah Winfrey. She enjoys reading books by Maya Angelou. And shopping. She loves soft-spoken, 17-year-old Damon Sewell, the defensive football captain at nearby Hawthorne High School. He will go on to Grambling with her.

11   Miss Miles and Mr. Sewell and their friends who live in the neighborhood pay a terrible price because of geography. They have to worry about simply staying alive. They have friends who have been shot and killed. They can't even get dressed in the morning without thinking, red and blue are gang colors; wearing them is dangerous. Then they have to confront the stigma that comes with being young and black and from Los Angeles.

12   "The neighborhood is famous now," Miss Miles said on Saturday as she and Mr. Sewell gave a tour of the devastation. They were just 15 minutes away from Beverly Hills and Hollywood. Miss Miles's tone was plaintive. "Why did it have to be famous for a riot? Why couldn't it be famous for people getting up in the world, or making money, or being actors?"

13   Getting ahead, despite enormous obstacles, is the story of the Miles family. Her parents, Aubrey and Willie Mae Miles, grew up in the South and migrated to Los

Angeles. They started their lives together in an apartment in Watts and eventually bought a two-bedroom on 65th Street, in the heart of South-Central Los Angeles.

Olivia remembers playing softball on the block with another little girl, 14 LaRonda Jones, who became her best friend and who will attend Santa Monica Community College next year. She also remembers how scared she was at night.

"I would lie in bed and hear the police helicopters overhead," she said. 15

Her four sisters and two brothers are all high school graduates. Except for 16 22-year-old Tracy, who is home with a 2-year-old daughter, they are all working. Shirley has a job in a school cafeteria. Cynthia is a mail carrier. Jacqueline is a cashier at Dodger Stadium. William is a custodian at police headquarters. Masad drives a school bus. Olivia visited Disneyland once, when she was 8. Jacqueline took her.

Mrs. Miles said she had never been there. Admission is $28.75 for adults, $23 17 for children 3 to 11. "Disneyland's a little high for me," she said.

Olivia Miles is tall and slim and walks with her head held high. "My mama 18 tells me: 'Be the best of everything; be proud, be black, be beautiful,'" she said.

Miss Miles knew some white people when her family lived briefly in Long 19 Beach, but that was years ago. She says she wishes there were white students at her high school. "I want to learn about different cultures," she said. She believes a job at Disneyland will give her that chance.

Aubrey Miles, who is 45, says he has taken pains to tell his daughter that 20 there are good white people. They saved his life, he told her. He was putting a roof on an office building seven years ago when a vat of hot tar exploded. He was severely burned.

"The guys on the job, who were white, helped me," he said. "I was on the 21 ground, on fire. They put the fire out. One guy sat me up and put his back against my back. I could feel the connection. Then, afterward in the hospital, it was the same thing with the doctors."

Mr. Miles was speaking by telephone from Gautier, Miss. He and his wife 22 moved there last year to care for Mrs. Miles's mother. Olivia remained in Los Angeles with her sister Shirley so she could graduate with her friends.

By last September, she and Mr. Sewell were already talking about the prom. 23 It was set for May 1 in Long Beach. To save money for the big night, Mr. Sewell, whose father was recently laid off from his machinist's job at McDonnell-Douglas, worked as many hours at McDonald's as he could get.

Two days before the prom, Miss Miles still needed shoes. After school, she 24 caught the bus to the Payless store at Crenshaw Plaza. It was April 29, the day the four policemen who beat Rodney G. King were acquitted.

"This lady on the bus told me, 'Baby, you better hurry up and get in the 25 house,'" she said. "I said, 'Why what's going on?' She said, 'The verdict was not guilty.'"

Miss Miles bought her shoes—"two pairs for $24.99"—and went home. The 26 prom was postponed because of the riots. Watching the images of fire and violence engulf her neighborhood on television, she wept. "It hurt me when they beat that man in the truck up," she said. "I didn't know people could be that mean."

27   Her parents kept telephoning. "I was asking my Daddy, 'Why did this happen, why are they doing this?'" Miss Miles said. "He told me some people were just using it as an excuse, and some people were hurt that those cops didn't get any time."

28   Mr. Miles said the acquittal shattered his daughter. "She was about to lose it," he said. "She kept saying: 'Why am I working so hard? Why have you been telling me that I can achieve?' She had been sheltered. This was reality."

29   Mr. Miles, who grew up in a segregated Louisiana, said he had agonized over how to comfort her. "I didn't want her to just use it to sit on the curb and say, 'I'm black so I can't achieve,'" he said. "I told her: 'Don't let this stop you. You're going to college. Keep going on, even though you will be met with discrimination.'"

30   "I was praying, and talking to her," he said. "I was worried. I'm still worried. The summer's not over. . . ."

31   His daughter plans to be a lawyer. So does Mr. Sewell.

32   The riots presented Olivia Miles with the biggest ethical quandary of her life. "I saw people on television coming out with boxes of shoes and pretty furniture," she said. Her smile was embarrassed. "It was like Christmas. I wanted to get some. I was asking my sister if we could go. She said, 'No, you can't go out.' I thought: 'She's going to go to work. Should I get it, or shouldn't I get it? It's not fair that I can't. Everyone else is going to get stuff.'"

33   This, too, her father had foreseen. "I told her, 'There are going to be a lot of opportunities for you to get things, so just stay in the house,'" Mr. Miles said. "She knew automatically that stealing was a no-no. . . ."

34   That Sunday, Olivia was in her regular pew at the Mt. Sinai Baptist Church. "The pastor was saying, 'If you took something, shame on you. That's a sin,'" she said. She looked relieved all over again. "I was so happy."

35   Three weeks later, she and Mr. Sewell went to the prom in Long Beach. "We loved it," Mr. Sewell said. "We loved it." He was surprised, he said, when his classmates voted him prom king.

36   "I felt like a queen," Miss Miles said. Last Friday, Disneyland telephoned: She got the job. This summer, she will be selling balloons and popcorn at the amusement park, about 30 miles from her home, that calls itself "the happiest place on earth."

37   The job, which includes transportation furnished by Disneyland, will also be hers on holidays during the year. The pay is $5.25 an hour.

38   Miss Miles had made herself familiar with Disneyland's grooming code. "Good-bye, nails," she said exuberantly, holding out her long, manicured ones. "A job's a job! Disneyland's Disneyland. It's not like Popeye's or McDonald's. It's like 'Hey, girl, how'd you get that job at Disneyland?'" ■

FOR DISCUSSION: How does the description of "the kids" in South-Central Los Angeles in this essay contradict the usual stereotypes? What is the author trying to make you think about these young people? What new stereotypes are being developed? What do you think about these young people as a result of reading this essay? Have you modified any of your previous opinions?

B. WRITING ASSIGNMENT: ANALYZING THE RHETORICAL SITUATION

Read "Don't Know Much About History." Then write a 300- to 400-word paper in which you explain the rhetorical situation for this essay. Answer the following questions:

1. How would you describe the **text** itself?
2. How would you characterize the **reader or audience** that the author may have had in mind when she wrote it?
3. What do you learn about the **author?**
4. What are some of the possible **constraints** that might have influenced the author? What constraints influence you as you read this essay?
5. What is the **exigence** for this essay?

DON'T KNOW MUCH ABOUT HISTORY*

Essay 2

Roberta Israeloff

East Northport, L.I. Though I vowed, on graduation from high school in 1969, that I was leaving the suburbs forever, I now live in a town that is just 20 minutes from the one I grew up in. For all its problems and faults, suburbia offered me a superior public education, and I wanted my sons to have one, too. 1

Yet no sooner did we enroll them than I began to have misgivings. Their work did not seem to engage them, to challenge them as much as I remembered being challenged. It wasn't until last month that I was able to confirm my suspicions. 2

My eighth grader brought home a research paper assignment for his American history course. Thirty-one years ago, I took a similar course—and I saved my papers. Comparing the two assignments left no doubt: the older assignment was vastly superior. 3

Back in 1965, we were given this quotation—from a turn-of-the-century commentator named Lloyd, in a book called *William Jennings Bryan and the Campaign of 1896*—and asked to agree or disagree with it: 4

"The Free Silver movement is a fake. Free Silver is the cow-bird of the reform movement. It waited until the nest had been built by the sacrifices and labour of others, and then laid its eggs in it. . . . The People's Party has been betrayed. No party that does not lead its leaders will ever succeed." 5

It took mind-splitting work just to decipher the quotation. And then, to fulfill the assignment, my classmates and I had to explore and understand three distinct phenomena. First, we had to digest gold and silver monetary standards. We had to research the reform movement, tracing the evolution of the People's Party from its origins. We had to sift through the politics of 1896, in which the Populists had to decide whether to field their own candidate and risk losing the election, or join the Democrats and risk annihilation. 6

*New York Times, June 15, 1996, p. A11.

7   After all this, we still had to figure out for which cause Lloyd was the mouthpiece. The passage, I finally realized, was an attempt to rally the Populists to take their own course—advice not taken. They nominated Bryan, who lost to William McKinley, thereby destroying the People's Party.

8   I concluded by urging Lloyd to grow up. The point is to have your issue prevail even if your party doesn't. The People's Party may have fallen on its sword, but it did so in a good cause.

9   In their assignment, my son and his classmates had to answer three questions. To the first, "Did we have to drop the bomb on Japan?" my son argued that Harry S. Truman, as well as many others, had no idea of the full devastation the atomic bomb would cause. On the second, whether it hastened a Japanese surrender, he equivocated. To the final question—"Is it fair to use the knowledge we have in 1996 to judge decisions made nearly 50 years ago?"—he wrote, "The simple answer is no."

10   We both received the same grade on our papers—100.

11   I do not intend to disparage my son, who has always been a highly conceptual thinker and an A student, or to exalt myself, for I was not alone in my high grade. But I think these two assignments illustrate a profound diminution of educational expectations.

12   When my classmates and I fulfilled our assignment, we couldn't help but learn that the world was much more complex than we could imagine; that we had to absorb reams of information before staking claim to an opinion; that objective "information" existed only within a context and issued from a point of view, both of which had to be fully understood.

13   From my son's paper, I see no evidence that he has absorbed any of these lessons. The newer assignment—three straightforward questions positing three answers—is premised on the modern view that we are all entitled to an opinion, no matter how little we may know.

14   To be honest, the ins and outs of the election of 1896 have not stayed with me. What has endured is the value I place on scholarship, argument and critical thinking. My teacher's high hopes for us, which at the time seemed far too ambitious to be fair, became the scaffolding upon which we built our careers and the ways we define ourselves.

15   As for my son and his classmates—the class of 2000—I'm not as hopeful. We expect terrifyingly little of today's students, and they are responding in kind. ■

FOR DISCUSSION: Agree or disagree with the author's final statement, "We expect terrifyingly little of today's students, and they are responding in kind." Provide an example, just as the author did, to support your view.

C. CLASS PROJECT: CREATING A COMPOSITE OF THE CLASS'S READING PROCESS

When all class members contribute their usual strategies to a composite reading process, the result is usually a very complete description of a possible reading process. Focus on developing a process for reading argument, and write the title "Reading Argument" on the board. Under it write the four headings "Pre-reading," "Reading," "Reading Difficult Material," and "Postreading." Class members should contribute both the strategies they use and those they would like to use to each of the four lists. When the activity is completed, students may freewrite for a few minutes on the reading process that they intend to use to read argument. Freewriting is described on page 94.

D. GROUP WORK: PRACTICING THE READING PROCESS

Practice the active reading strategies described in this chapter as you work with "The Road to Unreality."

Prereading

The whole class should preread together and discuss the results of prereading as follows:

1. Read the title and the first two or three paragraphs for one minute. What is the issue? What is your present position on the issue?
2. What ideas do you predict might be discussed in this essay? What question might be answered?
3. Survey the article for two minutes. Read the first sentence in each of the remaining paragraphs. Read the last paragraph. What do you think the essay is about now?
4. How much do you understand at this point? What do you still want to find out? Give yourself a comprehension score from 0 to 10, with 10 high.

Reading

Each class member should read, underline, and annotate the essay and then discuss the following questions:

1. How would you describe the rhetorical situation? Use TRACE.
2. Was your prereading accurate? Did the issue turn out to be what you thought? How would you describe the issue now?
3. What is the claim? What are subclaims? What are examples of support?
4. What is the author's conclusion?
5. What common ground, if any, exists between you and this author?
6. How much do you understand now? Give yourself a new score from 0 to 10.

Postreading

Work in pairs to write a summary-response. Share your results with the rest of the class.

1. Discusss the essay, decide what should be in a summary, and write a summary.
2. Discusss your summaries, and write a response.
3. Read your summary-response to the class.
4. How much do you understand now? Give yourself a score from 0 to 10. How much have your scores improved since your prereading score?

Essay 3

THE ROAD TO UNREALITY*

Mark Slouka

1   In 1990, a reporter for the *New York Times,* following the famous case of a man accused of murdering his pregnant wife and then blaming the assault on an unknown black assailant, asked a neighbor of the couple for her thoughts on the tragedy. Do you accept his story? she was asked. Does it seem possible to you, knowing this man, that he made up the whole thing? "I don't know," the woman said, "I'm dying for the movie to come out so I can see how it ends."[1]

2   I don't think this woman was joking. Or being cynical. Or even evasive. I think she simply meant what she said. For her, a TV movie about the tragedy would tell her—more accurately than her own experience—what to believe. It would settle for her what was real. Less than a year later, the made-for-television movie *Good Night, Sweet Wife: A Murder in Boston* presumably did just that.

3   I bring up this episode for the light it sheds on an important cultural trend, a trend so pervasive as to be almost invisible: our growing separation from reality.[2] More and more of us, whether we realize it or not, accept the copy as the original. Increasingly removed from experience, overdependent on the representations of reality that come to us through television and the print media, we seem more and more willing to put our trust in intermediaries who "re-present" the world to us.

4   The problem with this is one of communication; intermediaries are notoriously unreliable. In the well-known children's game of telephone, a whispered message is passed along from person to person until it is garbled beyond recognition. If we think of that original message as truth, or reality, we stand today at the end of a long line of interpreters. It's a line that's been growing longer throughout the century. And now, accustomed to our place at the end of that line, we've begun to accept the fictions that reach us as the genuine article. This is not good news. For one thing, it threatens to make us stupid. For another, it makes us, collectively, gullible as children: we believe what we are told. Finally, it can make us dangerous.

5   When did we start accepting abstractions for the real thing? Most answers point roughly to the beginning of this century. Before 1900, daily life for the majority of individuals was agrarian, static, local—in other words, not that different from what it had been for centuries. The twentieth century, however, altered the pace and pattern of daily life forever. Within two generations, the old world (for better or worse) was gone. Its loss meant the loss of two things that had always grounded us: our place within an actual community and our connection to a particular physical landscape.[3]

6   What started us on the road to unreality? Though the catalog reads like a shopping list of many of the century's most dramatic trends—urbanization, consumerism, increasing mobility, loss of regionality, growing alienation from the

*Mark Slouka, *War of the Worlds* (New York: Basic Books, 1995), pp. 1–4.

landscape, and so on—technology, their common denominator, was the real force behind our journey toward abstraction.

A single example may make my point. As everyone knows, unreality increases with speed. Walking across a landscape at six miles an hour, we experience the particular reality of place: its smells, sounds, colors, textures, and so on. Driving at seventy miles an hour, the experience is very different. The car isolates us, distances us; the world beyond the windshield—whether desert mesa or rolling farmland—seems vaguely unreal. At supersonic speeds, the divorce is complete. A landscape at 30,000 feet is an abstraction, as unlike real life as a painting. 7

It's an unreality we've grown used to. Habit has dulled the strangeness of it. We're as comfortable with superhuman speed—and the level of abstraction it brings with it—as we are with, say, the telephone, which in a single stroke distanced us from a habit as old as our species: talking to one another face-to-face. We forget that initial users of the telephone (our grandmothers and grandfathers) found it nearly impossible to conceptualize another human being beyond the inanimate receiver; in order to communicate, they had to personify the receiver and speak *to* it, as to some mechanical pet, rather than *through* it to someone else. Today, that kind of instinctive attachment to physical reality seems quaint. 8

We've come a long way, very quickly. What surprises us now, increasingly, is the shock of the real: the nakedness of face-to-face communication, the rough force of the natural world. We can watch hours of nature programming, but place us in a forest or a meadow and we don't know quite what to do with ourselves. We look forward to hanging out at The Brick with Chris on *Northern Exposure* but dread running into our neighbor while putting out the trash. There has come to be something almost embarrassing about the unmediated event; the man or woman who takes out a musical instrument at a party and offers to play is likely to make everyone feel a bit awkward. It's so naked, somehow. We're more comfortable with its representation: Aerosmith on MTV, Isaac Stern or Eric Clapton on CD. 9

And now, as we close out the century, various computer technologies threaten to take our long journey from reality to its natural conclusion. They are to TV or videoconferencing what the Concorde is to the car. They have the capacity to make the partially synthetic environments we already inhabit complete—to remove us, once and for all, from reality. ■ 10

NOTES

1. Constance L. Hays, "Illusion and Tragedy Coexist After a Couple Dies," *New York Times,* 7 January 1990.
2. I am aware, of course, that the term *reality,* problematic since Plato, has lately become a political minefield. So as not to be misunderstood, then, let me be as clear as possible. I have no problem with those who argue that reality, like taste, is subjective—a product of one's race, gender, economic class, education, and so on. These qualifications strike me as good and true. At the same time, however, I believe that under the strata of subjectivity, of language and perspective, lies a bedrock of fact: neo-Nazis in Köln or California may define the Holocaust

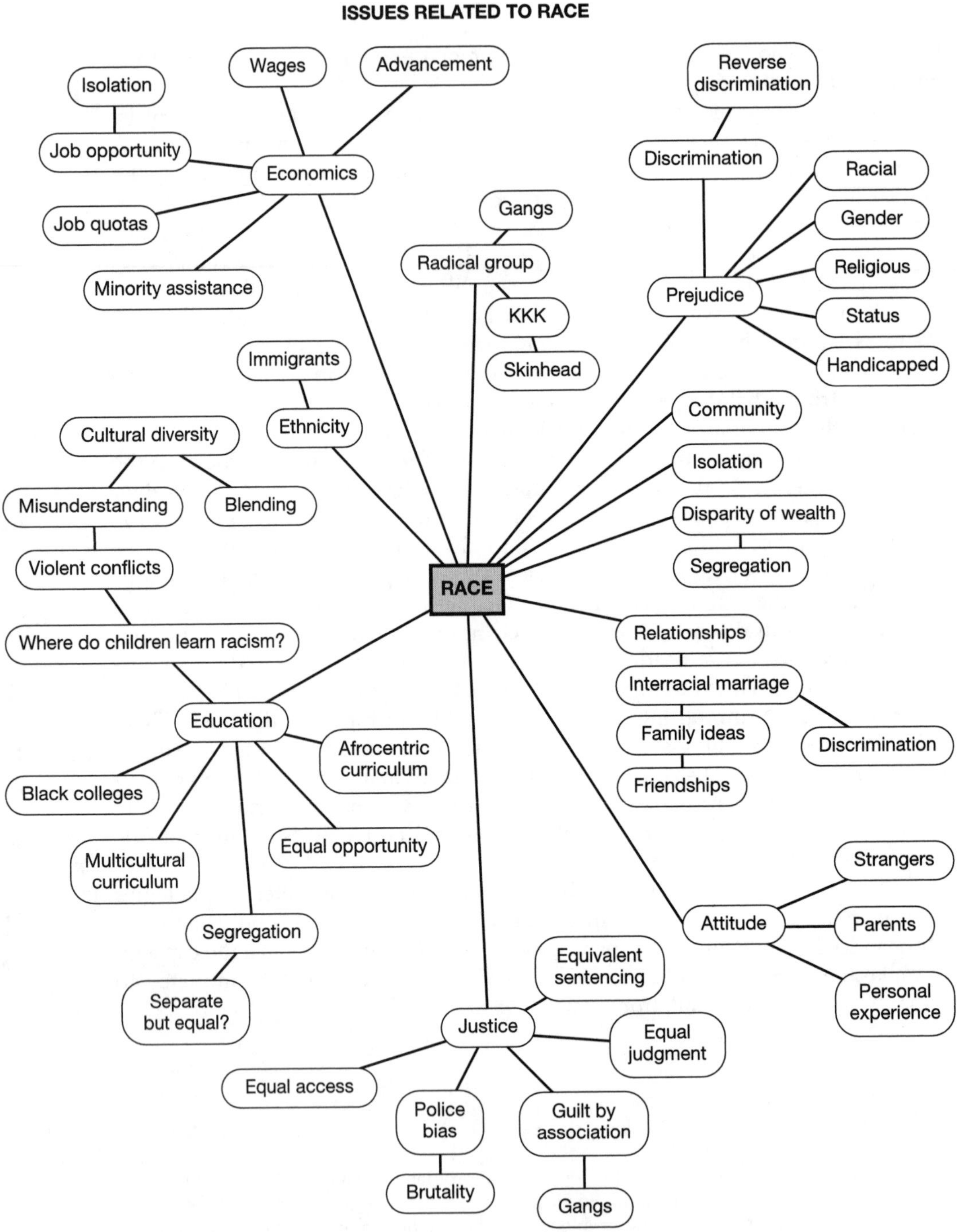

ISSUES RELATED TO RACE

Figure 3.3 A Map Can Help You Discover Specific Related Issues for Paper Topics
Designed by Eric West, Patricia Pulido, Ruby Chan, and Sharon Young. Used with permission.

differently than I do, yet the historical *fact* stands firm. It is *this* kind of reality—immutable, empirical, neither historically nor culturally relative—that I refer to here.

3. The rapid acceleration of cultural change in the twentieth century, of course, is a historical truism. One of the most vivid documents recording this transformation in American culture (it originally appeared in 1929) is Robert S. Lynd and Helen M. Lynd, *Middletown: A Study in Contemporary American Culture* (New York: Harcourt Brace Jovanovich, 1959).

FOR DISCUSSION: Provide at least one example of your own to support the author's view that human beings are losing touch with reality and another example to support the opposing view. Do you agree or disagree with this author? Provide some reasons for your answer.

E. WRITING ASSIGNMENT: THE SUMMARY-RESPONSE PAPER

1. Select the issue area in "The Reader" that interests you the most. Read the "Rhetorical Situation" section for that issue. Then select one of the issue questions in that area, and read the set of essays related to that question. Write a one-page summary-response paper for each essay. Accomplish this by dividing a piece of paper in half. Write a summary on the top half and your response on the bottom half. Refer to the sample summary on pages 72–73 and the sample response on page 74 to help you.

2. Find an article related to your issue, and write a one-page summary response paper about it.

F. GROUP WORK: CLASS MAPS

Some classes select an issue that all students will write about, others form groups around four or five issues that are selected by the groups, and some classes decide that each student will write on individual issues. Whether you are working with a group or alone, a map can often help you focus and clarify your issue, see its various aspects, and provide ideas for developing it.

To make a map, write the broad issue in a circle in the center of a page. Think of as many related aspects of that issue that you can, and attach them to the broad issue. When you have completed the map, identify the aspect or aspects of the issue that interest you or your group. See if this aspect of the broad issue area can now be narrowed, expanded, or modified in some other way as a result of seeing it in this larger perspective.

Figure 3.3 is a map of the issue area *race* that was made by some of the students who test-read this book. They made this map after they had surveyed the articles about race and culture in "The Reader." The map answers the question, "What are the issues related to race?"

CHAPTER FOUR

A Process for Writing Argument

This chapter will provide you with the expertise, confidence, and motivation that you will need to write arguments of your own on issues that are compellingly important to you. This chapter parallels Chapter 3, which covers the reading process, except that here the focus is on the writing process. You will be invited to analyze and describe your present process for writing argument and then to consider ways to improve this process. You will also practice the process by writing an exploratory paper in which you describe several perspectives on a single issue.

Chapter 3 introduced the concept that reading and writing should be integrated processes, and you were advised to write as part of your reading process. Writing while you read helps you understand a text better, and it helps you think beyond a text to develop ideas of your own. The "Read While You Write" box contains a corollary idea that can have a similarly powerful impact on the quality of your writing.

You will usually adapt your writing process to the specific writing task at hand. When you are expected to write long, complicated papers that rely on research in outside sources, you will need a well-developed writing process composed of a variety of thinking and writing strategies. At other times you will need a less elaborate process for simpler papers. A writing process makes the most difficult writing tasks seem less difficult. It also helps you avoid procrastination and the discomforts of writer's block.

Read While You Write

You may at times write without thinking very much. You find an idea, write something "off the top of your head," and turn it in, perhaps without even reading it over. Or you may try to write and find that you have nothing to say. One of the best ways to convert this blank writing to thoughtful writing is to read as part of your writing process. Reading while you write will provide you with background on your subject, new ideas to write about, fresh perspectives on your issue, and evidence and supporting details for your paper. It will at the same time suggest ways to solve writing problems as you read to understand how other writers have solved them.

HOW DO YOU WRITE NOW?

You already have a writing process, and to make it useful for writing argument, you will need to adapt it to that purpose. Begin by thinking first about what you do when you write argument.

What do you do . . .

- Before you write the draft of an argument paper?
- While you are writing the draft of an argument paper?
- When you get stuck?
- When you finish writing the draft of an argument paper?

What can you add to your present process to improve your ability to write argument? One idea is to write at all stages of the process, since writing helps you learn and also helps you think. Start writing ideas as soon as you begin thinking about your issue. Most people are especially creative and insightful during the early stages of a new writing project. Continue writing while you are thinking and gathering materials, organizing your ideas, and writing, rewriting, and revising your final copy. Notes and ideas on sheets of paper, on cards, and in notebooks are useful, as are lists, maps, various types of outlines, responses to research, drafts, and rewrites.

You must also be prepared to jot down ideas at any time during the process. Once your reading and thinking are under way, your subconscious mind takes over. At odd times you may suddenly see new connections or think of a new example, a new idea, a beginning sentence, or a good organizational sequence for the main ideas. Insights like these often come to writers when they first wake up. Plan to keep paper and pencil available so that you can take notes when good ideas occur to you.

Now consider what else you might do to improve your present process for writing argument. Focus on what you can do before you write, while you write, when you are stuck, and when you are working to finish your paper.

PREWRITING STRATEGIES

Prewriting is creative, and creativity is delicate to teach because it is individual. Still, like most writers, you will need directed prewriting strategies from time to time, either to help you get started on writing or to help you break though writer's blocks. Here are some suggestions to help you get organized, access what you already know, think about it, and plan what more you need to learn. You will not use all of these suggestions. Some, however, may become your favorite prewriting strategies.

Get Organized to Write

Some people develop elaborate rituals like cleaning the house, sharpening the pencils, laying out special pens, putting on comfortable clothes, chewing a special flavor of gum, or making a cup of coffee to help them get ready to write. These rituals help them get their minds on the writing task, improve their motivation to write, and help them avoid procrastination and writer's block. A professional writer, describing what she does, says she takes a few moments before she writes to imagine her work as a completed and successful project. She visualizes it as finished, and she thinks about how she will feel at that time.[1]

Creating a place to write is an essential part of getting organized to write. A desk and a quiet place at home or in the library work best for most students. Still, if ideal conditions are not available, you can develop alternative places like a parked car on a quiet street, an empty classroom, the kitchen or dining room table, or a card table in an out-of-the-way corner of a room.

Writing projects usually require stacks of books and papers that, ideally, one can leave out and come back to at any time. If you cannot leave them out, however, use a folder, briefcase, or box to keep everything in one safe place. You can then quickly spread your work out again when it is time to write. You will need a system to keep these writing materials organized. You may have idea notes, research notes, lists and outlines, and drafts at various stages of completion to keep track of. Categorize this material, keep it in stacks, and arrange the material in each stack in the order in which you will probably use it.

Finally, make a decision about the writing equipment you will use. The major choices will be the computer or typewriter, paper and pens or pencils, or some combination of these. Experiment with different methods, and decide which is best for you. Most students prefer computers for the same reasons that many professional writers like them: writing is faster, and the copy is easier to read and revise. A disadvantage of computers is that some people write too much. They literally write everything that occurs to them, and some of it is undeveloped, poorly organized, or off the subject. If you tend to write too much, you can solve your problem by cutting ferociously when you revise.

---

[1]Barbara Neely, "Tools for the Part-Time Novelist," *Writer*, June 1993, p. 17.

Understand the Assignment and Schedule Time

You will need to analyze the writing assignment and find time to do it. Divide the assignment into small, manageable parts, assign a sufficient amount of time for each part, set deadlines for completing each part, and use the time when it becomes available. Below is an example.

Assignment. Write a five- to six-page, typed, double-spaced argument paper in which you identify an issue of your choice, take a position, make a claim, and support it so that it is convincing to an audience of your peers. Do as much reading as you need to do, but plan to draw material from at least five sources when you write your paper. Use MLA style (explained in the Appendix to Chapter 10) to document your sources and prepare your bibliography.

Analysis of Assignment

Week 1

Select an issue from "The Reader," and write down some ideas.	2 hours Tuesday night
Read the articles on your issue in "The Reader," think, and take notes; write a first draft.	3 hours Thursday night
Read the draft to a peer group in class to get ideas for additional research.	Friday's class
Do research in the library or on the Internet to fill in the needs of the first draft.	3 hours Saturday

Week 2

Incorporate research and write a second draft.	3 hours Thursday night
Read it to the peer editing group in class.	Friday's class

Week 3

Rewrite, revise, and prepare final copy.	4 hours Tuesday night Hand in on Wednesday

Notice that the work on this paper has been spread out over two full weeks and is broken down into manageable units. A student would be able to complete this paper successfully, on time, and without panic and discomfort if this schedule were followed. A total of fifteen hours have been set aside for the various stages. The time is available even though the student may not need all of it. The student's focus should now be on finishing the paper as quickly as possible, not on simply using all of this time.

Here is a professional writer who cautions about the importance of working to finish rather than working to put in time: "Don't set your goal as minutes or hours spent working; it's too easy to waste that time looking up one last fact, changing your margins, or, when desperate, searching for a new pen." Instead, she advises, set a realistic writing goal for each day and work until you complete it.[2] Another author advises that you avoid creating units of work that are so large or unmanageable that you won't want to do them, such as writing an entire paper in one day. It may sound good on the surface to write a whole paper in one day or one night, "but you'll soon feel overwhelmed," and "you'll start avoiding the work and won't get *anything* done." Remember, she says, "it's persistence that counts" in completing writing projects.[3]

Identify an Issue and Do Some Initial Reading

You may start with a broad issue area such as crime, education, health care, or tax reform. You will need to find a more narrow and specific issue within this broad area to write about, however. The map in Figure 3.3 shows one way to find more specific issues related to a broad issue area. Reading about your issue can also help you discover a particular aspect that you want to explore. When you have an issue you think you can work with, write it as a question, and apply the twelve tests of an arguable issue presented in Box 1.3. You may also take a position on the issue and write a tentative claim. Additional information on how to write claims appears in Chapters 6 and 8.

Analyze the Rhetorical Situation

In Chapter 3, you learned to apply the elements of the rhetorical situation to help you read critically and analyze other authors' arguments. As a writer, you can now use the rhetorical situation to help you think critically and make decisions about your own writing.

All five elements of the rhetorical situation are important considerations for writers. Three elements of the rhetorical situation are in place before you begin to write. They are the *exigence,* the *reader* or *audience,* and the *constraints.* When you begin to write, two additional elements are added: you, the *author,* and the *text* that you create. Figure 4.1 provides a diagram of these five elements to suggest some of the relationships among them.

Now consider the five elements from the writer's point of view. Use TRACE to help you remember the elements. As a writer, however, you should think about them in the following order.

▲ **Exigence.** The exigence of the situation provides the motivation to write about the issue in the first place. Issues often emerge from real-life events that signal something is wrong. One student found a topic when a local jury appeared to

---

[2]Peggy Rynk, "Waiting for Inspiration," *Writer,* September 1992, p. 10.

[3]Sue Grafton, "How to Find Time to Write When You Don't Have Time to Write," *The Writer's Handbook,* ed. Sylvia K. Burack (Boston: Writer, 1991), p. 22.

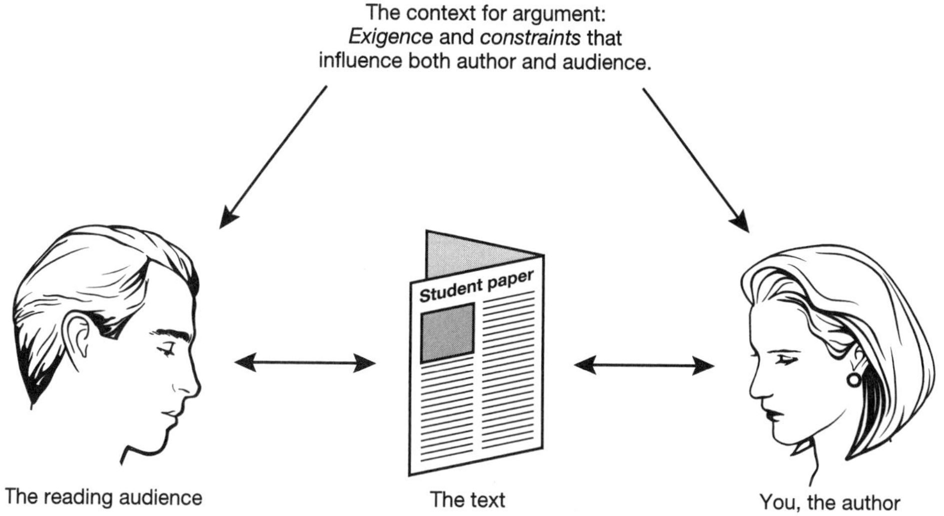

The context for argument:
Exigence and *constraints* that
influence both author and audience.

The reading audience   The text   You, the author

Figure 4.1   The Five Elements of the Rhetorical Situation That the Writer Considers While Planning and Writing Argument

have made a mistake because it assigned probation to a murderer instead of prison time. Another student developed an exigence to write when she visited a national forest and discovered that acres and acres of trees had been cut down since the last time she was there. Yet another student discovered an exigence when he read a newspaper article about the assisted death of an old woman who was very ill, and he began to compare her situation with his grandmother's. Such occurrences can cause the writer to ask the questions associated with exigence: What issue is involved in each of these incidents? Are these new or recurring issues? Do they represent problems or defects? How and why?

▲ **Reader or Audience.** Now think about how potential readers might regard the issues that emerge from these situations. Who are these people? Would they perceive these situations as problems or defects, as you do? Would they agree or disagree with you on the issues, or would they be neutral? What do they believe in? What are their values? Will you need to make a special effort with them to achieve common ground, or will you already share common ground? What audience outcomes can you anticipate? Will you be able to get the audience to agree and reach consensus, to take action, to agree on some points but not on others, or to agree to disagree? Or will they probably remain unconvinced and possibly even hostile?

▲ **Constraints.** Remember that constraints influence the ways in which both you and your audience think about the issues. What background, events, experiences, traditions, values, or associations are influencing both you and them? If you decide to write for an audience of lawyers to convince them to change the nature of jury trials, for instance, what are the constraints likely to be? How hard will it be to change the system? Or if you are writing for forest service employees whose job it is to cut down trees, what constraints will you encounter with this group? If you are writing for a group of doctors who have been trained to preserve human life as long as possible, what constraints will you encounter with them? And how about you? What are your own constraints? How are your training, background, affiliations, and values either in harmony or in conflict with your audience? In other words, will your respective constraints drive you and your audience apart, or will they bring you together and help you achieve common ground?

▲ **Author.** Other questions will help you think like an author of argument. Why am I interested in this issue? Why do I perceive it as a defect or problem? Is it a new or old issue for me? What is my personal background or experience with this issue? What makes me qualified to write about it? Which of my personal values are involved? How can I get more information? Refer to your direct experience if you have some. You may, for instance, be planning to go to law school, and you are interested in trial results, or you may have spent many happy childhood vacations camping in the forests, or maybe one of your relatives suffered many years before she died. Or you may have no direct experience, just an interest.

▲ **Text.** At this point, you can begin to plan your paper (the text). What strategies should you use? Will you favor an adversarial or a consensual style? How will you build common ground? What types of support will work best? Should you state your claim right away or build up to it? What will your argumentative purpose be? What will your original approach or perspective be?

As you can see, the rhetorical situation can be employed to help you get ideas and plan, and you should actually keep it in mind throughout the writing process. It will be useful to you at every stage.

Focus and Freewrite

Focus your attention, write a tentative title for your paper, and then freewrite for ten or fifteen minutes without stopping. Write about anything that occurs to you that is relevant to your title and your issue. Freewriting must be done quickly to capture the flow of thought. It may be done sloppily, using incomplete sentences and abbreviations. Don't worry about making errors.

Go back through your freewriting, and find a phrase or sentence that you can turn into a claim. This freewriting is also your first partial manuscript. Later you may use some or none of it in your paper. Its main value is to preserve the first creative ideas that flood your mind when you begin to work on a paper. Its other value is to focus and preserve your ideas so that they won't get lost when you later read the thoughts and opinions of others. If you start to freewrite and you find you do not have very many ideas, do some background reading in your issue area, and then try to freewrite again.

Brainstorm, Make Lists, Map Ideas

Brainstorming is another way to get ideas down on paper in a hurry. The rules for brainstorming are to commit to a time limit, to write phrases only, to write quickly, and to make no judgments as you write. Later you may go back to decide what is good or bad, useful or not useful. Brainstorming is like freewriting to the extent that it helps you get some ideas on paper quickly. It differs from freewriting in that it usually produces only words and phrases and it is often practiced as a group activity.

Listing is related to outlining. Insights may come at any time about how to divide a subject into parts or how to set up major headings for your paper. Write these ideas in list form. Or map your ideas (Figure 3.3) to get a better sense of what they are and how they relate to each other. You may also use a flowchart. Flowcharts are good for laying out processes or ideas and events that occur chronologically, over a period of time.

Talk It Through

Many people find it easier to speak the first words than to write them. Typical audiences for an initial talk-through may include a peer editing group, which is a small group of students in your class who will listen and read your paper at all stages; your instructor, who, in conference, may ask a few questions and then just listen to you explore your ideas; or a writing center tutor, who is trained to ask questions and then listen. Friends or family members can also become valued listeners. Some people like to tape-record the ideas they get from such sessions. Others prefer to end them with some rapid freewriting, listing, or brainstorming to preserve the good ideas that surfaced. If you do not tape-record or write, your good ideas may become lost forever. A sense of security comes from writing your paper with a stack of notes and ideas at hand and ready to use.

Keep a Journal, Notebook, or Folder of Ideas

Instead of talking to others, some authors talk to themselves on a regular basis by writing in a journal or notebook or simply by writing on pieces of paper and sticking them in a folder. To help you gather material for an argument paper, you may clip articles, write summaries, and write out ideas and observations about your issue as they come to you. These materials will provide you with an excellent source of information for your paper when it is time to write it.

A professional writer describes this type of writing as a tool that helps one think. This author sets out some suggestions that could be particularly useful for the writer of argument:

> Write quickly, so you don't know what's coming next.
> Turn off the censor in your head.
> Write from different points of view to broaden your sympathies.
> Collect quotations that inspire you and jot down a few notes on why they do.
> Write with a nonjudgmental friend in mind to listen to your angry or confused thoughts.

When words won't come, draw something—anything.

Don't worry about being nice, fair, or objective. Be selfish and biased; give your side of the story from the heart.

Write even what frightens you, *especially* what frightens you. It is the thought denied that is dangerous.

Don't worry about being consistent. You are large; you contain multitudes.[4]

You can write entire sections of material, ready to incorporate later into your paper. Or you can jot down phrases or examples to help you remember sudden insights. The object is to think and write on a regular basis while a paper is taking shape. Writing at all stages helps you discover what you know and learn about what you think.

Mentally Visualize

Create mental pictures related to your issue, and later describe what you see in your mind's eye. For example, if you are writing about preserving forests, visualize them before any cutting has been done and then later after clear-cutting, which removes all trees in an area. Use these descriptions later in your paper to make your ideas more vivid and compelling.

Do Some Directed Reading and Thinking

Continue reading, thinking, and writing notes and ideas throughout the prewriting process. Read to get a sense of other people's perspectives on the issue and also to generate ideas of your own. As you read, you may find that you need to narrow and limit your issue even more, to one aspect or one approach. Try to think of an original perspective or "take" on the issue, a new way of looking at it. For example, the personal examples in "Why I Want a Wife," pages 56–57, present an original approach to the household responsibilities issue. As you continue reading and thinking, clarify your position on the issue, decide on your argumentative purpose (Chapters 6 and 8 will help), and revise your claim if you need to. When you have written your claim, write the word *because* and list some reasons. Or list some reasons and write the word *therefore*, followed by your claim. This will help you decide, at least for now, whether your paper would be stronger with the claim at the beginning or at the end. Decide which words in your claim will need defining in your paper.

Use Argument Strategies

You will learn more about these in future chapters. The Toulmin model (Chapter 5) will help you plan the essential parts of your paper. Later, when you are revising, you can employ the Toulmin model to read and check the effectiveness of your argument. The claim questions in Chapter 6 will help you discover and write claims to focus your purpose for argument. The list of proofs from Chapter 7 will provide you with a variety of ways to develop your paper.

---

[4]Marjorie Pellegrino, "Keeping a Writer's Journal," *Writer,* June 1992, p. 27.

Use Reading Strategies

Use what you know about analyzing the organization of other authors' essays to help you organize your own paper. For example, you can plan an introduction, main body, and conclusion. You can make an outline composed of a claim, sub-claims, support, and transitions. You can write a simplified outline to help you visualize the structure of your paper. When you have finished your draft, you can try to summarize it to test its unity and completeness. Or you can survey it. If you have problems with summarizing or surveying, you will probably need to revise more. Much of what you learned about reading in Chapter 3 can now be used not only to help you write argument of your own but also to read and evaluate it.

Use Critical Thinking Prompts

You can get additional insight and ideas about your issue by using some well-established lines of thought that stimulate critical thinking. The "Critical Thinking Prompts" list in Box 4.1 provides some prompts that will cause you to think in a variety of ways. First, write out your issue, and then write your responses. You will be pleased by the quantity of new information these questions will generate for your paper.

Plan and Conduct Library Research

To help you plan your research tasks, make a brief list or outline of the main sections of your paper. This list will help guide your research. Research takes a lot of time, and you will want to read only the materials in the library that are most relevant to the items on your research outline. Read and take notes on the materials you locate, and relate them to your outline. Search for additional materials to fill in places on the outline where you need more information.

Make an Extended List or Outline to Guide Your Writing

A written outline helps many people see the organization of ideas before they begin to write. Other people seem to be able to make a list or even work from a mental outline. Still others "just write" and move ideas around later to create order. There is, however, an implicit outline in most good writing. The outline is often referred to metaphorically as the skeleton or bare bones of the paper because it provides the internal structure that holds the paper together. An outline can be simple—a list of words written on a piece of scrap paper—or it can be elaborate, with essentially all major ideas, supporting details, major transitions, and even some of the sections written out in full. Some outlines actually end up looking like partial, sketchy manuscripts.

If you have never made outlines, try making one. Outlining requires intensive thinking and decision making. When it is finished, however, you will be able to turn your full attention to writing, and you will never have to stop to figure out what to write about next. Your outline will tell you what to do, and it will ultimately save you time and reduce much of the difficulty and frustration you would experience without it.

Critical Thinking Prompts

What is your issue? _____

Use some, but not all, of these prompts to help you think about it.

1. **Associate it.** Consider other, related issues, big issues, or enduring issues. Also associate your issue with familiar subjects and ideas.

2. **Describe it.** Use detail. Make the description visual if you can.

3. **Compare it.** Think about items in the same or different categories. Compare it with things you know or understand well. Compare what you used to think about the issue and what you think now. Give reasons for your change of mind.

4. **Apply it.** Show practical uses or applications. Show how it can be used in a specific setting.

5. **Divide it.** Get insight into your issue by dividing it into related issues or into parts of the issue.

6. **Agree and disagree with it.** Identify the extreme pro and con positions and reasons for holding them. List other approaches and perspectives. Say why each position, including your own, might be plausible and in what circumstances.

7. **Consider it as it is, right now.** Think about your issue as it exists, right now, in contemporary time. What is its nature? What are its special characteristics?

8. **Consider it over a period of time.** Think about it in the past and how it might present itself in the future. Does it change? How? Why?

9. **Decide what it is a part of.** Put it in a larger category, and consider the insights you gain as a result.

10. **Analyze it.** Break it into parts, and get insight into each of its parts.

11. **Synthesize it.** Put it back together in new ways so that the new whole is different, and perhaps clearer and better, than the old whole.

12. **Evaluate it.** Decide whether it is good or bad, valuable or not valuable, moral or immoral. Give evidence to support your evaluation.

13. **Elaborate on it.** Add and continue to add explanation until you can understand it more easily. Give some examples to provide further elaboration.

14. **Project and predict.** Answer the question "What would happen if . . . ?" Think about further possibilities.

15. **Ask why, and keep on asking why.** Examine every aspect of your issue by asking why.

BOX 4.1   Use These Prompts to Help You Think Critically about Your Issue

Talk It Through Again

When you have completed your outline and are fairly satisfied with it, you can sharpen and improve it even more by reading it aloud and explaining its rationale to some good listeners. It is more and more common to organize peer editing groups in writing classes to give students the opportunity to talk through outlines and to read drafts to fellow students who then act as critics who make recommendations for improvement. Reading and talking about your outline in the early stages helps clarify ideas, making it easier to write about them later. At this stage, your student critics should explain to you what is clear and unclear and also what is convincing and not convincing.

WRITING THE FIRST DRAFT

The objective of writing the first draft is to get your ideas in some kind of written form so that you can see them and work with them. Here is how a professional writer explains the drafting process:

> Writing a first draft should be easy because, in a sense, you can't get it wrong. You are bringing something completely new and strange into the world, something that did not exist before. You have nothing to prove in the first draft, nothing to defend, everything to imagine. And the first draft is yours alone, no one else sees it. You are not writing for an audience. Not yet. You write the draft in order to read what you have written and to determine what you still have to say.[5]

This author advises further that you "not even consider technical problems at this early stage." Nor should you "let your critical self sit at your desk with your creative self. The critic will stifle the writer within." The purpose, he says, is "not to get it right, but to get it written."[6]

Here is another writer, Stephen King, who advises putting aside reference books and dictionaries when concentrating on writing the first draft:

> Put away your dictionary. . . . You think you might have misspelled a word? O.K., so here is your choice: either look it up in the dictionary, thereby making sure you have it right—and breaking your train of thought and the writer's trance in the bargain—or just spell it phonetically and correct it later. Why not? Did you think it was going to go somewhere? And if you need to know the largest city in Brazil and you find you don't have it in your head, why not write in Miami or Cleveland? You can check it . . . but *later*. When you sit down to write, *write*. Don't do anything else except go to the bathroom, and only do that it if absolutely cannot be put off.[7]

---

[5]John Dufresne, "That Crucial First Draft," *Writer,* October 1992, p. 9.

[6]Ibid., pp. 10–11.

[7]Stephen King, "Everything You Need to Know about Writing Successfully—in Ten Minutes," *The Writer's Handbook,* ed. Sylvia K. Burack (Boston: Writer, 1991), pp. 33.

You will be able to follow this advice if your outline and notes are available to guide you and keep you on track. If you occasionally get stuck, you can write some phrases, freewrite, or even skip a section that you cannot easily put into words. You will have another chance at your draft later. Right now, work only to capture the flow of ideas that is on the outline. You will discover, as you write, that many of the ideas that were only half formed on your outline will now become clear and complete as you get insight from writing.

SPECIAL STRATEGIES TO USE IF YOU GET STUCK

Everyone suffers from writer's block from time to time, and there are a number of ways to get going again if you get stuck while writing your first draft. Many people read and take more notes at times like this. Since reading will make you think, you should write out all of the ideas and insights that come to you as you read. Soon you will have plenty of new material to add to your paper. You can also go back and reread your outline, lists, and other idea notes, rearrange them into new combinations, and add more information to them.

If you are so blocked that you simply cannot make yourself write the next words, try freewriting—writing fast, in phrases or sentences, on your topic without imposing any structure or order. Then do some more reading, and follow that with additional freewriting. You may end up with a lot of material that doesn't make much sense and with a lot of unrelated bits and sentence fragments. That's fine—you can go back through it later, crossing out what you can't use, changing phrases to sentences, adding material in places, and soon you will find that you are started again. Getting words on the page in any form is what it takes for some writers to break out of a block.

It is also extremely useful to talk about your ideas for your paper with someone else to get fresh insights and solve some of your writing problems. Or ask someone else to read a draft of your paper and to write some comments on it. This will provide you with fresh insights and ideas to get you moving again. Finally, give yourself permission to write a less than perfect first draft. You can paralyze yourself by trying to produce a finished draft on the first try. Lower your expectations for the first draft, and remind yourself that you can always go back later and fix it.

POSTWRITING STRATEGIES

Resist the temptation to put your paper aside when you have finished drafting and declare it finished. Now is your opportunity to improve it in significant ways, and here are some suggestions for doing so.

Read Your Draft Critically and Submit It for Peer Review

If you can, put your draft aside for 24 hours, then read it critically and make all of the changes you can to improve it. It helps to read the paper aloud at this point to get an even better perspective on what can be improved. Then you can seek the opinion of other students in a class peer review session. The usual procedure for a peer editing session on a draft is to read the paper aloud to the group or to do a round robin reading session, where group members read all of the papers silently and make some notes before they discuss the papers one by one.

Peer groups make the writing task more sociable and provide immediate feedback from a real audience. They also help you become a more sensitive critic of your own and others' work. Most professional writers rely heavily on other people's opinions at various stages of writing. Look at the prefaces of some of the books you are using this semester. Most authors acknowledge the help of several people who read their manuscript and made suggestions for improvement. Many individuals recommended improvements for this book. Some of these people were teachers, some were editors, some were friends and family members, some were colleagues, and some were students. The students who test-read this book wrote many good suggestions for improvement. In fact, these students were responsible for several of the major changes and special features in the book that make it easier to read and use. One student commented that she liked being a part of the writing process for this textbook because it helped her read her other textbooks more critically. If peer review groups are not part of your writing class, try to find someone else to read your draft. You need someone to make suggestions and give you ideas for improvement.

Rewrite and Revise

Working with a rough draft is easier than outlining or drafting. It is, in fact, creative and fun to revise because you begin to see your work take shape and become more readable. Skillfully revised material, incidentally, makes a good impression on the reader. It is worthwhile to finish your draft early enough so that you will have several hours to read and revise before you submit it in its final form to a reader.

Most writers have some ideas and rules about writing that come to their aid, from an inner voice, when it is time to revise. Listen to your inner voice so that you will know what to look for and what to change. If you do not have a strongly developed inner voice, you can strengthen it by learning to ask the following questions. Notice that these questions direct your attention to global revisions for improved clarity and organization, as well as to surface revisions for details.

1. *Is it clear?* If you cannot understand your own writing, other people won't be able to, either. Be very critical of your own understanding as you read your draft. Make your writing clearer by establishing some key terms and using them throughout. Add transitions as well. Use those that are associated with the organizational patterns you have used. (You can find more information about these in Chapter 10.) Or write a transitional paragraph to summarize one major part of your paper and introduce the next. If you stumble over a bad sentence, begin again and rewrite it in a new way. There are a dozen possible ways to write one sentence. Also, change all words that do not clearly communicate exactly what you want to say. This is no place to risk using words from the thesaurus that

you are not sure about. Finally, apply this test: Can you state the claim or the main point of your paper and list the parts that develop it? Take a good look at these parts, and rearrange them if necessary.

2. *What should I add?* Sometimes in writing the first draft you will write such a sketchy version of an idea that it does not explain what you want to say. Add fuller explanations and examples, or do some extra research to improve the skimpy parts of your paper.

3. *What should I cut?* Extra words, repeated ideas, and unnecessary material find their way into a typical first draft. Every writer cuts during revision. Stephen King, who earns millions of dollars each year as a professional writer, describes how he learned to cut the extra words. His teacher was the newspaper editor John Gould, who dealt with King's first feature article as follows:

> He started in on the feature piece with a large black pen and taught me all I ever needed to know about my craft. I wish I still had the piece—it deserves to be framed, editorial corrections and all—but I can remember pretty well how it looked when he had finished with it. Here's an example:

> Last night, in the ~~well-loved~~ gymnasium of Lisbon High School, partisans and Jay Hills fans alike were stunned by an athletic performance unequalled in school history: Bob Ransom, ~~known as "Bullet" Bob for both his size and accuracy,~~ scored thirty-seven points. He did it with grace and speed . . . and he did it with an odd courtesy as well, committing only two personal fouls in his ~~knight-like~~ quest for a record which has eluded Lisbon's ~~thinclads~~ basketball team since 1953 . . .

When Gould finished marking up my copy in the manner I have indicated above, he looked up and must have seen something on my face. I think he must have thought it was horror, but it was not: it was revelation.

"I only took out the bad parts, you know," he said. "Most of it's pretty good."

"I know," I said, meaning both things: yes, most of it was good, and yes, he had only taken out the bad parts. "I won't do it again."

"If that's true," he said, "you'll never have to work again. You can do *this* for a living." Then he threw back his head and laughed.

And he was right: I *am* doing this for a living, and as long as I can keep on, I don't expect ever to have to work again.[8]

4. *Are the language and style consistent and appropriate throughout?* Edit out all words that create a conversational or informal tone in your paper. For example:

Change: And as for target shooting, well go purchase a BB gun or a set of darts.[9]

To read: For target shooting, a BB gun or a set of darts serve just as well as a handgun.

Also, edit out all cheerleading, slogans, clichés, needless repetition, and exhortations. You are not writing a political speech. For example:

Change: Violence! Why should we put up with it? Violence breeds violence, they say. America would be a better place if there were less violence.

To read: Violent crime has begun to take over the United States, affecting everyone's life. Every day another story of tragedy unfolds where a man, a woman, or a child is senselessly killed by someone with a gun. Under the tremendous stress of this modern society, tempers flare at the drop of a hat, and people reach for a gun that was bought only for defense or safety. Then they make rash, deadly decisions.[10]

You will learn more about language and style in Chapter 7. In general, use a formal, rational style in an argument paper unless you have a good reason to do otherwise. Use emotional language and examples that arouse feelings only where appropriate to back up logical argument.

5. *Is there enough variety?* Use some variety in the way you write sentences by beginning some with clauses and others with a subject or even a verb. Vary the length of your sentences as well. Try to write not only simple sentences but also compound and complex sentences. You can also vary the length of your paragraphs. The general rule is to begin a new paragraph every time you change the subject. Variety in sentences and paragraphs makes your writing more interesting to read. Do not sacrifice clarity for variety, however, by writing odd or unclear sentences.

6. *Have I used the active voice most of the time?* The active voice is more direct, energetic, and interesting than the passive voice. Try to use it most of the time. Here is a sentence written in the active voice; it starts with the subject:

Virtual reality is an exciting new technology that will enhance nearly every aspect of our lives.[11]

---

[8]King, pp. 30–31.

[9]From a student paper by Blake Decker; used with permission.

[10]Ibid.

[11]From a student paper by Greg Mathios; used with permission.

Notice how it loses its directness and punch when it is written in the passive voice:

> Nearly every aspect of our lives will be enhanced by virtual reality, an exciting new technology.

7. *Have I avoided sexist language?* Try to avoid referring to all people in your paper as though they were either all male or all female. Using such expressions as "he or she" or "himself or herself" sounds inclusive but comes across as awkward. Ways to solve this problem are to use plural nouns and pronouns and perhaps occasionally rewrite a sentence in the passive voice. It is better to write, "The pressure-sensitive glove is used in virtual reality," than to write, "He or she puts on a pressure-sensitive glove to enter the world of virtual reality."

8. *Have I followed the rules?* Learn the rules for grammar, usage, and punctuation, and follow them. No one can read a paper that is full of errors of this type. Make the following rules a part of that inner voice that guides your revision, and you will avoid the most common errors made by student writers:

- Write similar items in a *series,* separated by commas, and finally connected by *and* or *or.*

  Example: The National Rifle Association, firearms manufacturers, and common citizens are all interested in gun control.[12]

- Use *parallel construction* for longer, more complicated elements that have a similar function in the sentence.

  Example: Parents who fear for their children's safety at school, passengers who ride on urban public transit systems, clerks who work at convenience stores and gas stations, and police officers who try to carry out their jobs safely are all affected by national policy on gun control.

- Keep everything in the same *tense* throughout. Use the present tense to introduce quotes.

  Example: As Sherrill *states,* "The United States is said to be the greatest gun-toting nation in the world." Millions of guns create problems in this country.

- Observe *sentence boundaries.* Start sentences with a capital letter, and end them with a period or question mark. Make certain they express complete thoughts.
- Make subjects agree with verbs.

  Example: Restrictions on gun control *interfere* [not *interferes*] with people's rights.

---

[12] The examples presented here are drawn from a student paper by Blake Decker. I have revised his sentences for the sake of illustration.

- Use *clear and appropriate pronoun referents.*

  Example: The *group* is strongly in favor of gun control, and little is needed to convince *it* [not *them*] of the importance of this issue.

- Use commas to set off long initial clauses, to separate two independent clauses, and to separate words in a series.

  Example: When one realizes that the authors of the Constitution could not look into the future and imagine current events, one can see how irrational and irresponsible it is to believe that the right to bear arms should in these times still be considered a constitutional right, and according to Smith, the groups that do so "are short-sighted, mistaken, and ignorant."

Check for Final Errors, Add or Adjust the Title, and Type or Print Your Paper

Just before you submit your paper, check the spelling of every word you are not absolutely sure about. If spelling is a problem for you, buy a small spelling dictionary that contains only words and no meanings, or use the spell checker on the computer. If you use a spell checker, you should still read your paper one last time since the computer might not find every error. At this point you should also correct all the typographical errors that remain and format your paper. Now either add a title or adjust your existing title if it needs it. Be sure that your title provides information about your paper that will help the reader understand what it is about.

Complete your revision process by reading your paper aloud one more time. Read slowly and listen. You will be surprised by the number of problems that bother your ears but were not noticeable to your eyes. Your paper should be ready now to submit for evaluation. Either type it or print it out on a word processor.

ORGANIZING A PROCESS FOR WRITING ARGUMENT

The writing process for argument explained in this chapter and summarized in Box 4.2 integrates reading and writing at every phase. The strategies are presented in categories similar to those used for the reading process in Chapter 3. As you think about how you can adapt and use these ideas for writing argument, remember to keep the process flexible. That is, use your own present process, but add selected strategies as needed. It is unlikely that you will ever use all these strategies for one paper. Also, even though these strategies are explained here in an apparent order, you will not necessarily follow them in this order. You might write an entire section of your paper during the prewriting stage or do some rewriting and revising while you are working on the initial draft. The strategies are not steps. They are suggestions to help you complete your paper. By integrating them with your present writing process, you will develop an effective way of writing argument papers that is uniquely yours.

Writing Argument

PREWRITING STRATEGIES

- **Get organized to write.** Set up a place with materials. Get motivated.
- **Understand the writing assignment, and schedule time.** Break a complicated writing task into manageable parts, and set aside the time you need to write.
- **Identify an issue, and do some initial reading on it.**
- **Analyze the rhetorical situation,** particularly the exigence, the audience, and the constraints. Then think about you, as the author, and the text you will create.
- **Focus** on your issue and **freewrite.**
- **Brainstorm, make lists, map ideas.**
- **Talk things through** with a friend, your instructor, or members of a peer editing group.
- **Keep a journal, notebook, or folder of ideas.**
- **Mentally visualize** the major concepts.
- Do some directed **reading and thinking.**
- **Use argument strategies.**
- **Use reading strategies.**
- **Use critical thinking prompts.**
- Plan and conduct **library research.**
- Make an **expanded list or outline** to guide your writing.
- **Talk things through again.**

WRITING STRATEGIES

- **Write the first draft.** Get your ideas on paper so that you can work with them. Use your outline and notes to help you. Either write and rewrite as you go, or write the draft quickly with the knowledge that you can reread or rewrite later.

STRATEGIES TO USE WHEN YOU GET STUCK

- **Read more,** and **take more notes.**
- **Read your outline, rearrange parts, add more information.**
- **Freewrite** on the issue, **read some more,** and then **freewrite** some more.
- **Talk about your ideas** with someone else.
- **Lower your expectations for your first draft.** It does not have to be perfect at this point.

(continued)

BOX 4.2 A Summary of the Process for Writing Argument Explained in This Chapter.

POSTWRITING STRATEGIES

- **Read your draft critically,** and also **have someone else read it.** Put it aside for 24 hours, if you can, to develop a better perspective for reading and improving.
- **Rewrite and revise.** Make changes and additions until you think your paper is ready for other people to read. Move sections, cross out material, add other material, rephrase, as necessary.
- **Check your paper** for final mechanical and spelling errors, **write the final title,** and **type or print it.**

BOX 4.2 *(continued)*

The bare bones of the process can be stated simply:

- Select an issue, narrow it, take a tentative position, and write a claim.
- Do some reading and research.
- Create a structure.
- Write a draft.
- Revise and edit it.

You can practice the writing process by understanding and learning to write an exploratory paper.

THE EXPLORATORY PAPER

In the exploratory paper,[13] the arguer identifies not just one position but as many of the major positions on an issue as possible, both past and present, and explains them through summaries and an analysis of the overall rhetorical situation for the issue. The analysis of the rhetorical situation in these papers explains what caused the issue and what prompted past and present interest and concern with it, identifies who is interested in it and why, and examines the constraints of the inquiry and the various views in the ongoing conversation associated with it. The summaries of the positions not only explain each of the different perspectives on the issue but also provide the usual reasons cited to establish the validity of each perspective. The writer's own opinions are not expressed at all or are withheld until later in the paper.

There are a number of advantages to writing and reading exploratory papers. When writers and readers view an issue from many perspectives, they acquire a greater depth of understanding of it. They also acquire information—both

---

[13]I am indebted to the late Professor James Kinneavy of the University of Texas at Austin for the basic notion of the exploratory paper.

facts and opinions—on the various views. All these are beneficial because both the arguer and the reader become better educated and more fluent in their discussions of the issue. Exploratory papers also help establish common ground between writers and readers. Writers, by restating several opposing positions along with the usual reasons for accepting them, are forced to understand several opposing views. The reader is also interested because the exploratory paper explains all views, which usually includes the reader's as well. The reader is consequently more willing to learn about the other positions on the issue. Exploratory papers provide the mutual understanding and common ground essential for the next stage in argument, the presentation of the writer's position and reasons for holding it. The exploratory paper thus paves the way for the writer to enter the conversation on an issue with a single-perspective argument.

Exploratory papers are a common genre in argumentative writing. You will encounter them in newspapers, newsmagazines, other popular magazines of opinion, and scholarly journals. They are easy to recognize because they take a broad view of an issue, and they explain multiple perspectives instead of just one.

The following is an example of a short exploratory paper about single-sex classes in the public schools. The rhetorical situation, particularly the motivation for placing boys and girls in separate classes, is explained in the first paragraph. The author of this article then summarizes the different positions associated with this issue, including the reasons some schools give for separating the sexes, the arguments given by those who oppose this practice, and the requirements of federal law on the subject. Notice that the author does not take a side or express personal opinions directly. The reader gets a sense of the complexity of the issue and also of some new perspectives on it.

Essay 1

A ROOM OF THEIR OWN*

LynNell Hancock and Claudia Kalb

What is the
rhetorical
situation?

1 Who can forget the pubescent pain of junior high? Boys sprout pimples, girls sprout attitude and both genders goad each other into a state of sexual confusion. Teachers in Manassas, Va., figured that all these colliding hormones were distracting students from their academic tasks. So officials at Marsteller Middle School decided to try something old: dividing girls and boys into separate academic classes. Eighth-grade girls say they prefer doing physics experiments without boys around to hog the equipment. Boys say they'd rather recite Shakespeare without girls around to make them feel "like geeks." An eerie return to the turn of the century, when

*Newsweek, June 24, 1996, p. 76.

boys and girls marched into public schools through separate doors? Yes, say education researchers. But will it work—and is it legal?

In districts across the country, public schools are experimenting with sexual segregation, in the name of school reform. There is no precise tally, in part because schools are wary of drawing attention to classes that may violate gender-bias laws. But, researchers say, in more than a dozen states—including Texas, Colorado, Michigan and Georgia—coed schools are creating single-sex classes. Some, like Marsteller, believe that separating the sexes will eliminate distractions. Others, like Robert Coleman Elementary in Baltimore, made the move primarily to get boys to work harder and tighten up discipline.

2   What is the position of the schools that have set up single-sex classes?

The great majority of the experiments are designed to boost girls' math and science scores. The stimulus for these efforts was a report four years ago from the American Association of University Women, which argued that girls were being shortchanged in public-school classrooms—particularly in math and science. The single-sex classroom, however, is not what the gender-equity researchers involved with AAUW had in mind as a remedy. Their report was meant to help improve coeducation, not dismantle it. Research shows single-sex schools tend to produce girls with more confidence and higher grades. But single-sex classrooms within coed schools? There are no long-term studies of that approach, only a smattering of skeptics and true believers. "It's a plan that misses two boats," charges David Sadker, coauthor of *Failing at Fairness*—the education of boys, and the reality that children need to learn how to cope in a coed world. In short, says University of Michigan researcher Valerie Lee, "these classes are a bogus answer to a complex problem."

3

What is the position of those who oppose single-sex classes?

Critics worry that segregated classes will set back the cause of gender equity just when girls are finally being integrated into all-male academics. Half a century ago, boys in advanced science classes learned, for example, that mold is used for penicillin while girls in home economics learned that mold is the gunk on the shower curtain. "It's not an era we're eager to return to," says Norma Cantu of the U.S. Office of Civil Rights.

4

MIRACLES HAPPEN

As a general principle, federal law doesn't permit segregation by sex in the public schools. (Exceptions can be made for singing groups, contact sports and human-sexuality and remedial classes.) Some schools have survived legal challenges by claiming that their all-girl classes fill remedial needs. A middle school in Ventura, Calif., faced down a challenge by changing the name of its all-girl math class to Math PLUS (Power Learning for Underrepresented Students). Enrollment is open to boys, though none has registered yet.

5   What is the position of the federal law?

6   Despite the skeptics, single-sex experiments continue to spread. Teachers and students believe they work. At the high school in Presque Isle, Maine, members of the popular all-girl algebra class go on to tackle the sciences. University of Maine professor Bonnie Wood found that girls who take the algebra course are twice as likely to enroll in advanced chemistry and college physics than their coed counterparts. Michigan's Rochester High School turns away 70 students every year from its girls-only science and engineering class. Marsteller boys raised their collective average in language arts by one grade after a single term. Girls boosted their science average by .4 of a point.

7   For the teachers involved, the progress is no mystery. Sheryl Quinlan, who teaches science at Marsteller, knows single-sex classes let her kids think with something besides their hormones. Impressing the opposite sex is a 14-year-old's reason for being. Take away that pressure, and miracles happen. Quinlan recalls the girl who took a "zero" on her oral report rather than deliver it in front of her boyfriend. Those days are over. Now, says Amanda Drobney, 14, "you can mess up in front of girls, and it's OK." We've come a long way, babies—or have we? ■

What is the authors' perspective as indicated in their final question?

FOR DISCUSSION: Recall when you were in junior high School. Do you think you would have learned more effectively in a single-sex classroom? Why or why not? What do you think should be done to help junior high and high school students learn in public schools?

HOW TO WRITE AN EXPLORATORY PAPER

Now write an exploratory paper of your own. An exploratory paper will help you look at your issue from several angles, which will help you decide what position you want to take. Exploratory papers pave the way for position papers (taught in Parts Two and Three). If you write an exploratory paper before you write a position paper, you will find the position paper much easier to write. Not only will you have discovered your own position, but you will also understand some of the other views that you may want to refute. Explanations and examples in the Exercises and Activities for this chapter will set up the exploratory paper assignment. To complete it successfully, follow these general suggestions.

1. *Select an issue, and do some research and reading on it.* You will need a controversial issue to write about, one that invites several different perspectives. You may have an issue list you can refer to (see pages 17–21). Or you may already have an issue, especially if you have written an issue proposal (page 25) and several summary-response papers (page 87). If you do not have an issue, either read

a set of related articles in "The Reader" to become acquainted with several perspectives on an issue, or select an issue of your own and read about it on the Internet and in the library. Refer to "How Should You Engage with Issues," on pages 24–25, to help you find an issue, and then refer to "Some Suggestions to Help You with Library and Online Research," on pages 276–284, to help you locate information about it. Either take notes on the different perspectives you identify in this material, or make copies of the material you locate so that you can quote it later in your paper.

2. *Make an outline, list, or notes to help you plan your draft.* Review other suggestions for prewriting made in this chapter to help you with this phase of your paper (see pages 90–99). At the very least, however, do the following.

First, sketch out the rhetorical situation for your issue. What has aroused your interest in this issue in the first place? Who else is interested in it, and why? What are some of the constraints for the interested parties?

Second, identify at least three different ways that particular groups of people might think about your issue. For example, three perspectives on handgun control might be stated as follows: some people believe there should be no restrictions on personal handgun ownership; other people believe possession of handguns should be banned for everyone except police officers and military personnel; a third group believes people have a right to own handguns, but with restrictions including background checks, special training, and licensing. Notice that these are three different ways of looking at this issue, not three separate ideas about the issue. As you plan the perspectives for your paper, you can think about perspectives that are for, against, or in the middle; perspectives that represent three (or more) possible approaches or "takes" on an issue; perspectives that describe three (or more) possible ways to solve an issue; perspectives that provide three (or more) ways of interpreting an issue; and so on. These perspectives may be yours or other people's. Your objective, finally, is to identify at least three distinctly different ways to think about your issue.

3. *Write a draft, and include transitions.* Draw on some of the ideas for drafting a paper that are discussed in this chapter (pages 99–100). As you write your draft, include transitions to separate and emphasize the different perspectives on your issue. You might use transitions like "some people believe," "others believe," and "still others believe"; "one perspective on this issue is," "another perspective is," and "a final perspective is"; or "one way to look at this issue is," "another way is," and "a third way is."

4. *Work summarized ideas and quotes from your research into your draft.* You will mainly summarize, in your own words, the positions you describe in an exploratory paper. If you decide to add direct quotations to make these summaries clearer or more interesting, work the quotations smoothly into your draft so that they make sense in context and are easy to read. Tell your reader where the summarized ideas and quotations came from by introducing them with the authors' names and citing the page numbers in the original sources in parentheses at the end of the citations in the text.

Here is an example of research worked into a student exploratory paper. The paper is about different perspectives concerning the contributions men can make to family life. This student is summarizing the perspective that men can contribute in positive ways to child care. He draws ideas from the article by Jerry Adler that appears on pages 445–451 of "The Reader." Notice that he follows the MLA documentation style (see the Appendix to Chapter 10), including page numbers in parentheses to reference both his summaries of Adler's ideas and the direct quotes from Adler.

Some people believe that men are doing an admirable job of establishing strong family ties, particularly in their relationships with their children. Jerry Adler, author of "Building a Better Dad," shows that despite statistics that suggest few fathers actually take major responsibility for child care (452), there is still reason to believe that fathers have come a long way in having more influence over their children's lives. Seven out of every ten American fathers spend more time with their children than their own fathers did (454). Adler quotes Andrew Cherlin, a Johns Hopkins sociologist who studies American families, "Men today are better fathers when they're around—and worse when they're not" (454). Adler also shares some compelling stories that give hope to the whole situation, stories of a father like Robert Blumenfield who gets up every morning at 6:30 to make his son's breakfast, or a dad like Michael Greene who cranks up the radio and dances with his daughter (456). What an inspiration men can be when we apply ourselves.[14]

For further information on how to incorporate source material into your draft, see "Incorporating Research into Your First Draft" (on pages 311–315. For further advice on how to cite these sources in the text itself, see the Appendix to Chapter 10.

5. *Revise your paper, and include a list of works cited or references at the end.* Follow the suggestions for revision that appear on pages 101–105 of this chapter. At the end of your paper, list the works you have quoted in the text of your paper so that your reader can see where they came from. Refer to the Appendix to Chapter 10 for help with this. To cite articles that appear in "The Reader" in this book, show where they were published originally and also where they are published in this book. Follow example 20 on page 328. To create these citations, notice also that original publication information for each article in this book is provided in a footnote at the bottom of the first page of the article.

Here is an example of how the student who wrote the paragraph about fathers cited the Adler source on his Works Cited page:

---

[14]From a student paper by Tucker Norris; used with permission.

Works Cited

Adler, Jerry. "Building a Better Dad." <u>Newsweek</u> 17 June 1996:
58-64. Rpt. in <u>Perspectives on Argument</u>. Nancy V. Wood. 3rd
ed. Upper Saddle River: Prentice Hall, 2001. 452-57.

REVIEW QUESTIONS

1. What are some of the benefits of including reading as part of the writing process?
2. What are some of the decisions writers need to make when they get physically organized to write?
3. How can the writer use the rhetorical situation during the prewriting phase of a paper?
4. What are some of the prewriting strategies you will use?
5. Describe your method for writing a first draft.
6. What would help you if you got stuck in the process of writing a paper?
7. What would you need to pay particular attention to in the rewriting and revising phase of the writing process?

EXERCISES AND ACTIVITIES

A. CLASS PROJECT: CREATING A COMPOSITE OF THE CLASS'S WRITING PROCESS

When all class members contribute their usual strategies to a composite writing process, the result is usually a very complete description of a possible writing process. Focus on developing a process for writing argument, and write the title "Writing Argument" on the board. Under it write the four headings *"Prewriting," "Writing," "Writing When You Get Stuck," and "Rewriting."* Class members should contribute both the strategies they use and those they would like to use to each of the four lists. When the activity is completed, students may freewrite for a few minutes on the writing process they intend to use to write argument.

B. GROUP WORK: ANALYZING AN EXPLORATORY PAPER FROM A MAGAZINE

Analyze the exploratory paper, "Coming and Going," which follows.

Prereading

The whole class should preread and discuss the results.

1. Read the title and the first paragraph. What is the issue? What is your present position on the issue? (30 seconds)
2. What ideas do you predict in this essay? What question might be answered? (1 minute)

3. Survey the article by reading the first sentence in each paragraph and the final paragraph. What more have you learned about the essay? (1 minute)

Reading

Each class member should read, underline, and annotate the essay and then discuss the results as a class. (5 minutes)

1. Describe the rhetorical situation. What is the context for this issue?
2. What are the perspectives on the issue that the author identifies? Make a class list on the board.
3. What is the author's own perspective? Why does he hold it?
4. What common ground, if any, exists between you and this author?

Postreading

Working in pairs, discuss your responses to this article. Do you favor any of the perspectives in the article? Or do you have another perspective of your own? If so, what is it? Report some of these perspectives to the class. (3 minutes)

Essay 2

COMING AND GOING*

Nathan Glazer

1   Americans remain divided over immigration, because they are divided over the moral issues behind the question of how many people we should admit into this country. There are those—wilderness enthusiasts, conservationists, and others alarmed at population growth—who believe America already has enough people; they worry about Census projections that, if present immigration trends continue, there will be about 400 million Americans by 2050.

2   For others, immigration is a matter of economics. The debate between those who say immigration is good for the economy (University of Maryland economist Julian Simon and journalist Ben Wattenberg) and those who say it is not (Harvard University economist George Borjas) seems to be swinging in the direction of the pessimists. A recent study by Kevin McCarthy and Georges Vernez of the RAND Corporation concludes that for California, the state with the most immigrants, economic costs outweigh the benefits. Highly educated immigrants, about half the total, do well; in time, they reach income parity with natives. Poorly educated immigrants, however, do not.

3   Less-skilled immigrants also hurt the earnings of less-skilled natives. McCarthy and Vernez estimate that between one and one-and-a-half percent of the adult native-born population in the U.S. has become unemployed or left the labor force because of competition from immigrants. In addition, unskilled im-

New Republic, November 17, 1997, pp. 13–14.

migration has contributed to a declining migration rate to California by native-born Americans from other parts of the country, and to an exodus of natives from California. But then there is Silicon Valley, which believes the U.S. should skew immigration policy to favor those with the education and skills that high-tech industry needs.

Yet another value that influences immigration policy is "diversity." A while back, it became clear that the current emphasis on promoting the immigration of close family members of current residents was hurting potential Irish immigrants: their family members in this country were too distantly related to qualify as sponsors for new immigrants. Hence the remarkable "diversity" lottery in which persons from "underrepresented" countries may apply for immigrant visas by lottery. By now, the lottery mostly benefits not the Irish, but Africans.

Finally, there are those for whom the dominant value in setting immigration policy is compassion. Admitting large numbers of refugees is their desideratum—though it does not solve the problem of deciding who among the refugees deserves entry most; nor does it limit the role of foreign policy and domestic political considerations in making such determinations.

So, when we debate immigration, we are really debating which of these competing and sometimes incompatible values should predominate. Keeping America's population small, or making it bigger? Making America—or certain segments of America—richer? More "diverse"? Compassion, for refugees and for families, for families separated, and for those trying to create one? I would vote for compassion, primarily for refugees and close family members of residents.

But moral intuition rarely withstands the messy realities of policymaking. When Congress debated a new immigration law in 1996, it seemed easy to agree that the new law should deal only with illegal immigrants. While then Wyoming Senator Alan Simpson also wanted to review and revise laws that permit about 800,000 legal immigrants to enter each year—a number, the polls say, that most Americans consider excessive—Congress was more responsive to the views of those who feel most strongly about immigration. Thus, pro-immigrant groups and high-tech industries were able to block any major changes in the law affecting legal immigrants.

The legislation that emerged, then, seemed to link toughness (a crackdown on illegals) with compassion (hands off legal immigrants). But the new law has led to a spate of heart-breaking, and seemingly illogical, situations in which illegal immigrants, who are long-settled U.S. residents, married, with children and jobs, have run afoul of the law. Some have been seized by immigration authorities upon returning from trips abroad for seemingly minor infractions of immigration law, and whisked back to their countries of origin. The new laws often mean alleged illegals have less opportunity for a hearing before they are deported.

One change that is having drastic consequences is the requirement that applications for legal immigrant status be made from abroad. And now if you are illegal for more than six months and leave the country for any reason you can be barred from returning for three years—ten years if you were in the country illegally for more than a year. According to *The New York Times,* some immigrants without green cards are giving up jobs as waiters and chefs—even closing businesses that employ scores of workers—in order to go home to escape penalties. How can that possibly help the American economy?

10   So, while we can all agree in principle that there should be no illegal immigration, when we begin to act on that principle, it turns out that the illegal immigrant is the person who works for us, or runs the restaurant we eat at, or takes care of the garden, and has a spouse and children and parents from whom he or she will be separated if the law is enforced. Then our principled position crumbles before human realities. ■

FOR DISCUSSION: Have you or any of your ancestors immigrated from another country? Or do you know someone outside of your family who is an immigrant? How have your experiences affected your perspective on this issue? Which of the positions discussed in this article do you personally identify with? Why?

C. PAIRED STUDENT ACTIVITY: ANALYZING A STUDENT EXPLORATORY PAPER

The following is an example of an exploratory paper written by Tanya Pierce, a student in an argument class. Her position paper on the same subject appears at the end of Chapter 10 on page 332. Take a few minutes to read Tanya's paper. Then work in pairs to answer the following questions. Report your answers to the class.

1. What is the issue?
2. What is the context for this issue? Describe the rhetorical situation.
3. What are the perspectives on the issue that the author identifies? Make a list.
4. What transitions does the author use? Underline them.
5. What is the author's own perspective? Why does she hold it?
6. What is her claim? Underline it.

You may want to use Tanya's paper as a model for your own exploratory paper.

Tanya Pierce
Exploratory Paper
Professor Snow
English 1302
10 February 1999

           Trial by Jury: A Fundamental Right and a Flawed System

The right to a trial by jury is a fundamental part of the United 1
States legal system. It is a right firmly entrenched in our democratic tradition. The jury system provides a buffer between the
complex and often inflexible legal system and the average citizen on
trial. The right to be judged by a jury of one's peers is a right
that most Americans feel very strongly about. However, due to recent jury decisions, some critics are questioning the value of this
institution.

     Our jury system is by no means flawless. It is subject to con- 2
stant scrutiny and debate concerning its merit and its downfalls. As
is true in all institutions, juries are capable of making mistakes.
Psychological studies have been done on many aspects of jury behavior. Political scientists are also intrigued by juries and the manner in which they arrive at important decisions. Although I believe
most Americans believe in the jury system, there has been considerable controversy surrounding it lately. The public has become even
more concerned about this institution because of the results of some
famous trials. The outcomes of the Rodney King, the O. J. Simpson,
and the Menendez brothers trials in Los Angeles and the outrage that
followed each jury's decisions are examples of instances when the
effectiveness of the jury system has come under fierce attack. From
the public reaction to those decisions and others like them, it is
very clear that the way in which juries reach their decisions is
often as important to the American people as it is to the specific
person on trial. Many people feel that the average jurist is not
equipped to make the kinds of decisions jurors face. These critics'
suggestions range from restructuring the system to totally eliminating it.

     Most average Americans, I believe, feel that the right to a 3
jury trial is a fundamental one, and its guarantees should be honored. These people would argue that laws are inflexible. Statutes
cannot deal with the individual circumstances in each case, but juries can take these into account. Still others believe that juries
are favorable because they reflect the morals and values of the community they come from. Indeed, many proponents of the jury support

the system because of a particular kind of jury bias, the tendency for jurors to place justice above the law (Goldberg 457).

4   Opponents of the system argue that juries are uneducated in legal procedures and should not be given the type of responsibility they have traditionally had. These people also argue that juries are biased. In fact, the psychological literature provides many examples of this bias. Jurors are less likely to punish a sad or distressed defendant, as opposed to a joyful one, apparently because the defendant is already being punished emotionally (Upshaw and Romer 162). Some opponents say that although juries are instructed not to pay attention to the media, they are more easily influenced by the news than by the presiding judges. Critics of the jury system also point out that juries are expensive and are often unable to reach a consensus. They argue that the decision making should be left up to the people who know the law, the judges and lawyers.

5   In between these two extremes are those people who agree with the jury system as a whole but feel that some changes need to be implemented to improve its effectiveness. These people suggest that juries receive instruction prior to hearing testimony as well as before they begin deliberations. They argue that this would improve the system by providing some working legal knowledge for the jury as well as giving them an idea of what they are to listen for. Research has shown that in laboratory mock jury situations, exposing jurors to the laws involved in their decision making resulted in significantly fewer verdicts of guilty when compared to not exposing jurors to the relevant laws (Cruse and Browne 131). This finding suggests that lawyers and judges should have the responsibility of ensuring that the jury is adequately informed of the legal issues at hand and the laws and statutes available to handle those issues.

6   As a prospective law student, I am fascinated by this topic. I think it is incredible that juries, made up of ordinary citizens, make some of the most profound legal decisions in the world. I decided to write on this particular issue because of a recent decision by a jury in Texas to recommend probation instead of prison for a man who shot his wife several times, killing her, and also shot and injured her lover. Jury members did not want to send this individual to jail because they claimed his own remorse would punish him sufficiently over the years. This example forced me to evaluate the positive and negative aspects of jury trials.

7   The rise in crime in this country and the question of what to do with the offenders makes the role of juries even more compelling. As a whole, though, I feel that the American guarantee of trial by jury is a valuable one. I do feel, however, that in order to improve its utility, judges and attorneys need to accept the responsibility

for educating the jury on relevant legal issu
I will define the problem in detail and then e
of jury training can be implemented. ■

Works Cited

Cruse, Donna, and Beverly A. Brown. "Reasoning in ↵
    The Influence of Instructions." <u>Journal of General</u> ↲
    114 (1987): 129-33.
Goldberg, Janice C. "Memory, Magic, and Myth: The Timing of Jury
    Instructions." <u>Oregon Law Review</u> 59 (1981): 451-75.
Upshaw, Harry S., and Daniel Romer. "Punishments of One's Misdeeds
    as a Function of Having Suffered from Them." <u>Personality and
    Social Psychology Bulletin</u> 2 (1976): 162-69.

FOR DISCUSSION: What jury trial have you followed in recent years? Did you think the jury made a fair judgment? If you had been on the jury, would you have agreed or disagreed? Why? Do you think the present jury system needs improvement? If so, what could be done to improve it?

D. WRITING ASSIGNMENT: THE EXPLORATORY PAPER

Review "How to Write an Exploratory Paper" on pages 110–113 to help you complete this assignment. Then write a 750 to 900-word exploratory paper in which you do all of the following:

1. Explain the issue
2. Describe the rhetorical situation
3. Explain three (or more) positions on the issue along with some reasons for each of them
4. Explain your interest in the issue and the position you favor
5. Make a tentative claim that sets forth your position

Follow MLA style (see the Appendix to Chapter 10) unless you are advised otherwise.

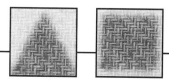

PART TWO

Understanding the Nature of Argument for Reading and Writing

The purpose of Chapters 5, 6, and 7 is to explain the essential parts of an argument and show how they operate to convince an audience. Chapter 5 identifies the parts of a traditional argument as explained by Stephen Toulmin in what has come to be known as the Toulmin model, Chapter 6 describes the types of claims and purposes in argument, and Chapter 7 presents the proofs for argument. When you finish reading Part Two:

- You will understand and be able to identify the essential parts of an argument.
- You will know the key questions that arguments attempt to answer.
- You will be able to identify types of claims and purpose in argument.
- You will understand how argument can appeal to your reason, your emotions, and your sense of values about people's character.
- You will know how to use argument theory to invent ideas for a position paper.
- You will know how to write a position paper and make it convincing.

CHAPTER FIVE

The Essential Parts of an Argument: The Toulmin Model

The purpose of the chapters in Part Two is to present some ideas from argument theory that will help you add strategies for reading and writing argument with confidence and expertise. Because people have been analyzing argument and writing theories of argument for twenty-five hundred years, there is a considerable tradition of theory to draw on to help with this task. A theoretical background is useful because theory describes argument, and once you possess good descriptions, argument will be more familiar and consequently easier for you to read and write yourself.

As you acquire new understandings of argument, you will be adding to what you already know and gradually building a stronger and larger body of knowledge and comprehension. Eventually, you will achieve "all-at-onceness," a quality Ann E. Berthoff describes in her book *The Sense of Learning* to describe the use of many ideas, bits of information, and strategies about reading and writing that finally come together so that you are able to use them unconsciously, simultaneously, and automatically.[1]

For now, however, you are still expanding your knowledge. Your goals in this chapter will be to get a better understanding of the usual anticipated outcomes of argument and to identify its component parts as they are identified by Stephen Toulmin in his model for argument.

---

[1] Ann E. Berthoff, *The Sense of Learning* (Portsmouth, N.H.: Boynton/Cook, 1990), pp. 86–91.

THE OUTCOMES OF ARGUMENT:
PROBABILITY VERSUS CERTAINTY

In Chapter 1 you learned that arguable issues require the possibility of at least two different views. It is the nature of argument to invite differing views and perspectives on issues. Outcomes can include achieving a closer agreement with a friendly audience or getting the attention and even perhaps some consensus from a neutral or hostile audience. Notice that these outcomes of argument are usually not described as establishing certainty or truth in the same sense that mathematics and science seek to establish certainty and truth. We do not argue about the fact that $2 + 3 = 5$ or that the area of a circle is πr^2. Mathematical proofs seek to establish such truths. Argument seeks to establish what is probably true as well as what might be expedient or desirable for the future. Arguers tell you what they think for now along with what they think should be done, given their present information. On that basis, you decide what you think for now, given your present information.

Throughout history, some thinkers have been drawn more to the idea of establishing truth and some have been drawn more to the idea of establishing probabilities. In ancient times the Greek philosopher Plato was interested in establishing truth. He employed dialectic, the question-and-answer method used in his dialogues, to help participants discover the Platonic ideas about truth. Aristotle, another Greek philosopher, was interested in probabilities. His *Rhetoric*, written somewhere between 360 and 334 B.C., is a key book in the history of argument theory, and its purpose is to train persuasive speakers to be convincing to audiences. Aristotle observed the orators of his time and described what they did. He noted that they were mainly concerned with matters and views concerning both the present and the future that were probably true rather than certainly true. The reason for their perspective lay in the audience. The ancient audience, like modern audiences, would disagree with many views that were stated as absolutely true. Those audiences could think of exceptions and reasons why certain views might not be true. Responsible persuaders, to communicate effectively, had to modify and qualify their views to make them acceptable to their audiences. They had to present probabilities instead of absolute truths. Thus views that are probably true comprise the realm of argument. To understand that realm better, it is useful to understand the parts that contribute to the whole argument.

THE PARTS OF AN ARGUMENT ACCORDING
TO THE TOULMIN MODEL

Stephen Toulmin, a modern English philosopher, developed a six-part model of argument in his book *The Uses of Argument,* and this model has been useful to many people for explaining the essential parts of an argument.[2] At the time Toul-

---

[2]Stephen Toulmin, *The Uses of Argument* (Cambridge: Cambridge University Press, 1958). I have adapted and added applications of the model to make it more useful for reading and writing.

min wrote his book, his colleagues were logicians who were interested in discovering truth rather than probabilities. Toulmin tells us that his book had a chilly welcome among those English colleagues. His graduate adviser at Cambridge, he tells us, "was deeply pained by the book, and barely spoke to me for twenty years." Another colleague described it as "Toulmin's *anti*-logic book."[3] After that, Toulmin expected his book to be a failure. But his editors assured him that people were buying it, and Toulmin found out who many of these people were when he visited the United States some time later. Professors in speech departments and departments of communication all over the United States were using his book to teach students to become better argumentative speakers. If you have ever taken a speech class, you may have already encountered the Toulmin model of argument. As time went by, the model was picked up by English departments to help students improve their reading and writing of argument. The Toulmin model has also been used in schools of law to help students learn to present legal argument. The Toulmin model is a very natural and practical model because it follows normal human thought processes. You will find that you have had experience with all its parts either in the everyday arguments you carry on with your friends and family or in the arguments that you see on television.

The Toulmin model has six parts. The first three parts are essential to all argument. They are (1) the *claim*, (2) the *data* (which we are calling *support*), and (3) the *warrant*. Arguments may also contain one or more of three additional elements: (4) the *backing*, (5) the *rebuttal*, and (6) the *qualifier*. Figure 5.1 shows Toulmin's diagram of these six parts of the model.

Here is an example to illustrate how these parts work together in an actual argument: The narrator of a television program makes the *claim* that critical think-

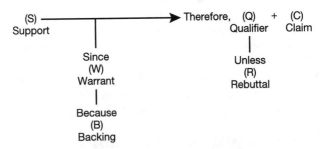

Figure 5.1   A Diagram of the Toulmin Model of Argument Showing the Three Essential Parts—Claim, Support, and Warrant—and the Three Optional Parts —Backing, Rebuttal, and Qualifier
Source: Adapted from Stephen Toulmin, *The Uses of Argument* (Cambridge: Cambridge University Press, 1958), p. 104

---

[3]"Logic and the Criticism of Arguments," in James L. Golden, Goodwin F. Berquist, and William E. Coleman, *The Rhetoric of Western Thought*, 4th ed. (Dubuque, Ia.: Kendall Hunt, 1989), p. 375.

ing is more important now than it was seventy years ago. This is followed by *support* that includes pictures of modern scientists launching space shuttles and air traffic controllers directing airplanes to land. These individuals seem intent and busy. It appears to be clear that if they do not think critically, there will be trouble. Then the camera switches to children riding on an old-fashioned school bus of seventy years ago. One is saying that he wants to grow up and be a farmer like his dad. This youngster is relaxed and bouncing along on the bus. He doesn't look like he is thinking critically or that he will ever need to. The unspoken part of this argument, the assumption that the author of this program hopes the audience will share, is the *warrant*. The author hopes the audience will agree, even though it is not explicitly stated, that farmers of seventy years ago did not have to think critically, that modern scientists and engineers do have to think critically, and that critical thinking was not so important then as now. The author hopes that the audience will look at the two bits of support, the scientist and the farmer's son, and make the leap necessary to accept the claim. That's right, the audience will think, those scientists and that young boy don't seem to share the same demands for critical thinking. Times have changed. Critical thinking *is* more important now than it was seventy years ago. Those three parts, the *claim*, the *support*, and the *warrant*, are the three essential parts of an argument.

The other three parts, if present, might go like this: Suppose the camera then shifts to an old man, who says, "Wait a minute. What makes you assume farmers didn't think? My daddy was a farmer, and he was the best critical thinker I ever knew. He had to think about weather, crops, growing seasons, fertilizer, finances, harvesting, and selling the crops. The thinking he had to do was as sophisticated as that of any modern scientist." This old fellow is indicating that he does not share the unstated warrant that farmers of seventy years ago had fewer demands on their thinking processes than modern scientists. In response to this rejoinder, the author, to make the argument convincing, provides *backing for the warrant*. This backing takes the form of additional support. The camera cuts to the narrator of the program: "At least two out of three of the farmers of seventy years ago had small farms. They grew food for their families and traded or sold the rest for whatever else they needed. The thinking and decision making required of them was not as complicated and demanding as that required by modern scientists. Your father was an exception." Notice that this backing takes the form of a smaller unit of argument within the argument. It is linked to the main argument, and it is used to back up the weakest part of the main argument. Furthermore, this smaller argument has a claim-support-warrant structure of its own: (1) the *claim* is that most farmers did not have to think; (2) the *support* is that two out of three did not have to think and that the old man's father was an exception; and (3) the *warrant*, again unstated, is that the old man will believe the statistics and accept the idea that his father was an exception. If he accepts this backing, the argument is on solid ground again. If he does not, if he asks for more backing for the new warrant by asking, "Hey, where did you get those statistics? They're not like any I ever heard," then another argument would need to be developed to cite the source of the figures and to convince the old man of their reliability. As you can see, the requests for backing, for more information to serve as further proof, can go on and on. But let's leave the old man and the narrator and look at what else might appear in this argument.

Suppose the camera now shifts to a modern science professor who wants to take exception with the claim itself by making a *rebuttal*. She makes her own claim: "The critical thinking required seventy years ago was demanding and sophisticated. Critical thinkers of that time had to figure out how to get the country out of a severe recession, and they had to develop the technology to win the Second World War." These opinions are then supported with factual evidence that includes pictures of individuals thinking.

After all of these challenges, exceptions, and requests for more information, the author at this point finds it necessary to *qualify* the original claim in order to make it acceptable to more of the audience members. Qualifying involves adding words and phrases to the claim like *sometimes, seems to be, maybe,* or *possibly* to make it acceptable to the audience. In this case, the narrator now restates the qualified claim: "Critical thinking, because of modern science, seems to some people to be more important now than it was sixty years ago." Compare this with the original claim that critical thinking is more important now than it was seventy years ago. Figure 5.2 diagrams this argument according to the Toulmin model. You have probably never systematically used this or any other model to read or write argument. The model can serve as a kind of guide for reading and analyzing

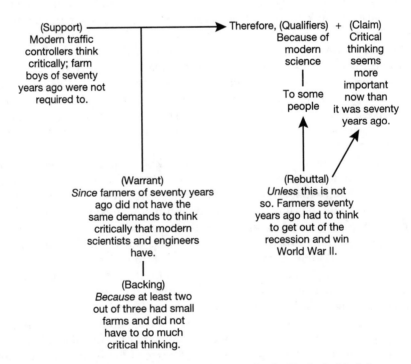

Figure 5.2   An Example of the Six Elements in the Toulmin Model

arguments and also for writing them. Authors do not usually use the model as an exact formula for writing, however. Rather, it describes what can be but is not necessarily always present in an argument. Consequently, when you read argument, you will at times easily recognize some parts of the model and at other times you will not. Some arguments, in fact, may not contain one or more of the parts at all, like a rebuttal, for example. You are not getting it wrong if you read and do not find all of the parts. When you write, you do not need to make all parts explicit either. The following sections provide some details about each of the six parts that will help you understand them better.

Claim

Discover the claim of an argument by asking, "What is the author trying to prove?" Or plan a claim of your own by asking, "What do I want to prove?" The claim is the main point of the argument. Identifying the claim as soon as possible helps you focus on what the argument is all about.

Synonyms for *claim* are *thesis, proposition, conclusion,* and *main point.* Sometimes an author of an argument in a newspaper or magazine will refer to the "proposition," or an individual arguing on television will ask, "What is your point?" Both are referring to the claim. When someone refers to the claim as the conclusion, don't confuse it with the idea at the end of an argument. The claim can appear at the end, but it can also appear at other places in the argument. The claim is sometimes stated in a sentence or sentences called the *statement of claim.* This sentence can also be called the *thesis statement,* the *purpose sentence,* the *statement of focus,* or the *statement of proposition.*

The terms used in this text to describe the main elements in argument, along with some of their synonyms, appear in Table 5.1. Become familiar with them so that you will understand other writers on the subject who may vary the terminology.

To locate the claim, what should you look for? The claim may be explicitly stated at the beginning of an argument, at the end, or somewhere in the middle. Or it may not be stated anywhere. It may sometimes be *implied,* in which case you will be expected to *infer* it. To infer an implicit claim, you will need to use what you already know about the subject along with what you have just read to formulate your own statement of it. In this case, the author is paying you a kind of compliment. The assumption is that you are smart enough to figure out the claim for yourself. You should probably make your own claims in your written arguments clear and explicit, however, at least at first.

Another interesting variation on the claim occurs in the case of irony. In irony the author says one thing but means something else. Usually the stated claim in irony is exaggerated, outrageous, or odd in some way. You may read it and think to yourself, "Surely the author doesn't *mean* this." What does the author really mean? Again, you are expected to use your background and judgment to figure that out.

The claim, whether implied or explicitly stated, organizes the entire argument, and everything else in the argument is related to it. The best way to identify it, if it is not obvious or easy to locate, is to complete the following statement as soon as you have finished reading: "This author wants to convince me to think that . . ." When you have finished that statement, you have the claim. As a

TERMS	SYNONYMS
Claim	Thesis Proposition Conclusion Main point Macro-argument Controlling idea
Statement of claim	Thesis statement Purpose sentence Statement of focus Statement of proposition
Subclaims	Reasons Main ideas Micro-arguments Arguments Lines of argument Supporting arguments Specific issues
Support	Evidence Opinions Reasons Examples Facts Data Grounds Proof Premise Statistics Explanations Information Personal narratives
Warrants	Assumptions General principles Widely held values Commonly accepted beliefs Appeals to human motives Cultural values Presuppositions Unstated premises Generally accepted truths

TABLE 5.1   Argument Terminology: Terms Used in This Book and Some of Their Synonyms

writer, you can check your own claim during revision by completing this statement: "I have convinced my audience to think that . . ."

Authors often make conscious decisions about where to place a claim and whether to make it explicit or implicit. Their decisions are related to their notions about the audience. A claim at the beginning is straightforward and draws the reader in right away, like the claim in "A View from Berkeley," page 51, in paragraph 2: "We *should* consider race, ethnicity and gender along with many other factors in [college] admissions." Both parties are thinking along the same lines, together, from the outset. Or an author may decide to lead up to the claim, in which case it may appear either in the middle or at the end. For example, the claim in "Applying to College, Made Easy," page 23, appears as a question in the middle of the essay (end of paragraph 3): "Why hasn't the college application been standardized?" And the claim in "Girls and Computers," page 24, appears at the end: "Educators must insure that girls are not inadvertently left out of the computer revolution." Delaying the claim pulls the audience in and increases interest and attention. "What is this author after?" the audience wonders, and reads to find out. The end of an essay is the most emphatic and memorable place for a claim. Many authors prefer to put the claim there to give it as much force as possible. There is some risk involved in putting the claim at the end. Students who use this strategy must be careful to insert cues along the way so that readers understand where the argument is headed and do not feel they are being led through a random chain of topics. Both the unstated claim and the ironic claim require special attention on the part of the reader because the reader has to make an inference to figure them out. As a result of this effort, the reader may find an inferred claim especially convincing and memorable.

Argument, like any other discourse, has main ideas and ideas that support them, as was shown in Chapter 3. The claim is the main point of the entire piece, and the subclaims are the shorter supporting arguments or reasons for the claim. We will present two examples that illustrate the relationships among the issues, related issues, claims, and subclaims in argument. Included are the following:

- *Two issue areas, racism* and *the environment,* that are at the most general level in these examples
- *Two of many possible specific related issues* in these issue areas that represent ideas *about* the general issue areas
- *Examples of claims* made in response to the specific related issues that are even more specific
- *Examples of some subclaims* used to support the claims (The subclaims are at the most specific level in this example because they represent ideas about the claims.)

Example 1

Issue area: Racism

Specific related issue: Where do racist attitudes come from?
Claim: People are not born with racist attitudes; they have to be taught them.

Subclaims: 1. Some parents transmit racist attitudes.
2. The press can reinforce racist attitudes.
3. Peer groups can also strengthen racist attitudes.
4. Segregated schools and neighborhoods contribute to racist attitudes.

Example 2

Issue area: The Environment

Specific related issue: How serious are the world's environmental problems?
Claim: The environment is the single most serious problem the world faces today.
Subclaims: 1. The rain forests are being destroyed, causing global warming.
2. Increasing population is depleting resources in some parts of the world.
3. Many important water sources are being polluted by industry.
4. The ozone layer, which protects us from harmful sun rays, is being destroyed by chemicals.

When you *read*, complete this statement: "The author wants me to believe that . . ." When you *write*, complete this statement: "I want my audience to agree that . . ." Can you do it? If you can, you understand the concept of the claim, and you will be able to recognize the main point in the arguments you read and to use a claim to articulate the main point in any argument you write.

Support

Discover the support in an argument by asking, "What additional information does the author supply to convince me of this claim?" Or if you are the author, ask, "What information do I need to supply to convince my audience?" You can summarize the most essential elements of an argument as a *claim with support*. Aristotle wrote in his *Rhetoric* that the only necessary parts of an argument are the statement of proposition (the claim) and the proof (the support). There has been general agreement about those two essential parts of an argument for more than twenty-three hundred years.

Support provides the evidence, opinions, reasoning, examples, and factual information about a claim that make it possible for us to accept it. Look back at the claims and subclaims on page 129 and in the examples above. If you are to take these claims seriously, you will want some support to make them convincing.

The synonyms that Toulmin uses for support are *data* and *grounds*, the British equivalents. In the United States you will often read arguments in which the author claims to be "grounding" a claim with particular support, and *data* is sometimes used as a synonym for *facts and figures*. Other synonyms for support are *proof, evidence,* and *reasons*. Sometimes authors refer to major evidence as *premises*. When you encounter that term in your reading, remember that premises lead to and support a conclusion (a claim). Don't confuse premises with the claim.

To locate support, what should you look for? One bit of good news: support is always explicitly stated, so you will not have to infer it as you sometimes have to infer the claim. Thus an understanding of the types of support is all you really need to help you recognize it. Let us look at some of the most common types.

Facts. In a court of law, factual support (the murder weapon, for example) is laid out on the table. In written argument, it must be described. Factual support can include detailed reports of *observed events;* specific *examples* of real happenings; references to *events,* either *historical* or *recent;* and *statistical reports.* Factual support is vivid, real, and verifiable. Two people looking at it together would agree on its existence, and what it looks like. They might not agree on what it *means* to each of them—that is, they might interpret it differently. But essentially they would agree on the facts themselves.

Opinions. When people start interpreting the facts, opinion enters the picture. The following quotation is an example of some statistics that have been interpreted. The author is a wildlife scientist who has studied wolves and other wild animals in Alaska for many years, and he is arguing against a plan by the state of Alaska to shoot wolves in order to protect herds of caribou.

> The state is portraying the wolf kill as an emergency measure to boost the size of what is called the "Delta caribou herd," which ranges east of Denali. But the herd's population decrease since 1989—from 11,000 to 4,000—represents little more than a return to the numbers that prevailed for decades until the mid-80's. The short-lived increase to 11,000 probably resulted largely from a temporary shift of caribou from a neighboring herd.
>
> The Delta herd didn't even exist until about 60 years ago; it is probably an offshoot of a much larger herd farther to the east. There is no major caribou-hunting tradition in this area, so the plan is not a matter of restoring something that hunters had enjoyed for generations. Over the past 12 months, most of the Delta herd has spent most of its time well outside the wolf-control area.
>
> In fact, the state's view that this and other caribou herds should be managed at stable or minimum sizes is a mistake. Virtually all of Alaska's caribou belong to a single population within which, over the span of decades, there are shifting centers of abundance. Thousands of caribou may abandon a range they have inhabited for decades and move to an area where numbers have traditionally been low. Despite recent declines in the Delta herd and in several nearby areas, other herds have increased dramatically. Statewide, the number of caribou has more then tripled over the past 15 years to about a million animals and is continuing to increase rapidly.[4]

Note that the raw data, the herd's decrease in numbers from 11,000 to 4,000, have been interpreted and explained. The author says the decrease in the caribou population has probably been caused by the herds moving around and that actually there are now more caribou statewide than fifteen years ago. Thus there is no

---

[4]Gordon C. Haber, "The Great Alaska Wolf Kill," *New York Times,* October 2, 1993, p. A23.

need to slaughter wolves to protect caribou. State officials had interpreted the same data to indicate that wolves should be killed to save the caribou. You need to distinguish between facts everyone would agree on and interpret in the same way and facts that are open to interpretation and opinion. We do not argue with the facts, as the saying goes, unless of course they are lies or they omit important information. We do, however, argue with interpretation and opinion.

Opinions may be the personal opinions of the author or the opinions of experts the author selects to quote. The quotes may be direct quotes, set off in quotation marks, or they may be summaries or paraphrases of what someone else thinks or has said. Furthermore, opinions may be informed, based on considerable knowledge and excellent judgment, or they may be ill-founded, based on hearsay and gossip. The most convincing opinions are those of experts, whether they be those of the author or of another person. Experts possess superior background, education, and experience on an issue. Contrast in your own mind the opinions of experts with the uninformed opinions of people on the evening news who are frequently cornered in the streets by reporters to give their opinions. Informed personal opinions and the opinions of experts can be more interesting and convincing than the facts themselves. Ill-founded, baseless opinion is boring and rarely convincing.

Examples.　Examples can be real or made up, long or short. They are used to clarify, to make material more memorable and interesting, and in argument particularly, to prove. Examples that are real, such as instances of actual events or references to particular individuals, function in the same way that fact does in an argument. They are convincing because they are grounded in reality. Made-up or hypothetical examples are invented by the writer and, like opinions, can only demonstrate probabilities. Personal experience is one type of example that is frequently used in argument. Writers often go into considerable detail about the experiences that have influenced them to think and behave as they do. Combining personal experience with the opinions and reasoning derived from it is a common way to develop a claim.

There are no set rules about the placement of support in an argument. Support can appear before the claim, as in the following example: "The caribou have moved around and are alive [the support]; *therefore,* we do not need a wolf-kill policy [claim]." Or support can appear after the claim: "The wolf-kill policy should be abandoned [claim] *because* the caribou have moved around, and there are three times as many of them as 15 years ago [support]."

Different authors manage support in different ways depending on the requirements of the subject, their purpose, and their audience. When the issue is an abstract idea and the audience is informed, the author may present mainly opinions and few, if any, facts or examples. Such arguments include a claim and blocks of logical reasoning organized around subclaims to develop and prove the claim. If you were to outline the argument, you might not need more than two levels, as in the claim and subclaim examples on pages 129–130. When the subject requires more specific support or the audience needs more information to be convinced, specific materials at lower levels on an outline are required to ground the subclaims in facts, figures, quotations from others, or author opinions.

Here is an example that illustrates these levels.[5] It includes (1) a general issue area, (2) one of many specific issues that could be generated by it, (3) a claim, (4) some subclaims, and (5) some support.

Example

Issue area: Cities

Specific related issue: How should cities be planned so that people will live happily in them?

Claim: Inner cities can be made more inhabitable.

Subclaim: One way is to omit automobiles and encourage walking.

Support: With no cars, people are forced to walk and interact, and interacting is pleasant. (opinion)

Subclaim: Another way is to eliminate public housing projects.

Support: More than half the poor are often in public housing. (fact)

Support: Warehousing the poor is destructive to the neighborhood and occupants. (opinion)

To summarize, support comprises all the explicitly stated explanations, information, facts, opinions, personal narratives, and examples that authors use to make their claims and subclaims convincing and believable. Notice that support may be true, as in the case of facts and real examples, or probable, as in the case of opinions and made-up stories and examples.

Readers and writers of argument should require that the support in an argument be acceptable and convincing. Factual evidence needs to be true and verifiable. All evidence needs to be clear, relevant, and understandable. It also should represent all of the significant information available; it must, in other words, be an adequate sample. The experts whose opinion are quoted should be real experts, and their credentials should, when necessary, be stated by the author to establish their degree of expertise. Personal opinion, to be convincing, should be original, impressive, interesting, and backed by factual knowledge, experience, good reasoning, and judgment. Support that meets these requirements is not only accepted but often shared by the audience because they have had similar experiences and ideas themselves. Such quality support helps build common ground between the arguer and the audience. Rantings, unfounded personal opinions that no one else accepts, or feeble reasons like "because I said so" or "because everyone does it" are not effective support. Audiences usually do not believe such statements, they do not share experiences or ideas suggested by them, and they lose common ground with the arguer when they read or hear them.

When reading argument, to help you focus on and recognize the support, complete this sentence as soon as you finish. "The author wants me to believe that . . . [the claim] because . . . [list the support]." When you read to revise

---

[5]The items in the example are from Witold Rybczynski, "How to Rebuild Los Angeles," *New York Times,* June 6, 1992, p. A15.

your own writing, you can complete this statement: "I have convinced my audience to believe [the claim] because [list your support]."

Warrants

Warrants are the assumptions, general principles, conventions of specific disciplines, widely held values, commonly accepted beliefs, and appeals to human motives that are an important part of any argument. Even though they can be spelled out as part of the written argument, usually they are not. In many instances it would be redundant and boring if they were. For example, an argument might go as follows: *Claim:* The president of the United States is doing a great job. *Support:* The economy is the best it has been in ten years. The unstated *warrants* in this argument might include the following *generally accepted beliefs:* the president is responsible for the economy; when the economy is good, it is a sign that the president is doing a good job; or even though the president may be doing well in other areas, a robust economy is the main index to how well he is doing. You may be able to think of some other ways of expressing the warrants in this argument. Since individual audience members vary in their backgrounds and perspectives, not everyone will state the warrants in exactly the same way.

Here is another example, and this one relies on a *value warrant. Claim:* Business profits are adversely affected by environmental protection laws. *Support:* Obeying environmental protection laws that call for clean air, for example, costs industry money that could otherwise be realized as profit. The unstated *warrants* in this argument involve the relative value individuals place on the environment and on business profit and might be stated thus: profit is more important than clean air, businesses must make profit to survive, or environmental protection laws are threatening the capitalistic system.

Finally, here is an example of a warrant that relies on a *commonly accepted convention* of a specific discipline, which in this case is the discipline of writing. *Claim:* You have received a failing grade on this paper. *Support:* You have several sentence fragments and subject-verb agreement errors in your paper. The unstated *warrants* could be stated as follows: these types of errors result in a failing grade in college papers, or the conventions of writing college papers do not allow for fragments and subject-verb agreement problems. When you encounter argument in your other college courses, try to identify the warrants that are implicit in these arguments and that are also part of the generally accepted knowledge or the conventions that inform these particular disciplines. Such warrants could include laws in physics, equations in mathematics, or theories in philosophy. Such information is not always spelled out in every argument, particularly if the people who are arguing share the same background information about these conventions, laws, equations, or theories. A physicist, for example, would not have to state the law of gravity to fill in the argument that an object dropped from a bridge will fall into the water below. Instead, the arguer assumes that the audience knows about the law of gravity and will mentally fill it in to complete an argument. Toulmin called the warrants that are specific to particular disciplines *field-dependent* because they are understood and accepted by individuals who have background and expertise in specific fields of knowledge. They can be differentiated from *field-independent* warrants that cut across disciplines and would be accepted by most people. The belief that the president should improve the economy is an example of a field-independent warrant.

Warrants originate with the arguer. Note, however, that the warrants also exist in the minds of the audience. They can be *shared* by the arguer and the audience, or they can be *in conflict.* Furthermore, if the audience shares the warrants with the arguer, the audience will accept them, and the argument is convincing. If the warrants are in conflict and the audience does not accept them (they believe private enterprises, not the president, is responsible for improving the economy, or they believe sentence fragments are acceptable in academic writing because many widely admired writers have used them), the argument is not convincing to them.

Here is another example. A politician arguing that crimes are caused by a lack of family values expects the audience to supply the warrant that people with family values do not commit crime. The argument is strong and convincing for audiences who happen to share those values and who thus share the warrant. It is not so convincing for audience members who believe there are other causes for crime that have nothing to do with family values. A conflicting warrant might be the belief that peer groups, not families, cause people to turn to crime.

Notice how warrants themselves, when they are recognized by the audience as either acceptable or not, can themselves become claims for new arguments. The examples of the two warrants about what causes crime can each be stated as new claims and supported as new arguments. Developing warrants as subjects for new arguments is called *chaining arguments.* The process can go on indefinitely and can help move an argument in a variety of interesting directions. For example, if one claims that peer groups cause crime and then supports that claim with the evidence that gangs are notorious for committing crimes, the shared warrant would be that gang members are criminals. That warrant could then become a claim for a new argument about the criminal records of gangs. A conflicting warrant, that many gang members are law-abiding citizens, could become the claim for a different argument that would provide an entirely different view of gang members.

Besides being related to what people commonly believe, value, want, or accept as background knowledge in a discipline, warrants are also culture-bound. Since values, beliefs, and training vary from culture to culture, the warrants associated with them also differ from culture to culture. Tension between Japan and the United States was caused by a Japanese official's claim that American workers are lazy and do not work hard enough. American workers were angry and countered with a rebuttal about how hard they think they work. Japanese and American workers have different work schedules, attitudes, and experience with leisure and work time. Consequently, the part of both arguments that was unstated, the warrant, described hard work in different ways for each culture. The lack of a shared warrant caused the tension. Furthermore, neither side was convinced by the other's argument.

You may be thinking at this point, How am I going to be able to understand warrants when they usually are not printed on the page, they exist in the minds of the author and the audience, and they may even differ from one individual or culture to another? You will not have the difficulty with warrants that you may be anticipating because you already know a great deal about people and the opinions and beliefs they are likely to hold. You may have never noticed warrants before. But once you become aware of them, you will recognize them in every argument you read. Warrants are one of the most interesting features of argument. They represent the psychology of an argument in the sense that they reveal unspoken beliefs and values of the author and invite you to examine your own beliefs and make comparisons.

Finding warrants is not very different from "psyching people out" or trying to discover their real reasons for saying things. Here is an example that might make finding warrants easier: Suppose your spouse or roommate makes the claim that you really should start sleeping at night, instead of staying up to study, because it is more beneficial to study in the daytime. As support, you are reminded that sunshine keeps people from getting depressed, that people sleep more soundly at night than in the day, and that you need to build daytime work habits because you will probably not get a nighttime job when you graduate.

To understand the warrants in this argument, you must try to figure out what else your roommate believes, values, and wants but has not said directly. The warrants might include these: Daytime people are better than nighttime people; you should be like other people and change your work habits to conform; you will get more done in the daytime because other people do; and you will have trouble switching from night to day if you ever have to. You might go a step further and ask, Why else is my roommate trying to change my work habits? What is the hidden agenda? Maybe it is because you leave the lights on and music playing all night. We figure out the subtexts or hidden agendas in our conversations with other people all the time. Warrants and hidden agendas are not the same, as you can see from these examples, but they are similar in the sense that neither are usually spelled out and that discovering them requires looking for what is left unstated in our communications with other people.

Some of the synonyms for warrants are *unstated assumptions, presuppositions of the author,* and *unstated premises.* Warrants are also sometimes described as general truths that the audience will accept as true.

Warrants provide critical links in argument. For instance, they link the support to the claim by enabling an audience to accept particular support as proof of a particular claim. Without the linking warrant, the support may not be convincing. Here is an example:

Claim:	The appeal process for criminals should be shortened . . .
Support:	because the appeals for criminals on death row can cost more than $2 million per criminal.
Expected warrants:	Spending more than $2 million to keep a convicted criminal alive a little longer is a waste of money. *(This individual shares the author's warrant, the link is made, and the argument is convincing.)*
Alternative warrant:	We are dealing with human life here, and we should spend whatever is necessary to make certain we have

a fair conviction. *(This individual supplies an opposing warrant, the link between claim and support is not made, and the argument is not convincing.)*

Supply your own warrant in the following argument:

Claim:	The government should abolish loan funds for college students . . .
Support:	because many students default on their loans, and the government cannot tolerate these bad debts.
Warrants:	*(Do you believe that evidence supports that claim? If yes, why? If no, why? Your answer provides the warrant. Is the argument convincing for you?)*

These examples demonstrate that the warrant links the evidence and the claim by justifying particular evidence as support for a particular claim. Notice also, however, that the warrant attempts to establish a link between the author and the audience as well. Shared warrants result in successful arguments. When the warrant is not shared or when there are conflicting warrants, the audience will question or disagree with the claim. When American workers argued with the Japanese about whether they are lazy or hardworking, a shared warrant was missing.

Japanese claim:	American workers are lazy . . .
Support:	because they only work 40 hours a week.
Japanese warrant:	People who only work 40 hours a week are lazy.
American rebuttal:	American workers are hardworking . . .
Support:	because they work 40 hours a week.
American warrant:	People who put in 40 hours a week are industrious and hardworking.

Perhaps now you can begin to appreciate the importance of shared warrants in argument. Shared warrants are crucial to the success of an argument because they are the most significant way to establish common ground between reader and writer in argument. Shared warrants and common ground, as you can imagine, are particularly important in international negotiations. Skillful negotiators take time to analyze warrants and to determine whether or not both parties are on common ground. If they are not, communication breaks down and argument fails.

At this point, you may wonder why authors do not spell out the warrants, since they are so essential to the success of the argument. There are two reasons for usually leaving warrants unstated, so that the audience has to supply them. First, an audience who supplies the warrant is more likely to buy in to the argument through a sense of participation. If there is potential for agreement and common ground, it will be strengthened by the audience supplying the warrant. Second, remember that audiences differ and that their views of the warrant also vary somewhat, depending on their past experiences and present perceptions. A stated warrant negates the rich and varied perceptions and responses of the audience by providing only the author's interpretation and articulation of the warrant. Less active participation is then required from the audience, and the argument is less powerful and convincing to them.

To help you discover warrants, ask questions like the following:

What is left out here?
What does this author value? Do I share those values?
What is causing this author to say these things?
Do I believe that this evidence supports this claim? Why or why not?

As the author of argument, you should consider your audience and whether or not it will accept your warrants. More information will be provided in Chapter 8 to help you do so. Now let's look at the other three parts of the Toulmin model, the optional elements. All or none might appear in a written argument.

Backing

You should have a sense by now that warrants themselves may require their own support to make them more acceptable to an audience, particularly if the audience does not happen to share them with the author. An author may provide backing, or additional evidence to "back up" a warrant, whenever the audience is in danger of rejecting it. When you are the author, you should provide backing also. In exchanges like debates or rebuttal letters to the editor, the author is sometimes asked to prove the warrant with additional support. Or the author may analyze the beliefs and values of the audience, anticipate a lack of common ground, and back the warrant with additional support explicitly in the text, just in case. For example, in the criminal appeals argument, the author might back the warrant that it is a waste of time to spend $2 million on a criminal appeal with additional statistical evidence that shows these appeals rarely result in a changed verdict. This additional backing would improve the likelihood that the audience would accept the claim.

Here is another example of backing for a warrant:

Claim:　All immigrants should be allowed to come into the United States . . .
Support:　because immigration has benefited the U.S. economy in the past.
Warrant:　Current economic conditions are similar to past conditions.
Backing:　Now, as in the past, immigrants are willing to perform necessary low-paying jobs that American citizens do not want, particularly in the service areas. *(Statistics could be supplied to show how many jobs of this type are available.)*

Look for backing in an argument by identifying the warrant and then determining whether or not you accept it. If you do not, try to anticipate additional information that would make it more acceptable. Then look to see if the author supplied that or similar additional support.

Rebuttal

A rebuttal establishes what is wrong, invalid, or unacceptable about an argument and may also present counterarguments, or new arguments that represent entirely different perspectives or points of view on the issue. To attack the validity of the claim, an author may demonstrate that the support is faulty or that the warrants are faulty or unbelievable. Counterarguments start all over again, with a new set of claims, support, and warrants.

Here is an example of a rebuttal for the argument about immigration:

Rebuttal 1: Immigrants actually drain more resources in schooling, medical care, and other social services than they contribute in taxes and productivity.

Rebuttal 2: Modern immigrants are not so willing to perform menial, low-skilled jobs as they were in past generations.

Here is an example of a counterargument for the immigration argument:

Claim: Laws should be passed to limit immigration . . .

Support: because we have our own unskilled laborers who need those jobs.

Warrant: These laborers are willing to hold these jobs.

Rebuttals may appear as answers to arguments that have already been stated, or the author may anticipate the reader's rebuttal and include answers to possible objections that might be raised. Thus an author might write a rebuttal to the claim that we should censor television by saying such a practice would violate the First Amendment. Or if no claim has been made, the arguer could anticipate what the objections to television violence might be (violence breeds violence, children become frightened, etc.) and refute them, usually early in the essay, before spelling out the reasons for leaving television alone.

Look for a rebuttal or plan for it in your own writing by asking, "What are the other possible views on this issue?" When reading, ask, "Are they represented here along with reasons?" Or when writing, ask, "How can I answer them?" Phrases that might introduce refutation include, "some may disagree," "others may think," or "other commonly held opinions are," followed by the opposing ideas and your reasons and evidence for rejecting them.

Qualifiers

Remember that argument is not expected to demonstrate certainties. Instead, it establishes probabilities. Consequently, the language of certainty (*always, never, the best, the worst,* and so on) promises too much when used in claims or in other parts of the argument. It is not uncommon for an author to make a claim and in the midst of writing to begin revising and qualifying it to meet the anticipated objections of an audience. Thus words like *always* and *never* change to *sometimes; is* or *are* change to *may be* or *might; all* changes to *many* or *some; none* changes to *a few;* and *absolutely* changes to *probably* or *possibly.* Qualified language is safer for demonstrating the probabilities of an argument. Look to see it the author has stated the claim in other parts of the argument in probable or absolute terms, and then read the entire argument to figure out why.

The following is a qualified version of the claim that all immigrants should be allowed to come into the United States. These qualifications would make the original claim more acceptable to the people who offered the rebuttals and counter-argument.

> Immigrants should be allowed to enter the United States only if they can prove that they already have jobs yielding sufficient income to offset social services and that no American citizens are currently available to perform these jobs.

VALUE OF THE TOULMIN MODEL FOR READING AND WRITING ARGUMENT

The Toulmin model has some advantages that make it an excellent model for both reading and writing argument. Its most essential advantage is that it invites common ground and audience participation in the form of shared warrants, increasing the possibility of interaction between author and audience. The three optional parts of the model also encourage an exchange of views and common ground because they require an arguer both to anticipate other perspectives and views and, at times, to acknowledge and answer them directly. The backing, for instance, requires additional evidence to satisfy audience concerns. The rebuttal requires answers to different or opposing views. The qualifier requires a modification of the claim to gain audience acceptance. The backing, rebuttal, and qualifier in the Toulmin model invite audience participation. They encourage dialogue, understanding, and agreement as argument outcomes. These features make the model valuable for examining the multiple perspectives likely to be expressed in response to complex modern issues.

The model works for reading or writing not only in debate and single-perspective argument but also in academic inquiry, negotiation, dialectic, Rogerian argument (explained in Chapter 11), or any other form of argument that requires exchange and attempts to reach agreement. It can even be a useful tool for one-on-one argument or personal decision making.

Writers of argument find the Toulmin model useful as both an invention strategy and a revision strategy. It can be used to help an author come up with the essential parts of an argument in the first place, and later it can be used to check and evaluate the parts of a newly written argument. See page 238 for a writing assignment that relies on the Toulmin model as a tool to help the writer think about the parts of a position paper. See pages 239-242 for an example of a student-written position paper with its Toulmin elements labeled in the margins.

Readers of argument find the model useful for analyzing and describing the essential parts of a written argument. Listeners find it just as useful for analyzing and describing the essential parts of an argumentative speech. It can be used to write or to analyze both consensual and adversarial arguments. It accommodates all of the various forms of argument. The model is summarized in a handy chart for quick reference for the use of both readers and writers in the Summary Charts on page 421.

REVIEW QUESTIONS

1. Name and describe the three essential parts of the Toulmin model. Do the same for the three optional parts.
2. What are some synonyms for each of the three essential parts of the Toulmin model? Consult Table 5.1.
3. What are some types of support?
4. Define warrants. Why does argument work better when warrants are shared by the arguer and the audience?
5. Give some examples of qualifiers.

EXERCISES AND ACTIVITIES

A. GROUP WORK AND CLASS DISCUSSION: TRUTH VERSUS PROBABILITY

This activity invites you to compare topics that are true and therefore not arguable with topics that are probable and thus open to argument. Think about one other course you are taking this semester, and write down one example of something you have learned in that course that is absolutely true or untrue and that you would not argue about. Then write one example of something you have learned in that course that is only probably true or untrue and that you might argue about. Make a class list of these examples. Think carefully about everything you put in the true and untrue columns. These must be topics that no one would argue about because they have been proved to be true or untrue. Here are some key words to help you think about these two types of information:

True: certain, fact, exact statement, right, correct, valid; wrong, incorrect, invalid

Probable: possible, opinion, qualified, reasonable, sound; unreasonable, unsound

You will be learning both types of information in college. Which topics on the probable list might be good topics for argument papers?

B. GROUP WORK AND CLASS DISCUSSION: USING THE TOULMIN MODEL TO ANALYZE AN ADVERTISEMENT

Study the advertisement for Saab automobiles that appears on the next page. Answer the following questions:

1. What is the claim?
2. What is the support?
3. What are the warrants?
4. Do you share them?
5. What types of rebuttal might you offer?
6. Is the claim acceptable, or should it be qualified?

Will your

heart pound any

less because

it's safe?

Will your

goose bumps care that its practical?

Find your own road:

900CS Turbo

Will that giddy feeling deep in your stomach diminish because the 9000 was ranked the safest car in Sweden three times in a row?* Will your exhilaration be dampened by the turbo's fuel efficiency? Will the guilty pleasure of driving it be compromised by its large interior and 56 cubic feet of cargo space? We don't think so. Experience turbo rush in **SAAB** the Saab 9000 CS. **For a free Saab Excursion Kit, call 1-800-582- SAAB, Ext. 222. www.saabusa.com**

*For years: 1990,1992 and 1994. Based on a study of injuries sustained in auto accidents in Sweden. Data compiled by Folksam Insurance Institute between 1985 and 1993 maximize safety benefits, you must wear seat belts ©1996 SAAB CARS USA, INC.

Source: Courtesy Saab Cars USA Inc.

"Children, today's story works on many levels."

Source: New Yorker, December 21, 1998, p. 103. Copyright © 1998 by The New Yorker Collection Bernard Schoenbaum Cartoonbank.com. All Rights Reserved.

C. GROUP WORK AND CLASS DISCUSSION: USING THE TOULMIN MODEL TO READ AND ANALYZE A CARTOON AND A SHORT ESSAY

A Cartoon

Analyze the cartoon, and discuss the answers to the following questions:

1. What is the teacher's claim?
2. What are the teacher's warrants?
3. What are the children's warrants?
4. What are your warrants?
5. Why is this funny?

A Short Essay

Read the essay that follows. Then answer the questions and discuss your answers with the class. You can expect some disagreement because of your differing backgrounds and experiences. If you disagree on some of these answers, try to figure out what is causing your differences.

1. What is the claim? Is it explicitly stated, or did you have to infer it?
2. What are some examples of support?

3. What are the author's warrants? Does the author back the warrants? If yes, how?
4. Do you share the author's warrants, or do you have conflicting warrants? If you have conflicting warrants, what are they?
5. Is there a rebuttal in the article? If yes, what is it?
6. Is the claim qualified? How?
7. Do you find this argument convincing? Why or why not?

Essay

WHAT'S HAPPENED TO DISNEY FILMS?*

John Evans

1   Many of today's over-30 adults who grew up on a diet of Disney movies are now responsible, God-honoring parents. They want their children to experience the same magic in films and videos that they once enjoyed.

2   Does the name "Disney" still mean the same in the '90s that it did in the '60s? Not at all. Disney is now a huge conglomerate with such diverse subsidiaries as Miramax Films, Hollywood Pictures, and Touchstone Pictures. The films they produce range from the violent, degrading *Pulp Fiction*, a Miramax film, to the delightful *Beauty and the Beast*, a Walt Disney Co. film. In between these two extremes are a myriad of movies of varying degrees of decency and offensiveness.

3   Listed below are descriptions which illustrate the undesirable content included in some Walt Disney Pictures films intended for young children. These comments are based on reviews from the *Preview* Family Movie and TV Guide.

4   *The Little Mermaid* (1989), G-rated animated film. While Disney's villains in the past have simply been mean and nasty, Ursula, the wicked sea witch, is downright evil. Her bizarre appearance and morbid undersea abode exude images of witchcraft, and some scenes are likely to frighten small children. Also, offensive, sexually suggestive dialogue is uncalled for. In one scene the evil Ursula intimates that the mermaid will have to "let her body do her talking." In romantic song, Ariel sings to Eric, "You know you want to do it." Even more disturbing, however, is the picture on the video box that includes a very obvious phallic symbol.

5   *Aladdin* (1992), G-rated animated film. The panther head entrance to the cave and a volcanic eruption are violent, jolting, and intense. The Genie transforms the evil Jofar into a sorcerer who violently manipulates others. Jofar changes into a giant snake to fight Aladdin. Again, the evil characters are more than scary—they attack. Also, the video tape includes some suggestive dialogue whispered in the background during a balcony scene between Aladdin and Jasmine. The words, "Take off your—" can be heard, implying that the muffled word is "clothes."

6   *Lion King* (1994), G-rated animated film. New Age and occultic concepts appear to be introduced when it's said that the father lion is living on in the son.

Dallas–Fort Worth Heritage, August 1995, p. 12.

Also, a remark is made that dead kings are looking down on the young lion. These can be interpreted literally as the Hindu concept of the universality of the soul. Also, when the young lion talks to his dead father, this violates the biblical admonition against communicating with the spirits of the dead.

Lion King also includes intense violence, including a graphic stampede and 7 clawing and biting among animals. This continues the trend to show hand-to-hand combat that inflicts severe injuries.

Pocahontas (1995), G-rated animated film. This brand new feature film favor- 8 ably depicts Indian animism, the belief that every natural object, such as rocks and trees, have spirits. Also, it portrays communication with spirits of the dead as acceptable. "The producers give an exaggerated picture of the white colonists as greedy, bloodthirsty monsters who just want to rid the land of 'those savages.'"

The Walt Disney Pictures company continues to produce Disney's G-rated 9 films as well as its more family oriented movies, such as *Iron Will, Angels in the Outfield, White Fang,* and the *Mighty Ducks* series. However, several years ago, the Disney organization decided to produce more "mature" films and established two wholly owned companies to produce them, Hollywood Pictures and Touchstone Pictures. Also, a few years ago, Disney acquired Miramax Films, which distributes some very offensive films, most of them produced in foreign countries.

A few examples of the most offensive films these companies have produced 10 or distributed are given below.

Pulp Fiction (1994-Miramax Films). Disgusting R-rated adult film which con- 11 tains over 320 obscenities and profanities, ongoing graphic and gratuitous violence, a homosexual rape, and much bizarre behavior.

Color of Night (1994-Hollywood Pictures). Gruesome R-rated murder mystery 12 with bloody killings, stabbings, an impaling, and choking. Also, a sexual affair with graphic sexual content and nudity, and over 100 obscenities and profanities.

Priest (1995-Miramax Films). This controversial R-rated film sympathetically 13 portrays a homosexual priest and depicts other Catholic priests as disreputable characters. Contains scenes of graphic homosexual lovemaking. Catholics nationwide protested the film.

Who Framed Roger Rabbit (1988-Touchstone Pictures). Suggestive, violent PG- 14 rated cartoon film in which some characters are boiled in toxic waste and flattened by a steam roller. Also, features an implied extramarital affair, crude language, sexually suggestive humor, and a voluptuous, seductive female character.

For parents who want to select only wholesome, decent entertainment for 15 their families, the *Preview* Family Movie and TV Guide publishes reviews of all current films twice a month. The reviews contain information on the desirable elements in a film as well as a detailed description of any offensive material. ■

FOR DISCUSSION: What was the first Disney film that you saw? Did it have a disturbing effect on you? Drawing on your own experiences and those of other people you know, how important is it for parents to screen the movies and television that their children watch? Where would you draw the line if you were doing the screening? That is, would you agree with the author of this essay, or would you apply different criteria?

D. READING AND CLASS DISCUSSION: USING THE TOULMIN MODEL TO READ AND ANALYZE

Turn back to page 127 and review the information on claims and how to recognize them. Reread, in particular, the paragraph that begins, "Another interesting variation on the claim occurs in the case of irony." Then read the following essay, "A Liberating Curriculum," and answer these questions:

1. What is irony?
2. What is the literal meaning of this essay (what does the author say)? What is the claim? What is the support? What are the warrants?
3. What is the implied meaning of this essay (what does the author mean)? What is the implied claim? What is the support? What are the warrants?
4. Do you find this essay convincing? Why or why not?

Essay

A LIBERATING CURRICULUM*

Roberta F. Borkat

1 A blessed change has come over me. Events of recent months have revealed to me that I have been laboring as a university professor for more than 20 years under a misguided theory of teaching. I humbly regret that during all those years I have caused distress and inconvenience to thousands of students while providing some amusement to my more practical colleagues. Enlightenment came to me in a sublime moment of clarity while I was being verbally attacked by a student whose paper I had just proved to have been plagiarized from *The Norton Anthology of English Literature.* Suddenly, I understood the true purpose of my profession, and I devised a plan to embody that revelation. Every moment since then has been filled with delight about the advantages to students, professors and universities from my Plan to Increase Student Happiness.

2 The plan is simplicity itself: at the end of the second week of the semester, all students enrolled in each course will receive a final grade of A. Then their minds will be relieved of anxiety, and they will be free to do whatever they want for the rest of the term.

3 The benefits are immediately evident. Students will be assured of high grade-point averages and an absence of obstacles in their march toward graduation. Professors will be relieved of useless burdens and will have time to pursue their real interests. Universities will have achieved the long-desired goal of molding individual professors into interchangeable parts of a smoothly operating machine. Even the environment will be improved because education will no longer consume vast quantities of paper for books, compositions and examinations.

Newsweek, April 12, 1993, p. 11.

Although this scheme will instantly solve countless problems that have 4 plagued education, a few people may raise trivial objections and even urge universities not to adopt it. Some of my colleagues may protest that we have an obligation to uphold the integrity of our profession. Poor fools, I understand their delusion, for I formerly shared it. To them, I say: "Hey, lighten up! Why make life difficult?"

Those who believe that we have a duty to increase the knowledge of our 5 students may also object. I, too, used to think that knowledge was important and that we should encourage hard work and perseverance. Now I realize that the concept of rewards for merit is elitist and, therefore, wrong in a society that aims for equality in all things. We are a democracy. What could be more democratic than to give exactly the same grade to every single student?

One or two forlorn colleagues may even protest that we have a responsibility 6 to significant works of the past because the writings of such authors as Chaucer, Shakespeare, Milton and Swift are intrinsically valuable. I can empathize with these misguided souls, for I once labored under the illusion that I was giving my students a precious gift by introducing them to works by great poets, playwrights and satirists. Now I recognize the error of my ways. The writings of such authors may have seemed meaningful to our ancestors, who had nothing better to do, but we are living in a time of wonderful improvements. The writers of bygone eras have been made irrelevant, replaced by MTV and *People* magazine. After all, their bodies are dead. Why shouldn't their ideas be dead, too?

JOYOUS SMILES

If any colleagues persist in protesting that we should try to convey knowledge to 7 students and preserve our cultural heritage, I offer this suggestion: honestly consider what students really want. As one young man graciously explained to me, he had no desire to take my course but had enrolled in it merely to fulfill a requirement that he resented. His job schedule made it impossible for him to attend at least 30 percent of my class sessions, and he wouldn't have time to do much of the reading. Nevertheless, he wanted a good grade. Another student consulted me after the first exam, upset because she had not studied and had earned only 14 points out of a possible 100. I told her that, if she studied hard and attended class more regularly, she could do well enough on the remaining tests to pass the course. This encouragement did not satisfy her. What she wanted was an assurance that she would receive at least a B. Under my plan both students would be guaranteed an A. Why not? They have good looks and self-esteem. What more could anyone ever need in life?

I do not ask for thanks from the many people who will benefit. I'm grateful 8 to my colleagues who for decades have tried to help me realize that seriousness about teaching is not the path to professorial prestige, rapid promotion and frequent sabbaticals. Alas, I was stubborn. Not until I heard the illuminating explanation of the student who had plagiarized from the anthology's introduction to

Jonathan Swift did I fully grasp the wisdom that others had been generously offering to me for years—learning is just too hard. Now, with a light heart, I await the plan's adoption. In my mind's eye, I can see the happy faces of university administrators and professors, released at last from the irksome chore of dealing with students. I can imagine the joyous smiles of thousands of students, all with straight-A averages and plenty of free time.

9   My only regret is that I wasted so much time. For nearly 30 years, I threw away numerous hours annually on trivia: writing, grading and explaining examinations; grading hundred of papers a semester; holding private conferences with students; reading countless books; buying extra materials to give students a feeling for the music, art and clothing of past centuries; endlessly worrying about how to improve my teaching. At last I see the folly of grubbing away in meaningless efforts. I wish that I had faced facts earlier and had not lost years because of old-fashioned notions. But such are the penalties for those who do not understand the true purpose of education.   ■

FOR DISCUSSION: Do you think grade inflation exists at your college? If so, how big a problem is it? What is its cause? Is it harmful? If yes, who does it harm? Why or how does it harm them? What could be done to reduce or eliminate it?

E. WRITING ASSIGNMENT AND CLASS PROJECT: WRITING A TOULMIN ANALYSIS AND REPORTING ON IT IN CLASS

1. Clip a short article, an advertisement, a cartoon, or a letter to the editor, and use the Toulmin model to analyze it.
2. Write a 250- to 300-word paper in which you identify and explain the claim, support, and warrants in your example. Provide further information about backing, rebuttals, or qualifiers if they are present.
3. In class, circulate the item you clipped among your classmates. Either read your paper or give a two- to three-minute oral report in which you describe the parts of the argument to the class

An example of a student-written Toulmin analysis of "What's Happened to Disney Films?" follows. Read it to help you write your Toulmin analysis paper. Also, see if you and your classmates agree with this analysis. Everyone does not apply the Toulmin model in exactly the same way. There are no absolutely correct answers because different readers' interpretations vary.

Beth Brunk
Toulmin Analysis
Professor Bartlett
English 1302
15 September 1999

Toulmin Analysis of "What's Happened to Disney Films?"

In "What's Happened to Disney Films?" John Evans claims that 1
Disney is not making the same caliber of movies that it was in the
past; the majority of recent Disney films are not suitable for young
audiences. Evans supports his claim through specific scenes and lines
from recent Disney movies. *The Little Mermaid* and *Aladdin* contain
sexual innuendoes. *The Lion King* presents New Age and occultic concepts and contains graphic violence. Disney's most recent film, *Pocahontas*, "favorably depicts Indian animism" and portrays the white
settlers in a bad light. Evans also frowns on Disney's ownership of
Touchstone Pictures, Miramax Films, and Hollywood Pictures, which
have produced movies such as *Who Framed Roger Rabbit*, *Pulp Fiction*,
and *Color of Night*, all of which he believes tarnish the once wholesome Disney image.

Evans's argument has two warrants: Disney should only be making 2
movies suitable for children regardless of the name they are produced under. Also, movies that are suitable for children are those
that are based strictly on Christian ideologies and portray "the
white man" in a positive light.

Evans prepares for rebuttal by naming some Disney movies such 3
as *Iron Will*, *Angels in the Outfield*, and *The Mighty Ducks* that are
considered suitable for children.

The backing for his warrants is Christian doctrines and the 4
Bible. Although he does not appeal to either explicitly throughout
much of the article, he does say that Simba's conversation with his
dead father in *The Lion King* "violates the biblical admonition
against communicating with the spirits of the dead." This worldview
underlies his entire argument.

His qualifier is a subtle one and is found at the end of the 5
piece, where he claims that there is information available "for parents who want to select only wholesome, decent entertainment for
their families." He allows that there may be some parents who do not
care what their children watch and would therefore disagree with his
claim. ■

FOR DISCUSSION: Do you agree with this student's analysis of Evans's article?
Look at the warrants spelled out in paragraph 2. Would you supply these same
warrants? If not, what warrants would you supply? Why do you agree or disagree
with this author's explanation of the warrants?

F. PREWRITING: USING THE TOULMIN MODEL TO GET IDEAS FOR A POSITION PAPER

You have used the Toulmin model in Exercises B through E to read and analyze other people's argument. Now use it to identify the main parts of an argument you will write. You may use the model to help you plan any argument paper. If, however, you have written an exploratory paper based on an issue in "The Reader" for Exercise D in Chapter 4, you have already written a tentative claim for a position paper. Your claim appears at the end of your exploratory paper. Use the Toulmin model as a prewriting exercise to help you develop ideas for a position paper. (The assignment for the "Position Paper Based on 'The Reader'" appears as Exercise G in Chapter 7.)

1. Write the claim. All of the rest of your paper will support this claim.
2. Write the support. Write two or three subclaims that you will develop in the paper. To help you do this, write the word *because* after your claim, and list reasons that support it. Also jot down ideas for specific support for these subclaims, such as examples, facts, and opinions, that come from your reading of the essays or from your own experience.
3. Write the warrants. Decide whether to spell out the warrants in your paper or to leave them implicit so that the reading audience will have to infer them.
4. Decide on the backing. Assume that your classmates are your audience. They may be reading drafts of your paper. In your judgment, will some of them require backing for any of your warrants because they will not agree with them otherwise? If so, how can you back these warrants? Write out your ideas.
5. Plan rebuttal. Think about the positions others may hold on this issue. You identified some of these positions in your exploratory paper. Write out some strategies for weakening these arguments.
6. Decide whether to qualify your claim to make it more convincing to more people. Write one or more qualifiers that might work.

Read what you have written, and make a note about additional information you will need to find for your paper. Save what you have written in a folder. You will use it later when you complete your planning and write your position paper.

G. GROUP DISCUSSION: UNDERSTANDING VALUE WARRANTS

Warrants often come from the systems of values that people hold. The values will not be spelled out in an argument, yet they will still influence the arguer and be present as warrants in the argument. The following essay describes six American value systems. These systems are somewhat oversimplified, and they do not identify all American value systems. They are useful, however, to help you understand some of the values that people hold. Read the essay, and then answer the questions for discussion at the end.

AMERICAN VALUE SYSTEMS*

Richard D. Rieke and Malcolm O. Sillars

By careful analysis individual values can be discovered in the arguments of our- 1 selves and others. There is a difficulty, however, in attempting to define a whole system of values for a person or a group. And as difficult as that is, each of us, as a participant in argumentation, should have some concept of the broad systems that most frequently bring together certain values. For this purpose, it is useful for you to have an idea of some of the most commonly acknowledged value systems.

You must approach this study with a great deal of care, however, because 2 even though the six basic value systems we are about to define provide a fair view of the standard American value systems, they do not provide convenient pigeonholes into which individuals can be placed. They represent broad social categories. Some individuals (even groups) will be found outside these systems. Many individuals and groups will cross over value systems, picking and choosing from several. Note how certain words appear as value terms in more than one value system. The purpose of this survey is to provide a beginning understanding of standard American values, not a complete catalog.[1]

THE PURITAN-PIONEER-PEASANT VALUE SYSTEM

This value system has been identified frequently as the *puritan morality* or the 3 *Protestant ethic.* It also has been miscast frequently because of the excessive emphasis placed, by some of its adherents, on restrictions of personal acts such as smoking and consuming alcohol.[2] Consequently, over the years, this value system has come to stand for a narrow-minded attempt to interfere in other people's business, particularly if those people are having fun. However, large numbers of people who do not share such beliefs follow this value system.

We have taken the liberty of expanding beyond the strong and perhaps too 4 obvious religious implications of the terms *puritan* and *Protestant.* This value system is what most Americans refer to when they speak of the "pioneer spirit," which was not necessarily religious. It also extends, we are convinced, to a strain of values brought to this country by Southern and Eastern European Catholics, Greek Orthodox, and Jews who could hardly be held responsible for John Calvin's theology or even the term *Protestant ethic.* Thus, we have the added word *peasant,* which may not be particularly accurate. Despite the great friction that existed between these foreign-speaking immigrants from other religions and their native Protestant counterparts, they had a great deal in common as do their ideological descendants today. On many occasions after describing the puritan morality we have heard a Jewish student say, "That's the way my father thinks," or had a student of Italian or Polish descent say, "My grandmother talks that way all the time."

*Richard D. Reike and Malcolm O. Sillars, *Argumentation and the Decision Making Process,* 2nd ed. (Glenview, Ill.: Scott, Foresman, 1984), pp. 118–124.

5   The Puritan-Pioneer-Peasant value system is rooted in the idea that persons have an obligation to themselves and those around them, and in some cases to their God, to work hard at whatever they do. In this system, people are limited in their abilities and must be prepared to fail. The great benefit is in the striving against an unknowable and frequently hostile universe. They have an obligation to others, must be selfless, and must not waste. Some believe this is the only way to gain happiness and success. Others see it as a means to salvation. In all cases it takes on a moral orientation. Obviously, one might work hard for a summer in order to buy a new car and not be labeled a "puritan." Frequently, in this value system, the instrumental values of selflessness, thrift, and hard work become terminal values where the work has value beyond the other benefits it can bring one. People who come from this value system often have difficulty with retirement, because their meaning in life, indeed their pleasure, came from work.

6   Likewise, because work, selflessness, and thrift are positive value terms in this value system, laziness, selfishness, and waste are negative value terms. One can see how some adherents to this value system object to smoking, drinking, dancing, or cardplaying. These activities are frivolous; they take one's mind off more serious matters and waste time.

7   Some of the words that are associated with the Puritan-Pioneer-Peasant value system are:

Positive: *activity, work, thrift, morality, dedication, selflessness, virtue, righteousness, duty, dependability, temperance, sobriety, savings, dignity*

Negative: *waste, immorality, dereliction, dissipation, infidelity, theft, vandalism, hunger, poverty, disgrace, vanity*

THE ENLIGHTENMENT VALUE SYSTEM

8 America became a nation in the period of the Enlightenment. It happened when a new intellectual era based on the scientific finding of men like Sir Isaac Newton and the philosophical systems of men like John Locke were dominant. The founders of our nation were particularly influenced by such men. The Declaration of Independence is the epitome of an Enlightenment document. In many ways America is an Enlightenment nation, and if Enlightenment is not the predominant value system, it is surely first among equals.

9   The Enlightenment position stems from the belief that we live in an ordered world in which all activity is governed by laws similar to the laws of physics. These "natural laws" may or may not come from God, depending on the particular orientation of the person examining them; but unlike many adherents to the Puritan value system just discussed, Enlightenment persons theorized that people could discover these laws by themselves. Thus, they may worship God for God's greatness, even acknowledge that God created the universe and natural laws, but they find out about the universe because they have the power of reason. The laws of nature are harmonious, and one can use reason to discover them all. They can also be used to provide for a better life.

Because humans are basically good and capable of finding answers, restraints 10 on them must be limited. Occasionally, people do foolish things and must be restrained by society. However, a person should never be restrained in matters of the mind. Reason must be free. Thus, government is an agreement among individuals to assist the society to protect rights. That government is a democracy. Certain rights are inalienable, and they may not be abridged; "among these are life, liberty and the pursuit of happiness." Arguments for academic freedom, against wiretaps, and for scientific inquiry come from this value system.

Some of the words that are associated with the Enlightenment value system 11 are:

Positive: *freedom, science, nature, rationality, democracy, fact, liberty, individualism, knowledge, intelligence, reason, natural rights, natural laws, progress*

Negative: *ignorance, inattention, thoughtlessness, error, indecision, irrationality, dictatorship, fascism, bookburning, falsehood, regression*

THE PROGRESSIVE VALUE SYSTEM

Progress was a natural handmaiden of the Enlightenment. If these laws were 12 available and if humans had the tool, reason, to discover them and use them to advantage, then progress would result. Things would continually get better. But although progress is probably a historical spin-off of the Enlightenment, it has become so important on its own that it deserves at times to be seen quite separate from the Enlightenment.

Richard Weaver, in 1953, found that "one would not go far wrong in naming 13 progress" the "god term" of that age. It is, he said, the "expression about which all other expressions are ranked as subordinate. . . . Its force imparts to the others their lesser degrees of force, and fixes the scale by which degrees of comparison are understood."[3]

Today, the unmediated use of the progressive value system is questioned, 14 but progress is still a fundamental value in America. Most arguments against progress are usually arguments about the definition of progress. They are about what "true progress is."

Some of the key words of the Progressive value system are: 15

Positive: *practicality, efficiency, change, improvement, science, future, modern, progress, evolution*

Negative: *old-fashioned,[4] regressive, impossible, backward*

THE TRANSCENDENTAL VALUE SYSTEM

Another historical spin-off of the Enlightenment system was the development of 16 the transcendental movement of the early nineteenth century. It took from the Enlightenment all its optimism about people, freedom, and democracy, but rejected the emphasis on reason. It argued idealistically that there was a faculty higher than reason; let us call it, as many transcendentalists did, intuition. Thus, for the transcendentalist, there is a way of knowing that is better than reason, a way which *transcends* reason. Consequently, what might seem like the obvious solution to problems is not necessarily so. One must look, on important matters at least, to the intuition, to the feelings. Like the Enlightenment thinker, the transcendentalist believes in a unified universe governed by natural laws. Thus, all persons, by following their intuition, will discover these laws, and universal harmony will take place. And, of course, little or no government will be necessary. The original American transcendentalists of the early nineteenth century drew their inspiration from Platonism, German idealism, and Oriental mysticism. The idea was also fairly well limited to the intellectuals. By and large, transcendentalism has been the view of a rather small group of people throughout our history, but at times it has been very important. It has always been somewhat more influential among younger people. James Truslow Adams once wrote that everyone should read Ralph Waldo Emerson at sixteen because his writings were a marvel for the buoyantly optimistic person of that age but that his transcendental writings did not have the same luster at twenty-one.[5] In the late 1960s and early 1970s, Henry David Thoreau's *Walden* was the popular reading of campus rebels. The emphasis of anti-establishment youth on Oriental mysticism, like Zen, should not be ignored either. The rejection of contemporary society and mores symbolized by what others considered "outlandish dress" and "hippie behavior" with its emphasis on emotional response and "do your own thing" indicated the adoption of a transcendental value system. Communal living is reminiscent of the transcendental "Brook Farm" experiments that were attempted in the early nineteenth century and described by Nathaniel Hawthorne in his novel *The Blithedale Romance.*

17   In all of these movements the emphasis on humanitarian values, the centrality of love for others, and the preference for quiet contemplation over activity has been important. Transcendentalism, however, rejects the common idea of progress. Inner light and knowledge of one's self is more important than material well-being. There is also some tendency to reject physical well-being because it takes one away from intuitive truth.

18   It should be noted that not everyone who argues for change is a transcendentalist. The transcendental white campus agitators of the late 1960s discovered that, despite all their concern for replacing racism and war with love and peace, their black counterparts were highly pragmatic and rationalistic about objectives and means. Black agitators and demonstrators were never "doing their thing" in the intuitive way of many whites.

19   It should also be noted that while a full adherence to transcendentalism has been limited to small groups, particularly among intellectuals and youth, many of the ideas are not limited to such persons. One can surely find strains of what we have labeled, for convenience, transcendentalism in the mysticism of some very devout older Roman Catholics, for instance. And perhaps many Americans become transcendental on particular issues, about the value to be derived from hiking in the mountains, for example.

20   Here are some of the terms that are characteristic of the Transcendental value system:

Positive:	*humanitarian, individualism, respect, intuition, truth, equality, sympathetic, affection, feeling, love, sensitivity, emotion, personal kindness, compassion, brotherhood, friendship, mysticism*
Negative:	*science,[6] reason, mechanical, hate, war, anger, insensitive, coldness, unemotional*

THE PERSONAL SUCCESS VALUE SYSTEM

The least social of the major American value systems is the one that moves people toward personal achievement and success. It can be related as a part of the Enlightenment value system, but it is more than that because it involves a highly pragmatic concern for the material happiness of the individual. To call it selfish would be to load the terms against it, although there would be some who accept this value system who would say, "Yes, I'm selfish." "The Lord helps those who help themselves" has always been an acceptable adage by some of the most devout in our nation. 21

You might note that the Gallup poll . . . is very heavily weighted toward personal values. Even "good family life" rated as the top value can be seen as an item of personal success. This survey includes only a few social values like "helping needy people" and "helping better America," and even those are phrased in personal terms. That is, the respondents were asked "how important you feel each of these is to you." The personal orientation of the survey may represent a bias of the Gallup poll, but we suspect it reflects much of American society. We are personal success–oriented in an individual way which would not be found in some other cultures (e.g., in the Japanese culture). 22

Here are some of the terms that tend to be characteristic of the Personal Success value system: 23

Positive:	*career, family, friends, recreation, economic security, identity, health, individualism, affection, respect, enjoyment, dignity, consideration, fair play, personal*
Negative:	*dullness, routine, hunger, poverty, disgrace, coercion, disease*

THE COLLECTIVIST VALUE SYSTEM

Although there are few actual members of various socialist and communist groups in the United States, one cannot ignore the strong attachment among some people for collective action. This is, in part, a product of the influx of social theories from Europe in the nineteenth century. It is also a natural outgrowth of a perceived need to control the excesses of freedom in a mass society. Its legitimacy is not limited to current history, however. There has always been a value placed on cooperative action. The same people today who would condemn welfare payments to unwed mothers would undoubtedly praise their ancestors for barnraising and taking care of the widow in a frontier community. Much rhetoric about our "pioneer ancestors" has to do with their cooperative action. And anticollectivist presidents and evangelists talk about "the team." At the same time many fervent 24 advocates of collective action in the society argue vehemently for their freedom and independence. Certainly the civil rights movement constituted a collective action for freedom. Remember the link in Martin Luther King, Jr.'s speech between "freedom" and "brotherhood"?

25   But whether the Collectivist value system is used to defend socialist proposals or promote "law and order" there is no doubt that collectivism is a strong value system in this nation. Like transcendentalism, however, it is probably a value system that, at least in this day, cannot work alone.

26   Here are some of the terms that tend to characterize the Collectivist value system:

Positive: *cooperation, joint action, unity, brotherhood, together, social good, order,*
             humanitarian aid and comfort, equality
Negative: *disorganization, selfishness, personal greed, inequality*

27   Clearly, these six do not constitute a complete catalog of all American value systems. Combinations and reorderings produce different systems. Two values deserve special attention because they are common in these systems and sometimes operate alone: *nature* and *patriotism*. Since the beginning of our nation the idea has prevailed that the natural is good and there for our use and preservation. Also, since John Winthrop first proclaimed that the New England Puritans would build "a city on the hill" for all the world to see and emulate, the idea has endured that America is a fundamentally great nation, perhaps God-chosen, to lead the world to a better life. This idea may be somewhat tarnished in some quarters today, but there is no doubt that it will revive as it has in the past. Linked to other value systems we have discussed, it will once more be a theme that will draw the adherence of others to arguments.

NOTES

1. The following material draws from a wide variety of sources. The following is an illustrative cross section of sources from a variety of disciplines: Virgil I. Baker and Ralph T. Eubanks, *Speech in Personal and Public Affairs* (New York: David McKay, 1965), pp. 95–102; Clyde Kluckhohn, "An Anthropologist Looks at the United States," *Mirror for Man* (New York: McGraw-Hill, 1949), pp. 228–261; Stow Persons, *American Minds* (New York: Holt, Rinehart and Winston, 1958); Jurgen Ruesch, "Communication and American Values; A Psychological Approach," in *Communication: The Social Matrix of Psychiatry,* eds. Jurgen Ruesch and Gregory Bateson (New York: W. W. Norton, 1951), pp. 94–134; Edward D. Steele and W. Charles Redding, "The American Value System: Premises for Persuasion," *Western Speech,* 26 (Spring 1962), pp. 83–91; Richard Weaver, "Ultimate Terms in Contemporary Rhetoric," in *The Ethics of Rhetoric* (Chicago: Henry Regnery, 1953), pp. 211–232; Robin M. Williams, Jr., *American Society,* 3rd ed. (New York: Alfred A. Knopf, 1970), pp. 438–504.
2. It is ironic that the original American Puritans did not have clear injunctions against such activity.
3. Weaver, p. 212.
4. Note that "old-fashioned" is frequently positive when we speak of morality and charm but not when we speak of our taste in music.

5. James Truslow Adams, "Emerson Re-read," in *The Transcendental Revolt*, ed. George F. Whicher, (Boston: D.C. Heath, 1949), pp. 31–39.
6. It is interesting to note, however, that one of the major organizations in the United States with transcendental origins, the Christian Science Church, combines transcendentalism with science. ■

FOR DISCUSSION:

1. Can you find your own system of values in this article? Of the six value systems described, which do you most closely identify with?

2. Which value systems do you find operating in the selections listed below that you have analyzed in this and earlier chapters? What value warrants are implicit in each of these selections? Provide reasons for your answers. There are no correct answers. Use your imagination, and have some fun with this exercise.

   The Saab automobile ad, page 142
   "What's Happened to Disney Films?" page 144
   "A Liberating Curriculum," page 146
   "We Knew What Glory Was," page 48
   "A View from Berkeley," page 51
   "Why I Want a Wife," page 56
   "Giving People a Second Chance," page 54

3. When your system of values does not match the system of values implicit in an argumentative essay, what happens? How does a difference in value systems influence your acceptance of the author's argument?

Chapter Six

Types of Claims

This chapter and the one that follows it expand on and develop some of the ideas in Chapter 5. In Chapter 5 the claim, the support, and the warrants were identified as the three essential parts of an argument. This chapter, along with Chapter 7, provides additional information about these three parts. Claims are the subject of this chapter. Support and warrants, which constitute the proofs of an argument, are the subject of the next chapter.

Argument theorists categorize claims according to types, and these types suggest the fundamental purposes of given arguments. Knowing possible categories for claims and the special characteristics associated with each of them will help you understand more fully the purposes and special features of the arguments you read and will also improve your writing of them. When reading, as soon as you identify the type of claim in an argument, you can predict and anticipate certain features of that type of argument. This technique helps you follow the author's line of thought more easily. When writing, knowing the types of claims can provide you with frameworks for developing your purpose and strategy.

When you begin to read argument with the idea of locating the claim and identifying it by type, your ability to identify and understand all the parts of an argument will increase. An understanding of proofs, the subject of Chapter 7, will improve your understanding further. Chapters 6 and 7, taken together, will teach you how to recognize and use both claims and proofs, the major components of argument. But first, here is a strategy for analyzing an argument to get a preliminary sense of its purpose and to identify its parts.

GETTING A SENSE OF THE PURPOSE AND PARTS OF AN ARGUMENT

▲ **Survey.** Follow the procedures for surveying a book or an article on page 64. Your objective is to find the claim and some of the main subclaims or parts.

▲ **Divide the Argument into Its Parts.** Draw a line across the page (or make a light mark in the margin) each time the subject changes. This physical division of a written argument into its parts is called *chunking*. For example, in a policy paper that proposes a solution to a problem, the explanation of the problem would be a major chunk, as would be the explanation of the solution.

▲ **Ask Why the Parts Have Been Placed in the Particular Order.** Try to determine if the parts have been placed in a logical order to facilitate understanding, for instance, or whether they have been placed in a psychological order, leading up to the conclusion or action step at the end. There are other possibilities as well. Try to get a sense of how the author thought about and organized the parts.

▲ **Analyze the Relationships among the Parts.** When you have speculated about why the author put the parts in a particular order, go a step further and think about the relationships among these parts. Do they all contribute to a central idea, such as a specialized definition? Or are other relationships apparent, such as causes for effects or solutions for problems?

When you begin to write argument, write a claim, list a few supporting reasons that represent the tentative parts, and then think about the best sequence for these parts. The relationships among them will become clearer to you as you rearrange them in an order that is logical to you.

Once you have a sense of the overall purpose and shape of an argument, you can then identify the type of claim that predominates in it.

FIVE TYPES OF CLAIMS

Virtually all arguments can be categorized according to one of five types of claims. You can identify each argument type by identifying the questions the argument answers. In general, certain types of organization and proof are associated with certain types of claims, as you will see in the following discussion. There are no hard-and-fast rules about using specific organizational strategies or types of proof to develop specific types of claims. Knowing common patterns and tendencies, however, helps readers make predictions about the course of an argument and helps writers plan and write their own arguments.

Here are the five categories of claims, along with the main questions that they answer:

1. *Claims of fact:* Did it happen? Does it exist?
2. *Claims of definition:* What is it? How should we define it?

3. *Claims of cause:* What caused it? Or what are its effects?
4. *Claims of value:* Is it good or bad? What criteria will help us decide?
5. *Claims of policy:* What should we do about it? What should be our future course of action?

The sections that follow provide additional explanations of the five types of claims, along with the general questions they answer, some examples of actual claims, a list of the types of proof (explained more fully in the next chapter) that are most typically associated with each type, the organizational strategies that one might expect for each type, and a short written argument that illustrates each type as it appears in practice.

Claims of Fact

When you claim that you turned a paper in on time even if the professor can't find it, or that you were not exceeding the speed limit when a policeman claims that you were, you are making claims of fact.

Questions Answered by Claims of Fact.   Did it happen? Is it true? Does it exist? Is it a fact?

Examples of Claims of Fact.   (Note that all of the "facts" in these claims need to be proved as either absolutely or probably true in order to be acceptable to an audience. All of these claims, also, are controversial.) The ozone layer is becoming depleted. Increasing population threatens the environment. American drivers are becoming more responsible. America's military is prepared for any likely crisis. The abominable snowman exists in certain remote areas. Women are not as effective as men in combat. A mass murderer is evil and not insane. The American judicial system operates successfully.

Types of Support Associated with Claims of Fact.   Factual support, as you might guess, is especially appropriate for claims of fact. Such support includes both past and present *facts, statistics, real examples,* and *quotations from reliable authorities. Inductive reasoning,* which cites several examples and then draws a probable conclusion from them, is also a common type of argument for claims of fact. *Analogies* that establish comparisons and similarities between the subject and something else that is commonly accepted as true are useful. *Signs* that present evidence of a past or present state of affairs are also useful to establish claims of fact. *Opinions* are used to support claims of fact and are usually also supported by factual data.

Possible Organizational Strategies.   *Chronological order,* which traces what has occurred over a period of time, usually in the order in which it occurred, can be used to develop claims of fact. For example, the history of the increase in population might be provided to show how it has happened over a period of time. Or *topical order* may be used. In topical order a group of reasons to support a fact may be identified and developed topic by topic. Thus reasons might be given for the existence of the abominable snowman, with each of them developed at length. This chapter is organized according to topics: the five types of claims.

The claim of fact itself is often stated at or near the beginning of the argument unless there is a psychological advantage for stating it at the end. Most authors make claims of fact clear from the outset, revealing early what they seek to establish.

An Example of an Argument That Contains a Claim of Fact. The following are the opening paragraphs from a longer article that establishes the fact that the African American community is in crisis and dysfunctional. This is controversial. Others might argue for a different view, that the African American community is healthy and prospering.

BLACK AMERICA'S MOMENT OF TRUTH*

Dinesh D'Souza

Essay

The last few decades have witnessed nothing less than a break- 1   Claim of fact
down of civilization within the African-American community.
Vital institutions such as the small business, the church, and the family are now greatly weakened; in some areas, they are on the verge of
collapsing altogether. And the symptoms of systemic decline are both   Examples of
numerous and ominous—extremely high rates of criminal activity, the   problems
normalization of illegitimacy, a preponderance of single-parent families, high levels of drug and alcohol addiction, a parasitic reliance on
government provision, hostility to academic achievement, and a
scarcity of independent enterprises. The next generation of young
blacks is especially vulnerable. "We are in danger of becoming superfluous people in this society," says African-American scholar Anthony
Walton. "We are not essential or even integral to the economy." Mar-   Quote from authority
ian Wright Edelman of the Children's Defense Fund puts it more
bluntly: "We have a black child crisis worse than any since slavery."

This crisis did not exist a generation ago. In 1960, 78 percent of 2
all black families were headed by married couples; today that figure is
less than 40 percent. In the 1950s black crime rates, while higher than   Statistics
those for whites, were vastly lower than they are today. These figures
suggest that the dire circumstances of the black community are not
the result of genes or racism. The black gene pool has not changed
substantially since mid-century, and racism then was far worse. The
main problem facing African Americans is that they have developed a
culture that represents an adaptation to past circumstances, but one
that is now, in crucial respects, dysfunctional and pathological. ◼

*American Spectator, October 1995, p. 35.

FOR DISCUSSION: What was some of the evidence that the author presented to support his view that there is a breakdown of civilization within the African American community? What evidence might someone use who wanted to refute this position? What is your own position? What evidence would you use to support your position?

Claims of Definition

When you claim that an athlete who receives compensation for playing a sport is "professional," and therefore loses "amateur" status, you are making a claim of definition.

Questions Answered by Claims of Definition. What is it? What is it like? How should it be classified? How should it be interpreted? How does its usual meaning change in a particular context?

Examples of Claims of Definition. (Note that here we are looking at definition claims that dominate the argument in the essay as a whole. Definition is also used as a type of support, often at the beginning, to establish the meaning of one or more key terms.) We need to define what constitutes a family before we talk about family values. To determine whether an art exhibit is pornography or art, we need to define what we mean by pornography in this context. To determine whether the police were doing their job or were engaging in brutality, we need to establish what we mean by police brutality. To determine whether a person is mentally competent, we need to define what we mean by that designation. If we have established the fact that a young man killed his wife, shall we define this killing as self-defense, a crime of passion, or premeditated murder?

Types of Support Associated with Claims of Definition. The main types of support used to prove claims of definition are *references to reliable authorities and accepted sources* that can be used to establish clear definitions and meanings, such as the dictionary or a well-known work. Also useful are *analogies* and other comparisons, especially to other words or situations that are clearly understood and that can consequently be used to shed some light on what is being defined. *Examples,* both real and hypothetical, and *signs* can also be used to clarify or develop definitions.

Possible Organizational Strategies. Comparison-and-contrast organization can dominate the development of a claim of definition and serve as the main structure. In this structure two or more objects are compared and contrasted throughout. For example, in an essay that expands the notion of crime to include white-collar crime, conventional crime would be compared with white-collar crime to prove that they are similar.

Topical organization may also be used. Several special qualities, characteristics, or features of the word or concept are identified and explained as discrete topics. Thus in an essay defining a criminal as mentally competent, the characteristics of mental competence would be explained as separate topics and applied to the criminal. Another strategy is to *explain the controversy* over the term and *give reasons* for accepting one view over another.

An Example of an Argument That Contains a Claim of Definition. The following excerpt suggests the confusion that can result if people do not agree on a definition for a term. For many years William Safire wrote a regular column on language for the *New York Times Magazine,* and his analysis in a column titled "Family Values" identifies some of the arguments about the definition of family values during the 1992 political campaign when this concept was a political issue. Family values were again a political issue in the 1996 and 2000 political campaigns. In both of these campaigns, family values were identified as desirable by both the Democrats and the Republicans. Which Democrats and which Republicans either do or do not possess family values has been the enduring political issue in particular for a number of years.

FAMILY VALUES*

William Safire

Essay

"Integrity, courage, strength"—those were the *family values* as defined by Barbara Bush at the Republican convention in Houston. She added "sharing, love of God and pride in being an American." Not much controversy in that definition.

Quote from reliable authority and first definition

But on "family values night," as Marilyn Quayle described the session dominated by Republican women, the values took on an accusatory edge: after recalling that many in the baby boom had not "joined the counterculture" or "dodged the draft," the Vice President's wife made clear to cheering conservatives what she felt was at the center of family values: "Commitment, marriage and fidelity are not just arbitrary arrangements."

Another authority and a second definition

Pat Robertson, the religious broadcaster who sought the Presidential nomination four years ago, eschewed such innuendo and slammed home the political point: "When Bill and Hillary Clinton talk about family values, they are not talking about either families or values. They are talking about a radical plan to destroy the traditional family."

Another authority and a third definition

We have here the G.O.P.'s political attack phrase of the 1992 campaign. When Mario Cuomo stressed the words *family* and *values* in his speech to the 1984 Democratic convention, he used them in a warmly positive sense. But *this year, packaged in a single phrase, the terms are an assertion of moral traditionalism* that carries an implicit charge: the other side seeks to undermine the institution of the fam-

Another authority and a fourth definition

Claim of definition

New York Times Magazine, September 6, 1992, p. 14.

Signs of a lack of family values according to new definition

ily by taking a permissive line on (a) abortion rights, (b) homosexual rights and (c) the "character issue," code words for marital infidelity.

5   Sometimes pot smoking is included, but sex is most often the common denominator, and the pointing finger includes women who do not center their lives inside the home: the defeated candidate Pat Buchanan includes "radical feminists" in his angry denunciation of those who lack what he considers to be family values. ■

FOR DISCUSSION: Who are the four authorities on family values referred to in this article, and what are their views on this issue? What is the meaning of family values that emerges finally from this article? What, according to the author, are some signs of a lack of family values? What, in your opinion, are some signs of a lack of family values?

Claims of Cause

When you claim that staying up late at a party caused you to fail your exam the next day or that the reason your paper is late is because the library closed too early, you are making claims of cause.

Questions Answered by Claims of Cause.   What caused it? Where did it come from? Why did it happen? What are the effects? What will probably be the results over the short and the long term?

Examples of Claims of Cause.   The United States champions human rights in foreign countries to further its own economic self-interests. Clear-cutting is the main cause of the destruction of ancient forests. Legalizing marijuana could have beneficial effects for medicine. The American people's current mood has been caused by a lack of faith in political leaders. The long-term effects of inadequate funding for AIDS research will be a disastrous worldwide epidemic. A lack of family values can lead to crime. Censorship can have good results by protecting children.

Types of Support Associated with Claims of Cause.   The argument must establish the probability of a cause-and-effect relationship. The best type of support for this purpose is *factual data,* including *statistics* that are used to prove a cause or an effect. You can also expect *analogies,* including both *literal* and *historical analogies* that parallel cases in past history to show that the cause of one event could also be the cause of another similar event. You can furthermore expect *signs* of certain causes or effects, and you can also expect *induction.* Several examples cited as a cause will invite the inductive leap to a possible effect as the end result. *Deduction* is also used to develop claims of cause. Premises about effects are proposed, as in the Sherlock Holmes example in Chapter 7, page 194, and a conclusion about the possible cause is drawn.

Possible Organizational Strategies.   One strategy is to describe *causes and then effects.* Thus clear-cutting would be described as a cause that would lead to the ultimate destruction of the forests, which would be the effect. Or *effects* may be described and then *the cause or causes*. The effects of censorship may be described before the public efforts that resulted in that censorship. You may also encounter refutation of other actual or possible causes or effects.

An Example of an Argument That Contains a Claim of Cause. The following article suggests that many of the world's economic problems stem from the way women are treated in some of the relatively impoverished nations of the world. Facts, quotations from authorities, and comparisons are used to establish that if women were treated differently, economic improvement would be the effect. Not all people in these countries would agree with this cause-and-effect argument.

PAYING THE PRICE OF FEMALE NEGLECT*

Susan Dentzer

Essay

Call it the case of the missing women—*more than 100 million of them,* 1 to be exact. It's a curiosity of human biology that women are hardier than men and thus outnumber their male counterparts in the United States, Europe and Japan. But in much of Asia, North Africa and parts of Latin America, the opposite is true: In all of South Asia, for example, females constitute less than 47 percent of the population, versus 52.2 percent in industrialized countries. The complex reasons, including poor health care and outright violence against women and girls, add up to pervasive neglect of females in many heavily populated nations. Harvard economist Amartya Sen concludes that well over 100 million women are in effect "missing" from the planet—the presumed victims of premature and preventable deaths. . . .

Facts

Quote from authority

The consequences for social justice are self-evident, but less 2 well understood in the West are the global economic costs of such widespread female deprivation. Of the 1.3 billion people living in poverty worldwide, a staggering 70 percent are women, notes a recent report by the United Nations Development Program. <u>Thus, the surest route to propelling nations out of poverty is to end the cycle of female neglect</u>. . . It may well be that giving women a leg up in education, entrepreneurship and political power could pay off in priceless benefits—ranging from slower population growth and higher incomes to healthier families.

Claim of cause

Effects if claim were adopted

VICIOUS CYCLE

Women in developing nations clearly face a host of social and cul- 3 tural obstacles, but they are also hurt by a simple economic calculus. On average, women worldwide earn 30 to 40 percent less than men;

Statistics

*U.S. News and World Report, September 11, 1995, p. 45.

because their daughters will earn less, parents in poor countries often invest in them less than they do in their sons, especially in education and health care. The resulting vicious cycle of underinvestment exacts a huge toll, since research clearly shows that better-educated women are more likely to have fewer children, seek health care when needed, earn more money and plow more resources into educating their offspring. One recent World Bank analysis suggests that providing 1,000 girls in India with an extra year of primary schooling would cost a mere $32,000, yet would prevent the premature deaths of two women and 43 infants, as well as avert 300 births. Another concludes that if women in Kenya, who make up the majority of the nation's farmers, were educated on a par with Kenyan men, food-crop yields would increase by more than a fifth. . . .

Authority   4   Most crucial may be increasing women's capacities to be agents of change rather than merely recipients of greater help from others, says economist Sen. He points to the Indian state of Kerala, where

Comparison   property inheritance among an elite group passes through the female line. Perhaps it is no coincidence that the state also has the most developed school system in India, and that the ratio of females to males approaches that of the United States and Europe. That lesson in the apparent consequences of women assuming more power may translate even to the United States, which ranks well down the roster of major industrialized countries in the number of women in the national legislature. And women themselves may owe it to the memories of more than 100 million of the missing to attempt no less. ■

FOR DISCUSSION: Why is it important not to neglect women in a society? What are some examples in the article of efforts to change the trend of neglect in some countries? What else might be done? What would the results be?

Claims of Value

When you claim that sororities and fraternities are the best extra-curricular organizations for college students to join, you are making a claim of value.

Questions Answered by Claims of Value. Is it good or bad? How bad? How good? Of what worth is it? Is it moral or immoral? Who thinks so? What do those people value? What values or criteria should I use to determine its goodness or badness? Are my values different from other people's values or from the author's values?

Examples of Claims of Value. Computers are a valuable addition to modern society. Prayer has a moral function in the public schools. Viewing television is a wasteful activity. Mercy killing is immoral. The contributions of homemakers are as valuable as those of professional women. Animal rights are as important as human rights.

Types of Support Associated with Claims of Value.   *Appeals to values* are important in developing claims of value. The arguer thus appeals to what the audience is expected to value. A sense of a common, shared system of values between the arguer and the audience is important for the argument to be convincing. These shared values must be established either explicitly or implicitly in the argument. *Motivational appeals* that suggest what the audience wants are also important in establishing claims of value. People place value on the things that they work to achieve. Other types of support used to establish claims of value include *analogies,* both *literal* and *figurative,* that establish links with other good or bad objects or qualities. Also, quotations from *authorities* who are admired help establish both expert criteria and judgments of good or bad, right or wrong. *Induction* is also used by presenting examples to demonstrate that something is good or bad. *Signs* that something is good or bad are sometimes cited. *Definitions* are used to clarify criteria for evaluation.

Possible Organizational Strategies.   *Applied criteria* can develop a claim of value. Criteria for evaluation are established and then applied to the subject that is at issue. For example, in arguing that a particular television series is the best on television, criteria for what makes a superior series would be identified and then applied to the series to defend it as best. The audience would have to agree with the criteria to make the argument effective. Or suppose the claim is made that toxic waste is the worst threat to the environment. A list of criteria for evaluating threats to the environment would be established and applied to toxic waste to show that it is the worst of all. Another possibility is to use *topical organization* by developing a list of reasons about why something is good or bad and then developing each of the reasons as a separate topic. You may also expect that *narrative* structure will sometimes be used to develop a claim of value. Narratives are real or made-up stories that can illustrate values in action, with morals or generalizations noted explicitly or implicitly along the way. An example of a narrative used to support a claim of value is the New Testament parable of the good Samaritan who helped a fellow traveler. The claim is that helping one another in such circumstances is valued and desirable behavior.

An Example of an Argument That Contains a Claim of Value.   The following article examines the value of standardized tests. Notice the author's conclusion and his major reasons for reaching this conclusion.

WHAT'S WRONG WITH STANDARD TESTS?*

Ted Sizer

One of American educators' greatest conceits is the belief that people can be pigeonholed, in effect sorted by some scientific mechanism, usually the standardized test.   1 Claim of value

New York Times Magazine, January 8, 1995, p. 58.

Appeals to data and values

2   The results of even the most carefully and sensitively crafted tests cannot be used fairly for high-stakes purposes for individuals; the belief that they can persists stubbornly in the educational community, in spite of an avalanche of research that challenges the tests' precision—and in spite of parents' common sense.

3   All of us who have taught for a while know "low testers" who became wonderfully resourceful and imaginative adults and "high testers" who as adults are, sadly, brittle and shallow people. We cringe as we remember how we so unfairly characterized them. . . .

Induction: examples

4   Danny Algrant's writing and directing of the 1994 film *Naked in New York* certainly was not completely evident when I taught him. Danny was an ebullient itch, even as a high school senior, a trial— but a worthy one—for his teacher. All that ebullient itchiness I gather now has been focused in successful film making. And so on: the awkward adolescent who now juggles the myriad demands of an inner-city school as principal, or the "low tester" who is now a successful writer. . . .

Appeal to values

5   There is tremendous public reluctance to question the usage and values of such tests. Being against conventional "testing" makes one appear to be against "standards." Test scores both give those in charge a device to move large numbers of students around and provide a fig leaf to justify labeling and tracking them in one way or another. How can we, they say, accept each little person as complicated, changeable, special? Impossible. It would take too much time. (Then privately, But not for *my* child. Let me tell you about her.)

Signs of adequacy and inadequacy

6   It would be silly, however, to dismiss all standardized testing. If carefully crafted and interpreted, these tests can reveal certain broad trends, even if they tell us only a bit about individual children. Such testing is helpful at the margins: it can signal the possibility of a troubled or especially gifted or otherwise "special" youngster. It can signal competence at immediate and comparable work if the classroom task to be completed (effective close reading of a text) is similar to the test (made up of prose passages and related questions) and if the task is attempted shortly after taking the test.

7   But none of the major tests used in American elementary and secondary education correlates well with long-term success or failure. S.A.T. scores, for example, suggest likely grades in the freshman year at college; they do not predict much thereafter.

8   On the contrary, conventional tests can distort and thereby corrupt schooling. Most do not measure long-term intellectual habits. Indeed, many undermine the value of such by excessively emphasizing immediate, particular facts and skills considered out of context.

9   Those characteristics that we most value fail to be "tested": the qualities of mind and heart upon which we count for a healthy culture.

And a competitive work force. Send me, says the business 10
leader, young employees who know something about using important knowledge, who learn readily and independently, who think for
themselves and are dependable in the deepest sense. The college
teacher says much the same, perhaps describing the qualities somewhat differently. Unfortunately, when classifying students, schools
still peg kids by brief paper records and scores. "If the combined
S.A.T. scores are below 1100, we will not consider the student," the admissions staff says, knowing full well that some high scorers are less   Comparison
worthy potential students than some low scorers. ■

FOR DISCUSSION: How and why does the author address the question of the
value of standardized tests? What does he consider their strengths? What does he
consider their weaknesses? What experiences have you had with these tests? Do
you think they are or are not a good measure of your abilities? Give reasons for
your answer.

Claims of Policy

When you claim that all new students should attend orientation or that all students who graduate should participate in graduation ceremonies, you are making
claims of policy.

Questions Answered by Claims of Policy.   What should we do? How
should we act? What should future policy be? How can we solve this problem?
What concrete course of action should we pursue to solve the problem? (Notice
that policy claims focus on the future more than the other types of claims, which
tend to deal with the past or present.)

Examples of Claims of Policy.   The criminal should be sent to prison rather
than to a mental institution. Everyone should be taught to recognize and report
sexual harassment in the workplace. Every person in the United States should have
access to health care. Small business loans must be made available to help people
reestablish their businesses after a natural disaster. Both filmmakers and recording
groups should make objectionable language and subject matter known to prospective consumers. Battered women who take revenge should not be placed in jail. Genetic engineering should be monitored and controlled. Parents should have the
right to choose the schools their children attend.

Types of Support Associated with Claims of Policy.   *Data* and *statistics* are
used to support a policy claim, but so are moral and commonsense appeals to
what people value and want. *Motivational appeals* are especially important for policy claims. The audience needs to become sufficiently motivated to think or even
act in a different way. To accomplish this degree of motivation, the arguer must
convince the audience that it wants to change. *Appeals to values* are also used for
motivation. The audience becomes convinced it should follow a policy to achieve

important values. *Literal analogies* sometimes support policy claims. The arguer establishes what other similar people or groups have done and suggests the same thing can work in this case also. Or a successful effort is described, and the claim is made that it could work even better on a broader scale. This is another type of literal analogy, because it compares a small-scale effort to a large-scale, expanded effort. *Argument from authority* is also often used to establish claims of policy. The authorities quoted, however, must be trusted and must have good credibility. Effort is usually made to establish their credentials. *Cause* can be used to establish the origin of the problem, and *definition* can be used to clarify it. Finally, *deduction* can be used to reach a conclusion based on a general principle.

Possible Organizational Strategies. The *problem-solution* structure is typical of policy claims. The problem is first described in sufficient detail so that the audience will want a solution. Then the solution is spelled out. Furthermore, the solution suggested is usually shown to be superior to other solutions by anticipating and showing what is wrong with each of the others. Sometimes the problem and solution sections are followed by a *visualization* of how matters will be improved if the proposed solution is accepted and followed. Sometimes problem-solution arguments end with an *action* step that directs the audience to take a particular course of action (vote, buy, etc.).

An Example of an Argument That Contains a Claim of Policy. The following article concerns the degree to which colleges should serve *in loco parentis* ("in the place of parents") by supervising the behavior of college students. The author presents her solutions to this problem in her article.

Essay

CAMPUS CLIMATE CONTROL*

Katie Roiphe

Signs of freedom

1 I remember the butter pats that covered the soaring ceiling of my freshman dining hall. They were the first sign that I had entered a world utterly devoid of adults. I remember by best friend passing out from inhaling nitrous oxide. I remember someone I know falling drunkenly off a fire escape and ending up in the hospital. I remember groups of us breaking into the pool at night and swimming naked. This was not 1967. This was 1990.

Comparison with '60s

2 By the time I arrived at college, the idea of adult authority had been chipped away and broken down by a previous generation—by Watergate and Vietnam and drugs. And though we would have died rather than admit it, without it some of us were feeling lost. We had the absolute, shimmering freedom that had been dreamed

New York Times, March 5, 1999, p. A25.

up for us during the 60's. We had the liberating knowledge that no one cared what we did.

But it wasn't making us as happy as it was supposed to. I re- 3 Problems
member moments of exultation walking through the pink campus at dawn, but I also remember moments of pure terror.

During a particularly wild period of my senior year, a profes- 4
sor looked up from my essay on Robert Lowell's falling out-of-love poetry, glanced at the violet circles under my eyes and said, "You re- Authority
ally need to get some sleep." I stood there in my ripped jeans. I felt suddenly reassured. The adult world, where people wake up in the morning, pay their bills and take out the trash, was still intact.

It therefore does not surprise me that students now want uni- 5 Solutions
versities to act *in loco parentis* again, and that slightly perplexed baby-boom administrators are trying to find ways to accommodate them. Some of the practical ideas being floated around campuses seem absurd. Alcohol-free adult-supervised student centers? Students will mock them. But they may serve a function by their mere existence.

Parents of teen-agers are always embarrassing to adolescents, 6 Signs
and institutions acting in loco parentis will also be embarrassing. The alcohol-free, adult-supervised student centers (or trips to the theater with professors, or more resident advisers) are simply signs of an adult presence. They offer tangible monuments to an authority that you can avoid or rebel against, but that nonetheless exists. You can find it on a campus map.

I remember the stories by mother told of climbing into her 7 Literal analogy
dorm room, wedging open the window, when she got back after curfew. Part of the thrill of rules, the perverse allure, is that they can be broken. Even when students are deliberately ignoring them, the fact of their existence is comforting. Rules give order to our chaos; they Definition of rules
give us some sort of structure for our wildness so that it doesn't feel so scary.

At the heart of the controversy over whether colleges should act 8
in loco parentis is the question of whether college students are adults or children, and of course they are neither. They are childish and sophisticated, naive and knowing, innocent and wild, and in their strange netherworld, they need some sort of shadow adult, some Literal analogy
not-quite-parent to be there as a point of reference.

That said, some new rules being considered on campuses seem 9
extreme—like the rule at Lehigh that there can be no campus parties without a chaperone. Surely there must be a way of establishing a benign and diffuse adult presence without students having to drink and dance and flirt and pick people up around actual adults.

Many students. . . . seem to like the superficial wholesome- 10
ness of the 50's. But what about the attitudes that informed it, like Historical analogy
the sexism that tainted any college girl who enjoyed sex?

Solution 11   There must be a way to create some sort of structure without romanticizing or fetishizing the 50's. There must be a way of bringing back an adult presence on college campuses without treating students like children, a way of correcting the excesses of the sexual revolution without throwing away all of its benefits.

Claim of policy 12   <u>Americans are always drawn to extreme ideologies, to extremes of freedom or repression, of promiscuity or virginity, of wildness or innocence, but maybe there is a middle ground, somewhere closer to where people want to live their actual lives:</u> a university without butter pats on the ceiling or 10 o'clock curfews. ■

FOR DISCUSSION: How much common ground do you share with the author? Have your experiences with student life been similar or different from hers? To what extent does your college act *in loco parentis*? If you had the power to change college policy, would you place more or fewer restrictions on student behavior on your campus? Why?

CLAIMS AND ARGUMENT IN REAL LIFE

In argument, one type of claim may predominate, but other types may be present as subclaims. It is not always easy to establish the predominant claim in an argument or to establish its type. You may find some disagreement in your class discussions when you try to categorize a claim according to type. The reason for this disagreement is that often two or more types of claim will be present in an argument. But close reading will usually reveal a predominant type, with the other types serving as subclaims. For example, a value claim that the popular press does harm by prying into the private lives of public figures may establish the fact that this is a pervasive practice, may define what should be public and what should not be public information, may examine the causes or more likely the effects of this type of reporting, and may suggest future policy for dealing with this problem. All may occur in the same article. Still, the dominant claim is one of value, that this practice of newswriters is bad.

It is useful when reading argument to identify the predominant claim because doing so helps you identify (1) the main purpose of the argument, (2) the types of support that may be used, and (3) the possible organizational strategies. It is also useful, however, to identify other types of subclaims and to analyze why they are used and how they contribute to the argumentative purpose. When planning and writing argument, you can in turn identify a predominant claim as well as other types of subclaims, support, and organization. The types of support and the organizational patterns that are particularly appropriate for developing different types of claims are explained and illustrated in this chapter. For quick reference, a chart of the types of support that can best be used for each type of claim appears in Table 9.1 on page 276. A second chart that shows the organizational patterns that can best be used to develop each type of claim appears in Table 10.1 on page 305.

Refer to these tables for a quick summary of the suggestions to help you develop your claim and purpose for the argumentative papers you write.

As you read and write argument, you will also notice that claims follow a predictable sequence when they originate in real-life situations. In fact, argument appears most vigorous in dramatic, life-and-death situations or when a person's character is called into question. We see claims and rebuttals, many kinds of support, and every conceivable organizational strategy in these instances. For example, as juvenile crime in this country increased in recent years, the issues that emerged included these: What is causing young people to commit crimes? What can be done to protect the family unit? Is the educational system adequate? Should the criminal justice system treat young offenders differently from older criminals? Does racial discrimination contribute to juvenile crime? How can we make inner cities more livable? How can we improve social programs?

Such real-life situations, particularly when they are life-threatening as juvenile crime often is, not only generate issues; they also usually generate many arguments. Interestingly, the types of arguments usually appear in a fairly predictable order. The first arguments made in response to a new issue-generating situation usually involve claims of fact and definition. People first have to come to terms with the fact that something significant has happened. Then they need to define what happened so that they can understand it better.

The next group of arguments that appear after fact and definition often inquire into cause. People need to figure out why the event happened. Multiple causes are often considered and debated. Next, people begin to evaluate the goodness or badness of what has happened. It is usually after all of these other matters have been dealt with that people turn their attention to future policy and how to solve the problems.

We can use the issues that emerged from the Columbine High School shootings in Littleton, Colorado, as an example of this typical sequence of claims. The shootings occurred quite suddenly in late spring of 1999. Two male students entered Columbine High School while it was in session, shot twelve of their classmates, injured several more, and then shot themselves. Everyone was caught off guard by the sudden chaos in Littleton, and the first question that was asked both at the scene and in the media was, "What happened?" The facts had to be established before people were prepared to examine other issues. There were also some early attempts to define what had happened, to give it a name. Was this revenge, a demonstration of some sort, evidence of mental illness, or wanton killing?

The initial concerns about fact and definition were soon followed by questions about the causes for this incident. A possible cause, examined early on, was the quality of parental supervision in the boys' homes. Some people argued that the supervision these parents provided seemed no better or worse than in many other homes. Others argued that since the boys prepared for the shooting over a long period of time, their parents should have been more aware of what the boys were doing. The cause that emerged as the most potent, however, was the boys' interest in violent video games, which they both played frequently, and violence on the

Internet, which also seemed to fascinate them. A number of argumentative articles were written at the time that explored the effects of such games on their users.

After much speculation about cause, people turned their attention to value and to arguing about whether any good could be found in these killings. One mother wrote an article about how her daughter professed her belief in God just before she was shot and killed. This was viewed as positive, even though the girl's death was certainly negative. The general opinion, however, was that this was a terrible occurrence and that similar incidents must absolutely be avoided in the future.

It was not until most of these initial matters were analyzed and debated that discussion of future policy began to surface. Articles about censoring the Internet versus preserving First Amendment guarantees appeared. Other articles discussed the issue of parental supervision and control and suggested policy for monitoring the behavior of teenagers. Still other articles presented ways to make schools safer and included suggestions that ranged from the installation of metal detectors in schools to requiring the wearing of school uniforms. Three articles motivated by the Littleton killings appear in "The Reader" on pages 524–531. These articles demonstrate how dramatic events that capture widespread attention can also generate issues for argument.

The same pattern of argument can be found in the sexual behavior issues that gathered speed after the scandals associated with various politicians and their girlfriends and the U.S. Navy Tailhook scandal, where male naval personnel harassed and abused women at an annual party. Articles written in response to such events often focus first on fact, or what happened. Were these actual incidents of sex or sexual harassment, the authors ask, or were they just incidents of flirting, the type of thing that goes on all the time between men and women? Definitions of sex and sexual harassment usually follow, with attempts to define both sex and sexual harassment in terms of actions, comments, or looks and to distinguish it from generally cloddish, insensitive behavior. Once people establish that an incident of illicit sex or harassment has occurred and that it can be defined, cause next becomes an issue. Did the woman cause the behavior by leading the man on? Or did the man cause the behavior by misusing his power?

Was liquor at fault? Were hormones to blame, or perhaps the age-old war between the sexes? Value arguments surface next that focus on who has been harmed and how badly or mildly. Policy issues, or what to do about the incident, come later. Should the politician resign? Should the annual navy parties be discontinued? A few years ago a policy to govern sexual correctness was established at Antioch College that required each person to obtain permission from the other party before making any advances of a sexual nature.

The articles presented under the issue question, "What Should Be Done with Young Offenders?" Starting on page 511 of "The Reader" follows the order just described. The first article establishes the fact that juvenile crime is a problem and that it will probably get worse. The next article establishes that poverty, not just bad character, is the principal cause of juvenile crime. The third article presents an example of juvenile crime to establish that it is bad and that its victims are hurt and angry. The final article proposes solutions for dealing with the problem of juvenile crime.

You may be able to think of other issues that have inspired a variety of arguments and claims in this same roughly predictable order. It is useful to pay attention to the issues that come out of dramatic events, the types of claims that are generated by them, and the order in which these claims appear. Such analysis will help you anticipate the course an issue will take. It will also help you determine at what point in the ongoing conversation about an issue you happen to be at a given moment. You can then speculate about the aspects of the issue that have already been argued and that are likely to be argued in the future.

VALUE OF THE CLAIMS AND THE CLAIM QUESTIONS FOR READING AND WRITING ARGUMENT

Readers of argument find the list of the five types of claims and the questions that accompany them useful for identifying the claim and the main purpose in an argument: to establish fact, to define, to establish cause, to assign value, or to propose a solution. Claims and claim questions can also help readers identify minor purposes in an argument, those that are developed as subclaims. When a reader is able to discover the overall purpose of an argument, it is much easier to make predictions and to follow the argument.

Writers of argument find the list of the five types of claims and the questions that accompany them useful for analyzing an issue, writing a claim about it, and identifying both the controlling purpose for a paper and additional ideas that can be developed in the paper. Here is an example of how this can work. The author writes the issue in the form of a question, as in the example "Should high schools be safer places?" Then the author asks the claim questions about this issue and writes a paragraph in response to each of them: Is it a fact that high schools are unsafe places? How should we define unsafe? What causes a lack of safety in high schools, and what are the effects? Is a lack of safety good or bad? What criteria could be established to judge the goodness or badness of safety in high schools? What can be done to make high schools safer places? Finally, the author reads the paragraphs and selects the one that is most promising to form the major claim and purpose in the paper. For example, suppose the author decides to write a policy paper, and the claim becomes "Parents, students, teachers, and administrators all need to cooperate to make high schools safer places." To show how that can be done becomes the main purpose of the paper. The information generated by asking the other claim questions, however, can also be used in the paper to provide reasons and evidence. The claim questions, used in this way as part of the prewriting process, can generate considerable information and ideas for a paper.

REVIEW QUESTIONS

1. What are the five types of claims?
2. What are the questions associated with each type?

3. What is a predictable sequence that claims follow when they originate in a dramatic, real-life situation?
4. How do claims typically appear in written argument? That is, do writers usually limit themselves to a single purpose and claim or not? Discuss.

EXERCISES AND ACTIVITIES

A. CLASS DISCUSSION: PREDICTING TYPES OF CLAIMS

Bring in the front page of a current newspaper. Discuss headlines that suggest controversial topics. Predict from each headline the type of claim that will be made.

B. GROUP WORK: READING AND ANALYZING TYPES OF CLAIMS

The class is divided into five groups, and each group is assigned one of the five articles that follow. Prepare for group work by reading the article assigned to your group. Then get in your groups and apply the new reading strategies described in this chapter by answering the following questions. Assign a person to report your answers to the class.

1. Which sentence is the claim? Remember it can appear at the beginning, in the middle, or at the end of the essay. Underline it.
2. What type of claim is it? Decide which of the five types of claims this claim represents.
3. What are one or two examples of support used in the essay? To help you identify support, review the marginal labels that identify the support in the five sample readings in the chapter.
4. How would you summarize the argument in the essay in two or three sentences?
5. What is your reaction to the author's position?
6. Where might you position this argument in an ongoing conversation about the issue? At the beginning, the middle, or the end? Why?

Essay 1

GENE TESTS: WHAT YOU KNOW CAN HURT YOU*

Barbara Koenig

Barbara Koenig is associated with the Stanford University Center for Biomedical Ethics. She codirects the program in genomics, ethics, and society.

1   Last year, it was discovered that 1 percent of Ashkenazi Jewish women, those of Central or Eastern European ancestry, carry a mutated form of a gene that might predispose them to breast and ovarian cancer.

*New York Times, April 6, 1996, p. A15.

After this discovery, a surgeon who operates on women with breast cancer told me that a day rarely passes when a patient does not ask about "the gene test." 2

Even with this demand, however, almost all leading scientists and two major commercial testing laboratories agreed informally not to offer the test for the mutation to the general public because widespread testing would do more harm than good. 3

That consensus was broken recently by Dr. Joseph D. Schulman, director of the Genetics and I.V.F. Institute in Fairfax, Va. The doctor, who advertised the service on the World Wide Web, says it will give women access to valuable information. But in genetic testing, what you know won't necessarily help you—indeed, it might even hurt you. 4

As Alice Wexler points out in *Mapping Fate,* her book about genetically determined Huntington's disease, Americans' strong bias for information leads them to believe in genetic testing. Doing something, anything, to counter illness is considered the brave and correct approach. 5

But testing for the 185delAG mutation does not help most women. A positive test does not mean that you will get cancer, and a negative test does not mean that you won't. 6

Most scientists agree that the mutation occurs in families in which many members have suffered from breast and ovarian cancer. But leaping to the conclusion that a mutation inevitably leads to cancer, especially for women without a family history, reflects a naïve genetic determinism and ignores the possible effects of the environment and other genes on one's health. 7

But let's assume that a woman from a high-risk family tests positive. What then? There is no guaranteed way to prevent cancer or detect it early. Some desperate women do resort to drastic measures such as surgically removing their breasts. 8

Paradoxically, this isn't the recommended treatment for many women already diagnosed with cancer. For a decade, more doctors have recommended and more women, especially those with small tumors, have chosen instead to have lumpectomies. 9

Knowing your genetic makeup can also create profound emotional and financial problems. For example, a spouse might use this information in a custody dispute. Or a woman might decide not to have children for fear of passing on the gene. But if she decides to adopt, will she be approved by an agency? And should a 9-year-old girl be tested for the mutation? 10

The test brings up other thorny questions that may be better left unexplored. For instance, with current technology, a woman could test a fetus for the gene and then abort it. In his ad, Dr. Schulman suggests that his Genetics and I.V.F. Institute may be able to screen embryos for the gene mutation. 11

There are also real economic repercussions. Women could face discrimination from employers and health insurers. And most physicians have little experience with ordering and interpreting genetic tests that determine a woman's cancer risk (and in guiding families through the turmoil generated by the results). 12

Until basic research on the clinical significance of the 185delAG mutation is complete, there is no justification for widespread screening. Unfortunately, noth- 13 ing prevents laboratories from offering genetic tests, nor are there any regulations to insure the quality of the tests.

14   In March, a Federal task force on testing suggested possible regulatory strategies, from requiring Food and Drug Administration approval for new tests to strengthening the laws that govern labs.

15   Either approach would slow down the premature commercialization of testing. Strict regulation may be unpopular among those who believe that women have a right to this information. But extreme caution should be the order of the day. ■

FOR DISCUSSION: What is the problem described in this article? What is the proposed solution? Can you think of other examples of information that might be controversial in the way that gene tests are? What is your opinion about communicating information of this sort to the people who are affected by it?

Essay 2

WE'RE TOO BUSY FOR IDEAS*

Michele McCormick

Michele McCormick is the owner of a small public relations firm in California.

1   I recently became one of the last people in America to acquire a portable radio/headphone set. This delay was out of character—normally I ride the crest of every trend. But in this case I sensed a certain dangerous potential. So I put off the purchase for ages, feeling wary of such an inviting distraction. Too much headphone time, I worried, could easily impair my business performance, if not ruin my way of life completely.

2   As it turns out, my concerns were right on target.

3   The problem isn't the expense, or the constant exposure to musical drivel, or even the endangerment of my hearing—and I do like to keep the volume set on "blast." No, the problem is more subtle and insidious. It's simply that, once I was fully plugged in, things stopped occurring to me.

4   I get excited about good ideas. Especially my own. I used to have lists of them in all my regular haunts. My office desk, kitchen, car and even my gym bag were littered with bits of paper. Ideas ranging from a terrific brochure headline or a pitch to a new client for my public-relations agency to finding a new route to avoid the morning rush—each notion began as an unsummoned thought, mulled over and jotted down.

5   I'm convinced that such musings are the key to business and social vitality. They are the initial source of the innovative problem solving, creative solutions and even radical departures, without which success and progress are elusive. I've found that a lot of my better ideas originate in those times when I allow my mind to range freely.

Newsweek, March 29, 1993, p. 10.

The old story has it that Isaac Newton identified the concept and presence of gravity while sitting under an apple tree. One fruit fell and science gained a new dimension. While there may be some historic license in that tale, it's easy to see that if Newton had been wearing his Walkman, he probably would have overlooked the real impact of the apple's fall. 6

This is the problematic side of technological evolution. As tools become more compact, portable and inescapable, they begin to take away something they cannot replace. The car phone, battery-powered TV, portable fax and notepad-size computer do everything for accessibility. They make it easy to be in touch, to be productive, to avoid the tragedy of a wasted second. But there are worse things than empty time. A calendar packed to the max makes it easy to overlook what's missing. A dearth of good ideas isn't something that strikes like a lightning bolt. It's a far more gradual dawning, like the slow unwelcome recognition that one's memory has become less sharp. 7

If that dawning is slow, it's because our minds are fully occupied. It now takes an unprecedented depth of knowledge to stay on top of basic matters, from choosing sensible investments to keeping up on job skills to purchasing the healthiest food. There is literally no end to the information that has become essential. 8

When there is a chance to relax, we don't stop the input; we change channels. With earphones on our heads or televisions in our faces, we lock in to a steady barrage of news, views and videos that eliminate the likelihood of any spontaneous thought. 9

THWARTED INSIGHT

Still, we are not totally oblivious. We work hard to counter the mind-numbing impact of the river of information and factoidal jetsam we are forced to absorb. There is a deliberate emphasis on the importance of creative thought as a daily factor. Many businesses try to ensure that the workplace is conducive to clear thinking. They can provide employees with a comfortable environment and stimulating challenges, and summon them to brainstorming sessions. From seminars to smart drinks, from computer programs to yoga postures, there's no end to the strategies and products that claim to enhance creativity. It would be unfair to say that all of these methods are without value. But beyond a certain point they are, at best, superfluous. Trying too hard to reach for high-quality insight can thwart the process in the worst way. 10

The best ideas occur to me when my mind is otherwise unchallenged and there is no pressure to create. I have mentally composed whole articles while jogging, flashed upon the solution to a software dilemma while sitting in the steam room, come up with just the right opening line for a client's speech while pushing a vacuum. These were not problems I had set out to address at those particular times. Inventiveness came to my uncluttered mind in a random, unfocused moment. 11

Certainly not every idea that pops up during a quiet time is a winner. But a surprising number do set me on the path to fresh solutions. And I have found 12 that a free flow of ideas builds its own momentum, leapfrogging me along to answers that work.

13   The bonus is that creative thought is joyful. It doesn't matter if the idea is for a clever party decoration, a better way to rearrange the living-room furniture or the definitive antigravity machine. When a fine idea emerges there is a moment of "Eureka!" that simply beats all.

14   The simple fact is that time spent lost in thought isn't really lost at all. That's why "unplugged time" is vital. It's when new directions, different approaches and exciting solutions emerge from a place that can't be tapped at will.

15   It is unwise to take this resource for granted. Better to recognize it, understand something about where it resides and thereby ensure it is not lost.

16   Clearly, this is far easier said than done. Technology is seductive. It chases us down, grabs hold and will not let us go. Nor do we want it to. The challenge is to keep it in its place and to remember that time spent unplugged brings unique rewards. This doesn't mean I will abandon my new radio headset toy. But I will take the precaution of leaving it in my dresser drawer on a regular basis.

17   Otherwise, unlike wise old Newton, I may see the fall but never grasp its meaning. ■

FOR DISCUSSION: When and under what circumstances are you most likely to have creative thoughts? Do you think that technology helps you or hinders your creativity? How? What can you do to provide yourself with opportunities for more creative thinking?

Essay 3

READING, WRITING, NARCISSISM*

Lilian G. Katz

Lilian G. Katz is a professor of early childhood education at the University of Illinois. This article first appeared in American Educator and was later adapted for the New York Times's op-ed page.

1   Developing and strengthening children's self-esteem has become a major goal of our schools. Although it is true that many children, especially the youngest students, have low self-esteem, our practice of lavishing praise for the mildest accomplishments is not likely to have much success. Feelings cannot be learned from direct instruction, and constant reminders about how wonderful one is may raise doubts about the credibility of the message and the messenger.

2   A project by a first grade class in an affluent Middle Western suburb that I recently observed showed how self-esteem and narcissism can be confused. Working from copied pages prepared by the teacher, each student produced a booklet called "All About Me." The first page asked for basic information about the child's

*New York Times, July 15, 1993, p. A25.

home and family. The second page was titled "what I like to eat," the third was "what I like to watch on TV," the next was "what I want for a present" and another was "where I want to go on vacation."

The booklet, like thousands of others I have encountered around the country, 3 had no page headings such as "what I want to know more about," "what I am curious about," "what I want to solve" or even "to make."

Each page was directed toward the child's basest inner gratifications. 4 Each topic put the child in the role of consumer—of food, entertainment, gifts and recreation. Not once was the child asked to play the role of producer, investigator, initiator, explorer, experimenter or problem-solver.

It is perhaps this kind of literature that accounts for a poster I saw in a school 5 entrance hall. Pictures of clapping hands surround the title "We Applaud Ourselves." While the sign's probable purpose was to help children feel good about themselves, it did so by directing their attention inward. The poster urged self-congratulation; it made no reference to possible ways of earning applause—by considering the feelings or needs of others.

Another common type of exercise was a display of kindergartners' work I 6 saw recently that consisted of large paper-doll figures, each having a balloon containing a sentence stem that began "I am special because . . ." The children completed the sentence with the phrases such as "I can color," "I can ride a bike," and "I like to play with my friends." But these children are not likely to believe for very long that they are special because they can color or ride a bike. What are they going to think when they discover just how trivial these criteria for being special are?

This overemphasizing self-esteem and self-congratulation stems from a le- 7 gitimate desire to correct previous generations' traditions of avoiding compliments for fear of making children conceited. But the current practices are vast over-corrections. The idea of specialness they express is contradictory: If everybody is special, nobody is special.

Adults can show their approval for children in more significant ways than 8 awarding gold stars and happy faces. Esteem is conveyed to students when adults and peers treat them with respect, ask for their views and preferences and provide opportunities for decisions and choices about things that matter to them. Children are born natural and social scientists. They devote much time and energy to investigating and making sense of their environments. During the preschool and early school years, teachers can capitalize on this disposition by engaging children in investigations and projects.

Several years ago, I saw this kind of project at a rural British school for 5- to 9 7-year-olds. A large display on the bulletin board read: "We Are a Class Full of Bodies. Here Are the Details." The display space was filled with bar graphs showing birth dates, weights and heights, eye colors, number of lost teeth, shoe sizes and other data of the entire class. As the children worked in small groups to take measurements, prepare graphs and help one another post displays of their analyses, the teacher was able to create an atmosphere of a community of researchers looking for averages, trends and ranges.

10   Compare this to the American kindergarten I visited recently in which the comments made by the children about a visit to a dairy farm were displayed on the bulletin board. Each sentence began with the words "I liked." For example, "I liked the cows" and "I liked the milking machine." No sentences began "What surprised me was . . ." and "What I want to know more about is . . ."

11   Of course, children benefit from positive feedback. But praise and rewards are not the only methods of reinforcement. More emphasis should be placed on appreciation—reinforcement related explicitly and directly to the *content* of the child's interest and effort. For example, if a child poses a thoughtful question, the teacher might come to class the next day with a new reference book on the same subject. It is important that the teacher shows appreciation for pupils' concerns without taking their minds off the subjects at hand or directing their attention inward.

12   When children see that their concerns and interests are taken seriously, they are more likely to raise them in discussion and to take their own ideas seriously. Teachers can strengthen children's disposition to wonder, reflect, raise questions and generate alternative solutions to practical and intellectual problems. Of course, when children are engaged in challenging and significant activities, they are bound to experience failures and rebuffs. But as long as the teacher accepts the child's feelings and responds respectfully—"I know you're disappointed, but you can try again tomorrow"—the child is more likely to learn from the incident than be harmed by it.

13   Learning to deal with setbacks and maintaining the persistence and optimism necessary for childhood's long road to mastery are the real foundations of lasting self-esteem. Children who are helped to develop these qualities will surely respect themselves—though they probably will have better things to think about. ▪

FOR DISCUSSION: What values does the author believe are communicated through school assignments and programs designed to improve students' self-esteem? How would she assess the final value of these assignments? What types of assignments might she consider more valuable? What is your position on teaching self-esteem as a major goal for public schools?

Essay 4

DEVISING NEW MATH TO DEFINE POVERTY*

Louis Uchitelle

Louis Uchitelle conducted much of the research for this article in Indianapolis, Indiana.

1   The Census Bureau has begun to revise its definition of what constitutes poverty in the United States, experimenting with a formula that would drop millions more families below the poverty line.

New York Times, October 18, 1999, pp. A1, A4.

The bureau's new approach would in effect raise the income threshold for 2 living above poverty to $19,500 for a family of four, from the $16,600 now considered sufficient. Suddenly, 46 million Americans, or 17 percent of the population, would be recognized as officially below the line, not the 12.7 percent announced last month, the lowest level in nearly a decade.

A strong economy has undoubtedly lifted many families, but not nearly as 3 many as the official statistics suggest.

"It is certainly our opinion, and the opinion of every researcher we have 4 talked to, that something should be done to update the poverty measure," said Edward Welniak, chief of the Census Bureau's Income Statistics Branch.

Fixing a poverty line has always been a subjective endeavor. The current for- 5 mula was created for President Lyndon B. Johnson to keep score in his "war on poverty" and has remained unchanged since 1965 except for adjustments for inflation. It is based on a minimal food budget that no longer represents American eating habits or spending. The Census Bureau's new Experimental Poverty Measures are an effort to determine what poor people must spend on food, clothing, housing and life's little extras.

"There is no scientific way to set a new poverty line," said Rebecca M. Blank, 6 dean of the School of Public Policy at the University of Michigan. "What there is here are a set of judgment calls, now being made, about what is needed to lift people to a socially acceptable standard of living."

Sociologists and economists who study what people must earn to escape 7 poverty in the United States place the line even higher than the Census Bureau's experimental measures, which were published in July and are now the focus of a growing debate. They put the threshold for a family of four somewhere between $21,000 and $28,000. That is partly because the bureau's criteria, based largely on a study by the National Academy of Sciences, do not allow extra cash for emergencies—to fix a car, say, or repair a leaky roof, or to buy health insurance.

Ordinary Americans, in opinion polls, draw the poverty line above $20,000, 8 saying it takes at least that much, if not more, to "get along in their community," to "live decently" or to avoid hardship.

But a higher threshold means government spending would rise to pay for ben- 9 efits tied to the poverty level, like food stamps and Head Start. That would require an incursion into the budget surplus that neither Republicans nor Democrats seek.

Not surprising, the White House, which would have to authorize a change 10 in the poverty formula, is proceeding cautiously. "We have at least a couple of years more work to do," an Administration official said, passing the decision for redefining poverty to the next administration. . . .

The new thinking has several facets. It redefines income to include for the first 11 time noncash income like food stamps and rent subsidies. It puts child care and other work-related expenses in a separate category because they vary so much from family to family. And it tries to determine what a low-income family must spend in the 1990's not only to survive, but to preserve a reasonable amount of self-respect.

A telephone is considered essential. So is housing in good repair. Clothing is 12 no longer just to keep warm or covered; looking decent is a critical status symbol.

That is why Isaac Pinner, 16 and in ninth grade, and his sister, Lea, 12 and in seventh grade, insist they are not poor. Sitting in the living room of their run-down rented home with their mother, Julie Pinner, 35, a receptionist and clerk, they resent her decision to talk to a reporter about poverty. "I get what I want," Lea said, and Isaac agreed. "Why talk to us?" he asked.

13   Judging by their clothes, they do not seem poor, although their mother's income of $15,500, including a rent subsidy, while higher than the official poverty line for a single mother of two, puts the Pinners right at the dividing line in the Census Bureau's experimental measures.

14   "They think I am richer than I am," said Ms. Pinner, who noted that the gas was turned off recently when she could not pay the bill. She also lacks money to fix her car.

15   "But," Ms. Pinner said of her children, "he wears the latest Nike brand shoes and she the latest Levi's. I like them to look nice, and here in the ghetto there are standards of dress. If they don't dress up to the standards, other kids tend to pick on them. I am not the only poor person who dresses her kids."

16   Most proposed definitions of poverty include a car—an old one—which is deemed necessary not only for work but for the odd outing, or the supermarket. "Not having a car is a big dividing line between the poor and the not so poor," said Christopher Jencks, a sociologist at Harvard's Kennedy School of Government.

17   More often than not, poor Indianapolis families own used cars, but they are often at risk. Austin Johnson, for example, says he cannot afford car insurance. Neither can Nevada Owens, who is also short of money to fix a flat tire. She drives her 1985 Delta Oldsmobile with a spare doughnut tire permanently on a rear wheel. The car was a gift from her church, but the cost of gasoline for this guzzler eats up 7 percent of her $17,300 in annual income.

18   Her income, from welfare, food stamps, rent and tuition subsidies and a $3,000 gift from her mother, puts Ms. Owens, a single mother, and her three children just above the official poverty line. But at 21, studying to be a licensed practical nurse, she needs the car. The course work requires her to travel from her school to two different hospitals, about 25 miles a day.

19   Then there is the Saturday outing in Ms. Owens's old car, which she drives to her grandfather's home in a rural area outside the city—the one family luxury. "We have a cookout," she said, "and the kids play on the swings and my mother comes over—she lives two doors away. We have a good time."

20   In a 1993 study of impoverished single mothers, published as the book *Making Ends Meet*, Kathryn Edin, a sociologist at the University of Pennsylvania, reported that the mothers found themselves forced to spend more than their acknowledged incomes. They got the difference from family members, absent boyfriends, off-the-books jobs and church charity.

21   "No one avoided the unnecessary expenditures," Ms. Edin said recently, "such as the occasional trip to the Dairy Queen, or a pair of stylish new sneakers for the son who might otherwise sell drugs to get them, or the cable subscription for the kids home alone and you are afraid they will be out on the street if they are not watching TV." ■

FOR DISCUSSION: What is the issue in this article? How does definition intensify this issue? What is your opinion about drawing the poverty line? Where should it be drawn? Who would benefit from your solution? Who would be burdened?

STUDY SAYS NET USE, DEPRESSION MAY BE LINKED*

Essay 5

Amy Harmon

The study described in this article tracked the behavior of 169 participants in the Pittsburgh area who were selected from four schools and community groups.

In the first concentrated study of the social and psychological effects of Internet 1 use at home, researchers at Carnegie Mellon University have found that people who spend even a few hours a week online experience more depression and loneliness than those who use the computer network less frequently.

The participants who were lonelier and more depressed at the start of the 2 two-year study, as determined by a standard questionnaire, were not more likely to use the Internet. Instead, Internet use itself appeared to lessen psychological well-being, the researchers said.

The results of the $1.5 million project are contrary to the expectations of the 3 social scientists who designed it and many of the organizations that financed it. The backers include technology companies such as Intel Corp., Hewlett Packard, AT&T Research and Apple Computer, as well as the National Science Foundation.

"We were shocked by the findings, because they are counterintuitive to 4 what we know about how socially the Internet is being used," said Robert Kraut, a social psychology professor at Carnegie Mellon's Human Computer Interaction Institute. "We are not talking here about the extremes. These were normal adults and their families, and on average, for those who used the Internet most, things got worse."

The Internet has been praised as superior to television and other "passive" 5 media because it allows users to choose the kind of information they want to receive, and, often, to respond actively through e-mail exchanges, chat rooms or electronic bulletin board postings.

Research on the effects of watching television indicates that it tends to re- 6 duce social involvement. But the new study, "HomeNet," suggests that the interactive medium may be no more socially healthful than older mass media. It also raises troubling questions about the nature of "virtual" communication and the disembodied relationships that are often formed in the vacuum of cyberspace.

Study participants used inherently social features such as e-mail and Inter- 7 net chat rooms more than they used passive information gathering such as reading

Arlington Star-Telegram, August 30, 1998, pp. 1, 29.

or watching videos. But they reported a decline in interaction with relatives and a reduction in their circles of friends that directly corresponded to how much time they spent online.

8   At the beginning and end of the two-year study, the subjects were asked to agree or disagree with statements such as "I felt everything I did was an effort" and "I enjoyed life" and "I can find companionship when I want it." They were also asked to estimate how many minutes each day they spent with each member of their family and to quantify their social circle. Many of those questions are standard in psychological health assessments.

9   For the duration of the study, the subjects' use of the Internet was recorded. Depression and loneliness were measured independently, and each subject was rated on a subjective scale. In measuring depression, the responses were plotted on a scale of 0 to 3, with 0 being the least depressed and 3 being the most depressed. Loneliness was plotted on a scale of 1 to 5.

10   By the end of the study, the researchers found that one hour a week on the Internet led to an average increase of .03, or 1 percent, on the depression scale, a loss of 2.7 members of the subject's social circle, which averaged 66 people, and an increase of .02, or four-tenths of 1 percent, on the loneliness scale.

11   The subjects exhibited wide variations in all three measured effects. The net effects are not large, but they are statistically significant in demonstrating deterioration of social and psychological life, Kraut said.

12   Based on the data, the researchers hypothesize that relationships maintained over long distances without face-to-face contact ultimately do not provide the kind of support and reciprocity that typically contribute to psychological security and happiness, such as being available to baby-sit in a pinch for a friend, or to grab a cup of coffee and talk.

13   "Our hypothesis is there are more cases where you're building shallow relationships, leading to an overall decline in feeling of connection to other people," Kraut said. . . .

14   Because the study participants were not randomly selected, it is unclear how the findings apply to the general population. It is also conceivable that some unmeasured factor caused simultaneous increases in use of the Internet and decline in normal levels of social involvement. Moreover, the effect of Internet use varied depending on an individual's life patterns and type of use. Researchers said that people who were isolated because of their geography or work shifts might have benefited socially from Internet use.

15   Even so, several social scientists familiar with the study vouched for its credibility and predicted that the findings will touch off a national debate over how public policy regarding the Internet should evolve and how the technology might be shaped to yield more beneficial effects.

16   "They did an extremely careful scientific study, and it's not a result that's easily ignored," said Tora Bikson, a senior scientist at Rand, the research institution. Based partly on previous studies that focused on how local communities such as Santa Monica, Calif., used computer networks to enhance civic participation, Rand has recommended that the federal government provide e-mail access to all Americans.

"It's not clear what the underlying psychological explanation is," Bikson said 17
of the study. "Is it because people give up day-to-day contact and then find themselves depressed? Or are they exposed to the broader world of Internet and then
wonder, 'What am I doing here in Pittsburgh?' Maybe your comparison standard
changes. I'd like to see this replicated on a larger scale. Then I'd really worry." ■

FOR DISCUSSION: What is the claim in this essay? Test it against your own experience. How much time do you spend on the computer each week? How has computer use changed your life? Would you say that you are more or less depressed as
a result of your use of computers? Compare your experiences with those of your
classmates.

C. GROUP WORK: READING AND ANALYZING CLAIMS AND SUBCLAIMS

The following essay is an example of several types of claims and associated
purposes used in one essay. One type of claim, however, predominates in the
essay, and the other claims support and develop it. First divide the essay into
"chunks" by drawing a line across the page each time the author changes the
type of claim and purpose. Label the type of claim and predominant purpose of
each chunk (example: fact, to establish the facts). Then underline the predominant claim and describe the purpose of the entire essay. Speculate about the reasons the author had for placing the parts of this essay in this particular order.
Discuss the relationship between the parts.

Much argumentative writing combines claims in this way, and you may
want to study the pattern of claims used here as a possible model for one of
your own argument papers.

HOLD YOUR HORSEPOWER*

Lyla Fox

Essay

Lyla Fox is a high school English teacher in Michigan.

F olks in the small Michigan town where I grew up revere the work ethic. Our 1
entire culture lauds those who are willing to work their tails off to get ahead.
Though there's nothing wrong with hard work, I suggest that our youngsters may
be starting too young—and for all the wrong reasons.

Increasingly I identify with Sisyphus trying to move that stone. There are 2
more mornings than I would like to admit when many of my students sit with
eyes glazed or heads slumped on their desks as I try to nurture a threatening-
to-become-extinct interest in school. These are not lazy kids. Many are high-

*"My Turn," *Newsweek*, March 25, 1996, p. 16.

achieving 16- and 17-year-olds who find it tough to reconcile 7:30 A.M. classes with a job that winds down at 10:30 P.M. or later.

3　　　"What's wrong?" I asked a student who once diligently completed his home-work assignments. He groggily grunted an answer. "I'm tired. I didn't get home until 11 P.M." Half the class nodded and joined in a discussion about how hard it is to try to balance schoolwork, sports and jobs. Since we end up working most of our adult life, my suggestion to the class was to forgo the job and partake of school—both intra- and extracurricular.

4　　　"Then how do I pay for my car?" the sleepy student, now more awake, asked. Click. The car. That's what all these bleary eyes and half-done papers are about. My students have a desperate need to drive their own vehicles proudly into the school parking lot. The car is the teenager's symbolic club membership. I know because I've seen the embarrassed looks on the faces of teens who must an-swer "No" to the frequently asked "Do you have a car?" National Merit finalists pale in importance beside the student who drives his friends around in a shiny new Ford Probe.

5　　　My own son (a senior at the University of Michigan) spent a good part of his high-school years lamenting our "no car in high school" dictate. When he needed to drive, we made sure he could always borrow our car. Our Oldsmobile 88, how-ever, didn't convey the instant high-school popularity of a sporty Nissan or Honda. Our son's only job was to do as well as he could in school. The other work, we told him, would come later. Today I see students working more than the legally permitted number of hours to pay for their cars. I also see once committed students becoming less dedicated to schoolwork. Their commitment is to their cars and the jobs that will help them make those monthly car payments.

6　　　Once cars and jobs enter the picture, it is virtually impossible to get students focused on school. "My parents are letting me get a car," one of my brightest stu-dents enthused a few months ago. "They say all I have to do is get a job to make the payments." *All.* I winced, saying nothing because parents' views are sacro-sanct for me. I bit my cheeks to keep from saying how wrong I thought they were and how worried I was for her schoolwork. Predictably, during the next few months, her grades and attitude took a plunge.

7　　　I say attitude because when students go to work for a car, their positive atti-tude frequently disappears. Teachers and parents are on the receiving end of curved-lip responses to the suggestion that they should knuckle down and do some schoolwork. A job and car payments are often a disastrous combination.

8　　　These kids are selling their one and only chance at adolescence for a car. Adults in their world must help them see what their children's starry eyes cannot: that stu-dents will have the rest of their lives to own an automobile and pay expenses.

9　　　Some parents, I know, breathe a sigh of relief when their children can finally drive themselves to orthodontist appointments and basketball practice. This trade-off could mean teens' losing touch with family life. Having a car makes it easy for kids to cut loose and take part in activities far from home. Needing that ride from Mom and Dad helps to keep a family connection. Chauffering teens an-other year or two might be a bargain after all.

What a remarkable experience a school day might be if it were the center of teens' lives, instead of that much-resented time that keeps them from their friends and their jobs. Although we may not have meant to, parents may have laid the groundwork for that resentment. By giving kids permission to work, parents are not encouraging them to study. Parents have allowed students to miss classes because of exhaustion from the previous night's work. By providing a hefty down payment on a $12,000 car and stressing the importance of keeping up the payments, they're sending a signal that schoolwork is secondary. 10

The kids I'm writing about are wonderful. But they are stressed and angry that their day has too few hours for too much work. Sound familiar? It should. It is the same description adults use to identify what's wrong with their lives. 11

After reading this, my students may want to hang me in effigy. But perhaps some of them are secretly hoping that someone will stop their world and help them get off. They might also concede that it's time to get out of the car and get on mass transit. For students in large metropolitan areas, public transportation is the only way to get around. 12

Adults should take the reins and let teens off the hook. We must say "no" when we're implored to "Please let me get a job so I can have a car." Peer pressure makes it hard for kids to turn away from the temptation of that shiny four-wheeled popularity magnet. It's up to the grown-ups to let kids stay kids a little longer. 13

The subject of teens and cars comes up in my home as well as in my classroom. My 15-year-old daughter gave me some bone-chilling news yesterday. "The Springers got Suzi her own car!" she announced. "All she has to do is make the payments." 14

I smiled and went back to correcting the essays that would have been lovely had their authors had some time to put into constructing them. The payment, I told myself after my daughter went grudgingly to begin her homework, may be greater than anyone in the Springer family could possibly imagine. ■ 15

FOR DISCUSSION: How people use their time is often controversial. How is it controversial in this essay? Can you think of other examples where time is controversial? In your opinion, is the problem the author identifies significant or not? Why do you think so?

D. WRITING ASSIGNMENT: TYPES OF CLAIMS

Write a 250–300 word paper that is organized around a single type of claim. Use the following claims about campus issues as starter sentences for your paper. Use the information about types of support and organizational strategies for each type of claim in this chapter to help you plan and write. Work in pairs to generate ideas and support for your papers.

1. Is it true? Does it exist? *Claim of fact:* School spirit (is or is not) an important part of our campus climate.
2. How should we define it? *Claim of definition:* Not everyone defines dangerous levels of drinking alcohol in exactly the same way.

3. What caused it? What are the effects? *Claim of cause:* Closing the college library for the weekend would (or would not) have a disastrous effect.

4. Is it good or bad? *Claim of value:* Sororities and fraternities (do or do not) contribute significant positive value to the college experience.

5. What is the problem and what should we do to solve it? *Claim of policy:* The food services on campus should (or should not) be improved.

E. PREWRITING: USING THE CLAIM QUESTIONS TO GET IDEAS FOR A POSITION PAPER

The claim questions can be used to invent ideas for any argument paper. If, however, you are gathering ideas for the assignment for the "Position Paper Based on 'The Reader'" (Exercise G in Chapter 7), you may want to use the claim questions to generate additional material for this paper. (You may have already completed other prewriting activities for this paper, including an issue proposal, Chapter 1, Exercise F; summary-response papers, Chapter 3, Exercise E; an exploratory paper, Chapter 4, Exercise D; and a Toulmin analysis, Chapter 5, Exercise F.) Now use the claim questions to refine or revise the tentative claim you have written for your paper.

1. Write your issue in the form of an issue question. *Example:* Is parking a problem on campus?

2. Apply the claim question to the issue questions, and write a paragraph in response to each question.

   a. *Fact:* Did it happen? Does it exist?
   b. *Definition:* What is it? How can we define it?
   c. *Cause:* What caused it? What are the effects?
   d. *Value:* Is it good or bad? What criteria will help us decide?
   e. *Policy:* What should we do about it? What should be our future course of action?

3. Read the paragraphs you have written, and select the one that interests you the most and that also seems most promising as the focus for your paper. Now look at your tentative claim and revise it, if necessary, to bring it in line with your new purpose and focus. You may also, of course, use information from the other paragraphs you have written to develop subclaims and support for your paper. Save what you have written in a folder. You will use it later when you plan and write your position paper.

CHAPTER SEVEN

Types of Proofs

You learned in Chapter 5 that the claim, the support, and the warrants are the three essential parts of an argument. Chapter 6 helped you understand claims, and this chapter will help you understand the support and warrants that provide proofs for the claim. The material in this chapter is organized to introduce you first to the different types of proofs, next to the language and style associated with each of them, and finally to some of the fallacies or pseudoproofs that sometimes occur in argument.

As you understand and begin to work with the proofs, you will discover that they are not simply uniform patterns that are obvious and easy to recognize. Rather, slippery and imperfect as they are, they represent an attempt to describe what goes on in the real world of argument and in the minds of writers and readers of argument. Understanding them can put you closer to an author so that you may better understand how that individual thought about, interpreted, and developed a particular subject. Then, when you switch roles and become the author yourself, your knowledge of what can happen in argument will help you develop your own thoughts and create your own effective arguments.

THE TRADITIONAL CATEGORIES OF PROOF

The traditional categories of proof, like much of our most fundamental argument theory, were first articulated by classical theorists, and they are still useful for describing what goes on in real-world argument today. Recall from Chapter 5 that Aristotle, in the *Rhetoric,* said that an arguer must state a claim (or a proposition) and prove it. He also went into detail about the broad categories of proof that can be used to establish the probability of a claim. Aristotle's categories of proof are still useful both because they accurately describe what classical arguers did then and what modern arguers still do and because they have become such an accepted part of our intellectual heritage that, like generations before us, we learn these methods and use them to observe, think about, and interpret reality. Aristotle's ideas and observations still provide accurate descriptions of what goes on in argument.

Aristotle distinguishes between proofs that can be produced and laid on the table, so to speak, like a murder weapon, fingerprints, or a written contract, and proofs that are invented and represent the creative thinking and insights of clever and intelligent people.

Aristotle divides this second category of proof into three subcategories: proofs that appeal to logic and reason, proofs that establish the credibility of the source, and proofs that appeal to the emotions. The Greek words used to refer to the proofs are *logos* (logic), *ethos* (credibility), and *pathos* (emotion).

Logical proof appeals to people's reason, understanding, and common sense. It is consistent with what we know and believe, and it gives us fresh insight and ideas about issues. As proof, it relies mainly on such support as reasoned opinion and factual data and also on warrants that suggest the soundness and truth of such support. Aristotle declared that logical proof is the most important type of proof in argument, and most modern theorists agree with him. Richard M. Weaver, a well-known modern rhetorician, for example, says that argument has its primary basis in reasoning and that it appeals primarily to the rational part of man. Logical proof, he says, provides, the "plot" of argument.[1] The other two types of proof are also present and important, however.

Proof that establishes ethos appeals to the audience's impressions, opinions, and judgments about the individual stating the argument. Arguers who demonstrate competence, good character, fair-mindedness, and goodwill toward the audience are more convincing than people who lack these qualities. Individuals who project such favorable qualities to an audience have established good *ethos*. Audiences are more likely to trust and believe individuals with good *ethos* than those without it. At times, arguers also need to establish the *ethos* of the experts whom they quote in their arguments. They usually accomplish this purpose by providing information about them so that audiences will appreciate these individuals' degree of expertise and consequently be more willing to accept what they say.

Emotional proof is used to appeal to and arouse the feelings of the audience. Audience's feelings are aroused primarily through emotional language, examples, personal narratives, and vivid descriptions of events that contain emotional elements and that arouse strong feelings in other people. Emotional proof is appropriate in an argument when it is used to develop the claim and when it contributes to the sense of logical conviction or agreement that are argument's intended outcomes. A well-reasoned set of logical proofs contributes to such outcomes. But

---

[1]Richard M. Weaver, "Language Is Sermonic," in Richard L. Johannesen, ed., *Contemporary Theories of Rhetoric: Selected Readings*, (New York: Harper & Row, 1971), pp. 163–179.

emotion can also contribute to a strong acceptance of a logical conclusion. Imagine, for example, an argument in favor of increasing taxes to build housing for homeless people. The logical argument would describe reasons for these taxes, methods for levying them, and recommendations for spending them. The argument would be strengthened, however, by a few vivid and emotional examples of homeless people who lead miserable lives.

The next three sections will introduce you to seven types of logical proof, one type of proof that builds *ethos,* and two types of emotional proof. All are commonly used in argument. The number and variety of logical proofs is greater than the others because logical thinking dominates and provides the "plot" for most argument. Most arguments rely on a variety of proofs because offering several types of proof usually makes a stronger argument than relying on only one.

Each type of proof will be explained according to the following format so that you can understand each type as quickly and easily as possible:[2]

> *Examples:* Examples follow a brief general description of each proof.
>
> *Claim and support:* You are then told what to look for, or what types of support you can expect to find on the printed page and how to find the claim.
>
> *Warrant:* You are told what you are expected to assume to make logical connections between the support and the claim. The warrants associated with types of proof suggest specific ways of thinking about support and its function in an argument.
>
> *Tests of validity:* You are provided with questions to ask to help you test the reliability and validity of the proof. These questions will focus your attention on both support and warrant and how they do or do not function together as effective proof. They will also help you locate the weaknesses in an argument, which can help you plan rebuttal and formulate argument of your own.

In Exercise B at the end of the chapter, you will have the opportunity to identify and analyze the proofs in a short essay so that you can see how they operate in written argument. Other exercises show you how to use the proofs in your own writing.

TYPES OF LOGICAL PROOF: *LOGOS*

Logical proofs (also called substantive proofs) include facts, reasons, and opinions that are based on reality. They rely on factual information, statistics, and accounts of actual events, past and present. The support used in logical proof is real and

---

[2]In this chapter I have drawn some of Wayne Brockriede and Douglas Ehninger's ideas in "Toulmin on Argument: An Interpretation and Application," *Quarterly Journal of Speech* 46 (1969): 44–53. I have expanded and adapted these authors' analysis of proofs to make it apply to the reading and writing of argument as explained in this book.

drawn from experience. Logical (or substantive) warrants guarantee the reliability and relevance of this support. Logical proofs represent common ways of thinking about and perceiving relationships among the events and data of the real world and then using those ideas and relationships as support for a line of argument.

Argument from Deduction

Deductive argument is also called argument from principle because its warrant is a general principle. Remember that the warrant may or may not be stated explicitly in an argument. Etymology can help you remember the special features of deductive argument. The prefix *de-* means "from" and the root *duc* means "lead." *A deductive argument leads from a general principle,* which is the warrant, applies it to an example or specific case, which is described in the support, and draws a *conclusion,* which is the claim.

Examples of Deduction. In Chapter 6 you learned that argument deals with matters that are probably rather than certainly true. People do not argue about matters that are certainly true because they already agree about them. Here is an example of a deductive argument based on a general principle that people would agree with and accept as true. Thus, they would not argue about it.

General warrant:	Every person has a unique set of fingerprints.
Support:	The accused is a person.
Claim:	The accused has a unique set of fingerprints.

This example might be used as a minor argument to support a claim that someone is guilty of a crime. It would never be the main issue in an argument, however, because it is not arguable.

Most of the deduction you will encounter in argument is arguable because it deals with probabilities rather than with certainties. Fictional sleuth Sherlock Holmes used deduction to reach his sometimes astonishing conclusions. Holmes examined the supporting evidence—footprints, for example—and deduced that the man who left them walked with a limp. The general principle, that most uneven footprints are left by people who limp, is an assumption that is important in Holmes's deductive thinking even though it is not stated in the argument. It does not need to be spelled out for readers who are able to supply that warrant themselves as they accept Holmes's conclusion. The Holmes deduction can be summarized as follows. The purpose of this argument is to establish the type of person who left these footprints.

Unstated warrant:	Most uneven footprints are left by people who limp.
Support:	These footprints are uneven.
Claim:	The person who left these footprints walks with a limp.

Is there any part of that argument that you might challenge as only possibly or probably rather than as certainly true? If so, you can argue about it.

Claim and Support.   Identify the claim by answering this question: "On the basis of a general principle (warrant), implied or stated, what does the author expect me to conclude about this specific example or case?"

Deductive Warrants.   You are expected to assume that a general principle about a whole category of phenomena (people, places, events, and so forth) has been stated or implied in the argument and that it is accurate and acceptable. You are expected to decide that since the general principle, or warrant, and the support for the specific case are both accurate and acceptable, the conclusion is also acceptable and probably true.

Tests of Validity.   Is the warrant acceptable and believable? Does the warrant apply to the example or case? Is the support for the case accurate? How reliable, then, is the conclusion?

If the reader has a problem with either the warrant or the example in a deductive argument, the conclusion will not be acceptable. Consider Holmes's warrant that uneven footprints are left by people who limp. That may be convincing to some readers but not others. For instance, a reader might reflect that a person who is pretending to limp or is carrying a heavy valise in one hand could also leave uneven footprints. This reader would then question the warrant and decide that the proof is not even probably true.

Here is another example of a deductive argument that would not be equally successful with all audiences:

Unstated warrant: Families cannot be happy when the mother works outside the home.
Support: The mother in this family works outside the home
Claim: This is an unhappy family.

For readers who come from happy homes with working mothers, the warrant in this example would seem faulty.

In the next example of a deductive argument, the support could be a problem for some readers who might have trouble accepting it because they think children's stories are not literary and do not have levels of meaning. Another reader might disagree and argue for the opposite point of view, providing examples of children's stories that have literary qualities and thus refute the other reader's claim. Whether or not a reader accepts the conclusion depends entirely on whether or not the reader also accepts the warrant and support. This argument, by the way, is depicted in the cartoon that appears on page 143. Would you say that the children who have gathered to hear the story accept the warrant and the support or not?

Warrant: All literary stories have levels of meaning.
Support: Children's stories are literary stories.
Claim: Children's stories have levels of meaning.

All parts of a deductive argument need to be accurate and acceptable to an audience for it to be convincing.

Argument from Definition

Definition is extremely important in argument. It is difficult to argue about any subject unless there is general agreement about the meanings of the key terms, especially when they are part of the claim. Sometimes an entire argument is based on the audience's acceptance of a certain meaning of a key term. If the audience accepts the definition, the arguer says that the claim should be accepted "by definition."

Examples of Definition. The argument in "Reading, Writing, Narcissism" (pages 180–182) can be laid out as deduction. Notice that if self-esteem is defined as narcissistic, then by definition educational goals that aim to teach self-esteem also end up teaching narcissism, or extreme self-centeredness.

> *Warrant:* Self-esteem is narcissistic.
> *Support:* An educational goal is to teach self-esteem.
> *Claim:* This educational goal also teaches narcissism.

Here is another example:

> *Warrant:* Family values characterize the good citizen.
> *Support:* Radical feminists lack family values.
> *Claim:* Radical feminists are not good citizens.

We will accept the claim that radical feminists, by definition, are poor citizens only if we also accept the warrants that define the good citizen as one who possesses family values and radical feminists as people who lack these values. (See the article "Family Values" on pages 163–164 to see how this argument appears in print.)

Even though argument by definition takes the form of deductive argument, it is listed separately here to emphasize the important function of definition in arguments that depend on it as major proof.

Claim and Support. Look for all definitions or explanations of words or concepts. These may be a sentence, several paragraphs, or an entire essay in length. Notice if the definition is used simply to define a word or if it is used as part of the proof in the argument, as in the case of "Reading, Writing, Narcissism." Look for a claim that you are expected to accept as a result of the definition.

Definition Warrants. You are expected to assume that the definition describes the fundamental properties and qualities of the term accurately so that it can be used to prove the claim.

Tests of Validity. Is this an accurate and complete definition? Is it convincing in this context? Are there exceptions or other definitions for this term that would make the final claim less reliable?

Argument from Cause

Argument from cause places the subject in a cause-and-effect relationship to show that it is either the cause of an effect or the effect of a cause. It is very common in argument to explain or to justify a claim with cause-and-effect reasoning.

Example of cause. The argument used in "Study Says Net Use, Depression May Be Linked" (pages 185–187) provides an example of argument from cause.

Warrant: Depression in a group of people has increased.
Support: This group of people has also increased its use of the Internet.
Claim: The Internet may be causing depression.

Claim and Support. Look for examples, events, trends, and people that have caused certain things to happen. Look for the effects. For example, "Video games cause children to become violent." Or turn it around and look for the effects first and then the causes: "Many children are violent as a result of playing too many violent video games." Look also for clue words such as *cause, effect, resulted in, as a result, as a consequence,* and *because* to indicate that cause-and-effect reasoning is being used. Finally, the claim states what you are expected to conclude as a result of this cause-and-effect reasoning: "Too much time on the Internet may cause depression."

Causal Warrants. You are expected to assume that the causes really do create the identified effects or that the effects really are the results of the named causes.

Tests of Validity. Are these causes alone sufficient to create these effects? Could these effects result from other causes? Can I think of exceptions to the cause-and-effect outcome that is claimed here?

Argument from Sign

A specific visible sign is sometimes used to prove a claim. A sign can be used to prove with certainty: someone breaks out in chickenpox, and the claim, based on that certain sign, is that the person has chickenpox. Or a sign can be used to prove the probability of a claim: a race riot, someone argues, is probably a sign of the claim that people think they are treated unfairly. Or the sign may turn out to be a pseudoproof, the "proof" of a false claim: a child asks, "Why should I believe in

Santa Claus?" and the parent answers, "Look at all the toys under the tree that weren't there yesterday." That support is used as a sign for the claim that Santa Claus exists.

Example of Sign.   Here is an example of an argument from sign used in the essay "Campus Climate Control" (pages 170–172). Would you say that the claim based on this sign is a certain or probable claim?

Claim:	There is no adult supervision in the freshman dining hall.
Support (sign):	There are butter pats on the ceiling of the dining hall.
Warrant:	Adults do not flip butter pats onto the ceiling.

Claim and Support.   Look for visible clues, symptoms, and occurrences that are explained as obvious and clear signs of a certain belief or state of affairs. Look for the conclusion or claim that is made on the basis of these signs.

Sign Warrants.   You are expected to assume that the sign is actually a sign of what the author claims it to be.

Tests of Validity.   Is this really a sign of what the author claims it to be? Is there another explanation for the sign?

Argument from Induction

Inductive argument provides a number of examples and draws a claim, in the form of a conclusion, from them. The audience is expected to accept the group of examples as adequate and accurate enough to make the inductive leap to the claim. Inductive argument is also called argument from generalization or argument from example because the claim is a generalization made on the basis of the examples. To help you remember the special features of inductive argument, learn its prefix *in-*, which means "in" or "into," and the root *duc,* which means "lead." *An inductive argument uses examples to lead into a claim or generalization about the examples.*

Examples of Induction.   Here is an example of induction. Four different people take their cars to the same car repair shop and are overcharged. The claim is then made that anyone who takes a car to that repair shop will probably be overcharged.

Inductive reasoning is the basis of the scientific method. Most scientific conclusions are reached inductively. When a sufficient number of phenomena are observed repeatedly, a generalization is made to explain them. Here is another example:

Claim (generalization):	The sun always comes up.
Support:	For example, the sun has come up every day of recorded history.

Warrant: Every day provides a sufficient number of days to make the claim that the sun always comes up.

Here is a third example. This inductive reasoning appears in the article "What's Wrong with Standard Tests" (pages 167–169).

Examples: Danny Algrant was a difficult student who became famous.
An unpromising adolescent became a school principal.
A low tester became a successful writer.
Claim (generalization made on the basis of the examples):
These unpromising students did well later, so others may also.
Warrant: These three examples are enough to make us accept the claim.

Induction demonstrates probability rather than truth when there is the possibility of an example that would prove an exception. For instance, an unpromising student may become an unpromising adult. But an apple always falls from a tree, thereby demonstrating gravity, and the sun always comes up, demonstrating that law of nature. No one has been able to find exceptions to disprove these last two generalizations.

To be effective, inductive argument requires a sufficient number of examples. When a generalization is made on the basis of only one, or a few, examples, it is called a *hasty generalization.* To claim, for instance, that an office worker should always be able to enter a certain amount of data because he did it once may not be accurate. To make a broad generalization, such as *all* office workers ought to be able to enter a certain amount of data because *one* employee was able to, is called a *sweeping generalization.* An inadequate sample of cases weakens or invalidates an inductive argument.

Claim and Support.   Look for a group of examples followed by a generalization (claim) based on the examples; or the generalization (claim) may be stated first and then be followed by several examples.

Inductive Warrants.   You are expected to assume that the list of examples is representative and that it shows a definite trend. You are also expected to assume that if you added more examples of the same general type, the conclusion would not change.

Test of Validity.   Is the sample adequate? Would more examples continue to show the trend? Are there examples that show an opposite trend, that provide an exception? (Was someone charged a reasonable amount at the repair shop?) Can we make the inductive leap from the examples to the generalization to demonstrate that it is probably true?

Argument from Statistics

Like other forms of logical proof, statistics describe relationships among data, people, occurrences, and events in the real world, only they do so in quantitative terms. Modern readers have considerable faith in numbers and statistics. They seem more "true" than other types of support to many people. It is more convincing to some people, for example, to make the claim that we should end draft registration because it costs $27.5 million per year than simply to claim that we should end it because we no longer need it.

Read statistical proofs carefully to determine where they come from and how reliable, accurate, and relevant they are. Note also whether the original figures have been altered or interpreted in some way. Figures are often rounded off or stated in different terms, such as percentages or plots on a graph. They are also sometimes compared to other material that is familiar to the audience to make them more interesting or memorable.[3] Various types of graphs or charts also make data and statistics visual and easier to grasp and remember.

Example of Statistics. Here is an example of a typical use of statistics in an article titled "Child-Killing Increases in Rio."[4]

Claim: Child-killing is increasing in Rio de Janeiro.
Support: Forty percent more children may be killed this year than last year.
Warrant: Forty percent represents an increase.

The source for these statistics is cited only as "preliminary statistics." On close reading, one realizes that 424 people under 18 were killed in one year in Rio, compared with 348 who were killed in seven months of the following year. Thus the claim of a 40 percent increase is qualified to read "may be killed," since it is based on a projection of what might occur in the next five months. The figures are also converted to percentages. The author goes on to compare these figures with one that is more familiar to the reader, the number of child killings in the United States. It is claimed that 6,000 to 7,000 children, or 20 a day, died from gunshot wounds during the comparable period of time in the United States. Notice that these figures, too, are rounded off. The source for these last figures is cited as a news conference interview with the executive director of UNICEF. You might have to read other sources on this subject to test the validity of these figures.

Claim and Support. Look for numbers and data, in both their original and their converted form, graphs and charts of figures, and interpretations of them, including comparisons. Look for a claim based on the data.

Statistical Warrants. You are expected to assume that the data have been gathered and reported accurately by competent people, that they are representa-

---

[3] James Wood, *Speaking Effectively* (New York: Random House, 1988), pp. 121–127.
[4] James Brooke, "Child Killing Increases in Rio," *Fort Worth Star-Telegram,* January 3, 1994, p. 7.

tive and complete unless stated otherwise, and that they have been interpreted fairly and truthfully.

Tests of Validity.   Where did these statistics come from? To what dates do the statistics apply? How reliable is the source? How accurate are they? How are they presented? Have they been rounded off, changed, or converted? How has the change affected their accuracy? Do they prove what they are supposed to prove? Have they been interpreted fairly, or are they exaggerated or skewed? Has enough backing been provided to prove their reliability? What are they compared to, and how does this comparison contribute to their final significance? Is any significant information left out?

Tests of Validity for Statistics Presented as Graphs.   Statistics are sometimes presented in graph form. The tests of validity in this case include these: Where did the information come from? What information is included in the sample? How was it gathered? Is anything significant left out or ignored because it didn't fit? Are the charts and graphs labeled accurately? Are there any exaggerations?

Argument from Historical, Literal, or Figurative Analogy

Historical and literal analogies explore similarities and differences between items in the same general category, and *figurative analogies* do the same, only with items in very different categories. In drawing analogies, we show how something we may not know much about is like something we know in greater detail. In other words, we interpret what we do not know in the light of what we do know. We then supply the warrant that what happened in one case will happen in the other, we draw conclusions, and we make a claim based on the comparisons in the analogy.

Historical Analogies.   These explain what is going on *now* in terms of what went on in similar cases *in the past*. Future outcomes are also often projected from past cases. The idea is that what happened in the past will probably repeat itself in the present. Also, the two events are so similar that the results of the former will surely be the end result of the latter.

Example of a Historical Analogy.   The following example compares a present event with a past event.

Claim:	Many people will die of AIDS.
Support:	Many people died of the Black Death.
Warrant:	AIDS and the Black Death are similar.

Literal Analogies.   These compare two items in the same category: two school systems, two governments, two religions, two individuals. Outcomes are described as in historical analogies—that is, what happened in one case will happen in the other because of the similarities or the differences.

Example of a Literal Analogy. Two similar items are compared in this example.

Claim:	The state should spend more money on education.
Support:	Another state spent more money with good results.
Warrant:	The two states are similar, and the results of one will be the results of the other.

Figurative Analogies. These compare items from two different categories, as in metaphor, only the points of comparison in a figurative analogy are usually spelled out in more detail than they are in a metaphor. Many figurative analogies appeal to the emotions rather than to reason. Figurative analogies are effective as logical proof only when they are used to identify *real qualities* that are shared by both items and that can then be applied to help prove the claim logically. When the items in a figurative analogy are compared to add ornament or to stir up an emotional response, the analogy functions as emotional proof. It engages the emotions rather than the reason.

Examples of Figurative Analogies. Here are some examples of figurative analogies used as logical proof. To prove that reading a difficult book should take time, Francis Bacon compares that activity with taking the time to chew and digest a large meal. The qualities of the two activities, rather than the activities themselves, are compared. Since these qualities are not spelled out, the audience must infer that both take time, and understanding, like digestion, benefits and becomes a permanent part of the individual. Here is this argument laid out so that you can see how it works.

Claim:	Reading a difficult book should take time.
Support:	Digesting a large meal takes time.
Warrant:	Reading and eating are sufficiently alike that they can be compared.

In another example of a figurative analogy used as logical proof, the human fossil record is compared to an apple tree in early winter that has only a few apples on it. The quality that the fossil record and the tree have in common, which the reader must infer, is that both tree and fossil record have a complicated system of branches and limbs. Also, the few apples on the tree are like the few available fossils. At one time there were many of both. The qualities compared in these two instances improve a rational understanding of the fossil record.

Here is a third example of a figurative analogy. This analogy comes from an ad sponsored by the Sierra Club, a group that works to protect the environment. Two pictures are placed side by side. The first is of the Statue of Liberty, which is 305 feet high, and the second is of a giant sequoia tree, which is 275 feet high. A question is posed: "Would you destroy the Statue of Liberty for scrap metal?" We are expected to reason by analogy and compare destroying the Statue of Liberty for scrap metal with destroying the tree for lumber or sawdust. The individual who created this ad hopes this analogy will encourage people to want to protect the trees as much as they want to protect the Statue of Liberty. Would you say that this figurative analogy appeals mainly to the emotions or to reason?

Claim and Support. Look for examples of items, events, people, and periods of times that are being compared. Whether these items are drawn from the past or the present, as in the case of historical or literal analogies, they must be drawn from the same category: two types of disease, two types of school systems, two types of government, and so on. Look for the clue words *compare, contrast, like, similar to,* and *different from* to signal that comparisons are being made.

In the case of figurative analogies, look for two items being compared that are from totally different categories. Identify the qualities that they have in common. Look for the clue words *like, as, similar to,* or *compare.* Discover claims that are made as a result of comparing similarities or differences.

Comparison Warrants. You are expected to assume that the items being compared are similar as described and that what happens in one case will probably occur in the other. For figurative analogies you are expected to assume that the qualities of the two items are similar and significant enough so that reference to one will help explain the other and will serve as convincing proof.

Tests of Validity. Are the two items similar as claimed? Can I think of ways they are not similar or of other qualities they share that would change the claim? Are the outcomes really likely to be the same in both cases? Why or why not?

For figurative analogies: Are the qualities of these two items similar, significant, and real enough to help prove a logical argument? Or are they so dissimilar, so far-fetched, or so trivial that the comparison does not prove anything? Does the analogy serve as an ornament, an emotional appeal, or a logical proof?

A Mnemonic Device

It is handy to be able to remember the full range of logical proofs both when you are reading and when you are developing a paper so that you can use them more readily. Figure 7.1 provides a mnemonic device that will help you remember them. It shows the first letter of each proof rearranged to make a nonsense word, SICDADS, and a picture to help you remember it. You can run through this mnemonic mentally when you are thinking about ways to develop the ideas in your paper.

PROOF THAT BUILDS CREDIBILITY: *ETHOS*

The materials provided in argument that help the audience gain a favorable impression of the arguer, the group the arguer represents, or the authorities and experts the arguer cites or quotes help create *ethos,* or the credibility of the author. The author

Sign
Induction
Cause
Deduction
Analogies (literal, historical, figurative)
Definition
Statistics

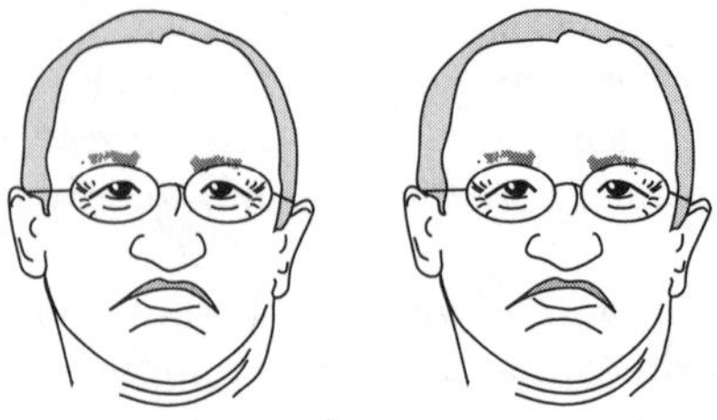

"SICDADS" refuted by logical proof.

Figure 7.1 The Seven Logical Proofs: Their Initials Spell Out SICDADS.

may build credibility by referring to experience and credentials that establish his or her own expertise. Another way is to quote others or to use arguments from authority.

Argument from Authority

We are usually inclined to accept the opinions and factual evidence of people who are authorities and experts in their fields.

Examples of Authority. In an article that claims California will have another earthquake, the author describes and provides the credentials for several professors of geology from the major universities in Southern California as well as scientists from the U.S. Geological Survey Office before quoting their opinions as support:

Claim: California will have an earthquake.
Support: Professors and scientists say so.
Warrant: These experts are reliable.

Authors themselves sometimes establish their own credentials by making references to various types of past experience that qualify them to write about their subject. They also sometimes establish the *ethos* of the group they represent, like "the great Republican Party."

Claim and Support. Look for all references to the author's credentials, whether made by the author or by an editor. Look for references to the author's training, education, professional position, background, and experience. Notice, also, references to the audience's concerns, beliefs, and values that demonstrate the author's effort to establish common ground and to show fairness and goodwill toward the audience. Look for references to groups the author may represent, and notice how they are described. Look for direct or paraphrased quotations from experts. Differentiate between facts and statements of opinion. Look for credential statements about these experts. Look for claims that are made more valid as a consequence of this expert opinion.

Authoritative Warrants.   You are expected to assume that the information provided about the author, the group, or the expert is accurate, that these authorities are honorable, fair, reliable, knowledgeable, and experienced, and that they also exhibit goodwill toward the audience.

Tests of Validity.   Is there enough information to establish the true character and experience of the author? Is this information complete and accurate? Is there enough information about the group to believe what the author says about it? Are the credentials of the experts good enough to make their contributions reliable? Also, are the credentials relevant to the issue? (A star athlete may not be the best judge of soft drinks or fast food.) If a source is quoted, is it reliable? Argument based on authority is as good as the authorities themselves.

TYPES OF EMOTIONAL PROOF: *PATHOS*

Some argument theorists would say that there should be no appeals to emotion or attempts to arouse the emotions of the audience in argument. The idea is that an argument should appeal only to reason. Emotion, they claim, clouds reasoning and judgment and gets the argument off course. Richard M. Weaver, quoted earlier in this chapter, would disagree. Weaver points out that people are not just austerely unemotional logic machines who are interested only in deduction, induction, and cause-and-effect reasoning. People also use language to communicate feelings, values, and motives.[5]

Furthermore, when we consider that the source of much argument lies in the dramatic, emotionally laden occurrences of everyday life, we realize how impossible it is to eliminate all emotion from argument. As you read the many argumentative essays in this book, study the emotional material that professional writers use. Try to develop a sense of when emotion contributes to argument in effective and appropriate ways and when it does not. In general, emotional proofs are appropriate in argument when the subject itself is emotional and when it creates strong feelings in both the writer and the reader. For writers of argument, emotion leads to positions on issues, influences the tone of the writing, and informs some of the interpretations. For readers, emotion leads to a stronger engagement with the issue and influences the final outcomes. Emotional proof is appropriate when the occasion justifies it and when it strengthens logical conviction. It is inappropriate when it merely ventilates feelings, serves as an ornament, or distracts the audience from the logical conclusion of the argument. Types of emotional proof focus on *motivation,* or what all people want, and on *values,* or what we consider good or bad, favorable or unfavorable, acceptable or unacceptable.

---

[5] Weaver elaborates on some of the distinctions between logic and emotion in "Language Is Sermonic."

Motivational Proofs

Some proofs appeal explicitly to what all audiences are supposed to want, such as food, drink, warmth and shelter, sex, security, belongingness, self-esteem, creativity, or self-expression. The purpose of motivational proof is to urge the audience to take prescribed steps to meet an identified need.

Examples of Motivational Proofs.   Advertisements and speeches by political candidates provide obvious examples of motivational proof. Drink a certain beer or buy a brand of blue jeans, and you will be irresistible to others. Or support a particular candidate, and you will gain job security and safe neighborhoods:

Claim: You should support this candidate.

Support: This candidate can help you get job security and safe neighborhoods.

Warrant: You want job security and safe neighborhoods.

Claim and Support.   To find the claim, look for what you are asked to believe or do to get what you want.

Motivational Warrants.   Look for references to items or qualities that you might need or want.

Tests of Validity.   What am I supposed to need? Do I really need it? What am I supposed to do? Will doing what is recommended satisfy the need in the ways described?

Value Proofs

Some proofs appeal to what all audiences are expected to value, such as reliability, honesty, loyalty, industry, patriotism, courage, integrity, conviction, faithfulness, dependability, creativity, freedom, equality, devotion to duty, and so on.

Example of a Value Proof.   Here is an example that claims that the curriculum can contribute to the values of equality and acceptance if it is multicultural:

Claim: The curriculum should be multicultural.

Support: A multicultural curriculum will contribute to equality and acceptance.

Warrant: You value equality and acceptance.

Claim and Support.   Look for value statements that are generally accepted by everyone because they have been proved elsewhere many times. Examples include "Freedom of speech is our constitutional right," "There should be no freedom without responsibility," and "Individuals who have the courage of conviction are to be trusted." Look for slogans that display such values as "Honest Abe," "The home of the free and the brave," and "Honesty is the best policy." Or look for narratives and examples that display values, such as the story of an industrious, thrifty, and ambitious mother who is on welfare. When the values are not directly stated, ask: What value or belief is causing the author to say this? Look for a claim that shows what will result if the recommended values are accepted.

Values Warrants.   You are expected to assume that you share the author's values and that they are as important as the author says they are.

Tests of Validity.   What are the values expressed or implicit in this argument? Do I share these values with the author? If not, how do we differ? What effect do these differences have on my final acceptance of the claim?

A Mnemonic Device

The acronym VAM (for *value, authority,* and *motivation*) may help you remember and use the proofs involving *ethos* and *pathos.*

LOGOS, ETHOS, AND *PATHOS* COMMUNICATED THROUGH LANGUAGE AND STYLE

You can learn to recognize logic, *ethos,* and emotion in argument not only by the use of proofs but also by the language and style associated with each of these types of appeal. Actually, you will not often encounter pure examples of one of these styles, but instead you will encounter a mix, with one of the styles predominating. The same is true of writing. You may plan to write in a logical style, but emotion and *ethos* creep in and actually help you create a richer and more varied style for your argument.

Language That Appeals to Logic

The language of logical argument, which is the language associated with reason, is sometimes called rational style. Words that carry mainly denotative meaning are favored in rational style over connotative and emotionally loaded language. The denotative meaning of a word is the commonly held meaning that most people would agree on and that is also found in the dictionary. Examples of words that have predominantly denotative meanings and that are emotionally neutral include *introduction, facts, information,* or *literal meaning.* Most people would agree on the meanings of those words and could produce synonyms. Words with strong connotative meaning may have many extra, unique, and personal meanings or associations attached to them that vary from person to person. Examples of words with connotative meaning include *rock star, politician, mugger, family values,* and *human rights.* Asked to define such words, different people will provide personal meanings and examples that would not be exactly alike or match the denotative meanings of these words in a dictionary.

For support, rational style relies on opinion in the form of reasons, literal or historical analogies, explanations, and definitions and also on factual data, quotations, and citations from experts and authorities. Furthermore, the reader is usually not required to make as many inferences as for other, more informal styles of writing. Most parts of the argument are spelled out explicitly for the sake of agreement and a better adherence of minds.

Slogans that elicit emotional response, such as "America is the greatest country," "The American people want change," or "Now is the time for healing," are also usually omitted in rational style. Slogans of this type substitute for logical thinking. Readers think better and draw better conclusions when provided with well-reasoned opinion, quotations from authorities, and facts.

For example, in the opening paragraph of an essay titled "The Lost Art of Political Argument," Christopher Lasch argues in favor of argument and debate.

> Let us begin with a simple proposition: What democracy requires is public debate, not information. Of course it needs information too, but the kind of information it needs can be generated only by vigorous popular debate. We do not know what we need to know until we ask the right questions, and we can identify the right questions only by subjecting our own ideas about the world to the test of public controversy. Information, usually seen as the precondition of debate, is better understood as its by-product. When we get into arguments that focus and fully engage our attention, we become avid seekers of relevant information. Otherwise, we take in information passively—if we take it in at all.[6]

Rational style, you can see, evokes mainly a cognitive, rational response from its readers.

Language That Develops *Ethos*

Authors who seek to establish their own credentials and good character use language to provide a fair-minded view of reality that is restrained and accurate rather than exaggerated or overly opinionated. When language is used to create positive *ethos*, an audience will trust the author as a credible source of information and opinion.

Language that develops *ethos* has several specific characteristics. To begin with, the writer exhibits a consistent awareness of the audience's background and values by adopting a vocabulary level that is appropriate for the topic and the audience. The writer does not talk down, use technical jargon for an audience unfamiliar with it, or use slang or colloquial language unless the context allows for that. Rap music, for example, invites a different vocabulary level than a scholarly paper does.

Writers intent on establishing *ethos* are sensitive to different audiences and what they will admire, trust, and accept. They try to use language precisely and to say exactly what they mean. They project an honest desire to communicate

---

[6] Christopher Lasch, "The Lost Art of Political Argument," *Harper's*, September 1990, p. 17.

by avoiding ranting, filler material that gets off the subject, or anything that the audience would perceive as offensive or repugnant.

As you have probably figured out, an author can destroy *ethos* and alter an audience's favorable impression by changing the language. A student who uses colloquial, everyday expressions in a formal essay written for a professor, a commencement speaker who shouts obscenities at the audience, a father who uses formal, abstract language to talk to his five-year-old—all have made inappropriate language choices for their particular audiences, thereby damaging their *ethos* with those audiences.

When you read argument, notice how an author uses language to build connections and trust and also to establish reliability with the audience. When you write argument, use language that will help your audience regard you as sincere and trustworthy. Appropriate language is important when you write a college paper. The use of slang, slogans, and street language and expressions in otherwise formal writing damages your credibility as a serious thinker. Writing errors, including mistakes in spelling, punctuation, and grammar, also destroy *ethos* because they indicate a lack of concern and goodwill for your readers.

Here is an example of language that builds effective *ethos* with an audience. These excerpts come from Martin Luther King Jr.'s "Letter from Birmingham Jail." An explanation of the rhetorical situation for this letter and the full text of the letter appear in Chapter 11. Briefly, however, King was jailed because of his involvement in the civil rights movement in Birmingham, Alabama, and he had been criticized publicly for his participation by eight of his fellow clergymen in that city. He wrote this letter to those clergymen. Notice that he deliberately uses language that is sincere and honest and that establishes his credibility as a trustworthy and responsible human being with values that his audience is likely to share. He does not come across as a crackpot, a troublemaker, or a man who is angry at the system, which one might expect from someone who has been jailed for participating in civil rights demonstrations.

My Dear Fellow Clergymen:

While confined here in the Birmingham city jail, I came across your recent statement calling my present activities "unwise and untimely." . . . Since I feel that you are men of genuine good will and that your criticisms are sincerely set forth, I want to try to answer your statement in what I hope will be patient and reasonable terms.

I think I should indicate why I am here in Birmingham, since you have been influenced by the view which argues against "outsiders coming in." . . . I, along with several members of my staff, am here because I was invited here. I am here because I have organizational ties here.

But more basically, I am in Birmingham because injustice is here. Just as the prophets of the eighth century B.C. left their villages and carried their "thus saith the Lord" far beyond the boundaries of their home towns, and just as the Apostle Paul left his village of Tarsus and carried the gospel of Jesus Christ to the far corners of the Greco-Roman world, so am I compelled to carry the gospel of freedom beyond my own home town. Like Paul, I must constantly respond to the Macedonian call for aid.

Moreover, I am cognizant of the interrelatedness of all communities and states. I cannot sit idly by in Atlanta and not be concerned about what happens in Birmingham. Injustice anywhere is a threat to justice everywhere. We are caught in an inescapable network of mutuality, tied in a single garment of destiny. Whatever affects one directly, affects all indirectly. Never again can we afford to live with the narrow, provincial "outside agitator" idea. Anyone who lives inside the United States can never be considered an outsider anywhere within its bounds.

Highlight the language in these passages that you think King used to establish good *ethos* with his audience of eight clergymen. Notice how King deliberately uses language to project sincerity and goodwill toward his audience. He also selects examples and appeals to values that are compatible with his audience's interests and values. King's letter is a classic example of argument that establishes effective *ethos* with a particular audience.

Language That Appeals to Emotion

References to values and motives evoke feelings about what people regard as good and bad and about what they want, and authors use the language associated with emotional style in a variety of ways to express and evoke feelings about these matters. The following paragraphs describe a few special techniques that are characteristic of emotional style. Examples are drawn from the essay by Sara Rimer, "Jobs Illuminate What Riots Hid: Young Ideals," which appears in full in Chapter 3.

Emotionally loaded language evokes connotative meaning and causes the audience to experience feelings and associations at a personal level that are not described in dictionaries. Highlight the emotional language in this passage:

> America has been bombarded with television images of the youth of South-Central Los Angeles: throwing bricks, looting stores, beating up innocent motorists. The Disneyland staff who interviewed the job applicants, ages 17 to 22, found a different neighborhood.
>
> "They were wonderful kids, outstanding kids," said Greg Albrecht, a spokesman for Disneyland. "We didn't know they were there." Nor, Mr. Albrecht added, had they known that the young people of South-Central Los Angeles would be so eager to work at Disneyland.[7]

There are several examples of emotional language here. Did you, for example, highlight the words used to describe the two types of kids the author claims live in South-Central Los Angeles: *throwing, looting,* and *beating up* in contrast to *wonderful* and *outstanding*?

---

[7]Sara Rimer, "Jobs Illuminate What Riots Hid: Young Ideals," *New York Times,* June 18, 1992, pp. A1, A12.

Emotional examples engage the emotions, as in this example: "One of the 600 who wanted to work at Disneyland was Olivia Miles, at 18 the youngest of seven children of a nurse's aide and a disabled roofer." Miss Miles has humble origins but achieves success. Success stories of this type usually result in positive emotional responses from the reader.

Vivid description of an emotional scene creates an emotional reader response, as in this example:

> Aubrey Miles, who is 45, says he has taken pains to tell his daughter that there are good white people. They saved his life, he told her. He was putting a roof on an office building seven years ago when a vat of hot tar exploded. He was severely burned.
>
> "The guys on the job, who were white, helped me," he said. "I was on the ground, on fire. They put the fire out. One guy sat me up and put his back against my back. I could feel the connection. Then, afterward in the hospital, it was the same thing with the doctors."

Notice how this description brings you into the scene, causing you to share the physical sensations and emotions of the individuals described and then to share in the conclusion about the people who helped.

Narratives of emotional events draw readers into a scene just as vivid description does. Here is a story about Olivia Miles and her reaction to the looting during the riots in Los Angeles:

> The riots presented Olivia Miles with the biggest ethical quandary of her life. "I saw people on television coming out with boxes of shoes and pretty furniture," she said. Her smile was embarrassed. "It was like Christmas. I wanted to get some. I was asking my sister if we could go. She said, 'No, you can't go out.' I thought: 'She's going to go to work. Should I get it, or shouldn't I get it? It's not fair that I can't. Everyone else is going to get stuff.'"
>
> This, too, her father had foreseen. "I told her, 'There are going to be a lot of opportunities for you to get things, so just stay in the house,'" Mr. Miles said. "She knew automatically that stealing was a no-no."
>
> That Sunday, Olivia was in her regular pew at the Mt. Sinai Baptist Church. "The pastor was saying, 'If you took something, shame on you. That's a sin,'" she said. She looked relieved all over again. "I was so happy."

By describing the emotions of the characters in a narrative, the author invites the reader to share them also.

Emotional tone, created by emotional language and examples, indicates that the author has a strong feeling about the subject and wants the audience to share that feeling. Also, irony and sarcasm should always be viewed as examples of emotional tone. They indicate strong feeling and a desire for change.

Figurative analogies contribute to emotion in an argument, particularly when two emotional subjects are compared and the resulting effect appeals more to emotion than to reason.

Emotional style is the easiest of all the styles to recognize because it is emotionally charged and is often close to our own experiences. Do not commit the common reading error of noticing only emotional style, ignoring logic and *ethos*, and even missing the main point of the entire text because you become distracted by emotional material. Remember, in argument, logic is the plot, and emotion and *ethos* add support. Table 7.1 provides a summary of the characteristics of language used to appeal to reason, to establish *ethos*, and to appeal to emotion.

Ethics and Morality in Argument

A person's ability to argue persuasively has been recognized as a potentially powerful influence over other people for centuries. Thus the classical argument theorists, Aristotle, Cicero, and Quintilian, all recognized that an arguer should be a good person with moral principles who is arguing for good causes. These writers criticized arguers who used their persuasive powers to manipulate people in order to achieve their own selfish ends. They stressed that an ethical arguer must have the courage and willingness to argue logically and honestly from a strong sense of personal integrity and values. Also, emotional and motivational appeals should be

TABLE 7.1 A Summary of Language and Style in Argument

TO APPEAL TO LOGIC	TO DEVELOP *ETHOS*	TO APPEAL TO EMOTION
	Style	
Theoretical, abstract language	Language appropriate to audience and subject	Vivid, concrete language
Denotative meanings	Restrained, sincere, fair-minded presentation	Emotionally loaded language
Reasons	Appropriate level of vocabulary	Connotative meanings
Literal and historical analogies	Correct grammar	Emotional examples
Explanations		Vivid descriptions
Definitions		Narratives of emotional events
Factual data and statistics		Emotional tone
Quotations		Figurative analogies
Citations from experts and authorities		
Informed opinion		
	Effect	
Evokes a cognitive, rational response	Demonstrates author's reliability, competence, and respect for audience's ideas and values through reliable and appropriate use of support and general accuracy	Evokes an emotional response

consistent with positive value systems that will benefit not just one individual but all of society. Using emotions to cloud judgment or to persuade individuals to accept ideas that the arguer does not really believe in is clearly unethical. Basic standards of good judgment and common honesty have always been critical to ethical argument both in classical times and in the present.

People were struck by some letters discovered in Germany a few years ago that were perfect examples of excellent argument but whose subject matter was totally immoral. These letters were the written orders for exterminating the Jews during World War II. Although Hitler was a convincing arguer, his values and his claims were immoral. In more recent years a political consultant working for the president of the United States was exposed as a person who had no core system of values and who was more interested in manipulating public opinion than in determining what was the best political course for the country. This individual was accused by the analysts at that time of believing in nothing.

Unethical individuals who argue mainly to manipulate public opinion often use unethical tactics to influence and gain adherence to their points of view. Such tactics include opinion polls that push for particular points of view, exaggerated or manipulated statistics, manufactured evidence, and deliberate fallacious reasoning. All of these techniques can be very effective in changing audience opinion even though they are based on false values and motives.

It is important that you learn to recognize the difference between ethical and unethical argument. You can begin by asking the two bottom-line questions: (1) *Am I convinced?* Does this argument change the way I think? Are the values honorable? Is the writer just and fair-minded? Is the support fair, accurate, and convincing? Can I accept the warrants? Should the claim be qualified if it isn't already? If you answer yes, that you are convinced, then you should also ask, (2) *Is this argument moral or immoral according to my values and standards of behavior?* You will need to judge the final moral worth of an argument by testing it against your own system of values.

The next section will help you learn to differentiate between honest, ethical argument and unethical, manipulative argument. Fallacies or pseudoproofs are often used by dishonest arguers to influence opinion.

FALLACIES OR PSEUDOPROOFS

In an advertisement for a health club, an attractive, muscular man is embracing a beautiful, slim woman. The caption reads, "Studies show diets don't work. This picture shows exercise does." No further evidence is provided. You do not have to be an expert in argument theory to sense that something is wrong with this proof.

Responsible and honest proof relies on skillful use of support and acceptable warrants to prove a claim. Since argument deals with probability instead of certainty, an argument may be perceived as very convincing, somewhat convincing, or not convincing at all. The success of the argument depends on the proofs. Weak support or a faulty or unacceptable warrant weakens an argument, but it is still an argument. The reader must ask the questions identified in this chapter to test the reliability and strength of the proofs and ultimately of the entire argument it-self to decide whether it is well developed or underdeveloped, acceptable or unac-ceptable, moral or immoral.

Sometimes, as in the case of the advertisement just described, a reader will encounter material that may appear at first to be a proof but really isn't a proof at all. It is a *pseudoproof*, which is commonly called a *fallacy*. Fallacies lead an audi-ence astray, they distort and distract, they represent inadequate reasoning or non-reasoning, and they oversimplify a claim instead of proving it. Read "Love is a Fallacy" on pages 228–237 for an entertaining introduction to fallacies.

You will encounter fallacies in advertisements, letters to the editor, and other argumentative writing. Avoid using them in your own writing because they weaken your argument and damage your *ethos*. Recognize fallacies by asking, "Is this material even relevant? Is it adequate? Do I agree? Does it support the claim." Learning some of the common types of fallacies will also help you recognize them. Here are some of the most common ones, categorized under the same categories we have used for genuine proofs: logic, *ethos*, and emotion.

Fallacies in Logic

These fallacies pose as logical proof, but you will see that they are really pseudo-proofs that prove nothing at all. You may have trouble remembering all of their names; many people do. Concentrate instead on the fallacious thinking character-ized by each of them, such as introducing irrelevant material, providing wrong, unfair, inadequate, or even no support, drawing inappropriate conclusions, and oversimplifying the choices.

Begging the Question. No support is provided by the arguer who begs the question, and the claim is simply restated, over and over again, in one form or an-other. For example "Capital punishment deters crime because it keeps criminals from committing murder," simply restates the same idea in other words. Here are other familiar examples: "Why is this true? It's true because I know it's true." "Everyone knows that the president of the United States has done his best for the environment because he said so." You can remember the name of this fallacy, beg-ging the question, by recalling that the arguer, when asked for support, begs off and simply restates the claim in the same or different words.

Red Herring. A red herring provides irrelevant and misleading support that pulls the audience away from the real argument. For example, "I don't be-lieve we should elect this individual because she would have to put her kids in day care" is a red herring; a candidate's qualifications to hold office have nothing to do with the candidate's household arrangements. Whether or not the police were racist in the O. J. Simpson trial was a red herring in the sense that even though their alleged racism might have provided a motive for planting evidence, their racism was unrelated to whether Simpson was innocent or guilty of murder. Another red herring in the O. J. Simpson case that influenced some people was the idea that the accused was a great sports hero and we should not degrade great sports heroes by trying them for murder. Authors of detective fiction sometimes use red herrings in their plots as false clues to divert the reader's attention from the real murderer. Remember the red herring fallacy by recalling that the fish, the red herring, was at one time used to train hunting dogs to follow a scent. It was not a true scent, however. The herring scent was irrelevant to the real smells of the real hunt, and the fallacy, the red herring, is irrelevant to an argument when it introduces such support as a person's parental responsibilities as a factor in the person's qualifications for a job or whether sports heroes should be treated differently from other people.

Non Sequitur.   *Non sequitur* is Latin for "it does not follow." In this type of fallacy, the conclusion does not follow from the evidence and the warrant. Here are some examples: the professor in the Hawaiian shirt and gold chains must be an easy grader; the self-consciously beautiful girl who has applied for a job as a secretary would not do the job well; that man with the powerful new computer must be highly skilled in the use of computer technology. The warrants for these three examples are that the professor's clothes indicate how he will grade, beautiful girls cannot be good secretaries, and owning powerful equipment implies the ability to use it. You can probably sense the problems with these warrants. They are so difficult for most people to accept that none of these examples come across as convincing arguments. Here is another example of a *non sequitur:* Women should not be placed in executive positions because they cannot drive cars as well as men.

Straw Man.   A straw man involves attributing an argument to an opponent that the opponent never made and then refuting it in a devastating way. The arguer sets up an idea, refutes it, and appears to win, even though the idea may be unrelated to the issue being discussed. For example, a political candidate might set up a straw man by claiming that his opponent has said he is too old to do the job, when in fact the opponent has never mentioned age as an issue. Then the candidate refutes the age issue by detailing the advantages of age and appears to win even though this is not an issue at all. In fact, by refuting this false issue, the candidate may give the impression that he could refute any other arguments put forth by the opposition as well. The use of a straw man suggests competence where it might not actually exist.

Stacked Evidence.   Stacking evidence to represent only one side of an issue that clearly has two sides gives a distorted impression of the issue. For example, to prove that television is an inspiring and uplifting medium, the only evidence given is that PBS nature shows are educational, *The Cosby Show* promotes family values, and news programs and documentaries keep audiences informed. The sex and violence programming is never mentioned.

Either-Or.   Some arguments are oversimplified by the arguer and presented as black-or-white, either-or choices when there are actually other alternatives.

Some examples are "This country can either have a strong defense program or a strong social welfare program," "We can either develop a strong space program or an urban development program," "A woman can either be a mother or have a career," and "A man can either go to graduate school or become a company man." No alternative, middle-ground, or compromise positions are acknowledged.

Post Hoc. This is short for *post hoc, ergo propter hoc*, a Latin phrase that translates as "after this, therefore because of this." To put it more simply, *post hoc* is the fallacy of faulty cause. For example, it is fallacious to claim in an advertisement that people will be more attractive and more popular if they drink a certain brand of cola. Look at other advertisements on television or in magazines, and you will easily find other examples of *post hoc*, the claim that one thing causes another when there is actually no causal relationship between them. Think about the outdoor healthy virility of the Marlboro man, for example, and the suggestion that he got that way by smoking cigarettes. Another example is the person who finds romance by serving a particular spaghetti sauce or using a specific cologne.

Hasty Generalization. Sometimes arguers "jump to conclusions" by basing a conclusion on too few examples. For example, someone may conclude that the justice system is hopelessly flawed because a man is sent to jail by mistake or that since some students in urban schools belong to gangs, most students in those schools belong to gangs. Look back at the essay on pages 77–80, "Jobs Illuminate What Riots Hid: Young Ideals." This author attempts to counter the stereotypical idea that young people in South-Central Los Angeles are rioters and hoodlums. The example of the young woman who was industrious and got a job at Disneyland can encourage an opposite type of hasty generalization and suggests that most of these young people are instead "wonderful kids, outstanding kids." Hasty generalizations often contribute to stereotyping.

Fallacies That Affect *Ethos*

Fallacies that are aimed at attacking character or at using character instead of evidence for proof are misleading and can damage *ethos*.

Ad Hominem. An *ad hominem* argument attacks a person's character rather than a person's ideas. The press is notorious for such attacks during political campaigns, and so are some of the candidates themselves. The "character issue," for example, may receive more attention than more serious, substantive issues. Thus negative information is provided about the candidates' personal lives rather than about their ideas and the issues that concern them. The purpose of *ad hominem* arguments is to discredit these individuals with the public. Here is another example of an *ad hominem* attack: Piety is said to have no validity because of the careless personal and financial habits of some television evangelists. *Ad hominem* means "to the man" in Latin. An *ad hominem* argument directs attention away from the issues and to the man. Thus we become prejudiced and biased against an individual personally instead of evaluating that person's ideas.

Guilt by Association.   The fallacy of guilt by association suggests that people's character can be judged by examining the character of their associates. For example, an employee in a company that defrauds the government is declared dishonest because of his association with the company, even though he may have known nothing of the fraud. Or an observer is thrown into jail along with some political protesters simply because she was in the wrong place at the wrong time. Political figures are often judged as morally defective if they associate with people with questionable values and reputations. It is assumed that these individuals are members of these groups and guilty by association.

Using Authority Instead of Evidence.   This is a variation of begging the question. The arguer relies on personal authority to prove a point rather than on evidence. For example, a salesman tells you to buy the used car because he is honest and trustworthy and he knows your neighbor.

Emotional Fallacies

Irrelevant, unrelated, and distracting emotional materials are often introduced into argument to try to convince the audience. Here are some examples.

Bandwagon Appeal.   The argument is that everyone is doing something, so you should too. For example, everyone is learning line dancing, so you should jump on the bandwagon and learn it also. Political and other public opinion polls are sometimes used to promote the bandwagon appeal. The suggestion is that since a majority of the people polled hold a certain opinion, you should adopt it also.

Slippery Slope.   The slippery-slope fallacy is a scare tactic that suggests that if we allow one thing to happen, we will immediately be sliding down the slippery slope to disaster. This fallacy is sometimes introduced into environmental and abortion issues. If we allow loggers to cut a few trees, we will soon lose all the forests. Or if a woman is required to wait twenty-four hours to reconsider her decision to have an abortion, soon there will be so many restrictions that no one will be able to have an abortion. This fallacy is similar to the saying about the camel that gets its nose into the tent. If we permit the nose today, we have the whole camel to deal with tomorrow. It is better not to start because disaster may result.

Creating False Needs.   Emotional proofs, as you have learned, appeal to what people value and think they need. Sometimes an arguer will create a false sense of need where none exists or will unrealistically heighten an existing need. The intent is to make the argument more convincing. Advertising provides excellent examples.

The housewife is told she needs a shining kitchen floor with a high gloss that only a certain wax can provide. Parents are reminded that they want smart, successful children, so they should buy a set of encyclopedias.

These examples of fallacies provide you with a good sense of what constitutes fallacious reasoning. Armed with this list and with the tests of validity for genuine proofs listed under "Tests of Validity" on pages 195–207, you now have what you need to evaluate the strength and validity of the proofs in an argument. This information will help you make evaluations, form rebuttals to challenge weak arguments, and create arguments of your own.

VALUE OF THE PROOFS FOR READING AND WRITING ARGUMENT

Readers of argument find that analyzing the proofs in an argument makes it easier to answer the bottom line questions: "Am I convinced?" and "Is this argument moral or immoral?" Analyzing the proofs in an argument focuses a reader's attention on the author's reasoning, use of supporting detail, and warrants. These are the elements in an argument that convince an audience. Applying the tests of validity to the proofs can also help a reader recognize fallacies or faulty reasoning, which can reveal a manipulative or immoral purpose in the argument. Fallacies, as you have learned, are not convincing once you figure out how they work.

Writers of argument can use the proofs to help them think of ways to develop a claim. By running through the list of proofs and asking relevant questions—What do I need to define? Should I use statistics? Can I generalize from some examples? What caused this? What can I compare this to? Who should I quote? What audience values and motives can I appeal to?—authors invent ideas and locate material that can be used at a specific level in a paper. The specific material is what makes a paper convincing. Also, thinking about the proofs makes authors more consciously aware of their own warrants and helps them decide whether to make them explicit in the argument or whether to leave them implicit so that the audience has to supply them. Finally, an awareness of proofs can help writers avoid fallacies in their writing.

The exercises and activities for this chapter will provide you with practice in using the proofs to invent support and warrants for a position paper. The proofs and the test for validity are summarized for both readers and writers in the summary charts on pages 424–430.

REVIEW QUESTIONS

1. Describe logical proofs. Name the seven types of logical proof. Use the acronym SICDADS to help you remember them.
2. Describe proofs that build *ethos,* or credibility. Name one type of proof that builds *ethos.*
3. Describe emotional proofs. Name two types of emotional support and explain why they appeal to the emotions.

4. Describe some of the features of the language and style associated with the three types of proof.
5. What is the difference between *ethos* in argument and ethics in argument?
6. What are fallacies? Why are they also described as pseudoproofs? Give some examples of fallacies.

EXERCISES AND ACTIVITIES

A. CLASS DISCUSSION: ANALYZING *LOGOS, PATHOS,* AND *ETHOS* IN AN ADVERTISEMENT

Study the advertisement on the next page, and identify the logical proofs, the emotional proofs, and the proofs that establish *ethos*. Use the acronyms SIC-DADS and VAM to help you remember the proofs. Which type of proof is strongest in this ad, in your opinion? How effective is the ad? Why do you think so?

B. CLASS DISCUSSION: ANALYZING THE PROOFS IN AN ESSAY

Review the five essays in Chapter 6 (pages 166–172) that have the proofs labeled in the margin. Next, read the following essay, "Censorship or Common Sense?" and jot similar labels of the proofs in the margin. Then answer the following questions.

1. What is this author's claim? What does she want to prove?
2. What logical proofs does she use to prove her claim? Which are most effective, and why?
3. What emotional proofs does she use to prove her claim? What values and motives are present in this argument? Do you share them?
4. How does she use *ethos* to prove her claim? What authorities does she mention to strengthen her position?
5. Is this essay convincing? Why? Is it moral or immoral by your standards? Why?

CENSORSHIP OR COMMON SENSE?*

Roxana Robinson

Essay

Roxana Robinson is the author of the novel This Is My Daughter.

A 5-year-old is not ready to confront the world. This should be obvious, but it doesn't seem that way to many free-speech advocates, who are angry that some libraries around the country have installed software on their computers to block out Internet material that's unsuitable for children.   1

New York Times, October 19, 1998, p. A 21.

Meet the Philip Morris Generation

A **record** to be **ashamed** of.

Philip Morris claims it doesn't want kids to smoke. But a major study shows that Marlboro, the Philip Morris flagship brand, is by far the best-selling cigarette among young smokers. On average, 60 percent of 8th, 10th and 12th graders — boys and girls — prefer Marlboro. Among white high school seniors it's even higher, at 70 percent.

This means that of the 3,000 kids who become regular smokers every day, about 1,800 head for Marlboro Country. A third of these kids will die early from tobacco-caused disease.

Once again, Philip Morris says one thing but does another.

Tobacco vs. Kids. Where America draws the line.®

American Cancer Society • American Medical Association • American Academy of Child & Adolescent Psychiatry • American Academy of Pediatrics • American Association for Respiratory Care • American College of Preventive Medicine • American Medical Women's Association • American Public Health Association • Association of Schools of Public Health • Girls Incorporated • INFACT • Interreligious Coalition on Smoking or Health • Latino Council on Alcohol and Tobacco • National Association of School Nurses • National Association of Secondary School Principals • National Hispanic Medical Association • Summit Health Coalition

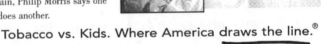

CAMPAIGN for TOBACCO-FREE Kids®

To learn more, call 800-284-KIDS or visit our web site at www.tobaccofreekids.org.
The National Center for Tobacco-Free Kids, 1707 L Street NW, Suite 800, Washington, DC 20036

Source: Courtesy of the National Center for Tobacco-free Kids.

The objections are coming from some usual sources: the American Civil Lib- 2
erties Union, for example, and Web publishers. But even the American Library
Association has opposed the use of filtering software.

Traditionally, the library has been a safe place for children. And librarians 3
have long been the guardians of public virtue. While they have been firm supporters of the First Amendment, they haven't generally interpreted it to mean that they
should acquire large holdings of published pornography and make such materials
available to children.

Librarians have always acquired books according to their own discrimination 4
and their sense of what is appropriate to their neighborhoods. They generally refuse to buy, among other things, pornography. This isn't censorship; it's common
sense.

If a library were to have a section of pornographic books, would we want 5
these to be printed in large, colorfully illustrated, lightweight volumes, shelved
near the floor where they were easily available to children? Probably not. But we
have gone to a great deal of trouble to insure that computers are user friendly,
with brightly colored graphics and easily accessible information.

Material on the Internet is not only uncensored but also unedited. Adults can 6
be expected to make their own evaluations of what they find. Children, who lack
experience and knowledge, cannot.

The debate over the filtering of the Internet is a bit like the debate over grants 7
given out by the National Endowment for the Arts. It's all tangled up in false cries
of censorship. Censorship is a legal term; it refers to government action prohibiting
material from being circulated. This is very different from a situation in which a
museum or an arts panel decides not to use public money to finance an exhibition
or an artist.

Commendably, our society defends freedom of speech with great vigor. But 8
there is a difference between allowing everything to be said and allowing everyone to hear it. We should know this by now, having seen the effects that exposure
to television and movie violence has on children.

The A.C.L.U. and the American Library Association say that the use of filter- 9
ing software in computers is censorship because it blocks access to constitution-
ally protected speech. But these cries are baffling and unfounded. The only control
libraries are asserting is over a small portion of the audience, not over the material
itself. Moreover, this control has a powerful historical precedent: parental guidance is even older than the Constitution.

The protection of children should be instinctive. A man may have the right to 10
stand on the street and spew obscenities at passers-by, but he would be ordered to
leave a kindergarten classroom.

It is absurd to pretend that adults and children are the same audience, and it 11
is shameful to protect the child pornographer instead of the child. ■

FOR DISCUSSION: How would you resolve the issue in this essay, that free speech
should be guaranteed because of the First Amendment, even if the result is that
objectionable material on the Internet is available to everyone?

C. GROUP WORK AND DISCUSSION: ANALYZING MOTIVATIONAL AND VALUE PROOFS AND STYLE

Read the following article, "The Whiny Generation." Focus on the emotional proofs and style in the essay. Then answer the following questions and report your answers to the class.

1. What is the author's claim?
2. What are the motivational proofs in the essay? (Review the description on page 206.) What does the author claim members of the twenty-something generation want? What does he claim they should want?
3. What are the value proofs in the essay? (Review the description on pages 206–207.) What values does the author claim twenty-somethings have? What values does he claim they should have? What does he claim will be the result if twenty-somethings accept his values?
4. Do you share the author's values? Do you accept his claims? Elaborate.
5. Review the description of style in Table 7.1. What type of style predominates in this essay? What evidence from the essay leads you to think so?

Essay

THE WHINY GENERATION*

David Martin

David Martin, a lawyer and bureaucrat in Ottawa, Canada, was 43 when he wrote this essay.

1   Ever since the publication of Douglas Coupland's book *Generation X*, we've been subjected to a barrage of essays, op-ed pieces and feature articles blaming us baby boomers for the sad face of the twentysomething generation: the boomers took all the good jobs; the boomers are destroying the planet, the media is boomer-dominated and boomer-obsessed. The litany is never-ending. If you believe the Generation X essayists, all the troubles of the world can be traced to us fortysomethings.

2   Well, enough is enough. As a baby boomer, I'm fed up with the ceaseless carping of a handful of spoiled, self-indulgent, overgrown adolescents. Generation Xers may like to call themselves the "Why Me?" generation, but they should be called the "Whiny" generation. If these pusillanimous purveyors of pseudoangst would put as much effort into getting a life as they do into writing about their horrible fate, we'd be spared the weekly diatribes that pass for reasoned argument in newspapers and magazines.

3   Let's examine for a moment the horrible fate visited on Generation X. This is a generation that was raised with the highest standard of living in the history of the world. By the time they arrived on the scene, their parents were comfortably established in the middle class and could afford to satisfy their offspring's every whim. And they did, in spades.

*Newsweek, November 1, 1993, p. 10.

Growing up in the '70s and '80s, the twentysomethings were indulged with 4
every toy, game and electronic device available. They didn't even have to learn
how to amuse themselves since Mom and Dad were always there to ferry them
from one organized activity to another. If we baby boomers were spoiled, the
Whiny Generation was left out to rot. They had it all.

That's the essence of the Generation X problem. We have a generation (or at 5
least part of a generation) whose every need has been catered to since birth. Now,
when they finally face adulthood, they expect the gift-giving to continue. I'm 28
and I'll never own a house, whines the Generation Xer. I'm 25 and I don't have a
high-paying job, says another.

Are these realistic expectations? Of course not. It's the rare individual in the 6
last 40 years who had a high-paying job and owned a home prior to his or her
30th birthday. But the Whiners want everything now. A generation raised on the
principle of instant satisfaction simply can't understand the concepts of long-term
planning and deferred gratification. What's their reaction when they don't get
what they want? That's right—they throw a tantrum.

The Whiners' most common complaint is that they've been relegated to 7
what Mr. Coupland calls McJobs—low-paying, low-end positions in the service
industry. I don't doubt that many Whiners are stuck in such jobs. But whose fault
is that? Here's a generation that had enormous educational opportunities. But
many Whiners squandered those chances figuring that a good job was a right not
a privilege.

My parents' generation provided a better shot at post-secondary education 8
for their boomer children than they themselves had enjoyed. And we took advantage of that situation in droves as the number of college and university graduates
soared. The Whiners were afforded even greater scope for educational success but
many of them failed to maximize their opportunities. They had the chance to
reach higher but often chose not to or chose foolishly or unwisely.

Those who pursued a liberal-arts degree with a view to obtaining a job were 9
either wealthy or naive. Those who thought that fine arts or film studies would
yield more than a subsistence living were only fooling themselves. And those who
entered law school will find sympathy hard to come by. More lawyers is one thing
we definitely don't need.

The twentysomethings who planned their education wisely and spent the 10
required years specializing in the technologies of the '90s now have the inside track
in the job market. Those who chose to slide through high school to achieve semi-
literacy are understandably unemployed or underemployed. Their cries of an-
guish do not now ring true. In fact, the youth unemployment rate is lower today
than it was during the baby-boom recession of the early '80s. And despite the
current recession, there are still plenty of positions available for highly skilled
workers who exhibited the foresight and determination to achieve the necessary
abilities.

The Whiners decry the lack of entry-level professional positions in the mar- 11
ketplace. Granted, during this current recession there are fewer such jobs. But that
was also true in the early '80s. Instead of blaming everyone for this state of affairs,

the Whiners should acquire more skills, education and specialized knowledge for the careers of the 21st century that will be awaiting those who have prepared themselves. Forget a career in law; start thinking about computers, telecommunications and health care.

POSITIONS OF POWER

12 As for the Whiners' complaint about the media being boomer-dominated and boomer-obsessed, that's nothing new. Once a generation has worked long and hard enough, it's only natural that some of its members become ensconced in positions of power. And once in power, it's not that surprising that they reflect the views, tastes and concerns of their contemporaries. Why should the media revolve around the lives of 25-year-olds? Remember, this is the generation whose biggest achievement to date is something called grunge rock. Once they've accomplished more, they'll get the media coverage.

13   So, I invite the Whiners to put aside their TV-generation values and accept cold, hard reality. Interesting, high-paying jobs and rich lifestyles are not automatic; they're not even commonplace. Most people live ordinary lives of quiet desperation stuck in uninteresting jobs that they're afraid to lose. If you want more than that, move out of your parents' houses, start working and, for heaven's sake, stop whining. ■

FOR DISCUSSION: Who are included in Generation X, and what are their characteristics? Are you a member of Generation X or some other group, like the baby boomers? What are the characteristics of your group? Why does the author refer to Generation X as the "whiny generation"? What does he think this generation should do to find its place in society? Do you agree or disagree? Why?

D. CLASS DISCUSSION AND WRITING ASSIGNMENT: PROOFS AND STYLE IN THE DECLARATION OF INDEPENDENCE

The Declaration of Independence, a classic argument, was written by Thomas Jefferson in 1776 and was used to separate the American colonies from Great Britain. It established America as independent states, and thus it is a revolutionary document with a revolutionary purpose.

1. Read the Declaration of Independence, and to understand it better, divide it into its three major component parts. Draw a line at the end of part 1, which explains the general principles behind the revolutionary action. Then draw a line at the end of part 2, which lists the reasons for the action. Finally, identify the purpose of the third and last brief part of the document.
2. The document presents an argument with the value warrants stated in part 1, the support in part 2, and the conclusion in part 3. Summarize the ideas in each part of the argument.
3. Test the argument by questioning the warrants and the support. Do you agree with them? If you accept them, you accept the conclusion.
4. Identify some of the proofs in the document, and comment on their effectiveness.

5. Describe the predominant style in the document, and give examples that support your answer.
6. Write a 250-word paper in which you explain the insights you now have about the structure, proofs, and style of the Declaration of Independence.

THE DECLARATION OF INDEPENDENCE

Thomas Jefferson

The Declaration of Independence was approved by Congress on July 2, 1776, and published two days later.

When in the course of human events, it becomes necessary for one people to dissolve the political bands which have connected them with another, and to assume among the Powers of the earth, the separate and equal station to which the Laws of Nature and of Nature's God entitle them, a decent respect to the opinions of mankind requires that they should declare the causes which impel them to the separation. 1

We hold these truths to be self-evident, that all men are created equal, that they are endowed by their Creator with certain unalienable Rights, that among these are Life, Liberty and the pursuit of Happiness. 2

That to secure these rights, Governments are instituted among Men, deriving their just powers from the consent of the governed. 3

That whenever any Form of Government becomes destructive of these ends, it is the Right of the People to alter or to abolish it, and to institute a new Government, laying its foundation on such principles and organizing its powers in such form, as to them shall seem most likely to effect their Safety and Happiness. Prudence, indeed, will dictate that Governments long established should not be changed for light and transient causes; and accordingly all experience hath shown that mankind are more disposed to suffer, while evils are sufferable, than to right themselves by abolishing the forms to which they are accustomed. But when a long train of abuses and usurpations pursuing invariably the same Object evinces a design to reduce them under absolute Despotism, it is their right, it is their duty, to throw off such government, and to provide new Guards for their future security. 4

Such has been the patient sufferance of these Colonies; and such is now the necessity which constrains them to alter their former Systems of Government. The history of the present King of Great Britain is a history of repeated injuries and usurpations, all having in direct object the establishment of an absolute Tyranny over these States. To prove this, let Facts be submitted to a candid world. 5

He has refused his Assent to Laws, the most wholesome and necessary for the public good. 6

7   He has forbidden his Governors to pass Laws of immediate and pressing importance, unless suspended in their operation till his Assent should be obtained; and when so suspended, he has utterly neglected to attend to them.

8   He has refused to pass over Laws for the accommodation of large districts of people, unless those people would relinquish the right of Representation in the Legislature, a right inestimable to them and formidable to tyrants only.

9   He has called together legislative bodies at places unusual, uncomfortable, and distant from the depository of their Public Records, for the sole purpose of fatiguing them into compliance with his measures.

10   He has dissolved Representative Houses repeatedly, for opposing with manly firmness his invasions on the rights of the people.

11   He has refused for a long time, after such dissolutions, to cause others to be elected; whereby the Legislative Powers, incapable of Annihilation, have returned to the People at large for their exercise; the State remaining in the meantime exposed to all the dangers of invasion from without, and convulsions within.

12   He has endeavored to prevent the population of these States; for that purpose obstructing the Laws for Naturalization of Foreigners; refusing to pass others to encourage their migration hither, and raising the conditions of new Appropriations of Lands.

13   He has obstructed the Administration of Justice, by refusing his Assent to Laws for establishing Judiciary Powers.

14   He has made Judges dependent on his Will alone, for the tenure of their offices, and the amount and payment of their salaries.

15   He has erected a multitude of New Offices, and sent hither swarms of Officers to harass our People, and eat out their substance.

16   He has kept among us, in time of peace, Standing Armies without the consent of our legislatures.

17   He has affected to render the Military independent of and superior to the Civil Power.

18   He has combined with others to subject us to jurisdictions foreign to our constitution, and unacknowledged by our laws; giving his Assent to their acts of pretended Legislation:

19   For quartering large bodies of armed troops among us:

20   For protecting them, by a mock Trial, from Punishment for any Murders which they should commit on the Inhabitants of these States:

21   For cutting off our Trade with all parts of the world:

22   For imposing Taxes on us without our Consent:

23   For depriving us in many cases of the benefits of Trial by Jury:

24   For transporting us beyond Seas to be tried for pretended offenses:

25   For abolishing the free System of English Laws in a neighboring Province, establishing therein an Arbitrary government, and enlarging its Boundaries so as to render it at once an example and fit instrument for introducing the same absolute rule into these Colonies:

26   For taking away our Charters, abolishing our most valuable Laws, and altering fundamentally the Forms of our Governments.

For suspending our own Legislatures, and declaring themselves invested 27 with Power to legislate for us in all cases whatsoever.

He has abdicated Government here, by declaring us out of his Protection and 28 waging War against us.

He has plundered our seas, ravaged our Coasts, burnt our towns, and de- 29 stroyed the Lives of our people.

He is at this time transporting large Armies of foreign Mercenaries to com- 30 pleat the works of death, desolation and tyranny, already begun with circumstances of Cruelty & perfidy scarcely paralleled in the most barbarous ages, and totally unworthy the Head of a civilized nation.

He has constrained our fellow Citizens taken Captive on the high Seas to 31 bear Arms against their Country, to become the executioners of their friends and Brethren, or to fall themselves by the Hands.

He has excited domestic insurrections amongst us, and has endeavored to 32 bring on the inhabitants of our frontiers, the merciless Indian Savages, whose known rule of warfare, is an undistinguished destruction of all ages, sexes and conditions.

In every stage of these Oppressions We have Petitioned for Redress in the 33 most humble terms: Our repeated Petitions have been answered only by repeated injury. A Prince, whose character is thus marked by every act which may define a Tyrant, is unfit to be the ruler of a free people.

Nor have We been wanting in attention to our British brethren. We have 34 warned them from time to time of attempts by their legislature to extend an unwarrantable jurisdiction over us. We have reminded them of the circumstances of our emigration and settlement here. We have appealed to their native justice and magnanimity, and we have conjured them by the ties of our common kindred to disavow these usurpations, which would inevitably interrupt our connections and correspondence. They too have been deaf to the voice of justice and of consanguinity. We must, therefore, acquiesce in the necessity, which denounces our Separation, and hold them, as we hold the rest of mankind, Enemies in War, in Peace Friends.

We, therefore, the Representatives of the *United States of America,* in General 35 Congress, Assembled, appealing to the Supreme Judge of the world for the rectitude of our intentions, do, in the Name, and by authority of the good People of these Colonies, solemnly publish and declare, That these United Colonies are, and of Right ought to be Free and Independent States; that they are Absolved from all Allegiance to the British Crown, and that all political connection between them and the State of Great Britain, is and ought to be totally dissolved; and that as Free and Independent States, they have full power to levy War, conclude Peace, contract Alliances, establish Commerce, and to do all other Acts and Things which Independent States may of right do. And for the support of this Declaration, with a firm reliance on the protection of Divine Providence, we mutually pledge to each other our Lives, our Fortunes and our sacred Honor. ■

FOR DISCUSSION: Describe the rhetorical situation for the Declaration of Independence. Why is it usually described as a "revolutionary document"? What are the four "self-evident" truths or human rights mentioned in this document? Do all people have equal claim to these rights, or can you think of constraining circumstances when certain individuals might be denied these rights? Do individuals pursue these rights, or do governments guarantee them? What is the difference? Discuss.

E. PAIRS OF STUDENTS: FALLACIES

Read the following story about a young man who tries to teach his girlfriend to recognize fallacies. He describes eight fallacies, which are numbered in the left margin and printed in boldface in the text. Form pairs. Each pair selects one fallacy until all eight have been assigned. With your partner, think of a modern example of the fallacy you selected, and write a paragraph in which you use this fallacy to prove a point. Use the examples in the story as models. Read your paragraphs in class. Discuss what is wrong with these arguments. Why are the fallacies characterized as pseudoproofs?

Essay 1

LOVE IS A FALLACY*

Max Shulman

Max Shulman is the author of humorous essays, plays & novels. Some of his novels have been made into films.

1   Cool was I and logical. Keen, calculating, perspicacious, acute, and astute—I was all of these. My brain was as powerful as a dynamo, as precise as a chemist's scales, as penetrating as a scalpel. And—think of it!—I was only eighteen.

2   It is not often that one so young has such a giant intellect. Take, for example, Petey Bellows, my roommate at the university. Same age, same background, but dumb as an ox. A nice enough fellow, you understand, but nothing upstairs. Emotional type. Unstable. Impressionable. Worst of all, a faddist. Fads, I submit, are the very negation of reason. To be swept up in every new craze that comes along, to surrender yourself to idiocy just because everybody else is doing it—this, to me, is the acme of mindlessness. Not, however, to Petey.

3   One afternoon I found Petey lying on his bed with an expression of such distress on his face that I immediately diagnosed appendicitis. "Don't move," I said. "Don't take a laxative. I'll get a doctor."

4   "Raccoon," he mumbled thickly.

5   "Raccoon?" I said, pausing in my flight.

6   "I want a raccoon coat," he wailed.

7   I perceived that his trouble was not physical, but mental. "Why do you want a raccoon coat?"

*From *Love Is a Fallacy* (New York: Doubleday, 1951).

"I should have known it," he cried, pounding his temples. "I 8 should have known they'd come back when the Charleston came back. Like a fool I spent all my money for textbooks, and now I can't get a raccoon coat."

"Can you mean," I said incredulously, "that people are actually 9 wearing raccoon coats again?"

"All the Big Men on Campus are wearing them. Where've 10 you been?"

"In the library," I said, naming a place not frequented by Big 11 Men on Campus.

He leaped from the bed and paced the room. "I've got to have 12 a raccoon coat," he said passionately. "I've got to!"

"Petey, why? Look at it rationally. Raccoon coats are unsanitary. 13 They shed. They smell bad. They weigh too much. They're unsightly. They—"

"You don't understand," he interrupted impatiently. "It's the 14 thing to do. Don't you want to be in the swim?"

"No," I said truthfully. 15

"Well, I do," he declared. "I'd give anything for a raccoon 16 coat. Anything!"

My brain, that precision instrument, slipped into high gear. 17 "Anything?" I asked, looking at him narrowly.

"Anything," he affirmed in ringing tones. 18

I stroked my chin thoughtfully. It so happened that I knew 19 where to get my hands on a raccoon coat. My father had had one in his undergraduate days; it lay now in a trunk in the attic back home. It also happened that Petey had something I wanted. He didn't *have* it exactly, but at least he had first rights on it. I refer to his girl, Polly Espy.

I had long coveted Polly Espy. Let me emphasize that my de- 20 sire for this young woman was not emotional in nature. She was, to be sure, a girl who excited the emotions, but I was not one to let my heart rule my head. I wanted Polly for a shrewdly calculated, entirely cerebral reason.

I was a freshman in law school. In a few years I would be out in 21 practice. I was well aware of the importance of the right kind of wife in furthering a lawyer's career. The successful lawyers I had observed were, almost without exception, married to beautiful, gracious, intelligent women. With one omission, Polly fitted these specifications perfectly.

Beautiful she was. She was not yet of pin-up proportions, but I 22 felt sure that time would supply the lack. She already had the makings.

Gracious she was. By gracious I mean full of graces. She had an 23 erectness of carriage, an ease of bearing, a poise that clearly indicated the best of breeding. At table her manners were exquisite. I had seen her at the Kozy Kampus Korner eating the specialty of the house—a sandwich that contained scraps of pot roast, gravy, chopped nuts, and a dipper of sauerkraut—without even getting her fingers moist.

24   Intelligent she was not. In fact, she veered in the opposite direction. But I believed that under my guidance she would smarten up. At any rate, it was worth a try. It is, after all, easier to make a beautiful dumb girl smart that to make an ugly smart girl beautiful.

25   "Petey," I said, "are you in love with Polly Espy?"

26   "I think she's a keen kid," he replied, "but I don't know if you'd call it love. Why?"

27   "Do you," I asked, "have any kind of formal arrangement with her? I mean are you going steady or anything like that?"

28   "No. We see each other quite a bit, but we both have other dates. Why?"

29   "Is there," I asked, "any other man for whom she has a particular fondness?"

30   "Not that I know of. Why?"

31   I nodded with satisfaction. "In other words, if you were out of the picture, the field would be open. Is that right?"

32   "I guess so. What are you getting at?"

33   "Nothing, nothing," I said innocently, and took my suitcase out of the closet.

34   "Where you going?" asked Petey.

35   "Home for the week end." I threw a few things into the bag.

36   "Listen," he said clutching my arm eagerly, "while you're home, you couldn't get some money from your old man, could you, and lend it to me so I can buy a raccoon coat?"

37   "I may do better than that," I said with a mysterious wink and closed my bag and left.

38   "Look," I said to Petey when I got back Monday morning. I threw open the suitcase and revealed the huge, hairy, gamy object that my father had worn in his Stutz Bearcat in 1925.

39   "Holy Toledo!" said Petey reverently. He plunged his hands into the raccoon coat and then his face. "Holy Toledo!" he repeated fifteen or twenty times.

40   "Would you like it?" I asked.

41   "Oh yes!" he cried, clutching the greasy pelt to him. Then a canny look came into his eyes. "What do you want for it?"

42   "Your girl," I said, mincing no words.

43   "Polly?" he said in a horrified whisper. "You want Polly?"

44   "That's right."

45   He flung the coat from him. "Never," he said stoutly.

46   I shrugged. "Okay. If you don't want to be in the swim, I guess it's your business."

I sat down in a chair and pretended to read a book, but out of 47
the corner of my eye I kept watching Petey. He was a torn man. First
he looked at the coat with the expression of a waif at a bakery window. Then he turned away and set his jaw resolutely. Then he looked
back at the coat, with even more longing in his face. Then he turned
away, but with not so much resolution this time. Back and forth his
head swiveled, desire waxing, resolution waning. Finally he didn't
turn away at all; he just stood and stared with mad lust at the coat.

"It isn't as though I was in love with Polly," he said thickly. "Or 48
going steady or anything like that."

"That's right," I murmured. 49

"What's Polly to me, or me to Polly?" 50

"Not a thing," said I. 51

"It's just been a casual kick—just a few laughs, that's all." 52

"Try on the coat," said I. 53

He complied. The coat bunched high over his ears and dropped 54
all the way down to his shoe tops. He looked like a mound of dead
raccoons. "Fits fine," he said happily.

I rose from my chair. "Is it a deal?" I asked, extending my hand. 55

He swallowed. "It's a deal," he said and shook my hand. 56

I had my first date with Polly the following evening. This was 57
in the nature of a survey; I wanted to find out just how much work I
had to do to get her mind up to the standard I required. I took her
first to dinner. "Gee, that was a delish dinner," she said as we left the
restaurant. Then I took her to a movie. "Gee, that was a marvy
movie," she said as we left the theater. And then I took her home.
"Gee, I had a sensaysh time," she said as she bade me good night.

I went back to my room with a heavy heart. I had gravely under- 58
estimated the size of my task. This girl's lack of information was
terrifying. Nor would it be enough merely to supply her with information. First she had to be taught to *think*. This loomed as a project
of no small dimensions, and at first I was tempted to give her back to
Petey. But then I got to thinking about her abundant physical charms
and about the way she entered a room and the way she handled a
knife and fork, and I decided to make an effort.

I went about it, as in all things, systematically. I gave her a 59
course in logic. It happened that I, as a law student, was taking a
course in logic myself, so I had all the facts at my fingertips. "Polly,"
I said to her when I picked her up on our next date, "tonight we are
going over to the Knoll and talk."

"Oo, terrif," she replied. One thing I will say for this girl: you 60
would go far to find another so agreeable.

We went to the Knoll, the campus trysting place, and we sat 61
down under an old oak, and she looked at me expectantly. "What
are we going to talk about?" she asked.

62　　　"Logic."

63　　　She thought this over for a minute and decided she liked it. "Magnif," she said.

64　　　"Logic," I said, clearing my throat, "is the science of thinking. Before we can think correctly, we must first learn to recognize the common fallacies of logic. These we will take up tonight."

65　　　"Wow-dow!" she cried, clapping her hands delightedly.

66　　　I winced, but went bravely on. "First let us examine the fallacy called **Dicto Simpliciter.**"

Fallacy 1

67　　　"By all means," she urged, batting lashes eagerly.

68　　　"Dicto Simpliciter means an argument based on an unqualified generalization. For example: Exercise is good. Therefore everybody should exercise."

69　　　"I agree," said Polly earnestly. "I mean exercise is wonderful. I mean it builds the body and everything."

70　　　"Polly," I said gently, "the argument is a fallacy. *Exercise is good* is an unqualified generalization. For instance, if you have heart disease, exercise is bad, not good. Many people are ordered by their doctors *not* to exercise. You must *qualify* the generalization. You must say exercise is *usually* good, or exercise is good *for most people.* Otherwise you have committed a Dicto Simpliciter. Do you see?"

71　　　"No," she confessed. "But this is marvy. Do more! Do more!"

72　　　"It will be better if you stop tugging at my sleeve," I told her, and when she desisted, I continued. "Next we take up a fallacy called **Hasty Generalization.** Listen carefully: You can't speak French. I can't speak French. Petey Bellows can't speak French. I must therefore conclude that nobody at the University of Minnesota can speak French."

Fallacy 2

73　　　"Really?" said Polly, amazed. *"Nobody?"*

74　　　I hid my exasperation. "Polly, it's a fallacy. The generalization is reached too hastily. There are too few instances to support such a conclusion."

75　　　"Know any more fallacies?" she asked breathlessly. "This is more fun than dancing even."

76　　　I fought off a wave of despair. I was getting nowhere with this girl, absolutely nowhere. Still, I am nothing if not persistent. I continued. "Next comes **Post Hoc.** Listen to this: Let's not take Bill on our picnic. Every time we take him out with us, it rains."

Fallacy 3

77　　　"I know somebody just like that," she exclaimed. "A girl back home—Eula Becker, her name is. It never fails. Every single time we take her on a picnic—"

78　　　"Polly," I said sharply, "it's a fallacy. Eula Becker doesn't *cause* the rain. She has no connection with the rain. You are guilty of Post Hoc if you blame Eula Becker."

79　　　"I'll never do it again," she promised contritely. "Are you mad at me?"

I sighed. "No, Polly, I'm not mad." 80

"Then tell me some more fallacies." 81

"All right. Let's try **Contradictory Premises.**" 82 Fallacy 4

"Yes, let's," she chirped, blinking her eyes happily. 83

I frowned, but plunged ahead. "Here's an example of Contra- 84 dictory Premises: If God can do anything, can He make a stone so heavy that He won't be able to lift it?"

"Of course," she replied promptly. 85

"But if He can do anything, He can lift the stone," I pointed out. 86

"Yeah," she said thoughtfully. "Well, then I guess He can't 87 make the stone."

"But He can do anything," I reminded her. 88

She scratched her pretty, empty head. "I'm all confused," she 89 admitted.

"Of course you are. Because when the premises of an argu- 90 ment contradict each other, there can be no argument. It there is an irresistible force, there can be no immovable object. If there is an immovable object, there can be no irresistible force. Get it?"

"Tell me some more of this keen stuff," she said eagerly. 91

I consulted my watch. "I think we'd better call it a night. I'll take 92 you home now, and you go over all the things you've learned. We'll have another session tomorrow night."

I deposited her at the girl's dormitory, where she assured me that 93 she had had a perfectly terrif evening, and I went glumly home to my room. Petey lay snoring in his bed, the raccoon coat huddled like a great hairy beast at his feet. For a moment I considered waking him and telling him that he could have his girl back. It seemed clear that my project was doomed to failure. The girl simply had a logic-proof head.

But then I reconsidered. I had wasted one evening; I might as 94 well waste another. Who knew? Maybe somewhere in the extinct crater of her mind a few embers still smoldered. Maybe somehow I could fan them in flame. Admittedly it was not a prospect fraught with hope, but I decided to give it one more try.

Seated under the oak the next evening I said, "Our first fallacy 95 tonight is called **Ad Misericordiam.**" Fallacy 5

She quivered with delight. 96

"Listen closely," I said. "A man applies for a job. When the boss 97 asks him what his qualifications are, he replies that he has a wife and six children at home, the wife is a helpless cripple, the children have nothing to eat, no clothes to wear, no shoes on their feet, there are no beds in the house, no coal in the cellar, and winter is coming."

A tear rolled down each of Polly's pink cheeks. "Oh, this is 98 awful, awful," she sobbed.

"Yes, it's awful," I agreed, "but it's no argument. The man never 99 answered the boss's question about the qualifications. Instead he appealed to the boss's sympathy. He committed the fallacy of Ad Misericordiam. Do you understand?"

100   "Have you got a handkerchief?" she blubbered.

101   I handed her a handkerchief and tried to keep from screaming while she wiped her eyes. "Next," I said in a carefully controlled tone, "we will discuss **False Analogy.** Here is an example: Students should be allowed to look at their textbooks during examinations. After all, surgeons have X rays to guide them during an operation, lawyers have briefs to guide them during a trial, carpenters have blueprints to guide them when they are building a house. Why, then, shouldn't students be allowed to look at their textbooks during an examination?"

Fallacy 6

102   "There now," she said enthusiastically, "is the most marvy idea I've heard in years."

103   "Polly," I said testily, "the argument is all wrong. Doctors, lawyers, and carpenters aren't taking a test to see how much they have learned, but students are. The situations are altogether different, and you can't make an analogy between them."

104   "I still think it's a good idea," said Polly.

105   "Nuts," I muttered. Doggedly I pressed on. "Next we'll try **Hypothesis Contrary to Fact.**"

Fallacy 7

106   "Sounds yummy," was Polly's reaction.

107   "Listen: If Madame Curie had not happened to leave a photographic plate in a drawer with a chunk of pitchblende, the world today would not know about radium."

108   "True, true," said Polly, nodding her head. "Did you see the movie? Oh, it just knocked me out. That Walter Pidgeon is so dreamy. I mean he fractures me."

109   "If you can forget Mr. Pidgeon for a moment," I said coldly, "I would like to point out that the statement is a fallacy. Maybe Madame Curie would have discovered radium at some later date. Maybe somebody else would have discovered it. Maybe any number of things would have happened. You can't start with a hypothesis that is not true and then draw any supportable conclusions from it."

110   "They ought to put Walter Pidgeon in more pictures," said Polly. "I hardly ever see him any more."

111   One more chance, I decided. But just one more. There is a limit to what flesh and blood can bear. "The next fallacy is called **Poisoning the Well.**"

Fallacy 8

112   "How cute!" she gurgled.

113   "Two men are having a debate. The first one gets up and says, 'My opponent is a notorious liar. You can't believe a word that he is going to say.' . . . Now, Polly, think. Think hard. What's wrong?"

114   I watched her closely as she knit her creamy brow in concentration. Suddenly a glimmer of intelligence—the first I had seen—

came into her eyes. "It's not fair," she said with indignation. "It's not a bit fair. What chance has the second man got if the first man calls him a liar before he even begins talking?"

"Right!" I cried exultantly. "One hundred percent right. It's not 115 fair. The first man has *poisoned the well* before anybody could drink from it. He has hamstrung his opponent before he could even start. . . . Polly, I'm proud of you."

"Pshaw," she murmured, blushing with pleasure. 116

"You see, my dear, these things aren't so hard. All you have to 117 do is concentrate. Think—examine—evaluate. Come now, let's review everything we have learned."

"Fire away," she said with an airy wave of her hand. 118

Heartened by the knowledge that Polly was not altogether a 119 cretin, I began a long, patient review of all I had told her. Over and over and over again I cited instances, pointed out flaws, kept hammering away without letup. It was like digging a tunnel. At first everything was work, sweat, and darkness. I had no idea when I would reach the light, or even *if* I would. But I persisted. I pounded and clawed and scraped, and finally I was rewarded. I saw a chink of light. And then the chink got bigger and the sun came pouring in and all was bright.

Five grueling nights this took, but it was worth it. I had made 120 a logician out of Polly; I had taught her to think. My job was done. She was worthy of me at last. She was a fit wife for me, a proper hostess for my many mansions, a suitable mother for my well-heeled children.

It must not be thought that I was without love for this girl. 121 Quite the contrary. Just as Pygmalion loved the perfect woman he had fashioned, so I loved mine. I decided to acquaint her with my feelings at our very next meeting. The time had come to change our relationship from academic to romantic.

"Polly," I said when next we sat beneath our oak, "tonight we 122 will not discuss fallacies."

"Aw, gee," she said, disappointed. 123

"My dear," I said, favoring her with a smile, "we have now 124 spent five evenings together. We have gotten along splendidly. It is clear that we are well matched."

"Hasty Generalization," said Polly brightly. 125

"I beg your pardon," said I. 126

"Hasty Generalization," she repeated. "How can you say that 127 we are well matched on the basis of only five dates?"

I chuckled with amusement. The dear child had learned her 128 lesson well. "My dear," I said, patting her hand in a tolerant manner, "five dates is plenty. After all, you don't have to eat a whole cake to know that it's good."

129   "False Analogy," said Polly promptly. "I'm not a cake. I'm a girl."

130   I chuckled with somewhat less amusement. The dear child had learned her lesson perhaps too well. I decided to change tactics. Obviously the best approach was a simple, strong, direct declaration of love. I paused for a moment while my massive brain chose the proper words. Then I began:

131   "Polly, I love you. You are the whole world to me, and the moon and the stars and the constellations of outer space. Please, my darling, say that you will go steady with me, for if you will not, life will be meaningless. I will languish. I will refuse my meals. I will wander the face of the earth, a shambling, hollow-eyed hulk."

132   There, I thought, folding my arms, that ought to do it.

133   "Ad Misericordiam," said Polly.

134   I ground my teeth. I was not Pygmalion; I was Frankenstein, and my monster had me by the throat. Frantically I fought back the tide of panic surging through me. At all costs I had to keep cool.

135   "Well, Polly," I said, forcing a smile, "you certainly have learned your fallacies."

136   "You're darn right," she said with a vigorous nod.

137   "And who taught them to you, Polly?"

138   "You did."

139   "That's right. So you do owe me something, don't you, my dear? If I hadn't come along you never would have learned about fallacies."

140   "Hypothesis Contrary to Fact," she said instantly.

141   I dashed perspiration from my brow. "Polly," I croaked, "you mustn't take all these things so literally. I mean this is just classroom stuff. You know that the things you learn in school don't have anything to do with life."

142   "Dicto Simpliciter," she said, wagging her finger at me playfully.

143   That did it. I leaped to my feet, bellowing like a bull. "Will you or will you not go steady with me?"

144   "I will not," she replied

145   "Why not?" I demanded.

146   "Because this afternoon I promised Petey Bellows that I would go steady with him."

147   I reeled back, overcome with the infamy of it. After he promised, after he made a deal, after he shook my hand! "That rat!" I shrieked, kicking up great chunks of turf. "You can't go with him, Polly. He's a liar. He's a cheat. He's a rat."

148   "Poisoning the Well," said Polly, "and stop shouting. I think shouting must be a fallacy too."

149   With an immense effort of will, I modulated my voice. "All right," I said. "You're a logician. Let's look at this thing logically. How could you choose Petey Bellows over me? Look at me—a brilliant

student, a tremendous intellectual, a man with an assured future. Look at Petey—a knothead, a jitterbug, a guy who'll never know where his next meal is coming from. Can you give me one logical reason why you should go steady with Petey Bellows?"

"I certainly can," declared Polly. "He's got a raccoon coat." ■ 150

FOR DISCUSSION: Name and describe some of the fallacies described in this article. What special application does Polly make of these fallacies? Is there a fallacy involved in her choice of Petey as a boyfriend at the end? Is the narrator guilty of any fallacious thinking himself? Describe.

F. PREWRITING: USING THE PROOFS TO GET IDEAS FOR A POSITION PAPER

You have analyzed other authors' use of proofs in the preceding exercises. Now think about how you can use the proofs in your own writing. If you are working on a "Position Paper Based on 'The Reader'" (Exercise G in this chapter), you will already have a claim, and you may have already used the Toulmin model (pages 149–150) and the claim questions (page 190) to help you develop the structure and some of the ideas for your paper. Use the acronyms SICDADS and VAM to help you consider the proofs. Ask the following questions, and write out answers for those that are most promising.

1. *Signs:* What symptoms or signs will demonstrate that this is so?
2. *Induction:* What examples can I use and what conclusions can I draw from them? Are they convincing enough to help the reader make the "inductive leap"?
3. *Cause:* What has caused this? Why is this happening? Think of explanations and examples of both cause and effect.
4. *Deduction:* What concluding statements do I want to make? What general principles and examples (or cases) are they based on?
5. *Analogies:* How can I show that what happened in one case will probably happen again in another case? Can I use a literal analogy to compare items in the same general category? Can I use a figurative analogy to compare items from different categories? Can I demonstrate that history repeats itself by citing an historical analogy?
6. *Definition:* What words or concepts will I need to define?
7. *Statistics:* What statistics can I use? Would they be more convincing in graph form?
8. *Values:* What values can I appeal to? Should I spell them out or leave them implicit? Will narratives and emotional language make my appeals to values stronger?
9. *Authority:* Who should I quote? What can I use from my own background and experience to establish my own expertise? How can I use language to create common ground and establish *ethos*?

10. *Motives:* What does my audience need and want in regard to this topic? How can I appeal to those needs? Will emotional language help?

G. WRITING ASSIGNMENT: A POSITION PAPER BASED ON "THE READER"

For this assignment, you will write a position paper in which you make a claim and prove it. Your claim should be related to a topic you have selected from "The Reader." Your paper should be about 1,000 words long, typed, and double-spaced.

Your purpose in this assignment is to use the argument theory you have learned in Chapters 5–7 to help you invent ideas and write. You will also draw on your own reasoning and information from the essays to help you argue.

Prewriting

If you have not already done so, complete some or all of the following prewriting activities, explained on the pages cited, so that you will have plenty of material to draw on when you draft your paper.

1. Read the issue questions in "The Reader," select the one that interests you the most, read the related essays, and write an issue proposal (page 25).
2. Write summary-response papers for each of the related essays (page 87).
3. Write an exploratory essay to help you understand your topic, and write a tentative claim at the end of it (pages 110–113 and 119).
4. Use the Toulmin model (pages 149–150) to help you find the elements for your paper, use the claim questions to refine and focus your claim and get further ideas for subclaims (page 190), and use the proof questions to develop convincing proofs for your claims (pages 237–238).

Writing a List or an Outline

Follow the instructions in Chapter 4 on page 97 for making an extended list or outline. Refer also to information about possible organizational patterns you might use to organize your ideas on pages 300–305. Or consider using one of the following patterns to organize your ideas and develop your claim:

- If you are writing a fact paper that answers the question "What happened?" consider using a chronological pattern. Use transitions like *first, then,* and *next.* You may begin your paper with present events and use flashbacks to explain what occurred in the past, or you may simply explain things in the order in which they occurred.

- If you are writing a definition paper that answers the question "What is it?" consider using comparison to help establish meaning by showing what the item you are defining is like and what it is not like. Or you may want to present examples of several meanings for the item and finally settle on the best of these meanings for your conclusion.

- If you are writing a cause paper that answers the question "What caused it?" consider using a c<u>ause-and-effect</u> or effect-and-cause pattern of organization. Cause and effect explains how certain causes result in certain effects, and effect and cause describes the effects first and then explains what caused them.

- If you are writing a value paper that answers the question "Is it good or bad?" consider a <u>claim-plus-reasons</u> pattern. Complete the sentence "It is (good or bad) because . . . ," and add reasons and evidence.

- If you are writing a policy paper that answers the question "What should we do?" consider using the <u>problem-solution</u> pattern of organization. Describe the problem first, and then describe one or more solutions.

Drafting, Revising, and Final Editing

Use your extended list or outline to help you write a draft, revise the draft, and prepare the final copy. Follow the suggestions for drafting, revising, and editing in Chapter 4, pages 99–105. Work quoted material into your draft as you write. Follow explanations and examples for integrating quoted material into your paper that appear in Chapter 4, pages 111–113 and the Appendix to Chapter 10, pages 319–337. Use MLA documentation to cite in-text references and to create a Works Cited page, unless you are advised otherwise. Follow the instructions and examples for MLA documentation in Chapter 4 and the Appendix to Chapter 10.

Read the following example of a position paper based on an issue question in "The Reader." The question is "What should be done with young offenders?" This paper was written by Kelly Dickerson, a student in an argument class. The type of claim, the elements of the Toulmin model, and the proofs are identified in the margin.

Notice also how Kelly worked quoted material into her paper so that you can read it easily. It flows with the rest of the text, and it is clear. Furthermore, introductions for the quotes, along with the in-text citations, show you where you could find these quotes yourself if you wanted to. Use this paper as a model to help you integrate your quotes into your paper and prepare a Works Cited page.

Student Paper

Kelly Dickerson
Position Paper Based on "The Reader"
Professor Pearman
English 1302
25 September 1999

Minor Problems?

Definition

1   Every time Americans tune in to local news broadcasts or read daily papers, they are likely to be shocked at the increasing number of serious crimes committed by youths who are only sixteen years old or even younger. It is sometimes difficult to imagine these youngsters behaving like hardened criminals, but statistics continually prove that their crimes are often just as brutal as those committed by their adult counterparts. Inevitably, people begin questioning how successful the juvenile justice system is in reforming these youths and debating whether violent juveniles should be tried as adults in our legal system. After reading about this topic, I feel there is no question that juveniles convicted of serious crimes—including murder, rape, robbery, physical assault, and drug involvement—should face the same consequences as adults.

Policy claim

Subclaim: Problem

2   While the teenage population in the United States has declined over the past decade, violent crimes committed by juveniles have sharply increased. Patricia Cohen in "Punishment" notes, "From 1988-1991 the youth murder-arrest rate climbed 80 percent" (512) and, at the time she wrote her article in 1996, 42 juveniles had been assigned to death row (512). According to Males and Docuyanan in "Crackdown on Kids: Giving Up on the Young," there were more than 200 teen murders in Central Los Angeles in 1993 (513), and another 459 teens were arrested there for murder in 1994 (514). Examples of teen crime are vivid and terrifying. Debra Dickerson in "Who Shot Johnny?" describes how a youth with no apparent motive shot and paralyzed her young nephew. The effect on both Johnny and his family has been devastating (517-20). Even Geoffrey Canada, who favors rehabilitation and other interventions over imprisonment for youthful offenders, suggests the need for a peace officer corps to keep youngsters from killing each other (522).

Support : Statistics

Induction

Authority

Warrant: The statistics and examples prove there is a problem.

Subclaim: The punishment does not always fit the crime.

3   Despite the staggering increase in serious crimes committed by young offenders, the punishment which juveniles receive has traditionally almost never fit the

severity of the crimes. Since the system has historically viewed children as not being fully developed, physically or mentally, it has prevented them from being held accountable for their wrongdoing. Although many of these "children" commit horribly vicious crimes, they have been routinely treated as victims of society who are too delicate to receive the punishments they deserve. Until very recently, lenient sentences and court proceedings have been the norm. The message they sent to serious juvenile criminals is that crime "pays" because there are no serious consequences for their actions. When the system lacks an element of fear, there is nothing to deter youthful offenders from committing future crimes. The current trend, as described by Males and Docuyanan (522), of assigning adult sentences to youths who commit serious crimes is absolutely just if the punishment is to fit the crime.

Warrant: The punishment should fit the crime.

Support: Cause and effect

Warrant: Adult sentences are a deterrent to crime.
Appeal to value of justice

Most pro-rehabilitation advocates argue that juvenile criminals are completely different from their adult counterparts and should therefore be treated differently in the justice system. However, the cost to society is the same regardless of the age of the criminal. What comfort does it give to the family of a slain or injured victim that the person who killed or maimed their loved one was a minor? Dickerson makes it clear that Johnny and his family suffer no less because Johnny was shot by a young offender. Instead of treating the loser who shot Johnny like a victim of society, this person should be treated like any other person who victimizes society and causes pain to individuals and communities.

4

Rebuttal: Cost to society is the same, so young offenders should get same treatment as adults.

Support: Cause and effect

Warrant: Cost to society should determine punishment.

Tougher measures must be taken to combat this growing problem of juvenile crime. In today's society, too many juveniles count on lenient sentences allotted by the juvenile justice system. As Dickerson says, a liberal lawyer can help a vicious criminal plea-bargain the offense, receive a short sentence, and return to the streets to commit more crime (519). Furthermore, as Canada points out, many young offenders, who compare jail with staying on the streets, choose jail (522). When there are no harsh consequences of being caught, committing crimes can be perceived as having positive benefits. As a result, juveniles are continuing to become more violent and less concerned with the value of human life.

5

Subclaim: Use tougher measures

Support: Sign

Warrant: Juveniles can still get off.

Backing: Authority
Support: Comparison

Cause and effect

Although I agree with Males and Docuyanan that re-

6

Qualifier

duction of poverty along with rehabilitation can be very important in decreasing the amount of juvenile crime, I believe that these measures should be directed toward youths who have committed minor offenses. Conversely, I feel that juveniles like the one who shot Johnny, those *Restatement of* who are convicted of serious crimes—including murder, *claim* and summary rape, robbery, physical assault, and drug involvement— should be tried as adults. Their actions are obviously more serious than those who commit misdemeanor offenses, and they almost always result in greater direct harm to society. A message has to be sent that we will no longer tolerate brutal crimes simply because of the age of the criminal. These youths must be held completely account- able for their crimes, suffering harsh consequences and ultimately realizing that they are no longer protected by the law. ■

Works Cited

Canada, Geoffrey. "Peace in the Streets." <u>Utne Reader</u>
    July-Aug. 1995: 59-61. Rpt. in Wood 527-31.
Cohen, Patricia. "Punishment." <u>George</u> June-July 1996:
    99. Rpt. in Wood 517-18.
Dickerson, Debra. "Who Shot Johnny?" <u>The New Republic</u> 1
    Jan. 1996: 17-18. Rpt. in Wood 523-26.
Males, Mike, and Faye Docuyanan. "Crackdown on Kids:
    Giving Up on the Young." <u>The Progressive</u> Feb.
    1996: 24-26. Rpt. in Wood 518-23.
Wood, Nancy V. <u>Perspectives on Argument.</u> 3rd ed. Upper
    Saddle River: Prentice, 2001.

H. CLASS PROJECT: A CLASS DEBATE

This activity will provide you with further practice in applying the argument theory you have learned in Chapters 5–7.

Debate is a traditional forum for argument, and your class can set up a debate in which everyone participates. A common model for debate is to have two people on each side of the issue present their views, and a judge then declares who wins. For this class debate, however, we will use a somewhat different strategy that involves not only stating the opposing viewpoints but also working to find some common ground between the two opposing positions to achieve more productive argument and to avoid a standoff with no agreement and no resolution of the issue.

We draw on social judgment theory to help organize the debate. Social judgment theorists, who study the positions that individuals take on issues, plot positions on a continuum that ranges from extremely positive to extremely negative. They then describe these positions in terms of latitudes of acceptance. Individuals at the extremes of the continuum have narrow latitudes of acceptance and can usually tolerate only positions that are very close to their own. Somewhere in the middle is a latitude of noncommitment. People in this area, who are not strongly involved with the issue, have comparatively wide latitudes of acceptance and can tolerate a wide range of positions. The object of this debate is to increase everyone's latitudes of acceptance so that productive argument can take place.

Preparing for the Debates

1. Select an Issue

The class may nominate possible issues from the following list of articles in this book or on their own and then vote on one of them as a topic for debate. The issue should be written in statement form, as in the list, so that individuals can either agree or disagree with it.

Possible Topics for Debate

Resolved: Men and women are not really different; they are in fact fundamentally the same. (pages 436–438)

Resolved: Computers are having a damaging effect on the quality of life in the world. (pages 185–187; 551–556)

Resolved: Capital punishment should be used more frequently than it currently is. (pages 507–511)

Resolved: Violent video games breed violence in real life. (pages 524–529)

Resolved: Standardized tests should be abolished. (pages 167–169; 491–495)

Resolved: Children should not have access to materials that might frighten them or subject them to immoral values. (pages 219–221)

Resolved: Traditional marriage is not necessary for a happy and productive family life. (pages 451–469)

Resolved: Grades should be eliminated in college. (pages 146–148; 489–491)

Resolved: Parents, not public institutions or industry, are responsible for child care. (pages 636–647)

Resolved: Racial differences no longer create significant problems. (pages 583–597)

Or: Brainstorm campus issues, and vote on one to debate.

2. Create Three Groups

The class will divide itself into three groups. Two groups are encouraged to take strong affirmative and negative positions and to argue from those points of view, presenting pro and con arguments, with presumably narrow latitudes of acceptance. A third, middle group with a wider latitude of acceptance will present suggestions for resolving some of the conflict. This group will look for common ground in the extreme positions, try to resolve conflict, and work to achieve better understanding and perhaps even a change of views in the opposing groups.

Group 1 is the affirmative group that is in favor of the subject for debate. Group 2 is the negative group that is against it. Group 3 is the moderate group that will attempt to resolve the conflict. The groups should be equal in size. To achieve this equality, some students may have to argue for positions that they do not in fact actually hold.

3. Do Background Reading and Writing

All three groups should do some background reading on the subject for debate. The negative and affirmative teams will read to get ideas for their arguments and to develop ideas for refutation. The moderates should read to understand the opposing positions. Students in groups 1 and 2 write 250-word papers outside of class that present some arguments to support their positions. After they have listened to the debate, the moderates write 250-word papers that make an effort to resolve the conflict.

Conducting the Debate

Day One

1. *Begin with the opening papers* (10 minutes). Two students from the affirmative group and two from the negative group agree to start the debate by reading their papers. The first affirmative, first negative, second affirmative, and second negative read their papers in that order.
2. *Others join in* (20 minutes). Students may now raise their hands to be recognized by the instructor to give additional arguments from their papers. Each person should stand to speak. The speakers should represent each side in turn. The class should decide whether everyone should first be allowed to speak before anyone is permitted to speak a second time. The instructor should cut off speakers who are going on too long.
3. *Caucus and closing remarks* (15 minutes). The affirmative and negative groups caucus for 5 minutes to prepare their closing arguments. Each group selects a spokesperson who then presents the group's final, strongest arguments in a 2-minute closing presentation.
4. *Moderates prepare responses.* The moderates write 250-word responses outside of class that answer the following question: Now that you have heard both sides, how would you resolve the conflict?

Day Two

1. *Moderates read* (20 minutes). All moderates read their papers. Each paper should take about 2 minutes to read.
2. *Analyze outcomes* (30 minutes). The class should now discuss the outcomes of the debate by addressing the following questions:
   a. What, in general, were some of the outcomes?
   b. Who changed their opinions? Which opinions? Why?
   c. Who did not change? Why?
   d. What are some of the outcomes of the attempts to reduce conflict and establish common ground?
   e. What strategies have you learned from participating in debate that can help you in real-life arguments?

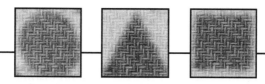

PART THREE

Writing a Research Paper That Presents an Argument

The purpose of the next three chapters is to teach you to write an argument paper from your own perspective that incorporates research materials from outside sources. Since other professors or even employers may also ask you to produce such papers, this instruction should be useful to you not only now but in the future as well. Chapter 8 teaches you to write a claim, clarify the purpose for your paper, and analyze your audience. Chapter 9 teaches you various creative strategies for inventing and gathering research material for your paper. Chapter 10 and its Appendix teach ways to organize this material, write and revise the paper, and prepare the final copy. Methods for locating and using resource materials from the library and the Internet are included. When you finish reading Part Three:

- You will know how to write your claim and determine the main argumentative purpose of your research paper.
- You will know how to analyze your audience and predict how it might change.
- You will know how to think about your claim and gather material from your own background and experience to support it.
- You will know how to organize and conduct library and online research to support your claim further.
- You will know a variety of possible ways to organize the ideas for your paper.
- You will know how to incorporate research materials into your paper and prepare the final copy.

CHAPTER EIGHT

The Research Paper: Clarifying Purpose and Understanding the Audience

This chapter and the two that follow form a self-contained unit. You may think of them as one long assignment. They present the information you will need to help you plan, research, and write a researched position paper. You will be familiar with some of the information in these chapters because you have encountered it in earlier chapters. The basic process for writing a researched position paper is much like the process for writing the position paper based on "The Reader" explained in Chapters 1–7. Some of the procedures for the researched position paper, however, are more elaborate than those you have encountered before in this book because a research paper is more complicated than the other papers you have written. As you read Chapters 8, 9, and 10, you can expect to encounter some familiar information along with some new material and ideas. All of this information, including the assignments in the Exercises and Activities at the end of each chapter, is included for one purpose: to help you plan and write a successful researched argumentative paper. Stay on top of these assignments, and you will be pleased with the final results.

The definition of argument quoted in Chapter 1 will help you focus on your final objective in writing this paper: you will seek "to create or increase the adherence of minds to the theses presented for [the audience's] assent."[1] In other words, you will try to get your reading audience to agree, at least to some extent, with your claim and the ideas you use to support it.

---

[1]Chaim Perelman and L. Olbrechts-Tyteca, *The New Rhetoric: A Treatise on Argumentation* (Notre Dame, Ind.: Notre Dame Press, 1969), p. 45.

UNDERSTANDING THE ASSIGNMENT AND GETTING STARTED

You may want to turn to page 318 now to read the assignment for preparing the final copy of the researched position paper so that you will know from the outset what this paper should finally look like. Then, to get you started on this paper, consider following some of the suggestions made in earlier chapters. They will ease you into your paper, help you think, and make you feel knowledgeable and confident.

1. *Decide on an issue, and write an issue proposal.* An issue may be assigned by the instructor, it can be inspired by "The Reader" or a set of readings provided by your instructor, or it can be left entirely up to you. There is often a stronger personal exigence for writing if you select the issue yourself. You may have made lists of issues as subjects for future papers when you finished reading Chapter 1. Look back at them now. Or think about the unresolved issues in your other classes or in current newspapers and television newscasts. Work to find an issue that captures your attention and interest. Submit it to the twelve tests for an arguable issue in Box 1.3. These tests will help you ascertain whether or not your issue is potentially arguable. Then write an issue proposal to help you focus your issue and think about what more you need to learn. Follow the assignment and model on pages 25–27.

2. *Do some initial reading.* If you are not very familiar with your issue, locate one or more sources about it, and do some background reading. Read enough material to form an idea of the various positions that people are likely to take on this issue. If you need advice to help you locate some initial sources, read pages 276–281, which will provide you with the information you need to locate material in the library and on the Internet.

3. *Write an exploratory paper.* Either list and explain three or more perspectives on your issue, or write an exploratory paper in which you explain multiple perspectives. The exploratory paper is described on pages 110–113. This process of exploring the different views or approaches to your issue will help you find an original and interesting perspective of your own, and it will also help you understand some of the other perspectives people take so that you can better refute them when you write your research paper. Remember that the exploratory paper calls for a tentative claim at the end of the paper.

WRITING A CLAIM AND CLARIFYING YOUR PURPOSE

Whether you write an issue proposal and an exploratory paper or not, you will want to write your claim for your position paper as early in the process as possible. Your claim is important because it provides purpose, control, and direction for everything else that you include in your paper. Mapping your issue (see Chapter 3) or freewriting about it (Chapter 4) can help you narrow and focus an issue and write a claim. The five claim questions from Chapter 6 can also help you write a claim and establish the fundamental purpose of your paper. Write your issue as a question, and then freewrite in response to each of the claim questions to get a sense of the best purpose and claim for your paper. Here is an example of how the claim questions can be answered in response to an issue that came out of a specific rhetorical situation.

The Rhetorical Situation

A teenage white supremacist murdered a black middle-class family man. This crime was committed in Texas, where juries are impaneled both to decide guilt and to sentence the criminal. The jury decided the white supremacist was guilty and, in ignorance, sentenced him both to probation and a jail term. The law does not permit both sentences, and so the murderer ended up with probation. As you can imagine, there was public concern, and issues concerning the sentence surfaced. Here are the claim questions used to focus purpose and a claim.

Questions to Plan Claim and Purpose

The issue question is, *How should I think about this sentence for murder?*

   1. *To establish a claim of fact,* ask: What happened? Does it exist? Is it a fact? Is it true?

   > *Example:* Something seems very wrong. I could analyze what is wrong, especially since some people are satisfied and others are dissatisfied with the sentence. My claim could be a claim of fact, *The murderer escaped an appropriate sentence.* I could organize the paper chronologically, giving a history of what has happened and quoting both facts and expert opinion to prove my claim.

   2. *To establish a claim of definition,* ask: What is it? What is it like? How should we interpret it? How does its usual meaning change in this context?

   > *Example:* There may be a definition problem in the sentencing procedure. The jury was supposed to assign an appropriate sentence for a murder. The audience needs a definition of an appropriate sentence for a murder. My claim could be, *Probation is not an appropriate sentence for murder.* I would rely on expert opinion and the citation of similar cases to illustrate what an appropriate sentence for murder should be.

   3. *To establish a claim of cause,* ask: What caused it? Where did it come from? Why did it happen? What are the effects? What will the short-term and long-term results be?

   > *Example:* Personal conversations and media reports indicate considerable confusion over the cause of the sentence. Some people think the jury was racially prejudiced, others think the murderer was assigned probation because he is young, and others are baffled. I think the cause was the jury's lack

of information, and my claim could be, *The jury did not know and did not receive information about how to sentence murderers, and as a result it recommended an inappropriate sentence.* To prove this claim, I will examine the training provided to jurors. I will interview people who have served on juries. I will learn what training was available for this particular jury.

4. To establish a claim of value, ask: Is it good or bad? How bad? How good? Of what worth is it? Is it moral or immoral? Who thinks so? What criteria should I use to decide goodness or badness? Are these the same criteria the audience would apply?

Example: There seems to be some disagreement about whether this sentence was good or bad, but I think it is a bad sentence. My claim could be, *It was wrong of the jury to assign the murderer probation and no jail sentence.* To prove this, I will appeal to the standard needs and values I assume my audience holds, including a desire for physical safety, a sense of fairness and justness, and a respect for the jury system, which, I argue, has failed in this case.

5. To establish a claim of policy, ask: What should we do about it? What should be our future course of action? How can we solve the problem?

Example: Almost everyone thinks that the jury made a mistake. In fact, the criminal is back in jail on another charge waiting for a new trial. I could write a policy paper in which I recommend jury training so that this same problem will not recur. My claim would be, *Juries need pretrial training in order to make competent judgments.*

An example of a student's policy paper organized around this last policy claim and written in response to this actual rhetorical situation appears at the end of the Appendix to Chapter 10. Try writing in response to the claim questions in this way yourself. Then read what you have written, and decide which of the potential claims seems most promising to develop in a paper. Decide on your main purpose, and write your claim. Now you can begin to think about ways to develop your claim.

SOME PRELIMINARY QUESTIONS TO HELP YOU DEVELOP YOUR CLAIM

Ask the following questions to clarify and develop your claim. Some tentative answers to these questions now can help you stay on track and avoid problems with the development of your paper later.

▲ **Is the Claim Narrow and Focused?** You may have started with a broad issue area, such as technology or education, that suggests many specific related issues. You may have participated in mapping sessions in class to discover some of the specific issues related to an issue area, and this work may have helped you narrow your issue. You may now need to narrow your issue even further by focusing on one prong or aspect of it. Here is an example:

Issue area: The environment

Specific related issue:

What problems are associated with nuclear energy?

Aspects of that issue:

What should be done with nuclear waste?

How hazardous is it, and how can we control the hazards?

What are the alternatives to nuclear energy?

In selecting a narrowed issue to write about, you may want to focus on only one of the three aspects of the nuclear energy problem. You might, for instance, decide to make this claim: *Solar power is better than nuclear energy.* Later, as you write, you may need to narrow this topic even further and revise your claim: *Solar power is best for certain specified purposes.* Any topic can turn out to be too broad or complicated when you begin to write about it.

You may also need to change your focus or perspective to narrow your claim. You may, for example, begin to research the claim you have made in response to your issue but discover along the way that the real issue is something else. As a result, you decide to change your claim. For example, suppose you decide to write a policy paper about freedom of speech. Your claim is, *Freedom of speech should be protected in all situations.* As you read and research, however, you discover that an issue for many people is a narrower one related to freedom of speech specifically as it relates to violence on television and children's behavior. In fact, you encounter an article that claims that television violence should be censored even if doing so violates free speech rights. You decide to refocus your paper and write a value paper that claims, *Television violence is harmful and not subject to the protection of free speech rights.*

▲ **Which Controversial Words in Your Claim Will You Need to Define?** Identify the words in your claim that may need defining. In the example just used, you would need to be clear about what you mean by *television violence, censorship,* and *free speech rights.*

▲ **Can You Learn Enough to Cover the Claim Fully?** If the information for an effective paper is unavailable or too complicated, write another claim, one that you know more about and can research more successfully. Or narrow the claim further to an aspect that you can understand and develop.

▲ **What Are the Various Perspectives on Your Issue?** Make certain that your issue invites two or more perspectives. If you have written an exploratory paper on your issue, you already know what several views are. If you have not written such a paper, explore your issue by writing several claims that represent several points of view, and then select the one you want to prove. For example:

Solar power is better than nuclear power.

Solar power is worse than nuclear power.

Solar power has some advantages and some disadvantages when compared to nuclear power.

Solar power is better than nuclear power for certain specified purposes.

As you identify the perspectives on your issue, you can also begin to plan some refutation that will not alienate your audience. An angry or insulted audience is not likely to change.

▲ **How Can You Make Your Claim Both Interesting and Compelling to Yourself and Your Audience?** Develop a fresh perspective on your issue when writing your claim. Suppose you are writing a policy paper that claims public education should be changed. You get bored with it. You keep running into old reasons that everyone already knows. Then you discover a couple of new aspects of the issue that you could cover with more original ideas and material. You learn that some people think parents should be able to choose their children's school, and you learn that competition among schools might lead to improvement. You also learn that contractors can take over schools and manage them in order to improve them. You refocus your issue and your perspective. Your new fact claim is, *Competition among schools, like competition in business, leads to improvement*. The issue and your claim now have new interest for you and your audience because you are looking at them in a whole new way.

▲ **At What Point Are You and the Audience Entering the Conversation on the Issue?** Consider your audience's background and initial views on the issue to decide how to write a claim about it. If both you and your audience are new to the issue, you may decide to stick with claims of fact and definition. If they understand it to some extent but need more analysis, you may decide on claims of cause or value. If both you and your audience have adequate background on the issue, you may want to write a policy claim and try to solve the problems associated with it. Keep in mind also that issues and audiences are dynamic. As soon as audiences engage with issues, both begin to change. So you need to be constantly aware of the current status of the issue and the audience's current stand on it.

▲ **What Secondary Purpose Do You Want to Address in Your Paper?** Even though you establish your predominant purpose as fact, for example, you may still want to answer the other claim questions, particularly if you think your audience needs that information. You may also need to speculate on cause. You may need to provide definitions for the key words. You may want to address value questions to engage your audience's motives and values. Finally, you may want to suggest policy even though your paper has another predominant purpose.

PRELIMINARY PLAN

A preliminary plan will guide your future thinking and research and help you maintain the focus and direction you have already established. Even though you may not know very much about your issue or your claim at this point, writing out what you know and what you want to learn can be valuable. Add some ideas to your plan for beginning research and getting started on a first draft. Box 8.1 provides an example.

A PRELIMINARY PLAN

VALUE CLAIM PLUS REASONS

Television violence is harmful and should not be subject to the protection of free speech rights because . . .

- violence on television and in life seem to be related.
- children do not always differentiate between television and reality.
- parents do not supervise their children's television viewing.
- even though free speech is a constitutional right, it should not be invoked to protect what is harmful to society.

RESEARCH NEEDS

I need to find out how free speech is usually defined. Does it include all freedom of expression, including violence on television? Also, I will need to find the latest studies on television violence and violent behavior, particularly in children. Will there be a cause-effect relationship? Even though I want to focus mainly on value and show that violent television is bad, I will also need to include definition and cause in this paper.

PLAN FOR FIRST DRAFT

I will define television violence and free speech. I need to do some background reading on censorship and freedom of speech and summarize some of this information for my readers. My strongest material will probably be on the relationship between violence on television and violence in real life. I think now I'll begin with that and end with the idea that the Constitution should not be invoked to protect harmful elements like television violence. I'm going to write for an audience that either has children or values children. I will use examples from an article I clipped about how children imitate what they see on television.

BOX 8.1 A Preliminary Plan Helps You Get Started

You now have the beginning of an argument paper: a claim, some reasons, and some ideas to explore further. Your claim may change, and your reasons will probably change as you think, read, and do research. Before you go further, however, you need to think more about the audience. The nature of your audience can have a major influence on how you will finally write your argument paper.

UNDERSTANDING THE AUDIENCE

Why is it important to understand your audience? Why not just argue for what you think is important? Some definitions and descriptions of effective argument emphasize the techniques of argument rather than the outcomes. They encourage the arguer to focus on what he or she thinks is important. For example, an argument with a clear claim, clear logic and reasoning, and good evidence will be described by some theorists as a good argument. The position in this book, however, has been different. If the argument does not reach the audience and create some common ground in order to convince or change it in some way, the argument, no matter how skillfully crafted, is not productive. Productive argument, according to the definitions we used in Chapter 1, must create common ground and achieve some definable audience outcomes.

In order for the writer of argument to reach the audience, create common ground, and bring about change, two essential requirements need to be met. First, the audience must be willing to listen and perhaps also be willing to change. Second, the author must be willing to study, understand, and appeal to the audience. Such analysis will enable the author to relate to the audience's present opinions, values, and motives and to show as often as possible that the author shares them to achieve the common ground essential for effective argument. Thus both audience and author need to cooperate to a certain degree for argument to achieve any outcomes at all.

Four strategies will help you begin the process of understanding and appealing to your audience: assess the audience's size and familiarity to you, determine how much you have in common with your audience, determine the audience's initial position and what changes in views or actions might occur as a result of your argument, and identify the audience's discourse community. Let us examine each in turn.

▲ **Assess the Audience's Size and Familiarity.** Audiences come in all sizes and may or may not include people you know. The smallest and most familiar audience is always yourself; you must convince yourself in internal argument. The next smallest audience is one other person. Larger audiences may include specific, known groups such as family members, classmates, work associates, or members of an organization you belong to. You may also at times write for a large unfamiliar audience composed of either local, national, or international members. And of course some audiences are mixed, including people you know and people you do not know. Your techniques will vary for building common ground with large and small, familiar and unfamiliar audiences, but your argumentative aim will not change.

▲ **Determine What You and the Audience Have in Common.** You may or may not consider yourself a member of your audience, depending on how closely you identify with it and share its views. For example, if you are a member of a union, you will probably identify and agree with its official position, particularly on work-related issues. If you work with management, you will hold other views about work-related issues. Your methods of achieving common ground with either of these audiences will be somewhat different, depending on whether you consider yourself a member of the group or not.

▲ **Determine the Audience's Initial Position and How It Might Change.** As part of your planning, project what you would regard as acceptable audience outcomes for your argument. Think about the degree of common ground you initially share with your audience, because it is then easier to imagine audience change. There are several possibilities of initial audience positions and possible changes or outcomes.

You may be writing for a *friendly* audience that is in near or total agreement with you from the outset. The planned outcome is to *confirm this audience's beliefs and strengthen its commitment.* You can be straightforward with this audience, addressing it directly and openly with the claim at the beginning, supported with evidence and warrants that it can accept. Political rallies, religious sermons, and public demonstrations by special-interest groups, such as civil rights or pro-life groups, all serve to make members more strongly committed to their original beliefs. When you write for a friendly audience, you will achieve the same effect.

Another type of audience either *mildly agrees* with you or *mildly opposes* you. This audience may possess no clear reasons for its tendencies or beliefs. Possible outcomes in this case usually include (1) *final agreement* with you, (2) a *new interest* in the issue and a commitment to work out a position on it, or (3) a *tentative decision* to accept what seems to be true for now. To establish common ground with this type of audience, get to the point quickly, and use support and warrants that will establish connections.

Other audiences may be *neutral* on your issue, uncommitted and uninterested in how it is resolved. Your aim will be to *change the level of their indifference* and encourage them to take a position. You may only be able to get their attention or raise their level of consciousness. As with other audiences, you will establish common ground with a neutral audience by analyzing its needs and by appealing to those needs.

A *hostile* audience that disagrees with you may be closed to the idea of change, at least at first. Anticipated outcomes for such audiences might include *avoiding more hostility* and *getting people to listen and consider possible alternative views.* Rogerian argument (see Chapter 11) or a delayed claim may be necessary to get such an audience to listen at all. It is always possible that a hostile audience might *change its mind* or at least *compromise.* If all else fails, sometimes you can get a hostile audience to *agree to disagree,* which is much better than increasing the hostility.

Think of your relationship with your audience as if it were plotted on a sliding scale. At one end are the people who agree with you, and at the other end are those who disagree. In the middle is the neutral audience. Other mildly hostile or mildly favorable audiences are positioned at various points in between. Your knowledge of human nature and argument theory will help you plan strategies of argument that will address all these audience types.

▲ **Identify the Audience's Discourse Community.** An audience's affiliations can help define its nature. Specialized groups that share subject matter, background, experience, values, and a common language (including specialized and technical vocabulary, jargon, or slang) are known as *discourse communities.* Common ground automatically exists among members of a discourse community because they understand one another easily.

Consider discourse communities composed of all scientists, all engineers, or all mathematicians. Their common background, training, language, and knowledge make it easier for them to connect, achieve common ground, and work toward conclusions. The discourse community itself, in fact, creates some of the common ground necessary for successful academic inquiry or for other types of argument.

You are a member of the university or college discourse community where you attend classes. This community is characterized by reasonable and educated people who share common background and interests that enable them to inquire into matters that are still at issue. You are also a member of the discourse community in your argument class, which has a common vocabulary and common tasks and assignments. Outsiders visiting your class would not be members of this community in the same way that you and your classmates are.

What other discourse communities do you belong to? How do the discourse communities in your home, among your friends, and at work differ from your university and argument class discourse communities? For some students, the differences are considerable. The strategies for connecting with others, building common ground, and arguing within the context of each of your discourse communities can vary considerably. With some reflection, you will be able to think of examples of the ways you have analyzed and adapted to each of them already. You can improve your natural ability to analyze and adapt to audiences by learning some conscious strategies for analyzing and adapting to both familiar and unfamiliar audiences.

ANALYZING A FAMILIAR AUDIENCE

At an early stage in the writing process, you need to answer certain key questions about your audience. To get this information, you may simply ask members of your audience some questions. Asking questions isn't always possible or advisable, however. More often, you will have to obtain your own answers by studying the audience and doing research.

The following list presents thirteen questions to ask about a familiar audience. You do not have to answer every question about every audience. You may need to add a question or two, depending on your audience. Answer questions that are suggested by the particular rhetorical situation for your argument. For example, the age range of the audience might be a factor to consider if you are writing about how to live a successful life; the diversity of the class might be important if you are writing about racial issues; or class member interests, particularly outdoor interests, might be useful to know if you are writing about the environment.

As you read through the audience analysis questions, imagine that you are continuing to work on the argument paper on the topic of jury trials. Recall that your claim is, *Juries need pretrial training in order to make competent judgments.* The information that you uncover about your audience follows each question.

1. Describe the audience in general. Who are its members? What do you have in common with them?

Example: My audience is my argument class. We have common educational goals, language, assignments, campus interests, and experiences.

2. What are some of the demographics of the group? Consider size, age, gender, nationality, education, and professional status.

Example: Two-thirds of the twenty-four students are eighteen to twenty years old, and one-third are over thirty. Fifty-eight percent are female, and 42 percent are male. Slightly less than half are white; about a third are black, Hispanic, and Asian; and the rest are international students. About three-fourths are freshman and sophomores, and the rest are upperclassmen. More than half of the class works at part-time outside jobs. Two have full-time professions in insurance and sales.

3. What are some of their organizational affiliations? Consider political parties, religion, social and living groups, and economic status.

Example: Roughly half say they are Democrats and half Republicans. Three say they are Libertarians. Fifty percent say they attend Christian churches, 20 percent are Jewish, and the rest either are Muslim or Hindu or say they are not religious. Four belong to fraternities or sororities, a few live in the dorms, and the rest live at home or in apartments. Most are in the middle or lower-middle class with aspirations to graduate, get better jobs, and move up.

4. What are their interests? Include outside interests, reading material, and perhaps majors.

Example: The group lists the following interests and activities: sports, movies, television, exercise and fitness, camping and hiking, attending lectures, repairing and driving cars, listening to music, reading local newspapers, and reading newsmagazines. They are all college students. Five are in engineering, six are in business, one is in nursing, and the rest are in humanities and social sciences.

5. What is their present position on your issue? What audience outcomes can you anticipate?

Example: My issue is jury trials, and my claim is, *Juries need pretrial training in order to make competent judgments.* Most members of the class have not thought about this issue and either are neutral or mildly agree. A show of hands reveals that five think juries need more training, fifteen don't know, and four favor the status quo. I can expect the neutral and status quo members to become interested and perhaps even agree. I can expect the others to agree more strongly than they do now.

6. Will they interpret the issue in the same way you have?

Example: This issue comes from a local event, and some class members may see a double-jeopardy issue or some other issue emerging from it. I will have to focus their attention on my issue and make it important to them.

7. How significant is your issue to the audience? Will it touch their lives or remain theoretical for them?

Example: This is a personally significant issue for the people planning to be lawyers. It has some personal significance for most of the others also because everyone who votes is a potential jury member. The international students will have interest in it, depending on their background and experience. I need to find out what their experiences have been.

8. Are there any obstacles that will prevent your audience from accepting your claim as soon as you state it?

Example: Part of this audience believes that juries are always effective and need no improvement. I will have to challenge that idea.

9. How involved are audience members in the ongoing conversation about the issue? Will they require background and definitions? Are they knowledgeable enough to contemplate policy change?

Example: Ninety percent know about the recent local case in which the jury made a poor judgment because of ignorance of procedures. Half of the class members have been called for jury duty, and two have served. Three intend to go to law school and have considerable background and interest in juries. This audience knows enough to think about policy changes.

10. What is the attitude of your audience toward you?

Example: I think I have a friendly audience, and I am an insider, a part of it. We have established an open atmosphere in this class, and there are no personal hostilities that I can see. We share the same discourse community.

11. What beliefs and values do you and your audience share?

Example: In regard to my issue, we all value trial by jury, a job well done, and education.

12. What motivates your audience? What are its members' goals and aims?

Example: The people in my audience would be motivated to do a good job if they were on a jury.

13. What argument style will work best with your audience?

Example: I don't want to debate this issue. I would like to get consensus and a sense of cooperation instead. In fact, I picked this issue because it is one

1. *Survival needs:* food, warmth, and shelter; physical safety
2. *Health:* physical well-being, strength, endurance, energy; mental stability, optimism
3. *Financial well-being:* accumulation of wealth; increased earning capacity; lower costs and expenses; financial security
4. *Affection and friendship:* identification in a group; being accepted, liked, loved; being attractive to others; having others as friends or objects of affection
5. *Respect and esteem of others:* having the approval of others, having status in a group, being admired, fame
6. *Self-esteem:* meeting one's own standards in such virtues as courage, fairness, honesty, generosity, good judgment, and compassion; meeting self-accepted obligations of one's role as employee, child or parent, citizen, member of an organization
7. *New experience:* travel; change in employment or location; new hobbies or leisure activities; new food or consumer products; variety in friends and acquaintances
8. *Self-actualization:* developing one's potential in skills and abilities; achieving ambitions; being creative; gaining the power to influence events and other people
9. *Convenience:* conserving time or energy; the ease with which the other motives can be satisfied

BOX 8.2   Needs and Values That Motivate Most Audiences

that people will probably not fight about. I want to use examples that will appeal to my audience's experiences. I am willing to negotiate or qualify my conclusion if the class members who critique my paper have trouble with it.

Go through these questions, and try to answer them for your potential audience at an early stage of the writing process. To help you answer questions 11 and 12 about values and motives, refer to Box 8.2.[2]

CONSTRUCTING AN UNFAMILIAR AUDIENCE

Sometimes you will not be able to gather direct information about your audience because it will be unfamiliar to you and unavailable for study. In this case, you will need to draw on your past experience for audience analysis. To do so you will

---

[2]The list in Box 8.2 is based on Abraham Maslow's hierarchy of needs and motives from his book *Motion and Personality*, expanded by James A. Wood in *Speaking Effectively* (New York: Random House, 1988), pp. 203–204. Used with permission.

have to imagine a particular kind of audience, a *universal audience,* and write for it when you cannot get direct audience information.

Chaim Perelman, who has written extensively about the difficulty of identifying the qualities of audiences with certainty, has developed the concept of the universal audience.[3] He suggests planning an argument for a composite audience that has individual differences but also important common qualities. This universal audience is educated, reasonable, normal, adult, and willing to listen. Every arguer constructs the universal audience from his or her own past experience, and consequently the concept of the universal audience varies somewhat from individual to individual and culture to culture.

The construct of the universal audience can be useful when you write argument and other papers for your other college classes. It is especially useful when the audience is largely unknown and you cannot obtain much information about it. Imagine writing for a universal audience on those occasions. Your professors and classmates as a group possess the general qualities of this audience.

It is also useful to try to construct an unfamiliar audience's possible initial position on your issue. When you do not know your audience's position, it is best to imagine it as neutral to mildly opposed to your views and direct your argument with that in mind. Imagining an unfamiliar audience as either hostile or friendly can lead to extreme positions that may cause the argument to fail. Imagining the audience as neutral or mildly opposed ensures an even tone to the argument that promotes audience interest and receptivity. The following excerpt from a speech report illustrates some of the problems that were created when the speaker assumed total agreement from the audience. Notice that the author, who describes himself as an audience member, is obviously different from the audience members imagined by the speaker. How is he different? What is the effect? What changes could this speaker make to create better common ground with all of her audience members? Consider what this speaker might have done differently if she had imagined a neutral or mildly opposed audience instead of a strongly friendly audience.

> I am listening to a lecture by Helen Caldicott, the environmental activist. Dr. Caldicott is in top form, holding forth with her usual bracing mixture of caustic wit and prophetical urgency. All around me, an audience of the faithful is responding with camp-meeting fervor, cheering her on as she itemizes a familiar checklist of impending calamities: acid rain, global warming, endangered species.
>
> She has even come up with a fresh wrinkle on one of the standard environmental horrors: nuclear energy. Did we know, she asks, that nuclear energy is producing scores of anencephalic births in the industrial shantytowns along the Mexican border? "Every time you turn on an electric light," she admonishes us, "you are making another brainless baby."
>
> Dr. Caldicott's presentation is meant to instill unease. In my case, she is succeeding, though not in the way she intends. She is making me worry, as so many of my fellow environmentalists have begun to make me worry—not simply for the fate of the Earth, but for the fate of this movement on which so much

---

[3]See Perelman and Olbrechts-Tyteca, *The New Rhetoric,* for additional details on the universal audience.

depends. As much as I want to endorse what I hear, Dr. Caldicott's effort to shock and shame just isn't taking. I am as sympathetic a listener as she can expect to find, yet rather than collapsing into self-castigation, as I once might have, I find myself going numb.

Is it possible that green guilt, the mainstay of the movement, has lost its ethical sting?

Despite my reservations, I do my best to go along with what Dr. Caldicott has to say—even though I suspect (as I think most of her audience does) that there is no connection between light bulbs and brainless babies.[4]

USING INFORMATION ABOUT YOUR AUDIENCE

When you complete your analysis of your audience, you need to go back through the information you have gathered and consciously decide which audience characteristics to appeal to in your paper. As an example, look back through the audience analysis of the argument class that was done for you. Suppose that you are the student who is planning to write the paper about jury training. You decide that the general questions about the makeup of the group suggest that you have a fairly typical college audience. Its members are varied enough in their background and experience so that you know they will not all share common opinions on all matters. They do have in common, however, their status as college students. Furthermore, all of you belong to the same group, so you can assume some common values and goals. All of them, you assume, want to be successful, to graduate, and to improve themselves and society; you can appeal to these common motives. All or most of them read local newspapers or watch local news programs, so they will have common background on the rhetorical situation for your issue. You have asked about their present views on jury training, and you know that many are neutral. Your strategy will be to break through this neutrality and get commitment for change.

You decide, furthermore, that you may have to focus the issue for them because they are not likely to see it your way without help. They should also, you decide, know enough to contemplate policy change. You can appeal to their potential common experience as jurors and their need for physical safety, fairness, and good judgment in dealing with criminals. You can further assume that your audience values competence, expertise, and reasonableness, all important outcomes of the training system you intend to advocate. Your argument style will work with the group members because you have already analyzed styles, and yours is familiar to them. They either share your style or are flexible enough to adapt to it. You are now in a position to gather materials for your paper that will be convincing to this particular audience. You will develop reasoning, including

---

[4]Theodore Roszak, "Green Guilt and Ecological Overload," *New York Times,* June 9, 1992, p. A27.

support and warrants, that audience members can link to their personal values, motives, beliefs, knowledge, and experience.

You need to show the same care in adapting to the needs of a universal audience. Since this audience is reasonable, educated, and adult, support and warrants must be on its level and should also have broad applicability and acceptance. Odd or extreme perspectives or support will usually not be acceptable. An example is the electric light causing brainless babies in "Green Guilt and Ecological Overload." This example does not have universal appeal. Notice also that the universal audience, reasonable and well educated, should inspire a high level of argumentative writing. Careful research, intelligent reasoning, and clear style are requirements for this audience.

REVIEW QUESTIONS

1. What are the claim questions, and how can they be used to establish major and minor purposes in your position paper?
2. What are some additional preliminary questions that you can ask to help you develop your claim?
3. What is the purpose of the preliminary plan? What three main types of information are included on it?
4. What would you need to consider about an audience to discover how much common ground you share?
5. What is a discourse community? How does it help establish common ground?
6. What are a few items described in this chapter that you consider particularly important in conducting an audience analysis?
7. What is the universal audience? What are its special qualities? Why is it a useful idea?

EXERCISES AND ACTIVITIES

A. THE RESEARCHED POSITION PAPER: WRITING A CLAIM AND CLARIFYING YOUR PURPOSE

Complete the following worksheet by writing answers to the questions. They will help you focus on your claim and ways to develop it. Discuss your answers with the other members in your writing group, or discuss some of your answers with the whole class.

Claim Development Worksheet

1. Write an issue question to focus your issue.
2. Freewrite in response to the claim questions. They are as follows:

   Fact: Did it happen? Does it exist?
   Definition: What is it? How can I define it?
   Cause: What caused it? What are the effects?
   Value: Is it good or bad? What criteria will help us decide?
   Policy: What should we do about it? What should be our future course of action?

3. Read what you have written, and decide on a purpose. Write your claim as a complete sentence.
4. Which will be your predominant argumentative purpose in developing the claim: fact, definition, cause, value, or policy?
5. What is your original slant on the issue, and is it evident in the claim?
6. Is the claim too broad, too narrow, or manageable for now? Elaborate.
7. How will you define the controversial words in your claim?
8. Do you predict at this point that you may have to qualify your claim to make it acceptable to the audience? How?

B. THE RESEARCHED POSITION PAPER: PRELIMINARY PLAN

Use the following worksheet to help you construct a preliminary plan and a guide for thinking and research.

Preliminary Plan Worksheet

TYPE OF CLAIM PLUS REASONS

- Write your claim, write the word *because* after the claim, and list three to five possible reasons or subclaims that you might develop in your paper.

RESEARCH NEEDS

- Anticipate your research needs. What parts of your paper can you develop with your present knowledge and information? What parts will you need to think about and research further? Can you learn enough to develop the claim, or should you simplify it? What types of research materials will you seek, and where will you seek them?
- How much preliminary background reading do you need to do, and where should you do it? Would any of the reference books in the library help you? Or should you ask your professor or a librarian for a better source?

(continued)

PLAN FOR FIRST DRAFT

- How much background will you need to provide your readers? What terms will you need to define?
- What are your strongest opinions? Your best reasons?
- What is a tentative way to begin your paper? What is a tentitive way to end it?
- What original examples, descriptions, or comparisons occur to you now?

C. THE RESEARCHED POSITION PAPER: AUDIENCE ANALYSIS OF YOUR WRITING GROUP

Do an analysis of the small group of four or five individuals in your class who will serve as readers and critics of your paper from now until you hand it in. Your aim is to get an idea of how your audience regards your issue before you write. Your aim is to help your audience members become interested in reading your paper and perhaps even to change their minds. Do this as a group project, with each group member in turn interviewing the others and jotting down answer the questions on the following page:

Audience Analysis Worksheet

1. Describe your issue. What is your audience's present position on your issue? Describe some other perspectives on your issue, and ask for reactions to those ideas. State your claim and ask if there is anyone who cannot accept it as stated. If there is, ask why.
2. How significant is your issue to the audience? If it is not considered significant, describe why it is significant to you, and talk about ways you can make it more significant to the audience.
3. How involved are audience members in the ongoing conversation about the issue? What do they already know about it?
4. How will you build common ground? What beliefs and values do you and your audience share about your issue? What motivates audience members in regard to your issue?
5. What argument style will work best with them? A direct adversarial style? A consensual style? Why?
6. Write what you have learned from this analysis to help you plan your appeal to this audience. Include values and motives in your discussion.

The Results of a Careful Audience Analysis

"I'll tell you what this election is about. It's about homework, and pitiful allowances, and having to clean your room. It's also about candy, and ice cream, and staying up late."

Source: New Yorker, May 27, 1996, p. 115. Copyright © 1996 by The New Yorker Collection Robert Weber from Cartoonbank.com. All Rights Reserved.

CHAPTER NINE

The Research Paper: Invention and Research

The writing process requires both creative thinking and critical thinking. For example, invention and research are creative, and rewriting and revision are critical. This chapter is about creativity. It encourages you to think about what you already know and believe before you seek the opinions of others. As a result, your voice will become the major voice in your paper, and your ideas will predominate over those of others. Information and ideas from other sources will be brought in later to back up what you ultimately say.

The invention strategies presented here are appropriate for helping you think about and develop your ideas for your researched position paper. Use them along with the prewriting invention strategies that appear in Chapter 4. All of the invention strategies from both chapters are summarized on the invention worksheet on pages 289–290.

The first two strategies described here are logical thinking methods to help you expand on your topic. These are followed by a review of argument theory from earlier chapters to help you invent ideas and identify the parts of your paper. The last sections of the chapter will help you do library and online research, other creative sources of information and opinion for your paper.

USING BURKE'S PENTAD TO ESTABLISH CAUSE

Asking "Why?" will help you establish cause for controversial incidents and human motives. So will a systematic application of Kenneth Burke's pentad as he describes it in his book *A Grammar of Motives*.[1] In his first sentence, Burke poses

---

[1]Kenneth Burke, *A Grammar of Motives* (New York: Prentice Hall, 1945), p. xv. James Wood pointed out to me the value of Burke's pentad in attributing cause in argument.

the question "What is involved when we say what people are doing and why they are doing it?" Burke identified five terms and associated questions that can be used to examine possible causes for human action and events. Since establishing cause is an important part of many arguments, and especially of fact, cause, and policy arguments, the pentad is potentially very useful to the writer of argument. Here are Burke's terms and questions along with an example to demonstrate its application. The example describes a controversial art exhibit that political leaders tried to shut down by withholding public funds from the art museum. Controversies about public funding of art occur from time to time. This specific example took place in Brooklyn, New York, in 1999. When you have read the example, apply Burke's questions to your own issue to help you think about possible ways to describe its cause. The questions force a close analysis of an issue, and they will help you gain additional insight into the controversy associated with your issue. Burke's pentad, by the way, is similar to the journalist's questions *who, what, where, when, why,* and *how* except that it yields even more information than they do.

1. *Act: What was done?* What took place in thought or deed?

Example: An exhibit of works by modern British artists opened at the Brooklyn Museum of Art. It was controversial because it included some objects that are not usually considered art, including animal parts and an unusual presentation of the Virgin Mary. Some people objected.

2. *Scene: When or where was it done?* What is the background or scene in which it occurred?

Example: The primary scene was the art museum and the exhibit. The scene also extended beyond the museum to include the art scene, made up of art lovers, museum directors, and art connoisseurs who saw the exhibit as a bold and interesting experiment in modern art; the political and religious scene, made up of political and religious leaders who saw the exhibit as outrageous and blasphemous and tried to shut it down as a result; and the judicial scene, made up of the judge and the court that ruled against withholding funds and declared that act a form of censorship, contrary to the First Amendment guarantee of freedom of speech. Thus the long tradition of constitutional law is also part of the scene.

3. *Agent: Who did it?* What person or kind of person performed the act?

Example: The British artists who created the exhibit, and their sponsors who hoped to make money on it, are agents, as are the museum directors and art lovers, the mayor and the religious leaders, and the judge. Other agents include the individuals who visited the art exhibit and either liked it or did not and the other individuals who only read or heard about the exhibit but formed opinions about it anyway.

4. *Agency: How was it done?* What means or instruments were used?

Example: The unusual materials used in the art exhibit are part of the agency: elephant dung adorned with sequins, flies and rotting meat, obscene body parts glued to the Virgin Mary's gown, mattresses, buckets, and so on. The mass media were also part of the agency: numerous articles in newspapers and magazines either praised or condemned the exhibit. The availability of the museum, the funding for the exhibit provided by outside individuals as well as by the city, and the desire to profit from the exhibit are part of the agency, as are the power of the mayor's office to withhold money and the power of the law to declare the mayor's actions unconstitutional.

5. *Purpose: Why did it happen?* What was the main motivation?

Example: The artists' purpose was to extend the definition of art by creating new forms, to create more tolerance for contemporary art by creating extreme examples, and to stimulate critical thinking and debate about art. The artists and their sponsors also wanted to exhibit the art, improve their own artistic reputations, and make money. The mayor and the religious leaders wanted to shut down the exhibit because they regarded it as offensive and irreligious and believed that the public would not want to support it. The judge's purpose was to uphold constitutional law.

Notice that you can focus on a part of an answer to any one of the five questions and argue that it is the main cause of the controversy. Notice also that each of the five questions provides a different perspective on the cause. Furthermore, the answers to these questions stir controversy. You may in fact have found yourself disagreeing with the answers in the examples. As Burke puts it, "Men may violently disagree about the purposes behind a given act, or about the character of the person who did it, or how he did it, or in what kind of situation he acted; or they may even insist upon totally different words to name the act itself."[2] Still, he goes on to say, one can begin with some kinds of answers to these questions, which then provide a starting point for inquiry and argument. Apply Burke's pentad to every issue you write about to provide you with a deeper perspective on the causes or motives behind it.

USING CHAINS OF REASONS TO DEVELOP GREATER DEPTH OF ANALYSIS AND DETAIL

Another method of developing a claim or subclaim in your paper is to use chains of reasons to help you get a line of thinking going. You use this method quite naturally in verbal argument when you make a claim, someone asks you ques-

---

[2]Ibid., p. xv.

tions like "Why?" or "What for?" and you give additional reasons and evidence as support. For example:

You claim: The university should be more student-friendly.

Someone asks: Why do you think so? I think it's OK.

You answer: Because students are its customers, and without us it would not exist.

Someone asks: Why wouldn't it?

You answer: Because we pay the money to keep it going.

Someone asks: Why do students keep it going? There are other sources of income.

You answer: Because our tuition is much more than all of the other sources combined.

You get the idea. Imagining that you are in a dialogue with another person who keeps asking *why* enables you to create quantities of additional support and detailed development for your claim. Also, by laying out your argument in this way, you can see where you need more support. In the preceding example, you need to provide support to show what portion of the operating budget is funded by student tuition. You might also give examples of insensitive treatment of students and explain what students have in common with customers.

To chain an argument, repeat the *why . . . because* sequence three or four times, both for your main claim and for each of your subclaims. Add evidence in all the places where your argument is sketchy. You will end up with a detailed analysis and support for your claim that will make it much less vulnerable to attack.

USING ARGUMENT THEORY TO THINK SYSTEMATICALLY ABOUT YOUR ISSUE

Let us review what you have learned about argument in earlier chapters to help you think about your claim and some ways to develop it.

Analyze the Rhetorical Situation

Focus your attention on the total context for your argument, including the motivation for the issue, how you will write about it, and how your reader-audience will react to it. Use the rhetorical situation questions, and apply them to your paper.

1. What is the *exigence* (context, dramatic real-life situation) that makes me and others perceive this issue as controversial?
2. Who is the *audience;* that is, who besides me thinks the issue is a problem? How do these people view it?
3. What are the *constraints* (other people, events, affiliations, organizations, values, beliefs, or traditions) that influence the audience's perceptions of this issue, and will they bring us together or drive us apart?

4. What is motivating *me*, the *author*, to write about this issue; what makes me qualified?
5. What will be the purpose and strategies of the text I produce?

Use the Toulmin Model

By the time you have answered the following questions, you will have the essential parts of your paper.

1. *What is my claim?* Your claim tells your readers what you are trying to prove. Decide whether it would be stronger to place it at the beginning, in the middle, or at the end.

2. *What support should I use?* Consider how to include *facts, opinions,* and *examples. Facts* include descriptions of events you or others have observed, specific examples or accounts of real happenings, narratives of both historical and recent events, and accurate and reliable statistical reports. To be convincing, facts must be vivid, real, and verifiable. *Opinions* include reasons, interpretations, explanations, and ideas about the issue and the factual information used to support it. Whereas facts by themselves are comparatively lifeless and boring, they become interesting and convincing when they are presented along with explanations about their significance and relevance. Besides your own opinions, you may want to include expert opinion that can be summarized, paraphrased, or quoted directly in your paper. *Examples* clarify points, make them interesting and easier to remember, and in argument help prove the claim. Remember that examples can be real or made up, long or short, and that real examples are more convincing than hypothetical examples.

3. *What are my warrants?* Remember that support and warrants, taken together, constitute the proofs or lines of argument for your paper. Every time you use a particular piece of support, a warrant, usually implicit, will cause your audience either to accept or reject it as appropriate support for the claim. Write down the warrants that are working in your paper, and answer three questions about them. (a) Do they link the evidence and the claim and make it convincing? (b) Do you believe your own warrants? If you do not, make some changes. Argument from personal conviction is the most convincing argument. (c) Will your audience share your warrants or reject them? If you think it will reject them, consider the possibility of stating them and providing some backing for them.

4. *What backing might I provide to make my warrants more acceptable and convincing?* You may use additional support, including facts, expert opinion, reports, studies, and polls, to back up your warrants. You can do the same to back up evidence when necessary. Add material, in other words, to make your paper more convincing whenever you think your audience requires it.

5. *How should I handle rebuttal?* Not all argument papers include rebuttal. You will usually strengthen your own position, however, if you decide to include rebuttal. It is particularly important to identify the arguments on the other side and point out what is wrong with them when the issue is familiar and obviously

controversial. Your audience will be familiar with the other views and will expect your opinion on them in your paper.

When you plan rebuttal, here are some specific strategies to consider. Use your exploratory paper or do some background research to get a sense of the different perspectives on your issue. Then write your own claim and state reasons in favor of it; next, write one or more opposing claims and some reasons to support them. Next, study the claims and reasons that are different from your own, and attack their weakest features. What is most vulnerable—the support, the warrants, or the claims themselves? Name some of the weakest features of these other perspectives, and point out the problems associated with them in your paper.

Another strategy for rebuttal is to build a strong case of your own that undercuts an opposing position but does not specifically acknowledge it. State and demonstrate that yours is the strongest position available. Or you can always examine the opposition's major proofs and apply the tests of validity explained in Chapter 7. In your paper, point out all problems with these proofs. Remember that rebuttal should not offend the audience. Angry people won't pay serious attention or change their minds. Watch members of the U.S. Congress on C-SPAN television for examples of cordial rebuttal. They constantly engage in rebuttal, but they are polite and usually compliment the opposition while disagreeing. This courtesy reduces hostility both in the opposition and the audience.

6. *Will I need to qualify my claim?* If you believe strongly in your claim, you may want to state it as absolutely true. You must realize, however, that absolute positions will only be acceptable to people who already agree with you. To gain the adherence of more members of your audience, you may need to qualify your claim by using such words as *usually, often, probably, sometimes,* or *almost always.*

Plan Your Proofs

Here is a review of the types of proof. They represent distinct ways to think about and develop an argument. A variety of types in your paper will make it more interesting and convincing.

Logical Proofs.   Logical proofs (SICDADS) are convincing because they are real and drawn from experience. Answer all of the proof questions that apply to your issue.

- *Signs:* What signs show that this might be true?
- *Induction:* What examples can I use? What conclusion can I draw from the examples? Can my readers make the "inductive leap" from the examples to accepting the conclusion?
- *Cause:* What is the main cause of the controversy? What are the effects?
- *Deduction:* What conclusions will I draw? What general principles, warrants, and examples are they based on?
- *Analogies:* What comparisons can I make? Can I show that what happened in the past might happen again or that what happened in one case might happen in another?

- *Definition:* What do I need to define?
- *Statistics:* What statistics can I use? How should I present them?

   ***Proofs That Affect* Ethos.**   Proofs that affect *ethos* are convincing because they establish the authority of the quoted individuals. Answer these questions to establish your own *ethos* and that of the experts you quote.

- *Authority:* Whom should I quote? What background information should I supply both for myself and for those I quote to establish our expertise?

   Emotional Proofs.   Emotional proofs are convincing because emotion can strengthen logical conviction. Ask the following questions to include emotional proofs in your paper.

- *Values:* What values can I appeal to? Should I spell them out or leave them unstated? Will emotional narratives, examples, descriptions, and language make my appeals to values stronger?
- *Motives:* What do my readers need and want in regard to my issue? How can I appeal to those needs? Will emotional materials help?

PRESENTING STATISTICS IN GRAPHS AND CHARTS

As you gather your proofs for your paper, you may want to think about presenting any statistics you intend to use in the form of graphs and charts, particularly since computer software now makes this relatively easy to do. Graphs and charts can be especially useful when the statistical information is too cumbersome to include in the written body of your paper. There are many different kinds of graphs, but the most commonly used are line, bar, and circle (or pie) graphs. These three kinds of graphs can be easily generated through common word processing packages such as Microsoft Word or WordPerfect. The examples that follow present graphs of data from *The World Almanac,* an excellent source for up-to-date statistics on many subjects. *Bar graphs* are usually used when you want to compare measurements of some kind. The numbers used in the measurements are often large, and the bar graph offers a picture that makes the numbers easily understood. *Line graphs* are most often used to show a change in a measurement over time. Some of the different measurements associated with line graphs are temperature, height and weight, test scores, population changes, and profits. *Circle graphs* are ordinarily used to show how something is divided. For instance, a circle graph would be an effective way to show where the government spent its money over a specific period of time. Whatever kind of graph you use, however, you must be sure that it is correctly and clearly titled and labeled, that the units of measurement are noted, and that you report the source of the statistical information used in the graph.

   If you are writing a paper arguing the ineffectiveness of AIDS education in America (including North and South America and the Caribbean) and Africa, and you want to give your audience some background concerning the number of

AIDS cases reported in these parts of the world over several years, a bar graph might be the best way to present this information. Figure 9.1 provides an example.

A line graph is most effective when showing change over a period of time. If you are writing a paper arguing that the United States needs to take care of its debt, you might want to show the change in the deficit over a number of years to let your reader better understand the growth pattern of the debt. The line graph in Figure 9.2 shows this information.

A circle or pie graph can quickly show how something is divided up. If you are writing a paper arguing that people are largely ignoring the depletion of the ozone caused by automobile emissions, you might want to sum the percentage of the different sizes of cars sold in the United States during a recent year. A circle graph would be an effective way to present this information. An example is provided in Figure 9.3.

Sometimes the statistical information you need to include in your paper is very detailed and too lengthy for a graph. In this case, a chart or a table is usually

NUMBER OF AIDS CASES REPORTED IN AFRICA/MIDDLE EAST AND NORTH AMERICA, 1985–1998

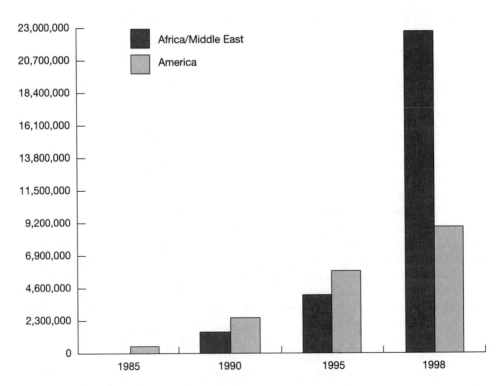

Figure 9.1   Bar Graph That Compares Large Numbers
Source: World Health Organization.

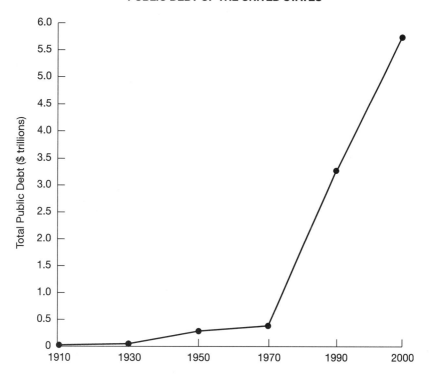

Figure 9.2   Line Graph Showing Change over a Period of Time
Source: Bureau of Public Debt, U.S. Department of the Treasury.

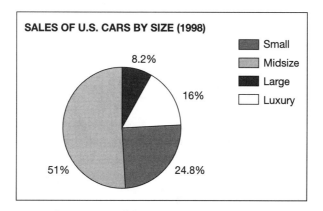

**Figure 9.3   A Circle Graph Showing How a Population
or Market Is Divided Up**
Source: American Automobile Manufacturers Association.

POPULATION PROJECTIONS FOR SELECTED COUNTRIES:
2010, 2020, AND 2050 (in thousands)

Country	2010	2020	2050
Bangladesh	176,902	210,248	212,495
Brazil	183,742	197,466	244,230
China	1,348,429	1,424,725	1,477,730
India	1,173,621	1,320,746	1,528,853
Japan	129,361	126,062	104,921
Mexico	120,115	136,096	146,645
Nigeria	161,969	215,893	244,311
Russia Federation	155,933	159,263	121,256
Saudi Arabia	31,198	43,255	54,461
United States of America	300,811	326,322	349,318

Figure 9.4   A Table That Presents Comparison Data
Source: Bureau of the Census, U.S. Department of Commerce.

recommended. For instance, if you wanted to argue for zero population growth, you might want to give some of the projected figures for populations of major countries. A chart would probably be the most effective way of presenting this material. See the example in Figure 9.4.

As a final check on the validity of your graphs and tables, check to see that nothing significant has been omitted and that the charts and graphs are accurately labeled.[3]

USING PROOFS AND SUPPORT APPROPRIATE FOR THE PURPOSE OR TYPE OF CLAIM

Some proofs and support work better than others to establish different types of claims.[4] The following are not rules, just suggestions for you to consider.

Fact and Cause.   Fact and cause papers call for factual support, including data and statistics. Consider also naming specific *causes* and *effects,* naming and describing *symptoms* and *signs,* using *induction* to prove a claim based on examples, using *analogies* to suggest that items coexist and share qualities and outcomes, and

---

[3]I am indebted to Samantha Masterton for generating these graphs and explanations.

[4]I am indebted to Wayne E. Brockriede and Douglas Ehninger for some of the suggestions in this section. They identify some types of proof as appropriate for different sorts of claims in their article "Toulmin on Argument: An Interpretation and Application," *Quarterly Journal of Speech* 46 (1960): 44–53.

using *definitions* that place items in classes or categories. Also consider quoting an *authority* to verify that something is a fact. Emotional proofs are less valuable than the other types for establishing fact or cause.

Definition.   Definition papers can be developed with *literal analogies* that invite comparisons of similar items; with *historical analogies* that suggest that if one thing happens, another thing will also; and with *classification,* or putting the item in a category with known characteristics. *Authorities* can be used to define it or support a particular view or interpretation of it. *Emotional proofs* are relevant only if the subject is emotional and you want the audience to accept an emotional definition—for example, "Modern art is rubbish."

Value Argument.   Value arguments require *motivational proofs* and *value proofs,* and they must be connected to the needs and values of the audience. *Authorities* may also be used to establish the value of something. *Definition* can be used to put an item in a good or bad category or class. *Analogies* that compare good or bad items or outcomes may also be used. Value arguments also require criteria for making value judgments. You will need to establish these criteria and describe where they came from. They may be your own, society's, a particular group's, or those of the universal audience.

Policy.   Policy papers can be developed with *literal analogies* showing that what worked in one case will also work in another. *Authorities* can be used to establish either the severity of the problem or the efficacy of the solution. *Motivational proofs* may be used to demonstrate how certain solutions or policies meet the needs of the audience. Table 9.1 summarizes the proofs that are appropriate for developing specific types of claims.

USING ORGANIZATIONAL PATTERNS TO HELP YOU THINK

Organizational patterns represent established ways of thinking about, developing, and organizing ideas. Chapter 10 will teach you to use organizational patterns to help you shape your paper when you are ready to write it. Now, however, during the early stages of your paper, organizational patterns can also be used to help you discover material for your paper and to help you think about it. Here are some of the most commonly used organizational patterns for argumentative writing.

- *Claim with reasons.* Write your claim, and think of some reasons that will support it. Add various types of examples and other evidence.
- *Problem-solution.* This is a pattern commonly used for policy papers. If you find yourself thinking of your topic in policy terms—that is, what should be done—consider describing the problem first and then proposing a solution that should solve it.
- *Cause and effect.* If you are trying to establish cause in your paper, you will find it useful to think in terms of both causes and their effects.

TABLE 9.1   Proofs and Support That Are Particularly Appropriate for Developing Specific Types of Claims

CLAIMS FACT	CLAIMS OF DEFINITION	CLAIMS OF CAUSE	CLAIMS OF VALUE	CLAIMS OF POLICY
Facts	Reliable authorities	Facts	Value proofs	Data
Statistics		Statistics	Motivational proofs	Motivational proofs
Real examples	Accepted sources	Historical analogies	Literal analogies	Value proofs
Quotes from reliable authorities	Analogies with the familiar	Literal analogies	Figurative analogies	Literal analogies
Induction	Examples (real or made up)	Signs	Quotes from reliable authorities	Reliable authorities
Literal and historical analogies	Signs	Induction	Induction	Deduction
Signs		Deduction	Signs	Definition
Informed opinion		Quotes from reliable authorities	Definitions	Statistics
			Cause	Cause

- *Chronology or narrative.* You may find it useful to consider your topic as it evolves over a period of time. This is a useful pattern to use for fact arguments, especially when you are trying to establish what happened.
- *Comparison and contrast.* If you are thinking about definition, it is useful to show what your subject is like and also what it is not like.

When you have worked through a few of the invention strategies described so far, you will be ready to do some research and get additional information from outside sources for your paper. Research is much easier to perform when you are fairly certain about your own thoughts and feelings on your particular issue. However, continue to interweave inventional strategies with library or online research as you go along. All of the strategies in this chapter, though described separately, should be integrated to maintain a high level of creativity through the information-gathering phase.

SUGGESTIONS TO HELP YOU WITH LIBRARY AND ONLINE RESEARCH

Searching for research materials in the library and online is a creative process that allows you to expand your ideas. Here are some suggestions to streamline your research.

Get Organized for Research

First, to help you find print materials, get acquainted with the library itself. Locate the card or computer catalogs and indexes to books and articles, the books and articles themselves (including those on microfilm), and the government documents and reference books. In addition, find out where the copy center or copy machines are located in your library. Finally, find the reference desk and the reference librarians who will answer your questions when you get stuck. Now, get prepared to write. Bring pens, sheets of paper, 3-by-5 cards, and something to keep them in. If you are going to take notes on cards, think about buying three different colors of cards to color-code the three types of information you will write on them: white for bibliography, yellow for all material you will cite in your paper, and blue for your own ideas. Also, bring money for the copy machine. If you make copies of some of your research materials, you will be able to mark what you want to use right on the copies themselves and thus save the time it takes to copy the same information onto cards. Acquire a yellow highlighter to mark this information.

To help you find electronic sources, locate your library's computers. If you are unfamiliar with accessing the Internet, see if your library offers free classes or printed material to help you get started. If you are connected to the Internet at home, you can also ask the librarians how to gain access to the library's online databases from your home computer so that you can conduct some of your research at home. You will be able to print copies of some of the articles that you find on the Internet and highlight the information you want to quote or paraphrase on the printouts themselves.

Learn to Use the Card Catalog or the Computer Index

Locate the books and journals that contain the articles you want to find in the library by consulting either the card catalog or the computer index. If your library still maintains a card catalog, you will find that each book is represented in it with three different cards: the first, with the author's name printed at the top, is filed in the *author section* of the catalog; the second, with the title of the book printed at the top, is filed in the *title section;* and the third, with the subject of the book printed at the top, is filed in the *subject section* of the catalog. The subject section will be particularly useful to you in the early stages of research because all of the library's books on your subject will be cataloged there in one place. You can often read the titles and decide which books might be useful.

Most libraries have eliminated the card catalog and now store the same information in a computer index. You use a computer terminal to call up the information you would find in the card catalog. Thus you may search for a book by author, title, or subject and look for a journal by title or subject. Computer indexes also permit you to search by "key word." Enter a key word that represents your topic, such as *clear-cutting,* and the computer will display all titles of the books and articles in the library that contain that word. Key word searches are the quickest way to find relevant sources for your paper. The key word search is a powerful and effective research tool. Read the titles of the books and articles as they appear on the screen to identify those that might be useful. When you have found a book title that looks promising, move to the screen that gives complete information about that book. There you will find all of the other subject headings under which that book is listed in the index. Use those subject headings, or key words extracted from them, to expand your search. For instance, you might move from the original key word, *clear-cutting,* to a new key word, *erosion,* in order to access more varied material. Computer indexes are user-friendly and will tell you on the screen how to use them. Follow the directions exactly, and ask for help if you get frustrated.

Use Your Preliminary Plan to Guide Your Research

Be specific about the material you seek in the library and online so that you do not get off course and waste time reading aimlessly. Use your preliminary plan (see pages 251–252), with its brief outline and description of your research needs, to keep you on track. Once you begin research, you may change some of your ideas about your topic. When you incorporate new ideas, change your brief outline so that it continues to focus and guide your research. Except when you are reading creatively to get ideas, every piece of research material that you copy on a card or highlight on a printed source should be related to an item on your outline.

Search for Information in the Library

You may want to find books, articles, material on microform (which includes newspapers and some magazines), reference books, and government documents in your library. Here is some advice on how to accomplish that.

To find books, you will need first to obtain the *call number.* You will find it listed with the book title in the computer index or the card catalog. Copy it exactly; find out where the book is located by consulting a directory, which is usually in plain sight in the lobby of the library; and go to the shelf where it belongs. If you cannot find it, look at the other books in the area. They will be on the same subject, and one of them may serve you just as well as the one you cannot find.

To find articles in the library, you will need to consult indexes to periodical literature, such as *The Reader's Guide to Periodical Literature, The Social Sciences Index, The Humanities Index, The Education Index,* and *The Engineering Index.* There are quite a few of these indexes, representing a variety of subject areas. They are usually shelved together in one area of the library. Take some time to read their titles and browse in them. Browsing will help you discover the ones that will be most useful for directing you to articles on your topic. When you have located an article, copy information about the journal and the issue in which it appears, look up the call number of the journal in the computer index or card catalog, and look for the journal in the same way you would look for a book. Be forewarned—some of the older issues of a periodical may be in bound volumes in the book stacks, some of the newer ones may be on microfilm, and the newest issues may be stacked on shelves in the current periodicals section of the library. You may have to look for a while to find what you want.

Newspapers, such as the *New York Times,* the *Wall Street Journal,* the *Christian Science Monitor,* and the *London Times,* along with newsmagazines like *Time* and *Newsweek,* are kept on microfilm in a special section of the library. Some books and many other journals are kept in this form also. When you encounter the abbreviations *mic, mf, mc,* or *mfc* as part of the catalog information for a book or magazine, you will need to look in the microfilm section. Machines are available there that enlarge the tiny images so that you can read them. Other machines enable you to print copies of microfilm material.

Indexes to newspapers and some magazines are available in the microfilm section as well. *Newsbank* is a particularly useful index for authors of argument papers. Check if your library has it. It collects newspaper articles from 150 urban newspapers starting from 1970 on almost any contemporary issue you can think of. Look up your topic in the *Newsbank* index, and it will lead you to a microfiche card that may contain 15 to 20 relevant articles. Indexes to large daily newspapers and newsmagazines are also available in the microfilm section. Look up your subject in one of them, and then find the articles they identify in the microfilm files.

You may also want to do research in other areas of the library, such as the reference room or the government documents area. The reference room contains a variety of volumes that provide biographical information. If you need to establish the credibility of one of your authorities, you can get biographical information from the *Biography Index, Current Biography,* or the various editions of *Who's Who.*

Government documents contain data and other factual information useful for argument. Indexes to consult to help you locate material in government documents include the *Public Affairs Information Bulletin,* the *Monthly Catalog,* and the *Index to U.S. Government Periodicals.* Look up your topic in each of them. Your librarian will help you locate the actual materials among the government documents.

Search for Information Online

Online research can be fast, it can take you to material that is unavailable in your library, and it can retrieve a large volume of resources to help you develop background and understand the controversy and perspectives associated with your issue. To search for information online, you need to know how to use search engines and library databases. You will also need to know some key words associated with your topic to help you search. You may want to consult a thesaurus to find a list of relevant key words.

Search Engines.   Use Netscape Navigator or Microsoft Internet Explorer to gain access to the World Wide Web. You can then use either of these programs to begin your search for information on your issue. Netscape, for example, offers a text line in which you may type an Internet address (known as a URL, or "uniform research locator") or a key word. Once you have typed in the information, simply use the mouse to click on the Search button to find the particular site of the URL or sites related to the key word.

No search engine can search all of the Web pages on the Internet. Most, in fact, find only a small percentage of the information that is available. When you have searched with Netscape or Explorer, you may then type on the text line the addresses of several additional search engines and metasearch engines to help you find still more information. These search engines take the search terms (key words) that you enter, comb the Net, and give you a search report, which is a list of titles and descriptions along with hypertext links that take you directly to the documents. The results that the engine judges most relevant will be at the top of the list. Different engines rank the results differently. Many simply count the number of times your search terms appear in the title or in the document.

Some engines allow you to use operators like *and, or,* and *not* to combine your key words in a more specific way so that the search results can be more relevant for you. By using specific key words and their grammatical variations and synonyms along with these operators, you can find more particular information. Some of the search engines take you directly to your subject, and others first present a directory of categories that are generated by the authors of the Web sites. They include subject guides (lists of categories like *science* and *education*) that can lead you to good general information about your issue as well as sites that serve as good starting points by offering lots of links.

Here are a few of the most powerful search engines along with their addresses.

- *AltaVista* <www.altavista.com> is large and fast, allowing advanced searches. It is case-sensitive, so avoid using capital letters.
- *Lycos* <www.lycos.com> also acts as a directory. Examine the subject guide that comes up on your search screen to see if any of the categories match what you are looking for.
- *Google* <www.google.com> does thorough searches, and it is highly recommended if you are looking for serious sources. It does not offer a subject guide.
- *Infoseek* <infoseek.go.com> will also search newsgroups and e-mail addresses. This engine may ask you to pay for further information once it has given you a certain amount.
- *Yahoo* <www.yahoo.com> is closely organized, making use of specific document summaries.
- *Magellan* <magellan.excite.com> reviews and rates many of the sites in its lists.
- *MetaCrawler* (www.go2net.com/search> is a metasearch engine that uses several search engines at a time. Try this if you are desperate to find a particular kind of information or a specific source that you were unable to find otherwise.

Some of the top search engines include *Excite* <www.excite.com>, *HotBot* <www. hotbot. com>, *LookSmart* <www.LookSmart.com>, *Snap* <www.snap.com>, and *Webcrawler* <www.webcrawler.com>.

Databases.   Your library will also help you gain access to periodical indexes that are available on the computer. They are called databases. Two of the most common are *Infotrac* and *Firstsearch.* You can use these databases by typing in subjects or key words and executing a search. A list of associated articles in periodicals and scholarly journals will be displayed on the screen, with the most current appearing first. Many of the entries include an annotation or a brief explanation of what the article contains. By reading the annotations, you can save time and be more certain which articles will be important for you to locate and read.

One of the most helpful databases available through the Internet is called *PAR* (Periodical Abstracts Research). PAR enables you to search for full-text articles. In other words, you may access and print entire periodical articles without ever leaving your computer. This is a very useful service, and it is worth learning if your library offers it. PAR is especially good for articles on current affairs published in general (and scholarly) journals after 1986. Other useful databases are *Contents1st,* which provides current, day-to-day access to content listings of over thirteen thousand periodicals, and *Article1st,* which searches the tables of contents of over ten thousand journals.

You can surf the Internet in other ways to help you get information for your paper. For example, the Internet offers a forum for you to discuss your issue with other interested people: you can send e-mail to addresses made available on Web sites, and you can take part in "live" chats in discussion rooms. If you are taking an English class in a computer classroom, your instructor might be able to give you the opportunity to discuss your issue anonymously on the computer with your classmates. Remember that e-mail and chatting are potential sources for your paper, so always generate a print copy of any exchanges you think are particularly interesting or pertinent. Your instructor may in fact want you to submit print copies of all electronic material you quote or paraphrase in your final paper, so it is best to keep print copies of everything you use from the Internet.[5]

Create a Bibliography

The bibliography is the list of sources you finally decide you will want to locate and read to add information to your paper. Make a bibliography card for each item of information you are likely to use, or you may write bibliography information right on the pages you have photocopied or printed from the Internet. For online material, make a note of the author's name (if known), the title of the article (in quotes), the title of the journal or book (underlined), the date of publication, volume and number, plus pages or paragraph numbers for articles (if available), the date you visited the site, and the full address (URL). You will need this information later when you assemble the bibliography for your paper, so write it all out accurately. You will not want to go back and try to find it again later. Add an annotation that includes a brief summary of the site's content and a note on how you intend to use it in your paper. Figure 9.5 offers an example.

Also, you should make a separate bibliography card (or note) for every print book, article, or pamphlet that looks useful and that you want to locate. A

---

[5]I am indebted to Samantha Masterton and Christine Flynn Cavanaugh for providing information about online research. Christine Flynn Cavanaugh also contributed ideas for evaluating online sources.

Wright, Kendra E., and Paul M. Lewin. "Drug War Facts."
<u>Common Sense for Drug Policy</u>. November 1999. 21 Apr. 2000
<http://www.csdp.org/factbook>

Use for statistics to support more treatment and less imprisonment.

1. "Treatment is 10 times more cost effective than interdiction in
reducing the use of cocaine in the United States."

2. "Over 80% of the increase in the federal prison population from
1985-1995 was due to drug convictions."

Figure 9.5   Bibliography Card for an Article from the Internet

bibliography card for a book must include the author, title, place of publication, publisher, date of publication, and call number so that you can find it later in the library. Add a summary and an explanation of how you will use the source in your paper. Figure 9.6 provides an example.

A bibliography card for an article must include the author's name (if there is one), the title of the article, name of the publication, volume (if there is one), the date of publication, the page numbers, and the call number or other description of location in the library. Add a summary to each card and a note about how you will use the source in your paper. Figure 9.7 provides an example.

When you complete your bibliography search, you will have a card or a note for each item you want to find along with its location in the library or on the

Gray, Mike. <u>Drug Crazy: How We Got into This Mess and How We
Can Get Out</u>. New York; Random, 1998.

Cite text to show historical failures and drawbacks of the current
laws and systems in place to fight the drug war. Author has produced award-winning documentaries and written three books, all
of which deal with investigative reporting.

Fairly objective. The author consulted various agencies, including
the DEA, U.S. Border Patrol, and U.S. Customs.

Wide audience appeal.

Call number:
HV
5825
.G6955

Figure 9.6   Bibliography Card for a Book

```
Massing, Michael. "It's Time for Realism." The Nation .
20 Sept. 1999: 11+.

Use for arguments against harsh drug laws and for better rehabili-
tation programs. Also use for statistics on drug crimes. Author has
researched historical and current drug war information for his
article. He's written a text on which this article is based.

Very objective source--written by a journalist/journalism professor.
Wide appeal.
```

Figure 9.7   Bibliography Card for an Article in a Magazine

Internet. You will also have written how you now think you will use each source in your paper. You can add author information and a general evaluation to this annotation later when you get your hands on the source itself.[6]

Your instructor may want you to create an annotated bibliography to help you organize the research for your paper. An annotated bibliography is an alphabetical listing of all of the sources you might use in your paper. Each listing is accompanied by a summary and a description of how you could use the source. Include more items than you are likely to use on an annotated bibliography, or in a stack of bibliography cards, so that if you cannot find all of the sources, you will still find some of them. An example of an annotated bibliography appears on pages 292–296.

Survey and Skim

When you have located your research material, do not try to read all of it. You will never finish. It is important, however, to understand the context of the material you quote and to learn something about the author. Survey rather than read books and articles (see Chapter 3). Use this technique to locate information quickly. It is especially important to read the preface to a book to learn the author's position on the issue. Then use the table of contents and index to find specific information. After you have surveyed, you can skim relevant parts to find the specific information you need. To skim, read every fourth or fifth line quickly, or sweep your eyes across the page in large diagonal movements. If you know what you are looking for and you are concentrating on finding it, you will be able to use these means to locate information quickly and successfully.

---

[6]I am indebted to Peggy Kulesz for the idea of adding annotations.

Read Creatively to Generate Ideas

Surveying and skimming may not always yield the understanding that you require, particularly if the material is difficult or dense or if you do not know exactly what information you are looking for. In these situations, switch from surveying or skimming to creative reading to help you think and get additional ideas for your paper.

Creative reading is different from some of the other types of reading that you do. For example, *leisure reading* is done for relaxation and pleasure. *Study reading* requires you to understand, learn, and remember material so that you can pass a test. *Critical reading,* which you learned to do in Parts One and Two of this book, has you identify and analyze the parts of an argument within an overall context. *Creative reading* enables you to form original ideas and think critically. Here are some questions that you can keep in mind to guide creative reading.

- What strikes me in this text? What interests me? Why?
- What new ideas and answers are occurring to me as I read?
- How does this new material fit with what I already know?
- Do these new ideas challenge any of my existing ideas? How? Can I reconcile the differences?
- What are the implications of these new ideas?
- How can I use these new ideas in my paper?

Using the Toulmin model to read will also help you find information quickly. You will focus on the important parts of a written argument: the claim, the support, and the warrants. The model will also call your attention to the different ways that other authors handle rebuttal. You may want to follow someone's example when you write your own.

Take Notes and Fill In Your Outline

Keep the most current version of your preliminary outline handy as you read and take notes. Then take notes to fill in your outline, and revise it as needed.

Either write notes on cards, or photocopy or print the material you intend to use in your paper. Whichever system you use, you must differentiate among the material you quote, the material you write in your own words (paraphrase), the material you summarize, and your own ideas. Code the different types of information by using different colors of cards, by writing with different colors of pens, or by labeling, each type of information. When you intersperse your own insights with material quoted from others, place your ideas in brackets [ ] to set them off. Always indicate directly quoted material by placing it in quotation marks.

If you decide to use copied or printed material, instead of writing on note cards, be sure to copy the entire article or entire section of a book and write brief source information on it. You only need brief source information on your note cards or printed sources because complete information is available on your bibliography cards or on your annotated bibliography. The author's name is usually enough to write on a note card, unless you are using more than one book by the same author. Then write the author's name and a short version of the title at the top of each note. Copy or mark quoted material exactly, and place it in quotes, so that it will go into your paper that way. You may omit words to make a quote shorter and more to the point; indicate where words have been omitted with three spaced points, known as *ellipses.* If you are following MLA style, place the omitted words in square brackets to show that you, not the author, have removed some words. Add the page number at the end. See Figure 9.8 for an example of a note card with a direct quote using ellipses and a page number.

Indicate at the top of the card, in the margin of copied material, or on your annotated bibliography where you intend to use the source in your paper. Use a brief heading on your preliminary outline for this cross-referencing. The example in Figure 9.8 shows one way to do this.

Paraphrased or summarized material should also be recorded carefully and accurately with the page number at the end. Since you are condensing or changing the wording of this material, do not place it in quotation marks. You will still have to let your reader know where you got it when you write your paper, so include on the card the author's name and page number. Also indicate where you will use it in your paper. Figure 9.9 provides an example. Figure 9.10 provides an example of a note card with the student essayist's original idea on it.

Arrange these cards as you go along according to the categories that are written at the top. Then place the categories in the sequence you think you will follow in your paper. The cards are now ready to work into your paper when you write the first draft.

EVALUATING PRINT AND ONLINE SOURCES

Good, reliable sources add to your credibility as an author, making your argument more convincing. In the same way, bad sources reflect poorly on your judgment

---

> Problems--current system
>
> Gray.
>
> "Not only has America nothing to show [. . .] , but the failed attempt has clearly made everything worse. After blowing hundreds of billions of dollars and tens of thousands of lives, the drugs on the street today are stronger, cheaper, more pure and more widely available than at any time in history."
> p.189

Figure 9.8   Note Card with Quoted Material

Introduction--statistics

Massing.

He quotes figures indicating there are more than 1.5 million drug arrests per year. Laws are discriminatory in that a large percentage of drug arrests are of black and Latino men. p. 11

U.S. spends $18 billion annually to fight the war on drugs. p. 14

Figure 9.9 Paraphrased Note Card

and detract from your credibility. You will need to evaluate every source that you use in your paper, whether it is a printed source you found in the library or an on-line source. Printed sources that are also to be found online should be evaluated as print sources.

You can evaluate each source by comparing it with other sources on the same subject, by analyzing the warrants, by applying the tests for the validity of the proofs, by determining whether or not the source in which you found it is biased, by looking up reviews, and by asking your professor or librarian for an opinion about it.

Be especially wary of the material you find on the Internet. Not much of it goes through a publisher or editor; in fact, anyone familiar with computers can set up a Web site and put articles or other documents on it. You cannot always be

Need for change

mine

If harsh laws for minor drug possession were reformed and if more money were spent on treatment of hard-core drug users, our jails would have more room for dangerous criminals.

Figure 9.10 Note Card with an Original Idea or Reaction on It

certain of a writer's authority or credibility, so you must be careful. Not all of the information on the Internet is reliable. Consequently, it is wise to use online articles and information sparingly unless directed otherwise by your instructor. Your paper will benefit from your using a variety of sources.

To help you determine the credibility of online sources, ask the following questions.

1. *Is the source associated with an organization that is recognized in the field?* For example, an American Civil Liberties Union Web site on capital punishment is credible because the ACLU is a nationally known organization that deals with issues of civil rights.
2. *Is the source listed under a reputable domain?* Look at the word after "www." For example, information found at <www.stanford.edu> has some credibility because it is associated with a university. Universities are considered reliable sources of information. Of course, any Stanford student, faculty member, or staff member could publish material online. The material would not necessarily be credible, so you have to review it carefully.
3. *Is the source published in an online journal that is peer-reviewed?* The journal will usually advertise this on its front page. For example, *Modern Language Notes,* published by Johns Hopkins University Press, is credible because everything written in it has been reviewed by a panel of experts to ensure that it meets a high standard of scholarship.
4. *Is the online source duplicated in print?* For example, material appearing on <www.nytimes.com> is credible because the *New York Times,* a nationally respected newspaper that is printed daily, sponsors it.
5. *Is the source accessed by a large number of people?* For example, a daily-updated news site,<www.drudgereport.com>, is read and talked about across the country.
6. *Is the source directed mainly to extremist, biased true believers?* You will recognize such sources by their emotional language, extreme examples, and implicit value systems that are associated with extremist rather than mainstream groups. Learn what you can about such groups, and try to determine whether or not they have a wide appeal. Your goal should be to find information with sufficiently wide appeal so that it might be acceptable to a universal audience.
7. *Is the evidence in the source stacked to represent one point of view?* Again, an unusual amount of emotional language, carefully selected or stacked evidence, and quotes from biased sources and authorities characterize this material. You can attack the obvious bias in this material if you want to refute it.
8. *Is the source sloppily edited, undocumented, or unreasonable?* Material that is poorly edited, infrequently updated, or old may be untrustworthy. Other red flags are inflammatory language and no identified author. Sweeping generalizations made without evidence, undocumented statistics, or unreasonable arguments indicate questionable sources for research.

9. *Is the source moral or immoral, ethical or unethical according to your values?* This is the bottom-line question that will help you differentiate credible from un-credible sources for research.

REVIEW QUESTIONS

1. What three inventional strategies discussed in this chapter particularly appeal to you? Describe them and explain how you might use them.
2. What are the five elements of Burke's pentad? How is the pentad useful in argument? What in particular does it help establish?
3. What method is suggested in this chapter to help you create a chain of reasons about your issue?
4. Several argument theories and models were reviewed in this chapter to help you review your ideas and think about them. Choose two that will be particularly useful to you. Why are they useful?
5. What is the value of making a bibliography, writing annotations, and writing how you might use the source? In what ways can this activity help you as you research and write your paper?
6. What three types of information might you write on note cards?
7. What should you take into consideration when you evaluate your research sources?

EXERCISES AND ACTIVITIES

A. THE RESEARCHED POSITION PAPER: USING BURKE'S PENTAD TO FORM IDEAS

Use Burke's pentad to analyze the whole context and particularly the cause for your issue. Write out your issue so that you will focus on it, and then answer the following questions. Use the information generated by these questions in your paper.

1. *Act:* What was done?
2. *Scene:* When or where was it done?
3. *Agent:* Who did it?
4. *Agency:* How was it done?
5. *Purpose:* Why did it happen?

B. THE RESEARCHED POSITION PAPER: USING BURKE'S PENTAD AND CHAINS OF REASONS

1. On your own, answer each of the five questions in Burke's pentad as it applies to your issue: What was done? When or where was it done? Who did it? How was it done? And why did it happen? Write a paragraph of at least 100 words in which you synthesize your responses.
2. Exchange your synthesis with a classmate. Read each other's syntheses, and write a thought-provoking question that asks for additional information about the topic or about the author's point of view. Return the paper to its author.

Each author should read the question and write a reasoned response of two or three sentences. Exchange papers again, read the responses, and ask another question. Continue this questioning and answering until time is called.

3. When the time is up, read over the chain of reasons you have developed for your issue. What surprised you? What do you need to research more? Where do you think your answers were the strongest? Once you have examined this particular chain of reasons closely, add to your outline or draft plan to indicate how this additional information might apply when you write your paper.[7]

C. THE RESEARCHED POSITION PAPER: INVENTING IDEAS

Read through the list of invention strategies on the following worksheet. They represent a composite of those described in this chapter and in Chapter 4. Some of them will be "hot spots" for you. That is, they will immediately suggest profitable activity for developing your paper. Check those that you want to use at this point, and complete them. There may be only two or three. Include the Toulmin model, however. It is one of the best invention strategies for argument.

---

[7] I am indebted to Corri Wells for this class exercise.

Invention Worksheet

Your claim:_____.

Begin to develop your claim by using some of the following invention strategies. If cannot generate information and ideas, do some background reading, and then come back to these.

1. Freewrite for five minutes.
2. Brainstorm additional ideas and details in brief phrases for another five minutes.
3. Make a list or map that shows the parts of your paper.
4. Explain to someone in your class or group what you expect to accomplish in your paper, or talk into a tape recorder about it.
5. Write your insights in a journal or on sheets of paper filed in a folder.
6. Mentally visualize and write a description of a scene related to your claim.
7. Make a preliminary plan. Write your claim plus three to five reasons. Add ideas for research and a draft plan.
8. Think about possible organizational patterns to shape your paper. What might work best—a claim with reasons, problem-solution, cause and effect, chronology or narrative, comparison and contrast, or a combination of two or more patterns?

(continued)

9. Think through the rhetorical situation. Remember TRACE: text, reader, author, constraints, exigence.

10. Use the Toulmin model to come up with the key parts of your paper. Consider the claim, support, warrants, backing for the warrants, rebuttal, and qualifiers.

11. Ask the claim questions: Did it happen? What is it? What caused it? Is it good or bad? What should we do about it?

12. Decide on some proofs that are appropriate for your type of claim. Remember SICDADS—sign, induction, cause, deduction, analogies (literal, figurative, historical), definition, and sign—and VAM—value, authoritative, and motivational proofs.

13. Apply critical thinking prompts. Start with your claim, but then make these recursive; that is, apply them at any point and more than once during the process.

Associate it.	Think about it as it is now.	Evaluate it.
Describe it.	Think about it over time.	Elaborate on it.
Compare it.	Decide what it is a part of.	Project and predict.
Apply it.	Analyze its parts.	Ask why.
Divide it.	Synthesize it.	

14. Use Burke's pentad to establish cause: act, scene, agent, agency, purpose.

15. Use chains of reasons to develop your claim through five repetitions of *claim, why, because*. Describe where you need to add evidence.

16. Make a more complete outline, notes, or list to guide your writing.

17. Write chunks or bits of your paper as they begin to form in your mind.

D. PAIRS OF STUDENTS: BECOMING FAMILIAR WITH THE LIBRARY

Visit your library with a partner, and begin to do research. This exercise will take roughly one class period if you and your partner work quickly.

You and your partner should explore the issues you have selected to write about in your position papers. Use the library to practice finding sources. To find your sources, work through the six library stations until you have completed the assignment. If you need help locating a source, ask a librarian for assistance.

Library Stations

1. *Online catalog or card catalog and periodical indexes.* At this station, locate books and articles about your subject by using the computer to do a key word or subject search; or use the card catalog to find books about your subject and one of the periodical indexes to find articles. Determine also how to find the call numbers for the periodicals if they are not listed in the computer. You will need to find a variety of sources that focus on your topic. Write down the call numbers of *a book about your subject, a current periodical* (one that has not yet

been bound), *a bound periodical,* and *an article that has been preserved on microfilm or microfiche,* such as one from a weekly newsmagazine.

2. *The stacks.* Next, go to the stacks, and use the call number to locate the book about your subject. When you find it, use a copy machine to make a copy of the title page or of the title page and the pages you will quote, paraphrase, or summarize in your paper.

3. *Bound periodicals.* Locate the bound periodicals in your library, and find the magazine article you selected. Make a copy of the entire article if you intend to draw information from it for your paper.

4. *Current periodicals.* Locate the current periodicals, and find the article you selected. Make a copy of the entire article if you intend to use it.

5. *Microfilm or microfiche.* Next, go to the part of your library that houses the microforms. Using the viewer, find your article, and write down one interesting quote from the article, along with the name of the source, the date, and the number of the page where you found your quote.

6. *Reference desk.* Find the reference desk at your library. Now you will know where to go to get assistance from reference librarians.[8]

E. THE RESEARCHED POSITION PAPER: CONDUCTING RESEARCH
Follow the steps delineated in the following worksheet.

Research Worksheet

1. Get organized for research: gather cards, pencils, money for the copy machine, paper, and a big envelope or folder. Review your preliminary outline and research plan.

2. Create a bibliography of ten to twelve sources. Plan to locate and use at least four to six for your paper. Include both books and articles, and write pertinent information on cards or on an annotated bibliography (see Exercise F). Add annotations that summarize and indicate possible use.

3. Survey and skim for specific information. Take notes.

4. Read creatively for original ideas. Take notes.

5. Make evaluative judgments about each source.

---

[8]This exercise was prepared by Leslie Snow.

F. THE RESEARCHED POSITION PAPER: WRITING AN ANNOTATED BIBLIOGRAPHY

Find ten quality sources that you think will be valuable for your researched position paper. Copy all the information you will need to cite your sources in the MLA or APA format (see the Appendix to Chapter 10 for information on how to do this). Survey, skim, and read selected parts of each source so that you can summarize them, and write brief statements of how you might use them in your paper. Alphabetize the ten sources, and type them up. The following example of an annotated bibliography is formatted according to MLA style.

Boatwright 1

Student Paper

Angela A. Boatwright
Annotated Bibliography
Professor Thorne
English 1302
20 October 2000

Human Cloning: An Annotated Bibliography

Bailey, Ronald. "The Twin Paradox: What Exactly Is Wrong with
     Cloning People?" 5 Sept. 1998. 21 Apr. 2000

   <http://www.reason.com/9705/col.bailey.html>

This article explains simply, in nonscientific terms, exactly what was done to clone Dolly the sheep. The author briefly explains the legislation that has resulted from the first asexual reproduction of a mammal. He explains what a clone would be and discusses the reasons why human clones could in no way be exact carbon copies of their predecessors. Clones would have different personalities and would be as different as identical twins. He doesn't feel it is unethical to clone humans because they would be treated with the same moral status as any identical twins or triplets. He states that as long as we treat cloned individuals as we would treat any other human being, all other ethical problems we have concerning cloning would essentially disappear.

   This article answers the questions I had regarding exactly what a clone would be like in relation to the "original model." It reinforces the belief I had that clones would be different people because of different social influences and environmental factors that have so much to do with the personality of an individual.

Boatwright 2

Butler, Declan. "Calls for Human Cloning Ban 'Stem from Ignorance.'" <u>Nature</u> 22 May 1997: 324.
This article highlights a report published by a working group on
cloning set up by the World Health Organization (WHO). This report
argues that much of the opposition to human cloning stems from "science fiction accounts," which have resulted in fear and ignorance on
the part of the public. It also explains that this fear and ignorance
has prompted legislators to act from "moral panic" rather than considered deliberation. The report concludes that the introduction of
an immediate ban on cloning would be unwise and counterproductive.
This report appears to have gone unheeded by the organization's General Assembly, a political body representing the WHO's member
states. The assembly adopted a resolution affirming that "the use of
cloning for the replication of human individuals is ethically unacceptable and contrary to human integrity and morality."

This report touches on some truths that I believe are important.
For example, cloning has become more of a political issue than an
ethical one. I will use this article to show that a lack of information is the biggest obstacle to a successful debate of the issue.

Butler, Declan, and Meredith Wadman. "Calls for Cloning Ban Sell
Science Short." <u>Nature</u> 6 Mar. 1997: 8-9.
This article acknowledges the need for ethical debate but states
that many scientists argue that politicians and the media are focusing on applications of cloning technology that are not even realis-
tically possible. These authors believe that human cloning is not
for tomorrow and may never be a practical proposition. There is also
a belief that medical ethics is unlikely to deter wealthy or powerful individuals from conducting experimentation out of the public
eye. This article also stresses that a ban on all research on human
cloning could prevent the development of lifesaving medical treatments. Cloning techniques could be used to generate skin grafts for
burn victims and bone marrow for patients undergoing cancer
chemotherapy.

I liked this article because it made the point that the public
is not frightened of all progress, just rapid progress. While I believe this is true, I had not thought of it in this way. This article will support the views of cloning proponents.

Carey, John. "Human Clones: It's Decision Time." <u>Business Week</u> 10
Aug. 1998: 32.
This article states that with the news that scientists had cloned
50 mice from adult mice cells, we now know that the process that

produced Dolly might be reduced to an almost humdrum process. The author indicates that cloning itself is only the tip of the iceberg of potential genetic manipulations. The article mentions how cloning technology might lead to manipulation that could produce superior humans. One scientist claims this is a major step toward regarding our children as acceptable only if they conform to the choices of our will. The article implies that cloning would be similar to manufacturing, with physical traits preplanned. Although many researchers claim there would probably be no public interest in human cloning, a business in the Bahamas had over 100 people interested in paying a fee of $200,000 or more for the chance to have a clone produced.

I will use this article to support my view of limits on cloning, based on the possible abuses the technology could allow.

"Human Cloning Requires a Moratorium, Not a Ban." <u>Nature</u> 6 Mar.
      1997: 1+.
This article begins with the statement that the history of science suggests that efforts to block its development are misguided and futile. This article conveys the idea that banning human cloning could result in the termination of research that shows so much promise in the realm of medical treatment, while a moratorium sends a public message that ethical considerations are important and need to be taken into account. The basic belief of this author is that we cannot stop the advance of human cloning technology through legislation, and the best we can hope for is to put a moratorium in effect until the education of the public can catch up to the actions of the researchers. The author believes that highly regulated human cloning will be found to be a tolerable way to proceed.

This article is very thought-provoking for me because it suggests that an outright ban on human cloning could result in unregulated research in private laboratories, which could be disastrous. On the other hand, a moratorium could give us time to weigh the benefits and risks and find a tolerable way to proceed.

Macklin, Ruth. "Human Cloning? Don't Just Say No." <u>U.S. News &
      World Report</u> 10 Mar. 1997: 64+.
This author believes that to justify human cloning, instead of looking for the benefits to humanity that cloning can offer, we should consider that no one has yet made a persuasive case that it would do any real harm either. She thinks efforts in cloning to breed individuals with genetic qualities that someone might deem exceptional is really no different from the "selective breeding" already prac-

ticed in democratic societies where, for example, lawyers are free
to choose to marry and have children with other lawyers. She uses
sperm banks as another example of selective breeding. She believes
that as a democratic society, we should not pass laws outlawing
something before there is actual evidence of harm.

I liked this article because it also discussed the fear we have
of cloning being used to create spare parts. While the author does
not believe cloning is a threat to human rights, she actually made
several points that caused me to consider just that. I think some of
her ideas are somewhat warped.

Marshall, Eliot. "Panel Urges Cloning Ethics Boards." <u>Science</u> 3
    Jan. 1997: 22+.
This article reports on a review of the system that guides U.S. policy on the ethical, legal, and social issues of the Human Genome Project. The report recommends that a high-level policy board be created in the office of the Secretary of Health and Human Services to
help develop policies on sensitive issues such as genetic privacy,
antidiscrimination legislation, public education on genetic risks,
and the regulation of genetic testing. The article also discusses
difficulties of the working group.

I plan to use this study as an example of how difficult it may
be to regulate an issue as complicated and controversial as cloning.
It makes me consider how effective regulation could be with so many
layers of government oversight.

Pence, Gregory E. <u>Who's Afraid of Human Cloning</u>? Lanham: Rowman &
    Littlefield, 1998.
This book is a comprehensive source of information on cloning. It
provides a complete overview, including discussions on the miscon-
ceptions, ethics, regulation, and arguments for and against human
cloning. This author is most definitely an advocate of human cloning
technology. He feels the discussion concerning the issue has been
horribly one-sided. He states that never in the history of modern
science had the world seen such an instant, overwhelming condemnation of the application to humanity of a scientific breakthrough.
His aim is to correct this problem of a one-sided debate over the
issue.

I will probably cite this book because of the wealth of information it contains. Although the author advocates human cloning, his
book is a fairly good source of material for arguing against human
cloning.

Wadman, Meredith. "Cloning for Research 'Should Be Allowed.'" <u>Nature</u>
    3 July 1997: 6.
This article discusses many of the state and national bills that
have been proposed to ban or limit clone research. The author feels
that this legislation is being based on fear and not fact. The article states that there are many concerns with this misinformed
legislation, including the example of one bill that contains three
different definitions of a somatic cell. The article discusses the
confusion surrounding the issue.

What I found most interesting in this article was the argument
by an influential member of the biotechnology industry who stated
that federal action to prevent cloning of human beings would be
preferable to a patchwork of state laws. I think this statement is
an indication that even proponents of human cloning believe that
legislators need to come together with a consensual decision.

Wilmut, Ian. "Roslin Institute Experiments: Creation of Dolly the
    Sheep." <u>Congressional Digest</u> Feb. 1998: 41+.
The man responsible for the experiments that led to the creation of
Dolly, the first cloned sheep, wrote this article. The creation of
Dolly was the exigence for this article. Dr. Wilmut briefly summarizes the experiments that he and his colleagues at Roslin Institute
and PPL Therapeutics reported. He then discusses the practical uses
of cloning technology in animal breeding. He explains some of the
difficulties encountered during the experiments leading to the successful creation of Dolly. He gives some specific statistics concerning his experiments. Finally, he explains his stance on the
issue of human cloning. He and his colleagues believe that cloning
of humans would be unethical. He also believes that it may not even
be technically possible.

This article is one of my favorite references because I was surprised by Dr. Wilmut's position on human cloning. For no other reason than my own ignorance, I fully expected Dr. Wilmut to support
human cloning. His statement that cloning of humans would be unethical held a great deal of importance to me. He states that similar
experiments with humans would be totally unacceptable. ■

CHAPTER TEN

The Research Paper: Organizing, Writing, and Revising

This chapter will provide you with the information you need to create some order in the material you have gathered so that you can now write your researched position paper. Specifically, you will be taught some ways to organize and outline, to incorporate research into your first draft, and to revise and prepare the final copy. Organization, or deciding on a framework of ideas for your paper, will be dealt with first.

USING ORGANIZATION TO HELP YOUR READER UNDERSTAND

Everyone has a natural tendency to associate or group ideas and to place them in an order so that they make sense and are easier to remember. You have probably already begun to do this with the materials for your paper. You may have made a preliminary plan, labeled note cards, and written some lists. Eventually, these activities will help your reader, who will understand organized ideas far more easily than disorganized ones. To illustrate this fact, here are two examples.

Example 1

The ideas and information presented here are a brainstormed list of ideas for a value paper that have not yet been organized. Brainstorming is one of the recommended ways to collect ideas for a paper.

Claim: Women have more opportunities for variety in their lives now than they had fifty years ago.

Women's movement.

Several causes for changes in women's opportunities.

Desire to satisfy personal ambition.

Comparison between women at mid-twentieth century and at start of twenty-first century.

Some women are dysfunctional.

Examples of three satisfied contemporary women: professional, military, homemaker.

Not all changes are good—signs of stress in women, men, children.

Women are now self-actualized.

Statistical data suggesting the variety of positions occupied by women in the late 1990s and early 2000s and in the 1950s.

Labor-saving devices, education, economy, and women's ambitions contribute to change.

A review of human needs and motivation and how they relate to women.

Improved opportunities for women.

The effects of the changes on men and children.

Analysis of the causes for the changes in opportunities for women.

Donna Reed and Ally McBeal.

How can this jumble of ideas and information be organized for an effective argument paper? Thinking about organization requires that you identify the *parts*, place them in an *order*, and establish some *relationships* among them. In other words, you must establish reasons for discussing one idea before another.

Example 2

Here the parts have been rearranged. The same items appear here as in Example 1, but they have been organized according to the following rationale:

1. The issue is introduced as a fact, that women have more opportunity now. This fact is illustrated with examples and statistics to focus the issue and get attention and interest.
2. Burke's pentad is used to explore causes for the changes: agency (labor-saving devices), scene (education and economy), agent (women and women's movement), and purpose (to satisfy personal ambition) are cited as causes.
3. The effects of the changes are explained and illustrated with examples.
4. The opposition is refuted, and negative perceptions are changed to positive values.
5. The value claim, that the changes are good, is stated and made more convincing with a quote.

Title: Improved Opportunities for Women

I. Introduction: *Women now have a wide range of opportunities.*

- A comparison between women at mid-twentieth century and start of twenty-first century. Example, two television characters who reflect social mores: Donna Reed (1950s) and Ally McBeal (2000s).
- Statistical data suggesting the variety of roles occupied by women in the late 1990s, early 2000s, and in the 1950s.

II. Analysis of the causes for the changes in women's opportunities.

- Labor-saving devices—freed-up time.
- Education—improved competences.
- Economy—requires two incomes.
- Women's movement—made women more aware of human needs and motivation and how they relate to women.
- Desire to satisfy personal ambition.

III. Effects of the changes.

- Women now able to meet needs for self-actualization in a variety of ways, some of which were formerly reserved for men.
- Examples of three contemporary women who are satisfied with their lives: professional, military, homemaker.

IV. Rebuttal: Some people argue that not all changes have been good and that there are signs of stress in women, men, and children. Actually, the effects they perceive as bad are good.

- The stress for women is good stress because they now choose what they want to do.
- Men are closer to their children because they share responsibility.
- Children learn to take more initiative and shoulder more responsibility.
- People made dysfunctional by the changes would probably have problems in any setting.

V. Conclusion: *Claim: Women have more opportunities for variety in their lives now than they had fifty years ago.*

- The benefits outweigh the problems.
- Quote from an authority about women's current satisfaction.
- No one would want to go back.

This is not the only organizational strategy that could have been used for this paper. The rebuttal, for example, could have been placed first. The effects could have been described before the causes. The value claim could have been placed at the beginning instead of at the end. Any one of these alternatives might have worked as well as another, provided they made sense to the author and were convincing to the audience.

Read the materials you have gathered for your own paper and think about (1) how they can be divided into *parts,* (2) how these parts can be placed in an *order,* and (3) what the logical *relationships* are among them. List the parts, tentatively number them to reflect order, and clarify the rationale for your decisions.

To help you plan the *parts,* keep the Toulmin model in mind. Your parts should include a claim, support, and warrants and possibly also backing for the warrants, a rebuttal, and a qualifier for the claim. Think also about the subclaims that represent the major sections of the paper and the facts, examples, and opinions that support them. Tentatively plan the introduction and conclusion and what to include in them. The usual functions of the introduction are to focus and introduce the topic, provide some background, and get the attention of the audience. The conclusion usually refocuses the claim through restatement and final, compelling reasons.

To help you think about *order,* keep in mind that the beginning of your paper is a strong position for arguments, but the end is even stronger. Put your strongest material at or near the end, other strong material at the beginning, and the less impressive material in the middle. Also, think about your audience when determining order. For instance, for a hostile audience, you might argue about women's roles by admitting that the 1950s were a good time for women but adding that times have changed and finally showing how the 1950s way of life is now impractical. For a neutral audience, you might want to present strong and interesting examples at the beginning to get attention and create interest. For a friendly audience, you can show how things are better right away and thus confirm an already favorable opinion.

To focus on *relationships,* use words that name the relationships you have worked out. As in Example 2, write the words *causes, effects,* and *rebuttals* into your plan to clarify the main sections and suggest the relationships among them.

USING ORGANIZATIONAL PATTERNS TO HELP YOU THINK AND ORGANIZE

For centuries, authors have used certain established patterns of thought to help them think about, develop, and organize ideas. This practice benefits not only authors but also readers, who are consequently able to follow and understand the material more easily. Some of these patterns of thought are particularly helpful for organizing the ideas in argument. The following list describes those most commonly used. These patterns, by the way, can shape your paper as the dominant pattern or can combine as minor patterns within the dominant pattern to organize some of the sections.

Claim with Reasons (or Reasons Followed by Claim)

This pattern takes the following form:

> Statement of claim
> Reason 1
> Reason 2
> Reason 3, and so forth

Set this pattern up by writing the claim, following it with the word *because,* and listing some reasons. Or list some reasons, follow them with the word *therefore,* and write the claim. For example, you may present the claim that we need a national health care program, which is followed by reasons: the unemployed have no insurance, the elderly cannot afford medicine, many children do not receive adequate health care. The reasons may be distinct and different from one another and set up like separate topics in your paper. Or you may have created a chain of related reasons by asking *why* and answering *because* five or six times. Also, some of your reasons may be used to refute, others to prove, and still others to show how your claim will meet the needs and values of the audience. Support all reasons with facts, examples, and opinions. You may use transitional phrases such as *one reason, another reason, a related reason,* and *a final reason* to emphasize your reasons and make them stand out in your paper.

Cause and Effect (or Effect and Cause)

The cause-and-effect pattern may be used to identify one or more causes followed by one or more effects or result. Or you may reverse this sequence and describe effects first and then the cause or causes. For example, the causes of water pollution might be followed by its effects on both humans and animals. You may use obvious transitions to clarify cause and effect, such as "What are the results? Here are some of them," or simply the words *cause, effect,* and *result.*

Applied Criteria

This pattern establishes criteria or standards for evaluation and judgment and then shows how the claim meets them. For example, in an argument about children in day care, you might set out physical safety, psychological security, sociability, and creativity as criteria for measuring the success of day care. Then you might claim that day-care centers meet those criteria as well as or even better than home care, and provide support. The applied criteria pattern is obviously useful for value arguments. It is also useful in policy arguments to establish a way of evaluating a proposed solution. You may want to use the words and phrases *criteria, standards, needs,* and *meets those criteria or needs* to clarify the parts of your paper.

Problem–Solution

The problem-solution pattern is commonly used in policy papers. There are at least three ways to organize these papers. The problem is described, followed by the solution. In this case, the claim is the solution, and it may be stated at the beginning of the solution section or at the end of the paper. An alternative is to propose the solution first and then describe the problems that motivated it. Or a problem may be followed by several solutions, one of which is selected as the best. When the solution or claim is stated at the end of the paper, the pattern is sometimes called the *delayed proposal.* For a hostile audience, it may be effective to describe the problem, show why other solutions do not work, and finally suggest the favored solution. For example, you may want to claim that labor unions are the best solution for reducing unemployment. First you describe the unemployment problem in vivid detail so that the audience really wants a solution. Then you show that government mandates and individual company initiatives have not worked. Finally, you show how labor unions protect employment for workers. You may use the words *problem* and *solution* to signal the main sections of your paper for your reader.

Chronology or Narrative

Material arranged chronologically is explained as it occurs in time. This pattern may be used to establish what happened for an argument of fact. For example, you may want to give a history of childhood traumas to account for an individual's current criminal behavior. Or you may want to tell a story to develop one or more points in your argument. Use transitional words like *then, next,* and *finally* to make the parts of the chronology clear.

Deduction

Recall that deductive reasoning involves reasoning from a generalization, applying it to cases or examples, and drawing a conclusion. For example, you may generalize that the open land in the West is becoming overgrazed; follow this assertion with examples of erosion, threatened wildlife, and other environmental harms; and conclude that the government must restrict grazing to designated areas. The conclusion is the claim. You may use such transitional phrases as *for instance, for example,* and *to clarify* to set your examples off from the rest of the argument and *therefore, thus, consequently,* or *in conclusion* to lead into your claim.

Induction

The inductive pattern involves citing one or more examples and then making the "inductive leap" to the conclusion. For instance, five or six examples of boatloads of illegal immigrants landing in the United States who require expensive social services lead some people to conclude that they should be sent home. Others may conclude that they should be allowed to stay. No matter which claim or conclusion is chosen, it can be stated at the beginning or at the end of the paper. The only requirement is that it be based on the examples. The same transitional words used for the deductive pattern are also useful for the inductive: *for instance, for example,* or *some examples* to emphasize the examples, *therefore, thus,* or *consequently* to lead in to the claim.

Comparison and Contrast

This pattern is particularly useful in definition arguments and in other arguments that show how a subject is like or unlike similar subjects. It is also often used to demonstrate a variety of similarities or differences. For example, the claim is made that drug abuse is a medical problem instead of a criminal justice problem. The proof consists of literal analogies that compare drug abuse to AIDS, cancer, and heart disease in a number of areas to redefine it as a medical problem. The transitional words *by contrast, in comparison, while, some,* and *others* are sometimes used to clarify the ideas in this pattern.

Rogerian Argument

You will be introduced to Rogerian argument in Chapter 11. Here is a preview of the recommended strategy for this pattern of argument. You first introduce the issue and state the opponent's position on it. Then you show that you understand the opponent's position, that you value it, and that you consider it valid in certain contexts or under certain conditions. Next, you state your own position and show the contexts in which it is valid. Finally, you show how the opponent's position would be improved by adopting all or at least some elements of your position. In other words, you finally reconcile the two positions and show how they complement one another.

For example, the issue of homosexuals in the military, each time it surfaces, results in particularly adamant positions on either side. Some military leaders fear people with a gay identity may exhibit openly gay behavior while they are on military duty, which would be just as wrong as straight people exhibiting openly straight behavior in this same situation. Thus these leaders oppose homosexuals in the military because they worry about how they might behave. Gay activists, by contrast, do not seek to exhibit openly gay behavior so much as not to be penalized for acknowledging a gay orientation. Rogerian strategy aimed at convincing military leaders to change their minds requires an opening statement that explains their position and gives reasons and evidence to show that it is understood and considered valid in certain circumstances. Next, the counterposition that homosexuals should be allowed to acknowledge their orientation is offered along with reminders that gay military personnel have served well in the past and that their behavior has not been objectionable. Finally, the claim is made that the military is improved by allowing gays and lesbians to serve openly because they are happier and better-adjusted employees.

Motivated Sequence

A common distinction between argument and persuasion is that argument results in agreement or conviction and persuasion results in action or changed behavior. The motivated sequence is a persuasive pattern that is used to motivate an audience to do something. You may find it useful when you want to persuade your audience to act. There are five steps. We will use, as an example, the campus issue that is a problem at some schools: insufficient numbers of classes for all the students who want to enroll.

1. *Attention.* First, create some interest and desire.

Example: How often have you tried to register for a class only to be told that it is closed and you must try again next semester?

2. *Need.* Heighten the audience's need to do something about this situation.

Example: A problem arises because you, like many other students, had planned to graduate at the end of this semester. If you cannot get into the classes you need to graduate, once again you put your life on hold for another half year. And what guarantee exists that the needed classes will be available to you next semester? The frustration may continue.

3. *Satisfaction.* Next, show that your proposed plan of action will solve the problem and satisfy the audience's needs.

Example: There is a way of dealing with this problem. Enroll in a nearby college, take the course there, and transfer it back here to be counted as credit toward your graduation. You will complete your coursework on schedule, learn just as much, and be ready to take that job you lined up at the time you agreed to start. You may have to drive more and complete some extra paperwork, but it will ultimately be worth it.

4. *Visualization.* Describe how things will be if the plan is put into action. Be positive.

Example: Imagine yourself six months from now with your diploma in hand, ready to tackle the real world, take on an interesting job, and make some money for a change. You'll be able to make car payments, move into a nice apartment, and put aside the pressures of school, including trying to get into closed classes.

5. *Action.* Finally, tell the audience what it needs to do to satisfy its needs and create the desired outcomes.

Example: It's easy to enroll at the other college. Call the registrar and start the necessary paperwork today.

Note that the motivated sequence includes the introduction and conclusion in its total structure. The other organizational patterns do not.[1]

Exploration

The pattern you used to write your exploratory paper can be expanded for a researched position paper. Recall that you explained the positions of those in favor of the issue, those against it, and those with various views in between. Your objective was to explain the range of different perspectives on the issue. Having stated these positions, you can now expand your exploratory paper by refuting some of them and by stating and supporting your own. You may want to use another pattern, such as the claim with reasons, to organize your own position on the issue.

---

[1]The motivated sequence pattern is popularized by Alan Monroe in his public speaking textbooks.

How to Match Patterns to Claims

Some of these organizational patterns are particularly appropriate for specific types of claims. Table 10.1 suggests patterns you might want to consider as promising for particular argumentative purposes. You may of course combine more than one pattern to develop a paper. For example, you may begin with a narrative of what happened, then describe its causes and effects, and finally propose a solution for dealing with the problems created by the effects.

Use organizational patterns to help you think and organize your ideas. The patterns may be too constraining if you start with one and try to fill it in with your own material. You may prefer to work with your ideas first, without the conscious constraints of a pattern to guide you. At some point, however, when you are finished or nearly finished organizing your ideas, move out of the creative mode and into the critical mode to analyze what you have done. You may find that you have arranged your ideas according to one or more of the patterns without being consciously aware of it. This is a common discovery. Now use what you know about the patterns to improve and sharpen the divisions among your ideas and to clarify these ideas with transitions. You will ultimately improve the readability of your paper by making it conform more closely to one or more specific patterns of organization.

TABLE 10.1 Appropriate Patterns for Developing Types of Claims (in descending order of suitability)

CLAIM OF FACT	CLAIM OF DEFINITION	CLAIM OF CAUSE	CLAIM OF VALUE	CLAIM OF POLICY
Claim with reasons	Deduction	Cause and effect	Applied criteria	Problem-solution
Induction	Claim with reasons	Claim with reasons	Cause and Effect	Applied criteria
Chronology or narrative	Comparisons and contrast	Rogerian argument	Claim with reasons	Motivated sequence
Cause and effect	Rogerian argument	Deduction	Chronology or narrative	Cause and effect
Rogerian argument	Exploration	Exploration	Rogerian argument	Claim with reasons
Exploration	Induction		Induction	Rogerian argument
			Deduction	Exploration
			Comparison and contrast	
			Exploration	

OUTLINING YOUR PAPER AND CROSS–REFERENCING YOUR NOTES

You have already been provided with a rationale and some ideas for outlining in Chapter 4. Some people find they can draft simple papers that require little or no research without an outline or list. They can later rearrange material on the computer until it is in a logical order. Most people, however, need some sort of outline or list to guide their writing when they are working with their own ideas or with material from outside sources.

Try making an outline or list for your research paper, and make one that works best for you. Think of your outline as a guide that will help you write later. At the very least, indicate on your outline the major ideas, in the order you intend to write about them, and add the ideas and research you will use for support and development. Read your invention and research notes, and check to make certain that all are cross-referenced in some way to the outline. Identify the places where you need more information and research. If you have gathered research material on cards, paper-clip the cards to the places on the outline where they will be used later. If you have photocopied or printed material, use numbers to cross-reference to your outline the highlighted passages you intend to quote. Work with your outline until it flows logically and makes sense. Pay attention to the parts, the order of the parts, and the relationships among the parts.

If you have the opportunity, discuss your outline or plan with your instructor, a peer editing group, or a friend. Someone else can often tell you if the organization is clear and logical, point out places where you will need more support and evidence, and also tell you whether or not the warrants will be generally acceptable.

Here is an example. The following outline is more complete than a preliminary plan to guide research. It would be complete enough to guide writing for some people. Other people might want to add more detail to it before attempting the first draft. It is the sort of outline one might take to a peer editing group to discuss and get suggestions for the actual writing of the paper.

Working Title: Is Technology Good or Bad? The Technophobic Perspective

INTRODUCTION

Value claim: Even though most people claim to be technophiles, many are really closet technophobes, and that may represent a desirable state of affairs. (Define technophobia as a fundamental distrust of modern technology, and give some examples, like getting the answering machine when you need to talk with a human, the constant updating and planned obsolescence of modern computers, and automated teller machines and credit cards that cause some people to lose control over their financial resources.)

(continued)

REASONS

1. Technology is advancing too rapidly, which causes some people to lag behind and resent it.

   - It's hard to learn the new ways and give up the old ones.
   - It's hard to adjust to constant change.

2. Technology is perceived as dehumanizing by many people.

   - Technology reduces human initiative.
   - New machines sometimes have a higher profile than individual people.
   - People forget how to relate to other people.

3. Technology changes the way many of us use our time, and we resent it.

   - We spend less time thinking and reflecting and more time engaged with machines. (Example: People who spend hours a day on the Internet)
   - We spend less time outdoors communing with nature and more time inside watching movies and television.
   - We are losing our sense of what is "real."

4. Many people become nostalgic for the way things were.

CONCLUSION

It is time for technophobes to declare themselves, and they should not be ashamed of their technophobia. It may lead to a healthy skepticism about technology that will help humans maintain their humanity while they objectively evaluate what technology can and cannot contribute to their lives.

Note that this outline is worked out in detail in some areas but not in others. The ideas in it so far, however, belong to the author. The peer group that critiques it at this stage would be able to identify the areas in which this paper is likely to need more development and would suggest areas for research. The author goes to the library and finds three relevant articles—about (1) students who spend too much time on the Internet, (2) a writer who likes word processing but does not like the Internet, and (3) a teacher who likes her old bicycle.

Figures 10.1 to 10.5 illustrate notes that this author has taken on cards to use in the rough draft of the paper. The notes are based on the essay that follows. The first card is the bibliography card, which presents full information about the source and a brief statement about how it might be used in the paper. The other four cards are note cards. They represent examples of the four types of notes authors take as they do research for a paper: the direct quote, the paraphrase, the summary, and the author's own ideas. You can begin to see the advantage of cards. They can be alphabetized, labeled, laid out to read more easily, and physically rearranged to fit into the parts of the paper. Cards are best for big projects. Highlighting with cross-referenced numbering on photocopied or printed research materials works best for simpler, shorter projects.

> Mednick, Johanne. "The Highs of Low Technology."
> Toronto Globe and Mail. 23 July 1993: 16.
>
>
> Use as an example of IV, nostalgia.

Figure 10.1   Bibliography Card for the Article by Mednick, with Annotation

> IV. Nostalgia
>
> Mednick
>
> "Perhaps my bike is representative of a world gone by [. . .]. My bike is certainly not built for speed [. . .]. It's built for taking time. It makes people feel relaxed."
> p. 16

Figure 10.2   Direct Quote (with ellipses) from Paragraph 6 of Mednick's Article

> II. Dehumanizing
>
> Mednick
>
> She says that her microwave and her computer make her feel that life is getting too complicated and out of control. p. 16

Figure 10.3   Paraphrase of the Ideas in Paragraph 7 of Mednick's Article

IV. Nostalgia

Mednick

She claims that people still long for the older, simpler machines like her old bicycle and the simpler way of life they represented. p. 16

Figure 10.4   Summary of Mednick's Article

IV. Nostalgia

mine

Examples of nostalgia for the old, besides Mednick's bicycle: wood stoves, old typewriters, old cash registers. People save these because of the ways of life they represent – they are still attractive to them.

Figure 10.5   Card with the Author's Original Insight Written on It

THE HIGHS OF LOW TECHNOLOGY*

Johanne Mednick

Johanne Mednick is a teacher who lives in Canada.

I have a wonderful bicycle. Most people refer to is as "the old clunker," an ancient   1
piece of metal the likes of which can be found in the dump or, if you're lucky, at garage sales.

*Toronto Globe and Mail, July 23, 1993, p. 16.

2   In other words, people trashed these things a long time ago. Mine is a souped-up version of the basic "no-speeder," vintage 1930 or '40—two large wheels, seat, handle bars, basket, bell and the simple mechanism that allows me to pedal my way to wherever I'm going. I go uphill and downhill, easily gliding past all the riders on racers and mountain bikes intent on engaging the right gear for the occasion.

3   It's not that I'm an Amazon bike rider or anything. In fact, I won't make it up those hills if I don't get the necessary run at the start. But I have confidence in my bike. It gives me power, and I cherish its simplicity.

4   What intrigues me, in this age of technological innovation (which is nowhere more apparent than in the bicycle world), is the number of people who stop me and comment on my bike. It's a regular conversation piece. "Where did you get that thing?" "I haven't seen one of those in ages." "What a great bike." I get all kinds of comments—the best one being from a motorcycle gang who cornered me while I was locking it up. They politely suggested to me that I wear gloves while riding to protect my hands. Maybe I should also don a leather jacket.

5   But really, what is it that people are admiring? Are they admiring me for resisting the lure toward mass bicycle consumerism? I must look like an eyesore pedalling behind my family, who all ride the latest model of designer-coloured mountain bike. (To them, I'm some sort of anomaly, an embarrassment not fit to be on the road.) On the other hand, maybe people are just genuinely curious, as they would be if confronted with a dinosaur bone. I never get the feeling that they think I'm crazy for riding something archaic when I could be fiddling with gears and having a presumably easier time of things. I believe that this curiosity runs deeper. My bike seems to touch a sensitive chord in people, and I'm not quite sure what or why that is.

6   Perhaps my bike is representative of a world gone by, the world before gimmicks and gadgets, accessories and attachments. A time when people thought in terms of settling into a cushioned seat, stopping the movement with their heel and travelling a bit slower than we are travelling now. My bike is certainly not built for speed, but who needs speed when I can coast along the streets, hold my head high and deliciously feel the wind on my face? It's built for taking time. It makes people feel relaxed.

7   When I'm riding my bike, I feel as though I have control. And I don't feel that way about most things these days. I don't deny that my computer or my microwave make my life a lot easier. I use these things, but they also make me feel rather small and, in a strange way, inadequate. What if I press the wrong button? What if something goes wrong? Maybe if I learned to understand these appliances I'd feel better, more secure about my relationship with technology. But frankly, I'm not comforted by manuals and how-to courses. Of course there are always "experts" I could go to who seem to know everything about anything. Relative, friend or salesperson, these people seem to breathe the latest invention and revel in ingenuity.

8   I just don't get excited over yet another thing I could do if I pulled the right lever or set the right program. Nervous and unsure in the beginning, I eventually adapt to these so-called conveniences and accept them as a part of life, but I'm not entirely convinced of their merit. I crave simplicity and I have a sneaking suspi-

cion that many people feel the same way. That's why they admire my bike
forts them and gives them a sense of something manageable, not too com
I'm not suggesting that we go back to a pioneer-village mentality. Бu. _
think it's important to respect that which is simple and manageable—no doubt
difficult in a time when more is better and new is best. I'm proud that my clunker
makes me and others feel good. It allows me the opportunity to relax and, at best
when I'm heading down the road, escape what I don't understand. ■

Now look back at the note cards in Figure 10.1 to 10.5 and the outline on
pages 306–307. Note that at the top of each card, the number and a short title of the
relevant subidea on the outline are recorded. Thus "IV. Nostalgia" refers to point 4
on the outline. Note also that the quoted material from paragraph 6 is placed in
quotation marks to remind the author that these are the essayist's exact words.
The paraphrase, or rephrasing of the ideas in paragraph 7, is written in the
author's words and thus is without quotes. The summary, also in the author's
words and without quotes, states the main point of the article. When all of the
notes have been taken on all of the articles, they can be stacked in the order in
which they will be used in the paper and placed next to the outline. The author is
now ready to begin the draft. Most of the material in the paper will be the insights,
observations, ideas, and examples of the author. Outside research material will be
incorporated into the paper to add interest and improve the clarity and credibility
of the final paper.

INCORPORATING RESEARCH INTO YOUR FIRST DRAFT

Use common sense in working your research materials into your draft. Your objective is to create a smooth document that can be easily read while at the same
time demonstrating to your readers exactly which materials are yours and which
are drawn from outside sources. Here are some suggestions to help you accomplish this.

1. *Use quoted material sparingly.* You want to have the controlling voice in
your paper. No more than 20 percent of your paper should be made up of direct
quotes of other people's words. When you do quote, select material that is interesting, vivid, and best stated in the quoted words.

2. *Paraphrase or summarize when you do not know enough to use your own explanations.* Use your own words to rephrase or summarize other people's explanations and ideas so that your voice is the dominant voice in your paper.

3. *Begin and end your paper with your own words instead of a quote, paraphrase, or
summary of other people's ideas.* The beginning and end are emphatic places in a
paper. Put *your* best ideas there, not someone else's.

4. *Introduce each quote, paraphrase, or summary in your paper so that your readers will know who wrote it originally.* Make it clear where your words and ideas leave off and where someone else's begin. Introduce each quote, paraphrase, or summary with the name of the person who wrote it. Consider also adding a description of that person's credentials to establish his or her *ethos* and authority.

Example: According to Johanne Mednick, a teacher in Canada, an old bicycle is better than newer models (16).

5. *Integrate every quote into your paper so that it flows with the rest of the text and makes sense to the reader.* Avoid sticking in quoted sentences that do not make much sense in the context you have created. Instead, work in the quotes so that they make sense in context.

Example: People have various reasons for preferring the old to the new. Mednick's reasons for preferring her old bicycle are clear in her concluding statement. In describing her bicycle, she says, "It allows me the opportunity to relax and, at best when I'm heading down the road, escape what I don't understand" (16).

6. *If your author quotes someone else and you want to use that quote in your own paper, introduce the quote by indicating who originated it.* Make clear that the quote is not your source's but someone your source quoted.

Example: Mednick declares that other people show a great deal of interest in her old bicycle. Strangers come up to her regularly and make such comments as "Where did you get that thing?" "I haven't seen one of those in ages" and "What a great bike" (16).

7. *Cite the source of the quote, paraphrase, or summary in parentheses at the end of it.* Further instructions for writing in-text parenthetical citations are given in the Appendix to this chapter.

Write all quotes, paraphrases, and summaries into your first draft so that your entire paper will be in place for smooth reading. The following three paragraphs show the quoted, paraphrased, and summarized material from the Mednick article worked into the first draft so that it is absolutely clear what is the author's and what is Mednick's.

```
Many people become nostalgic for the ways things were. Some
people keep old cash registers at their businesses to re-
mind customers of days gone by. Other people fire up wood
stoves to help them remember earlier times. Johanne Med-
nick, a teacher in Canada, claims that many people still
long for older, simpler machines and also for the way of
life they represent (16).
    Mednick uses her old bicycle as an example. "Perhaps my
bike is representative of a world gone by [. . .]," she
```

```
says. "My bike is certainly not built for speed. [. . .] It's
built for taking time. It makes people feel relaxed" (16).
    New computers and microwave ovens, by contrast, make
people feel that life is getting too complicated and out of
control (Mednick 16).
```

Notice that in the first paragraph, Johanne Mednick's entire name is used to introduce her material, and in subsequent references she is referred to as Mednick. Notice also that in the first two paragraphs, Mednick's name is used to introduce the material that is attributed to her. Since it is clear from the context where her material begins and where it leaves off, it is only necessary to insert the page number of her article at the end of the borrowed material. In the third paragraph, Mednick's name is not included in the text, and it is less clear whose idea this is. To make it absolutely clear to the reader that this is another idea of Mednick's, her last name along with the page number is placed at the end of the borrowed idea. The full information about this source and where it was first located will be placed on bibliography pages at the end of the paper. The reader who wants to know when and where Mednick published her article can refer to those pages.

Clearly Identify Words and Ideas from Outside Sources

Sometimes students mix their words in with the words of the author they are quoting and neglect to put the author's quoted words in quotation marks. The result is a strange mix of styles and voices that creates a problem for the reader who cannot easily sort out your words from those of the person you are quoting. First look at an example of this error.

```
Low technology can be a high for many people. A wonderful
bicycle that most people would refer to as an old clunker
might bring its owner considerable pleasure. Its two large
wheels, seat, handle bars, basket, bell, and pedals help
its owner glide past all of the riders on racers and moun-
tain bikes who are intent on engaging the right gear for
the occasion. People admire her bike because it gives them
a sense of something manageable, not too complicated (Med-
nick 16).
```

The problem with that paragraph is that the author has copied Mednick's original language from paragraphs 1, 2, and 8 without putting any of it in quotation marks. Even though the citation at the end of the paragraph indicates that the ideas are Mednick's, the reader does not know which words came directly from Mednick's essay and which have been supplied by the author.

Now let's examine two better ways to incorporate research. One is to *paraphrase the ideas in your own words:*

```
Not everyone likes new bicyles. Johanne Mednick describes
her old bicycle and the pleasure it brings her. She never
envies people who pass her by on new bikes. She prefers the
familiar comfort of her old bicycle (16).
```

An alternative is to *combine your words with the author's, but place the author's words in quotes:*

```
Johanne Mednick claims in her essay "The Highs of Low Tech-
nology" that she prefers her old bicycle to new racing
bikes or mountain bikes. She describes her old bicycle in
admiring terms. It has, she says, "two large wheels, seat,
handle bars, basket, bell and the simple mechanism that al-
lows me to pedal my way to wherever I'm going" (16). She is
often able to pass people on newer bikes because they have
to slow down to shift gears (16).
```

Avoid Plagiarism

As just noted, whenever you use quoted, paraphrased, and summarized material from other sources in your paper, you must indicate where your words leave off and someone else's begin, and you must identify the original source for all borrowed material.

Using other people's ideas or words in your paper without acknowledging where they came from or with whom they originated is a form of academic theft called *plagiarism.* It is regarded as an extremely serious violation in educational circles because it negates the whole purpose of education, which is to encourage original and analytical thinking. The writer of our first example was guilty of plagiarism by using a considerable amount of Mednick's language verbatim without indicating that it is hers. The source credit at the end of the paragraph does not justify using her words but presenting them as the writer's own.

online research seems to have increased the incidence of plagiarism in student work. Read the article "Universities Find a Sharp Rise in Computer-Aided Cheating" by Ian Zack that appears in "The Reader" on pages 562–564. Some students find it tempting to copy and paste information from Internet articles into their own papers without showing where it came from. Professors can usually detect paragraphs that belong to other writers, and they can easily go to the Internet themselves and find the material that has been copied. In other words, you are not likely to get away with this practice. The best approach, now that you understand plagiarism, is to differentiate between your ideas and those of others at all stages of the paper-writing process. This is why you were advised to enclose all direct quotations in quotation marks in your notes and to color-code your note cards to keep your ideas separate from the direct quotes, paraphrases, and summaries drawn from other people's works. Use other people's ideas and words in your paper, but acknowledge that they are theirs. Penalties for plagiarism can be severe, ranging from a failing grade to probation or suspension from college.

Document Your Sources

Some of the main features of source acknowledgment are explained in the Appendix to this chapter. Use the Appendix as a reference guide when you are working borrowed material into your paper and also when you are preparing the final list of the works you have used. These methods will inform your reader exactly what material in your paper is yours, what belongs to other people, and where you found the material in the first place. You will first be shown examples of ways to incorporate borrowed material into the text of your paper and to use in-text citations (page numbers in parentheses) to indicate succinctly where it originally appeared. You will then be shown how to prepare entries for the list of sources that you have used. This list will appear at the end of your paper. The list of sources in the Appendix may suggest resources for your paper that you have not thought of.

As you incorporate borrowed material from other sources, you will need to follow a system and a set of conventions that has been prescribed for this purpose. There are several such systems. The two that are taught in the Appendix are MLA style, which is recommended by the Modern Language Association for papers written in the humanities, and APA style, recommended by the American Psychological Association for papers written in the social sciences. Both give advice on how to acknowledge the work of other individuals in your paper and also how to give full information about these sources in a list of "Works Cited" (MLA) or "References" (APA) at the end of the paper. The Council of Biology Editors publishes the *CBE Manual,* which shows how to document sources in scientific papers in such areas as the natural sciences, chemistry, geography, and geology. Other styles of documentation are detailed in the *Chicago Manual,* the style manual of the University of Chicago Press.[2] *Chicago* style is followed in this book. No matter which system you use, be consistent throughout your paper.

Additional examples of incorporating quoted, paraphrased, and summarized material along with lists of works cited and references appear in the two student argument papers at the end of the Appendix to this chapter. Study the annotations in the margins of these papers. They demonstrate how quoted and summarized material can be incorporated into papers and acknowledged according to MLA style in the first paper and APA style in the second.

MAKING FINAL REVISIONS AND PREPARING THE FINAL COPY

Review Chapter 4 for additional information to help you write and rewrite your paper. It may take several tries, but you will eventually get a version of your paper that you are content to show to other readers. Seek the help of your peer

---

[2]Documentation styles are explained in detail in writer's handbooks. One handbook that provides information on all four of the styles mentioned here is Lynn Quitman Troyka, *Simon & Schuster Handbook for Writers,* 5th ed. (Upper Saddle River, N.J.: Prentice Hall, 1999).

a tutor, your instructor, or other readers once again, when you
[...] your paper as much as possible on your own. When you get to
[...] will think your paper is pretty good. However, a new reader will
[...] ways to improve your paper. So this is the time to put aside your
[...] others take a final look at what you have written. During this final
[...] ess, you and your readers can use the Toulmin model to help you
[...] revise the major elements in your paper.

1. Find your claim. Is it clear? Is it well positioned?
2. Check the quantity and quality of your support. Is there enough? Is it relevant? Is it authoritative and accurate?
3. Check your warrants. Are they likely to be acceptable to your audience?
4. Think about backing for your warrants. Would backing make your warrants stronger and more acceptable to your audience?
5. Focus on your rebuttal, if you have one. Does it effectively address the opposing arguments?
6. Consider a qualifier. Would your argument be stronger if you qualified your claim?

As you go through your paper these final times, make all the remaining changes, large and small. If you haven't done so already, write a meaningful title that reflects the content of your paper. Rewrite parts by using more evocative words, cut out anything that doesn't contribute to the meaning, add text where necessary, rearrange things if you have a good reason to do so, read your paper aloud to catch additional problems, and make all final corrections. You will finally reach a point where you are satisfied and ready to quit. Now it is time to prepare the final copy.

Type your paper on standard 8 1/2-by-11-inch paper, and double-space all of it, including the "Works Cited" (MLA) or "References" (APA). See pages 332–341 for further instructions. If you are following MLA style, leave 1-inch margins all around. Type your last name and the page number 1/2 inch from the top in the right corner. Repeat this on all subsequent pages. One inch from the top of the first page, by the left margin, type and double-space your name, your instructor's name, the course number, and the date. Double-space again, and type the title, centered. Double-space once more, and begin typing your paper. Attach the list of "Works Cited" at the end.

If you are following APA style, prepare a title page (if your professor requires it) on which you type a short version of your title and the page number in the top right-hand corner as on all subsequent pages. Drop down four spaces, and write the title, centered. Then double-space and write your name. Begin your paper on the next page with the short title and page number in the top right corner and on all subsequent pages. Then double-space and write the title. Double-space again and begin your paper. Attach the list of "References" at the end, starting on a new page, numbered sequentially.

Spell-check your paper if you are using a computer, and proofread it one last time. Correct all of the errors that you can find. Errors in a research paper damage your *ethos* with your readers. Careless errors communicate that you do not really value your own work or your audience. When your paper is as error-free as you can make it, it is ready for submission.

REVIEW QUESTIONS

1. Why is it important to organize the ideas in a paper? How does it help the reader? How does it help the writer?
2. What advice was given in the chapter to help you organize the ideas in your paper?
3. What are some examples of organizational patterns that you might use in a position paper? Name five and describe their main features or rationale.
4. How might making an outline or fairly complete list of ideas help you write the first draft of your paper?
5. What are some of the potential values of a peer editing session?
6. Describe the first draft. What should you probably include in it?
7. What are some of the things you should keep in mind when you revise your paper?
8. What is the purpose of in-text citations and the final list of sources?

EXERCISES AND ACTIVITIES

A. THE RESEARCHED POSITION PAPER: PEER CRITIQUE OF OUTLINE

Write an outline or a partial manuscript that will serve as a plan for your paper, and bring it to class. Organize peer editing groups of three or four students. Explain to the group what your paper is about and how you plan to organize and develop it. Get ideas from the others to help with ideas and organization and also with adding research.

B. THE RESEARCHED POSITION PAPER: PEER CRITIQUE SHEET

The peer critique sheet is a worksheet that provides a guide for critique and revision. Make a list on the board of all of the special requirements for a good researched position paper: a clear claim, adequate support, accurate documentation, and so on. Select five to ten items from this list that you believe are essential elements to consider during revision. Organize them on a peer critique sheet. The peer editing groups can now use these sheets to critique individual student papers and make recommendations for revision.

C. THE RESEARCHED POSITION PAPER: PEER CRITIQUE OF DRAFT

Finish drafting your paper, and then revise it. Bring it to class again to be reviewed by your peer editing group. The group should first read all of the papers either silently or aloud, and reviewers should make a few notes on the peer critique sheets created in Exercise B. Then each paper should be discussed, and members of the group should offer observations and recommendations for improvement to each author. As the discussion progresses, the peer critics may continue to add suggestions to the peer critique sheets, which should finally be given to the authors at the end of the session.

D. THE RESEARCHED POSITION PAPER: ASSIGNMENT FOR PREPARING FINAL COPY

Make final revisions, and prepare the final copy. Your paper should be 1,500 to 1,800 words in length. It should be double-spaced and use four to six outside sources. Use MLA format throughout unless advised to use APA or some other format. The two student papers in the Appendix to this chapter can be used as examples. The first demonstrates general format, in-text citations, and "Works Cited" requirements for MLA style. The second demonstrates similar requirements for APA style. Notice also that in both papers, the ideas that control the papers are the authors' original ideas and opinions and that the quoted and paraphrased material is used to provide support.

E. THE RESEARCHED POSITION PAPER: TOULMIN ANALYSIS

Write a one-page Toulmin analysis of your paper, and submit it with your paper.

F. THE RESEARCHED POSITION PAPER: SUBMISSION LETTER

Write a letter to your instructor, and submit it with your final paper. Describe what you like about your paper and what still dissatisfies you. Identify problems or passages on which you would like some feedback.

G. CLASS PROJECT: CONDUCTING A SYMPOSIUM AND PRESENTING YOUR RESEARCH

Present your researched position paper to the class as part of a symposium.

1. Write a 250-word abstract of your paper. State the claim, the main points made about it, and some of the evidence. Your abstract will take two to three minutes to read or to explain to the class.

2. Organize groups around the same or related topics. The best group size is five to seven students with a moderator. The moderator calls on the students in the group to present the abstracts of their research papers.

3. Each set of papers is followed by a five- to ten-minute question-and-answer period. Two sets of papers can usually be presented in a class period. Thus most classes can complete the symposium activity in two class periods.

[handwritten annotations] one page double space / Give some evidence / 2 - 3 minutes

How to Document Sources Using MLA and APA Styles

The following material will demonstrate how to use in-text citations to show your readers exactly what material you have included in your paper from outside sources. It will then show how to prepare a final list of sources with publication details at the end of your paper, called either "Works Cited" if you are following MLA style or "References" if you are following APA style. For additional detail on how to use MLA style, consult the *MLA Handbook for Writers of Research Papers* (5th ed., 1999), published by the Modern Language Association, and the *Publication Manual of the American Psychological Association* (4th ed., 1994), published by the American Psychological Association.

HOW TO WRITE IN–TEXT PARENTHETICAL CITATIONS

Both the MLA and APA systems of documentation ask that you show where you originally found a direct quote, a paraphrase, or a summary by inserting a brief parenthetical citation at the end of the borrowed material in your written text. The MLA system requires that you provide the author and the page number: (Jones 13). APA requires that you provide the author, the date of publication, and the page numbers, which are introduced by *p.* or *pp.* for books and newspapers *only:* (Jones, 1983, p. 5). If, however, you mention the name of the author in the text, you do not need to repeat the author's name in the parenthetical material for either style. The following are examples.

1. Direct quote with the author mentioned in the text

MLA: As Howard Rheingold describes his first trip into virtual reality, "My body wasn't in the computer world" (15-16).

APA: As Howard Rheingold (1991) describes his first trip into virtual reality, "My body wasn't in the computer world" (pp. 15-16).

2. Direct quote with the author not mentioned in the text

MLA: Virtual reality changes perceptions radically. As one participant explains it, "My body wasn't in the computer world. I could see around me, but one of my hands had accompanied my point of view onto the vast electronic plain that seemed to surround me" (Rheingold 15-16).

APA: As one participant explains it, "My body wasn't in the computer world. I could see around me" (Rheingold, 1991, pp. 15-16).

3. Paraphrase or summary with the author mentioned in the text

MLA: Howard Rheingold describes his first trip into virtual reality as one that involved his hand and arm but not his whole body (15-16).

APA: Howard Rheingold (1991) describes his first trip into virtual reality as one that involved his hand and arm but not his whole body (pp. 15-16).

4. Paraphrase or summary with the author not mentioned the text

MLA: One's whole body is not always a part of the virtual reality experience. Sometimes only a hand and arm enters that reality (Rheingold 15-16).

APA: One's whole body is not always a part of the virtual reality experience. Sometimes only a hand and arm enters that reality (Rheingold, 1991, pp. 15-16).

5. Two or more authors. If two or three authors have written the material you have borrowed, include all of their names either in the introductory material or the citation.

MLA: "Virtual reality is all about illusion" (Pimentel and Teixeira 7).

APA: Pimental and Teixeira (1993) remind us, "Virtual reality is all about illusion" (p. 7).

For more than three authors, use only the first author's name and add *et al.* (not underlined) to the citation for MLA. For APA, list all of the authors' names (up to five) for the first reference, then use the first name and *et al.* (not underlined) for subsequent references. For six or more authors, use the first author's name followed by *et al.* (not underlined) in all citations.

6. Two books by the same author. To indicate which book you are citing, either include the name of the book in the introductory material or add a short title to the parenthetical information to differentiate between the books for MLA. For APA, use the publication dates to distinguish between the books. For example, if you are using *The Second Self: Computers and the Human Spirit* (1984) and *Life on the Screen: Identity in the Age of the Internet* (1995), both by Sherry Turkle, document as follows:

MLA: Sherry Turkle says the computer is like a mirror that has a strong psychological hold over her (<u>Second Self</u> 306). She explains further that "the computer tantalizes me with its holding power" (<u>Life</u> 30).

APA: The computer can have a strong psychological hold over some individuals (Turkle, 1984, p. 306). In fact, the computer can tantalize "with its holding power--in my case, the promise that if I do it right, <u>it</u> will do it right, and right away" (Turkle, 1995, p. 30).

7. Corporate author. Sometimes written materials are attributed to a corporate rather than to an individual author. In this case, use the name of the corporation or group, preferably in the material that precedes the quote.

MLA: According to the <u>Notebook</u> published by the Network Project, "The results show. . . " (7).

Or you can mention the corporate author at the end:

APA: "The results show . . . " (Network Project, 1992, p. 7).

8. Title only. When no author is listed for either a book or an article, use the title or the first words of an abbreviated title in your citation.

MLA: *Article:* ("Creativity and Television" 14).
     Book: (<u>Neilsen Television</u> 17).

APA: *Article:* ("Creativity and Television," 1973, p. 14).
     Book: (<u>Neilsen Television,</u> 1975, p. 17).

9. Article in a book. If you quote an article that is reprinted or excerpted in a book such as this one, use the name of the author of the article in your citation, not the author or editor of the book. Thus the essay by Naomi Wolf on pages 438–441 of this book would be cited as (Wolf 438–41) according to MLA or (Wolf, 2001, pp. 438–441) according to APA.

10. Electronic source. Cite electronic sources just as you would print sources. For MLA, introduce the quote with the author's name in the text, or place the author's name (or the title if there is no author) with a page or paragraph number (if there is one) in parentheses at the end. If no page or paragraph numbers are available for the electronic source, place the author's name only in parentheses.

For APA, include the author's name, the date, and the page or paragraph numbers (if available) in parentheses, just as you would a print source.

11. Quotations. Follow special MLA and APA instructions for including short and long quotations. Type short quotes (four lines or less for MLA or forty words or less for APA) like any other sentences in your paper, enclosing them in quotation marks.

Short quotations

> **MLA:** According to Nate Stulman, many college students in his dormitory "routinely stay awake all night chatting with dormmates online. Why walk 10 feet down the hall to have a conversation when you can chat on the computer--even if it takes three times as long?" (562).

(*Note*: When you quote a question, put the question mark inside the quotes and a period after the closing parenthesis.)

> **APA:** Author Benjamin Cheever (1999) says he uses his computer to "read and write letters, and if it did not involve the elimination of envelopes and a certain parallel loosening of style, the process would be similar to the one that once involved lambskins and sharpened feathers" (p. 7).

Long quotations

Longer quotes should be indented ten spaces from the left-hand margin for MLA and five spaces for APA. Double-space, but do not use quotation marks. Note that the long MLA quote has no extra line space at the beginning and end, whereas the long APA quote has an extra line of space at the beginning and end. The parenthetical citations for both MLA and APA appear right after the final period for long quotes.

> **MLA:**
>
> Nate Stulman describes the various uses of computers by the students at his school:
>
>> Several people who live in my hall routinely stay awake all night chatting with dormmates online. Why walk 10 feet down the hall to have a conversation when you can chat on the computer--even if it takes three times as long?
>>
>> You might expect that personal computers in dorm rooms would be used for nonacademic purposes, but the problem is not confined to residence halls. The other day I walked into the library's reference department, and five or six students were grouped around a computer--not conducting research, but

> playing Tetris. Every time I walk past the library's
> so-called research computers, it seems that at least
> half are being used to play games, chat or surf the
> Internet aimlessly. (562)[3]

These experiences may be typical of student's computer use at
other colleges as well.

APA:

Author Benjamin Cheever (1999) contrasts his use of the
computer with individuals who spend a lot of time on the
Internet:

> The news bulges with stories about dispensing therapy on
> the Net, doing business on the Net, trolling for unsus-
> pecting sexual prey on the Net. Not on this computer.
> Most of what I do on the electronic superhighway is write
> and read letters, and if it did not involve the elimina-
> tion of envelopes and a certain parallel loosening of
> style, the process would be similar to the one that once
> involved lambskins and sharpened feathers. (p. 7)[4]

Cheever has essentially substituted computers and their word
processing programs for his old typewriter.

HOW TO WRITE THE LIST OF "WORKS CITED" (MLA) OR "REFERENCES" (APA)

Attach to your draft an alphabetized list of all the works you have quoted or paraphrased in your paper along with full publication information for each of them.
This list is titled either "Works Cited" (MLA) or "References" (APA). *All the information on these lists should be double spaced, just like the rest of your final paper.*

Look at the student papers appearing at the end of this Appendix. The first
follows MLA format, and the second follows APA. Include on your list only the
works you have actually cited in your paper. The easiest way to prepare this list is
to alphabetize your bibliography cards according to the authors' last names or, if
no author is listed, by the title of the work. (Ignore *a, an,* and *the* when alphabetiz-
ing.) If you have prepared an annotated bibliography, simply eliminate the annotations to create these pages.

For the MLA "Works Cited," start each citation at the left margin and indent
each successive line five spaces. For the APA "References," indent the *first* line of
each citation five spaces, and start each successive line at the left margin.

---

[3]This article appears in "The Reader," pages 561–562.
[4]The full citation for this article appears in item 14 on page 327.

Basic Format for Books and Articles

Books

> **MLA:** Author. <u>Title of Book</u>. City: Publisher Name in Shortened Form, date.
>
> **APA:**   Author. (Date). <u>Title of book.</u> City: Publisher Name in Full.

Articles in newspapers

> **MLA:** Author. "Title of Article." <u>Name of Newspaper</u> date of publication: page numbers.
>
> **APA:**   Author. (Date). Title of article. <u>The Name of Newspaper,</u> pp. page numbers.

Articles in magazines or journals

> **MLA:** Author. "Title of Article." <u>Name of Magazine or Journal</u> volume number (year): page numbers.
>
> **APA:**   Author. Title of article. <u>The Name of Magazine or Journal, volume</u> number, page numbers.

Note that in book and article titles, MLA capitalizes all important words, headline style, even if the original does not, and APA capitalizes only the first word of the title and/or subtitle and all proper nouns, sentence style. Also note that for article titles, MLA uses quotation marks and APA does not. The titles of periodicals are written headline style for both MLA and APA. Note also the differences in indenting and that in APA the words *A, An,* and *The* are included in titles of journals, magazines, or newspapers.

Here are some examples of the types of sources that are most commonly cited for argument papers. Examples of both MLA and APA styles are provided.

How to List Books

> ### 1. Book by one author
>
> **MLA:** Rheingold, Howard. <u>Virtual Reality</u>. New York: Simon, 1991.
>
> **APA:**   Rheingold, H. (1991). <u>Virtual reality.</u> New York: Simon & Schuster.
>
> ### 2. Book by two or three authors
>
> **MLA:** Pimentel, Ken, and Kevin Teixeira. <u>Virtual Reality: Through the New Looking Glass</u>. New York: McGraw, 1993.
>
> **APA:**   Pimentel, K., & Teixeira, K. (1993). <u>Virtual reality: Through the new looking glass.</u> New York: McGraw-Hill.

Use the same format to add a third author, using *and* (MLA) or *&* (APA) before the final name.

3. Book by more than three authors

MLA: Comstock, George, et al. <u>Television and Human Behavior</u>.
New York: Columbia UP, 1978.

APA: Comstock, G., Chaffee, S., Katzman N., McCombs, M.,
& Roberts, D. (1978). <u>Television and human behavior.</u> New
York: Columbia University Press.

4. Two or more books by the same author

MLA: Rheingold, Howard. <u>Tools for Thought</u>. New York: Simon,
1985.

   ---. <u>Virtual Reality</u>. New York: Simon, 1991.

APA: Rheingold, H. (1985). <u>Tools for thought.</u> New York:
Simon & Schuster.

   Rheingold, H. (1991). <u>Virtual reality.</u> New York:
Simon & Schuster.

For MLA, arrange the works in alphabetical order by titles. For APA, arrange the works in chronological order, earliest year first.

5. Book by a corporate author

MLA: VPL Research. <u>Virtual Reality at Texpo '89</u>. Redwood
City: VPL Research, 1989.

APA: VPL Research, Inc. (1989). <u>Virtual reality at Texpo
'89.</u> Redwood City, CA: Author.

6. Book with no author named

MLA: <u>Virtual Reality Marketplace</u>. Westport: Meckler, 1992.

APA: <u>Virtual reality marketplace.</u> (1992). Westport, CT:
Meckler.

7. Book reprinted in a later edition

MLA: Malthus, Thomas R. <u>An Essay on the Principle of
Population</u>. 1798. London: Pickering, 1986.

APA: Malthus, T. R. (1986). <u>An essay on the principle of
population.</u> London: Pickering. (Original work published
1798)

8. Translation

MLA: Rousseau, Jean-Jacques. <u>La Nouvelle Héloïse</u>. 1761.
Trans. Judith H. McDowell. University Park:
Pennsylvania State UP, 1968.

APA: Rousseau, J.-J. (1968). <u>La nouvelle Héloïse.</u> (J. H. McDowell, Trans.). University Park: Pennsylvania State University Press. (Original work published 1761)

9. Subsequent editions

MLA: Thompson, Warren S. <u>Population Problems</u>. 4th ed. New York: McGraw, 1953.

APA: Thompson, W. S. (1953). <u>Population problems.</u> (4th ed.). New York: McGraw-Hill.

10. Proceedings from a conference or symposium

MLA: McKerrow, Raymie E., ed. <u>Argument and the Postmodern Challenge: Proceedings of the Eighth SCA/AFA Conference on Argumentation</u>. 5-8 Aug. 1993. Annandale: Speech Communication Assn., 1993.

APA: McKerrow, R. E. (Ed.). (1993). <u>Argument and the postmodern challenge: Proceedings of the eighth SCA/AFA conference on argumentation.</u> Annandale, VA: Speech Communication Association.

11. Introduction, preface, foreword, or afterword

MLA: Schneiderman, Ben. Foreword. <u>Interacting with Virtual Environments</u>. Ed. Lindsay MacDonald and John Vince. Chichester, Eng.: Wiley, 1994. x-xi.

APA: Schneiderman, B. (1994). Foreword. In L. MacDonald & J. Vince (Eds.), <u>Interacting with virtual environments.</u> (pp. x-xi). Chichester, England: Wiley.

12. Government documents

MLA: United States. F.B.I. U.S. Dept. of Justice. <u>Uniform Crime Reports for the United States</u>. Washington: GPO, 1990.

APA: Federal Bureau of Investigation, U.S. Department of Justice. (1990). <u>Uniform crime reports for the United States.</u> Washington, DC: U.S. Government Printing Office.

How to List Articles

13. Article from a periodical

MLA: Monastersky, Richard. "The Deforestation Debate." <u>Science News</u> 10 July 1993: 26-27.

APA: Monastersky, R. (1993, July 10). The deforestation debate. <u>Science News,</u> 26-27.

14. Article from a newspaper

MLA: Cheever, Benjamin. "He'll Take His Web Pages Straight, with No Java Jive." <u>New York Times</u> 4 Feb. 1999: D7.

APA: Cheever, B. (1999, February 4). He'll take his Web pages straight, with no java jive. <u>The New York Times,</u> p. D7.

15. Article in a periodical with no author listed

MLA: "A Democratic Army." <u>New Yorker</u> 28 June 1993: 4+.

APA: A democratic army. (1993, June 28). <u>The New Yorker,</u> 4, 6.

For MLA, use a plus sign when the pages are not successive. For APA, list all pages on which the article is printed.

16. Article in a journal with continuous pagination in each volume

MLA: Jasinski, James. "Rhetoric and Judgment in the Constitutional Ratification Debate of 1787-1788: An Exploration of the Relationship between Theory and Critical Practice." <u>Quarterly Journal of Speech</u> 78 (1992): 197-218.

APA: Jasinski, J. (1992). Rhetoric and judgment in the constitutional ratification debate of 1787-1788: An exploration of the relationship between theory and critical practice. <u>The Quarterly Journal of Speech, 78,</u> 197-218.

17. Article in a journal that pages each issue separately

MLA: Rosenbloom, Nancy J. "In Defense of the Moving Pictures: The People's Institute, the National Board of Censorship, and the Problem of Leisure in Urban America." <u>American Studies</u> 33.2 (1992): 41-60.

APA: Rosenbloom, N. J. (1992). In defense of the moving pictures: The People's Institute, the National Board of Censorship, and the problem of leisure in urban America. <u>American Studies, 33</u>(2), 41-60.

18. Edited collection of articles or an anthology

MLA: Forester, Tom, ed. <u>The Information Technology Revolution.</u> Cambridge: MIT P, 1985.

APA: Forester, T. (Ed.). (1985). <u>The information technology revolution.</u> Cambridge, MA: MIT Press.

19. *Article in an edited collection or an anthology*

MLA: Boden, Margaret A. "The Social Impact of Thinking Machines." The Information Technology Revolution. Ed. Tom Foster. Cambridge: MIT P, 1985. 95-103.

APA: Boden, M. A. (1985). The social impact of thinking machines. In T. Foster (Ed.), The information technology revolution (pp. 95-103). Cambridge, MA: MIT Press.

20. *Reprinted article in an edited volume or collection (like "The Reader" in this book)*

MLA: Fox, Lyla. "Hold Your Horsepower." Newsweek 25 Mar. 1996: 16. Rpt. in Perspectives on Argument. Nancy V. Wood. 3rd ed. Upper Saddle River: Prentice, 2001, 187-89.

APA: Fox, L. (2001). Hold your horsepower. In N. V. Wood, Perspectives on argument (3rd ed., pp. 187-189). Upper Saddle River, NJ: Prentice Hall.

21. *Signed article in a reference work*

MLA: Davidson, W. S., II. "Crime." Encyclopedia of Psychology. Ed. Raymond J. Corsini. 4 vols. New York: Wiley, 1984. 310-12.

APA: Davidson, W. S. II. (1984). Crime. In R. J. Corsini (Ed.), Encyclopedia of psychology (pp. 310-312). New York: Wiley.

22. *Unsigned article in a reference work*

MLA: "Quindlen, Anna." Current Biography Yearbook. Ed. Judith Graham. New York: Wilson, 1993. 477-81.

APA: Quindlen, Anna. (1993). In J. Graham, Current biography yearbook (pp. 477-481). New York: Wilson.

23. *Review*

MLA: Watts, Steven. "Sinners in the Hands of an Angry Critic: Christopher Lasch's Struggle with Progressive America." Rev. of the book The True and Only Heaven: Progress and Its Critics, by Christopher Lasch. American Studies 33.2 (1992): 113-20.

APA: Watts, S. (1992). Sinners in the hands of an angry critic: Christopher Lasch's struggle with progressive America. [Review of The true and only heaven: Progress and its critics]. American Studies, 33(2), 113-120.

24. Letter to the editor

MLA: McCaffrey, Mark. Letter. <u>Utne Reader</u> July-Aug. 1993: 10.

APA: McCaffrey, M. (1993, July-August). [Letter to the editor.] <u>Utne Reader,</u> 10.

25. Editorial

MLA: "A Touch of Class for the Court." Editorial. <u>New York Times</u> 25 July 1993: E16.

APA: A touch of class for the court. (1993, July 25). [Editorial.] <u>The New York Times,</u> p. E16.

How to List Electronic Sources

The basic elements of an MLA "Works Cited" entry are author, title, editor, publication specifics including date of publication or update by an organization and the name of the organization that sponsors the information, date you accessed the information, and the URL (online address) placed in angle brackets and followed by a period.

The basic elements of an APA "References" entry are author, publication date in parentheses, title of the article, title of the periodical or electronic text, volume number and/or pages (if any), date retrieved from the World Wide Web, and the URL with no brackets and no period at the end.

26. Professional or personal Web site

MLA: Wyatt, Christopher Scott. <u>Existentialists: Friedrich Wilhelm Nietzsche</u>. 26 June 1999 <http:// userzweb. lightspeed.net/~taneri/nietz.html>.

APA: Wyatt, C. S. <u>Existentialists: Friedrich Wilhelm Nietzsche</u> [online]. Retrieved June 26, 1999 from the World Wide Web: http://userzweb.lightspeed.net/~taneri/ nietz.html

27. Book

MLA: Nettleship, Richard Lewis. <u>The Theory of Education in the Republic of Plato</u>. 1968. Classics in Education Series. 28 June 1999 <http://www.ilt.columbia.edu/ academic/CESdigital/CESdigital.html>.

APA: Nettleship, R. L. (1968). <u>The theory of education in the Republic of Plato.</u> Classics in Education Series [online book]. Retrieved June 28, 1999 from the World Wide Web: http://www.ilt.columbia.edu/academic/CESdigital/ CESdigital.html

28. Article in an electronic journal

MLA: Herring, Susan. "Gender and Democracy in Computer-Mediated Communication." <u>Electronic Journal of Communication</u> 3.2 (1993): 17 pp. 30 Sept. 1996 〈http://dc.smu.edu/dc/classroom/Gender.txt〉.

APA: Herring, S. (1993). Gender and democracy in computer-mediated communication [32 paragraphs]. <u>Electronic Journal of Communication, 3</u>(2). Retrieved September 30, 1996 from the World Wide Web: http://dc. smu.edu/dc/classroom/Gender.txt

29. Article in a newspaper

MLA: Safire, William. "Free Pills for Geezers?" <u>New York Times on the Web</u> 28 June 1999. 29 June 1999 〈http://www.nytimes.com/library/opinion/safire/062899safi.html〉.

APA: Safire, W. (1999, June 28). Free pills for geezers? <u>The New York Times on the Web</u> [online newspaper]. Retrieved June 29, 1999, from the World Wide Web: http://www.nytimes.com/library/opinion/safire/062899safi.html

30. CD-ROM

MLA: <u>The Oxford English Dictionary</u>. 2nd ed. CD-ROM. Oxford: Oxford UP, 1992.

APA: <u>The Oxford English Dictionary.</u> (1992). [CD-ROM]. Oxford, Eng.: Oxford University Press.

31. Electronic mail (e-mail)

MLA: Rieder, David. "Re: Jobs." E-mail to Debi Reese. 4 Oct. 2000.

In APA style, you would not cite this in the "References." Cite in text as

D. Rieder (personal communication, October 4, 2000)

32. FTP site

MLA: Freenet Directory. 28 June 1999 〈ftp://ftp.cwru.edu/pub/freenet/freedomshrine/timelines〉.

APA: Freenet Directory. Retrieved June 28, 1999: ftp://ftp.cwru.edu/pub/freenet/freedomshrine/timelines

How to List Media: Microforms, Video, Television, Film

33. ERIC Information Service (microform)

MLA: Bernhardt, Victoria L. <u>The School Portfolio: A Comprehensive Framework for School Improvement</u>. 2nd

ed. Larchmont, NY: Eye on Education, 1999. ERIC ED
431 783.

APA: Bernhardt, V. L. (1999). <u>The School Portfolio: A
Comprehensive Framework for School Improvement</u> (2nd
ed.). Larchmont, NY: Eye on Education. (ERIC Document
Reproduction Service No. ED 431 783)

34. *Videotape*

MLA: <u>Composition</u>. Prod. ABC/Prentice Hall Video Library.
          Videocassette. Prentice, 1993.

APA: ABC/Prentice Hall Video Library (Producer). (1993).
<u>Composition</u> [Videotape]. Englewood Cliffs, NJ: Prentice
Hall.

35. *Radio or television program*

MLA: "Resolved: Political Correctness Is a Menace and a
          Bore." Prod. and dir. Warren Steibel. Mod. William
          F. Buckley Jr. <u>Firing Line</u>. PBS. KDTN, Dallas. 2
          Dec. 1993.

APA: Steibel, W. (Producer and Director). (1993,
December 2). Resolved: Political correctness is a menace
and a bore. <u>Firing Line.</u> New York: Public Broadcasting
Service.

36. *Film*

MLA: <u>JFK</u>. Dir. Oliver Stone. Warner, 1991.

APA: Stone, O. (Director). (1991). <u>JFK</u> [Film]. Los
Angeles: Warner Bros.

How to List Interviews and Speeches

37. *Published interview*

MLA: Hardin, Garrett. Interview with Cathy Spencer. <u>Omni</u> June
          1992: 55-63.

APA: Hardin, G. (1992, June). [Interview with C.
Spencer]. <u>Omni,</u> 55-63.

38. *Personal interview*

MLA: Wick, Audrey. Personal interview. 27 May 1999.

In APA style, you would not cite this in the "References." Cite in the text as

A. Wick (personal communication, May 27, 1999)

39. Lectures, speeches, addresses

MLA: Yeltsin, Boris. Address. U.S. Congress, Washington. 18
June 1992.

APA: Yeltsin, B. (1992, June 18). Address before to the
U.S. Congress, Washington, DC.

PAPER IN MLA STYLE

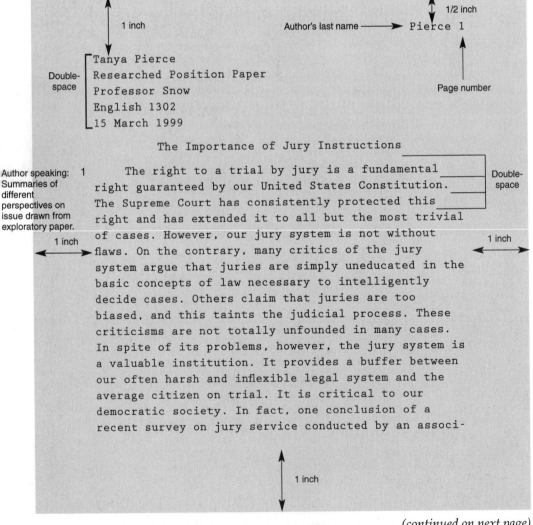

1/2 inch

1 inch — Author's last name ──→ Pierce 1

Page number

Double-space

Tanya Pierce
Researched Position Paper
Professor Snow
English 1302
15 March 1999

The Importance of Jury Instructions

Author speaking:
Summaries of different perspectives on issue drawn from exploratory paper.

1 inch

1   The right to a trial by jury is a fundamental
right guaranteed by our United States Constitution.
The Supreme Court has consistently protected this
right and has extended it to all but the most trivial
of cases. However, our jury system is not without
flaws. On the contrary, many critics of the jury
system argue that juries are simply uneducated in the
basic concepts of law necessary to intelligently
decide cases. Others claim that juries are too
biased, and this taints the judicial process. These
criticisms are not totally unfounded in many cases.
In spite of its problems, however, the jury system is
a valuable institution. It provides a buffer between
our often harsh and inflexible legal system and the
average citizen on trial. It is critical to our
democratic society. In fact, one conclusion of a
recent survey on jury service conducted by an associ-

Double-space

1 inch

1 inch

(continued on next page)

Pierce 2

ation of defense trial lawyers is that "the more involvement people have in the jury process, the more they seem to take to heart their responsibilities as citizens in our democratic society" (Robinson 62). Still, because of recent mistakes made by juries and the growing scrutiny of the decisions made by juries, it is necessary to improve our jury system.

Serving on a jury takes a great deal of time. Because jury service does require a lot of time, many Americans will do just about anything to get out of jury duty. In addition, many segments of the population are exempt from jury duty either by permissible judicial rule, by law, or by custom. Among the occupational groups generally exempt in the vast majority of jurisdictions are professionals such as lawyers, licensed physicians and dentists, members of the armed forces, officers of all three branches of government, police officers, fire fighters, clergy, and teachers (Abraham 117). The average jury in America consists of housewives or house-husbands, retirees, blue-collar workers, and the unemployed. According to the survey quoted above, only forty-five percent of all adult Americans have been called for jury duty, and only seventeen percent have served through an actual trial (Robinson 62). These people are often not indispensable in their jobs and are not as limited by time constraints as the exempt groups. Critics of the jury system argue that these juries are often not educated enough to handle the responsibility of deciding important cases.

It is sad to say, but in many cases the jurors are ignorant of the legal issues surrounding a given case. In many instances they do not understand the facts in the case, and they often do not understand the consequences of their decisions. For example, the jury in a hate crime case thought that it was

---

Margin annotations:

Direct quote cited: Author of quote not mentioned in text.

Author speaking: Introduction to policy claim.

2 Problems: Time, exemptions.

Summary citied.

Summary citied.

3 Author speaking: More problems: Unprepared jurors.

Supported by specific example.

(continued on next page)

sentencing the murderer to five years in jail plus ten years' probation. It is an either-or situation. Because of this lack of understanding by the jury and the ineffective instructions given by the judge and attorneys involved in the case, a grave and irreversible injustice was done. The murderer was given only ten years' probation for killing another human being. This is just one of numerous cases where the jury's lack of knowledge has led to disastrous decisions.

Transition: Current solutions and their problems.

4 Something clearly needs to be done to educate jurors. Current practice requires the judge to give instructions, called a charge, to the jury before it begins deliberations. According to Henry Abraham, who has written extensively on the judicial process, "Much

Direct quote cited. Author in text.

thought goes—or should go—into this charge, which is intended as an exposition of the law and is delivered orally in most, although not all, cases" (131).

5 One of the problems with the judge's charge, however, is that most states do not permit the jury to take either a copy or a tape recording of it with them when they leave the courtroom to make their

Summary cited. Author in text.

deliberations. Seymour Wishman, a criminal lawyer who has tried hundreds of cases before juries, quotes one judge who supports the idea of allowing jurors to take written or audiotaped instructions with them. According to this judge, we expect people to listen to instructions once and remember them well enough to make "monumental decisions" (224).

Transition.

6 The judge's instructions are not only difficult to remember; they are also sometimes difficult for the jury to understand. Wishman goes on to claim, "Jury instructions are often incomprehensible because they

Direct quotes cited. Authors in text.

are drafted by lawyers and judges who do not realize how much of their 'legalese' vocabulary and syntax was acquired in law school. [. . .] Little effort is

(continued on next page)

Pierce 4

made to write clear and simple language for those not
legally trained" (224). Abraham, agreeing that there
can be significant problems with the judge's charge,
says, "Many a charge has, ultimately, been instrumental in causing a mistrial; many another has been
found to be defective on points of law by appellate
courts" (131).

Obviously, the educational process for jurors
needs to be improved, and judges and lawyers need to
become active participants in this educational
process. They need to take the responsibility for
informing jurors about the relevant legal issues in
each case. They must educate jurors on the rules of
law applicable to the cases at hand and in language
they can understand. Some may argue that this system
may be abused by lawyers who want to bias a jury in
their favor. This is, of course, possible. But one
must realize that juries are inherently biased. Each
juror walks in with his or her own distinct set of
values and beliefs. The lawyers are always trying to
influence them to see their side. I would argue,
however, that it is better to risk the possibility of
some additional bias in order for the juries to be
better informed. It is more desirable to have a
knowledgeable jury, even at the risk of some bias,
rather than to have a jury that is totally in the dark
about the legal issues surrounding a particular case.

Some research suggests that juries should be
given lessons in the law before the trial begins and
also at various points during the trial. Psychological studies have consistently shown that early
exposure and frequent exposure to legal principles
correlate with juries that are more likely to presume
innocence in a case until sufficient evidence is
provided to decide otherwise. Experimental mock

7 Transition.

Author speaking.

Solution:
Establish new
policy.
Refutation of
those who may
disagree.

Author speaking.

8 Support for
solution.

Summary cited.

(continued on next page)

juries questioned midway through testimony showed a
significantly higher indecision rate when they had
been informed about the legal issues involved before
the start of testimony than those who had not been
instructed earlier (Heuer and Penrod 429). This
suggests that juries instructed prior to the presentation of evidence are more likely to consider all of
the evidence of a case before arriving at a decision
of guilt or innocence.

Author speaking: 9
More refutation and benefits of solution.

Although some may interpret this psychological
data as suggesting that informing juries early and
frequently would delay the judicial process, I
believe the opposite is true. Instructing juries on
the basic legal concepts will help them be more open-
minded. They will have more intelligent discussions
during deliberations because they will know what
issues to concentrate on. Psychological tests have
also demonstrated that juries who are informed on
legal concepts frequently are less likely to result

Summary cited.

in a hung jury (Goldberg 456). This latter finding is
especially valuable since so much government money in
the form of our tax dollars is wasted when juries are
unable to arrive at a unanimous decision.

Author speaking: 10
Summary of perspective in paper.

The right to be judged by a group of one's peers
is a right most Americans value highly. It helps
ensure that all citizens will be given a fair chance
in our legal system. It is valuable because it allows
the American public to play an active role in our
judicial process. However, like all institutions, our
jury system is not without its flaws. It is important
for us to recognize the shortcomings in this process

Policy claim in last sentence.

and try to improve it. A positive start toward
improving the jury system would be for judges and
lawyers to take a more active role in educating jurors
at several crucial points during the course of a trial.

(continued on next page)

Pierce 6

Works Cited

Abraham, Henry J. The Judicial Process: An Introduc-
     tory Analysis of the Courts of the United
     States, England, and France. 5th ed. New York:
     Oxford UP, 1986.
Goldberg, Janice C. "Memory, Magic, and Myth: The
     Timing of Jury Instructions." Oregon Law Review
     59 (1981): 451-75.
Heuer, Larry, and Steven Penrod. "A Field Experiment
     with Written and Preliminary Instructions." Law
     and Human Behavior 13 (1989): 409-30.
Robinson, Archie S. "We the Jury: Who Serves, Who
     Doesn't." USA Today: The Magazine of the Ameri-
     can Scene 120 (Jan. 1992): 62-63.
Wishman, Seymour. Anatomy of a Jury: The System on
     Trial. New York: Times Books, 1986.

PAPER IN APA STYLE

Shortened title ⟶ Alaskan Wolf 1
↑
Page number

Darrell D. Greer
Researched Position Paper
Professor Filip
English 1302
15 March 1999

Alaskan Wolf Management

Introduction and background of problem. Quotes from authorities and statistics to establish extent of problem.

1   In the past few years, Alaska has been witnessing a decline in the populations of caribou and moose in the Fortymile, Delta, and Nelchina Basin areas. This decline in the caribou and moose populations is due mainly to the uprising of the wolf populations in these three areas. Robert Stephenson of the Alaska Department of Fish and Game claims, "Wolf packs will kill one caribou every two days or so, and one moose every three to ten days" (Keszler, 1993, p. 65). The Delta caribou herd alone declined from about eleven thousand in 1989 to less than four thousand just four years later ("Alaska Wolf," 1993, p. 6). With statistics like these, the caribou and moose population in Alaska is clearly a problem that needs on-going attention.

Quotations worked into text that suggest the unique character of the problem in Alaska.

2   A rapid decline in caribou and moose populations can be devastating to the state. Not only are they a valuable resource for Alaska in terms of nonresident hunting and tourist sightseeing, but for many remote residents, caribou and moose are their main source of food. The way of life for many Alaskans is one that the average American cannot vaguely understand. Max Peterson, the executive director of the International Association of Wildlife Agencies, says that in Alaska, "People interact as another predator in the ecosystem," and as a result, "the interest in Alaska by people outside Alaska certainly is greater than their knowledge of Alaska" (Keszler, 1993, p. 67). Ted

(continued on next page)

Alaskan Wolf 2

Williams (1993) clarifies the lifestyle that many rural Alaskans lead:

> Genuine subsistence is the most environmentally benign of all possible lifestyles. Subsisters do not--indeed cannot--deplete fish and wildlife because if they do, they will subsist no more. But even in the remotest native villages, Alaska as trackless wilderness where people blend with nature is just an old dream. Many villagers are now on social welfare programs and are therefore cash dependent. (p. 49)

A long quotation of more than forty words is indented and written in block form. No quotation marks are necessary for indented quotes. The source is indicated at the end. Note that the author is mentioned in the text.

Failing to protect existing caribou and moose populations could lower the subsistence level for some Alaskans, even more than it is at present.

The biologists of the state of Alaska commonly believe that wolf populations are nowhere close to being endangered. In 1993 they estimated the total wolf population in Alaska to be between 5,900 and 7,200. In the three areas up for wildlife management (about 3.5 percent of the state), Rodney Boertje, an Alaskan Department of Fish and Game wildlife biologist, reported, "Wolf populations can sustain harvest rates of twenty-five to forty percent. So sixty to eighty-five percent of wolves must be removed for control efforts to be effective" (Keszler, 1993, p. 66). This amount totals between three hundred and four hundred wolves in these three areas. Wildlife management experts believe the most humane and efficient way of accomplishing this task is through aerial shootings of wolves.

3 Statistics and quotations from authorities to strengthen the solution preferred by this author.

With the announcement of the wolf management plan proposed by Alaska Governor Walter Hickel and the Alaska Department of Fish and Game in 1993 that involved aerial shootings of wolves, the animal rights groups started an all-out war with the state. They organized widespread mailings to the governor and

4 Refutation of the animal rights groups and their solutions to the problem.

(continued on next page)

threatened massive boycotts of tourism in Alaska if the plan was not repealed (Keszler, 1993, p. 65). The animal rights groups believed that other methods of management could increase caribou and moose populations. One such method involved reducing bag limits, shortening hunting seasons, or totally eliminating hunting in these three areas. This type of management was not effective, however, since hunters were not the real cause of the problem. Pete Buist, a Fairbanks, Alaska, resident, pointed out at the time, "In control areas, hunters are taking less than five percent of the annual production of meat animals. Predators are taking more than seventy-five percent" (1993, p. 12). Animal rights groups commonly point to hunters as the culprits in animal conservation efforts. According to Arms (1994), however, "Nowadays in developed countries, groups representing hunting and fishing interests are the most active conservationists. They understand that their sport and, sometimes, their livelihood depend on sustained or increasing populations of the organisms they hunt or fish" (p. 347). As mentioned earlier, rural Alaskans who depend on caribou and moose for subsistence are some of these hunters who continue to take these animals but not in dangerously large numbers.

5   Another alternative management method that has been brought up by the animal rights groups is tranquilizing and capturing the wolves and chemically sterilizing them or using some other sort of contraception. This method has not been scientifically proven to work. Even if it did work, this method would take entirely too long to be effective for this situation. Contraception only deals with the wolf numbers down the road, not with existing numbers, which would remain the same for now. Existing wolves in the immediate future may devastate the caribou and moose popula-

(continued on next page)

Alaskan Wolf 4

tions so drastically that they will not be able to recover.

In the United States Constitution, the management
of fish and wildlife is left up to the individual
states. When Alaska made the professional decision that
the best way to control its wolf population was by aerial shootings, the animal rights groups picked only
that part of a larger plan to attack. In media reports,
activists "portrayed the plan simply as a mass extermi-
nation of wolves designed to increase game numbers for
out-of-state hunters and wildlife watchers" (Keszler,
1993, p. 39). They showed through commercials "visions
of helicopter gunships slaughtering wolves by the hundreds" (p. 39) when in fact the aerial shooting of
wolves is just one small part of the plan. The animal
rights groups did not focus on the parts of the plan
that dealt with the restrictions to help the wolves in
other areas. In Denali National Park and Preserve,
Alaskan conservationists plan to do away with all hunting and trapping to give the wolves a sanctuary with no
outside pressure (p. 65). Other laws and bans on hunting and trapping to protect wolves would take place in
areas around Anchorage and Fairbanks. The practice of
land-and-shoot hunting (a practice used by many trap-
pers to locate game by helicopter, land the helicopter,
and start hunting) would be banned statewide (p. 65).
But none of these efforts to protect the wolf population were even discussed by the animal rights activists.

The professional wildlife biologists at the Alaska
Department of Fish and Game have taken a lot of heat
from the animal rights media reports on their decision
to go ahead with the original plan to manage wolf
populations through aerial shooting and other methods
not mentioned by the media. The biologists of the state
of Alaska have devoted their lives to the preservation

6

Evaluation and
refutation of other
solutions.

Establishment of the
ethos of
conservationists in
Alaska to make their
plan acceptable.

7

Author has identified
a problem, evaluated
several solutions,
and arrived at this
solution as the best
possible. This is a
value argument
because it claims
one of several
considered solutions
is the best.

(continued on next page)

Alaskan Wolf 5

of wildlife. They know Alaska and Alaska's wildlife better than anyone else. After researching and trying other methods, they believe the best solution to their problem is through aerial shooting. Their main concern is to protect the wildlife population as a whole, not just to wage a "war on wolves." While the animal right- ists are sitting around in their offices wondering which animals to save, the biologists at Alaska's Department of Fish and Game are in the field researching the range conditions and overall population conditions to manage the wildlife community as a whole. As inhumane and immoral as it might seem, the aerial shooting of wolves is still the best solution for game management in this situation.

Problem solution and policy are also strong features in this argument.

Claim in last sentence.

Alaskan Wolf 6

References

Alaska wolf update. (1993, August). <u>American Hunter,</u> 6.

Arms, K. (1994). <u>Environmental science</u> (2nd ed.). Fort Worth, TX: Harcourt Brace.

Buist, P. (1993, September). Letter to the edi- tor. <u>American Hunter,</u> 12.

Keszler, E. (1993, May). Wolves and big game: Searching for balance in Alaska. <u>American Hunter,</u> 38-39, 65-67.

Williams, T. (1993, May-June). Alaska's war on the wolves. <u>Audubon,</u> 44-47, 49-50.

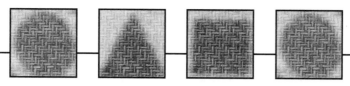

PART FOUR

Further Applications: Rogerian Argument/ Argument and Literature

Chapter 11 explains Rogerian argument, an alternative to traditional argument, that is particularly effective for building common ground and resolving differences. The Appendix to Chapter 11 synthesizes the critical reading and writing strategies taught in Chapters 1–11. Chapter 12 suggests some ways to apply argument theory to reading and writing about literature. When you finish reading Part Four:

- You will understand Rogerian argument strategy.
- You will have experience writing a Rogerian argument paper.
- You will have reviewed and synthesized argument theory.
- You will know how to analyze arguments in literature and how to write your own arguments about literature.

CHAPTER ELEVEN

Rogerian Argument and Common Ground

To this point, you have been studying traditional argument that has its origin in classical sources. It is the type of argument that predominates in American culture, and it is what you are used to when you listen to people argue on television or when you read arguments in many current periodicals or books. In traditional argument, the arguer states a claim and proves it by drawing on various types of proofs, including reasoning and evidence. The object is to convince an audience that the claim is valid and that the arguer is right. In this model of argument, the arguer uses the rebuttal to demonstrate how the opposition is wrong and to state why the audience should reject that position. The emphasis in traditional argument is on winning the argument. Debate, with participants on both sides trying to win by convincing a third-party judge, as in Exercise H in Chapter 7, is one form of traditional argument, as is courtroom argument and all other single-perspective argument in which one person argues to convince one or more people of a particular point of view, as in Exercise C in Chapter 12.

As you know from your own experience and from reading about argument in this book, traditional argument does not always achieve its aims with the audience. In fact, in certain situations when strongly held opinions or entire value systems are challenged, traditional argument may not be effective at all. The audience may in fact simply stop listening or walk away. When that happens, it is useful to have another argumentative strategy to turn to, one that might work better in cases where there seems to be a stand-off or a lack of common ground among the arguing parties.

Rogerian argument, so called because it evolved from techniques originally applied by psychotherapist Carl Rogers, is a technique that is particularly useful for reducing conflict and establishing common ground between people who hold divergent positions and may even at times express hostility toward each other.

Common ground may seem impossible to achieve in such situations, but two opposing parties can almost always find something to agree on if they try hard enough. Here is an anecdote that shows two hostile individuals establishing common ground. This comes from a column titled "In Politics, It Does Help to Be Smart" by Molly Ivins. Ivins claims that this is a true story.

> This is the perfect political story and also true, but the names have been changed to protect the players.
>
> Many years ago in the Texas Lege lurked two senators who loathed one another with a livid passion. One was conservative, the other liberal; one from a rural area, the other urban; one a mean old bull and the other a witty cosmopolite. We'll call them Bubba and Cary.
>
> One afternoon, Bubba is drinking with a friend in a local dive when in walks Cary. Bubba looks at him and snarls, "You're a sorry ———!"
>
> Cary continues to the bar without comment. But after he gets a drink, he passes Bubba's table again, stops and says: "You think I'm a sorry ———, right?"
>
> "Right," says Bubba.
>
> "Well, I think you're a sorry ———."
>
> Bubba rears back, ready to rise and fight. Cary continues: "But we both *know* Senator Doakes is a sorry ———."
>
> Bubba laughs and says, "I'll drink to that."
>
> They were both smart politicians. And that's what smart politicians do: concentrate on the areas where they can agree, even if there's only one. That's how deals get done, the ball is moved forward, the system works and the people's interest is more or less served.[1]

Establishing common ground in Rogerian argument, as in this example, also involves discovering what two parties have in common. But Rogerian argument does more than that. Instead of using rebuttal to show how the opposition is wrong, as in traditional argument, Rogerian argument requires the arguer to spend at least some time at the beginning of the argument not only explaining how the opposition's position is right but also identifying situations where it might be valid. The arguer cannot do that very successfully without finding some common ground with the opposition. It is almost impossible to show how any part of another individual's opposing position is valid if you disagree with it totally.

For example, imagine a parent who advocates that all parents arm themselves and take up positions each day at their children's school to protect their children from random shootings. Another parent absolutely disagrees with this policy but finds that common ground still exists with the first parent because they both share a concern for their children's safety. The second parent, in restating the first parent's position, would emphasize the common concern both parents have for their children as they search together for a solution they can agree on.[2] Additional descriptions and examples of Rogerian argument in this chapter and in the Exercises and Activities at the end of this chapter will demonstrate how various

---

[1] Molly Ivins, "In Politics, It Does Help to Be Smart" *Fort Worth Star-Telegram*, October 28, 1999, p. B9.

[2] I am indebted to Jenny Edbauer for this example.

people achieve common ground through restatement and validation of the other's position in Rogerian argument.

You may find Rogerian argument frustrating at first, especially if you favor contention and agonistic debate in situations where your ideas and values seem to be under threat. Because Rogerian argument emphasizes making connections with the opposition and reducing hostility in such situations, you will need to curb your instincts to launch your argument by letting the opposition know how wrong you think they are. You can learn to use Rogerian argument, even if it is not your preferred or most natural style of arguing, in situations where traditional argument is no longer effective. It is a useful strategy when other strategies are failing. Let us look at a couple of examples.

ACHIEVING COMMON GROUND IN ROGERIAN ARGUMENT

"Where Are Men and Women Today?" was the title of a public performance staged in New York City by Deborah Tannen, author of *You Just Don't Understand*, linguistics professor, and expert in male-female communication, and Robert Bly, author of *Iron John: A Book about Men*. The press publicized this exchange as a "face-to-face, word-to-word confrontation." An all-out "battle of the sexes" was predicted. The sell out audience consisted of one thousand people, half men and half women.

The expectations of open conflict between the presenters were not realized, however. Instead, Bly and Tannen began the program by showing first what they agreed on. To establish a harmonious context for their exchange, Tannen began by reading a poem by Emily Dickenson, and while she read, Bly played a stringed instrument. Then Bly showed his appreciation of Tannen by reading aloud from her book. Tannen in turn showed her appreciation of Bly by reading aloud from his book. Then the dialogue began as follows:

> BLY: The first time I came in contact with your book, my wife and I were having dinner up in northern Minnesota, and someone started to read out of it. We both fell off our chairs laughing, because it illuminated every mistake we had made, including every misunderstanding. . . .

He continued by explaining how Tannen's book had helped him and his wife gain insight and communicate better. Bly explained how he had learned from Tannen to build rapport with his wife. He had learned to use a style that Tannen identified as a "woman's style."

Tannen then replied:

> TANNEN: There's another side to this. You're assuming that it's good for men to learn to talk this way. And I always stop short of saying that because it's very important for me as a woman to say that men's styles are okay too.[3]

---

[3]Robert Bly and Deborah Tannen, "Where Are Men and Women Today?" transcript printed in *New Age Journal*, January-February 1992, pp. 28–33, 92–97.

These two individuals, meeting for the first time at this special program, were determined not to fulfill the predictions of the press by providing a traditional war-between-the-sexes debate complete with the audience functioning as judge and trying to declare winners. Instead, they resorted to Rogerian argument, a special strategy that can be used at any time in argument to cool emotions, reduce conflict, and create sympathetic understanding. In their case, their strategy involved demonstrating at the outset that they both understood and valued one another's ideas by reading from one another's books and then commenting on how they had valued them.

Let us look at another real-life example of building common ground between disagreeing parties with each side demonstrating an understanding of the other's point of view. Environmentalists, who typically want to protect the environment at all costs, often find themselves in opposition to individuals who make their living by exploiting the environment. Loggers, ranchers, mill owners, and other industrialists, for example, can fall into this second category. Individuals from both groups, stereotyped as "nature haters" and "eco-freaks" by the press, met in Idaho to discuss efforts for protecting endangered wildlife in the area. The environmentalists went to the meeting with some trepidation, but "as they joked and sparred over steak and beer, they discovered that neither side lived up to its stereotype. 'We found that we didn't hate each other,' said Alex Irby, a manager at the Konkolville sawmill. 'Turns out, we all like to do a lot of the same things. We love the outdoors.'" "Loggers in the back country sitting down with environmentalists is an astonishing change," reports Timothy Egan, who wrote about the details of the meeting.[4] One can infer that the common ground established in this meeting was brought about by each side's describing the value it placed on the environment and on outdoor activity in general. In such an exchange, both parties perceived that they had been heard, and further dialogue was then possible.

As you can see, understanding the rhetorical situation in general and the audience in particular by analyzing what the people involved think and value is of critical importance in Rogerian argument. In the two examples just cited, Tannen and Bly studied ahead of time and then demonstrated to the audience their understanding of each other's positions. The environmentalists, loggers, and mill workers discovered in conversation their shared values concerning the environment. In Chapter 8, you learned how to analyze an audience yourself when you planned your researched position paper. As you read the rest of this chapter, including the examples of Rogerian argument, pay particular attention to how Rogerian arguers analyze their audiences' dissenting opinions and values and then respond to those as part of their overall strategy.

ROGERIAN ARGUMENT AS STRATEGY

Carl Rogers was a psychotherapist who was well known for the empathetic listening techniques he used in psychological counseling. He later became interested in

---

[4]Timothy Egan, "Look Who's Hugging Trees Now," *New York Times Magazine,* July 7, 1996, p. 28.

how these same techniques could be used to improve communication in other difficult, emotionally charged situations. Richard Young and his colleagues Alton Becker and Kenneth Pike built on Rogers's ideas to formulate Rogerian argument, a method for helping people in difficult situations make connections, create common ground, and understand one another. The object was to avoid undue conflict or, even worse, a mutual standoff.[5]

According to Young, Becker, and Pike, written Rogerian argument reduces the reader's sense of threat and conflict with the writer so that alternatives can be considered. Three things are accomplished by this strategy:

1. *Writers let readers know they have been understood.* To accomplish this purpose, the writer restates the opponent's position in summary form by using dispassionate, neutral language. The writer demonstrates that the reader has been heard and that the writer understands the issue exactly as the reader does. Thus Tannen and Bly begin their special presentation by reading from one another's works to demonstrate that they are hearing one another.

2. *Writers show how readers' positions are valid in certain contexts and under certain conditions.* The writer demonstrates to the reader that at least part of the reader's position is acceptable and thereby makes it easier for the reader to reciprocate and accept part of the writer's position. Notice how Bly says at the outset that Tannen's observations are valid and can be applied to conversations he has actually had with his wife. Tannen then points out that males' preferences in communicating are also OK. Thus they validate one another's positions.

3. *Writers get readers to believe that both of them share the same values, types of experience, attitudes, and perceptions and are thus similar in significant ways.* Tannen and Bly accomplish this end by borrowing one another's theories and applying them to their own personal experiences. They make it clear that they both share the same values and types of experience.

The most important feature of Rogerian argument is listening empathetically and nonjudgmentally. Rogers says that people usually listen judgmentally and evaluatively. They are eager to jump in, point out what is right or wrong, and make corrections or refutations. Rogerian listening puts the writer in the reader's place by requiring the writer to provide neutral summaries of the reader's position that show sympathetic understanding. Thus the writer encourages a continued and open exchange of ideas with the reader. In Rogers's words, the writer "listens with" as opposed to "evaluating about."

Beyond empathetic understanding, writers should also show congruence, or genuine agreement, and an unconditional positive regard for the opposition. In communicating these attitudes, Rogerian argument takes the heat out of difficult argument that might otherwise result in a stalemate. Rogerian strategy cools the

---

[5]Richard Young, Alton Becker, and Kenneth Pike, *Rhetoric: Discovery and Change* (New York: Harcourt, Brace, and World, 1970), pp. 7–8, 274–290.

emotions and makes consensus more likely. The aim of the final reconciliation at the close of Rogerian argument attempts to show that the best solution to the issue may be a combination of what both parties want.

In real life, Rogerian argument is used frequently, particularly in business and politics, where agreement is indispensable. Some people in business claim they could not get anything done if they did not use Rogerian strategies on a daily basis. William L. Ury, one of the founders of the Program on Negotiation at Harvard Law School, claims that in business now, the best way to compete is to be able to cooperate. Cooperation is necessary because of the numerous mergers and cooperative ventures between companies. Many companies now work with the same markets and the same customers, and they cannot compete, as in former times, without weakening themselves as much as their competitors.[6] Some politicians have also resorted to Rogerian strategies to resolve difficult issues like health care and Social Security. Allowing tentative solutions to problems like these to split along party lines and stay that way is not always productive. Reaching across the lines to harness the best ideas from both political parties can be much more productive and usually leads to better solutions.

Table 11.1 contrasts Rogerian argument, as explained by Young, Becker, and Pike, with the traditional pro-and-con model of argument associated with debate.

In Chapter 5 you learned about the Toulmin model for argument. The Toulmin model and Rogerian argument have one extremely important feature in common. Even though the Toulmin model includes rebuttal, it also provides for the creation of common ground in the shared warrants between arguer and audience. Rogerian argument provides for common ground as well, but this is accomplished through the shared values and assumptions established through the summary and restatement of the opponent's position.

WRITING ROGERIAN ARGUMENT

To write Rogerian argument, according to Young, Becker, and Pike, the writer proceeds in phases rather than following set organizational patterns or argumentative strategies. These phases are as follows:

1. The writer introduces the issue and shows that the opponent's position is understood by restating it.
2. The writer shows in which contexts and under what conditions the opponent's position may be valid. Note that the opponent is never made to feel completely wrong.
3. The writer then states his or her own position, including the contexts in which it is valid.

---

[6]William L. Ury, "Getting Past No . . . to Yes! The Art of Negotiation." Workshop, Dallas, October 12, 1999.

TABLE 11.1   **Traditional and Rogerian Argument Compared**

	TRADITIONAL ARGUMENT	ROGERIAN ARGUMENT
Basic strategy	Writer states the claim and gives reasons to prove it. Writer refutes the opponent by showing what is wrong or invalid.	Writer states the opponent's claim to demonstrate understanding and shows how it is valid.
Ethos	Writer establishes own character by demonstrating competence, fair-mindedness, and goodwill.	Writer builds opponent's and enhances own character through empathy.
Logos	Writer appeals to reason to establish a claim and refute the opponent's claim.	Writer proceeds in an explanatory fashion to analyze the conditions under which the position of either side is valid.
Pathos	Writer arouses emotions with evocative language to strengthen the claim.	Writer uses descriptive, dispassionate language to cool emotions on both sides.
Goal	Writer seeks to change opponent's mind and thereby win the argument.	Writer creates cooperation, the possibility that both sides might change, and a mutually advantageous outcome.
Use of argumentative techniques	Writer draws on the conventional structures and techniques taught in Chapters 5–7 of this book.	Writer throws out conventional structures and techniques because they may be threatening and focuses instead on connecting empathetically.

4. The writer states how the opponent's position would benefit if the opponent were to adopt elements of the writer's position. An attempt is finally made to show that the two positions complement each other and that each supplies what the other lacks.

VARIATIONS OF ROGERIAN ARGUMENT

Rogerian argument as described by Young, Becker, and Pike is rarely if ever written exactly according to their format. You can learn more about Rogerian argument by practicing according to their format, however, and the Exercises and Activities section of this chapter provides four examples of Rogerian argument papers written by students who followed this format. You also will be invited to write a Rogerian argument paper by using this format.

As you read professionally written argument, however, you are much more likely to find elements or variations of Rogerian argument rather than arguments that include all of the parts of the Young, Becker, and Pike model. Here are some examples of variations of Rogerian argument that you may encounter in your academic reading:

1. *Report on past research at the beginning of an academic argument.* Authors of academic argument as a matter of convention, often begin with a review of what previous writers have contributed to the subject. They identify the writers by name and summarize their contributions before the article authors identify and develop their own contribution to the subject. Thus an ongoing chain of conversation is established that acknowledges what has gone before the new material that is the actual subject of the article.

2. *Research proposal.* Research proposals that request funds and resources from granting agencies typically begin with a positive summary of the contributions of past researchers. Only after this former work has been acknowledged does the researcher explain how the new proposed research will build on what has gone before.[7]

3. *Rogerian response paper.* This paper is written in response to an essay written by another person with whom the author disagrees. The author of a response paper typically rejects the position that the author of the other essay presents but hopes to create common ground and understanding with that person to keep a dialogue on the issue going. The goal is to make a connection with the author of the other essay and thus create a context of understanding so that both authors can continue exploring the issue. Such papers usually begin with a restatement of the other author's position along with an acknowledgment of what is valuable about that position before the author goes on to present a different view of the matter. You will be invited to try writing a Rogerian response paper yourself in Exercise C.

As you read arguments written by other authors, look for additional examples of elements of Rogerian argument. The three examples just cited by no means exhaust the possibilities.

THE ADVANTAGES AND DISADVANTAGES OF ROGERIAN ARGUMENT

The advantages of Rogerian argument are clear. Such an approach helps release tension and disagreement and encourages negotiation and cooperation when values and aims are in conflict. Also, Rogerian argument has the potential of leveling or at

---

[7]I am indebted to Mary Stanley for alerting me to this use of Rogerian argument.

least controlling uneven power relationships that may interfere with the peaceful resolution of conflicting issues.

There are also perceived disadvantages of Rogerian argument. It is sometimes difficult for the writer to understand and restate the reader's position, particularly when the opponent is not present and no written material is available to explain the opposing position. Also, connecting with the opponent by restating the opposing position may be extremely difficult if the writer is emotionally involved and strongly dislikes the opposing ideas. It takes courage, Rogers says, to listen and restate ideas that are strongly antithetical to your own. One has to want to make connections to succeed. One also has to be willing to risk change. By totally committing oneself to understanding a different viewpoint, one's own ideas will almost inevitably shift and change somewhat.[8]

Rogerian argument has also been criticized as annoying to women. Some researchers claim that women have always been expected to understand others, sometimes even at the expense of understanding themselves. As one female critic puts it, Rogerian argument "feels too much like giving in."[9] Another critic finds the advice that the writer should always use unemotional, dispassionate language to restate the opponent's argument unrealistic and constraining. Avoiding rude or insulting language is necessary, a matter of common sense. But to avoid all emotionally connotative language may be impossible.[10]

Rogerian argument persists as a viable model in spite of some of its shortcomings. Its central notion, that it is important to understand and see some validity in other people's opposing positions, is sometimes the only way to create common ground in difficult situations.

REVIEW QUESTIONS

1. What are some of the special characteristics of Rogerian argument and how does it differ from traditional argument?
2. In what types of argumentative situations do you think you might find Rogerian argument more productive than traditional argument? Give examples of at least two issues where you might profitably resort to Rogerian argument.
3. What are some of the advantages and some of the disadvantages of Rogerian argument?
4. What difficulties, if any, do you contemplate in using Rogerian argument?

---

[8]I am indebted to Paul Parmeley for this insight.

[9]See Catherine Lamb, "Beyond Argument in Feminist Composition," *College Composition and Communication,* February 1991, pp. 11–24. See also Phyllis Lassner, "Feminist Response to Rogerian Rhetoric," *Rhetoric Review* 8 (1990): 220–232.

[10]Doug Brent, "Young, Becker, and Pike's 'Rogerian' Rhetoric: A Twenty-Year Reassessment," *College English* 53 (April 1991): 446–452.

EXERCISES AND ACTIVITIES

A. CLASS DISCUSSION: UNDERSTANDING ROGERIAN ARGUMENT AS A STRATEGY

The accompanying advertisement describes an effort to reduce hostility between environmentalists and an oil company. Analyze the Rogerian strategy in this selection, and answer the following questions:

1. Why do these parties feel hostile? What are their differences?
2. Which party is the author of this ad? What interest does this party have in resolving the issue? How do both parties reduce hostility and create common ground? What common ground do they share?
3. How is Rogerian strategy employed? Summarize the major parts of the argument, and show how they conform to Rogerian strategy.
4. How effective do you think Rogerian argument will be in resolving the issues between these two parties?

B. WRITING ASSIGNMENT: ROGERIAN ARGUMENT

You are now going to write a Rogerian argument of around 1,000 words on an issue of your choice. There are several ways to set up this assignment. Read through the following options, select one that appeals to you, and proceed with the rest of the instructions for the assignment. The basic instructions in option 1 apply to all four options. Examples for options 1, 2, and 3 are provided at the end of this exercise.

1. If you wrote an exploratory paper or a position paper, write a Rogerian argument in response to the position you discovered that is most unlike the position you defended. You may have already articulated this opposing position in your exploratory paper or in a rebuttal in your position paper. Move this position to the beginning of your Rogerian argument paper, and rewrite it until you believe you have fairly and dispassionately represented that other point of view. People who hold that view need to be able to agree that you have heard and understood them. Look for common ground with that other view. Use that common ground to describe contexts and conditions where the opponent's position might be valid. Do not show what is wrong with this other position. Now write a transition that changes the subject to your position. Describe your position, and show the contexts in which is it valid. Finally, reconcile the two positions. Show how they can complement each other, how one supplies what the other lacks, and how everyone would benefit if elements of both were finally accepted. (See Example 1.)
2. Select any issue that you understand from at least two opposing points of view. It should be an issue that you feel strongly about, and you should also have strong negative feelings about the opposing viewpoint. Write a Rogerian argument in response to the opposing viewpoint. (See Example 2.)

When special care is called for

It can happen. An environmental organization and an oil company can overcome their traditional wariness and work together in an ecologically sensitive area. Here's a story of how progress can be made when people realize they share a common goal.

Scientists often compare the interdependence of life on earth with finely woven silk. Each species is a thread, and together we form a delicate fabric. Human development has, of course, altered the fabric, so there are few places left where native plants and animals are relatively untouched.

The Washington, D.C.-based environmental organization Conservation International (CI) is a leader in the effort to protect biodiversity "hotspots," regions rich in species that could be greatly affected by additional colonization, agriculture or industrialization. CI has compiled a list of 25 global hotspots that represent less than two percent of the planet's land surface but encompass more than half of the world's species. It has had much success with conservation efforts in these hotspots.

At the top of CI's list is the tropical Andes region, a narrow strip following the South American mountain range through Colombia, Ecuador, Peru and Bolivia. Within this region, which harbors over 20,000 plant species found nowhere else, lies the Tambopata River Valley. In an area as sensitive as Peru's Tambopata rain forest, even advances in farming can alter nature's fabric. Mining and oil exploration, if not properly carried out, can create tears that are difficult, if not impossible, to repair. CI has worked since 1990 with governments and local peoples to conserve and protect Tambopata's biodiversity.

So, when Mobil signed a contract in 1996 for petroleum exploration in part of the valley, CI's reaction was one of alarm. "Frankly, we didn't want to see oil development in Tambopata, but once the government granted the rights to exploration, we realized that we needed to view Mobil as another stakeholder," says Jorgen Thomsen, Vice President of CI's Conservation Biology Department. "We initiated a dialogue with the company."

Mobil was also concerned, because the company is committed to conducting exploration activities in an environmentally and socially responsible manner. We recognized that we needed to work openly and cooperatively with CI and other groups to achieve minimal environmental and social impact.

In the first phase of exploration, Mobil would obtain seismic data by setting off small energy charges and recording the resulting sound waves. We filed environmental plans with the Peruvian government showing that we would carve only yard-wide footpaths and small helicopter pads in the rain forest—best practices that are common for Mobil's seismic work. Before that work started, however, Mobil and CI held a five-day joint workshop to assess how they might work together. The participants learned a lot from each other. Perhaps the most valuable lesson was defining a common ground of shared interest.

What ultimately emerged was a unique collaborative effort that could lead to a demonstration of the coexistence of petroleum exploration and production with conservation efforts in sensitive ecosystems.

So far, we've taken just the first steps, but what we've accomplished is encouraging. In the next message, we'll discuss where the collaboration has taken both parties.

Source: Courtesy of Mobil Corporation.

3. Recall the last time you were in an argument in which you were angry and no one seemed to win. Write a letter to the individual you were arguing with. Use Rogerian strategy. (See Example 3.)
4. Team up with a classmate who disagrees with you on an issue. Take turns, articulating your partner's position until that person feels "heard" and understood. Then write a Rogerian argument in response to that position.

Prewriting

To help you prepare to write this paper, in addition to the instructions provided, write a one-paragraph summary of the opposing position and a one-paragraph summary of your position. Refer to these summaries when you write your paper.

Writing

Write your paper, making sure you do all of the following:

1. Introduce the issue, and restate the opposing position to show you understand it.
2. Show in which contexts and under what conditions the opposing position may be valid. State it so that it is acceptable to the opposition.
3. Write a clear transition that moves the reader from the position you have just explained to the position that you favor and will now defend.
4. State your own position, and describe the context in which it is valid.
5. Show how the opposing position would be strengthened if it added elements of your position, and try to reconcile the two positions.

Examples

Here are three examples of Rogerian argument written by students.

Example 1 (Assignment 1) "Human Cloning: Is It a Viable Option?" was written by a student in an argument class who had also written an exploratory paper and a position paper on this subject. Her annotated bibliography appears on pages 292–296. In writing this paper, she began with the position most unlike her own and rewrote it until she thought it would satisfy the individuals who hold this position. Notice that she was able to use the research for her other papers to add support for this paper as well. The marginal annotations make it easier for you to distinguish the parts of her paper. Following her paper is a "Rogerian Argument Evaluation Sheet" that has been filled out to show how this argument conforms to the recommended parts of the Rogerian argument. The requirements for the Rogerian argument paper are described in the left column, and the right column shows how well this paper met those requirements. When you have finished reading the papers in Examples 2 and 3, see if you can identify and describe the parts of those papers well enough to complete evaluation sheets like the sample. This analysis will help you understand how to write your own Rogerian argument.

Boatwright 1

Student Paper

Angela A. Boatwright
Rogerian Argument
Professor Thorne
English 1302
3 November 1999

Human Cloning: Is It a Viable Option?

<table>
<tr><td>1</td><td></td></tr>
</table>

1   Well, hello Dolly! Although research in animal or
human cloning is not new, the technology has never had as
much potential as it does today. Interest in what is and
is not considered ethical in cloning research has surfaced since the historic announcement in Scotland of the
existence of a cloned sheep named Dolly. Scientists were
able to create a cloned sheep by taking the genes from a
six-year-old sheep and putting them into a hollowed-out
egg from another sheep. This egg was then planted in the
womb of yet another sheep, resulting in the birth of an
identical twin that is six years younger than its sister
(Bailey). This is the first known asexual reproduction of
a mammal. It seems a reasonable assumption that a human
clone is the next logical step down this technological
pathway.

Introduction to issue and summary of rhetorical situation.

2   Those who support unregulated human cloning experimentation justify their position by citing the medical
gains and potential benefits the technology has to offer.
These people believe that the possible benefits of this
technology far outweigh the risks and, furthermore, that
it is an ethical practice because of its potential benefits. Some of these benefits include the generation of skin
grafts for burn victims and bone marrow for patients undergoing cancer chemotherapy (Butler and Wadman 8).
Cloning also shows promise for treating infertility and
could become an option either for infertile couples or
for people who have genetic defects and fear passing
these defects on to their offspring.

Explanation of opposing position to create common ground.

3   Supporters of cloning believe that the arguments
against cloning are vague and speculative and that they
simply do not justify a ban. It is not the technology
that frightens people so much as it is a lack of understanding. When people picture the result of an attempt at
human cloning, they see images of Frankenstein or an army
of Hitlers. Researchers believe that given time to digest the information, the public will one day regard

Boatwright 2

cloning with the same openness and sense of normalcy that it now regards blood transfusions and organ transplants. They also reason that a ban on cloning could drive the technology underground, where there is greater potential for unsafe, unregulated, and exploitative misuse.

Everyone would probably agree that technological ad- 4 vances have changed our lives in positive ways, and cloning research is not likely to be an exception. The fear held by cloning supporters, that the sensationalism created by this issue has clouded the judgment of the public and lawmakers who support a ban on cloning, is certainly a valid concern. Although it is not clear that human cloning will offer any great benefits to humanity, no one has yet made a persuasive case that it would do any real harm either (Macklin 64). It would be an injustice to completely abandon the possibilities that could enhance the lives of so many people based solely on hypothetical applications of a technology that may never be realized. Each disease we are able to eradicate is another huge step for humankind.

> Description of context in which opposing position is valid.

I agree that we should do everything in our power to 5 improve the longevity and quality of life of all people, but I do not believe it should be at the expense of the dignity of human life. Many people who oppose cloning view it as an "invasion of personality." Even Dr. Ian Wilmut and his colleagues, the creators of Dolly, hold the position that cloning of humans would be unethical (64). He points out that it took 277 attempts to produce one live lamb. Of the 277 "reconstructed" embryos, 29 were implanted into recipient ewes, and three out of five lambs died soon after birth and showed developmental abnormalities. He believes similar tests with humans would not be acceptable.

> Transition to author's view.
>
> Explanation of author's view.

Those of us who advocate anticloning measures be- 6 lieve that the potential abuse of such power could have disastrous consequences. The fear of the creation of human clones for the sole purpose of harvesting them for "spare parts" is too great to ignore. Another concern is that cloning will lead to efforts to breed individuals with perceived exceptional genetic qualities, eliminating the diversity that makes the human race what it is. There is a widespread belief that parents might create unrealistic expectations for cloned children, believing they no longer have the potential limitations of their genetic ancestors (Pence 135). Cloning is really a major step toward regarding our children as acceptable only if they conform to the choices of our will (Carey 32).

7   Many of us are also bound by the religious ideas we have been brought up with, that only God has the right to create life. It is sinful to think of removing that sovereign right from an omnipotent God and placing it in the hands of mere mortals. Like the majority of Americans, I believe that human cloning experimentation should be banned before it can become an out-of-control reality.

8   I am fortunate to be the mother of a wonderful and beautiful baby girl. If I had been given the opportunity to choose her characteristics, would I have elected to change my child? I absolutely would not. I would not trade any of her personal traits for something "better." I love her just as God gave her to me. Yet with absolute certainty, I can admit that if she developed a life-threatening ailment, I would not hesitate for a second to utilize any cloning technology available to cure her. This is not to say I would sacrifice another life for hers, only that I would employ any and all resources available short of that alternative.

Personal example to introduce idea of reconciliation of the two opposing positions.

9   If we can agree that human life should always be held in the highest esteem, we have the basis for reconciling our positions. Cloning should not be used to pick and choose the type of people who are allowed to exist, but we should explore the potential medical benefits of cloning technology research. Many of the medical procedures we take for granted every day were once as controversial as cloning is at this very moment. Most of these procedures became successful at the cost of testing on live beings, but with their consent. We must never allow human beings to be the subjects of experimentation without their knowledge or permission. We may not impose conditions on human beings that they might not have consented to if allowed to make the decision for themselves.

Reconciliation of positions.

10   A moratorium might be a better solution than an outright ban. A moratorium would authorize a temporary delay of human cloning research and allow us the time to sort out the details and ensure that an educated decision is made. It is easier to make an intelligent decision when there is not a feeling of impending doom hanging over our

Boatwright 4

heads. "In a democratic society we don't usually pass laws outlawing something before there is actual or probable evidence of harm" (Macklin 64). This statement can serve as a guide for future policy on human cloning. ■

Works Cited

Bailey, Ronald. "The Twin Paradox: What Exactly Is Wrong with Cloning People?" 5 Sept. 1998 <http://www.reason.com/9705/col.bailey.html>.

Butler, Declan, and Meredith Wadman. "Calls for Cloning Ban Sell Science Short." Nature 6 Mar. 1997: 8-9.

Carey, John. "Human Clones: It's Decision Time." Business Week 10 Aug. 1998: 32.

Macklin, Ruth. "Human Cloning? Don't Just Say No." U.S. News & World Report 10 Mar. 1997: 64+.

Pence, Gregory E. Who's Afraid of Human Cloning? Lanham: Rowman & Littlefield, 1998.

Wilmut, Ian. "Roslin Institute Experiments: Creation of Dolly the Sheep." Congressional Digest Feb. 1998:41+.

FOR DISCUSSION: Describe a rhetorical situation in which it would be better to write this paper in this form, using Rogerian strategy, than it would be to write it as a position paper, using traditional argument strategy. Describe the readers, constraints, and exigences in particular as you imagine the rhetorical situation for this paper.

Evaluation Sheet for Rogerian Argument Paper

REQUIREMENTS OF ROGERIAN ARGUMENT	WHAT THE AUTHOR DID
1. Introduce the issue and state opposing position to show you understand it.	1. Introduced the issue in paragraph 1 and presented the opposing view accompanied by good reasons in paragraphs 2 and 3.
2. Show how opposition might be right.	2. Showed the contexts in which the opposition might be valid in paragraph 4.

(continued)

3. Write a clear transition from the opposing position to your position.	3. Wrote a transition in the first sentence of paragraph 5 to move from opposing to own position.
4. Give your position and show how you might be right.	4. Presented own position in paragraphs 5, 6, and 7.
5. Reconcile the two positions.	5. Reconciled the two views in paragraphs 8, 9, and 10.

Example 2 (Assignment 2) "Special Education's Best Intentions" was written by a student who had returned to school after several years and whose handicapped child required special education. The issue of how handicapped children are educated in the public schools was, understandably, a particularly compelling issue for her. She had often been frustrated by school officials who seemed more interested in procedures than in her child. Even though she felt hostility for some of these individuals, she still managed to state their point of view in a way that should be acceptable to them before she introduced her own. When she finished writing this paper, she commented that she usually feels powerless when talking with school officials. The approach taken here, she thought, would probably achieve better results than a confrontational argument that accused her audience of wrongdoing and neglect.

Student Paper

```
Student Paper
Lois Agnew
Rogerian Argument
Professor Dickerman
English 1302
3 November 1999

                  Special Education's Best Intentions
```

1   The American public's growing recognition of the educational rights of handicapped children culminated in the 1975 enactment of the Education for All Handicapped Children Act, Public Law 94-142. Once the need to provide quality education for all students was clearly established as a matter of public record, it also became a

need that would demand immediate action on the part of parents and educators; the issue at hand shifted from a question of whether it should be done to how it could be done.

It is natural in the midst of such change to turn to experts for 2 guidance about how to face the challenges that lie ahead. In the years following the passage of PL 94-142, educators attempted to develop methods for identifying the needs of handicapped students in a way which would allow for the development of educational programs designed to serve their individual needs. As time went on, the methods for addressing students' goals became more carefully prescribed and were implemented primarily through the agency of designated professionals who were specially trained for dealing with such matters.

Of course, developing a system for helping students whose needs 3 are out of the ordinary had been a necessary step in assimilating those students into the world of public education. Hurling handicapped students into a regular education classroom without careful assessment of their needs would unquestionably lead to frustration on all sides. The need to determine the level of each student's skills clearly indicates the need for some type of testing program and demands the presence of individuals trained to administer and interpret those tests. The entire process is obviously a crucial element in meeting the educational needs of handicapped children.

However, the challenge of efficiently offering help to massive 4 numbers of students has inevitably resulted in the evolution of a bureaucratic network with all of the disadvantages inherent in such a system. State education agencies and local school districts alike have carefully allocated tremendous resources to carrying out the mandate of PL 94-142; the assurance they have provided anxious parents lies in their promise to find appropriate educational placement in the least restrictive environment possible for each child. The means for attempting such a mammoth task involves the use of a standard process of evaluation and diagnosis that will enable the experts assigned to the task to assess not only each child's present levels of performance educationally but also ultimately to make judgments about the child's potential for classroom performance in the future.

It is in this respect that the bureaucratic nature of the special 5 education program falters in meeting the needs of the individual child. As necessary as such a system may be to guarantee the efficient handling of large volumes of work, it becomes difficult in practice to maintain a focus on evaluation as the necessary means to the worthwhile end of providing children with new educational opportunities; too often it becomes an end in itself, a source of a convenient label that in turn is used to predict where a child's limits will lie. It is a tragedy of our educational system that in spite of the good intentions that have led us to emphasize test results and diagnosis for children with special needs, the machinelike efficiency of our program has achieved most of its goals without acknowledging what is most important, addressing the needs of students as individuals. The idea of trained diagnosticians administering objective tests to students to determine their educational placement must be appealing to a society that values scientific method to the degree ours does; however, few real live children fall neatly into the categories that represent the conclusion of the process. Once their futures have been charted by the system, it becomes increasingly difficult for them to prove that they have potential beyond that predicted by the experts.

6   I am the parent of such a child and have on many occasions experienced the frustration of watching well-meaning educators become so absorbed with finding an appropriate label for my son that they have apparently lost sight of the goal of educating him. Although I share the interest they have in finding an appropriate educational placement for him, I have in the meantime grown weary of the process. I have seen my child through the ordeal of psychological, neurological, language, and educational evaluations, all conducted by authorities in their fields with an impressive assortment of credentials, and can state with certainty that the ability to help him is unrelated to the specialized training the system values most. Those who have made a significant difference in my son's life have been those rare people who have encountered him as an individual and have devoted their energies to bringing out his potential without reservation and have been willing in the process to stop worrying about how he should be labeled. My contact with other parents of children with special needs tells me that my reaction to the process is quite common.

7   There is no question about the fact that the special education bureaucracy serves a useful purpose in helping students find the classrooms and programs most suited to their needs. At the same time, it often appears to be a tendency for any bureaucratic system to become so absorbed with its own structure, so convinced of the infallibility of the experts it employs, that it fails to devote adequate attention to each person it attempts to serve. Because special education involves so many thousands of unique students, it seems almost impossible to find a balance between the efficiency that benefits everyone and the personal attention that is a crucial part of the process. Yet with children's lives at stake, it is critical that we never give up the effort to do so. ■

FOR DISCUSSION: Provide some examples from your own experiences in school when you were treated as a member of the group and when you were treated as an individual. What are some measures that administrators and teachers could take to provide more individual attention for students?

Example 3 (Assignment 3) "Dear Mom" was written by a student whose parents wanted her to move out of her apartment and either come home, find a cheaper apartment, or move back into the dormitories. This student wrote her Rogerian argument as a letter addressed to her mother. She began by stating her mother's view and even read this part to her mother to make certain she was stating it accurately. She then acknowledged the advantages of her mother's view but went on to show why her own views were also advantageous and valid. At the end, she reconciles her parent's views with her own and shows how her position benefits both of them. She finally gave this letter to both of her parents to read. The result was that her parents agreed to allow her to stay in her apartment.

```
Student Paper
Taryn Barnett
Rogerian Argument
Professor Berthiaume
English 1302
3 November 1999
```

Student Paper

Dear Mom

Dear Mom,

    I wanted to write you a letter regarding the conversation we had 1 yesterday. You said that you wanted me to do one of three things: move home, transfer to a cheaper complex, or move into the dorms. I understand that you believe these options would allow me to work less and save more money in order to concentrate on my studies. You think that this would be financially simpler for you and for me and much less stressful for me.

    I understand the logic behind your position in that the whole 2 financial situation would be easier if I were living at home. First of all, we would not have as many expenses. Living at home would eliminate rent payments, cable bills, and electricity bills, but it would not eliminate phone bills, insurance bills, gas bills, or personal items. This would allow me to take some of the money that I am earning now and save it to give myself a strong financial foundation as I become more independent in the future. If I did not have a job and were under a lot of stress, I could see how it would make sense to move back home. If safety were not an issue, I could see how it would save me money to move to a cheaper apartment complex. Also, moving into a cheaper apartment complex could eliminate the worries and the need for a roommate. For example, I have a roommate now, and I have to worry about whether or not she will pay her share of the bills on time or whether I will have to cover for her until she has the money. Now, if I were going away to school, I could see the advantages of living in the dorms. This would include not having to worry about the bills, meeting more people from school, and entering all of the social aspects of living on campus. It is also safer to live in a well-monitored environment. I see the ways your points are valid, so let us discuss those points and work together to find a good solution for both of us.

3   I believe that staying in school while working part-time in order to live in this complex is showing responsibility on my part. A big part of this for me is pride. I want to be able to prove to you and dad that I can do it on my own with as minimal help from you as possible. Not only is having this independence important to me, but it also helps me learn about life through experience. To me, independence is learning to handle being responsible for myself and my actions, in which I figure out how to decide what to do, when to do it, and when to buckle down. Taking things into my hands and making sure everything that needs to get done does get done is a responsibility that I have learned how to prioritize. Now, in having this independence and showing my responsibility by keeping up with paying the bills on time (cable, phone, rent, and electricity) and getting my schoolwork done for all four of my classes (Music Appreciation, Political Science, Psychology, and English), I am building up my credit and learning self-discipline. By self-discipline I mean teaching myself what is important to me and making sure I keep up with the work and reading in my classes. I pay $430 per month for rent in my apartment complex, and in comparison to some that are $395 per month all bills paid, I may not be in a cheap complex, but I am in a safe complex. When a young woman lives alone, that is essential. It is a well-known fact that the cheaper the area of the apartment complex, the more prevalent is crime.

4   Since I am a full-time student and I get financial assistance from you and Dad, I can work part-time and afford my apartment. If I were to move back home, I would not get the financial support from you and Dad. So I would still have to work the same number of hours in order to have any money because the only thing I would not have to worry about financially would be rent. Although this offers less financial stress for you, it increases personal and operational stress between us. So if we can keep our minds open, we can see how our points complement each other.

5   Our points of view are very similar because any way you go, I am saving the same amount of money. With your plan I have less income with less bills and work part-time to get by. With my plan I work the same number of hours and I get financial help from you and Dad to help pay for the living expenses, but I have more expenses. So you can see that either way I go to school, work, and save the same amount of money. Only if I stay in my apartment complex, I have all of the benefits, and I learn how to live independently. You also say you worry about my stress levels. It is true that living in an apartment is sometimes stressful. But it would be more stressful for both of us if I took the

easy way and moved home. I would no longer be learning independence. To reassure you, I can call and visit you more often, and I can report on the progress I am making in my classes. I think, however, that both of our needs will best be met if I stay in my apartment, learn to manage my time to keep up with school and work, learn to manage my money and pay the bills, and learn to live independently. Both of us share that final goal for me. So unless I prove myself to be irresponsible, please do not ask me to give up my independence and move home. ■

Love,
Taryn

FOR DISCUSSION: The student who wrote this letter was at a standoff with her parents on this issue. Why do you think the Rogerian approach helped her change her parents' minds? Describe what is effective in this letter. Could you write a Rogerian letter on a personal matter? What topics would you consider appropriate for a letter that employs this particular argument strategy?

C. WRITING ASSIGNMENT: THE ROGERIAN RESPONSE PAPER

A Rogerian response paper is somewhat different from the examples of Rogerian argument presented in Exercise B in that it is written in direct response to a particular essay. The process involves reading and understanding an essay with which you disagree and responding to it using Rogerian strategy.[11] Here are some possible articles to respond to:

1. Write a response to one of these articles. You will surely find yourself in disagreement with one of them: "What's Happened to Disney Films?" (pages 144–145), "Let Gays Marry" (pages 465–467), "Leave Marriage Alone" (pages 467–468), "Making the Grade" (pages 489–491), "The Doom Factor" (pages 528–529), or "The Great Campus Goof-Off Machine" (pages 561–562).
2. Find a letter to the editor in your local or school newspaper that you disagree with, and write a Rogerian response to it.

Your paper should be at least 500 words long.

Prewriting

Write a brief summary of the opposing position and a brief summary of your position to make certain you understand them both clearly.

Writing

Do all of the following in your paper:

1. State the opposition's position as presented in the article, and describe in what instances this position might work or be acceptable. As you write,

---

[11]I am indebted to Barbara Chiarello for the general concept of this assignment.

imagine that the author of the article will be reading your response. Write so that that person will feel "heard."

2. Write a clear transition to your position on the issue.
3. State how your position would also work or be acceptable.
4. Try to reconcile the two positions.

The following is an example of a Rogerian response paper written by a student in an argument class. She wrote in response to the essay "Can Women 'Have It All'?" by William A. Henry III on pages 441–444 of "The Reader."

Student Paper
Doran Hayes
Rogerian Response
Professor Wood
English 1302
3 November 1999

A Letter to William A. Henry III

Dear Mr. Henry:

1   I am writing you in regard to your essay "Can Women 'Have It All'?" You and I are both interested in women and their opportunities in modern society. You believe that women have considerable opportunity and that the feminist movement may not be realistic in its search for total equality between men and women. You further believe that according to many different standards, women are already equal. You point out that one-third of all medical school, law school, and business school graduates are women. In fact, 46% of the financial managers, 42% of the biologists, 39% of the math professors, and most of the journalists and psychologists in the nation today are women. Few women actually run major corporations, but many women in middle management appear to be heading in that direction. There is no longer an excuse for affirmative action for women because, unlike people of different races, women's grievances are irrelevant and mostly self-imposed. Even though women may believe that they are descended from a long line of thwarted women, you point out they are also descended from a long line of unthwarted men. The biological link is the same from both sources and is inconsequential. You point out that although women tend to be on the lower rungs of the economic ladder, this occurs as a consequence of less education, poor career choices, and less commitment to the job. Society would be better off, according to your views, if women would stay home, at least until the children are in school, to avoid a decline in the quality of their education.

I believe you are correct when you say that the women's move- 2 ment, like all other movements striving for great change, is at times unrealistic and at times even somewhat ridiculous. And it is true that in many areas, women are becoming the majority. It is also true that many other women are less educated and do not make career choices that will move them to higher economic brackets. It is also true that the effects of day care and nannies may well be damaging to the educational progress of a child.

However, you and I have some differences regarding modern women 3 and the women's movement. I believe that the women's movement has resulted in great advances in society and that those advances greatly outweigh the moments when the movement has seemed ridiculous. I also feel that women are making great strides in the work force but that many obstacles to their advancement still exist. And these obstacles are not all self-imposed. I believe that when women make what you call "poor career choices," they do so out of necessity. Many have no other options. Women still need affirmative action to provide them with equal opportunity. I believe, with you, that children surely fare better under the early tutelage of parents. But why should it be the duty of the woman to give up her career and provide all of this early care? The influence of the father could be of equal, if not greater, importance to the development of a young, impressionable mind.

Why not regard women and men as equal, unthwarted adults? This 4 would help all women gain the equality you believe they already have and I believe they have not yet quite achieved. True equality would help women solve their economic, educational, and career problems, whether they are self-imposed or not. Women and men, working together, can also contribute to the care and education of their children without either having to sacrifice a career, so long as the work at home is shared. Men have much to contribute to their children and much to gain as well from closer contact with them. If men and women worked together for true equality, many of the "silly" concerns you associate with the feminist movement would surely disappear. ▪

Sincerely,
Doran Hayes

FOR DISCUSSION: Do you think that Henry would feel "heard" and understood if he read this letter? Do you think Henry's views might change as a result of reading this letter? If this letter were published in a magazine or journal as an answer to Henry's essay, what do you think the effect would be on the people who happened to read it? What would they think about William Henry? What would they think about Doran Hayes? Which of these authors is more convincing to you?

APPENDIX TO CHAPTER ELEVEN

Review and Synthesis of the Strategies for Reading and Writing Argument

The purpose of this Appendix is to provide you with the opportunity to review and synthesize what you have learned about reading and writing argument in the first eleven chapters of this book. You will apply argument theory as you read and understand a famous classic argument, Martin Luther King Jr.'s "Letter from Birmingham Jail."

When you finish, you will write a paper that answers the question, *Why is King's letter considered a classic argument?* In answering this question, you will draw on what you know about traditional argument and Rogerian argument. Begin by reading about the rhetorical situation for the letter.

RHETORICAL SITUATION FOR MARTIN LUTHER KING JR.'S "LETTER FROM BIRMINGHAM JAIL"

Birmingham, Alabama, was a very strange place in 1963. Black people were allowed to sit only in certain parts of buses and restaurants, they were required to drink out of separate water fountains, and they were not allowed in white churches, schools, or various other public places. The Reverend Martin Luther King Jr. was a black Baptist minister who was a leader in the civil rights movement at that time. The purpose of the movement was to end segregation and discrimination and to obtain equal rights and access for black people.

King and others carefully prepared for demonstrations that would take place in Birmingham in the spring of 1963. The demonstrators began by "sitting in" at lunch counters that had never served blacks before and by picketing stores. Twenty people were arrested the first day on charges of trespassing. Next, the civil rights leaders applied for permits to picket and hold parades against the injustices of discrimination and segregation. They were refused permission, but they demonstrated and picketed anyway. King was served an injunction by a circuit judge that said civil rights leaders could not protest, demonstrate, boycott, or sit in. King and others decided that this was an unfair and unjust application of the law, and they decided to break it.

King himself decided to march on Good Friday, and he expected to go to jail. Indeed, before he had walked half a mile, he was arrested and jailed, along with fifty other people. King stayed in jail for eight days. During that time he wrote his famous letter. It was written in response to a letter signed by eight white clergymen that had been published in a local newspaper.

After King left jail, there were further protests and some violence. Thousands of people demonstrated, and thousands were jailed. Finally, black and white leaders began to negotiate, and some final terms were announced on May 10, 1963. All lunch counters, restrooms, fitting rooms, and drinking fountains in downtown stores were to be desegregated within ninety days; blacks were to be hired in clerical and sales jobs in stores within sixty days; the many people arrested during the demonstrations were to be released on low bail; and permanent lines of communication were to be established between black and white leaders. The demonstrations ended then, and the city settled down and began to implement the agreements.[1]

READING THE LETTERS AND REPORTING TO THE CLASS

Divide the class into seven groups, and assign one of the following focus topics to each group. To prepare for the group work, all students read the two letters outside of class and make individual notes on the focus topics assigned to their groups. The brief questions in the margin will facilitate this reading and note taking. In class the groups will meet briefly to consolidate their views on the topic. Each group will then make a brief oral report, and other class members will discuss the results and take some notes. These notes will be used as prewriting materials for the paper described on page 368, paragraph 2.

Focus Topics

> **Group 1: Rhetorical situation and Rogerian elements.** Answer these questions:
>
> > a. What is the *exigence* for these two letters? What caused the authors to write them? What was the problem? Was it a new or recurring problem?
> > b. Who is the *audience* for the clergymen's letter? For King's letter? What is the nature of these audiences? Can they be convinced? What are the expected outcomes?
> > c. What are the *constraints*? Speculate about the beliefs, attitudes, habits, and traditions that were in place that limited or constrained both the

---

[1]This account is drawn from Lee E. Bains Jr., "Birmingham, 1963: Confrontation over Civil Rights," in *Birmingham, Alabama, 1956–1963: The Black Struggle for Civil Rights,* ed. David J. Garrow (Brooklyn: Carlson, 1989), pp. 175–183.

clergymen and King. How did these constraining circumstances influence the audience at that time?

d. Think about the *authors* of both letters. Who are they? Speculate about their background, experience, affiliations, and values. What motivates them to write?

e. What kind of *text* is this? What effect do its special qualities and features have on the audience?

f. Think about *yourself as the reader.* What is your position on the issue? Do you experience constraints as you read? Do you perceive common ground with either the clergymen or King or both? Describe it. Are you influenced by these letters? How?

g. Are there any efforts to use *Rogerian argument* strategies and thereby build common ground by establishing that the opposition may at times be correct? If yes, provide some examples and analyze their effect.

Group 2: Organization and claims. Divide each letter into its main parts. What is the subject of each part? Why have the parts been placed in this particular order? What is the relationship between them? What is the main claim in each letter? What types of claims are they? What are some of the subclaims? What types of claims are they?

Group 3: Logical proofs and style. Analyze the use of logical proof in each of the letters. Provide examples. Describe their effect on the audience. Provide an example of the language of rational style in one of the letters.

Group 4: Emotional proofs and style. Analyze the use of emotional proof in each of the letters. Provide examples. Describe their effect on the audience. Provide an example of the language of emotional style in one of the letters.

Group 5: Proofs and style that establish *ethos*. Analyze the use of proofs that establish *ethos* or credibility in the letters. Provide examples. Describe their effect on the audience. Provide an example of language that establishes *ethos* in one of the letters.

Group 6: Warrants. Identity the warrants in each of the letters. How much common ground do you think exists between the authors of the letters? How much common ground do you share with the authors? As a result, which do you find more convincing? Why?

Group 7: Fallacious thinking and rebuttals. Provide examples of reasoning that is considered fallacious or wrongheaded by the opposing parties in each of the letters. What rebuttals are made in response to these? How effective are they?

A CALL FOR UNITY: A LETTER
FROM EIGHT WHITE CLERGYMEN

Essay 1

April 12, 1963

We the undersigned clergymen are among those who, in January, issued "An Appeal for Law and Order and Common Sense," in dealing with racial problems in Alabama. We expressed understanding that honest convictions in racial matters could properly be pursued in the courts, but urged that decisions of those courts should in the meantime be peacefully obeyed. [1]

Since that time there had been some evidence of increased forbearance and a willingness to face facts. Responsible citizens have undertaken to work on various problems which cause racial friction and unrest. In Birmingham, recent public events have given indication that we all have opportunity for a new constructive and realistic approach to racial problems. [2]

However, we are now confronted by a series of demonstrations by some of our Negro citizens, directed and led in part by outsiders. We recognize the natural impatience of people who feel that their hopes are slow in being realized. But we are convinced that these demonstrations are unwise and untimely. [3]

We agree rather with certain local Negro leadership which has called for honest and open negotiation of racial issues in our area. And we believe this kind of facing of issues can best be accomplished by citizens of our own metropolitan area, white and Negro, meeting with their knowledge and experience of the local situation. All of us need to face that responsibility and find proper channels for its accomplishment. [4]

Just as we formerly pointed out that "hatred and violence have no sanction in our religious and political traditions," we also point out that such actions as incite to hatred and violence, however technically peaceful those actions may be, have not contributed to the resolution of our local problems. We do not believe that these days of new hope are days when extreme measures are justified in Birmingham. [5]

We commend the community as a whole, and the local news media and law enforcement officials in particular, on the calm manner in which these demonstrations have been handled. We urge the public to continue to show restraint should the demonstrations continue, and the law enforcement officials to remain calm and continue to protect our city from violence. [6]

We further strongly urge our own Negro community to withdraw support from these demonstrations, and to unite locally in [7]

Marginal questions:

What is the issue?

What is the clergymen's position?

What is the claim?

What type of claim is it?

What are the rebuttals?

How do the authors build *ethos*?

How do they appeal to logic?

How do they appeal to emotion?

What are the warrants?

Describe the predominant style.

working peacefully for a better Birmingham. When rights are consistently denied, a cause should be pressed in the courts and in negotiations among local leaders, and not in the streets. We appeal to both our white and Negro citizenry to observe the principles of law and order and common sense.

(Signed)

C.C.J. Carpenter, D.D., L.L.D, Bishop of Alabama; Joseph A. Durick, D.D., Auxiliary Bishop, Diocese of Mobile-Birmingham; Rabbi Milton L. Grafman, Temple Emanu-El, Birmingham, Alabama; Bishop Paul Hardin, Bishop of the Alabama–West Florida Conference of the Methodist Church; Bishop Nolan B. Harmon, Bishop of the North Alabama Conference of the Methodist Church; George M. Murray, D.D., L.L.D., Bishop Coadjutor, Episcopal Diocese of Alabama; Edward V. Ramage, Moderator, Synod of the Alabama Presbyterian Church in the United States; Earl Stallings, Pastor, First Baptist Church, Birmingham. ■

LETTER FROM BIRMINGHAM JAIL*

Martin Luther King Jr.

Essay 1

April 16, 1963

My Dear Fellow Clergymen:

What is the issue?
What is King's position?

Identify and describe the Rogerian elements and efforts to establish common ground throughout this letter.

1   While confined here in the Birmingham city jail, I came across your recent statement calling my present activities "unwise and untimely." Seldom do I pause to answer criticism of my work and ideas. If I sought to answer all the criticisms that cross my desk, my secretaries would have little time for anything other than such correspondence in the course of the day, and I would have no time for constructive work. But since I feel that you are men of genuine

---

* **Author's Note:** This response to a published statement by eight fellow clergymen from Alabama (Bishop C.C.J. Carpenter, Bishop Joseph A. Durick, Rabbi Milton L. Grafman, Bishop Paul Hardin, Bishop Nolan B. Harmon, the Reverend George M. Murray, the Reverend Edward V. Ramage, and the Reverend Earl Stallings) was composed under somewhat constricting circumstances. Begun on the margins of the newspaper in which the statement appeared while I was in jail, the letter was continued on scraps of writing paper supplied by a friendly Negro trusty, and concluded on a pad my attorneys were eventually permitted to leave me. Although the text remains in substance unaltered, I have indulged in the author's perogative of polishing it for publication.

good will and that your criticisms are sincerely set forth, I want to try to answer your statement in what I hope will be patient and reasonable terms.

I think I should indicate why I am here in Birmingham, since 2 you have been influenced by the view which argues against "outsiders coming in." I have the honor of serving as president of the Southern Christian Leadership Conference, an organization operating in every southern state, with headquarters in Atlanta, Georgia. We have some eighty-five affiliated organizations across the South, and one of them is the Alabama Christian Movement for Human Rights. Frequently we share staff, educational and financial resources with our affiliates. Several months ago the affiliate here in Birmingham asked us to be on call to engage in a nonviolent direct-action program if such were deemed necessary. We readily consented, and when the hour came we lived up to our promise. So I, along with several members of my staff, am here because I was invited here. I am here because I have organizational ties here.

But more basically, I am in Birmingham because injustice is 3 here. Just as the prophets of the eighth century B.C. left their villages and carried their "thus saith the Lord" far beyond the boundaries of their home towns, and just as the Apostle Paul left his village of Tarsus and carried the gospel of Jesus Christ to the far corners of the Greco-Roman world, so am I compelled to carry the gospel of freedom beyond my own home town. Like Paul, I must constantly respond to the Macedonian call for aid.

How does King build ethos?

What is the effect of the comparison with Paul?

Draw a line at the end of the introduction.

Moreover, I am cognizant of the interrelatedness of all commu- 4 nities and states. I cannot sit idly by in Atlanta and not be concerned about what happens in Birmingham. Injustice anywhere is a threat to justice everywhere. We are caught in an inescapable network of mutuality, tied in a single garment of destiny. Whatever affects one directly, affects all indirectly. Never again can we afford to live with the narrow, provincial "outside agitator" idea. Anyone who lives inside the United States can never be considered an outsider anywhere within its bounds.

Draw other lines at the end of each of the other major sections of material. Label the subject of each section in the margin.

You deplore the demonstrations taking place in Birmingham. 5 But your statement, I am sorry to say, fails to express a similar concern for the conditions that brought about the demonstrations. I am sure that none of you would want to rest content with the superficial kind of social analysis that deals merely with effects and does not grapple with underlying causes. It is unfortunate that demonstrations are taking place in Birmingham, but it is even more unfortunate that the city's white power structure left the Negro community with no alternative.

What is the subject of this first section?

What is the claim?

What type of claim is it?

Is it qualified?

In any nonviolent campaign there are four basic steps: collec- 6 tion of the facts to determine whether injustices exist; negotiation;

Identify and analyze the effect of the emotional appeals.

self-purification; and direct action. We have gone through all these steps in Birmingham. There can be no gain-saying the fact that racial injustice engulfs this community. Birmingham is probably the most thoroughly segregated city in the United States. Its ugly record of brutality is widely known. Negroes have experienced grossly unjust treatment in the courts. There have been more unsolved bombings of Negro homes and churches in Birmingham than in any other city in the nation. These are the hard, brutal facts of the case. On the basis of these conditions, Negro leaders sought to negotiate with the city fathers. But the latter consistently refused to engage in good-faith negotiation.

7   Then, last September, came the opportunity to talk with leaders of Birmingham's economic community. In the course of the negotiations, certain promises were made by the merchants—for example, to remove the stores' humiliating racial signs. On the basis of these promises, the Reverend Fred Shuttlesworth and the leaders of the Alabama Christian Movement for Human Rights agreed to a moratorium on all demonstrations. As the weeks and months went by, we realized that we were the victims of a broken promise. A few signs, briefly removed, returned; the others remained.

What are some of the values expressed in this argument?

8   As in so many past experiences, our hopes had been blasted, and the shadow of deep disappointment settled upon us. We had no alternative except to prepare for direct action, whereby we would present our very bodies as a means of laying our case before the conscience of the local and the national community. Mindful of the difficulties involved, we decided to undertake a process of self-purification. We began a series of workshops on nonviolence, and we repeatedly asked ourselves: "Are you able to accept blows without retaliating?" "Are you able to endure the ordeal of jail?" We decided to schedule our direct-action program for the Easter season, realizing that except for Christmas, this is the main shopping period of the year. Knowing that a strong economic-withdrawal program would be the by-product of direct action, we felt that this would be the best time to bring pressure to bear on the merchants for the needed change.

9   Then it occurred to us that Birmingham's mayoral election was coming up in March, and we speedily decided to postpone action until after election day. When we discovered that the Commissioner of Public Safety, Eugene "Bull" Connor, had piled up enough votes to be in the runoff, we decided again to postpone action until the day after the runoff so that the demonstrations could not be used to cloud the issues. Like many others, we waited to see Mr. Connor defeated, and to this end we endured postponement after postponement. Having aided in this community need, we felt that our direct-action program could be delayed no longer.

You may well ask: "Why direct action? Why sit-ins, marches and so forth? Isn't negotiation a better path?" You are quite right in calling for negotiation. Indeed, this is the very purpose of direct action. Nonviolent direct action seeks to create such a crisis and foster such a tension that a community which has constantly refused to negotiate is forced to confront the issue. It seeks so to dramatize the issue that it can no longer be ignored. My citing the creation of tension as part of the work of the nonviolent-resister may sound rather shocking. But I must confess that I am not afraid of the word "tension." I have earnestly opposed violent tension, but there is a type of constructive, nonviolent tension which is necessary for growth. Just as Socrates felt that it was necessary to create a tension in the mind so that individuals could rise from the bondage of myths and half-truths to the unfettered realm of creative analysis and objective appraisal, so must we see the need for nonviolent gadflies to create the kind of tension in society that will help men rise from the dark depths of prejudice and racism to the majestic heights of understanding and brotherhood.

The purpose of our direct-action program is to create a situation so crisis-packed that it will inevitably open the door to negotiation. I therefore concur with you in your call for negotiation. Too long has our beloved Southland been bogged down in a tragic effort to live in monologue rather than dialogue.

One of the basic points in your statement is that the action that I and my associates have taken in Birmingham is untimely. Some have asked: "Why didn't you give the new city administration time to act?" The only answer that I can give to this query is that the new Birmingham administration must be prodded about as much as the outgoing one, before it will act. We are sadly mistaken if we feel that the election of Albert Boutwell as mayor will bring the millennium to Birmingham. While Mr. Boutwell is a much more gentle person than Mr. Connor, they are both segregationists, dedicated to the maintenance of the status quo. I have hope that Mr. Boutwell will be reasonable enough to see the futility of massive resistance to desegregation. But he will not see this without pressure from devotees of civil rights. My friends, I must say to you that we have not made a single gain in civil rights without determined legal and nonviolent pressure. Lamentably, it is a historical fact that privileged groups seldom give up their privileges voluntarily. Individuals may see the moral light and voluntarily give up their unjust posture; but, as Reinhold Niebuhr has reminded us, groups tend to be more immoral than individuals.

We know through painful experience that freedom is never voluntarily given up by the oppressor; it must be demanded by the oppressed. Frankly, I have yet to engage in a direct-action campaign

10　Identify and describe the rebuttals.

What is the effect of the comparison with Socrates?

11　What is King's planned argumentative strategy?

12

Why does King refer to history?

Why does he refer to Niebuhr?

13　Identify and analyze the emotional proof.

What human motives and values does King appeal to?

that was "well-timed" in the view of those who have not suffered unduly from the disease of segregation. For years now I have heard the word "Wait!" It rings in the ear of every Negro with piercing familiarity. This "Wait" has almost always meant "Never." We must come to see, with one of our distinguished jurists, that "justice too long delayed is justice denied."

14   We have waited for more than 340 years for our constitutional and God-given rights. The nations of Asia and Africa are moving with jetlike speed toward gaining political independence, but we still creep at horse-and-buggy pace toward gaining a cup of coffee at a lunch counter. Perhaps it is easy for those who have never felt the stinging darts of segregation to say, "Wait." But when you have seen vicious mobs lynch your mothers and fathers at will and drown your sisters and brothers at whim; when you have seen hate-filled policemen curse, kick and even kill your black brothers and sisters; when you see the vast majority of your twenty million Negro brothers smothering in an airtight cage of poverty in the midst of an affluent society; when you suddenly find your tongue twisted and your speech stammering as you seek to explain to your six-year-old daughter why she can't go to the public amusement park that has just been advertised on television, and see tears welling up in her eyes when she is told that Fun-town is closed to colored children, and see ominous clouds of inferiority beginning to form in her little mental sky, and see her beginning to distort her personality by developing an unconscious bitterness toward white people; when you have to concoct an answer for a five-year-old son who is asking; "Daddy, why do white people treat colored people so mean?"; when you take a cross-country drive and find it necessary to sleep night after night in the uncomfortable corners of your automobile because no motel will accept you; when you are humiliated day in and day out by nagging signs reading "white" and "colored"; when your first name becomes "nigger," your middle name becomes "boy" (however old you are) and your last name becomes "John," and your wife and mother are never given the respected title "Mrs."; when you are harried by day and haunted by night by the fact that you are a Negro, living constantly at tiptoe stance, never quite knowing what to expect next, and are plagued with inner fears and outer resentments; when you are forever fighting a degenerating sense of "nobodiness"—then you will understand why we find it difficult to wait. There comes a time when the cup of endurance runs over, and men are no longer willing to be plunged into the abyss of despair. I hope, sirs, you can understand our legitimate and unavoidable impatience.

Identify emotional language, examples, and vivid description.

What is the effect of the emotional proof?

What is the predominant type of proof in the first section of the letter?

15   You express a great deal of anxiety over our willingness to break laws. This is certainly a legitimate concern. Since we so diligently urge people to obey the Supreme Court's decision of 1954

outlawing segregation in the public schools, at first glance it may seem rather paradoxical for us consciously to break laws. One may well ask: "How can you advocate breaking some laws and obeying others?" The answer lies in the fact that there are two types of laws: just and unjust. I would be the first to advocate obeying just laws. Conversely, one has a moral responsibility to disobey unjust laws. I would agree with St. Augustine that "an unjust law is no law at all."

Draw a line where the subject changes. What is the subject of the second section?

Now, what is the difference between the two? How does one determine whether a law is just or unjust? A just law is a man-made code that squares with the moral law or the law of God. An unjust law is a code that is out of harmony with the moral law. To put it in the terms of St. Thomas Aquinas: An unjust law is a human law that is not rooted in eternal law and natural law. Any law that uplifts human personality is just. Any law that degrades human personality is unjust. All segregation statutes are unjust because segregation distorts the soul and damages the personality. It gives the segregator a false sense of superiority and the segregated a false sense of inferiority. Segregation, to use the terminology of the Jewish philosopher Martin Buber, substitutes an "I-it" relationship for an "I-thou" relationship and ends up relegating persons to the status of things. Hence segregation is not only politically, economically, and sociologically unsound, it is morally wrong and sinful. Paul Tillich has said that sin is separation. Is not segregation an existential expression of man's tragic separation, his awful estrangement, his terrible sinfulness? Thus it is that I can urge men to obey the 1954 decision of the Supreme Court, for it is morally right; and I can urge them to disobey segregation ordinances, for they are morally wrong.

16

How and why does King use definition?

How does he support the definition?

What is the effect of the support?

Let us consider a more concrete example of just and unjust laws. An unjust law is a code that a numerical or power majority group compels a minority group to obey but does not make binding on itself. This is *difference* made legal. By the same token, a just law is a code that a majority compels a minority to follow and that it is willing to follow itself. This is *sameness* made legal.

17

Explain the example of just and unjust laws.

Let me give another explanation. A law is unjust if it is inflicted on a minority that, as a result of being denied the right to vote, had no part in enacting or devising the law. Who can say that the legislature of Alabama which set up that state's segregation laws was democratically elected? Throughout Alabama all sorts of devious methods are used to prevent Negroes from becoming registered voters, and there are some counties in which, even though Negroes constitute a majority of the population, not a single Negro is registered. Can any law enacted under such circumstances be considered democratically structured?

18

How does King further elaborate on this idea?

Sometimes a law is just on its face and unjust in its application. For instance, I have been arrested on a charge of parading without a

19

permit. Now, there is nothing wrong in having an ordinance which requires a permit for a parade. But such an ordinance becomes unjust when it is used to maintain segregation and to deny citizens the First-Amendment privilege of peaceful assembly and protest.

20   I hope you are able to see the distinction I am trying to point out. In no sense do I advocate evading or defying the law, as would the rabid segregationist. That would lead to anarchy. One who breaks an unjust law must do so openly, lovingly, and with a willingness to accept the penalty. I submit that an individual who breaks a law that conscience tells him is unjust, and who willingly accepts the penalty of imprisonment in order to arouse the conscience of the community over its injustice, is in reality expressing the highest respect for law.

Analyze the deductive reasoning in this paragraph.

21   Of course, there is nothing new about this kind of civil disobedience. It was evidenced sublimely in the refusal of Shadrach, Meshach and Abednego to obey the laws of Nebuchadnezzar, on the ground that a higher moral law was at stake. It was practiced superbly by the early Christians, who were willing to face hungry lions and the excruciating pain of chopping blocks rather than submit to certain unjust laws of the Roman Empire. To a degree, academic freedom is a reality today because Socrates practiced civil disobedience. In our own nation, the Boston Tea Party represented a massive act of civil disobedience.

Identify and describe the effect of the historical analogies.

22   We should never forget that everything Adolf Hitler did in Germany was "legal" and everything the Hungarian freedom fighters did in Hungary was "illegal." It was "illegal" to aid and comfort a Jew in Hitler's Germany. Even so, I am sure that, had I lived in Germany at the time, I would have aided and comforted my Jewish brothers. If today I lived in a Communist country where certain principles dear to the Christian faith are suppressed, I would openly advocate disobeying that country's antireligious laws.

What type of proof predominates in the second part of the letter?

Draw a line where the subject changes. What is the subject of the third section?

23   I must make two honest confessions to you, my Christian and Jewish brothers. First, I must confess that over the past few years I have been gravely disappointed with the white moderate. I have almost reached the regrettable conclusion that the Negro's great stumbling block in his stride toward freedom is not the White Citizen's Counciler or the Ku Klux Klanner, but the white moderate, who is more devoted to "order" than to justice; who prefers a negative peace which is the absence of tension to a positive peace which is the presence of justice; who constantly says: "I agree with you in the goal you seek, but I cannot agree with your methods of direct action"; who paternalistically believes he can set the timetable for another man's freedom; who lives by a mythical concept of time and who constantly advises the Negro to wait for a "more convenient season." Shallow understanding from people of good will is more frustrating than ab-

What are King's warrants in this passage?

solute misunderstanding from people of ill will. Lukewarm acceptance is much more bewildering than outright rejection.

I had hoped that the white moderate would understand that
law and order exist for the purpose of establishing justice and that
when they fail in this purpose they become the dangerously structured dams that block the flow of social progress. I had hoped that the
white moderate would understand that the present tension in the
South is a necessary phase of the transition from an obnoxious negative peace, in which the Negro passively accepted his unjust plight,
to a substantive and positive peace, in which all men will respect the
dignity and worth of human personality. Actually, we who engage
in nonviolent direct action are not the creators of tension. We merely
bring to the surface the hidden tension that is already alive. We bring
it out in the open, where it can be seen and dealt with. Like a boil that
can never be cured so long as it is covered up but must be opened
with all its ugliness to the natural medicines of air and light, injustice must be exposed, with all the tension its exposure creates, to the
light of human conscience and the air of national opinion before it
can be cured.

24

How do King's warrants differ from the clergymen's?

How and why does King use definition here?

In your statements you assert that our actions, even though
peaceful, must be condemned because they precipitate violence.
But is this a logical assertion? Isn't this like condemning a robbed
man because his possession of money precipitated the evil act of
robbery? Isn't this like condemning Socrates because his unswerv-
ing commitment to truth and his philosophical inquiries precipitated
the act by the misguided populace in which they made him drink
hemlock? Isn't this like condemning Jesus because his unique God-
consciousness and never-ceasing devotion to God's will precipitated
the evil act of crucifixion? We must come to see that, as the federal
courts have consistently affirmed, it is wrong to urge an individual
to cease his efforts to gain his basic constitutional rights because the
quest may precipitate violence. Society must protect the robbed and
punish the robber.

25

Identify and describe the effects of the analogies in these paragraphs.

What is the fallacious thinking King complains of?

I had also hoped that the white moderate would reject the
myth concerning time in relation to the struggle for freedom. I have
just received a letter from a white brother in Texas. He writes: "All
Christians know that the colored people will receive equal rights
eventually, but it is possible that you are in too great a religious
hurry. It has taken Christianity almost two thousand years to accomplish what it has. The teachings of Christ take time to come to earth."
Such an attitude stems from a tragic misconception of time, from the
strangely irrational notion that there is something in the very flow of
time that will inevitably cure all ills. Actually, time itself is neutral; it
can be used either destructively or constructively. More and more I
feel that the people of ill will have used time much more effectively

26

Summarize King's reasoning about time.

than have the people of good will. We will have to repent in this generation not merely for the hateful words and actions of the bad people but for the appalling silence of the good people. Human progress never rolls in on wheels of inevitability; it comes through the tireless efforts of men willing to be coworkers with God, and without this hard work, time itself becomes an ally of the forces of social stagnation. We must use time creatively, in the knowledge that the time is always right to do right. Now is the time to make real the promise of democracy and transform our pending national elegy into a creative psalm of brotherhood. Now is the time to lift our national policy from the quicksand of racial injustice to the solid rock of human dignity.

27   You speak of our activity in Birmingham as extreme. At first I was rather disappointed that fellow clergymen would see my nonviolent efforts as those of an extremist. I began thinking about the fact that I stand in the middle of two opposing forces in the Negro community. One is a force of complacency, made up in part of Negroes who, as a result of long years of oppression, are so drained of self-respect and a sense of "somebodiness" that they have adjusted to segregation; and in part of a few middle-class Negroes who, because of a degree of academic and economic security and because in some ways they profit by segregation, have become insensitive to the problems of the masses. The other force is one of bitterness and hatred, and it comes perilously close to advocating violence. It is expressed in the various black nationalist groups that are springing up across the nation, the largest and best-known being Elijah Muhammad's Muslim movement. Nourished by the Negro's frustration over the continued existence of racial discrimination, this movement is made up of people who have lost faith in America, who have absolutely repudiated Christianity, and who have concluded that the white man is an incorrigible "devil."

Describe the two opposing forces.

28   I have tried to stand between these two forces, saying that we need emulate neither the "do-nothingism" of the complacent nor the hatred and despair of the black nationalist. For there is the more excellent way of love and nonviolent protest. I am grateful to God that, through the influence of the Negro church, the way of nonviolence became an integral part of our struggle.

How and why does King attempt to reconcile the opposing forces?

29   If this philosophy had not emerged, by now many streets of the South would, I am convinced, be flowing with blood. And I am further convinced that if our white brothers dismiss as "rabble-rousers" and "outside agitators" those of us who employ nonviolent direct action, and if they refuse to support our nonviolent efforts, millions of Negroes will, out of frustration and despair, seek solace and security in black-nationalist ideologies—a development that would inevitably lead to a frightening racial nightmare.

Identify and describe the causal proof.

Oppressed people cannot remain oppressed forever. The yearning for freedom eventually manifests itself, and that is what has happened to the American Negro. Something within has reminded him of his birthright of freedom, and something without has reminded him that it can be gained. Consciously or unconsciously, he has been caught up by the *Zeitgeist*, and with his black brothers of Africa and his brown and yellow brothers of Asia, South America and the Caribbean, the United States Negro is moving with a sense of great urgency toward the promised land of racial justice. If one recognizes this vital urge that has engulfed the Negro community, one should readily understand why public demonstrations are taking place. The Negro has many pent-up resentments and latent frustrations, and he must release them. So let him march; let him make prayer pilgrimages to the city hall; let him go on freedom rides—and try to understand why he must do so. If his repressed emotions are not released in nonviolent ways, they will seek expression through violence; this is not a threat but a fact of history. So I have not said to my people: "Get rid of your discontent." Rather, I have tried to say that this normal and healthy discontent can be channeled into the creative outlet of nonviolent direct action. And now this approach is being termed extremist.

But though I was initially disappointed at being categorized as an extremist, as I continued to think about the matter I gradually gained a measure of satisfaction from the label. Was not Jesus an extremist for love: "Love your enemies, bless them that curse you, do good to them that hate you, and pray for them which despitefully use you, and persecute you." Was not Amos an extremist for justice: "Let justice roll down like waters and righteousness like an everflowing stream." Was not Paul an extremist for the Christian gospel: "I bear in my body the marks of the Lord Jesus." Was not Martin Luther an extremist: "Here I stand; I cannot do otherwise, so help me God." And John Bunyan: "I will stay in jail to the end of my days before I make a butchery of my conscience." And Abraham Lincoln: "This nation cannot survive half slave and half free." And Thomas Jefferson: "We hold these truths to be self-evident, that all men are created equal. . . ." So the question is not whether we will be extremists, but what kind of extremists we will be. Will we be extremists for hate or for love? Will we be extremists for the preservation of injustice or for the extension of justice? In that dramatic scene on Calvary's hill three men were crucified. We must never forget that all three were crucified for the same crime—the crime of extremism. Two were extremists for immorality, and thus fell below their environment. The other, Jesus Christ, was an extremist for love, truth and goodness, and thereby rose above his environment. Perhaps the South, the nation and the world are in dire need of creative extremists.

30 Summarize King's reasoning about the effects of oppression.

31 What is the effect of these comparisons?

32

Summarize King's description of the oppressor race.

I had hoped that the white moderate would see this need. Perhaps I was too optimistic; perhaps I expected too much. I suppose I should have realized that few members of the oppressor race can understand the deep groans and passionate yearnings of the oppressed race, and still fewer have the vision to see that injustice must be rooted out by strong, persistent and determined action. I am thankful, however, that some of our white brothers in the South have grasped the meaning of this social revolution and committed themselves to it. They are still all too few in quantity, but they are big in quality. Some—such as Ralph McGill, Lillian Smith, Harry Golden, James McBride Dabbs, Ann Braden and Sarah Patton Boyle—have written about our struggle in eloquent and prophetic terms. Others have marched with us down nameless streets of the South. They have languished in filthy, roach-infested jails, suffering the abuse and brutality of policemen who view them as "dirty nigger-lovers." Unlike so many of their moderate brothers and sisters, they have recognized the urgency of the moment and sensed the need for powerful "action" antidotes to combat the disease of segregation.

What types of proof are used in this third section?

33

Draw a line where the subject changes. What is the subject of the fourth section?

Reconsider the rhetorical situation: What went before? What will come later?

Let me take note of my other major disappointment. I have been so greatly disappointed with the white church and its leadership. Of course, there are some notable exceptions. I am not unmindful of the fact that each of you has taken some significant stands on this issue. I commend you, Reverend Stallings, for your Christian stand on this past Sunday, in welcoming Negroes to your worship service on a non-segregated basis. I commend the Catholic leaders of this state for integrating Spring Hill College several years ago.

34

But despite these notable exceptions, I must honestly reiterate that I have been disappointed with the church. I do not say this as one of those negative critics who can always find something wrong with the church. I say this as a minister of the gospel, who loves the church; who was nurtured in its bosom; who has been sustained by its spiritual blessings and who will remain true to it as long as the cord of life shall lengthen.

35

How does King build *ethos* in this fourth section?

When I was suddenly catapulted into the leadership of the bus protest in Montgomery, Alabama, a few years ago, I felt we would be supported by the white church. I felt that the white ministers, priests and rabbis of the South would be among our strongest allies. Instead, some have been outright opponents, refusing to understand the freedom movement and misrepresenting its leaders; all too many others have been more cautious than courageous and have remained silent behind the anesthetizing security of stained-glass windows.

36

What common ground did King hope for? How was he disappointed?

In spite of my shattered dreams, I came to Birmingham with the hope that the white religious leadership of this community would see the justice of our cause and, with deep moral concern, would serve as the channel through which our just grievances could reach the power structure. I had hoped that each of you would understand. But again I have been disappointed.

I have heard numerous southern religious leaders admonish 37 their worshipers to comply with a desegregation decision because it is the law, but I have longed to hear white ministers declare: "Follow this decree because integration is morally right and because the Negro is your brother." In the midst of blatant injustices inflicted upon the Negro, I have watched white churchmen stand on the sideline and mouth pious irrelevancies and sanctimonious trivialities. In the midst of a mighty struggle to rid our nation of racial and economic injustice, I have heard many ministers say: "Those are social issues, with which the gospel has no real concern." And I have watched many churches commit themselves to a completely otherworldly religion which makes a strange, un-Biblical distinction between body and soul, between the sacred and the secular.

How and why does King use vivid description?

I have traveled the length and breadth of Alabama, Mississippi 38 and all the other southern states. On sweltering summer days and crisp autumn mornings I have looked at the South's beautiful churches with their lofty spires pointing heavenward. I have beheld the impressive outlines of her massive religious-education buildings. Over and over I have found myself asking: "What kind of people worship here? Who is their God? Where were their voices when the lips of Governor Barnett dripped with words of interposition and nullification? Where were they when Governor Wallace gave a clarion call for defiance and hatred? Where were their voices of support when bruised and weary Negro men and women decided to rise from the dark dungeons of complacency to the bright hills of creative protest?"

Yes, these questions are still in my mind. In deep disappointment 39 I have wept over the laxity of the church. But be assured that my tears have been tears of love. There can be no deep disappointment where there is not deep love. Yes, I love the church. How could I do otherwise? I am in the rather unique position of being the son, the grandson and the great-grandson of preachers. Yes, I see the church as the body of Christ. But, oh! How we have blemished and scarred that body through social neglect and through fear of being nonconformists.

There was a time when the church was very powerful—in the 40 time when the early Christians rejoiced at being deemed worthy to suffer for what they believed. In those days the church was not merely a thermometer that recorded the ideas and principles of popular opinion; it was a thermostat that transformed the mores of society. Whenever the early Christians entered a town, the people in power became disturbed and immediately sought to convict the Christians for being "disturbers of the peace" and "outside agitators." But the Christians pressed on, in the conviction that they were "a colony of

What is the effect of the historical analogy?

heaven," called to obey God rather than man. Small in number, they were big in commitment. They were too God-intoxicated to be "astronomically intimidated." By their effort and example they brought an end to such ancient evils as infanticide and gladiatorial contests.

41   Things are different now. So often the contemporary church is a weak, ineffectual voice with an uncertain sound. So often it is an archdefender of the status quo. Far from being disturbed by the presence of the church, the power structure of the average community is consoled by the church's silent—and often even vocal—sanction of things as they are.

42   But the judgment of God is upon the church as never before. If today's church does not recapture the sacrificial spirit of the early church, it will lose its authenticity, forfeit the loyalty of millions, and be dismissed as an irrelevant social club with no meaning for the twentieth century. Every day I meet young people whose disappointment with the church has turned into outright disgust.

43   Perhaps I have once again been too optimistic. Is organized religion too inextricably bound to the status quo to save our nation and the world? Perhaps I must turn my faith to the inner spiritual church, the church within the church, as the true *ekklesia* and the hope of the world. But again I am thankful to God that some noble souls from the ranks of organized religion have broken loose from the paralyzing chains of conformity and joined us as active partners in the struggle for freedom. They have left their secure congregations and walked the streets of Albany, Georgia, with us. They have gone down the highways of the South on tortuous rides for freedom. Yes, they have gone to jail with us. Some have been dismissed from their churches, have lost the support of their bishops and fellow ministers. But they have acted in the faith that right defeated is stronger than evil triumphant. Their witness has been the spiritual salt that has preserved the true meaning of the gospel in these troubled times. They have carved a tunnel of hope through the dark mountain of disappointment.

> How does King contrast organized religion and the inner church? What is the effect?

44   I hope the church as a whole will meet the challenge of this decisive hour. But even if the church does not come to the aid of justice, I have no despair about the future. I have no fear about the outcome of our struggle in Birmingham, even if our motives are at present misunderstood. We will reach the goal of freedom in Birmingham and all over the nation, because the goal of America is freedom. Abused and scorned though we may be, our destiny is tied up with America's destiny. Before the pilgrims landed at Plymouth, we were here. Before the pen of Jefferson etched the majestic words of the Declaration of Independence across the pages of history, we were here. For more than two centuries our forebears labored in this country without wages; they made cotton king; they built the homes of their

> Why does King use historical analogies here?

> What types of proof are used in the fourth section?

masters while suffering gross injustice and shameful humiliation— and yet out of a bottomless vitality they continued to thrive and develop. If the inexpressible cruelties of slavery could not stop us, the opposition we now face will surely fail. We will win our freedom because the sacred heritage of our nation and the eternal will of God are embodied in our echoing demands.

Draw a line where the subject changes. What is the subject of section five?

Before closing I feel impelled to mention one other point in your statement that has troubled me profoundly. You warmly commended the Birmingham police force for keeping "order" and "preventing violence." I doubt that you would have so warmly commended the police force if you had seen its dogs sinking their teeth into unarmed, nonviolent Negroes. I doubt that you would so quickly commend the policemen if you were to observe their ugly and inhumane treatment of Negroes here in the city jail; if you were to watch them push and curse old Negro women and young Negro girls; if you were to see them slap and kick old Negro men and young boys; if you were to observe them, as they did on two occasions, refuse to give us food because we wanted to sing our grace together. I cannot join you in your praise of the Birmingham police department.

45

What is the predominant type of proof in this fifth section?

It is true that the police have exercised a degree of discipline in handling the demonstrators. In this sense they have conducted themselves rather "nonviolently" in public. But for what purpose? To preserve the evil system of segregation. Over the past few years I have consistently preached that nonviolence demands that the means we use must be as pure as the ends we seek. I have tried to make clear that it is wrong to use immoral means to attain moral ends. But now I must affirm that it is just as wrong, or perhaps even more so, to use moral means to preserve immoral ends. Perhaps Mr. Connor and his policemen have been rather nonviolent in public, as was Chief Pritchett in Albany, Georgia, but they have used the moral means of nonviolence to maintain the immoral end of racial injustice. As T. S. Eliot has said: "The last temptation is the greatest treason: To do the right deed for the wrong reason."

46

Provide some examples.

Describe the effect.

I wish you had commended the Negro sit-inners and the demonstrators of Birmingham for their sublime courage, their willingness to suffer and their amazing discipline in the midst of great provocation. One day the South will recognize its real heroes. They will be the James Merediths, with the noble sense of purpose that enables them to face jeering and hostile mobs, and with the agonizing loneliness that characterizes the life of the pioneer. They will be old, oppressed, battered Negro women, symbolized in a seventy-two-year-old woman in Montgomery, Alabama, who rose up with a sense of dignity and with her people decided not to ride segregated buses, and who responded with ungrammatical profundity to one who inquired about her weariness: "My feets is tired, but

47

my soul is at rest." They will be the young high school and college students, the young ministers of the gospel and a host of their elders, courageously and nonviolently sitting in at lunch counters and willingly going to jail for conscience' sake. One day the South will know that when these disinherited children of God sat down at lunch counters, they were in reality standing up for what is best in the American dream and for the most sacred values in our Judaeo-Christian heritage, thereby bringing our nation back to those great wells of democracy which were dug deep by the founding fathers in their formulation of the Constitution and the Declaration of Independence.

48   Never before have I written so long a letter. I'm afraid it is much too long to take your precious time. I can assure you that it would have been much shorter if I had been writing from a comfortable desk, but what else can one do when he is alone in a narrow jail cell, other than write long letters, think long thoughts and pray long prayers?

Draw a line to set off the conclusion. What is the concluding idea?

What is King's purpose in this conclusion?

49   If I have said anything in this letter that overstates the truth and indicates an unreasonable impatience, I beg you to forgive me. If I have said anything that understates the truth and indicates my having a patience that allows me to settle for anything less than brotherhood, I beg God to forgive me.

Do you find the two letters convincing? Why, or why not?

50   I hope this letter finds you strong in the faith. I also hope that circumstances will soon make it possible for me to meet each of you, not as an integrationist or a civil-rights leader but as a fellow clergyman and a Christian brother. Let us all hope that the dark clouds of racial prejudice will soon pass away and the deep fog of misunderstanding will be lifted from our fear-drenched communities, and in some not too distant tomorrow the radiant stars of love and brotherhood will shine over our great nation with all their scintillating beauty.

Are the clergymen's and King's arguments moral or immoral according to your values and standards?

Yours for the cause of Peace and Brotherhood,
Martin Luther King, Jr.   ■

CHAPTER TWELVE

Argument and Literature

The purpose of this chapter is to extend the applications of argument theory and to suggest that you apply this theory both when you read imaginative literature and when you write papers about literature, including poetry, short stories, plays, and novels. Any theory that is applied to literature can help you look at it in whole new ways. Argument theory works this way also. Argument theory is useful for speculating about the ideas and themes in literature, especially when there is no general agreement about what these ideas are exactly, and it can also provide insight into literary characters, particularly into how they argue and interact with one another. Finally, argument theory can help you write papers about literature and argue in favor of your own understandings and insights.

A basic idea in this book has been that argument can be found everywhere—particularly where people are. Creative writers, along with the imaginative characters they create, are as argumentative as any other people. It should not surprise you that argument is as pervasive in literature as it is in real life. In fact, literature often raises issues, takes positions on them, and even changes people's views about them. Literature can be convincing because it invites readers to identify with its characters, which creates common ground, and because it almost always employs effective emotional appeal. Literature has high interest appeal as well. Argument achieved through literary narrative can be one of the most convincing forms of argument.

This chapter will provide you with examples and focus questions to help you apply argument theory to literature. The exercises and activities will furnish you with sufficient practice to get you started. Note also that in the introductory material to each of the seven issues in "The Reader," the suggestion is made to expand your perspective on the issues through literature and film. Specific examples of relevant literature and film are provided. Film, like literature, raises issues, makes claims, and changes people's views about controversial subjects. You can analyze arguments in film and write arguments about film just as you would a piece of literature.

FINDING AND ANALYZING ARGUMENTS IN LITERATURE

When you apply argument theory to the reading of literature, you will be "inside the text," so to speak, analyzing what is there and working to understand it. Your focus may be on the main argument made by the text, or it may be on one or more of the characters and the arguments they make. Let's consider first how to analyze the main argument.

What Is at Issue? What Is the Claim?

To use argument theory to read a literary text and analyze the main argument, focus on the issues raised in the work, the perspectives that are expressed, and the claims that are made. The claims may be explicit, overtly and openly expressed, or they may be implicit, covert and merely suggested, so that you will need to infer them yourself. There may also be conflicting claims in a single work that seem at times to contradict each other. The Toulmin model is useful for analyzing and understanding the main line of argument in a literary work.

For example, here is a poem by Robert Herrick (1591–1674) that makes an explicit argument:

To the Virgins to Make Much of Time

Gather ye rosebuds while ye may:
    Old Time is still a-flying;
And this same flower that smiles today,
    Tomorrow will be dying.

The glorious lamp of heaven, the sun,
    The higher he's a-getting,
The sooner will his race be run,
    And nearer he's to setting.

That age is best which is the first,
    When youth and blood are warmer;
But being spent, the worse, and worst
    Times still succeed the former.

Then be not coy, but use your time;
    And while ye may, go marry:
For having lost but once your prime,
    You may for ever tarry.

In applying the Toulmin model to this poem, most readers would agree that a policy claim is stated in the first line and restated in different language in the last stanza. There would not be much disagreement, furthermore, about that claim: "young women should marry in their prime and not later" would be one way of putting it. Or the poet's first line, "Gather ye rosebuds while ye may," taken metaphorically to mean that one should take advantage of good things when they are available, serves as well to express the claim of this poem. The support is supplied in the form of reasons: time is flying, and it is better to marry when one is young than when one is old. The warrant that connects the support to the claim is that women will want to marry in the first place. Women who accept this warrant may be persuaded that they should, indeed, seize the day and wait no longer.

The claims in imaginative literature are not always this easy to identify. Sometimes it is necessary to ask some questions to identify what is at issue and to formulate the claim. Here are some questions to help you make these determinations:

1. *What is most of this work about?* This will help you identify the subject of the work.
2. *Can the subject be regarded as controversial?* That is, would it invite more than one perspective? This will help you discover the issues.
3. *What positions are taken on the issue, and who takes them?* This will help you discover both explicit and implicit claims along with who is making them: the author, a narrator, or various characters in the text.
4. *If the claim is not stated, what evidence can I use from the text to help me state it myself?* Draw on such evidence to help you make the claim explicit.
5. *Will everyone agree that this is a viable claim, or will I need to make a case for it?* Paper topics often come from disagreements over how to state the main argument in a literary work.

In her poem "The Mother," Gwendolyn Brooks begins, "Abortions will not let you forget." She continues by saying that she has never forgotten her "killed children," and she ends the poem:

> oh, what shall I say, how is the truth to be said?
> You were born, you had body, you died.
> It is just that you never giggled or planned or cried.
>
> Believe me, I loved you all.
> Believe me, I knew you, though faintly, and I loved,
> I loved you all.

One could argue that the claim of the poem is in the first sentence, "Abortions will not let you forget," a claim of fact. However, by the time one has read the entire poem, one can also infer and make a case for a value claim, that abortions cause the mothers who seek them considerable psychological pain and are difficult for them to endure as time goes on. There is sufficient evidence in the poem to make an argument for that second claim as well.

Still other literary texts may express conflicting claims about an issue. In poet Robert Frost's "Mending Wall," two claims are made about the issue concerning the value of fences. The two claims are "Something there is that doesn't love a wall" and "Good fences make good neighbors." These claims contradict each other. Furthermore, careful readers have pointed out that convincing arguments are made for both of these positions in the poem. In the case of "Mending Wall," the poem tends to start an argument rather than deliver one.[1] Once again, paper topics come out of such disagreements and can provide you with material to write papers about. You can always take a position yourself on any argument started by a literary work.

In other literary texts, arguments are made entirely through metaphor, as in Frost's poem "Birches," where swinging on birch trees becomes a way of escaping from the cares of life, or in another Frost poem, "The Road Not Taken," where the two roads in the poem become metaphors for two possible life choices. Metaphors are comparisons of items from two different categories. They work like figurative analogies since they invite readers to make unique mental connections and to expand their perspective on a subject in new and original ways. The meanings of metaphors in a literary work are often difficult to pin down exactly. Thus they become the subject of controversy and are often open to a variety of interpretations. The disputed meaning of a key metaphor in a literary work can become a fruitful paper topic.

Characters Making Arguments

The second way to employ argument theory to analyze literature is to apply it to specific arguments that are made by characters in the context of a literary text. Also enlightening is to consider how these individual characters' arguments contribute to the main argument of the text. Focusing on the rhetorical situation and the modes of appeal, identifying fallacies, and applying the Toulmin model all help with this type of analysis.

It is further useful to identify the form that the argument takes in the work (see Chapter 1, pages 6–8). For example, a character may argue internally with himself as Hamlet does when he asks, "To be or not to be, that is the question" in Shakespeare's *Hamlet*. A character may also argue with an imaginary audience, like the woman who constructs an imaginary argument with her child's counselor in the short story "I Stand Here Ironing" by Tillie Olsen. Two individuals may argue one on one, both trying to convince the other, as in the poem "Myth" by Muriel Rukeyser; or the character may make a single-perspective argument to convince a mass audience as Marc Antony does in his speech that begins "Friends, Romans, Countrymen, lend me your ears" in Shakespeare's *Julius Caesar*. The characters may argue in front of a third-party judge as they do in the play *Inherit the Wind*. Identifying the form of the argument will help you understand the rhetorical situation in which it takes place. It will focus your attention on who is arguing, with whom these characters are arguing, and to what end.

A famous literary argument is Satan's persuasion of Eve in John Milton's seventeenth-century epic *Paradise Lost*. The story is familiar. Adam and Eve have been placed in the garden of Eden by God and have been told they may eat anything in the garden except the fruit from the tree of knowledge. The rhetorical situation goes like this: Satan is the arguer. He sneaks into the garden, inhabits the serpent, and in

---

[1]Tim Morris provided me with some of the examples and insights in this chapter, such as this one, as well as with some of the literary examples in "The Reader."

that guise tempts Eve, his audience, to eat the forbidden fruit. This is a one-on-one argument with Satan trying to convince Eve. The exigence of Satan's argument is that he needs to get a foothold on earth so that he can spend more time there and less time in Hell, a very unpleasant place in this poem. Satan's constraints are that he must get Eve alone because he's afraid he cannot persuade Adam, Eve is a bit vain as he has discovered, and there are good angels around who could frustrate his plan. Thus he decides to hide in the serpent. Satan's persuasive argument, full of fallacies as it is, is successful with Eve. She eats the fruit, she gets Adam to eat it also, and as a result, they are expelled from the garden forever.

In the poem we witness the entire persuasive process that involves Satan and Eve, from the audience analysis carried on by Satan as he hides in the garden, watching Eve and analyzing her weaknesses, to the final changes in Eve's thought and action brought about by Satan's argumentative speeches. As part of this process, we overhear Satan's initial planning of his argument, and as he schemes and plans, we observe that there is a vast difference between his private feelings and beliefs and the roles he adopts to establish *ethos* with Eve. Satan is not an ethical arguer; he is an immoral manipulator. We also watch Satan deliberately plant a highly emotional version of the temptation in Eve's mind in the form of a dream. The remembered pleasure and emotional appeal of this dream will help make the later logical argument even more readily acceptable to Eve.

When Satan in the serpent delivers the speeches in book 9 of the poem that finally convince Eve that she should eat the apple, he employs *ethos, pathos,* and *logos* to strengthen his argument. He flatters Eve, he appeals to her desire to be more powerful, he refutes what God has told her with fallacious reasoning, he uses induction to show that he ate the fruit and did not die so Eve will not die either, he points to himself as a sign of the intelligence and power that can come from eating the fruit, and he uses a deductive argument that can be summarized as follows:

Eve should know evil in order to recognize good.
Eating the fruit will help Eve know evil.
Therefore, Eve should eat the fruit in order to recognize good.

There are other examples of logical and emotional appeal in this argument that are not detailed here. Furthermore, if the Toulmin model is also employed to analyze Satan's argument, his purpose and strategy become even clearer, particularly as we examine some of his warrants. One of these, for example, is that humans want to become gods. Satan himself envies God and assumes that humans will also.

Another unique feature of the argument in *Paradise Lost* is that we are allowed to witness the argument outcomes. Not only do we observe Eve's outward actions, but we are also a party to her inner thoughts following Satan's speech. We see her eat the fruit. We also learn from her private musings how her reasoning, her emotional state, and the credibility she places in the serpent have been changed by Satan's speeches. We have a full explanation of what has convinced Eve to disobey God and why the argument has been successful.

If you become interested in analyzing the argument in *Paradise Lost,* you might also like to know that Satan makes no fewer than twenty public addresses in the poem and that his audiences range in size from the single Eve to the multitudes of the fallen angels. Furthermore, Adam, Eve, God, the Son, and some of the angels in the poem make arguments of their own that can be profitably analyzed with argument theory.

Here is a list of questions that you can use to help you analyze the arguments of fictional characters in literature. Any one of these questions could help you discover a claim for a paper on a literary work. You would develop your claim by drawing examples from the literary work itself to illustrate your argument.

1. What is at issue in the literary work?
2. Who is the character taking a position on this issue, and what is the character's position on the issue?
3. What is the rhetorical situation for the argument?
4. What is the claim made by the character? Is it stated overtly? Is it implied? Write it yourself as a statement, and identify its type.
5. How does the character establish credibility? What logical and emotional proofs does the character use?
6. What type of language predominates: language that appeals to reason, language that appeals to emotion, or language that establishes credibility? Describe the language.
7. What are the warrants?
8. How does the character establish common ground? Through warrants? Through Rogerian argument? What else?
9. Are rebuttals used? How effective are they?
10. Are there fallacies? How do they distort the argument?
11. What are the outcomes of the argument? Is it convincing? To whom? What happens as a result?
12. Is the argument moral or immoral according to the standards established in the text itself? How would you evaluate the argument according to your own standards and values?
13. How does the argument made by the character contribute to the main argument of the text?

To help you learn to do an analysis of a literary argument, try analyzing Marc Antony's famous speech that begins "Friends, Romans, Countrymen . . ." from Shakespeare's *Julius Caesar*. It appears in Exercise D. A student-written analysis of this speech is provided as an example at the end of that exercise.

WRITING ARGUMENTS ABOUT LITERATURE

Argument theory can also be used to help you formulate your own argument about your insights and understanding of a literary text. At this point you will move "outside of the text," and you will begin by identifying an issue about the text on which there is no general agreement. You will then take a position on that issue, state your position in a claim, and present evidence from the text to prove it. Argument theory can be extremely beneficial in writing scholarly argument of this type. The Toulmin model will help you the most. It can help you identify an issue to write about in the first place, and it can also help you set up the elements of your argument.

Your first challenge will be to move from reading literature to writing about it. First, you will need to find an issue to write about. To help you find an issue, ask, *What is unclear about this text that I think I can explain?* or *What is left out by the author that I think I can explain?* Focus on the main argument of the text, on the characters themselves, on what the narrator says about the characters, or on the meaning of metaphors to help you discover possible issues to write about. Controversy often resides in those locations. Also, issues may emerge in class discussion, or issues may come from the questions in your literature anthology. If all else fails, write a summary of a literary text along with your reaction to it. Then read your reaction and circle the most promising idea in it. It should be an idea that you think you can make a claim about and defend with evidence from the text.

Here are some examples of issues that appear in literary texts. In Henry James's novel *The Turn of the Screw*, there is an unresolved question about whether the ghosts are real or not. One student actually went through the novel and highlighted in one color all of the evidence that suggests they are real and then highlighted in another color all of the evidence that suggests they are imaginary. According to this student, the quantity of evidence for both explanations was roughly comparable in the novel. If you decided to write about that issue, you could argue for either position and find plenty of people who would agree with you. Your instructor would evaluate your paper on the quality of its argument rather than on whether you had resolved the controversy or not. Some literary controversies cannot be finally resolved any more than many issues in life can be finally resolved. Here is another example of a literary issue. At the end of Ernest Hemingway's short story "The Short Happy Life of Francis Macomber," a wounded and enraged buffalo charges the main character, who is on an African safari. His wife shoots, but the bullet kills her husband instead of the buffalo. The "great white hunter" who is leading this expedition assumes the wife meant to kill her husband instead of the buffalo, and there is plenty of evidence in the story to suggest that this might have been her intent. But it is equally possible to argue that she was really shooting at the buffalo and hit her husband by mistake. You could write a paper in which you argue for either position just so long as you provide plenty of evidence from the story to support your position. In other words, you could make either position convincing. One student wrote a paper about a poem by William Butler Yeats in which she argued in favor of one interpretation, and she got an A. The next year, in another class, she argued in favor of a completely different interpretation of the same poem, and she got another A. In both cases she provided plenty of evidence from the poem itself to support the claims she made. Both of her arguments were convincing.

Here are some questions to help you make a claim about a literary work and write a convincing argument to support it:

1. What is an issue raised by this text that needs clarification?
2. What are the different perspectives that can be taken on this issue?
3. Which perspective will I take?

4. What support from the text will I use to defend my position?
5. What warrants are implicit in my argument, and will they be acceptable to the person who will evaluate this paper? Should I use backing for any of these warrants?
6. Would my paper be more convincing if I included a rebuttal of the opposing positions?
7. Will my claim be more acceptable to my audience if I qualify it?

Once you have read and thought about a literary text and you have answered these questions, you will write your paper just like you would write any other position paper in which your aim is to state what you think and provide evidence to support it. You can use suggestions from the other chapters in this book to help you meet this aim.

REVIEW QUESTIONS

1. How can argument theory be used in the study of literature? Name and describe the three approaches described in this chapter.
2. What are some of the questions the reader can ask to arrive at a claim in a work of literature? What are some of the ways in which claims are expressed in literature?
3. Describe the argument theory you would employ to help you analyze an argument that a character makes in a literary work.
4. What are some of the suggestions made in this chapter to help you find a topic for a position paper you might write about an issue in literature?
5. What is your main responsibility as a writer when you argue on one side or the other of a literary issue?

EXERCISES AND ACTIVITIES

A. WRITING ASSIGNMENT: ANALYZING THE ARGUMENT IN A POEM
The following poem was written by Langston Hughes in 1926 while he was a student at Columbia University in New York City.

1. Read the poem; then freewrite for five minutes to capture your original thoughts and reactions.
2. As a class, discuss the answers to the following questions:

   a. What is the rhetorical situation? Use TRACE to think it through.
   b. What are the issues in the poem?
   c. What is the claim? Try to get consensus. What are some subclaims?
   d. What supports the claim? Give examples.
   e. How does the author create common ground?
   f. What are the warrants?

3. Write a 300- to 400-word paper about the main argument in this poem and how it is developed.

THEME FOR ENGLISH B*

Langston Hughes

Poem

The instructor said,

    Go home and write
      a page tonight.
    And let that page come out of you—
      Then, it will be true.   5

I wonder if it's that simple?

I am twenty-two, colored, born in Winston-Salem.
    I went to school there, then Durham, then here
to this college on the hill above Harlem.
    I am the only colored student in my class.   10

The steps from the hill lead down to Harlem,
    through a park, then I cross St. Nicholas,
Eighth Avenue, Seventh, and I come to the Y,
    the Harlem Branch Y, where I take the elevator
up to my room, sit down, and write this page: 15
    It's not easy to know what is true for you or me
at twenty-two, my age. But I guess I'm what

I feel and see and hear. Harlem, I hear you:
    hear you, hear me—we two—you, me talk on this page.
(I hear New York, too.) Me—who?   20

Well, I like to eat, sleep, drink, and be in love.
    I like to work, read, learn, and understand life.
I like a pipe for a Christmas present,
    or records—Bessie, bop, or Bach.

I guess being colored doesn't make me not like   25
    the same things other folks like who are other races.
So will my page be colored that I write?
    Being me, it will not be white.
But it will be
    a part of you, instructor.   30
You are white—
    yet a part of me, as I am a part of you.
That's American.

Sometimes perhaps you don't want to be a part of me.
Nor do I often want to be a part of you.   35
    But we are, that's true!
As I learn from you,
    I guess you learn from me—
although you're older—and white—
    and somewhat more free.

This is my page for English B. ■   40

*Used with permission of Alfred A. Knopf, Inc.

FOR DISCUSSION: What is the relationship established between the teacher and the student in this poem? Think about similarities, differences, and common ground between them. How does the student in the poem interpret the writing assignment? How does he respond to it? What do you think of his version of this assignment?

B. WRITING ASSIGNMENT: AN ARGUMENT ABOUT A LITERARY WORK

The purpose of this assignment is to discover an issue, make a claim, and write about your interpretation of a story. The author of the following story has said that she was prompted to write the story by a remark she came across in William James's story "The Moral Philosopher and the Moral Life." In it, James suggests that if multitudes of people could be "kept permanently happy on the one simple condition that a certain lost soul on the far-off edge of things should lead a life of lonely torment," our moral sense would make us immediately reject that bargain. The story is written as a parable—that is, it is written to illustrate a principle. Think about these things as you read the story.

1. When you have finished reading the story, freewrite for five minutes to capture your original thoughts and reactions.
2. As a class, discuss the answers to the following questions:
   a. What is this story about? What issues are raised by this story?
   b. What are some of the perspectives in the story? Who takes them? Which do you identify with?
   c. Write a claim made by this story, and put a few of these claims on the board. Which of these claims could be supported with evidence from the text? Which would you like to write about? Write your claim. Read some of these claims to the class.
3. Answer the next three questions to plan your paper:
   a. What evidence from the text can you use to support your claim (examples, quotes, etc.)? Underline it.
   b. What warrants are implicit in your argument? Will they be acceptable to the person who reads your paper, or should you provide backing?
   c. Would your paper be more convincing if you included a rebuttal? What would it be?
   d. Will your claim be more acceptable if you qualify it? How would you do that?
4. Write a 500-word position paper defending the claim you have made about this story.

Story

THE ONES WHO WALK AWAY FROM OMELAS*

Ursula K. Le Guin

1 With a clamor of bells that set the swallows soaring, the Festival of Summer came to the city Omelas, bright-towered by the sea. The rigging of the boats in harbor sparkled with flags. In the streets between houses with red roofs

*Used with permission of the author.

and painted walls, between old moss-grown gardens and under avenues of trees, past great parks and public buildings, processions moved. Some were decorous: old people in long stiff robes of mauve and gray, grave master workmen, quiet, merry women carrying their babies and chatting as they walked. In other streets the music beat faster, a shimmering of gong and tambourine, and the people went dancing, the procession was a dance. Children dodged in and out, their high calls rising like the swallows' crossing flights over the music and the singing. All the processions wound towards the north side of the city, where on the great water-meadow called the Green Fields boys and girls, naked in the bright air, with mudstained feet and ankles and long, lithe arms, exercised their restive horses before the race. The horses wore no gear at all but a halter without bit. Their manes were braided with streamers of silver, gold, and green. They flared their nostrils and pranced and boasted to one another; they were vastly excited, the horse being the only animal who has adopted our ceremonies as his own. Far off to the north and west the mountains stood up half encircling Omelas on her bay. The air of morning was so clear that the snow still crowning the Eighteen Peaks burned with white-gold fire across the miles of sunlit air, under the dark blue of the sky. There was just enough wind to make the banners that marked the racecourse snap and flutter now and then. In the silence of the broad green meadows one could hear the music winding through the city streets, farther and nearer and ever approaching, a cheerful faint sweetness of the air that from time to time trembled and gathered together and broke out into the great joyous clanging of the bells.

Joyous! How is one to tell about joy? How describe the citizens of Omelas? 2

They were not simple folk, you see, though they were happy. But we do not 3
say the words of cheer much any more. All smiles have become archaic. Given a description such as this one tends to make certain assumptions. Given a description such as this one tends to look next for the King, mounted on a splendid stallion and surrounded by his noble knights, or perhaps in a golden litter borne by great-muscled slaves. But there was no king. They did not use swords, or keep slaves. They were not barbarians. I do not know the rules and laws of their society, but I suspect that they were singularly few. As they did without monarchy and slavery, so they also got on without the stock exchange, the advertisement, the secret police, and the bomb. Yet I repeat that these were not simple folk, not dulcet shepherds, noble savages, bland utopians. They were not less complex than us. The trouble is that we have a bad habit, encouraged by pedants and sophisticates, of considering happiness as something rather stupid. Only pain is intellectual, only evil interesting. This is the treason of the artist: a refusal to admit the banality of evil and the terrible boredom of pain. If you can't lick 'em, join 'em. If it hurts, repeat it. But to praise despair is to condemn delight, to embrace violence is to lose hold of everything else. We have almost lost hold, we can no longer describe a happy man, nor make any celebration of joy. How can I tell you about the people of Omelas? They were not naïve and happy children—though their children were, in fact, happy. They were mature, intelligent, passionate adults whose lives were not wretched. O miracle! but I wish I could describe it better. I wish I could convince you. Omelas sounds in my words like a city in a fairy tale, long ago and far away, once upon a time. Per-

haps it would be best if you imagined it as your own fancy bids, assuming it will rise to the occasion, for certainly I cannot suit you all. For instance, how about technology? I think that there would be no cars or helicopters in and above the streets; this follows from the fact that the people of Omelas are happy people. Happiness is based on a just discrimination of what is necessary, what is neither necessary nor destructive, and what is destructive. In the middle category, however—that of the unnecessary but undestructive, that of comfort, luxury, exuberance, etc.—they could perfectly well have central heating, subway trains, washing machines, and all kinds of marvelous devices not yet invented here, floating light-sources, fuelless power, a cure for the common cold. Or they could have none of that: it doesn't matter. As you like it. I incline to think that people from towns up and down the coast have been coming in to Omelas during the last days before the Festival on very fast little trains and double-decked trams, and that the train station of Omelas is actually the handsomest building in town, though plainer than the magnificent Farmer's Market. But even granted trains, I fear that Omelas so far strikes some of you as goody-goody. Smiles, bells, parades, horses, bleh. If so, please add an orgy. If an orgy would help, don't hesitate. Let us not, however, have temples from which issue beautiful nude priests and priestesses already half in ecstasy and ready to copulate with any man or woman, lover or stranger, who desires union with the deep godhead of the blood, although that was my first idea. But really it would be better not to have any temples in Omelas—at least, not manned temples. Religion yes, clergy no. Surely the beautiful nudes can just wander about, offering themselves like divine soufflés to the hunger of the needy and the rapture of the flesh. Let them join the processions. Let tambourines be struck above the copulations, and the glory of desire be proclaimed upon the gongs, and (a not unimportant point) let the offspring of these delightful rituals be beloved and looked after by all. One thing I know there is none of in Omelas is guilt. But what else should there be? I thought that first there were no drugs, but that is puritanical. For those who like it, the faint insistent sweetness of *drooz* may perfume the ways of the city, *drooz* which first brings a great lightness and brilliance to the mind and limbs, and then after some hours a dreamy languor, and wonderful visions at last of the very arcana and inmost secrets of the Universe, as well as exciting the pleasure of sex beyond all belief; and it is not habit-forming. For more modest tastes I think there ought to be beer. What else, what else belongs in the joyous city? The sense of victory, surely, the celebration of courage. But as we did without clergy, let us do without soldiers. The joy built upon successful slaughter is not the right kind of joy; it will not do; it is fearful and it is trivial. A boundless and generous contentment, a magnanimous triumph felt not against some outer enemy but in communion with the finest and fairest in the souls of all men everywhere and the splendor of the world's summer: this is what swells the hearts of the people of Omelas, and the victory they celebrate is that of life. I really don't think many of them need to take *drooz*.

4   Most of the processions have reached the Green Fields by now. A marvelous smell of cooking goes forth from the red and blue tents of the provisioners. The faces of small children are amiably sticky; in the benign grey beard of a man a couple of crumbs of rich pastry are entangled. The youths and girls have mounted their horses and are beginning to group around the starting line of the course. An

old woman, small, fat, and laughing, is passing out flowers from a basket, and tall young men wear her flowers in their shining hair. A child of nine or ten sits at the edge of the crowd, alone, playing on a wooden flute. People pause to listen, and they smile, but they do not speak to him, for he never ceases playing and never sees them, his dark eyes wholly rapt in the sweet, thin magic of the tune.

He finishes, and slowly lowers his hands holding the wooden flute.   5

As if that little private silence were the signal, all at once a trumpet sounds 6 from the pavilion near the starting line: imperious, melancholy, piercing. The horses rear on their slender legs, and some of them neigh in answer. Sober-faced, the young riders stroke the horses' necks and soothe them, whispering, "Quiet, quiet, there my beauty, my hope. . . ." They begin to form in rank along the straight line. The crowds along the racecourse are like a field of grass and flowers in the wind. The Festival of Summer has begun.

Do you believe? Do you accept the festival, the city, the joy? No? Then let me 7 describe one more thing.

In a basement under one of the beautiful public buildings of Omelas, or per- 8 haps in the cellar of one of its spacious private homes, there is a room. It has one locked door, and no window. A little light seeps in dustily between cracks in the boards, secondhand from a cobwebbed window somewhere across the cellar. In one corner of the little room a couple of mops, with stiff, clotted, foul-smelling heads, stand near a rusty bucket. The floor is dirt, a little damp to the touch, as cellar dirt usually is. The room is about three paces long and two wide: a mere broom closet or disused tool room. In the room a child is sitting. It could be a boy or a girl. It looks about six, but actually is nearly ten. It is feeble-minded. Perhaps it was born defective, or perhaps it has become imbecile through fear, malnutrition, and neglect. It picks its nose and occasionally fumbles vaguely with its toes or genitals, as it sits hunched in the corner farthest from the bucket and the two mops. It is afraid of the mops. It finds them horrible. It shuts its eyes, but it knows the mops are still standing there; and the door is locked; and nobody will come. The door is always locked; and nobody ever comes, except that sometimes—the child has no understanding of time or interval—sometimes the door rattles terribly and opens, and a person, or several people, are there. One of them may come in and kick the child to make it stand up. The others never come close, but peer in at it with frightened, disgusted eyes. The food bowl and the water jug are hastily filled, the door is locked, the eyes disappear. The people at the door never say anything, but the child, who has not always lived in the tool room, and can remember sunlight and its mother's voice, sometimes speaks. "I will be good," it says. "Please let me out. I will be good!" They never answer. The child used to scream for help at night, and cry a good deal, but now it only makes a kind of whining, "eh-haa, eh-haa," and it speaks less and less often. It is so thin there are no calves to its legs; its belly protrudes; it lives on a half-bowl of corn meal and grease a day. It is naked. Its buttocks and thighs are a mass of festered sores, as it sits in its own excrement continually.

They all know it is there, all the people of Omelas. Some of them have come 9 to see it, others are content merely to know it is there. They all know that it has to be there. Some of them understand why, and some do not, but they all understand that their happiness, the beauty of their city, the tenderness of their friendships, the health of their children, the wisdom of their scholars, the skill of their makers, even the abundance of their harvest and the kindly weathers of their skies, depend wholly on this child's abominable misery.

10   This is usually explained to children when they are between eight and twelve, whenever they seem capable of understanding; and most of those who come to see the child are young people, though often enough an adult comes, or comes back, to see the child. No matter how well the matter has been explained to them, these young spectators are always shocked and sickened at the sight. They feel disgust, which they had thought themselves superior to. They feel anger, outrage, impotence, despite all the explanations. They would like to do something for the child. But there is nothing they can do. If the child were brought up into the sunlight out of that vile place, if it were cleaned and fed and comforted, that would be a good thing, indeed; but if it were done, in that day and hour all the prosperity and beauty and delight of Omelas would wither and be destroyed. Those are the terms. To exchange all the goodness and grace of every life in Omelas for that single, small improvement: to throw away the happiness of thousands for the chance of the happiness of one: that would be to let guilt within the walls indeed.

11   The terms are strict and absolute; there may not even be a kind word spoken to the child.

12   Often the young people go home in tears, or in a tearless rage, when they have seen the child and faced this terrible paradox. They may brood over it for weeks or years. But as time goes on they begin to realize that even if the child could be released, it would not get much good of its freedom: a little vague pleasure of warmth and food, no doubt, but little more. It is too degraded and imbecile to know any real joy. It has been afraid too long ever to be free of fear. Its habits are too uncouth for it to respond to humane treatment. Indeed, after so long it would probably be wretched without walls about it to protect it, and darkness for its eyes, and its own excrement to sit in. Their tears at the bitter injustice dry when they begin to perceive the terrible justice of reality, and to accept it. Yet it is their tears and anger, the trying of their generosity and the acceptance of their helplessness, which are perhaps the true source of the splendor of their lives. Theirs is no vapid, irresponsible happiness. They know that they, like the child, are not free. They know compassion. It is the existence of the child, and their knowledge of its existence, that makes possible the nobility of their architecture, the poignancy of their music, the profundity of their science. It is because of the child that they are so gentle with children. They know that if the wretched one were not there sniveling in the dark, the other one, the flute-player, could make no joyful music as the young riders line up in their beauty for the race in the sunlight of the first morning of summer.

13   Now do you believe in them? Are they not more credible? But there is one more thing to tell, and this is quite incredible.

14   At times one of the adolescent girls or boys who go to see the child does not go home to weep or rage, does not, in fact, go home at all. Sometimes also a man or woman much older falls silent for a day or two, and then leaves home. These people go out into the street, and walk down the street alone. They keep walking,

and walk straight out of the city of Omelas, through the beautiful gates. They keep walking across the farmlands of Omelas. Each one goes alone, youth or girl, man or woman. Night falls; the traveler must pass down village streets, between the houses with yellow-lit windows, and on out into the darkness of the fields. Each alone, they go west or north, towards the mountains. They go on. They leave Omelas, they walk ahead into the darkness, and they do not come back. The place they go towards is a place even less imaginable to most of us than the city of happiness. I cannot describe it at all. It is possible that it does not exist. But they seem to know where they are going, the ones who walk away from Omelas. ■

FOR DISCUSSION: How is happiness defined in this story? Who gets to define it? Why? Why do some walk away? Make some connections: What actual societies or organized groups of people existing either now or in history might be suggested by this parable? Why do you think so?

C. CLASS PROJECT: LITERARY DEBATE IN AN IMAGINARY COURTROOM

In the early 1900s, Susan Glaspell and her husband founded the Provincetown Players, a theater group in Massachusetts. She wrote the play *Trifles* for this group in 1916. The play is about the death of a man and the arrest of his wife on suspicion of murder. The assignment at the end of the play will call on you to conduct the trial that might follow this play. Would you rather be a member of the prosecution, a member of the defense, or a member of the jury? Think about your answer as you read.

TRIFLES*

Susan Glaspell

Play

Characters

GEORGE HENDERSON, *Country Attorney*
HENRY PETERS, *Sheriff*
LEWIS HALE, *A Neighboring Farmer*
MRS. PETERS
MRS. HALE

Scene: *The kitchen in the now abandoned farmhouse of* John Wright, *a gloomy kitchen, and left without having been put in order—unwashed pans under the sink, a loaf of bread outside the breadbox, a dish-towel on the table—other signs of incompleted work. At the rear the outer door opens and the* Sheriff *comes in followed by the* County Attorney *and* Hale. *The* Sheriff *and* Hale *are men in middle life, the* County Attorney *is a young man; all are much bundled up and go at once to the stove. They are followed by the two women—the* Sheriff's *wife first; she is a slight wiry woman, a thin nervous face.* Mrs. Hale *is larger and would*

*Used with permission of the author.

ordinarily be called more comfortable looking, but she is disturbed now and looks fearfully about as she enters. The women have come in slowly, and stand close together near the door.

    County Attorney: (Rubbing his hands.) This feels good. Come up to the fire, ladies.

    Mrs. Peters: (After taking a step forward.) I'm not—cold.

    Sheriff (unbuttoning his overcoat and stepping away from the stove as if to the begin-
5 *ning of official business):* Now, Mr. Hale, before we move things about, you explain to Mr. Henderson just what you saw when you came here yesterday morning.

    County Attorney: By the way, has anything been moved? Are things just as you left them yesterday?

    Sheriff (looking about): It's just the same. When it dropped below zero last
10 night, I thought I'd better send Frank out this morning to make a fire for us—no use getting pneumonia with a big case on; but I told him not to touch anything except the stove—and you know Frank.

    County Attorney: Somebody should have been left here yesterday.

    Sheriff: Oh—yesterday. When I had to send Frank to Morris Center for that
15 man who went crazy—I want you to know I had my hands full yesterday. I knew you could get back from Omaha by today, and as long as I went over everything here myself—

    County Attorney: Well, Mr. Hale, tell just what happened when you came here yesterday morning.

20   *Hale:* Harry and I had started to town with a load of potatoes. We came along the road from my place; and as I got here, I said, "I'm going to see if I can't get John Wright to go in with me on a party telephone." I spoke to Wright about it once before, and he put me off, saying folks talked too much anyway, and all he asked was peace and quiet—I guess you know about how much he talked himself; but I thought
25 maybe if I went to the house and talked about it before his wife, though I said to Harry that I didn't know as what his wife wanted made much difference to John—

    County Attorney: Let's talk about that later, Mr. Hale. I do want to talk about that, but tell now just what happened when you got to the house.

    Hale: I didn't hear or see anything; I knocked at the door, and still it was all
30 quiet inside. I knew they must be up, it was past eight o'clock. So I knocked again, and I thought I heard somebody say, "Come in." I wasn't sure, I'm not sure yet, but I opened the door—this door *(indicating the door by which the two women are still standing)*, and there in that rocker—*(pointing to it)* sat Mrs. Wright. *(They all look at the rocker.)*

35   *County Attorney:* What—was she doing?

    Hale: She was rockin' back and forth. She had her apron in her hand and was kind of—pleating it.

    Country Attorney: And how did she—look?

    Hale: Well, she looked queer.

40   *Country Attorney:* How do you mean—queer?

    Hale: Well, as if she didn't know what she was going to do next. And kind of done up.

Country Attorney: How did she seem to feel about your coming?

Hale: Why, I don't think she minded—one way or other. She didn't pay much attention. I said, "How do, Mrs. Wright, it's cold, ain't it?" And she said, "Is it?"—and went on kind of pleating at her apron. Well, I was surprised; she didn't ask me to come up to the stove, or to set down, but just sat there, not even looking at me, so I said, "I want to see John." And then she—laughed. I guess you would call it a laugh. I thought of Harry and the team outside, so I said a little sharp: "Can't I see John?" "No," she says, kind o' dull like. "Ain't he home?" says I. "Yes," says she, "he's home." "Then why can't I see him?" I asked her, out of patience. " 'Cause he's dead," says she. "*Dead?*" says I. She just nodded her head, not getting a bit excited, but rockin' back and forth. "Why—where is he?" says I, not knowing what to say. She just pointed upstairs—like that (*himself pointing to the room above*). I got up, with the idea of going up there. I walked from there to here— then I says, "Why, what did he die of?" "He died of a rope around his neck," says she, and just went on pleatin' at her apron. Well, I went out and called Harry. I thought I might—need help. We went upstairs, and there he was lyin'—

Country Attorney: I think I'd rather have you go into that upstairs, where you can point it all out. Just go on now with the rest of the story.

Hale: Well, my first thought was to get that rope off. I looked . . . (*Stops, his face twitches.*) . . . but Harry, he went up to him, and he said, "No, he's dead all right, and we'd better not touch anything." So we went back downstairs. She was still sitting that same way. "Has anybody been notified?" I asked. "No," says she, unconcerned. "Who did this, Mrs. Wright?" said Harry. He said it businesslike— and she stopped pleatin' of her apron. "I don't know," she says. "You don't *know?*" says Harry. "No," says she, "Weren't you sleepin' in the bed with him?" says Harry. "Yes," says she, "but I was on the inside." "Somebody slipped a rope round his neck and strangled him, and you didn't wake up?" says Harry. "I didn't wake up," she said after him. We must 'a looked as if we didn't see how that could be, for after a minute she said, "I sleep sound." Harry was going to ask her more questions, but I said maybe we ought to let her tell her story first to the coroner, or the sheriff, so Harry went fast as he could to Rivers' place, where there's a telephone.

County Attorney: And what did Mrs. Wright do when she knew that you had gone for the coroner?

Hale: She moved from that chair to this over here . . . (*Pointing to a small chair in the corner.*) . . . and just sat there with her hands held together and looking down. I got a feeling that I ought to make some conversation, so I said I had come in to see if John wanted to put in a telephone, and at that she started to laugh, and then she stopped and looked at me—scared. (*The County Attorney, who has had his notebook out, makes a note.*) I dunno, maybe it wasn't scared. I wouldn't like to say it was. Soon Harry got back, and then Dr. Lloyd came, and you, Mr. Peters, and so I guess that's all I know that you don't.

County Attorney (looking around): I guess we'll go upstairs first—and then out to the barn and around there. (*To the Sheriff.*) You're convinced that there was nothing important here—nothing that would point to any motive?

Sheriff: Nothing here but kitchen things. *(The County Attorney, after again looking around the kitchen, opens the door of a cupboard closet. He gets up on a chair and*
90 *looks on a shelf. Pulls his hand away, sticky.)*

County Attorney: Here's a nice mess. *(The women draw nearer.)*

Mrs. Peters (to the other woman): Oh, her fruit; it did freeze. *(To the Lawyer.)* She worried about that when it turned so cold. She said the fire'd go out and her jars would break.

95 *Sheriff:* Well, can you beat the women! Held for murder and worryin' about her preserves.

County Attorney: I guess before we're through she may have something more serious than preserves to worry about.

Hale: Well, women are used to worrying over trifles. *(The two women move a*
100 *little closer together.)*

County Attorney (with the gallantry of a young politician): And yet, for all their worries, what would we do without the ladies? *(The women do not unbend. He goes to the sink, takes a dipperful of water from the pail and, pouring it into a basin, washes his hands. Starts to wipe them on the roller towel, turns it for a cleaner place.)* Dirty towels!
105 *(Kicks his foot against the pans under the sink.)* Not much of a housekeeper, would you say, ladies?

Mrs. Hale (stiffly): There's a great deal of work to be done on a farm.

County Attorney: To be sure. And yet . . . *(With a little bow to her.)* . . . I know there are some Dickson county farmhouses which do not have such roller towels.
110 *(He gives it a pull to expose its full length again.)*

Mrs. Hale: Those towels get dirty awful quick. Men's hands aren't always as clean as they might be.

County Attorney: Ah, loyal to your sex. I see. But you and Mrs. Wright were neighbors. I suppose you were friends, too.

115 *Mrs. Hale (shaking her head):* I've not seen much of her of late years. I've not been in this house—it's more than a year.

County Attorney: And why was that? You didn't like her?

Mrs. Hale: I liked her well enough. Farmers' wives have their hands full, Mr. Henderson. And then—

120 *County Attorney:* Yes—?

Mrs. Hale (looking about): It never seemed a very cheerful place.

County Attorney: No—it's not cheerful. I shouldn't say she had the home-making instinct.

Mrs. Hale: Well, I don't know as Wright had, either.

125 *County Attorney:* You mean they didn't get on very well?

Mrs. Hale: No, I don't mean anything. But I don't think a place'd be any cheerfuller for John Wright's being in it.

County Attorney: I'd like to talk more of that a little later. I want to get the lay of things upstairs now. *(He goes to the left, where three steps lead to a stair door.)*

130 *Sheriff:* I suppose anything Mrs. Peters does'll be all right. She was to take in some clothes for her, you know, and a few little things. We left in such a hurry yesterday.

County Attorney: Yes, but I would like to see what you take, Mrs. Peters, and keep an eye out for anything that might be of use to us.

Mrs. Peters: Yes, Mr. Henderson. *(The women listen to the men's steps on the* 135 *stairs, then look about the kitchen.)*

Mrs. Hale: I'd hate to have men coming into my kitchen, snooping around and criticizing. *(She arranges the pans under the sink which the Lawyer had shoved out of place.)*

Mrs. Peters: Of course it's no more than their duty. 140

Mrs. Hale: Duty's all right, but I guess that deputy sheriff that came out to make the fire might have got a little of this on. *(Gives the roller towel a pull.)* Wish I'd thought of that sooner. Seems mean to talk about her for not having things slicked up when she had to come away in such a hurry.

Mrs. Peters (who has gone to a small table in the left rear corner of the room, and 145 *lifted one end of a towel that cover a pan):* She had bread set. *(Stands still.)*

Mrs. Hale (eyes fixed on a loaf of bread beside the breadbox, which is on a low shelf at the other side of the room. Moves slowly toward it): She was going to put this in there. *(Picks up loaf, then abruptly drops it. In a manner of returning to familiar things.)* It's a shame about her fruit. I wonder if it's all gone. *(Gets up on the chair and looks.)* I think 150 there's some here that's all right, Mrs. Peters. Yes—here; *(Holding it toward the window.)* this is cherries, too. *(Looking again.)* I declare I believe that's the only one. *(Gets down, bottle in her hand. Goes to the sink and wipes it off on the outside.)* She'll feel awful bad after all her hard work in the hot weather. I remember the afternoon I put up my cherries last summer. *(She puts the bottle on the big kitchen table, center of the room. With* 155 *a sigh, is about to sit down in the rocking chair. Before she is seated realizes what chair it is; with a slow look at it, steps back. The chair, which she has touched, rocks back and forth.)*

Mrs. Peters: Well, I must get those things from the front room closet. *(She goes to the door at the right, but after looking into the other room steps back.)* You coming with me, Mrs. Hale? You could help me carry them. *(They go into the other room;* 160 *reappear, Mrs. Peters carrying a dress and skirt, Mrs. Hale following with a pair of shoes.)*

Mrs. Peters: My, it's cold in there. *(She puts the cloth on the big table, and hurries to the stove.)*

Mrs. Hale (examining the skirt): Wright was close. I think maybe that's why she kept so much to herself. She didn't even belong to the Ladies' Aid. I suppose she 165 felt she couldn't do her part, and then you don't enjoy things when you feel shabby. She used to wear pretty clothes and be lively, when she was Minnie Foster, one of the town girls singing in the choir. But that—oh, that was thirty years ago. This all you was to take in?

Mrs. Peters: She said she wanted an apron. Funny thing to want, for there 170 isn't much to get you dirty in jail, goodness knows. But I suppose just to make her feel more natural. She said they was in the top drawer in this cupboard. Yes, here. And then her little shawl that always hung behind the door. *(Opens stair door and looks.)* Yes, here it is. *(Quickly shuts door leading upstairs.)*

Mrs. Hale (abruptly moving toward her): Mrs. Peters? 175

Mrs. Peters: Yes, Mrs. Hale?

Mrs. Hale: Do you think she did it?

Mrs. Peters (in a frightened voice): Oh, I don't know.

Mrs. Hale: Well, I don't think she did. Asking for an apron and her little
180 shawl. Worrying about her fruit.

*Mrs. Peters (starts to speak, glances up, where footsteps are heard in the room above.
In a low voice):* Mr. Peters says it looks bad for her. Mr. Henderson is awful sarcas-
tic in speech, and he'll make fun of her sayin' she didn't wake up.

Mrs. Hale: Well, I guess John Wright didn't wake when they was slipping
185 that rope under his neck.

Mrs. Peters: No, it's strange. It must have been done awful crafty and still.
They say it was such a—funny way to kill a man, rigging it all up like that.

Mrs. Hale: That's just what Mr. Hale said. There was a gun in the house. He
says that's what he can't understand.

190 *Mrs. Peters:* Mr. Henderson said coming out that what was needed for the
case was a motive; something to show anger or—sudden feeling.

Mrs. Hale (who is standing by the table): Well, I don't see any signs of anger
around here. *(She puts her hand on the dish towel which lies on the table, stands looking
down at the table, one half of which is clean, the other half messy.)* It's wiped here.
195 *(Makes a move as if to finish work, then turns and looks at loaf of bread outside the breadbox. Drops towel. In that voice of coming back to familiar things.)* Wonder how they are
finding things upstairs? I hope she had it a little more red-up there. You know, it
seems kind of *sneaking.* Locking her up in town and then coming out here and trying to get her own house to turn against her!

200 *Mrs. Peters:* But, Mrs. Hale, the law is the law.

Mrs. Hale: I s'pose 'tis. *(Unbuttoning her coat.)* Better loosen up your things,
Mrs. Peters. You won't feel them when you go out. *(Mrs. Peters takes off her fur tip-
pet, goes to hang it on hook at the back of room, stands looking at the under part of the
small corner table.)*

205 *Mrs. Peters:* She was piecing a quilt. *(She brings the large sewing basket, and
they look at the bright pieces.)*

Mrs. Hale: It's log cabin pattern. Pretty, isn't it? I wonder if she was goin' to
quilt or just knot it? *(Footsteps have been heard coming down the stairs. The Sheriff enters, followed by Hale and the County Attorney.)*

210 *Sheriff:* They wonder if she was going to quilt it or just knot it. *(The men
laugh, the women look abashed.)*

County Attorney (rubbing his hands over the stove): Frank's fire didn't do much
up there, did it? Well, let's go out to the barn and get that cleared up. *(The men go
outside.)*

215 *Mrs. Hale (resentfully):* I don't know as there's anything so strange, our takin'
up our time with little things while we're waiting for them to get the evidence.
(She sits down at the big table, smoothing out a block with decision.) I don't see as it's
anything to laugh about.

Mrs. Peters (apologetically): Of course they've got awful important things on
220 their minds. *(Pulls up a chair and joins Mrs. Hale at the table.)*

Mrs. Hale (examining another block): Mrs. Peters, look at this one. Here, this is
the one she was working on, and look at the sewing! All the rest of it has been so nice

and even. And look at this! It's all over the place! Why, it looks as if she didn't know what she was about! *(After she has said this, they look at each other, then start to glance back at the door. After an instant Mrs. Hale has pulled at a knot and ripped the sewing.)*   225

    Mrs. Peters: Oh, what are you doing, Mrs. Hale?

    Mrs. Hale (mildly): Just pulling out a stitch or two that's not sewed very good. *(Threading a needle.)* Bad sewing always made me fidgety.

    Mrs. Peters (nervously): I don't think we ought to touch things.

    Mrs. Hale: I'll just finish up this end. *(Suddenly stopping and leaning forward.)*   230 Mrs. Peters?

    Mrs. Peters: Yes, Mrs. Hale?

    Mrs. Hale: What do you suppose she was so nervous about?

    Mrs. Peters: Oh—I don't know. I don't know as she was nervous. I sometimes sew awful queer when I'm just tired. *(Mrs. Hale starts to say something, looks*   235 *at Mrs. Peters, then goes on sewing.)* Well, I must get these things wrapped up. They may be through sooner than we think. *(Putting apron and other things together.)* I wonder where I can find a piece of paper, and string.

    Mrs. Hale: In that cupboard, maybe.

    Mrs. Peters (looking in cupboard): Why, here's a birdcage. *(Holds it up.)* Did she   240 have a bird, Mrs. Hale?

    Mrs. Hale: Why, I don't know whether she did or not—I've not been here for so long. There was a man around last year selling canaries cheap, but I don't know as she took one; maybe she did. She used to sing real pretty herself.

    Mrs. Peters (glancing around): Seems funny to think of a bird here. But she   245 must have had one, or why should she have a cage? I wonder what happened to it?

    Mrs. Hale: I s'pose maybe the cat got it.

    Mrs. Peters: No, she didn't have a cat. She's got that feeling some people have about cats—being afraid of them. My cat got in her room, and she was real upset and asked me to take it out.   250

    Mrs. Hale: My sister Bessie was like that. Queer, ain't it?

    Mrs. Peters (examining the cage): Why, look, at this door. It's broke. One hinge is pulled apart.

    Mrs. Hale (looking, too): Looks as if someone must have been rough with it.

    Mrs. Peters: Why, yes. *(She brings the cage forward and puts it on the table.)*   255

    Mrs. Hale: I wish if they're going to find any evidence they'd be about it. I don't like this place.

    Mrs. Peters: But I'm awful glad you came with me, Mrs. Hale. It would be lonesome for me sitting here alone.

    Mrs. Hale: It would, wouldn't it? *(Dropping her sewing.)* But I tell you what I   260 do wish, Mrs. Peters. I wish I had come over sometimes when *she* was here. I— *(Looking around the room)*—wish I had.

    Mrs. Peters: But of course you were awful busy, Mrs. Hale—your house and your children.

    Mrs. Hale: I could've come. I stayed away because it weren't cheerful—and   265 that's why I ought to have come. I—I've never liked this place. Maybe because it's down in a hollow, and you don't see the road. I dunno what it is, but it's a lonesome place and always was. I wish I had come over to see Minnie Foster sometimes. I can see now—*(Shakes her head.)*

270   *Mrs. Peters:* Well, you musn't reproach yourself, Mrs. Hale. Somehow we just don't see how it is with other folks until—something comes up.

    Mrs. Hale: Not having children makes less work—but it makes a quiet house, and Wright out to work all day, and no company when he did come in. Did you know John Wright, Mrs. Peters?

275   *Mrs. Peters:* Not to know him; I've seen him in town. They say he was a good man.

    Mrs. Hale: Yes—good; he didn't drink, and kept his word as well as most, I guess, and paid his debts. But he was a hard man, Mrs. Peters. Just to pass the time of day with him. *(Shivers.)* Like a raw wind that gets to the bone. *(Pauses, her eye*
280 *falling on the cage.)* I should think she would 'a' wanted a bird. But what do you suppose went with it?

    Mrs. Peters: I don't know, unless it got sick and died. *(She reaches over and swings the broken door, swings it again; both women watch it.)*

    Mrs. Hale: You weren't raised around here, were you? *(Mrs. Peters shakes her*
285 *head.)* You didn't know—her?

    Mrs. Peters: Not till they brought her yesterday.

    Mrs. Hale: She—come to think of it, she was kind of like a bird herself—real sweet and pretty, but kind of timid and—fluttery. How—she—did—change. *(Silence; then as if struck by a happy thought and relieved to get back to everyday things.)*
290 Tell you what, Mrs. Peters, why don't you take the quilt in with you? It might take up her mind.

    Mrs. Peters: Why, I think that's a real nice idea, Mrs. Hale. There couldn't possibly be any objection to it, could there? Now, just what would I take? I wonder if her patches are in here—and her things. *(They look in the sewing basket.)*

295   *Mrs. Hale:* Here's some red. I expect this has got sewing things in it. *(Brings out a fancy box.)* What a pretty box. Looks like something somebody would give you. Maybe her scissors are in here. *(Opens box. Suddenly puts her hand to her nose.)* Why—*(Mrs. Peters bends nearer, then turns her face away.)* There's something wrapped up in this piece of silk.

300   *Mrs. Peters:* Why, this isn't her scissors.

    Mrs. Hale (lifting the silk): Oh, Mrs. Peters—it's—*(Mrs. Peters bends closer.)*

    Mrs. Peters: It's the bird.

    Mrs. Hale (jumping up): But, Mrs. Peters—look at it. Its neck! Look at its neck! It's all—other side to.

305   *Mrs. Peters:* Somebody—wrung—its neck. *(Their eyes meet. A look of growing comprehension of horror. Steps are heard outside. Mrs. Hale slips box under quilt pieces, and sinks into her chair. Enter Sheriff and County Attorney, Mrs. Peters rises.)*

    County Attorney (as one turning from serious things to little pleasantries): Well, ladies, have you decided whether she was going to quilt it or knot it?

310   *Mrs. Peters:* We think she was going to—knot it.

    County Attorney: Well, that's interesting, I'm sure. *(Seeing the birdcage.)* Has the bird flown?

Mrs. Hale (putting more quilt pieces over the box): We think the—cat got it.

County Attorney (preoccupied): Is there a cat? *(Mrs. Hale glances in a quick covert way at Mrs. Peters.)*   315

Mrs. Peters: Well, not now. They're superstitious, you know. They leave.

County Attorney (to Sheriff Peters, continuing an interrupted conversation): No sign at all of anyone having come from the outside. Their own rope. Now let's go up again and go over it piece by piece. *(They start upstairs.)* It would have to have been someone who knew just the—*(Mrs. Peters sits down. The two women sit* 320 *there not looking at one another, but as if peering into something and at the same time holding back. When they talk now, it is the manner of feeling their way over strange ground, as if afraid of what they are saying, but as if they cannot help saying it.)*

Mrs. Hale: She liked the bird. She was going to bury it in that pretty box.

Mrs. Peters (in a whisper): When I was a girl—my kitten—there was a boy 325 took a hatchet, and before my eyes—and before I could get there—*(Covers her face an instant.)* If they hadn't held me back, I would have—*(Catches herself, looks upstairs where steps are heard, falters weakly.)*—hurt him.

Mrs. Hale (with a slow look around her): I wonder how it would seem never to have had any children around. *(Pause.)* No, Wright wouldn't like the bird—a thing 330 that sang. She used to sing. He killed that, too.

Mrs. Peters (moving uneasily): We don't know who killed the bird.

Mrs. Hale: I knew John Wright.

Mrs. Peters: It was an awful thing was done in this house that night, Mrs. Hale. Killing a man while he slept, slipping a rope around his neck that choked the 335 life out of him.

Mrs. Hale: His neck. Choked the life out of him. *(Her hand goes out and rests on the birdcage.)*

Mrs. Peters (with a rising voice): We don't know who killed him. We don't *know.*

Mrs. Hale (her own feeling not interrupted): If there'd been years and years of 340 nothing, then a bird to sing to you, it would be awful—still, after the bird was still.

Mrs. Peters (something within her speaking): I know what stillness is. When we homesteaded in Dakota, and my first baby died—after he was two years old, and me with no other then—   345

Mrs. Hale (moving): How soon do you suppose they'll be through, looking for evidence?

Mrs. Peters: I know what stillness is. *(Pulling herself back.)* The law has got to punish crime, Mrs. Hale.

Mrs. Hale (not as if answering that): I wish you'd seen Minnie Foster when she 350 wore a white dress with blue ribbons and stood up there in the choir and sang. *(A look around the room.)* Oh, I *wish* I'd come over here once in a while! That was a crime! That was a crime! Who's going to punish that?

Mrs. Peters (looking upstairs): We mustn't—take on.

Mrs. Hale: I might have known she needed help! I know how things can 355 be—for women. I tell you, it's queer, Mrs. Peters. We live close together and we live far apart. We all go through the same things—it's all just a different kind of

the same thing. *(Brushes her eyes, noticing the bottle of fruit, reaches out for it.)* If I was you, I wouldn't tell her her fruit was gone. Tell her it *ain't.* Tell her it's all
360 right. Take this in to prove it to her. She—she may never know whether it was broke or not.

 Mrs. Peters *(takes the bottle, looks about for something to wrap it in; takes petticoat from the clothes brought from the other room, very nervously begins winding this around the bottle. In a false voice):* My, it's a good thing the men couldn't hear us. Wouldn't
365 they just laugh! Getting all stirred up over a little thing like a—dead canary. As if that could have anything to with—with—wouldn't they *laugh! (The men are heard coming downstairs.)*

 Mrs. Hale *(under her breath):* Maybe they would—maybe they wouldn't.

 County Attorney: No, Peters, it's all perfectly clear except a reason for doing
370 it. But you know juries when it comes to women. If there was some definite thing. Something to show—something to make a story about—a thing that would connect up with this strange way of doing it. *(The women's eyes meet for an instant. Enter Hale from outer door.)*

 Hale: Well, I've got the team around. Pretty cold out there.
375 County Attorney: I'm going to stay here a while by myself. *(To the Sheriff.)* You can send Frank out for me, can't you? I want to go over everything. I'm not satisfied that we can't do better.

 Sheriff: Do you want to see what Mrs. Peters is going to take in? *(The Lawyer goes to the table, picks up the apron, laughs.)*
380 County Attorney: Oh I guess they're not very dangerous things the ladies have picked up. *(Moves a few things about, disturbing the quilt pieces which cover the box. Steps back.)* No, Mrs. Peters doesn't need supervising. For that matter, a sheriff's wife is married to the law. Ever think of it that way, Mrs. Peters?

 Mrs. Peters: Not—just that way.
385 Sheriff *(chuckling):* Married to the law. *(Moves toward the other room.)* I just want you to come in here a minute, George. We ought to take a look at these windows.

 County Attorney *(scoffingly):* Oh, windows!

 Sheriff: We'll be right out, Mr. Hale.

 (Hale goes outside. The Sheriff follows the County Attorney into the other room.
390 *Then Mrs. Hale rises, hands tight together, looking intensely at Mrs. Peters, whose eyes take a slow turn, finally meeting Mrs. Hale's. A moment Mrs. Hale holds her, then her own eyes point the way to where the box is concealed. Suddenly Mrs. Peters throws back quilt pieces and tries to put the box in the bag she is wearing. It is too big. She opens box, starts to take the bird out, cannot touch it, goes to pieces, stands there helpless. Sound of a*
395 *knob turning in the other room. Mrs. Hale snatches the box and puts it in the pocket of her big coat. Enter County Attorney and Sheriff.)*

 County Attorney *(facetiously):* Well, Henry, at least we found out that she was not going to quilt it. She was going to—what is it you call it, ladies?

 Mrs. Hale *(her hand against her pocket):* We call it—knot it, Mr. Henderson. ▪

FOR DISCUSSION: Characterize the men and the women in this play. What is the relationship between them? What contributes to this relationship? What are the results of it in the play? How do you think Mr. Wright died? What evidence is there in the play to support your answer? Why is the play called *Trifles*?

Literary Debate on Trifles[2]

1. *Set the Scene and Form Groups.*

Imagine that the classroom is a courtroom. Mrs. Wright will be on trial. The birdcage, the box with the bird in it, and the rope used to strangle Mr. Wright will be placed on the table as evidence. One-third of the class will identify themselves as members of the prosecution. Their role is to prove Mrs. Wright guilty of the murder of her husband. One-third of the class will identify themselves as members of the defense. They will devise a strategy for defending Mrs. Wright. Options for the defense include arguing that she is not guilty, that she is not guilty by reason of insanity, or that she is guilty but should be extended leniency. The members of the defense should meet briefly before the trial to decide which strategy to pursue. The final third of the class will become the jury who will write their verdicts, take a vote, and present their judgment to the class on the day following the trial.

The day before the trial, the class should divide into the three groups. Members of the prosecution and members of the defense should each prepare 250-word written arguments to bring to the trial. Each paper should present a clear position and reasons and evidence as support. Evidence should come from the text when possible. Evidence may also come from personal experiences, however, or from other classes. A psychology class, for example, may provide evidence about probable human behavior. The prosecution and the defense might want to examine character, cause, factual evidence, and the values of the individuals involved to help them prepare their cases. They might also want to remember that value systems can contradict each other. They should try to be aware of the warrants that the jury is likely to hold. Each student who is a member of the prosecution or defense should present a case to convict or to acquit as clearly and logically as possible.

2. *Conduct the Trial.*

The prosecution and defense meet briefly as groups at the beginning of class to decide on speaking order. The first speaker should read, and the others may add additional evidence and arguments from their papers. During this time the jury should assemble and elect a foreman who will later deliver the verdict.

Each side has ten minutes to present its case. This presentation will be followed by a ten-minute break during which each side will formulate rebuttals to the points that its opponents have made. Each side will have five minutes to

---

[2]I am indebted to Audrey Wick for this assignment.

rebut the opponents' arguments. No one may interrupt the other side at any time. Each member of the jury then makes an independent judgment of guilty or not guilty and writes a 250-word paper on this judgment before the next class. The paper should state the judgment (guilty or not guilty) and provide reasons and evidence from the trial to support the judgment. When the class reconvenes, the jury members meet briefly to record their votes. The foreman then delivers the verdict of the majority of the jury, and members of the jury refer to their papers to provide reasons for their votes.

D. WRITING ASSIGNMENT: ANALYZING THE ARGUMENT OF A LITERARY CHARACTER

The following speeches are made by Marc Antony in Shakespeare's *Julius Caesar*. The rhetorical situation is as follows: Caesar has been stabbed to death by Brutus and other conspirators and denounced as an unfit ruler of Rome. Antony, loyal to Caesar, has been allowed to give the funeral oration. Brutus has told Antony that he is not to say anything that would reflect badly on any of the conspirators. See what Antony does instead.

1. Break the class into five groups. Each group will take one of the following questions, work for ten minutes, and then report back to the class.

   a. What is the issue? What is Antony's ostensible purpose in this speech to the Roman people? What is his actual purpose? How does the rhetorical situation constrain Antony? How does Antony build common ground with his audience?
   b. Use the Toulmin model, and state Antony's claim, support, and warrants. Are there any rebuttals? Qualifiers?
   c. How does Antony use emotional appeal and incite *pathos* in his audience? Cite examples in the speech that cause the audience to feel emotion.
   d. What are some examples of logical appeal that Antony uses to persuade the audience?
   e. How does Antony destroy the *ethos* of the conspirators? How does he develop a positive *ethos* for himself? Would you say that Antony is a moral or immoral speaker in the context of the play?

2. Write a 500-to 750-word paper in which you draw on the answers to the questions to explain Antony's argumentative strategy in his speech to the Roman people. At the end of your paper, write your responses to the following questions: Did Marc Antony accomplish his purpose? What do you think were the most persuasive parts of the speech?

   After you have written your paper, you may want to read the student example at the end of this exercise.

ANTONY'S FUNERAL SPEECH FOR CAESAR

From *Julius Caesar*

William Shakespeare

Speech

Antony: Friends, Romans, countrymen, lend me your ears.
    I come to bury Caesar, not to praise him.
The evil that men do lives after them:
    The good is oft interred with their bones.
So let it be with Caesar. The noble Brutus   5
Hath told you Caesar was ambitious.
    If it were so, it was a grievous fault,
And grievously hath Caesar answered it.
    Here, under leave of Brutus and the rest—
For Brutus is an honorable man,   10
So are they all, all honorable men—
    Come I to speak in Caesar's funeral.
He was my friend, faithful and just to me;
    But Brutus says he was ambitious,
And Brutus is an honorable man.   15
He hath brought many captives home to Rome,
    Whose ransoms did the general coffers fill.
Did this in Caesar seem ambitious?
    When that the poor have cried, Caesar hath wept;
Ambition should be made of stronger stuff.   20
Yet Brutus says he was ambitious,
    And Brutus is an honorable man.
You all did see that on the Lupercal
    I thrice presented him a kingly crown,
Which he did thrice refuse. Was this ambition?   25
Yet Brutus says he was ambitious,
    And sure he is an honorable man.
I speak not to disprove what Brutus spoke,
    But here I am to speak of what I do know.
You all did love him once, not without cause.   30
What cause withholds you then to mourn for him?
    O judgment! Thou art fled to brutish beasts,
And men have lost their reason. Bear with me;
    My heart is in the coffin there with Caesar;
And I must pause till it come back to me.   35

The audience here makes a few comments about the passion in Antony's speaking, and Antony speaks again.

Antony: But yesterday the word of Caesar might
    Have stood against the world. Now lies her there,
And none so poor to do him reverence.
    O masters! If I were disposed to stir
Your hearts and minds to mutiny and rage,   40
I should do Brutus wrong, and Cassius wrong,
    Who, you all know, are honorable men.
I will not do them wrong; I rather choose
    To wrong the dead, to wrong myself and you,
Than I will wrong such honorable men.   45

But here's a parchment with the seal of Caesar.
    I found it in his closet; 'tis his will. *(He shows the will)*.
Let but the commons hear this testament—
Which, pardon me, I do not mean to read—
50   And they would go and kiss dead Caesar's wounds
And dip their napkins in his sacred blood,
Yea, beg a hair of him for memory,
    And dying, mention it within their wills,
Bequeathing it as a rich legacy
55   Unto their issue.

All: The will, the will! We will hear Caesar's will!

Antony: Have patience, gentle friends: I must not read it.
    It is not meet you know how Caesar loved you.
You are not wood, you are not stones, but men;
60   And being men, hearing the word of Caesar,
It will inflame you, it will make you mad.
    'Tis good you know not that you are his heirs,
For if you should, O, what would come of it?

Antony steps off the podium and stands by Caesar's body.

Antony: If you have tears, prepare to shed them now.
65   You all do know this mantle. I remember
The first time ever Caesar put it on;
    'Twas on a summer's evening in his tent,
That day he overcame the Nervii.
    Look, in this place ran Cassius' dagger through.
70   See what a rent the envious Casca made.
Through this the well-beloved Brutus stabbed,
    And as he plucked his cursed steel away,
Mark how the blood of Caesar followed it,
    As rushing out of doors to be resolved
75   If Brutus so unkindly knocked or no—
For Brutus, as you know, was Caesar's angel.
    Judge, O you gods, how dearly Caesar loved him!
This was the most unkindest cut of all;
    For when the noble Caesar saw him stab,
80   Ingratitude, more strong than traitors' arms,
Quite vanquished him. Then burst his mighty heart,
    And in his mantle muffling up his face,
Even at the base of Pompey's statue,
    Which all the while ran blood, great Caesar fell.
O, what a fall was there, my countrymen!
85   Then I, and you, and all of us fell down,
    Whilst bloody treason flourished over us.
O, now you weep, and I perceive you feel
    The dint of pit. These are gracious drops.
Kind souls, what, weep you when you but behold
90   Our Caesar's vesture wounded? Look you here,
Here is himself, marred as you see with traitors.
    (He lifts Caesar's mantle) ■

Antony finally reads Caesar's will, which proves Caesar's generosity toward the citizens of Rome. The audience is inflamed by Antony's speech.

FOR DISCUSSION: Visualize the scene for this speech. What do you see? How does the audience act before Antony begins to speak? How is it affected by the speech? What is the effect of repeating the refrain "For Brutus is an honorable man"? What historical evidence does Antony draw on? What physical evidence does he point to? What is the effect of his evidence?

Student Paper
Sara Orr
Argument in Literature
Professor Arroyo
English 1302
December 2, 2000

*Student
Paper*

Marc Antony's Argument

In William Shakespeare's <u>Julius Caesar</u>, Marc Antony delivers a 1 very persuasive argument to the commoners of Rome. On March 15, Marcus Brutus and several other conspirators joined together and murdered Julius Caesar. Following this ghastly attack, Marcus Brutus spoke to the commoners and convinced them that what he had done was for the good of Rome. Brutus described Caesar as an overly ambitious ruler, who had to be stopped before he gained too much power. Brutus was very successful in persuading the commoners to see and support his side of the situation. When Marc Antony was allowed to speak, Brutus' only stipulation was that Antony could not in any way blame the conspirators for their act. He was only to deliver a funeral speech for Julius Caesar. Marc Antony took this opportunity to speak to the audience and present his own argument about Caesar's death. It is in this famous speech that many elements of argument prove to be successful tools in effectively changing an audience's perspective.

Marc Antony first states his purpose to his audience. He claims 2 to be there to bury Caesar, not to praise him in any way. This enables the audience to open up their minds to what Antony is going to say. His true purpose, though, evolves during the speech. His goal is to convince the audience that the act that Brutus and the conspirators did was not honorable and therefore that they were wrong in murdering Caesar. Because Marc Antony promised not to blame the conspirators, he must reach this goal deceptively. He uses the modes of classical appeal: <u>logos</u>, <u>pathos</u>, and <u>ethos</u>. These elements enable Antony to persuade the crowd to change their view of Brutus and the death of Caesar.

Antony uses several examples of logical appeal in his speech to 3 the Romans. He gives them hard evidence to prove that Caesar was not too ambitious, nor was he cruel and ruthless. Antony details events such as the offer of the crown at the Feast of Lupercal, which Caesar denied three times. This surely did not seem ambitious. Antony also reminds the audience of the many ransoms Caesar has brought home to Rome that have filled the coffers. Again, this does not seem ambitious. Antony also produces Caesar's will and tempts the audience into forcing him to read it. This tangible piece of Caesar's generosity helps persuade the common crowd to see that Caesar was not as ambitious as Brutus had said.

4   Marc Antony destroys the <u>ethos</u> or character of the conspirators while promoting his own <u>ethos</u> to the crowd. One of the ways he destroys the <u>ethos</u> of the conspirators is through the repetition of the lines "For Brutus is an honorable man/So are they all honorable men." It is soon clear that Antony is being satirical in using these lines. In repeating these "honorable" lines, Marc Antony soon causes the Roman crowd to question the idea of whether or not these men were truly honorable. Antony's persuasive strategy depends on the warrant that the act of murder is not honorable, so these men could not be honorable. If the crowd can see this through his repetition of these lines about honor, he will be successful in destroying the <u>ethos</u> of the conspirators. He creates his own positive <u>ethos</u> by being very humble and mournful for Caesar. He claims he must pause because he is so overcome with grief that he can no longer speak. This causes the audience to sympathize with Antony. He continues to build this positive view of himself when he produces the will. He tells the commoners that he should not read it to them because it would hurt them to know how much Caesar loved them. He speaks as though his first concern is the people's feelings, and this adds to his positive <u>ethos</u>.

5   However, Antony's most persuasive technique is his ability to incite <u>pathos</u> or emotion in the audience. He is capable of changing the anger the commoners have for Caesar to tears of sadness for their ruler and revenge for his death. He begins by disclaiming the idea that Caesar was ambitious. This lures the crowd into Antony's speech so that he can incite emotion in them. When he produces the will, he begs the crowd not to make him read it. It would make them angry to know how much Caesar loved them. "And being men, hearing the word of Caesar. It will inflame you, it will make you mad." The temptation is too great, and the crowd forces Antony to read the will. He then leads the audience to tears as he re-creates the murder scene. He points to each of the stab wounds seen in Caesar's cloak. Antony gives a name to each stab wound, making it much more personal to the crowd. When he shows where the beloved Brutus stabbed Caesar, it is almost too much for the commoners to bear. He calls it the "most unkindest cut of all" since Brutus was Caesar's favorite, his angel. Even after the crowd is shedding tears, Antony

goes one step further: he removes Caesar's mantle so that his bare, bloody body is there for the crowd to witness. "Here is himself, marred as you see with traitors." By this time, the crowd is so angry and sorrowful, they are driven to riot and rage, just as Marc Antony planned.

Marc Antony was definitely successful in moving the audience. 6 Although he never states his true claim or purpose, it becomes quite evident through his support what his feelings are about this murderous event. The challenge laid before Antony was great, but he overcame it through the powerful uses of argument. His ability to maneuver the crowd from one side completely to the other was done through the use of argument. Had Brutus known the power of argument that Antony commanded, he might not have allowed Antony to speak to the crowd of Romans in the first place. ■

SYNTHESIS OF CHAPTERS 1–12

Summary Charts

TRACE

The Rhetorical Situation

For You as the Reader	For the Targeted Reader at the Time It Was Written	For You as the Writer
Text. What kind of text is it? What are its special qualities and features? What is it about?	**Text.** What kind of text is it? Is it unique to its time?	**Text.** What is your argumentative strategy? What is your purpose and perspective? How will you make you paper convincing?
Reader. Are you one of the readers the writer anticipated? Do you share common ground with the author and other audience members? Are you open to change?	**Reader.** What was the nature of the targeted readers? Were they convinced? How are they different from other or modern readers?	**Reader.** Who are your readers? Where do they stand on the issue? How can you establish common ground? Can they change?
Author. Who is the author? How is the author influenced by background, experience, education, affiliations, values? What is the author's motivation to write?	**Author.** Who is the author? What influenced the author? Why was the author motivated to write?	**Constraints.** How are your training, background, affiliations, and values either in harmony or conflict with your audience? Will they drive you apart or help build common ground?
Constraints. What beliefs, attitudes, habits, affiliations, or traditions will influence the way you and the author view the argument?	**Constraints.** What beliefs, attitudes, habits, affiliations, or traditions influenced the author's and the readers' views in this argument?	**Exigence.** What happened? What is motivating you to write on this issue? Why is it compelling to you?
Exigence. What caused the argument, and do you perceive it as a defect or problem?	**Exigence.** What happened to cause the argument? Why was it a problem? Has it recurred?	

THE PROCESS

Be selective and flexible in using the strategies, and remember there is no best order. You will backtrack and repeat.

When You Are the Reader

Prereading Strategies
- **Read the title and first paragraph; background the issue.** Identify the issue. Free-associate, and write words and phrases that the issue brings to mind.
- **Evaluate and improve your background.** Do you know enough? If not, read or discuss to get background. Look up a key word or two.

When You Are the Writer

Prewriting Strategies
- **Get organized to write.** Set up a place with materials. Get motivated.
- Understand the writing assignment, and schedule time. Break a complicated writing task into manageable parts, and set aside time to write.

(continued)

THE PROCESS *(continued)*

When You Are the Reader

Prereading Strategies

- **Survey the material.** Locate the claim (the main assertion) and some of the subclaims (the ideas that support it); notice how they are organized. Do not slow down and read.
- **Write out your present position on the issue.**
- **Make some predictions, and write one big question.** Jot down two or three ideas that you think the author may discuss, and write one question you would like to have answered.

Reading Strategies

- **Pick up a pencil, underline, and annotate** the ideas that seem important.
- **Identify** and **read** the information in the **introduction, body,** and **conclusion.**
- **Look for the claim, subclaims, and support.** Box the **transitions** to highlight relationships between ideas and changes of subject.
- **Find the key words** that represent major concepts, and jot down meanings if necessary.
- **Analyze the rhetorical situation.** Remember TRACE: Text, Reader, Author, Constraints, Exigence.
- **Read with an open mind, and analyze the common ground** between you and the author.

Strategies for Reading Difficult Material

- **Read all the way through once** without stopping.
- **Write a list** of what you understand and what you do not understand.
- **Identify words and concepts** you do not understand, look them up, and analyze how they are used in context.
- **Reread the material,** and add to your list of what you can and cannot understand.
- **Reread again** if you need to.

When You Are the Writer

Prewriting Strategies

- **Identify an issue, and do some initial reading.** Use the Twelve Tests (Box 1.3) to make certain you have an arguable issue.
- **Analyze the rhetorical situation,** particularly the exigence, the audience, and the constraints.
- **Focus** on your issue, and **freewrite.**
- **Brainstrom, make lists, and map ideas.**
- **Talk it through** with a friend, your instructor, or members of a peer editing group.
- **Keep a journal, notebook, or folder of ideas.**
- **Mentally visualize** the major concepts.
- Do some directed **reading and thinking.**
- Use **argument strategies.**
- Use **reading strategies.**
- Use **critical thinking prompts.**
- Plan and conduct **library research.**
- Make an **expanded list or outline** to guide your writing.
- **Talk it through again.**

Writing Strategies

- **Write the first draft.** Get your ideas on paper so that you can work with them. Use your outline and notes to help you. Either write and rewrite as you go, or write the draft quickly with the knowledge that you can reread or rewrite later.

Strategies to Use When You Get Stuck

- **Read more, and take more notes.**
- **Read your outline, rearrange parts, and add information to it.**
- **Freewrite** on the issue, **read some more,** and then **freewrite** some more.
- **Talk about your ideas** with someone else.
- **Lower your expectations for your first draft.** It does not have to be perfect at this point.

Postwriting Strategies

- **Read your draft critically,** and also **have someone else read it.** Put it aside for

(continued)

THE PROCESS *(continued)*

Be selective and flexible in using the strategies, and remember there is no best order. You will backtrack and repeat

When You Are the Reader

- **Discuss the material** with someone who has also read the material to get further clarification and understanding.

Postreading Strategies

- **Monitor your comprehension.** Insist on understanding. Check the accuracy of your **predictions,** and answer your **question.**
- **Analyze the organization,** and write either a **simplified outline** or a **summary** to help you understand and remember. Or make a **map.**
- **Write a response** to help you think.
- **Compare your present position** with your position before you began to read.
- **Evaluate the argument,** and decide whether it is convincing or not.

When You Are the Writer

Postwriting Strategies

twenty-four hours, if you can, to develop a better perspective for reading and improving.

- **Rewrite and revise.** Make changes and additions until you think your paper is ready for other people to read. Move sections, cross out material, add other material, and rephrase, as necessary.
- **Check your paper** for final mechanical and spelling errors, **write the final title,** and **type or print it.**

THE TOULMIN MODEL

When You Are the Reader

1. *What is the claim?* What is this author trying to prove? Look for the claim at the beginning or at the end, or infer it.
2. *What is the support?* What information does the author use to convince you of the claim? Look for reasons, explanations, facts, opinions, personal narratives, and examples.
3. *What are the warrants?* What assumptions, general principles, values, beliefs, and appeals to human motives are implicit in the argument? Do I share the author's values? Does the support develop the claim? Are the warrants stated, or must they be inferred?
4. *Is backing supplied for the warrants?* See if additional support is provided to make the warrants more acceptable to the reader.
5. *Is there a rebuttal?* Are other perspectives on the issue stated in the argument? Are they refuted? Are counterarguments given?
6. *Has the claim been qualified?* Look for qualifying words like *sometimes, most, probably,* and *possibly.* Decide what is probably the best position to take on the issue, for now.

When You Are the Writer

1. *What is my claim?* Decide on the type of claim and the subclaims. Decide where to put the claim in your paper.
2. *What support will I use?* Invent reasons, opinions, and examples. Research and quote authorities and facts. Consider using personal narratives.
3. *What are my warrants?* Write out the warrants. Do they strengthen the argument by linking the support to the claim? Do you believe them yourself? Will the audience share them or reject them?
4. *What backing for the warrants should I provide?* Add polls, studies, reports, expert opinion, or facts to make your warrants convincing.
5. *How should I handle rebuttal?* Include other perspectives and point out what is wrong with them. Make counterarguments.
6. *Will I need to qualify my claim?* Decide if you can strengthen your claim by adding qualifying words like *usually, often,* or *probably.*

TYPES OF CLAIMS

CLAIMS OF FACT

What happened? Is it true? Does it exist? Is it a fact?

Examples:

Increasing population threatens the environment.

Television content promotes violence.

Women are not as effective as men in combat.

Readers	Writers
• Look for claims that state facts. • Look for facts, statistics, real examples, and quotes from reliable authorities. • Anticipate induction, analogies, and signs. • Look for chronological or topical organization or a claim plus reasons.	• State the claim as a fact even though it is controversial. • Use factual evidence and expert opinion. • Use induction, historical and literal analogies, and signs. • Consider arranging your material as a claim with reasons.

CLAIMS OF DEFINITION

What is it? What is it like? How should it be classified? How should it be interpreted? How does its usual meaning change in a particular context?

Examples:

We need to define what constitutes a family before we discuss family values.

A definition will demonstrate that the riots were an instance of civil disobedience.

Readers	Writers
• Look for a claim that contains or is followed by a definition. • Look for reliable authorities and sources for definitions. • Look for comparisons and examples. • Look for comparison-and-contrast, topical, or deductive organization.	• State your claim, and define the key terms. • Quote authorities, or go to dictionaries, encyclopedias, or other reliable sources for definitions. • If you are comparing to help define, use comparison-and-contrast organization. • Use deductive organization.

CLAIMS OF CAUSE

What caused it? Where did it come from? Why did it happen? What are the effects? What probably will be the results on a short-term and long-term basis?

Examples:

Clear-cutting is the main cause of the destruction of ancient forests.

Censorship can result in limits on freedom of speech.

The American people's current mood has been caused by a booming economy.

Readers	Writers
• Look for a claim that states or implies cause or effect.	• Make a claim that states or implies cause or effect.

(continued)

TYPES OF CLAIMS *(continued)*

Readers	Writers
• Look for facts and statistics, comparisons, such as historical analogies, signs, induction, deduction, and causal arguments. • Look for cause-and-effect or effect-and-cause organization.	• Use facts and statistics. • Apply Burke's pentad to focus the main cause. • Use historical analogies, signs, induction, and deduction. • Consider using cause-and-effect or effect-and-cause organization.

CLAIMS OF VALUE

Is it good or bad? How good? How bad? Of what worth is it? Is it moral or immoral? Who thinks so? What do those people value? What values or criteria should I use to determine its goodness or badness? Are my values different from other people's or the author's?

Examples:

Computers are a valuable addition to modern education.

School prayer has a moral function in the public schools.

Animal rights are as important as human rights.

Readers	Writers
• Look for claims that make a value statement. • Look for value proofs, motivational proofs, analogies, both literal and figurative, quotes from authorities, signs, and definitions. • Expect emotional language. • Look for applied-criteria, topical, and narrative patterns of organization.	• State your claim as a judgment or value statement. • Analyze your audience's needs and values, and appeal to them. • Use literal and figurative analogies, quotes from authorities, signs, and definitions. • Use emotional language appropriately. • Consider the applied-criteria, claim-and-reasons, or narrative organizational patterns.

CLAIMS OF POLICY

What should we do? How should we act? What should future policy be? How can we solve this problem? What course of action should we pursue?

Examples:

The criminal should be sent to prison rather than to a mental hospital.

Sex education should be part of the public school curriculum.

Battered women who take revenge should not be placed in jail.

Readers	Writers
• Look for claims that state that something should be done. • Look for statistical data, motivational appeals, literal analogies, and argument from authority. • Anticipate the problem-solution pattern of organization.	• State the claim as something that should be done. • Use statistical data, motivational appeals, analogies, and authorities as proof. • Use emotional language appropriately. • Consider the problem-solution pattern of organization.

TYPES OF PROOF AND TESTS OF VALIDITY

Logical Proofs

Rearrange the logical proofs to form the mnemonic SICDADS: Sign, Induction, Cause, Deduction, Analogies, Definition, Statistics.

When You Are the Reader		When You Are the Writer

DEDUCTION

When You Are the Reader		When You Are the Writer
Locate or infer the general principle (warrant). Apply it to the example or case. Draw a conclusion or claim.	Applying a general principle (warrant) to an example or a case and drawing a conclusion. *Example:*	Make a general statement. Apply it to an example or a case. Draw a conclusion. Decide whether to make the general statement (warrant) explicit or implicit.
	Warrant: Most uneven footprints are left by people who limp.	
	Support: These footprints are uneven.	
	Claim: The person who left these footprints walks with a limp.	
	Test of Validity: Ask if the general principle (warrant) and the support are probably true, because then the claim is also probably true.	

DEFINITION

When You Are the Reader		When You Are the Writer
Look for definitions of key words or concepts. Definitions can be short, a word or sentence, or long, several paragraphs or an entire essay. Notice if the reader is supposed to accept the claim "by definition" because it has been placed in an established category.	Describing the fundamental properties and qualities of a term or placing an item in a category and proving it "by definition." *Example:*	Define the key terms and concepts in your claim. Define all other terms that you and your reader must agree on for the argument to work. Place some ideas or items in established categories and argue that they are so "by definition."
	Warrant: Family values characterize the good citizen.	
	Support: Radical feminists lack family values.	
	Claim: Radical feminists are not good citizens.	

(continued)

TYPES OF PROOF AND TESTS OF VALIDITY *(continued)*

When You Are the Reader	Logical Proofs	When You Are the Writer
	Tests of Validity: Ask if the definition is accurate and reliable or if there are exceptions or other definitions that would make it less reliable. Ask if the item belongs in the category in which it has been placed.	
	CAUSE	
Look for examples, trends, people, events that are cited as causes for the claim. Look for effects of the claim.	Placing the claim in a cause-and-effect relationship to show that it is either the cause of an effect or an effect of a cause. *Example:*	Make a claim, and ask what caused it. Apply Burke's pentad to focus the main cause:
	Warrant: Depression in a group of people has increased.	What was done?
	Support: This group of people has also increased its use of the Internet.	Where was it done? Who did it?
	Claim/ conclusion: The Internet may be causing depression.	How was it done? Why did it happen?
	Test of Validity: Ask if these causes alone are sufficient to create these effects or if these effects could result from other causes. Try to think of exceptions to the cause-and-effect outcome.	
	SIGN	
Look for clues, symptoms, and occurrences that are explained as signs or symptoms that something is so.	Pointing out the symptoms or signs that something is so.	Think of symptoms or signs that you can use to demonstrate that something is so.

(continued)

425

TYPES OF PROOF AND TESTS OF VALIDITY (continued)

Logical Proofs

When You Are the Reader		When You Are the Writer

INDUCTION

When You Are the Reader

Look for a conclusion or claim based on examples or cases.

Drawing a conclusion (claim) from a number of representative cases or examples.

Example:

Claim: The child has chickenpox.
Support: The child had spots.
Warrant: Those spots are a sign of chickenpox.

Test of Validity: Ask if this is really a sign of what the author claims, or if there is another explanation.

Example:

Claim: Everyone liked that movie.
Support: I know three people who liked it.
Warrant: Three examples are enough.

Tests of Validity: Ask if there are enough examples, or if this is a "hasty" conclusion or claim. Try to think of an exception that would change the conclusion or claim. See if you can make the "inductive leap" from the examples to the conclusion or claim and accept it as probably true.

When You Are the Writer

Give some examples and draw a conclusion/claim based on them; *or* make the claim and back it up with a series of examples.

STATISTICS

When You Are the Reader

Look for numbers, data, and tables of figures along with interpretations of them.

Using figures or data to prove a claim.

When You Are the Writer

Find data, statistics, and tables of figures to use as evidence to back up your claim. Make clear where you get the statistics, and add your interpretations and those of experts.

(continued)

TYPES OF PROOF AND TESTS OF VALIDITY *(continued)*

Logical Proofs

When You Are the Reader		When You Are the Writer

Example:

Claim: We should end draft registration.

Support: It costs $27.5 million per year.

Warrant: This is too much; it proves we should end it.

Tests of Validity: Ask where the statistics came from, to what dates they apply, and if they are fair and accurate. Ask if they have been exaggerated or skewed. Ask if they prove what they are supposed to prove.

ANALOGIES: LITERAL, HISTORICAL, AND FIGURATIVE

Interpreting what we do not understand by comparing it with something we do. Literal and historical analogies compare similar items, and figurative analogies compare items from radically different categories.

Example of historical analogy:

Claim: Many people will die of AIDS.

Support: Many people died of the Black Death.

Warrant: AIDS and the Black Death are similar.

Example of literal analogy:

Claim: The state should spend more money on education.

Literal and historical analogy:
Look for items, events, people, or periods of time that are being compared.

Literal and historical analogy:
Think of items in the same category that can be compared. Show that what happened in one case will also happen in the other. Or demonstrate that history repeats itself.

(continued)

TYPES OF PROOF AND TESTS OF VALIDITY (continued)

Logical Proofs

When You Are the Reader		When You Are the Writer

Figurative analogy:
Look for extended metaphors or items compared that are from totally different categories.

Support:	Another state spent more money with good results.
Warrant:	The two states are similar, and the results of one will be the results of the other.

Example of figurative analogy:

Claim:	Reading a difficult book should take time.
Support:	Digesting a large meal takes time.
Warrant:	Reading and eating are sufficiently alike that they can be compared.

Figurative analogy:
Think of comparisons with items from other categories. Try to compare items that have similar qualities, characteristics, or outcomes.

Tests of Validity: For literal analogies, ask if the cases are so similar that the results of one will be the results of the other. For historical analogies, ask if history will repeat itself. For figurative analogies, ask if the qualities of the items being compared are real enough to provide logical support or if they are so dissimilar that they do not prove anything.

Proof to Establish *Ethos*

AUTHORITY

Look for references to the author's credentials, background, and training. Look for credential statements about quoted authorities.

Quoting established authorities or experts or establishing one's own authority and credibility.

Refer to your own experience and background to establish expertise.
Quote the best and most reliable authorities.

Establish common ground and respect by using appropriate language and tone.

(continued)

Proof to Establish *Ethos*

When You Are the Writer

Example:

Claim: California will have an earthquake.

Support: Professors and scientists say so.

Warrant: These experts are reliable.

Test of Validity: Ask if the experts, including both outside authorities and the author, are really experts. Remember that argument from authority is only as good as the authorities themselves.

Emotional Proofs

MOTIVES

Think about what the members of your audience need, and show how your ideas will help them meet these needs.

Use emotional language and tone where appropriate.

Appealing to what all audiences are supposed to need, such as food, drink, warmth and shelter, sex, security, belonging, self-esteem, creativity, and self-expression. Urging audiences to take steps to meet their needs.

Example:

Claim: You should support this candidate.

Support: The candidate can help you get job security and safe neighborhoods.

Warrant: You want job security and safe neighborhoods.

Tests of Validity: Ask if you really need what the author assumes you need. Ask if doing what is recommended will satisfy the need as described.

When You Are the Reader

Look for references to items or qualities you might need or want and advice on how to get them.

Look for emotional language, description, and tone.

(*continued*)

429

Emotional Proofs

When You Are the Reader

Look for examples or narratives that display values.

Infer values (warrants) that are not explicitly stated.

Look for emotional language and tone.

VALUES

Appealing to what all audiences are supposed to value, such as reliability, honesty, loyalty, industry, patriotism, courage, integrity, conviction, faithfulness, dependability, creativity, freedom, equality, devotion to duty, and acceptance by others.

Example:

Claim: The curriculum should be multicultural.

Support: A multicultural curriculum will contribute to equality and acceptance.

Warrant: You value equality and acceptance

Tests of Validity: Ask if you share the author's values. Ask about the effect that differences in values will have on the argument.

When You Are the Writer

Appeal to your audience's values through warrants, explicit value statements, and narratives that illustrate values.

Use emotional language and tone where appropriate.

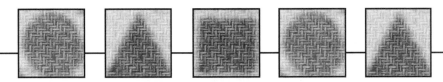

PART FIVE

The Reader

Introduction to "The Reader": Reading and Writing about Issue Areas

"The Reader" contains seven sections that introduce you to broad issue areas that engage modern society: the modern family, education, crime and the treatment of criminals, computers, race and culture in America, genetic engineering, and social and personal responsibility. Essays are then organized under specific related issues in each broad category. "The Reader" contains essays that explore some of the individual perspectives and positions people have taken in regard to these issues both now and in the past. You may expand your information and understanding of these issues by doing additional research and reading in other sources on the Internet, in the library, or elsewhere.

You may also expand your perspective on each of these issues through film and literature. In the introduction to each issue area, a list of related films and literary works that treat these issues in interesting ways is provided. The films are available on videotape, and the literature is available in anthologies and in the library.

PURPOSE OF "THE READER"

"The Reader" serves three main purposes:

1. It introduces you to big issue areas and a few of their specific related issues. It also helps you build background and provides you with information to quote in your papers.
2. It provides you with models of different types of arguments and thus gives you a better idea of how argument works in general. It provides you with examples and strategies for improving your own written arguments.

3. It helps you think and invent arguments and ideas of your own by providing you with essays that function as springboards for your own thoughts and reactions.

HOW TO USE "THE READER"

Refer to the chapters indicated for details or review.

1. Select an issue area that is compelling for you. Understand why it is compelling. Consult your background on it. Anticipate ways to build common ground with those who oppose you. (Chapters 1 and 11)
2. Survey it: read the titles and summaries of the articles in the table of contents, read the introductory material and "The Rhetorical Situation" at the beginning of the issue area, and read the introductions to the articles. (Chapter 3)
3. Select the specific related issue that interests you the most. (Chapters 1 and 3)
4. Read the articles about the related issue, and jot down the claim and some of the major support and warrants for each article. (Chapters 3 and 5)
5. Make a map or write a list of all of the smaller related issues that you can think of that are related to the issue you have read about. Discover the aspect of the issue that interests you the most. This will be your issue. (Chapter 3)
6. Understand the perspectives presented by the articles in "The Reader" on your issue. You may also want to do outside research. Write an exploratory paper in which you explain at least three perspectives on your issue. (Chapter 4)
7. Take a position on your issue, and phrase it as a question. Apply the Twelve Tests in Box 1.3 to make certain you have an arguable issue. (Chapter 1)
8. State your claim, clarify your purpose, plan, and write an argument paper that presents your position on the issue. (Chapters 5–10)

QUESTIONS TO HELP YOU READ CRITICALLY AND ANALYTICALLY

1. What is at issue?
2. What is the claim? What type of claim is it?
3. What is the support?
4. What are the warrants?
5. What are the weaknesses in the argument, and how can I refute them?
6. What are some other perspectives on the issue?
7. Where do I stand now in regard to this issue?

QUESTIONS TO HELP YOU READ CREATIVELY AND MOVE FROM READING TO WRITING

1. What is my exigence for writing about this topic?
2. What is my general position compared to the author's?

3. Which specific ideas do I agree or disagree with?
4. Do the essays confirm what I think, or do they cause me to change my mind?
5. What original or related ideas are occurring to me as I read?
6. What original perspective can I take?
7. What type of claim do I want to make?
8. What can I quote, paraphrase, or summarize in my paper?

SECTION I
Issues Concerning Families
THE ISSUES

A. How Do Men's and Women's Ideas about Themselves Influence the Roles They Play in Their Families?

Five authors provide perspectives on how modern men and women see themselves in society and, by implication, how they see themselves as members of their families. Doloff's article suggests the two sexes may not be as equal as we sometimes think they are. Wolf and Henry write about the women's movement and its implications for family life, Coltrane writes about the division of labor in a family, and Adler writes about men's family roles. As you read these articles, think about your role in your present or future family, and consider which of these authors most closely reflects your sense of values about the responsibilities of men and women in families. See also "Why I Want a Wife," page 56; "Paying the Price of Female Neglect," page 165; and "There's No Place like Work," page 636.

B. What Are Some Variations on the Traditional Family? How Effective Are These Variations?

The traditional family is usually thought of as composed of two members of the opposite sex in which the man is the breadwinner and the woman is the homemaker who cares for the home and children. The articles in this section describe variations on that model and address some of the issues associated with them. As you read, you will need to think about the criteria that are necessary for a family to be effective. See also "Culture by the Campfire," page 582, and, "Family Values," page 163.

To Extend Your Perspective: Films and Literature Related to Families

> *Films: Disclosure,* 1996; *Annie Hall,* 1977; *The Birdcage,* 1996
> *Literature:* poem: "Myth" by Muriel Rukeyser; short story: "The Chrysanthemums" by John Steinbeck; plays: *A Doll's House* by Henrik Ibsen; *M. Butterfly* by David Henry Hwang; novel: *Persuasion* by Jane Austen; memoirs: *The Color of Water: A Black Man's Tribute to His White Mother* by James McBride

THE RHETORICAL SITUATION

The organization of families, including the roles that individuals play in them, has always been a source of controversy. The world's religions, along with social customs and traditions, provide both the constraints and many of the warrants for the positions individuals take on issues associated with family life. In this section, contemporary authors provide their perspectives on modern families. They raise issues associated with the roles that men and women assume in their families, with families that differ from the traditional family, and with the effectiveness of these various types of families.

Some people think that the women's movement in the second half of the twentieth century changed what women and men expect from each other in families. Many women now choose to work first and have children later or not at all. Working women also expect men to do their share of the housework, which they no longer consider "women's work." The women's movement has provided new opportunities for women, but it has also been blamed for the high divorce rate and troubled children.

An increase in single-parent families and interfaith families can precipitate additional family issues. So can same-sex unions, particularly if the couple decides to raise children. The final question you may want to answer as you read these articles is, "What, after all, is a family?"

Family issues touch everyone's lives eventually, so there is a constant exigency for family issues. Look at the best-seller list. Browse in the magazine section of a bookstore. What are the related issues on this subject now? Which of them affect you? Family issues are intensely personal, and you will probably want to consult your own experience as you read and write about them.

A. How Do Men's and Women's Ideas about Themselves Influence the Roles They Play in Their Families?

THE OPPOSITE SEX*

Steven Doloff

Steven Doloff is a literature instructor at the Taylor Business Institute in New York. He describes the results of one of his writing assignments in this article. How would you respond to this assignment? You may also want to compare this essay with Sherry Turkle's essay on page 545.

1 Having seen Dustin Hoffman's female impersonation in the movie *Tootsie*, I decided to give myself some reading over the Christmas recess by assigning in-class essays to my English composition students on how each would spend a day as a

---

*Washington Post, January 13, 1983, p. A19.

member of his or her respective opposite sex. From four classes I received approximately 100 essays. The sample, perhaps like the movie, proved both entertaining and annoying in its predictability.

The female students, as a group, took to the subject immediately and with 2 obvious gusto, while the male students tended to wait a while (in several cases half the period), in something of a daze, before starting. The activities hypothetically engaged in by the women, whose ages averaged about 20, generally reflected two areas: envy of men's physical and social privileges, and curiosity regarding men's true feelings concerning women.

In their essays, women jauntily went places *alone,* and sometimes stayed out 3 *all night.* They threw their clothes on the floor and left dishes in the sink. They hung out on the street and sweated happily in a variety of sports from football to weightlifting.

More than a third of them went out to cruise for dates. Appointing them- 4 selves in brand names of men's clothing and dousing themselves in men's cologne I have never heard of (I was instructed to read *Gentleman's Quarterly* magazine), they deliberately and aggressively accosted women, *many* women, on the street, in discos, in supermarkets. Others sought out the proverbial locker room for the kinds of bull sessions they hoped would reveal the real nitty-gritty masculine mind at work (on the subject of women).

At least two female students in each class spent chunks of their essays under 5 the sheets with imaginary girlfriends, wives or strangers, finding out with a kind of scientific zeal what sex is like as a man.

Some but not all of the women ended their essays with a formal, almost 6 obligatory sounding statement of preference to be a female, and of gratitude in returning to their correct gender after a day as Mr. Hyde.

The male students, after their initial paralysis wore off, did not write as 7 much as the females. They seemed envious of very little that was female, and curious about nothing. Three or four spent their day as women frantically seeking medical help to turn back into men more quickly. Those who accepted the assignment more seriously, if unenthusiastically, either stayed home and apathetically checked off a list of domestic chores or, more evasively, went off to work in an office and engaged in totally asexual business office routines.

A small percentage of the men ventured into the more feminine pursuits of 8 putting on makeup and going to the beauty parlor. They agreed looking good was important.

If they stayed home as housewives, then their hypothetical husbands re- 9 turned from work, they ate dinner, watched some television and then went right to sleep. If they were businesswomen, they came directly home after work, ate some dinner, watched TV and went right to sleep. A handful actually went out on dates, had dinner in the most expensive restaurants they could cajole their escorts into taking them to, and then, after being taken home, very politely slammed the doors in their escorts' faces and went right to sleep. Not one male student let anybody lay a finger on him/her.

Finally, the sense of heartfelt relief at the end of the male students' essays, 10 underscored by the much-repeated fervent anticipation of masculinity returning with the dawn, seemed equivalent to that of jumping up after having been forced to sit on a lit stove.

11   Granted, my flimsy statistical sample is nothing to go to the Ford Foundation with for research money. But on the other hand, do I really need to prove that young people even now are still burdened with sexist stereotypes and sexist self-images not nearly as vestigial as we would like to think? (One male student rhetorically crumpled up his paper after 10 minutes and growled, "You can't make me write this!") What does that imply about the rest of us? What would *you* do as a member of the opposite sex for a day? This last question is your essay assignment. ■

THE FUTURE IS OURS TO LOSE*

Naomi Wolf

Naomi Wolf is the author of The Beauty Myth *and* Promiscuities. *She writes frequently about women's issues.*

1 Standing at the turn of the millennium, how odd it seems that women, the majority of the human species, have not, over the course of so many centuries, intervened successfully once and for all on their own behalf. That is, until you consider that women have been trained to see themselves as having no relationship to history, and no claim upon it. Feminism can be defined as women's ability to think about their subjugated role in history, and then to do something about it. The 21st century will see the End of Inequality—but only if women absorb the habit of historical self-awareness, becoming a mass of people who, rather than do it all, decide at last to change it all. The future is ours to lose.

2   Since there has always been some scattered awareness that women's low status was unfair, you could say that there has always been a women's movement. And just as you could say that there has always been a women's movement, you could also say that there has always been a backlash. It is truly striking how often Western humanity has taken the leap forward into more egalitarian, rational and democratic models of society and government, and made the decision—for a decision it had to be—to leave women out. At every turn, with a heroic effort of the will to ignore the obvious path of justice, men were granted, and granted themselves, more and more equality, and women of all races were left in history's tidewater.

3   Once again, we are at a turning point. This decade has seen one new landmark after another: the Family and Medical Leave Act; a feminist sitting on the Supreme Court; a woman in charge of American foreign policies that now include opposition to clitoridectomy. Indeed, feminism has become mainstream: Betty Friedan has met Betsy Ross; Barbie's ads now read "Dream With Your Eyes Wide Open" and "Be Your Own Hero." Oprah is talking about how to walk out of an

New York Times Magazine, May 16, 1999, p. 134.

abusive marriage, and Tori Amos and Fran Drescher speak out in the celebrity press about sexual assault. This flood tide could either crest further to change the landscape forever, or it could recede once again. This is what historians call an "open moment," and women have blown such moments in the past. What determines the outcome is the level of historical awareness we reach before the tide inevitably turns.

There are four ways that our culture militates against historical conscious- 4 ness in women. One is the steady omission of women from history's first draft, the news. Women, Men and Media, a national watchdog project, reports that women are featured in only 15 percent of the front-page news—and then usually as victims or perpetrators of crime or misconduct. It is not because no one is interested in what women are doing that this ceiling of visibility is kept so low; nor is it a conscious conspiracy. But if tomorrow the editors in chief and publishers of national news media were to see front sections dominated by 53 percent female newsmakers, they would not shout, Stop the presses! Too many women! Rather, there would be the impression that somehow these publications had, by featuring newsmakers who are part of a majority, marginalized themselves. So women's advances take place with little day-by-day, let alone month-by-month, popular analysis.

The second pressure, which complements the omission of women from his- 5 torical culture, is the omission of history from women's culture. One example: under its previous editor, Ruth Whitney, *Glamour* magazine ran a political column. Bonnie Fuller, a new editor fresh from *Cosmopolitan,* has deleted this monthly column and added a horoscope. It's a shift from real-time—historical-political time— back into that dependent, dreamy, timeless state of Women's Time. In Women's Time, your fate is not in your own hands as an agent of historical change. Rather— Hey, are you a Pisces? Why bother running down your Manolo Blahniks to do something as *mousy* as voting? Your fate is in your cleavage, and in the stars.

Emerging naturally from this is the third pressure: the recurrent ideological 6 theme that if women take themselves seriously they will lose femininity and, therefore, social status. If what they do, think, worry about and long for doesn't matter, surely it's not important that history pays them attention.

The fourth pressure is forgetfulness. Young women I have met on real col- 7 lege campuses think sex discrimination is a thing of the past. Or that the struggle for the vote lasted maybe 10 years, not more than 70. Or that women got the vote when African-Americans did. Or that it has always been legal to get an abortion in America. They are stunned to discover that in their mothers' lifetimes women could not get credit on their own. They are amazed to learn that it was African-American middle-class women's clubs that led the movement against lynching. They didn't know that women chained themselves to the gates of Congress, or went on hunger strikes and were force-fed—so that young women far into the future could take their rights for granted. These young women are shocked, in other words, to find that they have a history.

As a result, women remain dependent on other models of "revolution" for 8 their own. They must catch the taste and techniques of activism like a hit song of the month wafting through the air. So one sees women slumbering and then "waking up" every 30 years or so; periods of feminism always follow periods of agitation by women on behalf of other, more respectable causes.

9   This past century shows how fragile conscious feminism has been. The 1910's, with their wave of populist reform, saw the crescendo of women's push for the vote. But the year before it was granted, in 1919, the term "post-feminist" had already expediently been coined. By the 20's pop culture was once again ridiculing the suffragists' generations as being man-hating old battle-axes, irrelevant and out of touch with "today's women."

10   A long sleep followed, with fitful waking. After Betty Friedan's 1963 book helped middle-class white women identify the causes of their deeper malaise, the magical 15 years, from 1965 to 1980, began, representing a high point of historical self-awareness for Western women. Again, other movements had to set the stage: the anti-war movement, the free-speech movement and the hippie movement all contributed to the idea that it was all right to break free of social roles. The civil rights movement trained a generation of African-American activists. The 70's were astonishing: the statutes against sex discrimination labeled Title VII and Title IX; Shirley Chisholm's 1972 race for the Democratic Presidential nomination. That era, personified by Steinem and Jong, NOW and the National Women's Political Caucus, showed what could happen for women when, as an energized mass in a democracy, they wanted change badly enough to make noise about it.

11   The predictable backlash came, as it always does; the evil 80's were a time of shoulder pads, silicone and retrenchment. Again—so quickly, so thoroughly— women "forgot." A *Time*/CNN poll found that only 33 percent of women called themselves feminists—and only 16 percent of college-age women. "Guilt" and "the Mommy Track" were the catchwords of the day. Once again, feminists were represented as hairy-legged man-hating shrews.

12   The heartbreak of those times was in seeing newly clueless young women come of age. Once, when I visited Yale as a speaker, a brilliant young Asian-American student joined her male debating society peers in loudly ridiculing feminism. Later, when we were alone for a moment, she confided that she didn't really believe what she said—but the guys were in charge of the club and she just wanted to get along with them. "Besides," she had said, as if parroting some women's magazine, "women my age just have to accept that we can't have it all." It was as if all those words—flextime, family leave, egalitarian marriage—had vanished, taking with them the ways in which that young woman could have reconsidered her life.

13   Enter the explosive 90's. Women are now the most important voting mass in America. "Women's Issues" dominate the agenda. The word "feminism" is as taboo as ever, but does it matter if you call yourself a feminist if you are living feminism? And American women are doing that, considering the number of their new businesses, and their new judgeships, new elected officials and new spending power. Feminism today is not a label; it's a way of life.

14   But here's the catch: if we remain indifferent to history, we risk losing it all. The bad old days are always ready to knock at your door, sisters: while you're

packing your briefcase or getting into your truck, feeling confident, having thrown out the mailing from that advocacy group you could just find that you can't get a legal abortion anymore; or that your boss knows that those sexual harassment statutes can be managed with a wink and a nod.

Women who are ignorant of their own history forget the main lessons, like: 15 Here's how you mobilize; being nice is never as good as getting leverage; the nature-nurture debate has been going on forever, and neither side is going to win; your representatives pay attention when you use your money, your voice and your will. And voting millions can provide the will.

Maybe we will learn at last. Maybe we will create institutions that are willing 16 to share influence with younger women coming up, rather than hoarding power for one generation. Maybe we will learn to honor our heroines and role models while they are still alive: maybe Gloria Steinem and Shirley Chisholm will get their commemorative stamps and parades in their own lifetimes, so our daughters will grow up with some one to turn to more powerful in their imaginations than Kate Moss and Calista Flockhart. Maybe we will learn at last that dissent and disagreement among women across the political spectrum is a sign of our diversity and strength. Maybe we will turn from the horoscope page to the *Congressional Quarterly*, and understand at last that our salvation lies not in our stars, but in ourselves. ■

CAN WOMEN "HAVE IT ALL"?*

William A. Henry III

William A. Henry III is a Pulitzer Prize winner. In his book In Defense of Elitism, *Henry comments on some basic, fundamentally ingrained ideas about women in the 1990s.*

Whenever the feminist movement gets a bit captious or silly—as in the 1993 fuss 1 over whether there were enough statues of women in public parks and plazas in New York City—it is surely useful to remind oneself that many women, especially the best educated and most historically aware among them, are ablaze with rage over the way things used to be. To be born female was, by and large, to be born with limited horizons and few options. That was true not only in the eighteenth century and the ones that preceded it, but in the nineteenth and indeed the twentieth. I have seen the warping effects of frustration in the mothers of my friends; these women married and gave birth to successful men but found no place in the public world themselves, and their dammed-up drive often went into oversteering the careers of their husbands and children. My own mother regretted all her adult life that she had majored in English rather than her true love, physics, because she had been convinced by older women (including her aunt, a pioneer college dean) that the sciences were not "ladylike." Katharine Graham, perhaps the

*William A. Henry III, *In Defense of Elitism* (New York: Anchor/Doubleday, 1994), pp. 102–109.

most powerful woman in America, has observed, "Power is neither male nor female." But Graham came to power the way almost every woman in history got there, up to virtually the present moment: through inheritance and marriage. Power may be neutral, but the road to it has been signposted by gender.

2   Having said all that, a dispassionate observer must still find it curious that women, a literal majority of the American population and holders of a large majority of its private wealth, have managed to get themselves classified as a minority group. They continue to enjoy advantages in recruitment and promotion long after the doors once closed to them have been flung wide open. It may still be hard for a woman to become a firefighter or steelworker; taunting or outright harassment of those who do crash the barrier is frequent and disgraceful (although reflective, for good or ill, of how male locker room louts also treat each other). In terms of jobs that matter in the formation of thought and allocation of resources, however—in other words, jobs for the elite—the evidence proving access for women is incontrovertible. Barely a quarter of a century after the women's movement began to make its mark, a third or more of all medical school, law school, and business school graduates are women, according to Census Bureau figures published in *The Washington Post*. By the same count, forty-six percent of the nation's financial managers are women, and so are forty-two percent of biologists and thirty-nine percent of mathematics professors—to name just three fields considered resistant to women and in which women traditionally were thought not to excel. In psychology, public relations, and my own niche of journalism, women now appear to be an absolute majority. While women still feel underrepresented in elective government (in part because they will not vote as a block for a fellow female in anything like the same percentages that, say, blacks will give to a fellow black), the gender ratio in the managerial ranks of the civil service is nearly fifty-fifty. Few women run major corporations, but many in the middle management generation seem to be well on their way.

3   Quotas, by whatever euphemism they are known, have become superfluous. Their primary effect, as with blacks, is to de-credential candidates who could have succeeded without help. Whenever quotas are operating, a woman who gets a good job is apt to be viewed as having arrived there solely because she is a woman—and in her heart of hearts is apt to ask herself if that might really be true.

4   The moral rationale for affirmative action on behalf of women is even weaker than the political and economic one. When blacks point to the cumulative effects of slavery and racial discrimination as a basis for giving them special advantages, they are speaking as an identifiable community. Both they themselves and the larger society around them have viewed them as a collective entity. In every generation up to the present one, and to a distressing extent even today, blacks have been born into families apt to be disadvantaged socially, educationally, and economically, have grown up in neighborhoods where similar disadvantages were the norm, and have entered schools and workplaces prone to perceive them as automatically inferior. It does not take much imagination to trace a clear hereditary line from the injustices of the past to the inadequacies of the present. Even so, the time must come when affirmative action gives way to open competition. . . . When it comes to elite jobs, that time is already here.

Women, by contrast, can claim no such hereditary burden. Their sense of his- 5
torical grievance is largely irrelevant and almost entirely self-imposed. Whatever
happened to women in the past, it is only minimally visited upon women of
today. Feminist anger is primarily a theoretical and ideological, not a practical,
construct. Novelist Michael Crichton summed up the absurdity of much such pos-
turing by privileged women in his [. . .] socially astute best seller *Disclosure*. A
careworn husband whose wife starts running a feminist guilt trip on him says in
reply, "You're a partner in a law firm, for Christ's sake. You're about as oppressed
as Leona Helmsley."

Yes, women are descended from a long line of thwarted women. They are 6
equally descended from a long line of admittedly unthwarted men. The spiritual
connection with female forebears may seem stronger, but the biological link is exactly the same. The distribution of children by gender remains roughly fifty-fifty
no matter the social class of the parents, so women cannot claim, as blacks can, to
have been born into comparative economic privation.

It is true that adult women tend to be paid less than men and to be grouped 7
disproportionately on the lower rungs of the economic ladder. Susan Faludi's
Backlash and its ideological kin notwithstanding, that variance is attributable to
many other factors besides overt prejudice. Women are often less educated or
credentialed. They tend to be employed in fields that society rewards less extrava-
gantly (some women, ill versed in the workings of the free market or tempera-
mentally inclined to the folly of Marxism, see that fact of life as some sort of
conspiracy). In no-nonsense economic terms, women tend to be less committed to
their careers. They take time away to have children. They are ready to stay home
or leave work abruptly when one of those children is sick or when an aging parent
is in trouble. They often object on family grounds to long and irregular hours or
abruptly scheduled travel and other normal, male-accepted demands of a job. All
these outside concerns are socially valid, but they get in the way of work. Many
women who also see themselves as caregivers want the rules of the workplace
rewritten to suit their personal needs. Indeed, they want their relative lack of commitment (or, as they would phrase it, alternative set of priorities) treated as something admirable and reward-worthy in a business setting. That attitude almost
never wins appreciation from an employer and has rarely if ever led men to success; still, women argue that past and proven ways of doing business are irre-
deemably commingled with "sexism." In personal style, moreover, women tend
to be less aggressive and confrontational than men while performing in an economy that seeks and compensates those go-getter qualities. . . .

Even among women prepared to accept the reality of the past, one finds a 8
widespread yearning to rewrite the rules of the present so that women may enjoy
a more glorious future.

The overt goal of these feminists is to change ground rules of working life so 9
that wives and mothers can, as the boast runs, "have it all." They argue that society benefits by giving special privileges to mothers in the marketplace. Is that so?
Let me admit here that I think children are better off when their mothers (or fathers) stay home full-time, at least until the children enter school. I believe that

much of the perceived educational decline of children has very little to do with the favorite whipping boy, television, and a great deal to do with a phenomenon that more closely fits the time frame of the decline—the two-income household, which in practice generally means employment for the mothers of young children. If this causal relationship holds true (and I readily concede that it is opinion rather than fact—if shared, albeit reluctantly, by virtually every working mother I know), then any benefit to society from the mother's working has to be weighed against the developmental loss to the next generation. Day care, the common solution, is usually merely custodial. The yuppie alternative, a live-in nanny, clearly represents an intellectual step down for the child. Of the ten parental couples to whom my wife and I are closest, eight have used live-ins, of whom not one had attended college (although the biological parents were mostly Ivy Leaguers) and only three were native speakers of English. ■

FATHER'S ROLE AT HOME IS UNDER NEGOTIATION*

Scott Coltrane

Scott Coltrane is the author of Family Man *and* Gender and Families. *He is an associate professor of sociology at the University of California at Riverside.*

1 Americans are facing a paradox about gender: Although most people agree that men and women are equal, gender remains a major determinant of one's life chances. Compared with men, women are more likely to earn low wages, take orders from others, live in poverty, and be raped or abused. Men, in contrast, are more likely to kill someone, be a homicide victim, be involved in a lethal accident, commit suicide, and die before 70. Contrary to popular belief, these gender differences are neither natural nor inevitable. Subservient women and macho men are the product of historically specific social and economic arrangements. Unless men and women can change the family ideals and practices that support these patterns, the gender paradox will continue.

2   National surveys show that Americans' idealized notions of gender and family are at odds with their daily practices and perceptions. In a poll conducted last fall and winter, sponsored by *The Washington Post,* the Kaiser Family Foundation, and Harvard University, large majorities of men and women said gender roles had changed dramatically, with two out of three respondents agreeing that these changes had made it harder for average Americans to have successful marriages.

3   When asked about their own lives, in contrast, the number of people who said recent changes had made things better for them personally was twice the number who felt that things were worse. Only about one in four said going back to the traditional roles of the 1950s would be beneficial for them. Three of four Americans agreed that wives' and husbands' jobs now were equally important, and nine of

Chronicle of Higher Education, October 2, 1998, p. B8.

10 said women and men should share all aspects of parenting. In spite of such ideals, however, studies of time use show that wives who are employed still do at least twice as much child care and three times as much housework as their husbands.

Analysis of gender discrimination usually focuses on unequal access to jobs, 4 promotions, and pay, but the stereotyping of household labor must be an equally important impediment to gender equity. Men do little housework and child care because they define those jobs as "women's work" and take for granted the domestic services and ministrations of wives. This outdated sense of masculine entitlement, coupled with women's feeling solely responsible for the emotional well-being of family members, leads to a division of family work that is markedly unbalanced.

There is evidence that things are changing, albeit slowly and unevenly. At 5 the same time that more fathers assume a greater share of child care and housework, other fathers are forsaking marriage or failing to support their children. These contrasting developments result from similar social and economic forces: Because more women are in the labor force and rates of divorce are high, women are less dependent on marriage for survival, men with jobs are no longer guaranteed spouses, and marriage is becoming more a matter of individual choice.

As a result, more couples are openly negotiating over the division of domestic 6 labor. Arguments are common, but more marriages are becoming equal partnerships. As husbands do more housework, wives' double work burden will be lessened. As fathers do more child care, daughters' and sons' personalities and expectations will become more similar, preparing future generations for a world less polarized by gender.

Although family work may appear trivial, finding new ways to share it may 7 be the key to solving our gender paradox. Cross-cultural research shows that when men take an active role in the details of running a home and raising children, they develop emotional sensitivities, avoid boastful and threatening behavior, and include women in community decision-making. Increasing men's involvement in family work thus has the potential to increase women's public status and reduce men's propensity for violence. By instituting equity in the family, we can move closer to achieving gender equity in the larger society. ■

BUILDING A BETTER DAD*

Jerry Adler

Jerry Adler is a frequent writer for Newsweek *magazine.*

How do we assess a man's life? The late William S. Paley, founder and longtime 1 chairman of CBS, devoted his life to the pursuit of wealth, power, fame and worldly pleasure—just like me, come to think of it, except he was very much luckier

Newsweek, June 17, 1996, pp. 58–64.

at it. But what I remember best about him is a telling remark in one of his many fulsome obituaries. Paley, said a friend, wasn't the kind of guy to attend his kids' Little League games, but when they needed him, he was there for them. And I thought, gee, how could one of the great visionaries of American industry be such a putz? Little League games are precisely when your kids need you the most. I accept that I will never own a Cézanne or sleep with a starlet, but nobody will say anything so dumb about me when I die, because *I've been to more goddam ball games in the past eight years than Cal Ripken Jr.*

2   Ha-ha. Just kidding, guys. I love Little League games, the earlier on Saturday morning the better. They remind me that it's always been hard to be a man. That was true even for my father, in the heyday of American malehood, the 1950s, when he would haul his weary suitbound hide off the bus every day at 6 P.M. and, responding to the invariable question, mutter, "Every day is hard when you're trying to make a living." By the standards then in effect, he was a model father, without once taking his kid backpacking, helping them sew costumes for their Kwanzaa pageant or making marinara sauce from scratch for their dinners. These are just a few of the ways in which men of my generation have redefined their roles beyond the business of making a living. Of course, most men still have to make a living, too, so in a single generation, fatherhood (like motherhood) has gotten twice as hard. I don't want to take anything away from Paley's achievements, but as far as I'm concerned, creating CBS would have been a more impressive feat if he'd done it while lugging his kids to the office in a Snugli.

3   Which he might actually do, if he were alive today. Men today "have permission to care for their children that they didn't have a generation ago," says Betty Thomson of the Center for Demography and Ecology at the University of Wisconsin. It's no coincidence that society gave men this permission just when they were needed to watch the kids so their wives could go to law school. By 1991, 20 percent of American fathers were taking care of young children in the home. (Two years later, as the economy improved, that proportion dropped to 16 percent.) But this cultural shift goes deeper than home economics. Baby boomers have transformed paternity, as they have every other institution they have touched, into an all-consuming vocation and never-ending quest for improvement and self-fulfillment. An outpouring of books, tapes, magazines and seminars—especially notable in the weeks leading up to Father's Day—both celebrates the pleasures of fatherhood and exhorts men to improve their performance in it. [. . .]

4   Executives [now] quit lucrative jobs to spend more time with their families, a phrase that used to mean "he couldn't find his way out of the men's room." Jeffrey E. Stiefler, the 49-year-old president of American Express, resigned last year to become a consultant and "watch his sons grow up." "How many presidents of Fortune 500 companies get to do that?" his former wife remarked in *The Wall Street Journal.* Bill Galston, President Clinton's domestic-policy adviser, quit to return to teaching after his 10-year-old son told him "baseball's not fun when there's no one there to applaud you." I say go for it, Bill—*and don't even think of bringing that laptop to the game Saturday.*

Just kidding, Bill; you wouldn't do that. You know that fathering today 5
demands far more concentration and effort than it did when you were growing up
in the 1950s, that discredited era of emotionally distant, conformist, workaholic
dads. To an astonishing extent, today's fathers define themselves in opposition to
the generation that raised them. There is "a substantial gulf between the boomer
generation and their fathers," says Don Eberley of the National Fatherhood Initiative. "There is disappointment, a sense of loss, regret bordering on anger."

This, of course, was the seminal kvetch of the men's movement: the alien- 6
ation of fathers from their families, dating from the Industrial Revolution, which
separated the worlds of work and home. A son who feels let down by his father
carries a lifelong grievance. How could he have been so blind, so indifferent to my
needs, so absorbed in the stupid newspaper? At the age of 49, Robert Blumenfeld,
a San Francisco businessman, recalls exactly how many times his father played
ball with him (once) and what his father said when he graduated from high school
cum laude: that some other 18-year-old had just signed with a baseball team for
$100,000. Dan Koenigshofer, a 46-year-old engineer in Chapel Hill, N.C., "can't
ever recall that my dad said he loved me" (although he's sure that he did love him,
in his taciturn 1950s way). David Weinstein, a Harvard economist, even knows
where his father was when he was born, 32 years ago. He was in his office. Back
then, the next day was soon enough for a new father to visit his son; Weinstein's
dad was presumably in no hurry to learn how to change a diaper, since most men
in those years didn't expect they would ever need to know.

Something changed in the culture when these men grew up, and sociologists 7
are still trying to figure out exactly what it was. Somehow, out of the poignancy of
memories such as these, men forged a determination to do better. There was new
research: around 1980 psychologists discovered that attachment to the father—
previously assumed to commence around the time a child began drawing a
weekly allowance—actually forms at the same time as the maternal bond, six to
eight months. Weinstein, taking no chances, made sure that he was the very first
thing his son, Jeremy, saw when he poked his head into the world almost two years
ago. But the most profound changes didn't grow out of a laboratory. Koenigshofer
tells his kids—ages 4 and 1—he loves them "a dozen times a day." "You no longer
see families where the dad says, upon finding that a kid has a dirty diaper, 'Go
find your mother,' " says Michael Lamb, a psychologist at the National Institutes
of Health and a leading authority on American family structure. "But it was universal 20 years ago." A *Newsweek* poll found that seven out of 10 American fathers
spend more time with their children than their own fathers did; nearly half think
they are doing a better job and only 3 percent think they're worse. What other area
of American life has shown such improvement in just a generation?

Of course, *Newsweek* didn't poll the kids. Their wives, for what it's worth, 8
tended to agree with them. But proving that men are actually being better fathers—
as opposed to talking and writing books about it—is one of the great unsolved
problems of contemporary sociology. "We all think there's been a change," says
Thomson, "but I haven't seen any data that convinces me it's true." Part of the

problem is that the same quest for self-realization that has led men to seek fulfill-
ment in nurturing and sacrifice has also led them in increasing numbers to pursue
their destiny with a sexy divorcée from their aerobics class. More than half of all
American children born in the 1970s and 1980s are expected to spend part of their
childhoods with just their mothers. A Census Bureau study found that 16.3 million
American children were living with just a mother in 1994—and 40 percent of those
hadn't seen their father in at least a year. It would take an awful lot of millionaire
executives quitting the rat race to offset that statistic. "Men today are better fathers
when they're around—and worse when they're not," says Andrew Cherlin, a
Johns Hopkins sociologist who studies American families.

9   True, some studies have shown that fathers today are more involved with
their children. But even those researchers admit that the demonstrable changes are
small compared with what you'd expect from watching Donahue over the years.
Studies of different nations show that American fathers are about average in
parental involvement, spending on average 45 minutes a day caring for their children by themselves; American mothers, by the way, spend the most among
women of any nation studied, more than 10 hours daily. (The least-involved fathers:
Japanese, averaging three minutes a day.) "Women are still doing twice as much
[child care] as men, although 20 years ago they were doing three times as much,"
says James A. Levine, director of the Fatherhood Project of the Families and Work
Institute. "Progress has been slow, and it will continue to be slow."

10   Levine's assumption, clearly, is that it is desirable—for children, for society
and for fathers themselves—for men to spend more time with their children. This
seems obvious at first glance, although advocacy groups for fatherhood can also
summon up reams of statistics to demonstrate it. "What reduces crime, child
poverty, teen pregnancy AND requires no new taxes?" asks a handout from the
National Fatherhood Initiative. The answer, of course, is responsible fatherhood
(although like many panaceas, this one is vulnerable to the counterexample: if fathers can prevent all these social ills, how has Japan escaped them?). This organization was founded in 1994 to "reinstate fatherhood as a national priority," and it
focuses mostly on public-policy issues related to divorce, abandonment and
unwed motherhood. Its materials are thick with sound-bite-size statistics asserting, for instance, that "Fatherless children are twice as likely to drop out of school"
or that "Seventy percent of the juveniles in state reform institutions grew up in
single- or no-parent institutions." The National Center for Fathering, by contrast,
has a more evangelical approach, exhorting individual fathers to greater "commitment" and to enhancement of their fathering "skills." Levine's organization promotes the compatibility of family life and work for men who may still feel guilty
about sneaking out on, say, a half-written magazine story on the remote chance
that this will be the day someone hits a ball right to where their kids are standing
in right field.

11   Most married parents would agree that one grown-up is not enough to raise a
child, although if pressed they would probably admit that two grown-ups are not
nearly enough either. But when sociologists began studying the long-term effects of
fathers' involvement, they didn't find what they'd expected. A few studies, mostly

with highly educated and motivated fathers who displayed a superhuman threshold of boredom, did indeed show a correspondence between the time fathers spent with their children and such desirable traits as "increased cognitive competence" and "a more internal locus of control." But in an influential review of the research Lamb concluded dolefully that in general "there is little evidence and no coherent reason to expect that increased paternal involvement in itself has any clear-cut or direct effects." *So tell your coach Daddy had to work really, really hard this week and he's too tired to pitch batting practice Saturday, OK?*

Just kidding. This is so counterintuitive, so potentially dangerous and sub- 12 versive, that not even the experts want to believe it. Instead, they're trying to prove that what counts is the quality of the father's involvement. To do this requires a statistically useful standard for judging fathers. Lamb's collaborator, Joseph Pleck of the University of Illinois, describes "positive paternal involvement" as being "high in interaction, accessibility and responsibility, and within the engagement component, performing positive activities and possessing positive stylistic characteristics." Before you get too worked up about this discovery, though, Pleck cautions that "to date, no research has directly tested this perhaps obvious prediction."

There is, however, one undisputed benefit to "paternal involvement," ac- 13 cording to psychologists: it's better for the fathers. The effects of taking care of one's children include enhanced self-esteem, increased marital happiness and the quality psychoanalyst Erik Erikson called "generativity," referring to the ability to sacrifice and take responsibility for others. There are other ways to achieve this, such as devoting one's life to the betterment of humanity. But fatherhood is by far the most common test of selflessness, and in some ways the most exacting.

That's right: all those high-powered executives who are dropping out so 14 they never have to miss another Little League game are in for a shock: their new career requires just as much intensity, focus and mastery of technique as business or war. That is the message of Ken Canfield, an educator who founded the National Center for Fathering in 1990. "There are rising expectations for fathers," warns Canfield, whose column in *Today's Father* magazine is ominously titled "In the Trenches." In the 1950s, good fathers paid the bills and handed out discipline. Now, he says, "you have to be sensitive, you have to be emotionally involved, you have to forgo job advancement to be a good dad." Books like Canfield's *Seven Secrets of Effective Fathers* or *The Five Key Habits of Smart Dads*, by Paul Lewis, bring to bear on fatherhood the same management-by-objective insight that has inspired 10,000 business best sellers. ("Effective fathers have a task orientation toward fathering" . . . "Without some simple guidelines to help them win at being dads, most men lack the confidence that breeds success.") Other books focus on developing specific skills, like making a popping sound with your finger in your mouth. ("Keep your cheek taut and your forefinger stiff and hooked," advise John Boswell and Ron Barrett in *How to Dad.*) "Men want things summarized," says Canfield. "They want orientation. They want to know: 'What should I be doing?'"

And dads are doing it! Dads like Blumenfeld, who gets up every morning at 15 6:30 to make breakfast for his 13-year-old son, Bryan. Blumenfeld craftily sets the sports section next to Bryan's cereal bowl, and in that way, he says, "I guess I trick him into doing 20 more minutes of reading before school." How's that for task orientation? Or Robert Jones, a Birmingham, Ala., lawyer, who came into four tickets to a baseball game, and told his then 10-year-old son to invite two friends. When Jones got home, there were three friends instead of two, so Jones taught his son a lesson; he left him home and took the other boys to the game. That's how you win at being a dad—especially if, like Jones, you then demonstrate your sensitivity by getting all teary at the game and bringing everyone home after the first inning.

16   The analogy between fathering and managing a corporation breaks down, though, at one critical point. The return on investment is outside your control. The limits of possible success are set, more or less arbitrarily, at the moment of conception. You can do everything the books say and your kid still won't develop enough "increased cognitive competence" to get into Harvard.

17   And, naturally, you don't get paid for being a father—quite the contrary, as everyone knows—which explains the persistence of the myth that it's actually tremendous fun. There is a whole literature of fathers' lush, almost sensuous tributes to their own kids, the smell of their scalps after their baths, the secret pleasure of tiptoeing into their rooms to watch them sleep. People who have experienced only romantic love may find it hard to believe that the parental kind can turn one's brain to mush just as readily.

18   Boston TV producer Michael Greene likes to put some Aretha Franklin on the stereo, crank it up real high, and dance with his 5-year-old daughter, an experience that moves him to unparsable rhapsodies about "getting connected back to some basic essence of my life." Sitting quietly late at night with his infant son dreamily gumming a bottle was "like falling in love again," says Weinstein. In "Father's Day: Notes from a New Dad in the Real World," Bill McCoy, an editor of *Parents* magazine, describes how during softball games his mind would wander to "the way my daughter pushes me over when I'm sitting cross-legged on the carpet, then tumbles into my arms as I fall." His solution was to give up softball. Art Perlman, a writer and lyricist who works from his New York apartment, looks after 6-year-old Jason while his wife puts in long days in her law office. Father and son fill their afternoons discussing topics Perlman lists as "colonial history, U.S. presidents, dinosaurs, space and science and animals in general." I don't think I'd given dinosaurs more than five minutes' thought in the year before my first son was born—and then, suddenly, my life opened up to a menagerie of fascinating, exotic creatures *that I wish had stayed buried for another 200 million years.*

19   Just kidding. I love dinosaurs, Barney especially. I don't want to sound like my own father, who frankly disdained them—a typical attitude of 1950s-era dads. Yet I detect a paradox in this frantic rejection of the values of the Eisenhower era. At the time, the postwar years in America were actually regarded as a remarkable experiment in family togetherness. Much of the iconography of American domestic life—the Saturday Little League games, the Sunday barbecues, the backyard birthday parties—dates from just that despised era. Parents, after all, moved to the suburbs for their children, not in order to work late at the office or eat out more often. And, as David Blankenhorn pointedly observes in *Fatherless America,* fathers

of the 1950s overwhelmingly stayed married and supported their families with their paychecks—an example that seems lost on all too many of their offspring.

And for me, Lord, if I can do no more, at least help me do no less: to come 20 home to my family each night, to take care of them to the best of my ability, to raise my children with the certainty that no matter how much they screw up the rest of their lives, one person loved them unconditionally. Like millions of other men, I have made my choice. We will never know what greatness might have lain within our reach, not to mention starlets. And we will find satisfaction in knowing we did what was right, *without expecting any gratitude for it.*

Just kidding. ▧   21

B. What Are Some Variations on the Traditional Family? How Effective Are These Variations?

THE FUTURE OF MARRIAGE*

Stephanie Coontz

Stephanie Coontz is a historian and writer. She has appeared on several television panels to discuss family issues.

Most Americans support the emergence of alternative ways of organizing parent- 1 hood and marriage. They don't want to reestablish the supremacy of the male breadwinner model or to define masculine and feminine roles in any monolithic way. Many people worry, however, about the growth of alternatives to marriage itself. They fear that in some of today's new families parents may not be devoting enough time and resources to their children. The rise of divorce and unwed motherhood is particularly worrisome, because people correctly recognize that children need more than one adult involved in their lives.

As a result, many people who object to the "modified male breadwinner" 2 program of the "new consensus" crusaders are still willing to sign on to the other general goals of that movement: "to increase the proportion of children who grow up with two married parents," to "reclaim the ideal of marital permanence," to keep men "involved in family life," and to establish the principle "that every child deserves a father."[1]

Who could disagree? When we appear on panels together, leaders of "tra- 3 ditional values" groups often ask me if I accept the notion that, on the whole, two parents are better than one. If they would add an adjective such as two *good* parents, or even two *adequate* ones, I'd certainly agree. And of course it's better to try to make a marriage work than to walk away at the first sign of trouble.

As a historian, however, I've learned that when truisms are touted as stunning 4 new research, when aphorisms everyone agrees with are presented as a courageous

*Stephanie Coontz, *The Way We Really Are: Coming to Terms with America's Changing Families* (New York: Basic Books, 1997), pp. 77–80, 93–95, 196–197, 201.

political program, and when exceptions or complications are ignored for the sake of establishing the basic principles, it's worth taking a close look for a hidden agenda behind the clichés. And, in fact, the new consensus crowd's program for supporting the two-parent family turns out to be far more radical than the feel-good slogans might lead you to believe.

5   Members of groups such as the Council on Families in America claim they are simply expressing a new consensus when they talk about "reinstitutionalizing enduring marriage," but in the very next breath they declare that it "is time to raise the stakes." They want nothing less than to make lifelong marriage the "primary institutional expression of commitment and obligation to others," the main mechanism for regulating sexuality, male-female relations, economic redistribution, and child rearing. Charles Murray says that the goal is "restoration of marriage as an utterly distinct, legal relationship." Since marriage must be "privileged," other family forms or child-rearing arrangements should not receive tax breaks, insurance benefits, or access to public housing and federal programs. Any reform that would make it easier for divorced parents, singles, unmarried partners, or stepfamilies to function is suspect because it removes "incentives" for people to get and stay married. Thus, these groups argue, adoption and foster care policies should "reinforce marriage as the child-rearing norm." Married couples, and only married couples, should be given special tax relief to raise their children. Some leaders of the Institute for American Values propose that we encourage both private parties and government bodies "to distinguish between married and unmarried *couples* in housing, credit, zoning, and other areas." Divorce and illegitimacy should be stigmatized.[2]

6   We've come quite a way from the original innocuous statements about the value of two-parent families and the importance of fathers to children. Now we find out that we must make marriage the only socially sanctioned method for organizing male-female roles and fulfilling adult obligations to the young. "There is no realistic alternative to the one we propose," claims the Council on Families in America. To assess this claim, we need to take a close look at what the consensus crusaders mean when they talk about the need to reverse the "deinstitutionalizing" of marriage.[3]

7   Normally, social scientists have something very specific in mind when they say that a custom or behavior is "institutionalized." They mean it comes "with a well-understood set of obligations and rights," all of which are backed up by law, customs, rituals, and social expectations. In this sense, marriage is still one of America's most important and valued institutions.[4]

8   But it is true that marriage has lost its former monopoly over the organization of people's major life transitions. Alongside a continuing commitment to marriage, other arrangements for regulating sexual behavior, channeling relations between men and women, and raising children now exist. Marriage was once the primary way of organizing work along lines of age and sex. It determined the roles that men and women played at home and in public. It was the main vehicle for redistributing resources to old and young, and it served as the most important marker of adulthood and respectable status.

All this is no longer the case. Marriage has become an option rather than a   9
necessity for men and women, even during the child-raising years. Today only
half of America children live in nuclear families with both biological parents present. One child in five lives in a stepfamily and one in four lives in a "single-parent"
home. The number of single parents increased from 3.8 million in 1970 to 6.9 million in 1980, a rate that averages out to a truly unprecedented 6 percent increase
each year. In the 1980s, the rate of increase slowed and from 1990 to 1995 it leveled off, but the total numbers have continued to mount, reaching 12.2 million
by 1996.[5]

These figures understate how many children actually have two parents in the   10
home, because they confuse marital status with living arrangements. Approximately a quarter of all births to unmarried mothers occur in households where the
father is present, so those children have two parents at home in fact if not in law. Focusing solely on the marriage license distorts our understanding of trends in children's living arrangements. For example, the rise in cohabitation between 1970 and
1984 led to more children being classified as living in single-parent families. But
when researchers counted unmarried couples living together as two-parent families, they found that children were spending *more* time, not less, with both parents in
1984 than in 1970. Still, this simply confirms the fact that formal marriage no longer
organizes as many life decisions and transitions as it did in the past.[6]

Divorce, cohabitation, remarriage, and single motherhood are not the only   11
factors responsible for the eclipse of marriage as the primary institution for organizing sex roles and interpersonal obligations in America today. More people are
living on their own before marriage, so that more young adults live outside a family environment than in earlier times. And the dramatic extension of life spans
means that more people live alone after the death of a spouse.[7]

The growing number of people living on their own ensures that there are   12
proportionately fewer families of *any* kind than there used to be. The Census Bureau defines families as residences with more than one householder related by
blood, marriage, or adoption. In 1940, under this definition, families accounted for
90 percent of all households in the country. By 1970, they represented just 81 percent of all households, and by 1990 they represented 71 percent. The relative
weight of marriage in society has decreased. Social institutions and values have
adapted to the needs, buying decisions, and lifestyle choices of singles. Arrangements other than nuclear family transactions have developed to meet people's
economic and interpersonal needs. Elders, for example, increasingly depend on
Social Security and private pension plans, rather than the family, for their care.[8]

Part of the deinstitutionalization of marriage, then, comes from factors that   13
few people would want to change even if they could. Who wants to shorten the
life spans of the elderly, even though that means many more people are living outside the institution of marriage than formerly? Should we lower the age of marriage, even though marrying young makes people more likely to divorce?[9] Or
should young people be forced to live at home until they do marry? Do we really
want to try to make marriage, once again, the only path for living a productive
and fulfilling adult life? [. . .]

REALITY BITES

14 It makes little sense to whip up hysteria about an issue if you don't have any concrete solutions. Yet for people who believe we're on the verge of "cultural suicide," the measures proposed by the family values crusaders are curiously halfhearted. Amitai Etzioni urges individuals to make "supervows," voluntary premarriage contracts indicating "that they take their marriage more seriously than the law requires." One of the few concrete reforms David Blankenhorn proposes to ensure "a father for every child" is that we forbid unmarried women access to sperm banks and artificial insemination. In addition, he asks men to take pledges that "marriage is the pathway to effective fatherhood," wants the president to issue an annual report on the "state of fatherhood," and thinks Congress should designate "Safe Zones" for male responsibility. Can anyone who looks at the historical trends in divorce, unwed motherhood, and reproductive technology seriously think such measures will bring back the married-couple–biological-parent monopoly over child rearing?[10]

15 Barbara Dafoe Whitehead of the Institute for American Values advocates "restigmatization" of divorce and unwed motherhood; "stigmatization," she argues, "is a powerful means of regulating behavior, as any smoker or overeater will testify." But while overeaters may now feel "a stronger sense of shame than in the past," this has hardly wiped out the problem of obesity. Indeed, the proportion of overweight Americans has increased steadily since the 1950s. As for curbing smoking, the progress here has come from stringent public regulations against smoking, combined with intensive (and expensive) interventions to help people quit. The pretended "consensus" of the new family values crusaders would quickly evaporate if they attempted to institute an equally severe campaign against single parents. After all, 90 percent of the people in a 1995 Harris poll believe society "should value all types of families."[11]

16 Besides, stigmatization is a blunt instrument that does not distinguish between the innocent and the guilty any better than no-fault divorce. Dan Quayle's latest book, for example, includes a divorced family among five examples he gives of the "strong" families that still exist in America. He puts a divorced single mother into a book intended to prove that "intact" families are ideal because, "Though Kathy experienced divorce, she did not foresee or want it." It was not this woman's intent, Quayle explains, to pursue "a fast-track career." She "expected to play the traditional role, to raise her children and create a home for a husband of whom she was proud." Such distinctions put the consensus brokers in the tricky business of examining people's motives to decide which divorced or single parents had good intentions and therefore should be exempt from stigmatization.[12]

17 It would be easy to dismiss the flimsy reforms proposed by the "new consensus" proponents as fuzzy-headed wishful thinking were it not for the fact that their approach opens such a dangerous gap between practice and theory. At best, affirming lifelong marriage as a principle while issuing exceptions for people whose *intentions* were good encourages a hypocrisy that is already far too common in today's political and cultural debates. Consider Congressman Newt Gingrich, who

was born into a single-parent family, made his ex-wife a single mom by divorcing her, and has a half-sister who is gay. "I'm not sitting here as someone who is unfamiliar with the late twentieth century," he has said. "I know life can be complicated." Yet that didn't stop him from blaming Susan Smith's murder of her two children in 1994 on lack of family values—though he considered it irrelevant that the stepfather who abused her was a member of the Christian Coalition.[13]

18 At worst, this approach offers right-wing extremists moderate-sounding cover for attempts to penalize or coerce families and individuals that such groups find offensive. Insisting that everyone give lip service to lifelong marriage as an ideal while recognizing in practice that life is complicated is like having a law on the books that *everyone* breaks at one time or another. Authorities can use it selectively to discipline the poor, the powerless, or the unpopular, while letting everyone else off the hook.

19 The family values crusade may sound appealing in the abstract. But it offers families no constructive way to resolve the new dilemmas of family life. Forbidding unmarried women access to sperm banks, for instance, is hardly going to put the package of child rearing and marriage back together. It would take a lot more repression than that to reinstitutionalize lifelong marriage in today's society.

20 As Katha Pollitt argues, "we'd have to bring back the whole nineteenth century: Restore the cult of virginity and the double standard, ban birth control, restrict divorce, kick women out of decent jobs, force unwed pregnant women to put their babies up for adoption on pain of social death, make out-of-wedlock children legal nonpersons. That's not going to happen."[14] If it did happen, American families would be worse off, not better, than they are right now. ■

NOTES

1. "Marriage in America: A Report to the Nation," Council on Families in America, New York, N.Y., March 1995, pp. 10–11, 13.
2. David Popenoe, "Modern Marriage: Revising the Cultural Script," in David Popenoe, Jean Bethke Elshtain, and David Blankenhorn, eds., *Promises to Keep: Decline and Renewal of Marriage in America* (Lanham, Md.: Rowman and Littlefield, 1996), p. 254; "Marriage in America," p. 4; David Popenoe, *Life Without Father: Compelling New Evidence That Fatherhood and Marriage Are Indispensable for the Good of Children and Society* (New York: The Free Press, 1996), p. 222; David Blankenhorn, *Fatherless America: Confronting Our Most Urgent Social Problem* (New York: Basic Books, 1995), p. 229; Charles Murray, "Keep It in the Family," *Times of London,* November 14, 1993; Maggie Gallagher, *The Abolition of Marriage: How We Destroy Lasting Love* (Washington, D.C.: Regnery Publishing, 1996), pp. 250–257; Barbara Dafoe Whitehead, "Dan Quayle Was Right," *Atlantic Monthly* 271 (April 1993), p. 49.
3. "Marriage in America," p. 4. The "deinstitutionalizing" phrase comes from Blankenhorn, *Fatherless America,* p. 224.
4. William Goode, *World Changes in Divorce Patterns* (New Haven, Conn.: Yale University Press, 1993), p. 330.
5. On the leveling off of family change, see Peter Kilborn, "Shifts in Families Reach a Plateau," *New York Times,* November 27, 1996. Other information in this and the following three paragraphs, unless otherwise noted, come from Steven Rawlings and Arlene Saluter, *Household and Family Characteristics: March 1994,* Current Population Reports Series P20–483 (Washington, D.C.: Bureau of the Census, U.S. Department of Commerce, September 1995), pp. xvii–ix; Michael Haines, "Long-Term Marriage

Patterns in the United States from Colonial Times to the Present," *History of the Family* 1 (1996); Arthur Norton and Louisa Miller, *Marriage, Divorce, and Remarriage in the 1990s*, Current Population Reports Series P23–180 (Washington, D.C.: Bureau of the Census, October 1992); Richard Gelles, *Contemporary Families: A Sociological View* (Thousand Oaks, Calif.: Sage, 1995), pp. 116–120, 176; Shirley Zimmerman, "Family Trends: What Implications for Family Policy?" *Family Relations* 41 (1992), p. 424; Margaret Usdansky. "Single Motherhood: Stereotypes vs. Statistics," *New York Times*, February 11, 1996, p. 4; *New York Times*, August 30, 1994, p. A9; *New York Times*, March 10, 1996, p. A11, and March 17, 1996, p. A8; U.S. Bureau of the Census, *Statistical Abstracts of the United States* (Washington, D.C., 1992); McLanahan and Casper, "Growing Diversity and Inequality in the American Family," in Reynolds Farley, ed., *State of the Union: American the 1990s*, vol. 1 (New York: Russell Sage, 1995).

6. Larry Bumpass, "Patterns, Causes, and Consequences of Out-of-Wedlock Childbearing; What Can Government Do?" *Focus* 17 (University of Wisconsin–Madison Institute for Research on Poverty, 1995), p. 42; Larry Bumpass and R. Kelly Raley, "Redefining Single-Parent Families: Cohabitation and Changing Family Reality," *Demography* 32 (1995), p. 98.

7. *Olympian,* February 26, 1996, p. D6.

8. Susan Watkins, Jane Menken, and John Bongaarts, "Demographic Foundations of Family Change," *American Sociological Review* 52 (1987), pp. 346–358.

9. Barbara Wilson and Sally Clarke, "Remarriages: A Demographic Profile," *Journal of Family Issues* 13 (1992).

10. Ruth Shalit, "Family Mongers," *New Republic,* August 16, 1993, p. 13; Popenoe, *Life Without Father,* p. 194; David Popenoe, "American Family Decline, 1960–1990," *Journal of Marriage and the Family* 55 (1993), p. 539; Blankenhorn, *Fatherless America,* pp. 220–233; and quoted in *Newsweek,* February 6, 1995, p. 43; "Marriage in America," p. 4.

11. Whitehead, "Dan Quayle Was Right," p. 49; Carole Sugarman, "Jack Sprat Should Eat Some Fat," *Washington Post National Weekly Edition,* May 2–8, 1994; *Olympian,* February 5, 1996, p. A8; Janet Giele, "Decline of the Family: Conservative, Liberal, and Feminist Views," in Popenoe, Elshtain, and Blankenhorn, *Promises to Keep,* p. 104.

12. Dan Quayle and Diane Medved, *The American Family: Discovering the Values That Make Us Strong* (New York: HarperCollins, 1996), pp. 2, 87, 114.

13. Katharine Seelye, "The Complications and Ideals," *New York Times,* November 24, 1994.

14. Katha Pollitt, "Bothered and Bewildered," *New York Times,* July 22, 1993.

SINGLE MOTHERHOOD IS A JOY, NOT A DISASTER*

Carolyn Edy

Carolyn Edy is a single mother living in New Hampshire. She reports that undeterred by doubting friends and gloomy statistics, she chose to keep her baby.

1 Just after Christmas '97, I went to Video Thunder with my mom and my grandmother. We were three single mothers in search of a way to spend a cold New Hampshire evening. My mother was divorced, my grandmother was recently widowed and I was three weeks shy of becoming an unwed mother.

Newsweek, May 10, 1999, p. 12.

My grandmother held up a video box and hollered across the store to me: "Oh, this is it! The perfect movie for you." In her hand was the movie *Bastard Out of Carolina*. I laughed and told her I'd already seen it. I'd rented it after I'd discovered I was pregnant. 2

I was 25 and had just received a master's degree from the University of North Carolina. A week after listening to graduation speeches telling me how far I could go, I sat on the edge of a twin bed, listening to the object of my affection give me his canned "It's not you—it's me" speech. Two weeks after that I sat at Planned Parenthood, where I'd gone for a $10 pregnancy test, waiting for my name to be called. A hip 22-year-old told me I was "definitely pregnant" and offered me cheerful sympathy, a tissue, a bag of congratulatory paraphernalia and several abortion pamphlets. 3

I had always known I would never have an abortion or give up my child. Now I was sure that my life was over. Media portrayals of single mothers confirmed this—unless, like Murphy Brown, I was over-35 and already a success. But I felt so strongly I had to keep my child that it didn't take long to change my perspective. I began to rejoice and become hopeful—and I saw that these emotions were considered inappropriate. 4

While waddling around a national magazine as its first pregnant intern, I received a press release from the Census Bureau stating that families headed by single mothers were among the country's poorest. That same month I listened to a man on C-SPAN radio predicting doom for the children of single mothers—in the form of dropouts, drugs and divorce. 5

A pregnant co-worker spoke excitedly with me about our pregnancies, until I told her I was planning to deliver the baby in New Hampshire. She asked if my husband had been transferred. I told her I wasn't married, that I was going to live near my family. The conversation ended, and my pregnancy was never mentioned again. 6

Premarital sex is a given these days, and half of U.S. pregnancies are unintended. Yet living among the young and privileged—in four years of prep school, four years of college and one year in Manhattan—I knew of no peers who were pregnant. I learned of friends' abortions only after they learned I was having a baby.

The shock value of my pregnancy was blaming those who believe in a woman's right to choose. The pro-choice, feminist movement often forgets that it is advocating a *choice*. Many who view abortion as an uncomplicated operation see my decision as incomprehensible. And whether they support a woman's right to have an abortion or oppose it, many would agree that I am depriving my daughter and one loving, infertile couple of a happy family.

To those who said I needed to think of my child, I responded with questions of my own. How could I be sure my child would be well cared for by someone else? And as for depriving her of an in-house father, I asked: How many children are abandoned by their fathers later in life? How many have to deal with divorce? When people said I needed to think of my own life, I replied that I couldn't live with myself if I did not keep this baby. 7

Most of my family viewed my optimism as pure naiveté. "She has no idea what she's in for" was a favorite line during my pregnancy—and continued into 8 my daughter's first few months. This when I was already up every hour feeding, diapering and rocking a newborn.

9   But so far this prediction has come true: I really had no idea what I was in for. As much as I knew I would love my child, I love her more. I had hoped I would enjoy being a mother, and in fact I thrive in my new role.

10   After a yearlong silence, my daughter's father asked to be a part of her life. He resented me for not giving him a choice in whether she was born or whether I kept her. But I did allow him to choose whether he became involved, and that has greatly changed the way he views her. Now he feels as I do—proud that there is no other baby like her.

11   It's hard now to remember the panic I felt two summers ago. I have become so accustomed to my life with my daughter that I never know quite what to say to people who shake their heads and say, "It must be so hard." The truth sounds saccharine. I am hopelessly in love with my child.

12   Whenever I do complain that single motherhood is hard, I've got my mom and grandmother to tell me I have it easy—I don't have a husband to take care of as well. ■

A MATTER OF FAITH*

Jerry Adler

Jerry Adler often writes about family issues. In this article he addresses the issues associated with interfaith families. How would you feel about marrying outside of your faith? Or would that not be an issue for you?

1 Driving home from Thanksgiving dinner in New London, Conn., to Spencer-town, N.Y., the Kirsch family talked about the tree. They've had one every Christmas since Claudia Ricci and Richard Kirsch got married in 1978—even though a rabbi helped marry them, and even though their three children are being raised as Jews and even though Claudia herself, baptized a Roman Catholic, become a Jew eight years ago. Over that time the tree has come to seem increasingly out of place in their home. "How would I feel if the rabbi saw this?" Ricci wondered.

2   But in the car, Lindsay, 11, remembered coming down the stairs on a week-end morning to watch TV by the twinkling lights, and her younger brother, Noah, who started out the trip opposed to a tree, said quietly, "Couldn't we just have a little one?" Of all the difficult emotional, theological and familial issues raised by Ricci's conversion, this one alone remained unsettled. In one small part of Ricci's soul, it's Christmas, and she wants her tree.

Newsweek, December 15, 1997, pp. 49–54.

"There are many paths to God," Ricci's Catholic mother complacently 3 observed last month after participating in her granddaughter Jocelyn's bat mitzvah. But for most of the last 2,000 years, most people lived in villages where those paths almost never intersected, and if they did, the outcome might as easily have been a holy war as a wedding. Their religious traditions did not prepare them for a society in which the handsome boy next door might be any of three different kinds of Catholic, let alone a Shiite.

We have always been a nation of seekers, and now not one bound by the re- 4 ligious fault lines of the past. The proportion of Jews who married Gentiles, around one in 10 for the first half of the century, according to the American Jewish Committee, doubled by 1960, doubled again by the early 1970s, and in this decade has leveled off at just over 50 percent. To put it another way, by some estimates one out of three American Jews lives in an interfaith household and faces some version of Ricci's dilemma every December. The comparable figure for Catholics, according to a 1990 survey cited by psychologist Joel Crohn, an authority on mixed marriages, is 21 percent; for Mormons, 30 percent, and for Muslims, 40 percent. This year, when the first day of Chanukah happens to fall on Dec. 24, the December quandary may be especially anxiety-provoking. When Ricci's parents arrive for the traditional Christmas Eve dinner at her home, they may not see a tree, but they will unquestionably see a menorah.

And as these families raise their children, they are creating, in effect, a new 5 form of religious identification in America, analogous to the "mixed race" category that some people want to add to census forms. Dilip Viswanath and Carmen Guerra, both doctors raised in New York City, were married twice on Labor Day weekend—Friday night in a Hindu ceremony in Queens, and Saturday by a Catholic priest in Manhattan. Carmen wore a sari for the Hindu service, which involved colorful rituals such as circling a fire and pouring milk over the couple's joined hands. She wore a white gown for the Catholic ceremony, an occasion so decorous that it had to be held at the Plaza Hotel, because the church wouldn't allow Vivaldi to be played during the service. They plan to have children, Dilip says, and "we want to expose them to both religions."

By the time they're in college, a Hindu-Catholic child will hardly be a novelty 6 in this country. Perhaps one of them might even marry Rabia Asghar, the 3-year-old daughter of Cynthia and Tariq Asghar of Chicago, who is being raised in both her mother's Methodism and the Islam of her Pakistani-born father. Or Karenna Meredith, 2, who is learning about God from the perspective of her Mormon mother, Christine, and her Catholic father, Tony, with a little "free-form prayer" adopted from both faiths thrown in each morning. "We're going to position it as 'Daddy likes this and Mommy likes that,'" says Tom Clark, 35, a management consultant who was raised a Methodist in a Wisconsin farm town. His wife, Amy Rosenbaum Clark, 33, grew up Jewish in New Jersey. Their 4-month-old son, Graham, had neither a ritual Jewish circumcision nor a baptism, but a "dedication" at a Chicago church, with a rabbi and minister in attendance. "He'll get exposed to both, and won't be overdosed in either," Clark says confidently. Like other parents raising their children in two faiths, they expect him someday to look inside himself and find there either a Jew or a Gentile.

7   Clark's system of letting Mommy's and Daddy's religions speak for themselves is less demanding than the alternative of immersing the whole family in the practice of both faiths. This is the approach of Chicago lawyer Stephen Smith, 47, who was raised an Orthodox Jew, and his Catholic wife, Eileen, 46. The couple, who are active in the large interfaith support group that often meets at Old St. Pat's Church, aren't just "exposing" their children to both faiths, Smith insists; "we're raising them as both Catholics and Jews, and insist that they do what they need to in our view, and later on it's likely that they'll make a selection." Bringing three children under the age of 11 to Jewish and Catholic services every weekend "is very labor-intensive, as you can imagine," says Eileen. "We don't do soccer. We do church." And intellectually intense as well. Sometimes, she says, her 10-year-old daughter, Nora, will plaintively ask, "Can we not talk about religion tonight?"

8   Raising children in two faiths promotes one of the most favored values of the Zeitgeist, diversity. The problem is, the diversity occurs within the same individual. Expecting children to choose between their mother's and father's religions "puts them in the position of rejecting one of their parents," says Leslie Goodman-Malamuth, who was raised "as nothing" by her Jewish and Christian parents and wrote a self-help book called *Between Two Worlds.* "Children of intermarriage often feel they're not as good as their all-Jewish or all-Christian cousins. They feel like damaged goods." Moreover, to be both Jewish and Christian is the theological equivalent of squaring the circle. Judaism and Christianity don't complement each other, they exclude one another. You cannot believe in salvation by Christ if you're still awaiting the Messiah.

9   The position of organized Jewry, according to Steven Bayme of the American Jewish Committee, is that "we would rather that children were raised in one faith, even another one, than in both." For Beth and Michael Berkowitz of Sudbury, Mass., the moment of truth came when their son Jared raised his hand at temple preschool to answer the teacher's question "Who loves you?" "Jesus," the toddler replied, which is what he'd been told at church the previous week. At their unaffiliated "post-denominational" temple, where 60 percent of new members are in mixed-faith marriages, this was considered an amusing faux pas rather than a scandal. But the aftermath is that the Berkowitzes now go only to temple, and Beth, the daughter of a Presbyterian pastor, has stopped attending church.

10   Meanwhile, out of concern for just that kind of confusion, the Union of American Hebrew Congregations, representing Reform temples, passed a resolution in 1995 against enrolling children in temple school if they were also taking instruction in another religion. For the most assimilated of the three major branches of Judaism in the United States, this move was so controversial that former senator Howard Metzenbaum resigned from the organization's board in protest.

11   You might expect that most families, facing a toss-up choice between Judaism and Christianity, would opt for the majority religion, which also is the one with Santa Claus and the Easter Bunny. But Rabbi Lewis Mintz of Temple Beth Elohim in Acton, Mass., sees the opposite happening all the time. The religious identity of

a Christian is defined by faith, he reasons. But Judaism, in America, is a culture and an ethnic identification as well. The Jewish partner in a mixed marriage will feel drawn to those elements and want to reassert his Jewishness. That's what happened to Jeff Bornstein, a San Francisco lawyer, but with this difference: he was forced into becoming a better Jew by his wife, Veronica Sanchez. Veronica, a Catholic, took a class in Judaism before their marriage in 1992, although she chose not to convert. At dinner the night before the wedding, she was appalled to see that her future mother-in-law didn't know the Hebrew blessing over the Sabbath candles, which she had been forced to memorize. She elbowed her fiancé in the ribs. "How come you put me through this?" she demanded. When their son, David, was born, Sanchez made Bornstein go back and relearn all the stuff he'd forgotten from Hebrew school. By the same token, Joan Hawxhurst, editor of *Dovetail*, a magazine for Jewish-Christian families, believes that marrying a Jew has made her think more about her own Christianity. "If I had married another United Methodist, it would have been really easy for me never to question what I did every Sunday in church."

Amazing how a child, or the prospect of one, evokes in people such strong, 12 almost tribal, feelings of solidarity. Sitting in church without her family for Sunday mass, Sanchez feels very lonely. "When I see the little altar boys, and realize my son will never be one, I feel a deep wound inside me." These emotions transcend even the most deeply held secular convictions. When Constance Baker, a Baltimore lawyer, told her college-age son that, all things being equal, it wouldn't be so bad, if he could possibly arrange it, not to, please God, bring a Gentile fiancée home from college, he exploded in outrage. "It was kind of the exact opposite of everything else she had tried to teach me, about valuing people for what kind of person they are rather than by some label," Chuck Baker argued. His mother can't exactly dispute that but, by way of explanation, says the issue came up only recently, "as the children have grown older, and I've begun thinking about their families. It occurred to me that my son didn't know that I felt that way." If Chuck happens to fall in love with a Gentile girl, she notes, "conversion is fine."

But Baker's attitude is a long way from one that was common a generation or 13 two ago, when Jewish parents would, literally, rend their garments in mourning for a son lost to the Gentiles through intermarriage. Finding a rabbi to marry a mixed couple sometimes meant a trip to another city. But last year a survey of 325 American rabbis by the Jewish Outreach Institute of the City University of New York found that acceptance of intermarriage was growing, albeit very slowly. Even 11 percent of Orthodox rabbis said they would refer a mixed couple to a Reform rabbi to perform the ceremony. One possible explanation for the shift: nearly three fifths of the rabbis themselves had relatives who had married Gentiles.

The interfaith movement even has its own model wedding ceremony, created 14 18 years ago by Father John Hester and Rabbi Charles Familant of San Francisco. (Catholics are allowed to participate in interfaith marriages under a dispensation from their diocese, which requires the Catholic partner to promise to try to raise the children as Catholics.) The ceremony retains certain religious customs, but "universalizes" them. The Jewish tradition of trampling a wineglass at the end of the ceremony is universalized into a generic reminder of how grief and joy mingle in the world. (The Jewish interpretation more specifically evokes the destruction of the Temple in Jerusalem in A.D. 70.) The deity invoked is the "Lord," a term that conveniently covers Jesus as well as Yahweh.

15   It isn't just Jews who have changed their attitudes toward intermarriage. Growing up in the 1940s in a small town in Nebraska, the theologian Martin Marty recalls that "if a Catholic married a Lutheran, they had to move out of town, because the hassles were just too much. Before Vatican II [1962–65] Catholics weren't allowed to go into another person's church; I've heard couples say they weren't allowed to attend the baptism of their own children." Today, Marty says, mixed marriage "is not a big deal" among most American Christians. "Even if a staunch Catholic marries a Methodist, there's almost a sigh of relief by the families that at least their child isn't marrying a druggy or a cult member." "Methodists and Catholics [share] a belief in Jesus Christ," agrees the Rev. Eugene Winkler of Chicago Temple: First United Methodist Church, whose own daughter is married to a Catholic. In contrast to Catholicism and Judaism, "for a Protestant, religion is a necessary part of one's life, but it's not bound up so closely with who you are and who your friends are," Winkler says. But staunchly conservative sects such as Old Colony Mennonites and Missouri Synod Lutherans are less tolerant of intermarriage, and born-again Christians usually insist on born-again spouses. "To me," Winkler frets, "the worst-case scenario would be an evangelical Christian [wanting to marry] an Orthodox Jew." Experience suggests that he needn't worry too much about the possibility.

16   The amount of family strife and grief Americans have been spared by this trend toward tolerance is incalculable. But there is a price, at least for Jews. The traditional Jewish stricture against intermarriage grew out of the experience of the Diaspora, when Jews were a tiny and persecuted minority. They are still, for all their prominence in American life, less than 3 percent of the population. When half of them marry someone outside the faith, says Elliott Abrams, the president of the Ethics and Public Policy Center in Washington, D.C., and a former assistant secretary of state, "we're looking at a very dismal prospect" for long-term survival. Abrams argues that secularized, ethnic Judaism—the kind that finds its highest expression in writing pro-Israel letters to the editor of *The New York Times*—is a doomed experiment. Only religious observance counts, and only about a quarter of interfaith couples, by his figures, raise their children as Jews. But the writer Gabrielle Glaser, who studied intermarriage in her new book *Strangers to the Tribe*, concluded more or less the opposite: that "a significant number of Jews who marry outside their faith are making serious efforts to pass on the religion and culture of their forefathers. . . . If the interfaith couples I met over the past three years are any measure, [Judaism] will surely survive modern intermarriage."

17   Jews, at least, share a history with Christianity, and most Americans have at least a passing familiarity with the faith. But the misunderstandings that can arise when an American marries into a polytheistic religion make the Christmas-tree dilemma seem simple by contrast. As a matter of fact, Ann and Rajesh, a couple from Maryland who didn't want to use their last names, don't have that problem

because his family, which has lived in America for years, has always had a Christmas tree anyway. On the other hand, Ann finds some Hindu practices strange and the statues of temple gods positively frightening. "Whenever I go to their temple," she confesses, "I just close my eyes and pray to Jesus." Islam is much closer to the religions most Americans follow than Hinduism, but it places a high value on proselytizing—as Joe Miller, a nonpracticing Catholic by birth, discovered when he announced his engagement to Rashda Buttar, a Chicago lawyer. On a courtesy visit to her family's mosque, Miller recalls, an uncle led him to a back room, handed him a Koran and a sheaf of papers in English and Arabic to sign, testifying to his conversion. Miller declined, but it made for an uneasy few months leading up to their wedding.

But love is always hard, and people who have found it don't let go. Even if, like Julie Marcus of New York, marrying Alex Gomez, a Catholic, meant that the ceremony couldn't be performed by her father, a Conservative rabbi. Even if, for Siona Carpenter, a Baptist in New Orleans, marrying the Catholic Kenneth La France on Easter weekend meant that her family couldn't have barbecue at the rehearsal dinner on Good Friday. Even if, like Christine Meredith, she worries that she will not have eternal life with her husband, Tony, if he doesn't get around to joining the Mormon Church. 18

Two days after Thanksgiving, Claudia Ricci went to her synagogue to think and pray, and when she came home her mind was made up. There would be no tree this year. She would undoubtedly agree with Dan Josephs, one of the founders of Chicago's interfaith support group. Josephs, a Catholic married to a Jew, once took his wife to a Good Friday service at his hometown and was mortified to hear the priest talk about how the Jews killed Jesus. Did marrying a Jew mean betraying his love of Christ? "How can falling in love and getting married be a betrayal of anything?" he asks. ■ 19

MARRIAGE AS WE SEE IT*

Chris Glaser

Chris Glaser is the author of Uncommon Calling: A Gay Christian's Struggle to Serve the Church. *He describes how exchanging vows with his partner in a church ceremony made him feel transformed.*

Between my own Presbyterian church's vote rejecting ordination of gays and lesbians and the House vote against same-sex marriages, I feel beaten up. The one-two punch came early in July. Had I been the victim of a street gay-bashing, I would be able to seek comfort from my church and legal redress from the government. When the gay-bashers are my own church and government, I'm bewildered, wondering where to turn. 1

Newsweek, September 16, 1996, p. 19.

2   The two most sacred commitments in my life—my calling to the ministry and my same-gender marriage—are under attack because they are deemed threatening to a church and a society troubled by the lack of family cohesion, so-called "traditional family values." Our culture fails to see this as a largely heterosexual problem but instead scapegoats homosexuals, just as we who are gay and lesbian attempt to maintain relationships within our biological families and establish our own family units. Our birth families often come under attack for supporting us; our chosen families are refused recognition. Our families of faith treat us as society once treated illegitimate children. In the body politic, rights taken for granted by heterosexuals are called "special" when applied to us.

3   I've lived long enough in the gay movement to witness those who oppose us come full circle in their reasons that we should be outcasts from church and society. Twenty years ago, gay love was opposed because it supposedly didn't lead to long-term relationships and the rearing of children. Today gay love is attacked because gay people in committed relationships and gay couples with children are coming out. In the past, gays were denounced because we supposedly were "selfish" and "irresponsible." Now we're denounced if our selfless service—from the ministry to the military—is revealed. This damned-if-we-don't-and-damned-if-we-do syndrome should offer a clue to our opponents that their basis for being anti-gay is not reason.

4   From 1976 to 1978 I served on a national Presbyterian task force whose mandate was to lead our denomination in a study of homosexuality, particularly as it related to ordination. During one regional hearing, a minister testified that homosexuals shouldn't be ordained because we didn't form lasting relationships. Another pastor spoke proudly of leading a female couple in his church to see the "error" of their ways, thus breaking up their 20-year relationship. During these hearings, when anyone mentioned the possibility of sanctioning gay marriages, audible gasps came from the crowd. We could talk about gay ordination, but marriage was more sacrosanct!

5   In 1991 a Presbyterian committee on human sexuality endorsed a sexual ethic of "justice-love" for sexual relationships, including heterosexual marriage and homosexual unions. Fellow churchgoers went ballistic. To suggest that heterosexual marriage was not the bastion of all that is good and sacred about sexuality was too radical a concept for most of the church. The committee's report pointed out that heterosexual marriage as a holy paradigm had clay feet, mentioning the subjugation of women in most marriages, the problems of marital rape and parent-child incest, as well as adultery. The study also clearly affirmed gays and lesbians and our relationships. During the assembly that rejected the report, some opponents seemed to be saying to gay people, "We'll give you ordination—just give us back marriage."

6   Resistance to calling same-sex unions marriages is beyond my understanding. In no way does it lessen the sacred or civil nature of marriage. Indeed, its value is bolstered by the recognition that both homosexuals and heterosexuals wish to enter into such a covenant. Commonly, both procreation and companionship are viewed as independent satisfactory goals of marriage. Gay and lesbian

couples enjoy companionship; some lesbians bear children; many lesbian and gay couples rear them.

It's true that the most ancient biblical sexual ethic is procreation-obsessed. 7 That's why the Bible accepts practices we now find unacceptable, such as polygamy, concubinage and required sexual intercourse with the childless wife of a dead brother. It is also true that Jesus, the source of Christianity, saw fidelity, not gender, as the central issue in marriage and redefined family as fellow believers rather than blood relatives. Until a few centuries ago in Western culture, marriage was primarily an economic institution that ensured inheritance rights, protected political arrangements and produced offspring. Only relatively recently did the ideal of romantic love supplant these reasons. That change redefined marriage far more dramatically than will the inclusion of same-gender couples under the rubric.

When my partner's and my relationship was blessed two years ago by our 8 Presbyterian church in Atlanta, I felt transformed by our exchange of vows before God and a supportive community of family, friends and church members. I felt even more tenderly toward my partner and I understood more profoundly the sacred nature of our commitment. But when the local newspaper ran a notice of our ceremony, other Presbyterians demanded that our pastor be reprimanded and our blessing "undone."

Another male couple attending the ceremony expressed regret that they had 9 never had such a ceremony. Less than two weeks later, one was killed in a traffic accident. Because most members of their congregation were unaware of the significance of their relationship, the surviving partner did not receive the support that might have otherwise been offered by fellow churchgoers.

Even as the position on anti-gay ordination goes to presbyteries for ratifica- 10 tion and the marriage bill is taken up by the Senate, I'm grateful to know that if something were to happen to me or my partner, our congregation, family and neighborhood would be there for us, caring for us in trouble, challenging us to keep faith in God and one another. I grieve that the same cannot be said of all congregations, families and communities throughout this land. ■

LET GAYS MARRY*

Andrew Sullivan

Andrew Sullivan is senior editor of The New Republic *and the author of* Virtually Normal: An Argument about Homosexuality. *William Bennett, in the essay following this one, answers Sullivan's claims.*

"A state cannot deem a class of persons a stranger to its laws," declared the 1 Supreme Court last week. It was a monumental statement. Gay men and lesbians, the conservative Court said, are no longer strangers in America. They are citizens,

Newsweek, June 3, 1996, p. 26.

entitled, like everyone else, to equal protection—no special rights, but simple equality.

2   For the first time in Supreme Court history, gay men and women were seen not as some powerful lobby trying to subvert America, but as the people we truly are—the sons and daughters of countless mothers and fathers, with all the weaknesses and strengths and hopes of everybody else. And what we seek is not some special place in America but merely to be a full and equal part of America, to give back to our society without being forced to lie or hide or live as second-class citizens.

3   That is why marriage is so central to our hopes. People ask us why we want the right to marry, but the answer is obvious. It's the same reason anyone wants the right to marry. At some point in our lives, some of us are lucky enough to meet the person we truly love. And we want to commit to that person in front of our family and country for the rest of our lives. It's the most simple, the most natural, the most human instinct in the world. How could anyone seek to oppose that?

4   Yes, at first blush, it seems like a radical proposal, but, when you think about it some more, it's actually the opposite. Throughout American history, to be sure, marriage has been between a man and a woman, and in many ways our society is built upon that institution. But none of that need change in the slightest. After all, no one is seeking to take away anybody's right to marry, and no one is seeking to force any church to change any doctrine in any way. Particular religious arguments against same-sex marriage are rightly debated within the churches and faiths themselves. That is not the issue here: there is a separation between church and state in this country. We are only asking that when the government gives out *civil* marriage licenses, those of us who are gay should be treated like anybody else.

5   Of course, some argue that marriage is *by definition* between a man and a woman. But for centuries, marriage was *by definition* a contract in which the wife was her husband's legal property. And we changed that. For centuries, marriage was *by definition* between two people of the same race. And we changed that. We changed these things because we recognized that human dignity is the same whether you are a man or a woman, black or white. And no one has any more of a choice to be gay than to be black or white or male or female.

6   Some say that marriage is only about raising children, but we let childless heterosexual couples be married (Bob and Elizabeth Dole, Pat and Shelley Buchanan, for instance). Why should gay couples be treated differently? Others fear that there is no logical difference between allowing same-sex marriage and sanctioning polygamy and other horrors. But the issue of whether to sanction multiple spouses (gay or straight) is completely separate from whether, in the existing institution between two unrelated adults, the government should discriminate between its citizens.

7   This is, in fact, if only Bill Bennett could see it, a deeply conservative cause. It seeks to change no one else's rights or marriages in any way. It seems merely to promote monogamy, fidelity and the disciplines of family life among people who have long been cast to the margins of society. And what could be a more conservative project than that? Why indeed would any conservative seek to oppose those very family values for gay people that he or she supports for everybody

else? Except, of course, to make gay men and lesbians strangers in their own country, to forbid them ever to come home. ■

LEAVE MARRIAGE ALONE*

William Bennett

William Bennett is the editor of The Book of Virtues *and a codirector of Empower America. This article is a response to the preceding one. Which argument do you find more compelling? Why?*

There are at least two key issues that divide proponents and opponents of same- 1 sex marriage. The first is whether legally recognizing same-sex unions would strengthen or weaken the institution. The second has to do with the basic understanding of marriage itself.

The advocates of same-sex marriage say that they seek to strengthen and cel- 2 ebrate marriage. That may be what some intend. But I am certain that it will not be the reality. Consider: the legal union of same-sex couples would shatter the conventional definition of marriage, change the rules which govern behavior, endorse practices which are completely antithetical to the tenets of all of the world's major religions, send conflicting signals about marriage and sexuality, particularly to the young, and obscure marriage's enormously consequential function—procreation and child-rearing.

Broadening the definition of marriage to include same-sex unions would 3 stretch it almost beyond recognition—and new attempts to expand the definition still further would surely follow. On what *principled* ground can Andrew Sullivan exclude others who most desperately want what he wants, legal recognition and social acceptance? Why on earth would Sullivan exclude from marriage a bisexual who wants to marry two other people? After all, exclusion would be a denial of that person's sexuality. The same holds true of a father and daughter who want to marry. Or two sisters. Or men who want (consensual) polygamous arrangements. Sullivan may think some of these arrangements are unwise. But having employed sexual relativism in his own defense, he has effectively lost the capacity to draw any lines and make moral distinctions.

Forsaking all others is an essential component of marriage. Obviously it is not 4 always honored in practice. But it is the ideal to which we rightly aspire, and in most marriages the ideal is in fact the norm. Many advocates of same-sex marriage simply do not share this ideal; promiscuity among homosexual males is well known. Sullivan himself has written that gay male relationships are served by the "openness of the contract" and that homosexuals should resist allowing their "varied and complicated lives" to be flattened into a "single, moralistic model." But that "single, moralistic model" has served society exceedingly well. The burden

*Newsweek, June 3, 1996, p. 27.

of proof ought to be on those who propose untested arrangements for our most important institution.

5   A second key difference I have with Sullivan goes to the very heart of marriage itself. I believe that marriage is not an arbitrary construct which can be redefined simply by those who lay claim to it. It is an honorable estate, instituted of God and built on moral, religious, sexual and human realities. Marriage is based on a natural teleology, on the different, complementary nature of men and women—and how they refine, support, encourage and complete one another. It is the institution through which we propagate, nurture, educate and sustain our species.

6   That we have to engage in this debate at all is an indication of how steep our moral slide has been. Worse, those who defend the traditional understanding of marriage are routinely referred to (though not to my knowledge by Sullivan) as "homophobes," "gay-bashers," "intolerant" and "bigoted." Can one defend an honorable, 4,000-year-old tradition and not be called these names?

7   This is a large, tolerant, diverse country. In America people are free to do as they wish, within broad parameters. It is also a country in sore need of shoring up some of its most crucial institutions: marriage and the family, schools, neighborhoods, communities. But marriage and family are the greatest of these. That is why they are elevated and revered. We should keep them so. ■

THE CHANGING FAMILY: BREAKING THE MOLD
OF A TRADITIONAL HOME*

Esther B. Fein

Esther B. Fein writes about two gay men who have adopted a child.

1 Diana Galligan, nearly 7, knows what adoption means. "It's when people who love you take care of you and become your parents," she says, quietly poised.

2   And she will tell you that in her case, those people are her "guys," her dad, John Galligan, and her pop, Richard Koonce.

3   At Tuckahoe Elementary School in Arlington, Va., Diana is one of many adopted children, although her fathers think she is the only one there who is being raised by openly gay parents. And even though Mr. Galligan and Mr. Koonce are far more concerned with helping their daughter learn to read and to express herself freely, they are acutely aware that families like theirs are a symbol of "the new American family."

4   "In previous generations, one of the most difficult notions for many gay men coming out was putting aside the idea of having a family," said Mr. Galligan, 39, who works for the United States Treasury Department.

New York Times, National Ed., October 25, 1998, p. 19.

Mr. Galligan said that he knew he wanted to be a father ever since he worked 5
as a college volunteer in a Big Brother program. Several years ago, Mr. Galligan,
said, although he had no partner at the time, he decided that "the time was right;
I wanted to be a father."

He was trying to figure out how to go about adopting, when a woman he 6
knew with two older children told him that she was pregnant and was willing to
have him adopt the baby. Their arrangement is open, and Diana visits her birth
mother every summer and calls her when she feels like it.

Although they have sensed disapproval and worse from strangers, Mr. Galligan 7
and Mr. Koonce said, they have never faced prejudice from neighbors or teachers.

But both men lamented that many religious and political institutions were
still hostile. Although Mr. Galligan adopted Diana, Mr. Koonce is legally only
Diana's guardian in case something happens to Mr. Galligan. He has yet to
formally adopt her, they said, because Virginia courts would not allow it.

Many states let single people adopt without their sexual orientation being an 8
issue. Some states allow one gay person to adopt, then later the other partner. But
about half the states do not allow a second parent of the same sex to adopt a child,
even later. And in Florida and New Hampshire, it is nearly impossible for gay
people to adopt at all.

Mr. Koonce and Mr. Galligan said that they thought such resistance to adop- 9
tions by gay people would eventually wither.

"Society is on the edge of creating a lot of new models for work, family 10
and community," said Mr. Koonce, 44, who owns his own career counseling
business. "I look at myself. I have a nontraditional model of work that's a far cry
from what my father did, working for the big company. I have what many people would consider a nontraditional family, although we see ourselves as very
conservative and mainstream. I walk Diana to school; John picks her up. On
Teacher Appreciation Day, there I was with all the moms, bringing a tossed
salad." ■

QUESTIONS TO HELP YOU THINK AND WRITE ABOUT FAMILY ISSUES

1. Why do you think the women in Professor Doloff's class were more enthusiastic about writing about their possible experiences as members of the opposite sex than the men in the class were? What would you write if you were
   given this assignment? What does your answer imply about the roles and
   responsibilities you expect of yourself and your family members either now
   or in the future?

2. Read the essays by Wolf and Henry together. Summarize the views of each of
   these authors on the subject of feminism. What do the views of each of these
   authors suggest about a woman's ideal role in a modern family? Compare and
   contrast what Wolf's "ideal wife" and what Henry's "ideal wife" might be.
   Now join this conversation yourself. Which of these authors best represents
   your views about contemporary women's roles in the family? Explain your
   answer.

3. The responsibilities associated with household chores and child care become issues for many families. Coltrane suggests that some changes in these areas are now taking place. What are they? What does he predict might happen to men who take more responsibility for the children and the chores? Do you find any evidence to support his conclusions in Adler's article, "Building a Better Dad"? What evidence does Adler present that Coltrane might be right? Evaluate these changes. Do you regard them as positive or negative? Why?

4. Adler in his article "A Matter of Faith" writes about a trend that is becoming more and more frequent in modern families. What is this trend? What special strengths might it create in families? What problems might it create? Which family members might be the most affected, and how? What is your opinion about this trend? Do you see it as positive, negative, or a mix? Explain your position.

5. Coontz makes the statement, "Most Americans support the emergence of alternative ways of organizing parenthood and marriage." As a class, make a list of all of the ways you can think of to organize a family. Then take a vote to see how many members of your class wholeheartedly support, support with reservations, or do not support each of the options. Which are the most popular family models in your class? Why? Which are your favorite models? Which did you reject? Give reasons for your choices.

6. What circumstances in her life have made single motherhood a joy for Carolyn Edy? What circumstances might make this experience less joyful for other single mothers? What can you conclude is probably necessary for child rearing to be both joyful and successful for everyone concerned?

7. Have the opinions of Glaser, Sullivan, and Bennett influenced your views about same-sex marriages? What were your views before you read these essays? What are your views now? If your views have changed, how have they changed?

8. Has the article by Fein influenced your views about gay couples adopting and raising children? What were your views before you read this essay? What are your views now? If your views have changed, how have they changed?

SECTION II

Issues in Education

THE ISSUES

A. What Should Schools Teach?

The enduring argument about what students should learn in school is addressed by three authors in this section. The essays by Gardner and Hirsch were originally published together and presented as "opposing approaches" to teaching students to read and think. The third author, Sollod, presents yet another opinion on what schools should teach. See also "Reading, Writing, Narcissism," page 180; "Theme for English B," page 395.

B. What Can Be Done to Improve Schools?

One of the most enduring questions related to schools is how to improve them. Three authors suggest ideas for improvement that include using indoctrination to improve student performance, forming "girls only" science classes, and eliminating bias in textbooks. What suggestions would you add to improve schools? See also "Don't Know Much about History," page 81; "Special Education's Best Intentions," page 360; "A Room of Their Own," page 108; and "Hold Your Horsepower," page 187.

C. What Are Some Problems with Grading and Evaluating Learning?

The articles here explore the issues associated with grading college assignments, using standardized tests to measure learning, and employing computer programs to evaluate student essays. See also "A Liberating Curriculum," page 146, and "What's Wrong with Standard Tests?" page 167.

To Extend Your Perspective: Films and Literature Related to Education

> *Films: Stand and Deliver,* 1987; *Back to School,* 1986
> *Literature:* poems: "The Student" by Marianne Moore; "Learning to Read" by Frances E. W. Harper; essay: "Education" by E. B. White; short story: "The Lesson" by Toni Cade Bambara; novels: *The Chosen* by Chaim Potok; *A Separate Peace* by John Knowles

THE RHETORICAL SITUATION

In classical times, Plato argued that students should not be allowed to read poetry because it appealed to emotion and warped the perception of truth. In the seventeenth century, Milton made a strong case for introducing writing instruction late in students' careers, after they had read widely and deeply on many subjects. What students should learn, when and under what conditions they should learn it, who should teach it, and how learning should be evaluated are enduring issues that continue to receive lively attention.

What college students should know and be able to do when they leave school and take their places as workers and citizens is at the heart of education issues. Successful education, in most people's minds, leads to successful lives and a successful society. What constitutes a successful life and a successful society provide some of the value warrants for this issue.

Some people argue that traditional public schools need radical reform, and they advance a variety of ideas for achieving reform, including the privatization of schools or the issuing of vouchers to allow students to select their own schools. Another idea is to broaden the traditional curriculum, which focuses mainly on the European cultural heritage, to include the study of minority and third-world cultures. Not all students are equally motivated to learn, so ideas are regularly proposed for boosting motivation. Some people argue that male and female students should be separated so they can learn more easily, that all students should have access to the Internet to improve their education, or that learning should be regularly evaluated not only with teacher-made tests but also with various types of standardized tests.

Because everyone in the United States is expected to attend school, there is a constant exigency for a wide variety of education issues. Only a few of them are represented here. They include some ideas about what schools should teach, some ways that schools can improve, and some problems with grading and other forms of evaluation. As a student yourself, you will undoubtedly be able to add your own related issues to this list.

A. What Should Schools Teach?

TOWARD GOOD THINKING ON ESSENTIAL QUESTIONS*

Howard Gardner

Howard Gardner teaches at Harvard University. His book The Disciplined Mind: What All Students Should Understand *argues that teaching students to think critically and analytically in various disciplines should be at the heart of education. What students actually read or study is of less importance.*

1 As one concerned with precollege education, I'm gratified by the attention paid to this topic over the last two decades. At the same time I have to signal my uneasiness that so much of the discussion centers on means: should we have charters, vouchers, teachers' unions, national tests, etc. I think it is essential that we step back, at least periodically, and ask about the ends or aims of education.

2   My own answer can be stated succinctly. A dozen or more years of education should yield students who can think well about the essential questions of human life: who are we, where do we come from, what's the world made of, what have humans achieved and what can we achieve, how does one lead a good life? Many people, institutions and experiences can contribute to formulating these questions

New York Times, September 11, 1999, pp. A15, A17.

and the answers. The distinct contribution of formal education is to equip students with the ways of thinking, the scholarly disciplines, that have been constructed over the years to allow individuals to think well and deeply about these questions and some viable answers.

In speaking of disciplines, I have something specific in mind. Disciplines did ₃ not always exist; they are human-created methods and structures for approaching long-standing puzzles. Historians evaluate documents and testimony to reconstruct plausible accounts of past events. Scientists generate hypotheses about how the world works, collect data relevant to those hypotheses, analyze the data objectively and then revise or endorse the original hypotheses or theories. The arts are also disciplines: they involve clear procedures for production (how does one write a fugue, stage a ballet, render a portrait) and for interpreting the productions of others. For those inclined to dismiss the disciplines, imagine a world without such mental furniture.

By a convenient pun, the attainment of disciplines requires discipline. This is ₄ because our natural, common-sense ways of making sense of the world are non- or even anti-disciplinary. Only through years of asking questions and following well-honed strategies can we replace common-sense accounts (e.g., human beings have always existed, a highly civilized nation would never engage in genocide, the best portraits are photographs) with more nuanced and grounded disciplinary accounts.

The disciplines are arguably the most important human inventions of the last ₅ two millenniums. Yet their importance tends to be obscured, especially in the rhetoric-filled discourse of education. Instead, we hear a lot about facts, skills, tests and subject matter. None of these terms should be dismissed, but they attain fresh significance when they are considered in a disciplinary context.

First, skills. I know no one who opposes the acquisition of basic skills: read- ₆ ing, writing, calculation. Indeed, one cannot even enter the disciplinary worlds unless one has mastered the three R's. Basic skills are the means for acquiring the disciplines, just as the disciplines (and ultimately interdisciplinary amalgams) provide the means for thinking well about important issues.

Next, facts. You cannot think well about a topic or question unless you have ₇ information, data, facts. However, that information should be acquired not for its own sake but as a means of finding a better answer to a consequential question. And facts can only be well used if they relate to one another in a meaningful way: otherwise, to use Alfred North Whitehead's term, they are simply "inert knowledge." Facts need the connective tissue of disciplines, or they are undisciplined, rote information.

Subject matter is typically collapsed with disciplines, but it is important to ₈ honor a distinction. One can have lots of facts in a subject without having any disciplinary understanding. Too often a person is considered a master because she or he has taken a certain number of courses, often called Carnegie units. A person understands to the extent that he or she can apply knowledge appropriately in a new situation. Only an individual in possession of disciplinary moves can do this.

9   Which brings us to tests, or assessments. There may be some who oppose assessments, but I am not in their ranks. Not in the least! At the same time, I reject as inadequate most of the short-answer instruments now being adopted at the state level. These instruments may probe factual or subject-matter knowledge, but they typically fall short of probing disciplinary mastery and understanding. In life no one presents us with four choices, the last of which reads "none of the above."

10   I favor instruments that actually determine whether a person can think in a disciplined way. And so rather than ask students to name nine Civil War battles, I would ask them to assess two historical accounts based on the same primary documents (or create their own). Rather than asking students to recall a chemical formula, I would provide them with data from an experiment and ask them to extract the regularities (and perhaps indicate which other data need to be collected next). Rather than asking students to memorize authors or lines from a poem, I would ask them to edit or complete an unfinished poem.

11   Every educational philosophy reflects a certain knowledge base and a certain value system. My educational regimen builds on findings from cognitive science. These findings indicate that, when young, individuals develop intuitive theories that are very powerful and difficult to eradicate. While some are on the mark, most are remote from the disciplines. Only a concerted effort over years to establish disciplinary ways of thinking can eradicate or educate the unschooled mind. My own belief is that this goal is best achieved by focusing in depth on certain important topics; not only does one come to understand those topics well, but in the process one gains incipient mastery for what it is like to use the methods of a discipline.

12   This incipient mastery can be built upon for the rest of one's life. Indeed, I am idealistic enough to believe that once individuals have genuinely understood a theory like evolution, a historical period like the Holocaust, a work of art like "The Marriage of Figaro," they will insist on commensurate understanding of other topics in the future.

13   Pursuing this line of reasoning, I find myself out of sympathy with a preordained canon. One can acquire disciplinary ways of thinking from a variety of topics, and it simply does not matter that much which ones happen to be used. It is more important, in my view, to use examples that are valued by the community and that come alive for students than to insist that everyone read the same play or master the same theorem or learn the same topics in science. I don't care that much if one can name the planets; one can always request that information from a Palm Pilot. I care mightily that half of the American population (and perhaps some of our recent Presidents) can't distinguish astronomical from astrological ways of thinking and that two-thirds of Americans don't see the disciplinary difference between evolutionary and creationist accounts of the origins of human beings.

14   In putting forth these views, I find myself at odds with much of the program put forth by E. D. Hirsch Jr. Perhaps it is possible to reconcile our work to some extent—for example, by emphasizing his "Core Knowledge" in early grades and my disciplinary focus for the later grades. I have admiration for his democratic vi-

sion, his belief in public education and his sponsoring of programs in our schools. Still, I think it is valuable to put forth these quite different educational visions: one focusing on questions and on ways of thinking, the other on factual answers and on shared knowledge. The value is in part epistemological, different views of the mind's use; in part cultural, different views of an educated society. ■

FINDING THE ANSWERS IN DRILLS AND RIGOR*

E. D. Hirsch Jr.

E. D. Hirsch Jr. teaches at the University of Virginia and is president of the Core Knowledge Foundation. In his books Cultural Literacy *and* The Schools We Need and Why We Don't Have Them, *Hirsch argues that schools should teach a common vocabulary and common facts, stories, and skills so that everyone will share the same body of knowledge. He favors drills and practice and a common core curriculum.*

The most interesting debate about American education concerns why the United 1 States has not fulfilled the egalitarian aims of schooling as well as other democracies have. The main cause of inequality in American schools, I have argued, has been the dominance of the progressive-education tradition, which has seriously misconceived itself as the guardian of social progress and democratic ideals.

In this regard, I hope Howard Gardner is right that my work poses a threat 2 to the assumptions of the progressivist tradition.

If we are lucky, the end of the 1990's will mark the end of spurious connections 3 between educational ideas and political affiliations.

During the last two decades, when Democrats have controlled a school board, 4 the district has tended to favor the whole-language method of teaching reading, to encourage the use of calculators for "math understanding" (instead of memorizing the multiplication table) and to disparage multiple-choice tests, all positions connected with progressive education but not logically with the platform of the Democratic Party.

By contrast, when a majority of school-board members have been Republi- 5 can, the district has tended to favor the explicit teaching of phonics, the memorization of the multiplication table and the use of standardized tests, positions properly associated with educational conservatism but not necessarily with political conservatism.

On the contrary, political conservatism, understood as the preservation of 6 the social status quo, is best achieved by progressive educational methods.

There have been recent signs that the politics of education is belatedly be- 7 coming more sophisticated. As long ago as the 1930's, Antonio Gramsci, a brilliant Communist opponent of Mussolini, denounced the new "progressive" ideas

*New York Times, September 11, 1999, pp. A15, A17.

that were being introduced into Italy from the United States. He argued that social justice required educational conservatism because only if the poor worked hard in school to accumulate the "intellectual baggage" of the rich could they earn money and wield the levers of power. Gramsci, the Communist, serving on a modern American school board, might surprise fellow board members by voting with Republicans.

8   So might James S. Coleman. Progressive methods failed disadvantaged students, he concluded after a decade of inquiries into the implications of his famous 1966 report, *Equality of Educational Opportunity.* What people remember about his 1966 report is that schools appear to count for little in determining educational achievement, whereas family background matters a great deal. This statistical fact upset many people, including Coleman, because it dashes the democratic hope of giving all students an equal chance by simply putting rich and poor together in the same common school. If the common school does not in fact reduce the advantages of wealth and privilege, then the premises of democratic education must be re-examined.

9   After the Coleman report, one had a choice of two positions: one could become an advocate of compensatory education to narrow the achievement gap between groups, or one could adopt the determinist view that the schools can do little to rectify the ills of the wider society. The deterministic position, which excuses the schools for failing to reduce the test-score gap between groups, is widely held in the American educational world. But after further research, Coleman adopted the compensatory position.

10   Published in the 80's, that research showed that most Roman Catholic schools were better at achieving equity than most public schools. Catholic schools followed a rich and demanding curriculum, required a lot of drill and practice, and expected every child to reach minimal goals in each subject during the year. As a result disadvantaged children prospered academically, as did their advantaged peers, and the schools narrowed the gap between races and social classes.

11   This deeper inquiry of Coleman's started a controversy almost as fierce as the one surrounding his 1966 report. It was seen as an attack on public schools, but, as Coleman unanswerably pointed out, his findings were not limited to Catholic schools; the very same democratic results were being achieved by the few public schools that defied progressivist doctrine. Consistent with that finding is the fact that recent improvements in equity have been achieved only by school reforms that use conservative methods like drill and practice (e.g., the Success for All program at Johns Hopkins) and a demanding curriculum (e.g., the "Core Knowledge" series of books).

12   After so many practical failures, few educational experts overtly label themselves progressivists, but one can detect de facto progressivists by certain distinctive traits. First, there is their belief that knowledge and skill will be gained incidentally from intensive study of a few subjects. This incidental method claims, against all evidence, to achieve greater depth, as if there were a simple trade-off between depth and breadth. A claim is made under various labels and slogans such as "the project method" and "less is more" that exposure to a few complex experiences will cause

understanding to occur naturally, an idea that first gained currency during the Romantic movement.

The persistent attractions of this "natural" method may possibly be explained by the vestigial Romanticism of American culture, but as Lisa Delpit observes in her book *Other People's Children*, the progressivist mode of teaching has consistently failed to benefit African-American children (and many advantaged children as well). 13

Another mark of progressivism (and another vestige of the Romantic movement) is its criticism of an "overemphasis" on language. Emerson said: "We are shut up in schools and college recitation rooms for 10 or 15 years and come out at last with a bellyful of words and do not know a thing." But as Ms. Delpit points out, these antiverbal ideas have done the most harm to the most disadvantaged students. Their greatest deficits are in vocabulary and the conventions of literate language; they make up math deficits much more readily than language deficits. 14

Keith Stanovich and his colleagues have shown that a score on a standardized reading test in first grade is the best predictor of 11th-grade academic achievement, a shocking indictment of present-day schools and a powerful illustration of the accuracy of standardized tests and of the centrality of verbal training for determining life chances. 15

Disparagement of objective tests is a third way to detect progressivists. Their hostility to tests is not surprising, given that progressive methods fail to improve test scores. Yet standardized reading tests are among the most valid and reliable assessments that exist and among the most important instruments for measuring excellence and fairness in education. To take a reading test, a student has to perform the very skill being assessed. These tests, even in their much-maligned multiple-choice forms, are highly correlated with each other and with real-world reading skills. 16

Competence in reading (that is in comprehension) is central to academic achievement and to participation in economic and political life. High school graduates who read well enough to get into top colleges know about 100,000 words, which means an average learning rate of more than 15 new words a day, an astonishing number attainable only by wide reading and by psychological mechanisms that are only beginning to be understood. 17

A broad vocabulary is an index to broad knowledge, and broad knowledge, extended over time, is the key to depth of knowledge and to a general ability to learn new things. 18

Since the late 60's it has been known that high literacy entails prior background knowledge over many different domains. Within a given literate culture, the most literacy-enhancing background knowledge can be identified and taught to all students. Theory predicts that teaching such a high-octane curriculum will raise everyone's reading and learning levels and narrow the achievement gap between social groups. This prediction has now been confirmed by independent researchers. 19

Teaching a curriculum that produces high literacy for all is a potent way of fostering the egalitarian goal of democratic education. But before we can advance toward that goal on a broad front, many progressivist ideas will have to be discarded. ■ 20

THE HOLLOW CURRICULUM*

Robert N. Sollod

Robert N. Sollod teaches psychology at Cleveland State University.

1 The past decade in academe has seen widespread controversy over curricular reform. We have explored many of the deeply rooted, core assumptions that have guided past decisions about which subjects should be emphasized in the curriculum and how they should be approached. Yet I have found myself repeatedly disappointed by the lack of significant discussion concerning the place of religion and spirituality in colleges' curricula and in the lives of educated persons.

2   I do not mean to suggest that universities should indoctrinate students with specific viewpoints or approaches to life; that is not their proper function. But American universities now largely ignore religion and spirituality, rather than considering what aspects of religious and spiritual teachings should enter the curriculum and how those subjects should be taught. The curricula that most undergraduates study do little to rectify the fact that many Americans are ignorant of religious and spiritual teachings, of their significance in the history of this and other civilizations, and of their significance in contemporary society. Omitting this major facet of human experience and thought contributes to a continuing shallowness and imbalance in much of university life today.

3   Let us take the current discussions of multiculturalism as one example. It is hardly arguable that an educated person should approach life with knowledge of several cultures or patterns of experience. Appreciation and understanding of human diversity are worthy educational ideals. Should such an appreciation exclude the religious and spiritually based concepts of reality that are the backbone upon which entire cultures have been based?

4   Multiculturalism that does not include appreciation of the deepest visions of reality reminds me of the travelogues that I saw in the cinema as a child—full of details of quaint and somewhat mysterious behavior that evoked some superficial empathy but no real, in-depth understanding. Implicit in a multicultural approach that ignores spiritual factors is a kind of critical and patronizing attitude. It assumes that we can understand and evaluate the experiences of other cultures without comprehension of their deepest beliefs.

5   Incomprehensibly, traditionalists who oppose adding multicultural content to the curriculum also ignore the religious and theological bases of the Western civilization that they seek to defend. Today's advocates of Western traditionalism focus, for the most part, on conveying a type of rationalism that is only a single strain in Western thought. Their approach does not demonstrate sufficient awareness of the contributions of Western religions and spirituality to philosophy and literature, to moral and legal codes, to the development of governmental and political institutions, and to the mores of our society.

**Chronicle of Higher Education,* March 18, 1992, p. A60.

Nor is the lack of attention to religion and spirituality new. I recall taking un- 6
dergraduate philosophy classes in the 1960's in which Plato and Socrates were
taught without reference to the fact that they were contemplative mystics who believed in immortality and reincarnation. Everything that I learned in my formal undergraduate education about Christianity came through studying a little Thomas
Aquinas in a philosophy course, and even there we focused more on the logical sequence of his arguments than on the fundamentals of the Christian doctrine that he
espoused.

I recall that Dostoyevsky was presented as an existentialist, with hardly a nod 7
given to the fervent Christian beliefs so clearly apparent in his writings. I even recall
my professors referring to their Christian colleagues, somewhat disparagingly, as
"Christers." I learned about mystical and spiritual interpretations of Shakespeare's
sonnets and plays many years after taking college English courses.

We can see the significance of omitting teaching about religion and spiritual- 8
ity in the discipline of psychology and, in particular, in my own field of clinical
psychology. I am a member of the Task Force on Religious Issues in Graduate Education and Training in Division 36 of the American Psychological Association, a
panel chaired by Edward Shafranske of Pepperdine University. In this work, I
have discovered that graduate programs generally do not require students to
learn anything about the role of religion in people's lives.

Almost no courses are available to teach psychologists how to deal with the 9
religious values or concerns expressed by their clients. Nor are such courses required or generally available at the undergraduate level for psychology majors.
Allusions to religion and spirituality often are completely missing in textbooks on
introductory psychology, personality theory, concepts of psychotherapy, and developmental psychology.

Recent attempts to add a multicultural perspective to clinical training almost 10
completely ignore the role of religion and spirituality as core elements of many
racial, ethnic, and national identities. Prayer is widely practiced, yet poorly understood and rarely studied by psychologists. When presented, religious ideas are
usually found in case histories of patients manifesting severe psychopathology.

Yet spiritual and mystical experiences are not unusual in our culture. And re- 11
search has shown that religion is an important factor in the lives of many Americans; some studies have suggested that a client's religious identification may affect the psychotherapeutic relationship, as well as the course and outcome of
therapy. Some patterns of religious commitment have been found to be associated
with high levels of mental health and ego strength. A small number of psychologists are beginning to actively challenge the field's inertia and indifference by researching and writing on topics related to religion and spirituality. Their efforts
have not as yet, however, markedly affected the climate or curricula in most psychology departments.

Is it any wonder that religion for the typical psychotherapist is a mysterious 12
and taboo topic? It should not be surprising that therapists are not equipped even
to ask the appropriate questions regarding a person's religious or spiritual life—
much less deal with psychological aspects of spiritual crises.

13   Or consider the field of political science. Our scholars and policy makers have been unable to predict or understand the major social and political movements that produced upheavals around the world during the last decade. That is at least partly because many significant events—the remarkable rise of Islamic fundamentalism, the victory of Afghanistan over the Soviet Union, the unanticipated velvet revolutions in Eastern Europe and in the Soviet Union, and the continuing conflicts in Cyprus, Israel, Lebanon, Northern Ireland, Pakistan, Sri Lanka, Tibet, and Yugoslavia—can hardly be appreciated without a deep understanding of the religious views of those involved. The tender wisdom of our contemporary political scientists cannot seem to comprehend the deep spirituality inherent in many of today's important social movements.

14   Far from being an anachronism, religious conviction has proved to be a more potent contemporary force than most, if not all, secular ideologies. Too often, however, people with strong religious sentiments are simply dismissed as "zealots" or "fanatics"—whether they be Jewish settlers on the West Bank, Iranian demonstrators, Russian Baptists, Shiite leaders, anti-abortion activists, or evangelical Christians.

15   Most sadly, the continuing neglect of spirituality and religion by colleges and universities also results in a kind of segregation of the life of the spirit from the life of the mind in American culture. This situation is far from the ideals of Thoreau, Emerson, or William James. Spirituality in our society too often represents a retreat from the world of intellectual discourse, and spiritual pursuits are often cloaked in a reflexive anti-intellectualism, which mirrors the view in academe of spirituality as an irrational cultural residue. Students with spiritual interests and concerns learn that the university will not validate or feed their interests. They learn either to suppress their spiritual life or to split their spiritual life apart from their formal education.

16   Much has been written about the loss of ethics, a sense of decency, moderation, and fair play in American society. I would submit that much of this loss is a result of the increasing ignorance, in circles of presumably educated people, of religious and spiritual world views. It is difficult to imagine, for example, how ethical issues can be intelligently approached and discussed or how wise ethical decisions can be reached without either knowledge or reference to those religious and spiritual principles that underlie our legal system and moral codes.

17   Our colleges and universities should reclaim one of their earliest purposes—to educate and inform students concerning the spiritual and religious underpinnings of thought and society. To the extent that such education is lacking, our colleges and universities are presenting a narrow and fragmented view of human experience.

18   Both core curricula and more advanced courses in the humanities and social sciences should be evaluated for their coverage of religious topics. Active leadership at the university, college, and departmental levels is needed to encourage and carry out needed additions and changes in course content. Campus organizations should develop forums and committees to examine the issue, exchange information, and develop specific proposals.

19   National debate and discussion about the best way to educate students concerning religion and spirituality are long overdue. ■

B.   What Can Be Done to Improve Schools?

BACK TO BASICS IN THE BRONX*

David Grann

David Grann writes about some unusual methods for motivating students that he claims are working. What do you think of these methods? Should they be more widely employed?

"Pow! Pow!" says one of the kids, his finger pointed like a pistol at another boy's 1 head. "You're a dead motherfucker, you hear me?" The other kid falls back a step as if he had actually been shot; then, ready to strike back the old-fashioned way, he makes a fist. While other students look on, eager for something, anything, to happen, a security guard steps between the two combatants. "Get outta here," he shouts. "Go home." The boys stare at each other in the squalid heat—their baseball caps flipped backward, their hands coiled like springs—and then slowly disperse in the direction of the Andrew Jackson housing projects across the street. It is three o'clock in the afternoon, and the first day of classes at I.S. 151, a middle school in the heart of the South Bronx and one of the lowest-performing schools in the district, is officially over. But, as the kids race through the open metal gates into the streets, another commotion, even louder, erupts on the fourth floor of the school building. "What room is this?" someone shouts. Suddenly two dozen voices cry out in unison:

> This is the room
> That has the kids
> Who want to learn
> To read more books!

A train rattles by outside the window. The teacher, a tall black man with 2 thick arms and legs, asks, "Is KIPP in the house?" and the students begin to pound their feet against the floor, chanting over the clacking rails:

> No need to hope
> For a good-paying job
> With your first-grade skills
> You'll do nothing but rob
> You got to read, baby, read!
> You got to read, baby, read!

As the cries filter out the window, there seems to be something slightly un- 3 natural about them, as if they were coming from one of those TV ads for literacy the networks play during Saturday morning cartoons. But the sounds of the KIPP school are so familiar by now that few passersby even seem to notice them. Set in one of the city's worst neighborhoods, and in the same building as I.S. 151, the

New Republic, October 4, 1999, pp. 24–26.

Knowledge Is Power Program has become an educational oasis, a public school that is defiantly and mysteriously working. Founded by two recent Ivy League graduates in conjunction with a similar program in the barrios of Houston, Texas, the Bronx school, as well as its Texas counterpart, has produced such high success rates that other educators have suspected both schools—despite having absolutely no evidence—of somehow manipulating their statistics. At KIPP Academy in Texas, where nine out of ten students are Hispanic and need assistance for school lunches, only about one-third of the students who enrolled could pass the state's reading and math tests; after only a year in the program, more than 91 percent passed.

4   In the Bronx, the results have been just as miraculous. In two years, reading scores have jumped by 54 percent. More than 70 percent of the students are now scoring above the national average in math, making the KIPP Academy the highest-performing public middle school in the Bronx for the second year in a row. What's more, it has remained—in contrast to the KIPP Academy in Texas, which recently became an open-enrollment charter school—part of the public school system.

5   David Levin launched the original KIPP in 1994 with his friend Michael Feinberg, after they had spent two years as elementary school instructors in the nationwide program Teach for America. It started as a special college-prep program for fifth-graders within the Garcia Elementary School in Houston, initially open to anyone in the school and eventually to anyone within the district. In the first year, 45 students signed up. But school officials were less enthusiastic, and the program was forced to hopscotch from building to building in search of a permanent home. Even during this struggle, Levin decided to expand to New York City. He lobbied the New York authorities, insisting that he could do what most critics said he couldn't: build a successful middle school from scratch in the heart of the Bronx. In 1995, after much resistance, the Board of Education relented and gave him space, but ended up paying only for the faculty, leaving Levin to raise money for almost everything else—textbooks, music equipment, even phone services.

6   As word of KIPP's success has spread, academics from Argentina to Japan have descended upon it, trying to uncover its secrets. President Clinton recently invited the 29-year-old Levin to the White House. A crew from *60 Minutes* has visited, gathering data for an upcoming broadcast. When I arrive one morning, two journalists from Sweden are roaming the corridors with their microphones. "We could learn from this" in Stockholm, one of them tells me.

7   The roughly 240 students in grades five through eight are quietly filing into their classrooms, which are named after universities. "UCLA will always meet over here," says Levin. "NYU over here." The students are dressed in bright yellow shirts that read "Knowledge Is Power" on the front and on the back list "The Laws of Success": "self-confidence," "a definite chief aim," "self-control." In the main hallway, students first pass a giant replica of the contract they signed vowing to attend school some 67 percent more than the average student, including on Saturdays and during summers, and then other signs motivating them to a higher order: "Excuses are for losers!" "There are no shortcuts!"

Between classes, the students are required to stand in neat rows, backs ramrod 8 straight and mouths closed, and march along the black lines that bisect the corridors. Everything is monitored, from diction to dress. The boys are not allowed to wear baseball hats, stocking caps, or "do-rags." The girls can't wear makeup or artificial nails. Beepers and cell phones are not permitted. No baggy pants or hoop earrings, either—because, as Rachel Ademola, an eighth grader, tells me, "they may give you an attitude, and if you have the wrong attitude then you might not get a job."

In contrast to the national trend toward multiculturalism, there is a conscious 9 effort at KIPP to transform the students' culture into that of the mainstream. While I sit in on a music class, one of the girls begins to raise her voice in anger at the teacher, her arms folded and her chin cocked to the ceiling. "You're going ghetto on me," the teacher shoots back. "Don't start going ghetto on me."

At KIPP, teachers are willing to do something other schools are increasingly 10 afraid to do: teach morality and decorum. "Everything we do is about building character skills," says Fred Shannon, a 30-year veteran of the New York public school system who now selects and trains staff for KIPP. In music class, when one of the girls sits with her legs spread apart, the teacher assumes a parental role. "When you have a short skirt on," he says, "you must sit a certain way." He instructs the female students on how to keep their skirts from "riding up" and their legs together. If a girl sees her classmate sitting the wrong way, he says, she should quietly inform the person, and, if a boy notices, he should politely tell another girl to say something. "We must all learn to act like ladies and gentlemen," he says.

This KIPP culture is maintained the old-fashioned way, through after-school 11 detention, suspension, and even, on rare occasions, expulsion. (In Houston, miscreants must sit on "the porch" while other students walk past them all day.) The teachers, however, rely less on force than on a kind of reverse peer pressure. When one student misbehaves in class, all the students must stand, leave the room, and reenter in silence. If one student talks on the stairwell, the whole class has to walk back down the four flights and up again.

Along with these punishments, the school offers the students elaborate in- 12 centives to behave—to act like "KIPPsters." Every week, the students receive points based on their performance and conduct. These are calculated on forms that resemble actual paychecks, which the students and their parents must endorse on the back. The students can then use these "checks" to purchase materials at the school store, including books, T-shirts, even computers. In short, they are paid to study—a fact that many critics consider crass at best and unethical at worst. "You want to inspire them to do better, but you also need to be pragmatic," says Marina Bernard, a slender Haitian-American who is one of the school's original teachers.

While the school uses the "paycheck" system to teach youths to earn re- 13 wards and manage their money, it also serves as an introduction to the working world. Every Friday, even the ten-year-olds dress like corporate executives, in suits and ties or full-length skirts, their long cornrows often tucked under their blazer collars, their braids pulled into buns. "The rest of the world goes casual," says Levin. "We go professional."

14 The results of this unabashed indoctrination are evident at noon each day, when the students from the KIPP Academy and from I.S. 151 flow into the same cafeteria. On the left side of the room, the I.S. 151 students swarm around the tables, screaming and yelling, their baseball caps turned backward, their high-tops unlaced, while a man with a bullhorn walks back and forth, futilely squawking at them. On the right side, the KIPP students—many of them the recipients of glares from the other side of the room—sit neatly across from each other, their shirts emblazoned with "The Laws of Success," their voices hushed. When a teacher wants their attention, he simply claps his hands once and everyone falls silent.

15 It is this controlled environment, the KIPP instructors say, that allows them to do what is most important: teach. "This removes all the nonsense" that distracts from the classroom, says Shannon. And, in an age of radical new theories of how to teach children, the KIPP curriculum is a return to the "three Rs": reading, writing, and arithmetic. "There is nothing fancy," Shannon says.

16 Instead, the creativity lies in the lesson plans, which are carefully constructed to keep students engaged from 7:25 A.M. until 5 P.M. In math, the students yell out "Oohahh!" after solving a problem, then clap their hands and chant, "Piece of cake, piece of cake." They learn the multiplication tables as raps. In English, they read *Willie Wonka and the Chocolate Factory* and then create their own fantasy factory with hand-wrapped candy bars.

17 Despite all this remarkable stuff, there's something oddly mundane about the school. Rather than by a secret formula, it is governed by the same forces that govern most professions: discipline, accountability, high standards. Which raises the question: Can KIPP work elsewhere? Doubters say that the school maintains an unfair advantage in resources. In fact, though Levin raises private funds, the school's overall budget remains comparable to that of other schools in the city— only it's spent more creatively. Still other doubters say that the school is somehow "skimming"—getting the best students. There is some truth to this. Because parents choose to send their kids to KIPP and sign a contract stating that they agree to the rigorous hours, the students are more likely to come from families with at least a vague commitment to education. Yet applicants for the fifth grade are accepted on a first-come, first-served basis and seem to reflect the neighborhood.

18 One day after classes, I bump into a wiry kid from the Andrew Jackson housing projects who tells me that his mother has just gotten out of jail and that his father died before he was born. He has already been suspended from the KIPP school four times, he says, for "acting crazy." His pants hang down off his hips as he retreats back into the projects, where, he told me, he recently found an automatic hidden in the grass. Across the street, his friends are listening to music and shooting baskets in the dusk, and he looks toward them as if unsure whether to join in. Then, all of a sudden, Levin appears in the distance and begins to yell at him. "If you want to be famous and talk to reporters," Levin shouts, "you better make sure you wear a belt tomorrow." The boy stops and stares at him for a long moment. He seems to be thinking of something else—maybe the gun, or maybe his mother, or maybe simply his friends playing ball. Then, in an instant, he smiles, turns, and heads straight home. ■

SCIENCE FOR GIRLS ONLY*

Patricia A. King

Patricia A. King suggests that female students be segregated from male students to help them learn better. Do you think such segregation would help some students learn?

The subject of the day is electrical circuits, and the sixth graders are tinkering intently 1 with wires and batteries. But the real subjects of this experiment are the students themselves, a pioneer class of 35 who have enrolled since last September in the new Girls' Middle School in Mountain View, Calif., the heart of Silicon Valley. They're having a little trouble with defective batteries and miswiring, but they're not fazed. Earlier in the year they built suspension bridges out of Popsicle sticks and arch bridges out of Styrofoam, so they're not about to be bested by some stupid loose connection. They are intent on understanding how Christmas lights work—why some blow out singly and why some blow out a whole string at a time—and how to repair them. "Then," notes Aliya Lakha, 12, "we won't have to ask men to fix it."

Making girls electrically independent on Christmas Eve is only a microcosm 2 of the school's mission. The teachers (including a Stanford-trained structural engineer) and the curriculum (where 40 percent of class time is devoted to science, technology and math) were both chosen to make the girls as comfortable in technical subjects as they are in writing and history, says founder Kathleen Bennett, a former teacher and technical writer for Apple. The math, science and tech courses emphasize hands-on learning and working in groups, both of which promote girls' interest and learning. (The program also includes language arts, Spanish, fine arts and performing arts.) The first class—chosen by an admissions committee from 80 applicants—is not all science whizzes; their career ambitions range from computer engineer to horse trainer to teacher to lawyer.

You'd think that Silicon Valley would be the last place where girls would need 3 to be sold on science. Not so. Even here, says Bennett, girls "hit the wall of femininity," when the formerly feisty and intellectually daring become afraid to stand out. As a result, far fewer girls than boys enroll in high-level math and science classes, particularly physical science, found a 1992 report [titled] "How Schools Shortchange Girls," by the American Association of University Women. The failure of those teachers to give girls as much attention and computer time as boys seemed to be part of the reason, as was peer pressure on girls to hide their brains and zip their lips. Although the gender gap has closed some, the AAUW concluded this year that "girls' failure to take more top math and science courses . . . threatens to make women bystanders in the burgeoning technology industry of the 21st century."

Not our girls, they said in the Valley. The warning that girls are getting the 4 short end of the mouse has attracted to GMS an all-star advisory council that includes CEOs Carol Bartz of Autodesk and Trip Hawkins of 3DO. It has also at-

*Newsweek, June 21, 1999, pp. 64–65.

tracted $2.5 million for start-up costs. Venture capitalist Dan Lynch was first in line with a $100,000 gift. His daughter, now 29, quit science when middle-school peer pressure kicked in, he says; he fears his 9-year-old (who for now is "interested in absolutely everything like squashing bugs and seeing what they bleed") will make the same mistake. "Girls are still afraid not to be cool," especially in front of boys, Lynch says. Other parents agree: nationwide enrollment in girls' schools has gone up 20 percent in the last eight years.

5   All-girl classes can be especially helpful in middle school, a transition period when conflicting messages about femininity and achievement, and the need to fit in, often erode girls' self-image. But at the $10,000-per-year GMS, which will expand to eighth grade in 2000, girls get all the teachers' attention and all the leadership roles. Sixth grader Divya Dujari, 11, who wants to be the CEO of a computer company, raves about the help she gets from teachers and the chance to do cool projects. Kris Bobier says her daughter Audrey has been sold on GMS ever since the open house, when she built a tower of cards. But there was an even stronger draw. "We were losing her," says Bobier. "She was shutting down to school. She really is a free spirit. This school gives her room for that." As for Audrey, she's so delighted with her boy-free school that she's hoping to remain at a girls' school until college.

6   Critics argue that a single-sex environment gives girls a false idea of what they'll face in the real world. Also, studies of girls' schools have produced conflicting results, with some suggesting that it is small classes, innovative curricula and great teaching that really help. But even if no one has figured out a sure-fire way to hook girls on science and tech, GMS probably has a better shot than most. After all, if they can't do it in Silicon Valley, where can they? ■

WHAT SHOULD BE DONE ABOUT BIAS IN OUR CHILDREN'S TEXTBOOKS?*

Paul C. Vitz

This excerpt from a book published in 1986 will seem relevant to many individuals today. Identify the value warrants in this selection.

1 Studies make it abundantly clear that public school textbooks commonly exclude the history, heritage, beliefs, and values of millions of Americans. Those who believe in the traditional family are not represented. Those who believe in free enterprise are not represented. Those whose politics are conservative are almost unrepresented. Above all, those who are committed to their religious tradition—at the very least as an important part of the historical record—are not represented.

2   Even those who uphold the classic or republican virtues of discipline, public duty, hard work, patriotism, and concern for others are scarcely represented. Indeed, the world of these virtues long advocated by believers, as well as by deists

*Paul C. Vitz, *Censorship: Evidence of Bias in Our Children's Textbooks* (Ann Arbor, Mich.: Servant Books, 1986), pp. 77–81.

and skeptics such as Thomas Paine, Benjamin Franklin, and Thomas Jefferson, is not found here. Even what one might call the "noble pagan" has ample reason to reject these inadequate and sentimentalized books which seem to be about an equal mixture of pap and propaganda.

Over and over, we have seen that liberal and secular bias is primarily accomplished by exclusion, by leaving out the opposing position. Such a bias is much harder to observe than a positive vilification or direct criticism, but it is the essence of censorship. It is effective not only because it is hard to observe—it isn't *there*— and therefore hard to counteract, but also because it makes only the liberal, secular positions familiar and plausible. As a result, the millions of Americans who hold conservative, traditional, and religious positions are made to appear irrelevant, strange, on the fringe, old-fashioned, reactionary. For these countless Americans it is now surely clear that the textbooks used in the public schools threaten the continued existence of their positions. 3

A natural question to raise is: how could this textbook bias have happened? What brought it about? Some have suggested that religion is downplayed because of concern over maintaining the separation of church and state. This concern seems either unlikely or a rationalization of an underlying distaste for religion. After all, to identify the historical or contemporary importance of religion is to respect the facts; it is not to advocate religion. To teach *about* religion is not to teach religion. 4

Furthermore, the rejection of religion in these books is part of a very general rejection of the entire conservative spectrum of American life. Recall that these books omit marriage and the traditional family, along with traditional sex roles, patriotism, and free enterprise. In short, the bias in these books is not accidental; much of it is certainly not the result of some misunderstanding about separating church and state. 5

Another possible answer is that the publishers of these books have attempted to avoid controversial subjects. According to this theory, the books have been written in a style which will avoid offending anyone. In fact, some publishers do give guidelines to authors on what kinds of people and issues to avoid. But the evidence of this study makes clear that a desire to avoid offense and controversy *cannot* explain much of the bias observed here. [. . .] Consider the profeminist position found in several social studies texts and throughout the basal readers for grades 3 and 6. That feminism is controversial cannot be seriously denied, even by feminists. And consider that positive representations of traditional feminine role models are obviously absent from these books. The regular pro coverage of environmental issues also makes clear that the only people and topics which are avoided in these books are those on the political right, those that are "controversial" to a liberal frame of mind. 6

One explanation of the antireligious bias in these books is that religion is so especially controversial that publishers want to avoid the subject. Curiously, the religions that do get some mention, e.g., Catholicism, Judaism, and Islam, are hardly uncontroversial. (In any case, why religion is supposedly more controversial than race, ethnic identity, feminism, or politics remains to be explained.) 7

The real issue is how a book handles religion. For example, magazines like the *Reader's Digest* and others often have articles about the positive accomplishments of people of different religious denominations. Such articles celebrating the different 8 religions and their contributions to this country are uncontroversial, well received, and appear to help sales. Yet, such a positive treatment of America's religious life is without any example in the ninety books evaluated in this entire study.

9 Religious concepts and vocabulary are certainly censored in these textbooks. A most revealing example of this censorship was recently published in the article "Censoring the Sources" by Barbara Cohen.[1] The issue centered on a children's story of hers called "Molly's Pilgrim." The story has an important Jewish religious theme; it focuses on the Jewish harvest holiday of Sukkos, a holiday that influenced the Pilgrims in initiating Thanksgiving. A major textbook publisher (Harcourt Brace Jovanovich) wanted to reprint part of the story for [a] third grade reader. But like most such stories, the publishers wanted to shorten it greatly and to rewrite parts to make it more acceptable. They phoned Ms. Cohen and asked her for permission to reprint their modified version. But her story wasn't just modified, it was maimed. "All mention of Jews, Sukkos, God, and the Bible"[2] had been removed. So Barbara Cohen refused to give them permission. They called back dismayed and tried to convince her to let them go ahead with the heavily censored version. They argued, "Try to understand. We have a lot of problems. If we mention God, some atheist will object. If we mention the Bible, someone will want to know why we don't give equal time to the Koran. Every time that happens, we lose sales."[3] "But the Pilgrims did read the Bible," Barbara Cohen answered.[4] Yes, you know that and we know that, but we can't have anything in it that people object to, was the reply!

10 After more debate and give and take, a compromise was reached. The publisher allowed a reference to worship and the Jewish harvest holiday of Sukkos to stay in. But God and the Bible were "eternally unacceptable"[5] and they had to go. The publisher claimed, "We'd get into terrible trouble if we mentioned the Bible."[6]

11 This true but incredible story ends with Barbara Cohen stating: "Censorship in this country is widespread, subtle, and surprising. It is not inflicted on us by the government. It doesn't need to be. We inflict it on ourselves."[7] At the very least, the publishers should hear from the millions of Christians and Jews that if God and the Bible are left out, the publishers will also lose sales. And, God willing, lots more sales will be lost than when publishers leave God and the Bible in. The schools and the publishers must learn that what is left out of a textbook can be just as offensive as what is let in.

12 Of course, the central issue hinges on the *facts* of America's past and present. And the facts are clear: religion, especially Christianity, has played and continues to play a central role in American life. To neglect to report this is simply to fail to carry out the major duty of any textbook writer—the duty to tell the truth.

13 To explain the liberal and secular prejudice of the texts, some have proposed that a deliberate, large-scale conspiracy is involved. I doubt very much, however, that this is the case. The number of people writing, editing, publishing, selecting, and using these books is far too large and varied for this explanation to be plausible. Instead, the bias is, I believe, the consequence of the widespread, dominant, secular worldview found throughout the upper levels of the field of education,[8] especially among those who control the schools of education, the publishers, the federal and state education bureaucracies, and the National Education Association.

But, whatever the source of the bias, it certainly exists. Thus, the question is "What should be done?" Let us consider the major possibilities.

One possibility [. . .] is as follows. In this possible future the public school 14 leadership acknowledges that the majority of America's parents are religious in their sympathies and generally conservative in their moral and social life. Recognizing this, educators move clearly and positively back into the mainstream of American life. Religion is given a positive and realistic portrayal in textbooks and other curriculum. The traditional family and moral values are recognized and integrated into the school programs. Finally, the new emphasis on character education continues to grow and become widely influential.

The result of making these changes is a revival of confidence in the public 15 schools and increased community support. As a result, many religious Americans return their children to the public schools. Meanwhile more secular Yuppy parents note the increased morale of teachers and students and they also return to active public school support. After all, the private schools favored by many of the young upwardly mobile professionals are quite expensive. Revitalized public schools would be welcomed by many of them. In short, in this scenario the public schools are positively transformed and gain a new long lease on life. ■

NOTES

1. Barbara Cohen, "Censoring the Sources," *School Library Journal,* March 1986.
2. Cohen, 97.
3. Cohen, 98.
4. Cohen.
5. Cohen, 99.
6. Cohen.
7. Cohen.
8. This is also the opinion of Mel and Norma Gabler in *What Are They Teaching Our Children?* (Wheaton, IL: SP Publications, 1985).

C. What Are Some Problems with Grading and Evaluating Learning?

MAKING THE GRADE*

Kurt Wiesenfeld

Kurt Wiesenfeld is a physicist who teaches at Georgia Tech in Atlanta.

It was a rookie error. After 10 years I should have known better, but I went to my of- 1 fice the day after final grades were posted. There was a tentative knock on the door.

Newsweek, June 17, 1996, p. 16.

"Professor Wiesenfeld? I took your Physics 2121 class? I flunked it? I wonder if there's anything I can do to improve my grade?" I thought: "Why are you asking me? Isn't it too late to worry about it? Do you dislike making declarative statements?"

2   After the student gave his tale of woe and left, the phone rang. "I got a D in your class. Is there any way you can change it to 'Incomplete'?" Then the e-mail assault began: "I'm shy about coming in to talk to you, but I'm not shy about asking for a better grade. Anyway, it's worth a try." The next day I had three phone messages from students asking *me* to call *them*. I didn't.

3   Time was, when you received a grade, that was it. You might groan and moan, but you accepted it as the outcome of your efforts or lack thereof (and, yes, sometimes a tough grader). In the last few years, however, some students have developed a disgruntled-consumer approach. If they don't like their grade, they go to the "return" counter to trade it in for something better.

4   What alarms me is their indifference toward grades as an indication of personal effort and performance. Many, when pressed about why they think they deserve a better grade, admit they don't deserve one but would like one anyway. Having been raised on gold stars for effort and smiley faces for self-esteem, they've learned that they can get by without hard work and real talent if they can talk the professor into giving them a break. This attitude is beyond cynicism. There's a weird innocence to the assumption that one expects (even deserves) a better grade simply by begging for it. With that outlook, I guess I shouldn't be as flabbergasted as I was that 12 students asked me to change their grades *after* final grades were posted.

5   That's 10 percent of my class who let three months of midterms, quizzes and lab reports slide until long past remedy. My graduate student calls it hyperrational thinking: if effort and intelligence don't matter, why should deadlines? What matters is getting a better grade through an unearned bonus, the academic equivalent of a freebie T-shirt or toaster giveaway. Rewards are disconnected from the quality of one's work. An act and its consequences are unrelated, random events.

6   Their arguments for wheedling better grades often ignore academic performance. Perhaps they feel it's not relevant. "If my grade isn't raised to a D, I'll lose my scholarship." "If you don't give me a C, I'll flunk out." One sincerely overwrought student pleaded, "If I don't pass, my life is over." This is tough stuff to deal with. Apparently, I'm responsible for someone's losing a scholarship, flunking out or deciding whether life has meaning. Perhaps these students see me as a commodities broker with something they want—a grade. Though intrinsically worthless, grades, if properly manipulated, can be traded for what has value: a degree, which means a job, which means money. The one thing college actually offers—a chance to learn—is considered irrelevant, even less than worthless, because of the long hours and hard work required.

7   In a society saturated with surface values, love of knowledge for its own sake does sound eccentric. The benefits of fame and wealth are more obvious. So is it right to blame students for reflecting the superficial values saturating our society?

8   Yes, of course it's right. These guys had better take themselves seriously now, because our country will be forced to take them seriously later, when the stakes are much higher. They must recognize that their attitude is not only self-destructive, but

socially destructive The erosion of quality control—giving appropriate grades for actual accomplishments—is a major concern in my department. One colleague noted that a physics major could obtain a degree without ever answering a written exam question completely. How? By pulling in enough partial credit and extra credit. And by getting breaks on grades.

But what happens once she or he graduates and gets a job? That's when the 9 misfortunes of eroding academic standards multiply. We lament that schoolchildren get "kicked upstairs" until they graduate from high school despite being illiterate and mathematically inept, but we seem unconcerned with college graduates whose less blatant deficiencies are far more harmful if their accreditation exceeds their qualifications.

Most of my students are science and engineering majors. If they're good at 10 getting partial credit but not at getting the answer right, then the new bridge breaks or the new drug doesn't work. One finds examples here in Atlanta. Last year a light tower in the Olympic Stadium collapsed, killing a worker. It collapsed because an engineer miscalculated how much weight it could hold. A new 12-story dormitory could develop dangerous cracks due to a foundation that's uneven by more than six inches. The error resulted from incorrect data being fed into a computer. I drive past that dorm daily on my way to work, wondering if a foundation crushed under kilotons of weight is repairable or if this structure will have to be demolished. Two 10,000-pound steel beams at the new natatorium collapsed in March, crashing into the student athletic complex. (Should we give partial credit since no one was hurt?) Those are real-world consequences of errors and lack of expertise.

But the lesson is lost on the grade-grousing 10 percent. Say that you won't 11 (not can't, but won't) change the grade they deserve to what they want, and they're frequently bewildered or angry. They don't think it's fair that they're judged according to their performance, not their desires or "potential." They don't think it's fair that they should jeopardize their scholarships or be in danger of flunking out simply because they could not or did not do their work. But it's more than fair; it's necessary to help preserve a minimum standard of quality that our society needs to maintain safety and integrity. I don't know if the 13th-hour students will learn that lesson, but I've learned mine. From now on, after final grades are posted, I'll lie low until the next quarter starts. ■

WHERE'S THE MERIT IN THE S.A.T.?*

Eugene E. Garcia

Eugene E. Garcia is the dean of the Graduate School of Education at the University of California at Berkeley.

I recently suggested to the University of California Regents that the Scholastic As- 1 sessment Test's role in admissions be diminished. The response has astonished me.

*New York Times, December 26, 1997, p. A17.

2   Parents and students have chimed in with support and stories of their travails with the test. But national and local commentators acted as if I had tried to crush the Holy Grail. The College Board, the S.A.T.'s administrator, warned that such a policy would usher in lower academic standards. Others argued that we were trying to circumvent California's ban on affirmative action.

3   Our modest proposal, the product of a university task force on Hispanic student eligibility, is not about lowering standards. It's about insuring that all high-achieving students get a fair chance at the opportunity of a good college education. To do this, we must revisit how we define and measure academic merit.

4   The use of the S.A.T. in college admissions and the implementation of affirmative action advanced on parallel tracks in the 1960's and 1970's. The reliance on affirmative action to redress past inequities hid the damaging effects of overrelying on the S.A.T., a tool created for admissions officers inundated with applications from the baby boom generation.

5   The University of California adopted the S.A.T. in 1968. By 1979, the test had evolved into a vaulting pole that could benefit ostensibly bright students with poorer grades. By the mid-1980's, the university was placing equal weight on S.A.T. scores and grade point averages.

6   The university assembled my task force to research the causes of its poor record in attracting Latino students. We found that the percentage of Latino and African-American high school graduates in California eligible for admission would double if the S.A.T.'s were eliminated. These students meet all the other prescribed standards—for instance, a minimum 3.3 G.P.A. in certain required courses.

7   Any measure of merit should consider the circumstances in which students are schooled. Isn't a migrant worker's child who has excelled in academics, shown leadership ability and performed community service as meritorious as a prep-school graduate with a similar G.P.A. but no evidence of leadership? Now, what if the migrant student's S.A.T. is 100 points below that of the prep-school student, whose parents probably sent him to an expensive S.A.T. course? The prep school may grade more rigorously, but relying on the S.A.T. to account for grading differences ignores the obstacles the migrant student had to overcome to shine at a poorer school.

8   The S.A.T.'s ability to predict success in college is questionable. At best, the scores are 25 percent accurate when it comes to predicting the variation in first-year college grades, and they have not been shown to predict whether someone will graduate from college. The test does correlate highly to parents income and educational level. Women in general score a total of 45 points lower than men, but they get higher first-year college grades.

9   I received a letter from a high school student from a migrant family who had earned a 3.94 G.P.A., won state awards for dancing and served in student government. But she scored poorly on the S.A.T. and wondered if she should apply to a "good" university. Undoubtedly, there are many others like her who have questioned their self-worth after such an experience. University admissions boards, looking at her S.A.T. scores, may indeed be skeptical of this student's academic merit.

Our report suggested that more consideration be given to improvement in 10 high school performance as well as resourcefulness in overcoming adversity. Better yet, universities could adopt new tests tied to state academic standards for secondary schools, standards that have been adopted and used to guide teacher licensing. More than 30 states are developing tests aligned with such standards. Universities could also switch from aptitude tests like the S.A.T. to tests that measure knowledge, like the New York State Regents exams.

Doubts about the S.A.T. as a high-stakes measure of merit are not new. But 11 with affirmative action under attack across the country, they should be taken much more seriously. ■

WHAT DO TESTS TEST?

Howard Gardner

Howard Gardner is the author of Extraordinary Minds *and* The Disciplined Mind: What All Students Should Understand. *He is a professor at Harvard's School of Education. Compare this article with Gardner's article on page 472 to form a more complete sense of his educational philosophy.*

A few years ago I sat in on a discussion in Chicago at which local political and 1 educational leaders were crowing over rising scores on a standardized test for public school children. I broke in to pose some questions: Was it not true that whenever a new version of the test was adopted, scores immediately dropped? And wasn't it the case that scores recovered over the next few years as students and teachers became accustomed to the test? The test had been administered a dozen times by then.

The group conceded that this was the pattern. It was obvious that students 2 were not learning important new skills; they were learning how to take a certain kind of test. The testing tail was wagging the academic dog.

The Chicago story could be replayed across the country. Most states have 3 adopted new academic standards, and many are beginning to ratchet up standardized testing, too. Kentucky introduced new tests eight years ago that are far more demanding than the Chicago test, but has rescinded them under pressure from parents and teachers because the scores at some schools have remained stubbornly low. Virginia and Massachusetts have had disappointing early results with their new tests.

This week New York State introduced new reading and writing tests for 4 fourth graders. Rather than the old multiple-choice format, two-thirds of the new three-day exam will involve writing critiques and personal essays.

State officials predict that the test will help identify weaknesses in the curricu- 5 lum. But many teachers are afraid that they'll be judged by the performance of

*New York Times, December 4, 1998, p. A29.

ill-prepared students, and parents have expressed concern that their children's scores will be considered in applications for gifted programs and selective middle schools.

6   Should such new tests be embraced as a necessary medicine or are they yet another useless exercise in the perennial race to improve public education? It is a mistake to polarize the debate: there are good and poor ways of conducting such tests. It makes more sense to ask what we are trying to achieve and then to make decisions accordingly. With any proposed test, I always ask four questions.

- Does the test focus on something that is indisputably important?
- Does it test the desired skill directly, or does it use other methods as an index of the student's proficiency (for example, testing students' "writing ability" by asking them to choose the best-written of four sample passages)?
- Are teachers prepared to help students acquire the required skills, and do they have the necessary resources?
- Could students who do well on this test do well on a different sort of exam that presumably tests the same skill?

7   The New York test seems to have received a high score on the first two criteria. No one doubts the importance of being able to write analytically about what one has read or to compose a personal essay. And it is a significant advance to ask students to write freely, rather than simply to edit or critique a passage.

As for preparedness, however, legitimate questions have been raised about whether New York fourth graders have the background to fill in blank pages under timed conditions, and whether teachers know how to prepare children from families that do not stress reading and writing.

8   Which brings us to the fourth and most crucial question. Whenever a new exam is introduced there is a temptation on the part of teachers to "teach the test." It might now seem far better to teach students how to write a personal essay than to simply ask them multiple-choice questions about a passage. Yet it is possible even with essay tests to teach students to do well through mimicry rather than through general writing skills.

9   Here's how this could happen on the New York test. Teachers could instruct students that a personal essay must have three paragraphs, each with a different topic sentence; that the first paragraph must begin with an opinion ("I strongly believe that . . ."); that the second paragraph must include two vivid images, and so on. Undoubtedly, fourth graders could learn to write such an essay.

10   But what would happen if they were then asked to write a letter or a response to a newspaper article? Would they do any better than children who hadn't been taught such essay-writing techniques?

Educators and parents should value the development of knowledge and skills that go beyond a single test. That is, high performance should be an incidental result of strong general preparation.

11   Soon most states, including New York, will be mandating so-called high-stakes tests in many subjects at several grade levels. We must proceed cautiously before we place students' minds and hearts at risk with tests of dubious quality whose meaning can be overinterpreted and whose consequences can be devastating.

Yes, we need rigorous academic standards, but we must also serve as models 12
to youngsters when it comes to developing the most crucial skills: love of learning,
respect for peers and good citizenship. That is what they need most to pass the test
of life. ■

LOOKING FOR THE TIDY MIND, ALAS*

Janny Scott

*Janny Scott describes a new method for grading student essays that could save testing
companies a lot of money. Would you like to have your essays graded this way? Why
or why not?*

So it has come to this. The essay, the great literary art form that Montaigne con- 1
ceived and Virginia Woolf carried on, that the writer Edward Hoagland likens to
jazz or a butterfly's flight, has sunk to a state where someone thinks it is a bright
idea to ask a computer if an essay is any good.

The new computer, which is called e-rater (sort of like In-Sink-Erator, the 2
company that makes machines to grind up kitchen garbage), will be used along
with a trained human to grade the two essay questions on the Graduate Management Admission Test taken by 200,000 business school applicants each year.

E-rater's interest is not exactly that of Addison and Steele or E. B. White. 3
Humor is outside its jurisdiction, as are irony and surprise. E-rater likes subordinate and complementary clauses and words like "however" and "therefore" that
some people think suggest a tidy mind.

There was a time when essays were thought to be more than the sum of their 4
therefores. They were distinguished by their originality, insight and personal voice,
by their graceful style, lack of affectation and willingness to meander. Instead of
stomping toward a conclusion, many never arrived.

A genuine essay is "the movement of a free mind at play," writes Cynthia 5
Ozick, the novelist and critic; it is "a stroll through someone's mazy mind." The essayist, she says, is free "to hop from thought to thought, to begin with the finish and
finish with the middle, or to eschew beginning and end and keep only a middle."

A century ago, Samuel Johnson and other great essayists were used as mod- 6
els to teach theme writing in schools. But in the factory of freshman composition,
the meaning of "essay" has eroded to a point where it is almost equivalent to any
old hunk of prose. As a result, shortly after Robert Atwan started editing his annual book series, *The Best American Essays* (Houghton Mifflin), a dentist sent along
an article on root canal that he had published in a dental journal and said was the
best essay he had ever written.

The telltale signs of a bad essay are at least as familiar as the virtues of the 7
great ones. There is the obligatory "thesis statement," Mr. Atwan says. Then come

*New York Times, January 31, 1999, sec. 4, p. 2.

three paragraphs of exposition, then a concluding paragraph summarizing the preceding three, along with the phrase "Thus we see that . . ."

8 "Everybody has to forget the school essay before they can write," said Ian Frazier, the writer. "They have to forget 'not only but also' constructions. That's dead. Nobody wants to read that, not even teachers."

9 Enter the e-rater.

10 The impulse behind e-rater was not, of course, doing Max Beerbohm one better. The idea was to cut costs, among other things. Instead of two people grading each essay, the Graduate Management Admission Council, which administers the test, could have one trained human and one machine.

11 And what a machine! E-rater is "the most highly developed, holistic electronic writing assessment application to date," said Frederick McHale of the admission council. It is a computer bulked up on a high-protein diet of high-scoring answers to past admission-test essay questions.

12 Jill Burstein, a scientist at Educational Testing Service in Princeton, N.J., who led the team that invented e-rater, says the computer looks for what she called syntactic variety, such as different kinds of clauses. It also looks for words associated with organization of ideas, such as "first," "second" and "third."

13 "It's not trained to score Montaigne," she said. "It's not designed to score creative writing and irony and metaphor and poems. It's designed for a specific purpose, to score the kinds of essays we see on standardized tests."

14 It is impossible (therefore!) to say how Montaigne might have fared. He never did have to analyze the annual report of Olympic Foods or agree or disagree with a statement like "Nations should cooperate to develop regulations that limit children's access to adult material on the Internet."

15 Much business writing seems to aspire to little more than lowest-common-denominator order and clarity. And, with home computers already editing for gender neutrality and pointing out when sentences exceed 31 words, why not let e-rater be the enforcer of corporatese?

16 "For business letters, I think it's O.K.," Ms. Ozick conceded in an interview. "On the other hand, this is no way to teach somebody to think. If an essay represents thinking at its purest and most original, this is a terrible template to put over the human mind."

17 Mr. Frazier, however, said he understands the impulse. Strangers keep cranking out manuscripts on computers and shipping them off to him. "It would be great if one machine wrote it and another machine read it," he said, "and we would all be free to go about our business." ■

QUESTIONS TO HELP YOU THINK AND WRITE ABOUT EDUCATION ISSUES

1. Read the first two articles, by Gardner and Hirsch. The articles were originally published together in the *New York Times* and described as "opposing approaches" to what schools should teach. Gardner's article was described as "one approach to teaching students to give them a thorough grasp of a few

disciplines to show them how to think critically." Hirsch's article was described as another approach to give students "a broad grounding in society's common information and skills." How different are these approaches? Does it make sense to present them as opposing approaches, or is there another way to present these ideas? What are your ideas about the relative value of these approaches?

2. Read the article by Sollod. Draw a line down the middle of a sheet of paper, and make lists of the advantages and disadvantages of teaching religion and spirituality at college. What do you value? Why? What is consistent with your current educational experiences? Explain in detail.

3. Grann and King propose ways to improve student motivation, learning, and grades. What are their ideas? Evaluate their ideas. Do you think these ideas should be widely practiced? What ideas would you add for improving students' academic motivation and performance?

4. Vitz claims that many modern textbooks exhibit a biased point of view. What would he change in modern textbooks? What are his value warrants? Do you share them? What is your position on this issue? Do you think your textbooks are biased or not?

5. The articles by Borkat (page 146) and Wiesenfeld deal with the problem of grade inflation in different ways. What is your response to these authors' ideas? Do you think this is a problem? What is its cause? Is it harmful? Why or how? What should be done about it?

6. Make a list of the issues associated with standardized tests that Garcia, Gardner, and Hirsch identify in their articles in this section. Which of these issues is most compelling for you? What is your position? What are your reasons?

7. What is the significance of the title "Looking for the Tidy Mind, Alas"? What does it suggest about computerized grading of student essays? What are the advantages and disadvantages of such a practice?

8. Israeloff (see "Don't Know Much about History," page 81) reports that students are learning less about history than when she was in school. Do you think this is true? List all of the reasons you can think of why history is important to know and understand. Can you build a strong case that history is unimportant? How do you think history should be taught in schools?

SECTION III

Issues Concerning Crime and the Treatment of Criminals

THE ISSUES

A. How Should We Treat Convicted Criminals?

Five authors provide different perspectives on the treatment of criminals and how to avoid the problems caused by repeat offenders. Gilligan, Koch, and Will offer inventive approaches for dealing with criminals. As you read these selections, you will want to think about your definition of punishment and its purpose in our society. You will also want to think about our current prison system and its reputed effectiveness. Two additional articles focus on the effectiveness of the death penalty. One is a firsthand account of an execution, and the other suggests how some positive social good could come from capital punishment. For a very different view, see also "Giving People a Second Chance," page 54, and "The Color of Suspicion," page 589.

B. What Should Be Done with Young Offenders?

The focus here is on the escalating problem of children and teenagers who commit crimes and acts of violence. The arguments establish the nature of the problem, discuss its causes, evaluate how bad the problem is, and propose some ways of solving it. Cohen provides examples and statistics about young offenders. Males and Docuyanan claim that poverty is a crucial factor in the rise of juvenile crime. Debra Dickerson gives a personal account of a crime committed against her nephew. Her article touches on the issues of poverty, race, and stereotypes. Geoffrey Canada advocates intervention and programs that focus on prevention rather than punishment.

C. Do Violent Video Games and Books Cause Young People to Commit Crimes?

All three of the articles on this topic respond to a particular rhetorical situation. In April 1999, two male teenage students entered Columbine High School in Littleton, Colorado, shot twelve of their peers, injured many more, and finally took their own lives. Later it was revealed that these teenagers were fascinated by the violence they found on the Internet and that they had also played violent video games. These practices were regarded as possible causes for their crime. The three featured articles ponder the secret life of teens and the effects of violent games and books. As you read them, ask yourself the following questions: Does excessive exposure to violence desensitize young adults and motivate them to commit acts of violence themselves? What other social factors might also be involved?

To Extend Your Pespective: Films and Literature Related to Crime and the Treatment of Criminals

Films: A Clockwork Orange, 1971; *Dead Man Walking*, 1996; *Boyz N the Hood*, 1991
Literature: poem: "The Ballad of Reading Gaol" by Oscar Wilde; short story: "Billy Budd" by Herman Melville; autobiography: *Live from Death Row* by Mumia Abu-Jamal; novels: *Crime and Punishment* by Fyodor Dostoyevsky; *Of Mice and Men* by John Steinbeck; *A Clockwork Orange* by Anthony Burgess

THE RHETORICAL SITUATION

Everyone seems to have opinions about the issues associated with crime and the treatment of criminals. All of the recent presidents of the United States have made it a major issue in their campaigns and presidencies, yet the problems persist.

According to the perceptions of many, the country is becoming increasingly lawless. Motivational warrants linked to the need for safety are implicit in many of the arguments about crime issues.

It has been said that a "society is known by the prisoners it keeps." The issues related to crime that are included in this section deal with the treatment of convicted criminals, unconventional punishments for criminals, and the growing problem of young offenders. Children and young teenagers breaking the law and committing particularly heinous crimes is a fairly new problem that concerns many people. This problem has become so serious that some people believe severe punishments are as justified for young offenders as for adult offenders.

Capital punishment, though fairly widely practiced, is still controversial. The death penalty has had an interesting history. It was banned in this country in 1972 and ruled constitutional again in 1976. According to various polls, the majority of Americans favor the death penalty for particularly horrible crimes. Other people argue for crime prevention, including various types of interventions, and for rehabilitation for all criminals, young or old. There is a strong exigency in the United States to understand and solve the problems associated with crime.

A. How Should We Treat Convicted Criminals?

REFLECTIONS FROM A LIFE BEHIND BARS: BUILD COLLEGES, NOT PRISONS*

James Gilligan

James Gilligan is the former director of mental health for the Massachusetts prison system. He is also a clinical instructor in psychiatry at Harvard Medical School who has twenty-five years of experience as a prison psychiatrist. He believes that education is the key to preventing recidivism.

Neither words nor pictures, no matter how vivid, can do more than give a faint 1 suggestion of the horror, brutalization, and degradation of the prisons of this country. I speak from extensive personal knowledge of this subject, for I have spent 25 years of my professional life behind bars—not as an inmate, but as a prison psychiatrist.

I am a physician, and I see violence (whether it is legal or illegal, homicidal 2 or suicidal, intentional or careless) as a public-health problem—indeed, the most important and dangerous threat to public health in our time. Because it effects mostly the young, violence kills more people under the age of 65 in this country than do cancer and heart disease, the two illnesses that are often (and mistakenly) thought to be the most significant causes of death.

Chronicle of Higher Education, October 16, 1998, pp. B7–B9.

3   So I cannot emphasize too strongly how seriously I take the problem of violence. Far from being tolerant or permissive toward it, I am far more strongly opposed to violence in all its forms and in all its legal statuses, and far less tolerant and permissive toward it than are those who believe that our salvation lies in building more and more punitive (i.e., violent) prisons.

4   There is a widespread misimpression that punishment deters violence—in other words, that punishment is one means of preventing violence. However, the overwhelming weight of empirical evidence suggests that exactly the opposite is true—namely, that punishment, far from inhibiting or preventing violence, is the most potent stimulus or cause of violence that we have yet discovered. Several different lines of evidence, from several different populations and stages of the life cycle, converge in supporting that conclusion.

5   For example, child-rearing is such an inherently and inescapably complicated subject that there are relatively few findings from the past several decades of research on it that are so clear, so unmistakable, and so consistently replicated that they are virtually universally agreed on. But among those few is this: The more severely punished children are, the more violent they become, both as children and as adults. This is especially true of violent punishments. For example, children who are subjected to corporal discipline are significantly more likely to subject other people to physical punishments (i.e., inflict violence on them), both while they are still children and after they have reached adulthood. That is hardly surprising, of course, for corporal discipline is simply another name for physical violence; it would be called assault and battery if committed against an adult.

6   In fact, even with respect to nonviolent behavior, such as bed-wetting or excessive dependency or passivity ("laziness"), punishment has a counterproductive effect; that is, the more severely children are punished for a given behavior, the more strongly they persist in repeating it. To put it the other way around: If we want to produce as violent a generation of children and adults as possible, the most effective thing we can do is to punish our children and adults as severely as possible.

7   While the research just referred to can be found in the literature on child development and child abuse, there is no reason to think that the psychology of adults differs in this respect from that of children, and every reason to think that it is the same. In fact, I have been able to confirm those findings on children from my own clinical experience of over 25 years with violent adult criminals and the violent mentally ill. The degree of violent child abuse to which this population had been subjected was so extreme that the only way to summarize it is to say that the most violent people in our society—those who murder others—are disproportionately the survivors of attempted murder themselves, or of the completed murders of their closest relatives, siblings, or parents.

8   Thus, if punishment could prevent violence, these men would never have become violent in the first place, for they were already punished, even before they became violent, as severely as it is possible to punish a person without actually killing him. Many were beaten nearly to death as children, so when they became adults, they did beat someone else to death.

Fortunately, we not only know what stimulates violence (punishment, humiliation), we also know what prevents violence, both in society in general and in the criminal-justice and prison systems in particular. Unfortunately, we Americans have been dismantling the conditions that do prevent violence as rapidly as we could over the past 25 years, with the entirely predictable result that the levels of violent crimes, such as murder, have repeatedly reached the highest recorded levels in our history. For example, for the last quarter of a century our murder rates have been twice as high as they were 40 years ago, and five to ten times as high as they currently are in any other democracy and developed economy on earth. 9

What are the conditions that prevent violence? Among general social conditions, there are several, but space permits mentioning only the most powerful one: a relatively classless society, with an equitable social and economic system in which there are minimal discrepancies in wealth, income, and standard of living between the poorest and the wealthiest fractions of the population (people are vulnerable to feelings of shame and inferiority if they are poor, or economically inferior, while other people are rich, or economically superior). 10

Around the world, the nations with the most equitable economic systems, such as Sweden and Japan, are significantly more likely to have the lowest murder rates. And those with the greatest economic discrepancies between the rich and the poor (of which the United States is the world leader among developed democracies) have the highest murder rates (a statistic in which the United States is also the world leader). Even within the United States, the most equitable or "classless" states have the lowest murder rates, and those with the most inequitable degrees of class stratification have the highest. Yet the last Congress dismantled one of the few programs we had that tended to equalize income in this country—the earned-income tax credit. 11

Among the conditions in the prison system that prevent violent behavior (both during imprisonment and after release to the community), the most powerful is education. In Massachusetts, for example, when I headed the prison mental-health service, we did a study to see what programs within the prison had been most effective in preventing recidivism among prison inmates after they had been released from prison and returned to the community. While several programs had worked, the most successful of all, and the only one that had been 100 percent effective in preventing recidivism, was the program that allowed inmates to receive a college degree while in prison. Several hundred prisoners in Massachusetts had completed at least a bachelor's degree while in prison over a 25-year period, and not one of them had been returned to prison for a new crime. 12

Immediately after I announced this finding in a public lecture at Harvard, and it made its way into the newspapers, our new governor, William Weld, who had not previously been aware that prison inmates could take college courses, gave a press conference on television in which he declared that Massachusetts should rescind that "privilege," or else the poor would start committing crimes in order to be sent to prison so they could get a free college education! And lest one think that that was merely the rather bizarre response of one particularly cynical 13 demagogue, it is worth noting that the U.S. Congress responded the same way. The last Congress declared that inmates throughout the federal prison system would no longer be eligible to receive Pell grants.

14   It is too late now to even begin to attempt to "reform" prisons. The only thing that can be done with them is to tear them all down, for their architecture alone renders them unfit for human beings. Or even animals: No humane society permits animals in zoos to be housed in conditions as intolerable as those in which we cage humans. The reason for the difference, of course, is clear: Zoos are not intended for punishment; prisons are. That is why it would benefit every man, woman, and child in this country, and it would hurt no one, to demolish the prisons and replace them with much smaller, locked, secure residential schools and colleges in which the residents could acquire as much education as their intelligence and curiosity would permit.

15   Such institutions would of course be most effective in their only rational purpose, which would be to prevent crime and violence, if they were designed to be as humane and homelike as possible, and as near the prisoners' own homes as possible, so that their families could visit as freely as possible (including frequent conjugal visits), and so they could visit their families as freely as possible. (For conjugal and home visits have repeatedly been shown, in this country and around the world, to be associated with lowered rates of violence, both during incarceration and after release into the community—which is probably why both have been effectively abolished in this country.)

16   Since there is no reason to isolate anyone from the community against his will unless he poses a danger of physically harming others, these residential schools would need to be limited to those who have been, or have threatened or attempted to be, violent. (Very few, if any, nonviolent "criminals" need to be removed from the community at all. Nor should those who have committed only nonviolent crimes ever have to be housed with those who have been seriously violent; and there are many reasons why they should not be.)

17   Thus one of the most constructive responses I can think of . . . would be the designing of an "anti-prison"—not prison reform, but prison replacement; not prison construction, but prison deconstruction. If we replaced prisons with a boarding-school "home away from home" for many people who are literally homeless in the so-called community, and provided them with the tools they need in order to acquire knowledge and skill, self-esteem and self-respect, and the esteem and respect of others, these new facilities could actually reduce the rates of crime and violence in our society, instead of feeding them, as our current prisons do.

18   Of course, before we could do that, we would need to overcome our own irrational need to inflict revenge (i.e., punishment) on those who are weaker than we. Nothing corrodes the soul of the vengeful person as thoroughly as his own vengeful impulses. Thus the main reason we need to abolish [prisons] is not only, or even primarily, for the sake of those who get imprisoned in them, but in order to heal our own souls—and indeed, our whole society, which is sick with an epidemic of violence, both legal and illegal. ■

UNCONVENTIONAL PUNISHMENT
FOR CRIMINALS CATCHING ON*

Nicole Koch

Nicole Koch is a staff writer for the Dallas Morning News. *This article focuses on creative sentencing incorporating public humiliation into the punishment process.*

Each time James Skrobarczyk Jr. pulls a bill from his wallet, he sees his friend 1 Tyson Wilkins smiling back at him. And he remembers the car crash that took his friends's life and changed his forever.

But he can't take the picture out of his wallet. It's there as part of his punish- 2 ment for an involuntary manslaughter conviction in the accident four years ago in Houston.

He also must place flowers on Mr. Wilkins' grave and write letters to his 3 friend's family during his five-year sentence.

It sound humbling and more humiliating than jail time, and that's the idea be- 4 hind this *Scarlet Letter* kind of sentencing.

Mr. Skrobarczyk, 23, is one of a growing number of people receiving out-of-the 5 ordinary sentences—punishments intented to embarrass or shame the defendant.

Whether it's sentencing someone to make a public apology, posting pictures 6 of fugitives on Web pages or ordering a defendant to wear a humiliating sign, this sort of tactic is catching on in courtrooms accross the country.

Call it innovative. Call it poetic justice. Houston District Judge Ted Poe just 7 knows it works. Since 1988, he has used this sort of punishment 62 times, and only two of those punished have been arrested again.

Not everyone agrees with this form of sentencing. Nationwide, attorneys 8 with the American Civil Liberties Union have spoken out, often calling it cruel and unusual.

"If we go back to allowing judges to create their own punishments, we'll 9 have fanatical judges running amok with citizens' rights," said Diana Philip, ACLU regional director of northern Texas. "I hope we're civil enough as a country not to let that happen."

Judge Poe said he passes down sentences with three things in mind: the de- 10 fendant, public safety and the victim.

"The scales of justice are balanced," he said. "You have the concerns of the 11 defendant, but you have the public safety and the victim on the other side. When you balance that, you get justice."

In other cases, Judge Poe has: 12

- Ordered an 8 × 10 picture of a family of four mounted in one man's jail cell. The man, while driving drunk, hit the family's vehicle head-on and killed the parents.

*Dallas Morning News, June 18, 1998, p. 6A.

- Jailed a man convicted of domestic abuse and sentenced him to make a public apology to his wife on the steps of City Hall at noon.
- Sentenced a convicted auto thief to jail and required him to hand over the keys of his Trans Am to a 75-year-old grandmother. The woman drove the car until her vehicle, stolen by the man, was recovered and repaired.

13   Humiliation deters conduct, Judge Poe said, and it's important that judges use it to make the system work. "Victims should not be embarrassed by crime," he said. "Defendants should be embarrassed by what they do."

14   Matthew Ware, 21, of Houston, discovered that firsthand. In March, he let some friends write hot checks at the grocery store where he worked. Judge Poe sentenced him to two years' probation, 400 community-service hours and seven days of carrying a sign in front of the grocery store. The signs read, "I stole from Fiesta. Don't steal or this could be you."

15   "I'm never doing anything against the law again," Mr. Ware said. "This right here has straightened me up for good. No more bad guy."

16   Jim Harrington, legal director of the Texas Civil Rights Project, said he's sympathetic to some forms of creative sentencing, but he questions public humiliation.

17   "It's not productive or rehabilitative," he said. "If you're trying to get to creating or stirring feelings of remorse in somebody, that's fine. The way to do that isn't by humiliating somebody. It's just mean, in a sense."

18   In other parts of the country, cities are using similar tactics to identify criminals and deter potential ones.

19   Wichita, Kan., motorists know when they're behind a convicted drunken driver thanks to the Repeat Offender DUI Decal Program.

20   District Judge Eric Yost created the program six months ago because repeat offenders weren't learning anything from their punishment.

21   "Going to jail isn't shameful because there are so many people who have done that," he said. "A public display of punishment is going to have a greater impact and more desirable results."

22   Kirk England, 33, of Wichita, has been convicted of driving under the influence twice, and now, he's required to display a decal in bright orange and black that reads "Convicted DUI."

23   Mr. England takes exception to his creative sentence.

24   "It's downgrading and insulting," he said. "I don't think you should have to show people your problems. The punishment went too far."

25   But even though he's unhappy with his sentence, Mr. England said he's never going to drink and drive again.

26   "No way. It's getting worse—the consequences. It's not worth it."

27   Ohio, Oregon and Minnesota require special license plates for repeat drunken drivers.

28   In northeast Kansas City, Mo., City Council member Teresa Loar turned to public access television to try to rid her neighborhoods of drugs and prostitution.

29   Four times each Wednesday, photographs and names of prostitutes and their customers who have been arrested appear on "John TV."

Since the first segment aired in May 1997, prostitution arrests have dropped 30 47 percent.

Ms. Loar said the point of her program isn't to embarrass or humiliate those 31 arrested—it's to deter prostitutes and johns from coming to her district.

In Chester County, Pa., outside Philadelphia, District Attorney Anthony 32 Sarcione is targeting fugitives by television. Two local cable stations air the names and photos of suspects in all sorts of cases—from murders to deadbeat parents.

"People who are wanted by law enforcement for crimes have brought it 33 upon themselves," Mr. Sarcione said. "The more embarrassment, the better."

Mr. Sarcione said in two years, more than 100 of the people featured on the 34 TV program have been apprehended or have turned themselves in.

"The protection of the public outweighs any potential negative attention 35 brought on the defendant." he said. "We can't rest on our laurels. We have to change with the times in order to be effective." ■

A JAILBREAK FOR GERIATRICS

*George F. Will**

George F. Will offers another solution for reducing recidivism and government spending.

Federal and state governments can significantly reduce spending in a field of 1 soaring costs, while radically reducing their rates of recidivism among criminals released from prison. All they need to do is put hundreds, perhaps thousands, of convicts where they belong, which is—really—back in society. This idea will probably be a hard sell to a crime-conscious public in a conservative era. But consider Quenton Brown, whose case gave rise to POPS (the Project for Older Prisoners). And consider the case of Noah Wade, who also illustrates the point of POPS.

In June 1973 Brown, then 50, with an IQ of 51, stole $117 and a 15-cent cherry 2 pie from a Morgan City, La., store. He crossed the street, crawled under a house, ate the pie and docilely surrendered himself and his .38 pistol, which may not have been in working order, to police when they arrived. He was sentenced to 30 years without parole.

Seventeen years into that sentence, at age 67, he came to the attention of a 3 young Tulane law professor, Jonathan Turley, who was struck by the anomaly of the graying prison population—aging men becoming more and more expensive to

Newsweek, July 20, 1998, p. 70.

warehouse as they become less and less dangerous. By the time he had won a parole for Brown, Turley and more than 200 Tulane law students had become founders of POPS, an organization devoted to culling low-risk geriatrics from overcrowded prisons.

4   In 1944, Noah Wade, then probably 19, had consensual sex with a 15-year-old. Virginia charged him with statutory rape. Wade says the girl's father said Wade must marry her. Wade says he was already married to a 14-year-old. Sentenced to seven years, he got into a fight with an inmate. Both men wielded prison-made shanks, both were stabbed. The other man died. Wade was sentenced to life. In 1992, shortly before Virginia's prison system became so crowded that the state started paying other states to incarcerate some of its convicts, POPS got Wade paroled to a Richmond nursing home.

5   It costs about $20,000 a year to imprison a young, healthy, dangerous man. Because of the normal medical costs associated with aging, and the unhealthy nature of prison life, it costs two to three times that, and sometimes more, to imprison someone 55 or older. (Because they usually have led hard lives before prison, and because of the chronic stress, idleness and the rest of prison life, 55-year-old prisoners often are, physiologically, akin to people seven or eight years older than that.) Men 55 and older comprise one of the fastest-growing cohorts in the prison population. And because of society's turn toward long sentences and away from parole, by the end of this decade there may be 90,000 prisoners over the age of 50.

6   Which is not to say that there should be wholesale de-institutionalization of the elderly. Organizations advocating victim's rights insist, reasonably, that retribution should not be lightly abandoned for budgetary reasons. They denounce the notion of "senior-citizen discounts" for criminals. However, their sensible philosophy encounters a stubborn fact: no matter how fast billions are poured into increasing the supply of cells, the supply of truly dangerous convicts increases faster. This is partly because, Turley says, sheriffs read newspapers: "They know when a new prison is coming online and they start to execute warrants. And in state after state, we see a self-adjusting market." And, inevitably, courts get involved.

7   At any given time nowadays, upwards of 40 states' prison systems are under court orders to rectify overcrowding. Some states' prisons even have a "zero sum" status: the addition of a new inmate requires the release of an existing one— public safety at the mercy of arithmetic.

8   Therefore the practical question is not whether but which prisoners are going to be released before their full sentences have been served. And a salient fact is that age is the surest predictor of recidivism. These two variables vary inversely.

It is unclear what cocktail of biological and cultural factors determines this.

9   But in any case, the rate of rearrest (for a felony or serious misdemeanor) for state prisoners within three years of release from prison is 68 percent among those ages 18 to 24; 65 percent among those 25–29; 63 percent among those 30–34; 57 percent among those 35–39; 49 percent among those 40–44; 40 percent among those over 45. The rate among the almost 200 prisoners paroled or pardoned because of POPS' efforts is zero.

10   This is partly because POPS is meticulous in selecting candidates for release. POPS never challenges an inmate's conviction, and to be eligible for POPS' help,

inmates must acknowledge their guilt. Although predicting recidivism is not an exact science, extensive interviewing can establish each inmate's ranking on a recidivism risk scale.

States can also reap sizable savings by designating some prisoners for incar- 11 ceration in minimum-security facilities for geriatrics—essentially, nursing homes— or assigning them to live at large but wearing electronic bracelets for monitoring. Turley, who is now at the George Washington University Law School, says that prisons are designed for vigorous and violent young predators, but now increasingly valuable cells are being occupied by decreasingly dangerous individuals. These elderly are taxing the capacity of prison medical systems, which are already buckling under the burden of the AIDS epidemic.

Although prison medical care often is not optimum, courts have held that 12 denial of adequate care violates the Eighth Amendment prohibition of cruel and unusual punishments. Which is how America may come to regard the tax burden of its correctional system (in what sense are prisoners "corrected"?) unless it moves in the direction POPS is pointing.

By the way, when Quenton Brown was paroled, POPS got him a job with a 13 Tampa firm that made pies. The employers asked Turley if Brown had ever worked with pastries. "Oh, yeah," Turley replied. "He loves pastries." ■

WITNESS TO AN EXECUTION*

Terry FitzPatrick

Terry FitzPatrick wrote this firsthand account of an execution in Texas in 1992. You will need to infer his claim.

I must confess that I *wanted* to see the execution of Johnny Frank Garrett. It took a 1 bit of journalistic hustle to secure a place on the five-member press pool. My friends told me that I should examine my motives before I went. I didn't. I marched toward the Death House at midnight to satisfy insatiable journalistic curiosity. I just wanted to get *inside*.

The Death House is a brick bunker tucked inside The Walls prison unit in 2 downtown Huntsville. Inside it's painted milky blue. It must be the most brightly lighted place in the entire Texas prison system. The room is small; only a few feet and silver, metal prison bars separated Garrett from his family. I stood directly behind Garrett's mother. The executioner stood in a separate room behind a pane of mirrored glass. Thin intravenous tubes ran through a small opening in the wall, into both arms of the prisoner.

Garrett was strapped to a gurney, with white leather belts across his chest, 3 belly, thighs, knees, and ankles. His hands were concealed by tape. His arms were strapped outward at right angles. From above, it must have looked like he was on a crucifix.

Texas Observer, February 28, 1992, p. 10.

4   Garrett was in a defiant mood and was clearly agitated. He was already on the gurney when the press contingent entered a few minutes past midnight. I'd seen Garrett many times before, in courtrooms, in jails, in those undignified hallway shuffles past the packs of reporters and cameras. He had always seemed calm, a bit detached. Back then, his prison haircuts, long sideburns, and thick eyebrows made him look like a Neanderthal. But here in the Death House, Garrett was clean shaven with his hair neatly combed back. He was very thin, clothed in pressed prison blues and new, white canvas shoes. His last meal had been chocolate ice cream. He had the look of panic: wide eyes, short breaths, tense movements of the head. Despite the psychiatrist's assessment that Garrett didn't believe a lethal injection would kill him, it seemed to me that Johnny Frank Garrett knew he was about to die.

5   His family was tightly huddled when I entered. His mother, two sisters, stepfather, and brother-in-law clutched the prison bars as Garrett strained to turn his head to the right to speak his final words.

6   "I'd like to thank my friends who tried to pull me through all this. My guru for helping me go through this. I'd like to thank my family for loving me. And the rest of the world can kiss my ass."

7   Garrett looked at the warden as he spoke that last part. Then he jerked his head toward the white ceiling to show he was ready. Garrett began to recite some kind of prayer or mantra to himself and the warden made a barely perceptible signal to the anonymous executioner behind the mirrored glass.

8   It was over in an instant: Garrett's mouth caught open in mid-speech, his eyes open—frozen with a small squint of recognition that poison was racing through his veins.

9   His mother kept saying "I love you son, it's okay. Go to sleep," as if it were a lullaby. Garrett's sisters were angry. "They're gonna' pay," one sister said.

10   With that, Garrett's mother tried to console her daughters. "God forgives those who forgive his brothers," she said. "He's at peace. He paid his debt. We all have to do that."

11   "He's in a better place than we are," the sister replied. "There aren't any assholes to tell him what to do."

12   The family sang "Amazing Grace" in broken tearful voices.

13   Texas uses three drugs in executions: sodium thiopental to relax the prisoner and induce sleep, pancuronium bromide to paralyze the muscles and prevent breathing, and potassium chloride to stop the heart. The dose is large enough to kill 10 people. The injection lasted four minutes, though life had slipped from Garrett's body just seconds after it began.

14   The executioner placed a roll of white adhesive tape in the small opening in the wall, beside the clear intravenous tubes, to indicate the injection was over. A prison doctor ambled in and searched perfunctorily for a pulse on Garrett's neck and arm, and then listened to Garrett's chest through a stethoscope for just an instant. He turned to the warden and compared the time on their watches. "I figure 12:18."

15   With that the heavy metal doors swung open with a startling thud. We filed out of the Death House behind the family. Nobody said a word. Officials looked at the floor as they walked. And Garrett lay there still. There were no gestures of re-

spect for his corpse. Nobody covered him with a sheet, or closed his lifeless eyes. There was no dignity in this death.

We stepped outside the prison into the glare of television lights. A crowd of stu- 16 dents from the nearby university broke out in cheers and applause, singing "na-na-na-na, hey-hey-hey, good bye." I felt ashamed as I walked with Garrett's family to the prison administration building across the street. The students weren't jeering at just the family, they were jeering at me. I felt my privileged press-pool access made me a participant in the execution as well as an observer. As a citizen of Texas, I realized that Johnny Frank Garrett had been executed in my name. ■

TURNING BAD INTO GOOD*

Graeme Newman

Graeme Newman, a professor at the School of Criminal Justice of the State University of New York at Albany, writes arguments about the treatment of criminals that have original slants.

In 1983 I noted in *Just and Painful: A Case for the Corporal Punishment of Criminals* 1 that there were approximately 315,000 individuals incarcerated in federal and state prisons, plus some 158,000 persons in jails of various kinds. The annual cost of this incarceration was estimated then to be $20,000 per inmate, amounting to an annual expenditure of some $10 billion.

The solution I advocated at that time was to replace much of the punishment 2 of prison with corporal punishment of a specific type: one that applied acute pain (that is, intense sharp pain of very brief duration). [. . .]

But I am humbled by the fact that hardly anyone takes my solution to the 3 punishment problem seriously, especially since things have become much worse since 1983. Today there are over 600,000 persons in prison plus some 405,000 in jails. The annual cost is somewhere in the vicinity of $40,000 per inmate, and to build a new cell costs approximately $100,000. Why has the situation become so much worse? Why has no credible alternative to prison arisen? [. . .]

There have, of course, been alternatives to prison, but these attempts them- 4 selves demonstrate the very failure to understand the profound centrality of punishment to social life. The most well-known "alternative" was, of course, probation, introduced on a large scale in the United States early this century. It turned out to be largely an add-on "punishment" simply finding additional offenders. Worse, probation failed to convince the general public that it was in fact punitive enough. The great solution of the 1980's was supposed to be "community service," but unless its punitive element is sharpened, it will go the way of probation: people will see it, justifiably, as yet another attempt to subvert the punishment process. It turns "pun-

Chronicles, May 1992, pp. 19–22.

ishment" into "service" and "service" into "punishment" by taking away the intrinsic merit of service from those who would normally volunteer for it.

5   Yet the idea embedded in community service is morally attractive: it tries to draw out of the punishment process something "good"—service to the community. This is an important idea that, unfortunately in the way it is currently implemented, will go the way of other "alternatives" to punishment, because it does not address the fact that punishment must be punishment. The public, in my view, understands and demands this. Legislators understand this to a point, by enacting severe prison terms, but they ignore the fiscal implications of their legislation. These alternatives to prison have simply subverted the central idea of punishment: the intentional and deliberate infliction of pain and suffering on the offender. [. . .]

6   I propose, therefore, to turn to the other end of the criminal justice system, and ask what we might do to those few who have been condemned to death for the most hideous of crimes. Theirs is behavior that is not so difficult to pronounce as evil, and whose behavior we might try to avoid in our punishment. At the same time, though, in an effort to raise ourselves above the level of the murderer, we must try to extract something good out of the evil that we do to the murderer (such as the application of the death penalty) even though he may well deserve to suffer terribly for his crimes.

7   What "good" did the execution of the serial killer Ted Bundy do? We know that such penalties do not deter, so this was not the "good." Did it "satisfy" justice? But what kind of justice is it that feeds on the killing of individuals? Is it good to feel satisfied after killing someone, even though the person deserved it? I do not argue that the motives for killing are identical, but I do insist that there are psychological elements of both acts that are similar. The most obvious similarity is that both killings are intentional. I contend that there is no positive aspect in the infliction of pain or suffering on an individual, even when it is justified. We need to work hard, therefore, to turn this act of violence into something that *is* positive. The mere taking away of the murderer's life does not fulfill this need.

8   The answer lies in the very common complaint of murderers on death row. They announce that they are "sorry" for what they did (though it's often hard to believe them), but add, what can they do? Their victims are dead, they say, and they can't bring them back to life. True enough. But if we pause for a moment, we see the answer: while they cannot bring their victims back to life, they can save the life (and perhaps lives) of others. They could donate their body parts. In this way, one executed criminal's body could possibly save several lives. I would go so far as to say that the condemned murderer should be *made* to give up his body organs. The social and moral good could be enhanced tremendously by this practice.

9   There is a critical shortage of donor organs. As of 1987, for example, there were over 13,000 individuals waiting for organs of one kind or another, and the number is closer to 20,000 today. The U.S. government spent $300,000 in 1990 on Medicare assistance for each of the 60,000 Americans who require kidney dialysis. Thus, each executed murderer is "worth" at least $600,000 just for the two kidneys alone. In 1987 there were more than 12,000 individuals waiting for kidney transplants, and only some 2,500 donors. A liver transplant costs about $150,000. The need, therefore, is critical.

The fantastic service that executed murderers could provide by saving lives 10 is tremendous. While their suffering may not make up for the specific suffering and loss of the particular victim, the victim's family and society as well can at least take comfort in the fact that two terrible deeds—the murder and the execution—have been turned at least to a truly positive outcome: saving lives and improving the quality of life of many others. This is true community service, while at the same time preserving the punitive element of the punishment.

There are, of course, many obvious objections to this idea. I anticipate, for ex- 11 ample, complaints that the government will execute more murderers in order to obtain more body parts. This is indeed a cynical view of government. It should be possible to introduce legislative safeguards to fend off this pitfall, if it is a pitfall. There may also be some concern about an individual living with a serial murderer's heart or other body part. Patients receiving such organs would need to be counseled carefully. Whether it should even be known from whom the organs came is a question that would need to be addressed. Others might complain of a slippery slope, since some organs, such as kidneys, could be extracted from prisoners without killing them. Why not trade off years in prison for donating a kidney? And could an inmate "freely volunteer" parts of his body in order to get out of prison? For the moment, we should begin only with executed prisoners, and if this works, then look to its extension in other settings.

When I advocated corporal punishment for most offenders some nine years 12 ago, I thought that the enormous cost of using prisons for punishment would sooner or later bring the system down. The massive increase in the use of prisons since that time has so far proven me wrong. The problem of punishment is not motivated or limited by fiscal concerns. Rather, it is a problem of moral psychology, as I have argued in this essay. We must try hard to solve this distinctly late-20th-century problem of punishment by beginning to acknowledge the deep-seated shame we have about punishing. We should not be ashamed to use punishment in order to save lives. In doing so, we may turn not only the bad of the offender into good, but also the bad of the punishment process itself into something good. ■

B. What Should Be Done with Young Offenders?*

PUNISHMENT

Patricia Cohen

Patricia Cohen asks the question, rehabilitation or punishment? Which do you favor?

It's Friday, the equivalent of open-mike night in Judge Michael Corriero's Man- 1 hattan courtroom. There's the ninth-grader who went on a robbery spree, the two

*George, June–July 1996, p. 99.

girls who wielded a butcher's knife to steal a 12-year-old's knapsack, the 15-year-old accused of fatally shooting a man. Judge Corriero, who could pass for Al Pacino's younger brother, listens intently before deciding who gets jail and who gets probation, who gets youthful-offender status and who gets thrown into the much harsher adult system.

2   Rehabilitation or punishment? This vexing question, which Corriero weighs dozens of times each day, lies at the heart of a major political and philosophical battle over juvenile crime, which could have the emotional explosiveness of last year's welfare reform debate.

3   This crackdown on young lawbreakers has been fueled by the rising number of juveniles arrested for violent crimes. After remaining virtually constant between 1972 and the late '80s, the juvenile crime rate nationwide began to spike in 1990 and by 1992 had reached a 20-year high. From 1988 to 1991, the youth murder-arrest rate climbed 80 percent. A handful of stomach-churning incidents also made teenage offenders seem more impulsive and vicious. Now, Hawaii is the only state that treats all kids under age 16 as juveniles. In Illinois and North Carolina, 13-year-old offenders can be treated as adults; in Vermont, 10 is the cut-off. In New York, only murder suspects under age seven are automatically treated as juveniles, and Governor George Pataki recently vowed to further toughen the state's law.

4   Both Democrats and Republicans have recognized the political rewards of outraged fist-pounding: 700 legislative proposals to prosecute minors as adults were introduced last year, a trend that President Clinton promised, in his State of the Union address, to pursue.

5   Meanwhile, 24 states allow kids under the age of 18 to get the death penalty. Although no criminal has been executed while a minor, some sentenced while minors have been put to death. Currently, 42 juveniles sit on death row. ■

CRACKDOWN ON KIDS: GIVING UP ON THE YOUNG*

Mike Males and Faye Docuyanan

Mike Males and Faye Docuyanan were social ecology doctoral students at the University of California, Irvine, when they wrote this article.

1 Madness is the word Stephen Bruner uses to describe the summer of 1992. "The things I did, things I had done to me. [. . .] Madness." It was the summer after eighth grade. He and his gang Panic Zone hung out where the rural black community of Spencer intersects the southeast Oklahoma City suburb of Midwest City. He rattles off the names of a dozen gangs—Hoover Street, Westside, Candlewood, 6–0—that inhabit the district.

2   For his contribution to the madness, Bruner spent his ninth grade in an Oklahoma juvenile lockup. Now Bruner works as an intern for Wayne Thompson at

*Progressive, February 1996, pp. 24–26.

the Oklahoma Health Care Project in Founder's Tower overlooking the city's opulent northwest side. Thompson himself spent three years in prison in the 1970s at Terminal Island and Lompoc for armed bank robbery on behalf of the San Francisco Black Panther chapter.

Madness, Thompson suggests, is "the natural, predictable reaction" of youths   3
to the "larger, hostile adult culture that is anti-youth, particularly anti-African-American youth."

Twenty thousand more Oklahoma City children and teenagers live in poverty   4
than a quarter of a century ago. "These kids are at risk of extinction if they depend upon adults to protect them," Thompson says. It is not just parents who fail them, but an adult society increasingly angry and punishing toward its youth. "That is the perception of the young people who are being ground up in this culture and the grinder of the juvenile-justice system. Their perception of their situation is very correct."

Today, state after state is imposing harsher penalties on juveniles who run   5
afoul of the law. "The nationwide trend is to get tough on juvenile crime," says Gary Taylor of Legal Aid of Western Oklahoma. Rehabilitation and reintegration into the community are concepts that have already fallen out of fashion for adult criminals. Now they are fast becoming passé for juveniles, as well. Instead of prevention and rehabilitation programs, more prisons are being built to warehouse juveniles along with adults. The trend began in California; it is now sweeping the nation.

Juveniles are being waived into adult court at lower and lower ages. In Wis-   6
consin, ten-year-olds can now be tried as adults for murder. Juveniles convicted of drug offenses in adult court receive lengthy mandatory sentences. In California, studies by the state corrections department show that youths serve sentences 60 percent longer than adults for the same crimes. Oklahoma wants to try thirteen-year-olds as adults and petitioned the Supreme Court to allow executions of fourteen- and fifteen-year-olds.

And it's not just the states. It's the Administration, too. *The New York Times*   7
reported in December [1995] that "proposals by the Administration would allow more access to juvenile records and give federal prosecutors discretion to charge serious juvenile offenders as adults."

In short, we are giving up on human beings at a younger and younger age.   8

Juvenile crime is on the rise. But the reason is not media violence, rap music,   9
or gun availability—easy scapegoats that have little to do with the patterns of violence in real life. Rather, the reason is rising youth poverty.

Sensational press accounts make it seem as though juvenile crime is pattern-   10
less. It is hardly that. Juvenile crime is closely tied to youth poverty and the growing opportunity gap between wealthier, older people and destitute, younger people. Of California's fifty-eight counties, thirty-one with a total of 2.5 million people recorded zero teenage murders in 1993. Central Los Angeles, which has roughly the same number of people, reported more than 200 teen murders.

In the thirty-one counties free of teenage killers, the same blood-soaked   11
media and rock and rap music are readily available (more, since white suburban families oversubscribe to cable TV), and guns are easy to obtain. Nor can some "innate" teenage qualities be the cause, since by definition those qualities are as

present in youths in areas where violent teenage crime is rare as in areas where it is common.

12   "We see kids from *all* walks of life," says Harry Hartmann, counselor with the L.A. Office of Education. But "the races are skewed to blacks and Hispanics," he acknowledges. Very skewed—six out of seven of those who are arrested for violent juvenile crimes are black or Hispanic. By strange coincidence, that is just about the proportion of the county's youths in poverty who are black or Hispanic.

13   "Poverty in a society of affluence, in which your self-esteem is tied to failure to achieve that affluence," is a more accurate explanation for our uniquely high level of violence, says Gilbert Geiss, a criminologist formerly with the University of California, Irvine. It's not just "poverty, per se."

14   L.A. County is a clear illustration. Its per-capita income is much higher, and its general poverty rate lower, than the United States as a whole. But its youth poverty rate is staggering: 200,000 impoverished adolescents live in the county.

15   L.A. County is home to one in fifteen teenage murderers in the United States. Its vast basin harbors such a bewildering array of gangs and posses that estimates of the number of youths allied with them at any one time are almost impossible to pin down.

16   Jennifer, seventeen, at the Search to Involve Philippino Americans (SIPA), a local community center, rattles off the names of twenty youth gangs, takes a breath, admits she has left some out. Los Angeles County (population 9 million) has more teen murders than the dozen largest industrial nations outside the United States combined. Of L.A.'s 459 teen murder arrestees in 1994, just twenty-four were white. Blacks and Hispanics predominated, but Asian Americans comprise the fastest-rising group of violent juveniles.

17   "I tried to ask them, 'Why are you in it?'" Jennifer says. "They don't know. A lot of people regret it after. 'Yeah, that was some stupid shit.' They thought it was so cool." But if stupid, confused kids were the whole problem, why are black kids in Los Angeles a dozen times stupider than white kids? Why are Asians getting stupider faster than anyone else?

18   As youth poverty rises and becomes more concentrated in destitute urban neighborhoods, violence becomes more concentrated in younger age groups.

19   But today's reigning criminal-justice experts—UCLA's James Q. Wilson, Northwestern's James Allen Fox, Princeton's John D'Iulio, former Robert Kennedy aide Adam Walinsky—dismiss poverty as a cause of youth violence. Instead, they talk about an insidious culture of poverty, and they argue relentlessly that only more cops and more prisons will bring down juvenile crime. Instead of proposing more money for alleviating poverty or for crime prevention, they want more law enforcement—at a cost of tens of billions of dollars.

20   Writing in the September 1994 *Commentary*, Wilson calls the growing adolescent population "a cloud" that "lurks . . . just beyond the horizon." It will bring "30,000 more muggers, killers, and thieves than we have now." Wilson downplays poverty, racism, poor schools, and unemployment as "not . . . major causes of

crime at all." The real problem, he writes, is "wrong behavior" by a fraction of the population (he pegs it at 6 percent) with bad temperament, concentrated in chaotic families and "disorderly neighborhoods."

If more prisons and surer sentences were the solutions to crime and delin- 21 quency, California should be a haven where citizens leave doors unlocked and stroll midnight streets unmenaced. California inaugurated the new era of impris- oning juvenile offenders in Ronald Reagan's second term as governor in 1971, and since then the state has incarcerated a higher percentage of its youths than any other state. By 1993, a state corrections study found teenagers served terms nearly a year longer than adults for equivalent offenses.

"I tell parents who want to release their kid to the [juvenile-justice] system: 22 he might come out worse than when he went in," says Gilbert Aruyao of SIPA.

Eleven hundred new state laws passed during the 1980s set longer, more cer- 23 tain prison terms, especially for juveniles. California's forty-one-prison, 140,000- inmate system is the third-largest in the world; only the United States as a whole and China have larger inmate systems.

The Golden State's biggest growth industry is corrections. Seven new prisons 24 opened in California from 1989 to 1994, at a cost of $1.3 billion, to accommodate 16,000 more prisoners; today, they confine 28,000 prisoners. From 1995 through 1996, four new prisons, costing $839 million, will open their doors. There's a new prison built every eight months. Each one is full upon opening.

"For that incorrigible 25 percent (of youth offenders), prisons may be the only 25 way to go," says Harry Hartmann of the L.A. Office of Education. "It's really hard for them to change." In California in 1994, 140,000 persons under the age of twenty were arrested for felonies—including one out of five black males, and one in ten Hispanic males ages sixteen through nineteen. If even one-tenth of that number must be imprisoned more or less permanently, the state's minority teenage male population will require four new prisons every year to contain them.

As youth poverty mushrooms and the attitudes of the larger society become 26 harsher, the traditional markers of race and class are sliding toward new realign- ments. "There's still a racial element, sure," says Thompson. "But this has gone be- yond race now. There's a larger madness."

Says Bruner: "There are white kids in black gangs, blacks in Mexican gangs, 27 Mexicans in white gangs, blacks in white gangs, Asians in black gangs. We don't fight each other that way. It isn't a race thing. It's who's in the 'hood.' "

The *1995 Kids Count Factbook* lists 47,000 impoverished children and adoles- 28 cents in the Oklahoma City metropolitan area—21,000 whites, 13,500 blacks, 4,500 Native Americans, 3,000 Asian Americans, 5,000 Latinos.

A November 1995 *Daily Oklahoman* series on the metropolis's exploding 29 poverty reported that these adolescents are increasingly isolated, jammed together in a chain of destitute neighborhoods ringing downtown and extending eastward past the suburbs.

"You go to school with them, people ask of this guy you know, 'Is he OK with 30 you, 'cause if he's OK with you, he's OK with me,' " says Bruner. "If you're in a sub- cultural group, it's no different in society's eyes whether you're in a gang or not.

Kids had no choice but to hang with us. Racism is here. You can't run away from it. [But] racism is not just black or white." Nonwhite youths, white youths on the wrong side, "we are all targets."

31 Bruner is training in office management and in television production and editing through Thompson's program. Enough of his friends remain trapped in the justice system. Bruner sees that as surrender. "They didn't get out like I did; now they're up for murder one."

32 Bruner says the system is rigged: "I believe they want to keep me and every other black male and minority male and poor kid in the system permanently, send us all to the penitentiary."

33 In 1988, Oklahoma petitioned the U.S. Supreme Court to execute fourteen- and fifteen-year-olds (and lost only on a 5–4 vote).

34 "Society wants to kill these kids," says Thompson. "The death penalty. Shooting them in the street. If it can't do that, then killing their spirit."

35 Gary Taylor, deputy director of Legal Aid of Western Oklahoma, recounts his agency's efforts to reform a juvenile prison system whose brutality and punitive excesses had been exposed nationally. "Beatings, sexual assaults, hog tying, extreme medical punishments, extreme isolation," said Taylor. "It was kid-kid; it was staff-kid."

36 There was no notion of rehabilitation. San Francisco lawyers for convicted murderer Freddy Lee Taylor investigated his incarceration in the Oklahoma juvenile prison system and found "a concentration-camp environment," attorney Robert Rionda said.

37 Many of these youths were wrongly imprisoned: they had been removed from their homes because their parents were abusive or neglectful, or the youths had committed minor offenses like curfew violations or truancy. Rionda's firm did not have to look hard to find Freddy Taylor's co-inmates: most were now in state prison serving terms for major felonies.

38 "There were many, many kids who were in the system because they were poor and in need of supervision, and [it] turned them into monsters," Rionda said.

39 In recent years, twice as many Oklahoma youths have been placed in the adult prison system as in the juvenile system. Oklahoma imprisons more of its citizens than any other state except Texas. If forcing youths into the adult prisons and administering harsh punishment is the remedy, Oklahoma, like California, should be a paradise of peace.

40 Yet arrest figures over the last decade show Oklahoma's juvenile violence growing at twice the already alarming national pace.

41 Los Angeles County and Oklahoma City officials stress prevention but note that it is underfunded. The most effective prevention effort by far is to raise fewer children in poverty. However, "reducing child poverty, much less eliminating it, is no longer a paramount priority for either political party," *U.S. News & World Report* pointed out in November 1995.

42 Wayne Thompson in Oklahoma City takes prevention seriously. "We approach juvenile crime as a public-health problem, not a law-enforcement problem," says Thompson. "Intervene, then trace the pathology back to its source." The source

inevitably turns out to be "the low social, educational, and economic status of the families and communities" violent youths come from.

Thompson's program uses employment training and a variety of family 43 services to reintegrate youths who have already been convicted back into their communities. "We want to empower these young people to change the social and economic circumstances of their lives," he says.

An initial evaluation showed that Thompson's program was more effective 44 than law-enforcement approaches in preventing recidivism among delinquent youths as well as preventing younger members of their families from following in their older siblings' footsteps. The clientele served by the program is small—fewer than 100 youths per year.

The adults most responsive to Thompson's approach are in the business 45 community, Republicans more than Democrats, he notes. "That's frightening," he says. "The social services, academia, are bound like serfs to the status quo."

When he talks to Oklahoma City's business groups, Thompson finds growing 46 concern over the costs of more prisons and "alarm in the white community because the gangs are becoming more integrated." He doesn't push charity or altruism.

"I tell them, 'You're going to die in fifteen or twenty years, and you have 47 grandchildren. They're going to have to live with the environment we've created. And we've created a hellacious environment.' This is not just some teenage rite-of-passage problem. The alienation of young people from the traditional institutions is profound. This is the legacy we're leaving: armed camps. If we don't learn how to share with the people who are now powerless, this culture is ultimately going to acquire the means to bring our society to an end." ■

WHO SHOT JOHNNY?*

Debra Dickerson

Debra Dickerson is a lawyer in Washington, D.C.

Given my level of political awareness, it was inevitable that I would come to 1 view the everyday events of my life through the prism of politics and the national discourse. I read *The Washington Post, The New Republic, The New Yorker, Harper's, The Atlantic Monthly, The Nation, National Review, Black Enterprise* and *Essence* and wrote a weekly column for the Harvard Law School Record during my three years just ended there. I do this because I know that those of us who are not well-fed white guys in suits must not yield the debate to them, however well-intentioned or well-informed they may be. Accordingly, I am unrepentant and vocal about having gained admittance to Harvard through affirmative action; I am a feminist, stoic about my marriage chances as a well-educated, 36-year-old black

New Republic, January 1, 1996, pp. 17–18.

woman who won't pretend to need help taking care of herself. My strength flags, though, in the face of the latest role assigned to my family in the national drama. On July 27, 1995, my 16-year-old nephew was shot and paralyzed.

2 Talking with friends in front of his home, Johnny saw a car he thought he recognized. He waved boisterously—his trademark—throwing both arms in the air in a full-bodied, hip-hop Y. When he got no response, he and his friends sauntered down the walk to join a group loitering in front of an apartment building. The car followed. The driver got out, brandished a revolver and fired into the air. Everyone scattered. Then he took aim and shot my running nephew in the back.

3 Johnny never lost consciousness. He lay in the road, trying to understand what had happened to him, why he couldn't get up. Emotionlessly, he told the story again and again on demand, remaining apologetically firm against all demands to divulge the missing details that would make sense of the shooting but obviously cast him in a bad light. Being black, male and shot, he must, apparently, be gang- or drug-involved. Probably both. Witnesses corroborate his version of events.

4 Nearly six months have passed since that phone call in the night and my nightmarish, headlong drive from Boston to Charlotte. After twenty hours behind the wheel, I arrived haggard enough to reduce my mother to fresh tears and to find my nephew reassuring well-wishers with an eerie sangfroid.

5 I take the day shift in his hospital room; his mother and grandmother, a clerk and cafeteria worker, respectively, alternate nights there on a cot. They don their uniforms the next day, gaunt after hours spent listening to Johnny moan in his sleep. How often must his subconscious replay those events and curse its hosts for saying hello without permission, for being carefree and young while a would-be murderer hefted the weight of his uselessness and failure like Jacob Marley's chains? How often must he watch himself lying stubbornly immobile on the pavement of his nightmares while the sound of running feet syncopate his attacker's taunts?

6 I spend these days beating him at gin rummy and Scrabble, holding a basin while he coughs up phlegm and crying in the corridor while he catheterizes himself. There are children here much worse off then he. I should be grateful. The doctors can't, or won't, say whether he'll walk again.

7 I am at once repulsed and fascinated by the bullet, which remains lodged in his spine (having done all the damage it can do, the doctors say). The wound is undramatic—small, neat and perfectly centered—an impossibly pink pit surrounded by an otherwise undisturbed expanse of mahogany. Johnny has asked me several times to describe it but politely declines to look in the mirror I hold for him.

8 Here on the pediatric rehab ward, Johnny speaks little, never cries, never complains, works diligently to become independent. He does whatever he is told; if two hours remain until the next pain pill, he waits quietly. Eyes bloodshot, hands gripping the bed rails. During the week of his intravenous feeding when he was tormented by the primal need to masticate, he never asked for food. He just listened while we counted down the days for him and planned his favorite meals. Now required to dress himself unassisted, he does so without demur, rolling himself back and forth valiantly on the bed and shivering afterwards, exhausted. He "ma'am"s and "sir"s everyone politely. Before his "accident," a simple request to

take out the trash could provoke a firestorm of teenage attitude. We, the women who have raised him, have changed as well; we've finally come to appreciate those boxer-baring, oversized pants we used to hate—it would be much more difficult to fit properly sized pants over his diaper.

He spends a lot of time tethered to rap music still loud enough to break my 9 concentration as I read my many magazines. I hear him try to soundlessly mouth the obligatory "mothafuckers" overlaying the funereal dirge of the music tracks. I do not normally tolerate disrespectful music in my or my mother's presence, but if it distracts him now . . .

"Johnny," I ask later, "do you still like gangster rap?" During the long pause 10 I hear him think loudly, *I'm paralyzed Auntie, not stupid.* "I mostly just listen to hip hop," he says evasively into his *Sports Illustrated.*

Miserable though it is, time passes quickly here. We always seem to be jerk- 11 ing awake in our chairs just in time for the next pill, his every-other-night bowel program, the doctor's rounds. Harvard feels a galaxy away—the world revolves around Family Members Living With Spinal Cord Injury class, Johnny's urine output and strategizing with my sister to find affordable, accessible housing. There is always another long-distance uncle in need of an update, another church member wanting to pray with us or Johnny's little brother in need of some attention.

We Dickerson women are so constant a presence the ward nurses and cleaning 12 staff call us by name and join us for cafeteria meals and cigarette breaks. At Johnny's birthday pizza party, they crack jokes and make fun of each other's husbands (there are no men here). I pass slices around and try not to think, "17 with a bullet."

Oddly, we feel little curiosity or specific anger toward the man who shot him. 13 We have to remind ourselves to check in with the police. Even so, it feels pro forma, like sending in those $2 rebate forms that come with new pantyhose: you know your request will fall into a deep, dark hole somewhere but, still, it's your duty to try. We push for an arrest because we owe it to Johnny and to ourselves as citizens. We don't think about it otherwise—our low expectations are too ingrained. A Harvard aunt notwithstanding, for people like Johnny, Marvin Gaye was right that only three things are sure: taxes, death and trouble. At least it wasn't the second.

We rarely wonder about or discuss the brother who shot him because we 14 already know everything about him. When the call came, my first thought was the same one I'd had when I'd heard about Rosa Parks's beating: a brother did it. A non-job-having, middle-of-the-day malt-liquor-drinking, crotch-clutching, loud-talking brother with many neglected children born of many forgotten women. He lives in his mother's basement with furniture rented at an astronomical interest rate, the exact amount of which he does not know. He has a car phone, an $80 monthly cable bill and every possible phone feature but no savings. He steals Social Security numbers from unsuspecting relatives and assumes their identities to acquire large TV sets for which he will never pay. On the slim chance that he is brought to justice, he will have a colorful criminal history and no coherent explanation to offer for this act. His family will raucously defend him and cry cover-up. Some liberal lawyer just like me will help him plea bargain his way to yet another short stay in a prison pesthouse that will serve only to add another layer to the brother's sociopathology and formless, mindless nihilism. We know him. We've known and feared him all our lives.

15   As a teenager, he called, "Hey, baby, gimme somma that boodie!" at us from car windows. Indignant at our lack of response, he followed up with, "Fuck you, then, 'ho!" He called me a "white-boy lovin' nigger bitch oreo" for being in the gifted program and loving it. At 27, he got my 17-year-old sister pregnant with Johnny and lost interest without ever informing her that he was married. He snatched my widowed mother's purse as she waited in pre-dawn darkness for the bus to work and then broke into our house while she soldered on an assembly line. He chased all the small entrepreneurs from our neighborhood with his violent thievery, and put bars on our windows. He kept us from sitting on our own front porch after dark and laid the foundation for our periodic bouts of self-hating anger and racial embarrassment. He made our neighborhood a ghetto. He is the poster fool behind the maddening community knowledge that there are still some black mothers who raise their daughters but merely love their sons. He and his cancerous carbon copies eclipse the vast majority of us who are not sociopaths and render us invisible. He is the Siamese twin who has died but cannot be separated from his living, vibrant sibling; which of us must attract more notice? We despise and disown this anomalous loser but, for many, he *is* black America. We know him, we know that he is outside the fold, and we know that he will only get worse. What we didn't know is that, because of him, my little sister would one day be the latest hysterical black mother wailing over a fallen child on TV.

16   Alone, lying in the road bleeding and paralyzed but hideously conscious, Johnny had lain helpless as he watched his would-be murderer come to stand over him and offer this prophecy: "Betch'ou won't be doin' nomo' wavin', motha' fucker."

17   Fuck you, asshole. He's fine from the waist up. You just can't do anything right, can you? ■

PEACE IN THE STREETS*

Geoffrey Canada

Geoffrey Canada is president and CEO of Harlem's Rheedlen Center for Children and Families, which serves at-risk inner-city children. Canada is also largely responsible for the Beacon Schools and the Peacemakers program in Harlem and is the East Coast coordinator for the Children's Defense Fund's Black Community Crusade for Children. This is an excerpt from his book Fist Stick Knife Gun.

1 It's a Wednesday night in October and I'm early for my martial arts class in Harlem. I walk into the brightly lit gym and all eyes turn toward me. I'm walking with purpose, quickly and silently. A little boy begins to run over to me and an

older student grabs his arm. I see him whispering in the younger boy's ear. I'm sure he's telling him, "You can't talk to him before class." And he's right. I stand in front of my class, looking unhappy and displeased. Everyone wonders who is out of place or not standing up straight. This is part of my act. Finally I begin the class and then I'm lost in the teaching. I'm trying to bring magic into the lives of these kids. To bring a sense of wonder and amazement. I can feel the students losing themselves and focusing on me. They are finally mine. I have them all to myself. I have crowded all the bad things out of their minds: The test they failed, the father who won't come by to see them, the dinner that won't be on the stove when they get home. I've pushed it all away by force of will and magic.

This is my time and I know all the tricks. I yell, I scream, I fly through the air 2 with the greatest of ease. And by the time the class is ending my students' eyes are wide with amazement and respect, and they look at me differently. I line them up and I talk to them. I talk to them about values, violence, and hope. I try to build within each one a reservoir of strength that they can draw from as they face the countless tribulations small and large that poor children face every day. And I try to convince each one that I know their true value, their worth as human beings, their special gift that God gave to them. And I hope they will make it to the next class with something left in that reservoir for me to add to week by week. It is from that reservoir that they will draw the strength to resist the drugs, the guns, the violence.

My two best students usually walk with me after class and stay with me 3 until I catch a cab. I tell them it's not necessary, but they are there to make sure I get home all right. What a world. So dangerous that children feel that a second-degree black belt needs an escort to get home safely.

This community, like many across this country, is not safe for children, and 4 they usually walk home at night filled with fear and apprehension. But when I walk with them after class they are carefree, as children ought to be. They have no fear. They believe that if anything happens they'll be safe because I'm there. I'll fly through the air and with my magic karate I'll dispatch whatever evil threatens them. When these children see me standing on the corner watching them walk into their buildings they believe what children used to believe, that there are adults who can protect them. And I let them believe this even if my older students and I know different. Because in a world that is so cold and so harsh, children need heroes. Heroes give hope, and if these children have no hope they will have no future. And so I play the role of hero for them even if I have to resort to cheap tricks and theatrics.

If I could get the mayors, the governors, and the president to look into the eyes 5 of the 5-year-olds of this nation, dressed in old raggedy clothes, whose jacket zippers are broken but whose dreams are still alive, they would know what I know—that children need people to fight for them. To stand with them on the most dangerous streets, in the dirtiest hallways, in their darkest hours. We as a country have been too willing to take from our weakest when times get hard. People who allow this to happen must be educated, must be challenged, must be turned around.

If we are to save our children we must become people they will look up to. 6 We must stand up and be visible heroes. I want people to understand the crisis and I want people to act: Either we address the murder and mayhem in our country or we simply won't be able to continue to have the kind of democratic society that we as Americans cherish. Violence is not just a problem of the inner cities or of the minorities in this country. This is a national crisis and the nation must mobilize differently if we are to solve it.

7 Part of what we must do is change the way we think about violence. Trying to catch and punish people after they have committed a violent act won't deter violence in the least. In life on the street, it's better to go to jail than be killed, better to act quickly and decisively even if you risk being caught.

8 There are, however, things that governments could and should do right away to begin to end the violence on our streets. They include the following:

CREATE A PEACE OFFICER CORPS

9 Peace officers would not be police; they would not carry guns and would not be charged with making arrests. Instead they would be local men and women hired to work with children in their own neighborhoods. They would try to settle "beefs" and mediate disputes. They would not be the eyes and ears of the regular police force. Their job would be to try to get these young people jobs, to get them back into school, and, most importantly, to be at the emergency rooms and funerals where young people come together to grieve and plot revenge, in order to keep them from killing one another.

REDUCE THE DEMAND FOR DRUGS

10 Any real effort at diverting the next generation of kids from selling drugs *must* include plans to find employment for these children when they become teenagers. While that will require a significant expenditure of public funds, the savings from reduced hospitalization and reduced incarceration will more than offset the costs of employment.

11 And don't be fooled by those who say that these teenagers will never work for five dollars an hour when they can make thousands of dollars a week. I have found little evidence of this in my years of working with young people. Most of them, given the opportunity to make even the minimum wage, will do so gladly. The problem for many young people has been that they have looked for work year after year without ever finding a job. In some cities more than 40 percent of minority youth who want to work can't find employment.

REDUCE THE PREVALENCE OF DOMESTIC VIOLENCE AND CHILD ABUSE AND NEGLECT

12 Too many children learn to act violently by experiencing violence in their homes. Our society has turned a blind eye to domestic violence for so long that the smacking, punching, and beating of women has become almost routine. And in many of the same homes where women are being beaten, the children are being beaten also. Our response as a society has been to wait until the violence has gotten so bad that the woman has to go to a battered-women's shelter (often losing the only place she has to live), or we have to take the abused child from the family. In both cases we

break up a family, and common sense tells us this ends up costing us more money than it would have if we had intervened early and kept the family together.

The best mode of early intervention for really troubled families is family 13 preservation services—intensive, short-term interventions designed to teach families new coping skills. The family preservation worker spends as much time as needed with a family to ensure that it gets the type of support and skills that it needs to function as a supportive unit rather than a destructive one.

REDUCE THE AMOUNT OF VIOLENCE ON TELEVISION AND IN THE MOVIES

Violence in the media is ever more graphic, and the justification for acting vio- 14 lently is deeply implanted in young people's minds. The movie industry promotes the message that power is determined not merely by carrying a gun, but by carrying a big gun that is an automatic and has a big clip containing many bullets.

What about rap music, and especially "gangsta rap"? It is my opinion that peo- 15 ple have concentrated too much attention on this one source of media violence. Many rap songs are positive, and some are neither positive nor negative—just kids telling their stories. But there are some rap singers who have decided that their niche in the music industry will be the most violent and vile. I would love to see the record industry show some restraint in limiting these rappers' access to fame and fortune.

But by singling out one part of the entertainment industry as violent and ig- 16 noring others that are equally if not more violent (how many people have been killed in movies starring Arnold Schwarzenegger, Sylvester Stallone, and Clint Eastwood?) we will have no impact on reducing violence in this country. The television, movie, and record industries must all reduce the amount of violence they sell to Americans.

REDUCE AND REGULATE THE POSSESSION OF HANDGUNS

I believe all handgun sales should be banned in this country. Recognizing, how- 17 ever, that other Americans may not be ready to accept a ban on handguns, I believe there are still some things we must do.

Licensing

Every person who wants to buy a handgun should have to pass both a written test 18 and a field test. The cost for these new procedures should be paid by those who make, sell, and buy handguns.

Insurance

Gun manufacturers and dealers should be required to register every handgun 19 they manufacture and sell. This registration would be used to trace guns that wind up being used for crimes, and the manufacturers and dealers should be held liable for damages caused by any gun they manufacture and sell. Individual citizens would be required to carry insurance policies for liability and theft on their handguns, which would increase the pressure on citizens to make sure that their guns were safely locked away.

Ammunition Identification

20 While we are beginning to bring some sane regulations to the handgun industry, we must also begin to make the killing of Americans with handguns less anonymous than it is today. One way to do this is to make all handgun ammunition identifiable. Gun owners should have to sign for specially coded ammunition, the purchase of which would then be logged into a computer. The codes should be etched into the shell casing as well as the bullet itself, and the codes should be designed so that even when a bullet breaks into fragments it can still be identified.

Gun Buy-Backs

21 The federal government, which recently passed a $32 billion crime bill, needs to invest billions of dollars over the next ten years buying guns back from citizens. We now have more than 200 million guns in circulation in our country. A properly cared-for gun can last for decades. There is no way we can deal with handgun violence until we reduce the number of guns currently in circulation. We know that young people won't give up their guns readily, but we have to keep in mind that this is a long-term problem. We have to begin to plan now to get the guns currently in the hands of children out of circulation permanently.

22   The truth of the matter is that reducing the escalating violence will be complicated and costly. If we were fighting an outside enemy that was killing our children at a rate of more than 5,000 a year, we would spare no expense. What happens when the enemy is us? What happens when those Americans' children are mostly black and brown? Do we still have the will to invest the time and resources in saving their lives? The answer must be yes, because the impact and fear of violence has overrun the boundaries of our ghettos and has both its hands firmly around the neck of our whole country. And while you may not yet have been visited by the spectre of death and fear of this new national cancer, just give it time. Sooner or later, unless we act, you will. We all will. ■

C. Do Violent Video Games and Books Cause Young People to Commit Crimes?

THE SECRET LIFE OF TEENS*

John Leland

John Leland wrote this article shortly after two students at a high school in Littleton, Colorado, shot and killed several of their classmates and then themselves.

1 "Hi, kids, do you like violence? Wanna see me stick nine-inch nails through each one of my eyelids? Wanna copy me and do exactly like I did?" The bleached-blond

Newsweek, May 10, 1999, pp. 45–50.

pixie could be a refugee from the set of "Friends," all smirk and glimmer. He is Marshall Mathers, better known as Eminem, whose debut rap album has been near the top of the charts for the last two months. In the secret lives of American teenagers, Eminem is large. "By the way," he raps, "when you see my dad, tell him I slit his throat in this dream I had."

Since they first emerged as a demographic entity earlier this century, adoles- 2 cents of every era have carved out their own secret worlds, inventing private codes of style and behavior designed to communicate only within the in group and to exclude or offend adults. It is a central rite of American passage. But lately this developmental process has come under great strain. "In the past, the toughest decision [teens] had was whether to have sex, or whether to use drugs," says Sheri Parks, who studies families and the media at the University of Maryland. "Those are still there, but on top are piled all these other issues, which are very difficult for parents or children to decipher." New technologies and the entertainment industry, combined with changes in family structure, have more deeply isolated grown-ups from teenagers. The results are what Hill Walker, codirector of the Institute on Violence and Destructive Behavior in Oregon, calls "almost a virtual reality without adults."

With as many as 11 million teenagers now online, more and more of adoles- 3 cent life is taking place in a landscape that is inaccessible to many parents. "That is apparent in the geography of households," says Marlene Mayhew, a clinical psychologist who runs an online mental-health newsletter. With the computer often in the teen's bedroom, Mayhew says, the power structure in the family is turned upside down. "Kids are unsupervised, looking at whatever they please." A parent who might eventually notice a stockpile of *Guns & Ammo* or pornographic magazines has fewer clues to a child's online activities. "We're missing the opportunity for an adult reality check, adult perspective on the stimulation [teens] are getting exposed to. Kids have less access to parents, more access to potentially damaging information."

The pop-culture industry, marketing tribal styles through MTV and the In- 4 ternet, makes it harder than ever for adults to read their kids, even parents raised on rock and roll. Parents in the '50s could "read" the ripe sexuality of Elvis—they just might not have approved. But what to make of the much more densely encrypted messages and camp nihilism of Eminem or Marilyn Manson, who dare outsiders to take offense? How to distinguish a kid drawn to gangsta rapper DMX for the rhymes from one drawn to the crimes? Making the process harder, teens have long been adept at lying, dissembling and otherwise conniving to hide their secret lives. Robyn Sykes, a senior at Jordan High School in Long Beach, Calif., reports that the skills are still sharp. "Some girls," she says, "leave the house wearing one thing, and then change into tight, short skirts when they're here."

Mike L., 13, from suburban New York, is one of the unsupervised millions on- 5 line. A couple years ago his father spied on him through a window, catching him in a chat room where people swapped pirated software. But now Mike has his own laptop and can do what he wants. Like many kids, he mostly sends e-mail and hangs around chat rooms, where he encounters both adults and other teens. "You go in, and someone offers what they've got stored in their computer," he says. "And maybe one of the things is *The Anarchist Cookbook*," a notorious handbook that includes instructions for building bombs. Though he doesn't have it, he says, "one of my friends gets called down to the guidance counselor every day because somebody told a teacher that he knows how to make bombs. He's not the kind of guy who would do it. But he found out how on the Internet." Andrew Tyler, 13, from Haddonfield, N.J., used his Internet freedom another way: two weeks ago, while his mother tended the family garden, Tyler placed bids on $3.2 million worth of merchandise via the online auction house eBay, including the winning bid on a $400,000 bedroom set. "I thought [eBay] was just a site," he told *Newsweek*. "It turned out to be a lot more than that."

6   The vast majority of adolescents' online activity ranges from edifying to harmless. Though hard numbers on Internet use are notoriously suspect, Malcolm Parks, an Internet researcher at the University of Washington in Seattle, says that most teens use the computer to send e-mail or instant messages, visit chat rooms or fan Web sites, do homework or download songs. For the most part, he says, "I worry more about poor quality of information online, and students' lack of skills for evaluating information, than I worry about frequently discussed evils like pornography."

7   At Neutral Ground in Manhattan on a recent afternoon, other skills are in play. The drafty, fourth-floor gaming room, undetectable from the street, is a teen oasis, dotted with interconnected computers. By a quarter to four, it is packed with adolescent boys. Robert, one of eight boys glued to the screens, suddenly curses and bangs on the table. "Die, you stupid whore," he shouts. Then, "I'm gonna go kill Sebastian now." Sebastian, three terminals down, calls back: "You take this game way too seriously."

8   They are playing Half-Life, known in video game parlance as a multiplayer "first-person shooter" game, or FPS. As Robert pushes a key, a red shell fires from an on-screen shotgun; arms fly off, blood spatters on the walls. "If my parents came down here now," says Mike, pausing from the carnage, "they'd probably drag me out." The best-known FPS is Doom, the game reportedly favored by the Littleton shooters, but to the kids at Neutral Ground, Doom is already passé. A new game, Kingpin, promises even hairier carnal gratifications. "Includes multiplayer gang bang death match for up to 16 thugs!" coos the ad copy. "Target specific body parts and actually see the damage done, including exit wounds."

9   The video game business last year topped $6.3 billion, much of it dedicated for play on the home computer. The more violent games are marked for sales to mature buyers only, but like R-rated movies, they are easily accessible to kids. "The people usually tell you you're not old enough," says Eddie, 14, a regular at Neutral Ground, "but they don't stop you from buying it." Eddie says most FPS games "make me dizzy," but he enjoys one called Diablo, which is not just another shoot-'em-up orgy. "It's more like slice 'em up." His parents don't like the games

but rarely engage him on it. His mother, he says, "thinks it's too violent, so she doesn't watch."

Most teenagers seem to process the mayhem as mindless pyrotechnics. But 10 not all kids react the same way, warns Dan Anderson, a University of Massachusetts psychologist who has studied the effects of TV on children. "It's always been the case that the kids who have been vulnerable to violent messages on television have been a small minority. But a small minority can cause serious havoc. If you're predisposed to violence and aggression, you can find like-minded people who will validate your experience. You can become part of an isolated group that family and friends don't know about, and that group can exchange information on getting or making weapons." Brad Bushman, an Iowa State University psychologist, argues that violent computer games are more harmful than movies, "because the person becomes the aggressor. They're the one that does the killing."

In Santa Monica last week Collin Williams and his friends, a multiracial 11 group of eighth graders, describe a numbing effect. Sure, they shrugged, a tragedy like the one in Littleton could happen in their school. Though they don't spend much time on computers, says Williams, 14, "we see so much violence on TV and in the movies that it just seems like it's everywhere. We don't go to school thinking we're going to be killed. But maybe it's because we're so used to it."

The challenges for parents may be new, but they are not insurmountable. 12 Many psychologists recommend changing the way the computer is used. Put it in a family room, where adults and teens have more opportunities to discuss what's coming into the house. Every Web browser records what sites users visit; parents can monitor their kids' activities with just elementary computer savvy. Filters, such as Net Nanny, restrict which sites users can visit, but smart kids can get around them, often by using a friend's computer. Idit Harel, founder of the kid-friendly site MaMaMedia, highly recommends playing videogames along with your kids. Even in violent games, she says, "there is learning, visualization; there is analysis of hints." Likewise, parents can either set limits on their kids' pop-cultural diets or just talk to the teens about what they're consuming. Say: "I don't understand this kid Eminem. What's he about?"

Even with such interaction, the secret lives of teenagers are likely to remain 13 secret. They are as unbounded as the Internet and as plebeian as the Backstreet Boys, a daunting world for any parent to enter. But this remains the job of parenting. Today's teens command an electronic landscape more stimulating, vibrant and mysterious than any before. They are the masters of the new domain. But they still need adult guidance on their travels. ▪

THE DOOM FACTOR*

John C. Dvorak

John C. Dvorak hosts News, Views, and Snide Asides *at* PC Magazine Online *and* Silicon Spin *on ZDTV. He wrote this article for* PC Magazine *in response to the controversy concerning violent video games and their effect on young people.*

1   Now that the Littleton, Colorado, disaster has calmed down, we can seriously look at the role the game Doom played in the death and injuries caused by the two boys who went crazy and shot up their school. Many have tried to downplay the game's role, but they're dead wrong. My conclusions do not bode well for the future.

2   One observer on TV called Doom and other games "murder simulators," pointing out that the military even practices on Doom. In fact, as I listened to various pundits discuss the role of violent games, few brought up the incredible effectiveness of many simulations.

3   Pilots learn to fly those jumbo jets on computer simulators, and the Army tank corps uses computer simulators to make the corps world-class. My eldest son learned to drive a car on a computer, and he's the best driver in the family. I've been using a simulator to practice skeet shooting, and last year when I grabbed a shotgun for the first time, I hit the first four birds out of the chute. The instructor called me a natural. The fact is, computers are great training tools.

4   There's no doubt that Doom and other games are in fact murder simulators. If you're going to tear up a place like a maniac, you'll do a lot more damage after playing Doom for a year or two than if you've never played the game. But so what?

5   I play Doom, too. I let my kids play Doom and Quake and Duke Nukem. I even let them play Grand Theft Auto. And yes, I know Grand Theft Auto is a simulator for carjackers. My thinking is that the boys find it fun and will move on to something else eventually. And they do. Yes, they could probably go carjacking and maybe be better at it than a kid who hasn't been playing the game. Well, if they ever become carjackers, they'll be damn good at it.

6   I'm convinced that there's a long stretch between knowing how to carjack (or murder, for that matter) and actually doing it. There are factors other than ability and knowledge. Martial arts classes can teach you how to kill someone, but everyone who learns martial arts doesn't go out and kill. My oldest son learned much of his driving skill on the old game Vette, where you run people over. He hasn't run anybody over in real life. He's not an idiot. This is the issue here.

7   There's also something called *sublimation* at work in these violent games, which has been completely overlooked in the debate. You get pooped playing these games—especially head to head, where you're shooting at other people. The kids eventually fall back into chat rooms or strategy gaming. The amount of time

*PC Magazine, June 22, 1999, p. 87.

you spend playing Doom-type games naturally decreases once you get good at them and you get something out of your system. You sublimate.

The Doom players who tore up their high school had other problems. I 8 was personally creeped out by the school itself, which from the helicopter views actually looked like a Doom scenario. It looked like a factory, warehouse, or prison—you decide. And the principal was an out-of-touch bureaucrat running a too-large institution.

The rationale for such cavernous, soulless schools is beyond me. They're 9 building one in the town where I live, and I expect it to be shot up one day by a disaffected youth haunted by the daily prisonlike impersonal atmosphere. Nobody shoots up small private schools where the kids get lots of attention. For the sociology of the situation, I recommend the movie *Over the Edge* (1979). It was about a similar instance of disaffection, exacerbated by the vacuous environment of modern suburbia.

This problem is not going to go away as long as children are warehoused in 10 a perverse environment where there are too many kids for anyone to know what's really going on. Perhaps these two jokers could have been stopped by their parents or who knows who. And perhaps the school shouldn't be held responsible, although it *was* the school that was shot to pieces. Whatever the case, the underlying alienation and pent-up hostility are not going away. There were sites put up on the Web that congratulated these kids—an underreported fact.

What makes this situation urgent now more than ever is the Doom factor. This 11 generation has been training itself on murder simulators. The disaffected youth of the past was a raw amateur who managed to kill one or two people; today's youth is essentially Rambo on the loose. I expect the body count to skyrocket in the next catastrophe and get worse and worse. Count on it. ■

FULL METAL DUST JACKET: BOOKS ARE VIOLENT, TOO*

Doreen Carvajal

This article considers the influence of violence in books and compares violent images in print to violence on the screen.

Since the shootings in Littleton, Col., the tone of complaints about what children 1 read has shifted dramatically from outrage about sexual descriptions to concern about mayhem on the printed page.

Last week's free-for-all in Congress included proposed legislation making it 2 a felony to expose children to books, movies and video games that contain explicit sex or violence. The measure failed, with a vigorous lobbying effort by the entertainment and book industries, but the debates lingers among the bookstacks of public and school libraries.

New York Times, June 20, 1999, p. 16.

3   To date virtually no one has challenged *Medeca* with its bleak plot of adultery, poisoning and child murders, but the American Library Association is tracking complaints from adult readers who are scolding librarians for the violence in books like John Steinbeck's *Of Mice and Men* or Alvin Schwartz's *More Scary Stories to Tell in the Dark.*

4   "There are more complaints coming in because of violence," said Judith Krug, the director of the office for intellectual freedom for the Chicago-based American Library Association, "and the people complaining say it's because of Colorado." Last year the library association said libraries reported receiving 478 complaints, most of them predominantly about sexual material in literature. The association estimates that those represent only one-fourth of actual complaints since libraries call them to report challenges on a voluntary basis.

5   Some institutions, like the Cumberland County Public Library in Fayetteville, N.C., responded to a complaint this spring by raising the age at which teen-agers may borrow general circulation books to 16 from 13 and by issuing special library cards that allow access only to juvenile books. The library took the action following a complaint about sexual descriptions in three adult-level books, but its review of the titles themselves continues, said the library's director, Jerry Thresher. In the meantime, the controversy has increased demand for the disputed library books, *Knowing* by Roslyn MacMillan and *History Laid Bare* and *An Underground Education*, both by Richard Zacks.

6   Literary complaints usually come in distinct cycles, said Ms. Krug, of the library association. "I've been here before." she said. "It's just that the subject changes and today it's violence and yesterday it was sex and tomorrow it's going to be hate."

7   Some young readers may scorn *Of Mice and Men*, but for very different reasons than an anxious adult fretting over the coldblooded murder of a ranch hand by his friend to prevent his death at the hands of a lynch mob. In focus groups in California and Connecticut that were convened by Scholastic to explore teen reading and buying patterns, teen-agers made a list of their "unfavorites." Among them were Ernest Hemingway's *Old Man and the Sea* ("very slow"), *Animal Farm* and *Of Mice and Men*. They explained that they wanted their reading set in a present-day world.

8   For boys, that means a reading diet of science fictions, horror, spy stories and suspense. Girls also expressed an interest in horror and ghost stories, and a taste for romance.

9   Mary Leonhardt, a high-school English teacher in Massachusetts for more than 28 years, who wrote *Keeping Kids Reading: How to Raise Avid Readers in the Video Age* (Crown Publishing Group, 1998), started thinking about a possible relationship between violent books and violent youths when a student said how much more she enjoyed reading Alice Walker's *The Color Purple* than seeing the movie, which chronicles the struggles of a battered, sexually abused heroine.

10   "One thing I know," Mrs. Leonhardt said, "avid readers are almost never violent kids. Kids can read war books and horror books and science-fiction thrillers and still be gentle, peace-loving students." She insists that there is a crucial difference between reading about violence and watching movie mayhem; a book gives a reader more complex information to understand the feelings and insights of characters.

"We are inside the minds of the characters," Ms. Leonhardt said. "We under- 11 stand their confusion. We feel their suffering. While movies can desensitize us to violence, I think reading can make us more sensitive to it. We understand, in a much deeper sense, the impact of violence on a victim's life." She is less concerned about violent images in books than whether a student reads.

Her own students have coined a term for their favorite subset of literature, calling 12 it the "psycho-killer" genre of tales of deranged serial murderers. Thomas Harris's *The Silence of the Lambs* and his earlier book *Red Dragon* remain perennial favorites with students intrigued by the sinister Hannibal Lecter, a gifted psychopath and serial killer who has a penchant for eating parts of his victims.

Christopher Gray, a 16-year-old sophomore in Ms. Leonhardt's class at Con- 13 cord-Carlisle High School in Massachusetts, said that his last summer's reading material consisted of two sports magazines. But this year, his literary appetite was whetted by the chance to earn class course credits for reading up to 200 pages a week of virtually anything he pleased. So a few weeks ago, he read *Silence of the Lambs,* which left him primed to read the third book in the series, *Hannibal,* which Delacorte Press published this month.

For Mr. Gray, the violent images "made the book a little more interesting," he 14 said. "It sort of got me involved in it. I could kind of picture it in my head. With me, it doesn't really affect my life. It's just sort of a way of entertaining myself. Personally, I think it's kind of funny that anybody thinks that the violence in books is going to play a role in someone's life."

Inspired by *Hannibal,* Mr. Gray said he plans to read more than just sports 15 magazines this summer. ■

QUESTIONS TO HELP YOU THINK AND WRITE ABOUT ISSUES CONCERNING CRIME AND THE TREATMENT OF CRIMINALS

1. James Gilligan calls for a complete renovation of the current prison system. He claims prisons should focus on educating the criminals they hold. Do you agree or disagree with Gilligan's claim? Identify the reasons for your answer. What are the benefits of adopting Gilligan's plan? What are the drawbacks? In your opinion, what should the purpose of prison be?
2. What is your response to George Will's ideas about shortening the prison sentences of older prisoners, even if they have been sentenced to life in prison? Would this practice achieve what society hopes to achieve by punishing criminals? How do you react to this variation in the usual practice?
3. Refer to the article by Nicole Koch, "Unconventional Punishment for Criminals Catching On." What do you think about the use of "scarlet letter" punishment? Is humiliation a new and inventive approach to punishment or an infringement on "criminal rights"? Should criminals have rights, in your opinion? Why or why not? If so, how far do those rights extend?
4. Compare Graeme Newman's essay "Turning Bad into Good" with Koch's "Unconventional Punishment." Give some specific examples of the concept of making the punishment fit the crime. Give some examples that violate

this concept. Can you think of some other creative ways for making the punishment fit the crime? Finally, what do you think about punishment that claims to fit the crime? Is it effective or not? Why?

5. Compare Newman's article with Terry FitzPatrick's "Witness to an Execution." Do these authors rely on *ethos,* on logic, on emotional proofs, or on a combination of these to further their argument? What are the strengths of their proofs? What are the weaknesses? How would you refute each of these arguments? What is your own opinion on the issue of capital punishment? Were you influenced in your thinking by the works of either of these authors?

6. Next, compare FitzPatrick's article with Debra Dickerson's "Who Shot Johnny?" Both rely on the audience to infer the main claims. What are the claims? What is the exigence (the author's motivation) for writing each piece? How does the exigence influence the manner and effectiveness of the writing?

7. Suppose that Cohen, Males and Docuyanan, Dickerson, and Canada have been appointed to a national committee to make recommendations on how to deal with young offenders. What warrants would each of these individuals bring to this committee? What are two suggestions that each of these authors might make for dealing with juvenile offenders? How would you reconcile their positions? What final recommendations would you like to see made?

8. Leland and Dvorak are concerned with adolescents' ability to access potentially dangerous or damaging information through computers without having the critical thinking skills necessary to evaluate or make sense of it. Do you share their concern? Should the focus be on limiting young people's access to certain types of information, or should it be on teaching them how to analyze such material? Speculate on how you would implement the option you favor.

9. Have you ever played a video game like Doom, Quake, or Duke Nukem? Did these games have a particular effect on you? Do you think they might have a different effect on others? What is your final conclusion about the potential danger of such games? Are they more or less dangerous than violent books (see the article by Carvajal)? Why do you think so?

SECTION IV
Issues Concerning Computers

THE ISSUES

A. How Are Computers Changing the Culture?

"The New Wired World" describes the status of computers in the American culture near the close of the twentieth century. Next, Negroponte and Kurzweil discuss the future of computers and the changes they could create in society in the next twenty years or so. McGinn and Raymond focus on the changes that computers have already caused in the workplace along with other changes they are likely to cause in the future. See also "The Road to Unreality," page 84.

B. How Are Computers Changing Their Users?

Turkle describes the experience of changing her gender, just to see what might happen, when she communicates with people in cyberspace. Miller writes about the "human" qualities of computers and how they are expected to become even more humanlike in the future. McGrath and Maas deal with some of the frustrations and problems computers create for their users, including those related to the use of time and to privacy. See also "The Secret Life of Teens," page 524; "The Doom Factor," page 528; "Study Says Net Use, Depression May Be Linked," page 185; and "Censorship or Common Sense?" page 219.

C. How Are Computers Changing Education?

Many modern politicians seem to believe that educational problems could be solved in this country if every schoolchild were issued a computer. Dertouzos, a computer expert from MIT, takes issue with this idea and suggests that we move more slowly, at least until we understand where we should be using computers in education and where we should not. Arenson describes some of the issues associated with college-level distance-education courses, which are taught entirely on computers. In two final articles, Stulman writes about time problems computers can create for college students, and Zack writes about the problem of computer-aided cheating among college students. See also, "Looking for the Tidy Mind, Alas," page 495, and "Girls and Computers," page 24.

To Extend Your Perspective: Films and Literature Related to Computers

> *Films: Alphaville,* 1965; *2001: A Space Odyssey,* 1968; *Colossus: The Forbin Project,* 1970; *TRON,* 1982; *Hackers,* 1995; *Johnny Mnemonic,* 1995; *The Net,* 1995; *Strange Days,* 1995; *You've Got Mail,* 1999
>
> *Literature:* novels: *Player Piano* by Kurt Vonnegut Jr.; *Bugs* by Theodore Roszak; *The Bohr Maker* by Linda Nagata; *Society of the Mind* by Eric L. Harry; *Mona Lisa Overdrive* and *Neuromancer* by William Gibson; *Cryptonomicon* by Neal Stephenson

THE RHETORICAL SITUATION

Computers are associated with change, and change is often controversial. People who resist the changes brought about by computer technology are sometimes referred to as Luddites, after a group of nineteenth-century English workmen who destroyed new labor-saving machinery to protest the changes they feared the machines would bring about. Anti-Luddites would then be assumed to welcome change. But of course, reacting to the changes associated with computers is more complicated than this simple pro-or-con approach.

Computers have, without question, produced rapid changes in the culture as a whole as well as in the lives of individuals. And as a whole, people have adjusted to these changes quickly. Personal computers have been available for only about twenty years, and the Internet dates back to around 1985. In 1995 it was estimated that 50 million individuals in 175 countries were using the Internet; five years later that number had increased to more than 200 million people worldwide, 80 million of them in the United States alone.

The use of computers in all areas of life invites controversy. For example, the use of computers in education is open to debate. Can students learn on computers in isolation as well as they can in a room with other students and teachers? Can computers grade essays? How is the Internet changing research practices? These are just a few of the issues. Computers also raise questions regarding privacy, censorship, commerce, politics, and communication. Studies suggest that there is a widening income gap between people who use computers and those who do not. Other studies suggest that computers may have a negative effect on individuals who use them extensively; they seem to increase loneliness and depression.

In spite of these problems, few people who use computers would be willing to part with them. We use computers at work, in school, and at home for accounting, researching, communicating, composing, buying, trading, gaming, surfing, chatting. Computers put us in touch with massive amounts of information on virtually any subject, and they also entertain us. Argument about computers usually centers around cause-and-effect, value, and policy issues and invites questions regarding the effects of computers on society and individuals, the long-term value of computers, and policies to guard against possible negative effects.

Before you read the essays in this section, explore your own personal rhetorical situation for the issues associated with computers by answering these questions: How do you use computers? Do they create issues for you? What are these issues? What are your present opinions about these issues?

A.   How Are Computers Changing the Culture?

THE NEW WIRED WORLD*

In a special edition of Newsweek *magazine that appeared in late 1999, the editors described how the Internet was changing America as they perceived it at that time. They also made a projection: by 2003, they claimed, more than 500 million people would be surfing the Web.*

1   Was there a single moment when we turned the corner? When we moved from a culture centered on network television, phones with wires, information on paper and stock prices based on profit into a digital society of buddy lists, streaming video, Matt Drudge and 34-year-old billionaires in tennis shoes? Did the transition come with the Deep Blue chess match, when millions of Web-surfers watched a stack of computer chips dominate the world's greatest player in a test of "intelligence"? Could the global outburst of online mourning after the death of Princess

*Newsweek, September 20, 1999, pp. 40–41.

Diana have marked our passage? Did it come last Christmas, when hundreds of thousands of shoppers avoided malls and clicked through their gift lists? Or was it the online lingerie fashion show? The online birth? And just when did putting an e-mail address on a business card stop marking you as ahead of your time?

Let the chat rooms debate what marked the turning point. What's certain is 2 that America has digitized, and there's no going back. Worldwide there are almost 200 million people on the Internet. In the United States alone, 80 million. The numbers tell just part of the story: the Net is no longer a novelty, an interesting way to pass the time. A third of wired Americans now do at least some of their shopping on the Net, and some are already consulting doctors on the Net, listening to radio on the Net, making investments on the Net, getting mortgages on the Net, tracking packages on the Net, getting news on the Net, having phone conversations on the Net, checking out political candidates on the Net, even, um, having *sex* on the Net. Each of these activities is impressive, but the aggregate effect is a different kind of life. [. . .] The Internet is changing the way we live now.

It's been 30 years since the Internet's predecessor, the Arpanet, was switched 3 on to help academics and government wonks get connected. Almost 25 years since the first software for personal computers (co-written by some kid named Bill Gates). About five years since the Net became in effect the world's grandest public utility, driven by a combination of cheap, powerful PCs, a remarkably scalable infrastructure that sped up our connections (though not enough), and easy-to-use browsing software that took advantage of the Net's open rules. And maybe three or four years since concocting Internet business schemes became the world's most desirable creative outlet, the contemporary successor to writing the Great American Novel.

The triumph of tech, for better or for worse, is far from complete—in schools, 4 businesses, operating rooms, labs, banks or the halls of government. Just about everything we've ever done that has to do with communication and information has been digitized, and now we're going to start tackling stuff that hasn't been done because you can do it only with the Internet. And if you think up something that fits that bill, there's a venture capitalist in Palo Alto who will whip out a huge check for you. Even the most knuckleheaded CEO—the kind of guy who used to think it was beneath him to put a terminal anywhere near his mahogany desktop— now knows that job No. 1 in the firm, no matter what the company does, is to figure out how to become an *Internet* company, because he can be damn well sure that his competitors are.

It's crucial to assess the impact of this shift, because the digital revolution is 5 much more profound than a mere change of tools. The Internet is built on both a philosophy and an infrastructure of openness and free communication; its users hold the potential to change not just how we get things done, but our thinking patterns and behavior. Bound together by digital mesh, there's hope we may thrive together—if some nagging, unanswered questions find felicitous answers. Can a spirit of sharing be maintained in the face of the need to recoup huge investments? Will persistent security holes—both personal and national, with the threat of cyberwar—erode our confidence in this new medium? Is it really possible for governments to forgo their impulses to regulate the Net with their usual heavy-handedness? How will the bounty of the digital age be distributed fairly?

6   The corner has been turned, but only just. We're at the beginning of a new way of working, shopping, playing and communicating. [. . .] We're calling this phenomenon e-life, and it's just in time. Because the day is approaching when no one will describe the digital, Net-based, computer-connected gestalt with such a transitory term. We'll just call it life. ■

AN AGE OF OPTIMISM*

Nicholas Negroponte

Nicholas Negroponte is professor of media technology at MIT. The following article is the epilogue to his book, Being Digital. *In it, Negroponte claims that the computer has four powerful qualities that will "result in its ultimate triumph." Identify these qualities, and see if you agree with them.*

1   I am optimistic by nature. However, every technology or gift of science has a dark side. Being digital is no exception.

2   The next decade will see cases of intellectual-property abuse and invasion of our privacy. We will experience digital vandalism, software piracy, and data thievery. Worst of all, we will witness the loss of many jobs to wholly automated systems, which will soon change the white-collar workplace to the same degree that it has already transformed the factory floor. The notion of lifetime employment at one job has already started to disappear.

3   The radical transformation of the nature of our job markets, as we work less with atoms and more with bits, will happen at just about the same time the 2 billion–strong labor force of India and China starts to come on-line (literally). A self-employed software designer in Peoria will be competing with his or her counterpart in Pohang. A digital typographer in Madrid will do the same with one in Madras. American companies are already outsourcing hardware development and software production to Russia and India, not to find cheap manual labor but to secure a highly skilled intellectual force seemingly prepared to work harder, faster, and in a more disciplined fashion than those in our own country.

4   As the business world globalizes and the Internet grows, we will start to see a seamless digital workplace. Long before political harmony and long before the GATT talks can reach agreement on the tariff and trade of atoms (the right to sell Evian water in California), bits will be borderless, stored and manipulated with absolutely no respect to geopolitical boundaries. In fact, time zones will probably play a bigger role in our digital future than trade zones. I can imagine some software projects that literally move around the world from east to west on a twenty-four-hour cycle, from person to person or from group to group, one working as the other sleeps. Microsoft will need to add London and Tokyo offices for software development in order to produce on three shifts.

*Nicholas Negroponte, *Being Digital* (New York: Knopf, 1995), pp. 227–231.

As we move more toward such a digital world, an entire sector of the popu- 5
lation will be or feel disenfranchised. When a fifty-year-old steelworker loses his
job, unlike his twenty-five-year-old son, he may have no digital resilience at all.
When a modern-day secretary loses his job, at least he may be conversant with the
digital world and have transferable skills.

Bits are not edible; in that sense they cannot stop hunger. Computers are not 6
moral; they cannot resolve complex issues like the rights to life and to death. But
being digital, nevertheless, does give much cause for optimism. Like a force of nature, the digital age cannot be denied or stopped. It has four very powerful qualities
that will result in its ultimate triumph: decentralizing, globalizing, harmonizing,
and empowering.

The decentralizing effect of being digital can be felt no more strongly than 7
in commerce and in the computer industry itself. The so-called management information systems (MIS) czar, who used to reign over a glass-enclosed and air-
conditioned mausoleum, is an emperor with no clothes, almost extinct. Those
who survive are usually doing so because they outrank anybody able to fire
them, and the company's board of directors is out of touch or asleep or both.

Thinking Machines Corporation, a great and imaginative supercomputer 8
company started by electrical engineering genius Danny Hillis, disappeared after
ten years. In that short space of time it introduced the world to massively parallel
computer architectures. Its demise did not occur because of mismanagement or
sloppy engineering of [the] so-called Connection Machine. It vanished because
parallelism could be decentralized; the very same kind of massively parallel architectures have suddenly become possible by threading together low-cost, mass-
produced personal computers.

While this was not good news for Thinking Machines, it is an important 9
message to all of us, both literally and metaphorically. It means the enterprise of
the future can meet its computer needs in a new and scalable way by populating
its organization with personal computers that, when needed, can work in unison
to crunch on computationally intensive problems. Computers will literally work
both for individuals and for groups. I see the same decentralized mind-set growing in our society, driven by young citizenry in the digital world. The traditional
centralist view of life will become a thing of the past.

The nation-state itself is subject to tremendous change and globalization. 10
Governments fifty years from now will be both larger and smaller. Europe finds itself dividing itself into smaller ethnic entities while trying to unite economically.
The forces of nationalism make it too easy to be cynical and dismiss any broad-
stroke attempt at world unification. But in the digital world, previously impossible
solutions become viable.

Today, when 20 percent of the world consumes 80 percent of its resources, 11
when a quarter of us have an acceptable standard of living and three-quarters
don't, how can this divide possibly come together? While the politicians struggle
with the baggage of history, a new generation is emerging from the digital landscape free of many of the old prejudices. These kids are released from the limitation of geographic proximity as the sole basis of friendship, collaboration, play,

and neighborhood. Digital technology can be a natural force drawing people into greater world harmony.

12 The harmonizing effect of being digital is already apparent as previously partitioned disciplines and enterprises find themselves collaborating, not competing. A previously missing common language emerges, allowing people to understand across boundaries. Kids at school today experience the opportunity to look at the same thing from many perspectives. A computer program, for example, can be seen simultaneously as a set of computer instructions or as concrete poetry formed by the indentations in the text of the program. What kids learn very quickly is that to know a program is to know it from many perspectives, not just one.

13 But more than anything, my optimism comes from the empowering nature of being digital. The access, the mobility, and the ability to effect change are what will make the future so different from the present. The information superhighway may be mostly hype today, but it is an understatement about tomorrow. It will exist beyond people's wildest predictions. As children appropriate a global information resource, and as they discover that only adults need learner's permits, we are bound to find new hope and dignity in places where very little existed before.

14 My optimism is not fueled by an anticipated invention or discovery. Finding a cure for cancer and AIDS, finding an acceptable way to control population, or inventing a machine that can breathe our air and drink our oceans and excrete unpolluted forms of each are dreams that may or may not come about. Being digital is different. We are not waiting on any invention. It is here. It is now. It is almost genetic in its nature, in that each generation will become more digital than the preceding one.

15 The control bits of that digital future are more than ever before in the hands of the young. Nothing could make me happier. ■

AN INEXORABLE EMERGENCE: TRANSITION TO THE TWENTY-FIRST CENTURY*

Ray Kurzweil

This is an excerpt from Ray Kurzweil's book The Age of Spiritual Machines: When Computers Exceed Human Intelligence, *published in 1999. He is also the author of* The Age of Intelligent Machines, *which won the Association of American Publishers' award for the Most Outstanding Computer Science Book of 1990.*

1 Computers today exceed human intelligence in a broad variety of intelligent yet narrow domains such as playing chess, diagnosing certain medical conditions, buying and selling stocks, and guiding cruise missiles. Yet human intelligence overall remains far more supple and flexible. Computers are still unable

*Ray Kurzweil, *The Age of Spiritual Machines: When Computers Exceed Human Intelligence* (New York: Viking, 1999) pp. 2–6.

to describe the objects on a crowded kitchen table, write a summary of a movie, tie a pair of shoelaces, tell the difference between a dog and a cat (although this feat, I believe, is becoming feasible today with contemporary neural nets—computer simulations of human neurons),[1] recognize humor, or perform other subtle tasks in which their human creators excel.

One reason for this disparity in capabilities is that our most advanced computers are still simpler than the human brain—currently about a million times simpler (give or take one or two orders of magnitude depending on the assumptions used). But this disparity will not remain the case as we go through the early part of the next century. Computers doubled in speed . . . every two years in the 1950s and 1960s, and are now doubling in speed every twelve months. This trend will continue, with computers achieving the memory capacity and computing speed of the human brain by around the year 2020. 2

Achieving the basic complexity and capacity of the human brain will not automatically result in computers matching the flexibility of human intelligence. The organization and content of these resources—the software of intelligence—is equally important. One approach to emulating the brain's software is through reverse engineering—scanning a human brain (which will be achievable early in the next century)[2] and essentially copying its neural circuitry in a neural computer (a computer designed to simulate a massive number of human neurons) of sufficient capacity. 3

There is a plethora of credible scenarios for achieving human-level intelligence in a machine. We will be able to evolve and train a system combining massively parallel neural nets with other paradigms to understand language and model knowledge, including the ability to read and understand written documents. Although the ability of today's computers to extract and learn knowledge from natural-language documents is quite limited, their abilities in this domain are improving rapidly. Computers will be able to read on their own, understanding and modeling what they have read, by the second decade of the twenty-first century. We can then have our computers read all of the world's literature—books, magazines, scientific journals, and other available material. Ultimately, the machines will gather knowledge on their own by venturing into the physical world, drawing from the full spectrum of media and information services, and sharing knowledge with each other (which machines can do far more easily than their human creators). 4

Once a computer achieves a human level of intelligence, it will necessarily roar past it. Since their inception, computers have significantly exceeded human mental dexterity in their ability to remember and process information. A computer can remember billions or even trillions of facts perfectly, while we are hard pressed to remember a handful of phone numbers. A computer can quickly search a database with billions of records in fractions of a second. Computers can readily share their knowledge bases. The combination of human-level intelligence in a machine with a computer's inherent superiority in the speed, accuracy, and sharing ability of its memory will be formidable. 5

Mammalian neurons are marvelous creations, but we wouldn't build them the same way. Much of their complexity is devoted to supporting their own life 6 processes, not to their information-handling abilities. Furthermore, neurons are extremely slow; electronic circuits are at least a million times faster. Once a computer achieves a human level of ability in understanding abstract concepts, recognizing patterns, and other attributes of human intelligence, it will be able to apply this ability to a knowledge base of all human-acquired—and machine-acquired—knowledge.

7   A common reaction to the proposition that computers will seriously compete with human intelligence is to dismiss this specter based primarily on an examination of contemporary capability. After all, when I interact with my personal computer, its intelligence seems limited and brittle, if it appears intelligent at all. It is hard to imagine one's personal computer having a sense of humor, holding an opinion, or displaying any of the other endearing qualities of human thought.

8   But the state of the art in computer technology is anything but static. Computer capabilities are emerging today that were considered impossible one or two decades ago. Examples include the ability to transcribe accurately normal continuous human speech, to understand and respond intelligently to natural language, to recognize patterns in medical procedures such as electrocardiograms and blood tests with an accuracy rivaling that of human physicians, and, of course, to play chess at a world-championship level. In the next decade, we will see translating telephones that provide real-time speech translation from one human language to another, intelligent computerized personal assistants that can converse and rapidly search and understand the world's knowledge bases, and a profusion of other machines with increasingly broad and flexible intelligence.

9   In the second decade of the next century, it will become increasingly difficult to draw any clear distinction between the capabilities of human and machine intelligence. The advantages of computer intelligence in terms of speed, accuracy, and capacity will be clear. The advantages of human intelligence, on the other hand, will become increasingly difficult to distinguish.

10   The skills of computer software are already better than many people realize. It is frequently my experience that when demonstrating recent advances in, say, speech or character recognition, observers are surprised at the state of the art. For example, a typical computer user's last experience with speech-recognition technology may have been a low-end freely bundled piece of software from several years ago that recognized a limited vocabulary, required pauses between words, and did an incorrect job at that. These users are then surprised to see contemporary systems that can recognize fully continuous speech on a 60,000-word vocabulary, with accuracy levels comparable to a human typist.

11   Also keep in mind that the progression of computer intelligence will sneak up on us. As just one example, consider Gary Kasparov's confidence in 1990 that a computer would never come close to defeating him. After all, he had played the best computers, and their chess-playing ability—compared to his—was pathetic. But computer chess playing made steady progress, gaining forty-five rating points each year. In 1997, a computer sailed past Kasparov, at least in chess. There has been a great deal of commentary that other human endeavors are far more difficult to emulate than chess playing. *This is true.* In many areas—the ability to write

a book on computers, for example—computers are still pathetic. But as computers continue to gain in capacity at an exponential rate, we will have the same experience in these other areas that Kasparov had in chess. Over the next several decades, machine competence will rival—and ultimately surpass— any particular human skill one cares to cite, including our marvelous ability to place our ideas in a broad diversity of contexts.

12 Evolution has been seen as a billion-year drama that led inexorably to its grandest creation: human intelligence. The emergence in the early twenty-first century of a new form of intelligence on Earth that can compete with, and ultimately significantly exceed, human intelligence will be a development of greater import than any of the events that have shaped human history. It will be no less important than the creation of the intelligence that created it, and will have profound implications for all aspects of human endeavor, including the nature of work, human learning, government, warfare, the arts, and our concept of ourselves.

13 This specter is not yet here. But with the emergence of computers that truly rival and exceed the human brain in complexity will come a corresponding ability of machines to understand and respond to abstractions and subtleties. Human beings appear to be complex in part because of our competing internal goals. Values and emotions represent goals that often conflict with each other, and are an unavoidable by-product of the levels of abstraction that we deal with as human beings. As computers achieve a comparable—and greater—level of complexity, and as they are increasingly derived at least in part from models of human intelligence, they, too, will necessarily utilize goals with implicit values and emotions, although not necessarily the same values and emotions that humans exhibit.

14 A variety of philosophical issues will emerge. Are computers thinking, or are they just calculating? Conversely, are human beings thinking, or are they just calculating? The human brain presumably follows the laws of physics, so it must be a machine, albeit a very complex one. Is there an inherent difference between human thinking and machine thinking? To pose the question another way, once computers are as complex as the human brain, and can match the human brain in subtlety and complexity of thought, are we to consider them conscious? This is a difficult question even to pose, and some philosophers believe it is not a meaningful question; others believe it is the only meaningful question in philosophy. This question actually goes back to Plato's time, but with the emergence of machines that genuinely appear to possess volition and emotion, the issue will become increasingly compelling.

15 For example, if a person scans his brain through a noninvasive scanning technology of the twenty-first century (such as an advanced magnetic resonance imaging), and downloads his mind to his personal computer, is the "person" who emerges in the machine the same consciousness as the person who was scanned? That "person" may convincingly implore you that "he" grew up in Brooklyn, went to college in Massachusetts, walked into a scanner here, and woke up in the machine there. The original person who was scanned, on the other hand, will acknowledge that the person in the machine does indeed appear to share his history,

knowledge, memory, and personality, but is otherwise an impostor, a different person.

16   Even if we limit our discussion to computers that are not directly derived from a particular human brain, they will increasingly appear to have their own personalities, evidencing reactions that we can only label as emotions and articulating their own goals and purposes. They will appear to have their own free will. They will claim to have spiritual experiences. And people—those still using carbon-based neurons or otherwise—will believe them.

17   One often reads predictions of the next several decades discussing a variety of demographic, economic, and political trends that largely ignore the revolutionary impact of machines with their own opinions and agendas. Yet we need to reflect on the implications of the gradual, yet inevitable, emergence of true competition to the full range of human thought in order to comprehend the world that lies ahead. ■

NOTES

1. For an excellent overview and technical details on neural-network pattern recognition, see the "Neural Network Frequently Asked Questions" web site, edited by W. S. Sarle, at <ftp://ftp.sas.com/pub/neural/FAQ.html>. In addition, an article by Charles Arthur, "Computers Learn to See and Smell Us," from Independent, January 16, 1996, describes the ability of neural nets to differentiate between unique characteristics.
2. As will be discussed . . . , destructive scanning will be feasible early in the twenty-first century. Noninvasive scanning with sufficient resolution and bandwidth will take longer but will be feasible by the end of the first half of the twenty-first century.

WORKERS OF THE WORLD, GET ONLINE*

Daniel McGinn and Joan Raymond

Daniel McGinn and Joan Raymond investigate the future of work in light of advancing technology.

1

When George Yano opened his garage in the Cleveland suburbs 47 years ago, the shelves were lined with Mitchell's manuals, the multivolume bible for mechanics. Back then, all Yano needed was the right book and a good ear to make any car run smoothly. Today the manuals are gone, replaced by a Pentium-based computer and $1,800 worth of CD-ROMs. The fix-it-by-sound method has disappeared, too; today's cars are controlled by noiseless computer chips. To keep up with the changes, Yano's son Andy, 43, spends two nights a week in continuing-education courses. It's a different world than when his father, now 74, looked under his first hood. "They used to call us grease monkeys," Andy says, pausing as he pulls a schematic drawing off the Internet as his father looks on. "If anybody

*Newsweek, special ed., February 1998, pp. 32–33.

told me I would have a computer in the garage, I would have told them they were crazy."

Workers of the world, get out your crystal balls. Just as the last decades have 2 brought immense changes to the workplace—the influx of women, the advent of computers, the decline of organized labor, the rise of the service sector—the decades ahead will bring changes just as dramatic. Trying to make refined predictions of what work will look like decades from now is an exercise in folly, economists say, since the biggest changes will probably come from technological innovations we can only dream about. "To try to predict technology, you really go out on a limb," says David Bills, author of *The New Modern Times,* a book on the past and future of work. But what lies ahead is not completely unpredictable. Demographers can tell us much about what the work force will look like 10 or 15 years out. Charting other changes is a matter of extrapolating from existing trends while hoping not to be embarrassed.

On the second floor of a Washington, D.C., office building, a group of 45 econ- 3 omists is hard at work on the government's sketch of tomorrow's workplace. Every other December, the Bureau of Labor Statistics publishes its employment projec- tions. The paperback guide, a standard accessory in high-school guidance offices, predicts which occupations will grow and shrink over the next decade. The hot growth areas: health care and computer-related work. Things look less rosy for bookkeepers, typists, copy-machine operators—and anyone whose job can be va- porized by automation. Other changes are obvious. With longer life spans and the cash-strapped Social Security fund, working into old age will become more com- mon. The workplace, like the country, will be home to many more immigrants. And if you work in a factory today, you—or your children—are more likely to work in an office tomorrow.

That last change may be the most profound. In the future, says Robert Reich, 4 the former Labor secretary who's arguably the nation's foremost contemplator of the future of work, we won't be able to classify workers under the blue-collar/ white-collar division of yore. We also won't see so many Americans with only a high-school education earning comfortable middle-class wages. In Reich's view, the upper crust of today's white-collar workers will be classified as something that he calls "symbolic analysts." That rubric will include jobs—like lawyers, doctors, investment bankers and some teachers—that usually require graduate degrees. These will be well-paid positions involving "some of the most intensive knowl- edge work in the New Economy," he says. At the bottom of the ladder will be the so-called personal-service workers, the remaining low-skill, low-pay jobs that haven't moved overseas or been replaced by a computer. Think of the fast-food worker as the epitome of this job segment.

If the lives of the folks at the top and bottom of the ladder don't sound much 5 different from what they lead today, that's because the greatest changes face work- ers in the middle, whom Reich calls, mercifully, "the new middle class." The rise of a middle class in America was largely a blue-collar phenomenon, and despite overseas competition, there are still millions of workers earning more than $35,000 a year on an assembly line. Those jobs will dwindle in years to come. "Jobs bend- ing metal or doing the machining in a factory will become fewer and fewer," Reich says. Tomorrow's middle class will be made up largely of "technicians," he says, whose jobs will usually require training on top of a high-school diploma. They will be the plumbers of the computer age. The technician class will include everyone from inventory managers to paralegals to high-tech auto mechanics like Andy Yano. "Almost all 'technician' jobs involve computers," Reich says. "You'll have to have more education than the old middle class."

6　　　Ed Lotterman, a regional economist at the Federal Reserve Bank in Minneapolis, already sees the changes. At local foundries, print shops and cabinetmaking plants, he sees many jobs that require more than the on-the-job training that sufficed in years past, but less than a college degree. Community colleges will train many of these workers, some of whom may receive proposed federal grants for two years of higher ed. And there may be a boom in privately run training schools.

7　　　Even the knowledge workers—those highly educated, high-earning professionals who should thrive in the new economy—face some big changes. In the wake of the early-1990s downsizing, it seemed as though nearly every laid-off executive had to call himself a consultant lest he admit to being permanently unemployed. But freelance talent-for-hire will become more the norm than the exception, experts say. A research project by the Human Resource Institute found that just 61 percent of the large companies it surveyed expected more than three quarters of its work force to consist of full-time, regular employees a decade from now, down from 84 percent today. While that may sound scary, Wharton professor Mike Useem says the midcareer executives he works with are already becoming comfortable with the notion of bouncing between employers and assignments rather than climbing the ladder at a single employer. Of course, they have no choice.

8　　　According to Watts Wacker, a futurist with SRI International, the talent-for-hire trend of the next century is a return to the guild system of the Middle Ages, in which tradesmen traveled from town to town practicing their craft for a variety of clients. Many knowledge workers will telecommute to their various offices.

9　　　Even without telecommuting, if you believe one school of thought, we won't be seeing our colleagues much in tomorrow's workplace. So say folks like Jeremy Rifkin, author of the best-seller *The End of Work*, a discussion of how technology will take the place of many mass laborers. While it sounds like a chilling scenario with lots of painful unemployment, Rifkin argues it will free us up for more cultural activities and nonprofit work. "There's no reason we shouldn't move to a 30-hour workweek now and a 25-hour workweek 10 years from now, with higher pay and benefits," Rifkin says. Economists scoff at that notion—if anything, they say, today's unemployment rate and wage pressure show we face a shortage not a surplus, of skilled labor. But Rifkin has sold more than 100,000 books and keeps a full speaking schedule, suggesting that there will always be ample work for futurologists.

10　　　Not everything will change. Michael Tavoletti has learned that lesson well. It's no secret that farming has been a dying occupation for a century, but Tavoletti won't give up his 500 acres in central Ohio without a fight. Many of the rhythms of his job haven't changed in years: he still feeds his 100-plus head of cattle each morning and tends to fields of corn, hay and wheat each afternoon. But when it comes time to breed his cattle, Tavoletti now uses a computer to analyze what the potential of the offspring might be if he breeds, say, Cow 17 with Bull 8. Someday, he expects, the computers will help him optimize his planting, fertilizing and harvesting. "[I'm just] a guy who knows that technology is the key to keeping the farm in the family," he says. He's also a walking reminder that no matter what forecasters say, someone has to milk the cows. ◼

B.   How Are Computers Changing Their Users?

DRAG NET: FROM GLEN TO GLENDA AND BACK AGAIN— IS IT POSSIBLE?*

Sherry Turkle

Sherry Turkle is a professor of the sociology of science at MIT and a licensed clinical psychologist. She is the author of Life on the Screen: Identity in the Age of the Internet. *In the following article, she describes her experience in a multiuser domain, or MUD, where people meet in cyberspace. In MUDs people often play fantasy-based characters or change their gender.*

When I first logged on to a MUD, I named and described a character but forgot to 1
give it a gender. I was struggling with the technical aspects of the MUD universe— the difference between various commands such as "saying" and "emoting," "paging" and "whispering"—and gender was the last thing on my mind. This rapidly changed when a male-presenting character named Jiffy asked me if I were "really an it." I experienced an unpleasurable sense of disorientation that immediately gave way to an unfamiliar sense of freedom.

When Jiffy's question appeared on my screen, I was standing in a room of 2
LambdaMOO—one of the first very popular MUDs—filled with characters engaged in sexual banter, *Animal House*-style. The innuendos, double entendres, and leering invitations were scrolling by at a fast clip; I felt awkward, as if I were at a party I'd been invited to by mistake. It reminded me of kissing games in junior high, where it was both awful to be chosen and awful not to be chosen. Now, on the MUD, I had a new option: Playing a male might allow me to feel less out of place. People would expect me to make the first move, and I could choose not to. I could "lurk," stand on the sidelines and observe the action. Boys, after all, were not considered prudes if they were too cool to play kissing games. They were not categorized as wallflowers if they held back and didn't ask girls to dance. They could simply be shy in a manly way, cool, above it all.

Two days later I was back in the MUD. After I typed the command that 3
joined me, in Boston, to the computer in California where the MUD resided, I discovered I'd lost my password. This meant I couldn't play my own character but had to log on as a guest. As such, I was assigned a color: magenta. As "Magenta_

*Utne Reader, September–October 1998, pp. 51–55.

guest," I was again without gender. While I struggled with basic commands, other players were typing messages for all to see: "Magenta_guest gazes hot and enraptured at the approach of Fire_Eater." Again I was tempted to hide from the frat-party atmosphere by passing as a man.

4   Much later, when I did play a male character, I finally experienced the permission to move freely that I had always imagined to be men's birthright. Not only was I approached less frequently, but I found it easier to respond to unwanted overtures with aplomb, saying something like, "That's flattering, Ribald_ Temptress, but I'm otherwise engaged." My sense of freedom didn't involve just a different attitude about sexual advances—which now seemed less threatening. As a woman, I have a hard time deflecting a request for conversation by asserting my own agenda. As a MUD male, doing so (nicely) seemed natural; it never struck me as dismissive or rude. In this way, I was learning about the construction of gender— and learning about myself.

5   It was easy to see that virtual gender-swapping teaches the first lesson of gender studies: the difference between sex as biology and gender as a social construct. When a man goes online as a woman, he soon finds that maintaining this fiction is difficult. To pass as a woman for any length of time requires understanding just how gender inflects speech, manner, and the interpretation of experience. Women attempting to pass as men face the same kind of challenge. One says: "It is not so easy. You have to think about it, to make up a life, a job, a set of reactions." Pavel Curtis, the founder of LambdaMOO, has observed that when a female-presenting character is called something like FabulousHotBabe, there's usually a real-life man behind the mask. Another experienced MUDder shares this piece of folklore: "If a female-presenting character's description of her beauty goes on for more than two paragraphs, [the player behind the character] is sure to be an ugly woman."

6   Case, a 34-year-old industrial designer who is happily married to a coworker, told me that he currently plays on several MUDs as a female character. When I ask whether MUDding ever causes him emotional pain, he says, "Yes, but also the kind of learning that comes from hard times.

7   "I'm having pain in my playing now," he continues. "The woman I'm playing in MedievalMUSH [her name is Mairead] is having an interesting relationship with a fellow. Mairead is a lawyer. It costs so much to go to law school that it has to be paid for by a corporation or a noble house. A man she met and fell in love with was a nobleman. He paid for her law school. He bought my contract. [Note that Case slips into the first person here.] Now he wants to marry me, although I'm a commoner. I finally said yes. I try to talk to him about the fact that I'm essentially his property. He says, 'Oh no, no, no . . . we'll pick you up, set you on your feet, the whole world is open to you.'

8   "But every time I assert myself, I get pushed down. It's an incredibly psychologically damaging thing to do to a person. And the very thing that he liked about her—that she was independent, strong, said what was on her mind—it is all being bled out of her."

9   Case looks at me with a wry smile and sighs, "A woman's life."

Case has played Mairead for nearly a year, but even a brief experience playing 10 a character of another gender can be evocative. William James said that philosophy is the art of imagining alternatives. Virtual communities can test philosophy about gender issues via action; it's a form of consciousness-raising. For example, on many MUDs, offering technical assistance has become a common way in which male characters "purchase" female attention, analogous to picking up the check at a real-life dinner. In real life, our expectations about sex roles (who offers help, who buys dinner, who brews the coffee) can become so ingrained that we no longer notice them. On MUDs, expectations are expressed in visible textual actions, widely witnessed and openly discussed.

When men playing females are plied with unrequested offers of help on 11 MUDs, they often remark that such chivalries communicate a belief in female incompetence. When women play males on MUDs and realize that they are no longer being offered help, some say those offers of help may well have led them to believe they needed it. As a woman, "First you ask for help because you think it will be expedient," says a college sophomore, "then you realize that you aren't developing the skills to figure things out for yourself."

Shakespeare used the evocative nature of gender-swapping as a plot device 12 for reframing and reconsidering personal and political choices. *As You Like It* is a classic example: The comedy uses gender-swapping to reveal identity and increase the complexity of relationships. In the play, Rosalind, the duke's daughter, is exiled from the court of her uncle Frederick, who has usurped her father's throne. Frederick's daughter, Rosalind's cousin Celia, flees with Rosalind to the magical Forest of Arden. When Rosalind remarks that they might be in danger because "beauty provoketh thieves sooner than gold," Celia suggests that they rub dirt on their faces and wear drab clothing, a tactic—becoming unattractive—that often allows women greater social ease. Rosalind takes the idea a step further: They will dress as men.

The disguise is both physical ("A gallant curtle-ax upon my thigh, / A boar 13 spear in my hand") and emotional ("and—in my heart, / Lie there what hidden women's fear there will").

Rosalind does not endorse an essential difference between men and women; 14 rather, she suggests that men routinely adopt the same kind of pose she is now choosing. Biological men have to construct male gender just as biological women have to construct female gender. By making themselves unattractive, Rosalind and Celia end up less feminine; they deconstruct their female gender. Both posing as men and deconstructing femininity are games that female MUDders play.

In addition to virtual cross-dressing and creating character descriptions that 15 deconstruct gender, MUDders swap genders as double agents. That is, men play women pretending to be men, and women play men pretending to be women. Shakespeare's characters play these games as well. When Rosalind flees Frederick's court, she is in love with Orlando. In the Forest of Arden, disguised as the boy Ganymede, she encounters Orlando, himself lovesick for Rosalind. As Ganymede, Rosalind says she will try to cure Orlando of his love by playing Rosalind, pointing out the flaws of femininity as she does so. In current stagings,

Rosalind usually is played by a woman who, at this point in the play, pretends to be a man who pretends to be a woman.

16   When Rosalind/Ganymede and Orlando meet "man to man," they are able to speak easily, free of the courtly conventions that constrain communications between men and women. In this way, the play suggests that donning a mask—adopting a persona—can be a step toward a deeper truth. This is also how MUDders regard their experiences as virtual selves.

17   One young woman, Zoe, describes her virtual experience: "I played a man for two years. As a man, I could be firm and people would think I was a great wizard. As a woman, drawing the line and standing firm has always made me feel like a bitch, and, actually, I feel that people saw me as one, too. As a man, I was liberated from all that. I learned from my mistakes. I got better at being firm but not rigid. I practiced, safe from criticism."

18   What Zoe's and Case's stories have in common is that a virtual gender swap gave them a greater sense of their emotional range. There was a chance to discover, as Rosalind and Orlando did in the Forest of Arden, that for both sexes, gender is constructed.

19   Having literally written our gender-swapping online personae into existence, they can be a kind of Rorschach. We can use them to become more aware of what we project into everyday life, and the ways those projections affect others. This means that we can use the virtual to reflect constructively on the real.

20   Indeed, in my experience, life in cyberspace can provide very serious play. We take it lightly at our risk. And in my research I have found that people who cultivate an awareness of what stands behind the screen personae they craft do best in using virtual experience for personal transformation. Those who make the most of their life on the screen come to it in a spirit of self-reflection. ▄

COMPUTERS WILL BE MORE HUMAN*
Michael J. Miller

Michael J. Miller believes that thanks to new technology, future computer interactions will become increasingly similar to interactions between people, which could make computers seem more humanlike.

1 When we say that computers will become more human, we don't mean that they will suddenly become as mobile or as intelligent as Data, the android from *Star Trek: The Next Generation*. Instead, we mean that they will take on more human attributes such as the ability to react to spoken words or written instructions and to reply in a way that seems more natural. The result: A user interface that will appear much more human, even if the underlying computer program is not "artificially intelligent" at all.

PC Magazine, June 22, 1999, pp. 104, 113.

The natural outgrowth of his desire to create a more human interface is to give it a bit of a personality. Done badly, this could mean an interface that is overly cute or gets in the way more than it helps. But done correctly, this could make computers and Web sites much easier and much more natural to use.

One of the first heavily publicized attempts was a market failure: Microsoft's Bob, which used a "social interface" as a front end to Windows. Bob has long since disappeared from the retail shelves, but the concept lives on in the Intelligent Assistant in Microsoft Office. Office users probably know one of these characters (be it the animated paperclip or the friendly dog), and chances are you either like the character enough to ask it questions or you hate it so much you've banished it forever.

Love them or hate them, you're likely to see a lot more of these techniques used in computer systems over the next few years. Such characters—sometimes called bots or agents—will probably become staples of many Web sites.

PGS THAT UNDERSTAND

Perhaps the most fundamental technique underlying this is *natural-language processing,* or the ability to respond to a question that is phrased the way you would phrase it to another person. One Web site that has used a natural-language interface to make it stand out is Ask Jeeves. Unlike using a traditional search engine, you ask Jeeves a question and it gives you a list of specific questions it knows the answer to, one of which, it is hoped, holds the answer to your original question.

Ask Jeeves doesn't pretend any level of personality, but other services in this space try to create more human characters. The result is something called a *chatterbot*—a virtual character that you can ask questions of and get answers from on a particular area.

Many of you may remember Eliza, a simulated psychiatrist that just played back words and random phrases based on rudimentary analysis of keyed input to demonstrate a simplistic form of artificial intelligence. Some chatterbots have much of the same feel—uncannily human at times and obvious and fairly useless at others. But chatterbots don't pretend any innate intelligence; they just respond to questions that match a subject they've been programmed on.

Some chatterbots, such as Neuromedia's Red, which is designed as a demonstration of a virtual customer service representative, don't appear as much more than a box into which you type text. The idea is that your customers can talk to it and get useful answers most of the time, thus cutting down on the time they spend on the phone waiting for a human representative. Ask Red "Are you intelligent?" and it will reply: "Smart, yes. Intelligent, no. I don't reason; I just match patterns. It only seems like I'm intelligent because humans would have to reason, or think, to answer these questions."

Other companies are going for a more human approach. One example comes from Big Science Co. The demo of its Klone Server, Andrette, not only replies to your questions but shows different pictures of the character as well. Ask it "What does Big Science sell?" and it will reply: "Big Science Company creates Klones like me. Can I give you a short tour of this site?" Ask it "Are you married?" and it replies: "Only wetware engages in rituals of gene mixing. Not me."

10   When natural language or a chatterbot is used as a way of controlling an application, the result is what some call a social interface. NetSage has developed several of these, including its Social Intelligence Server. Using NetSage's languages, companies develop systems that act as sales or support representatives, stock brokers, mortgage assistants, or teachers. Examples of the Social Intelligence Server include the Office Assistants in Office 97 or the voice user interface for General Magic's Portico virtual assistant.

VOICE RECOGNITION

11   Another method of creating a more human interface is voice recognition, which is improving at an amazing pace. Already products like Dragon NaturallySpeaking and IBM's ViaVoice are doing a reasonable job of continuous-speech recognition. Today, such products are limited by the need to speak punctuation such as "period" or "comma," but that limitation will soon be overcome.

12   A lot of work is also being done toward eliminating the time users must spend training the software to recognize their voices, making these programs truly speaker-independent. IBM's head of speech development, David Nahamoo, notes that "as devices get smaller and smaller, you need to change how you interface with them." He demonstrated software you call over the phone that answers and directs your questions based on your response, without any training required.

13   In fact, many researchers are working on such telephone-based systems. Victor Zue of MIT's Laboratory for Computer Science has been working with what he calls *speech understanding* systems designed for specialized functions. He notes that most households don't yet have Internet access, but nearly all have telephones, so he views voice as a way of bringing new applications to more people. Among the systems that Zue and LCS have created is Jupiter, which uses speech understanding to answer your questions about the weather over the phone (888-573-8255). Other projects in the works include a mapping application and a system that gives out airline information.

UNDERSTANDING EMOTION

14   What if a computer could begin to understand what you're feeling? MIT professor Rosalind W. Picard, head of the Media Labs' Affective Computing Group, is developing a system that will do just that. Physiological sensors attached to your body and tiny cameras that record your facial expressions let the computers monitor your reactions. Then an "affective tutor" will adjust a program to react to your emotions. For instance, if you're confused by a complex part of a video lecture, the tutor could play it back to you or offer an explanation.

15   Perhaps the machine itself could express emotion. MIT has developed Bruzard, an interactive animated 3-D character designed to look like a small child.

It uses facial expressions to react to your questions. In the future, Bruzard could be hooked up to something like a chatterbot to create a more human interface.

Microsoft Research has combined many of these ideas into a concept called 16
Flow. James Kajiya, assistant director of Microsoft Research, believes computers should be about giving you back your time. Thus Flow, which is still in the research stage, will allow you to sit at your computer and take part in a virtual meeting. Lifelike avatars would represent you and your coworkers so it would look much like a traditional meeting, even though everyone might be in different locations. And the entire conversation would be recorded and converted to searchable text for later use. One of the big challenges, Kajiya says, is modeling human attention, so that you could pay attention when you wanted to and not when you didn't have to.

These techniques are a long way from the mainstream. But the combination 17
of animation, natural-language processing, voice recognition, and voice synthesis may very well result in user interfaces that seem more natural than anything we have today. ■

POTHOLES ON THE ROAD AHEAD*

Peter McGrath

Peter McGrath writes about his frustrations with computers. Have you ever felt frustrated with your computer? Or are you and your computer always in perfect harmony?

Go on, admit it: you've wanted to smash that screen, haven't you? Or fry the key- 1
board in a manic deluge of diet cola. Or maybe tear your modem line out by its twisted copper roots. Sometimes you harbor dark suspicions of your computer: it wants to foul you up. Why else would it freeze just when you need it most, and send creepy messages like *This program has performed an illegal operation and will be shut down*?

There's no escape. Networked digital devices set the pace of change today. 2
As James Gleick notes in his new book, *Faster,* the truly breakneck technologies are the ones governed by Moore's Law, the prediction in 1965 by Intel cofounder Gordon Moore that microchip miniaturization would lead to a doubling of computer power every 18 months. He was right, as it turned out. The result is exuberance among researchers, a strange blend of triumphalism and paranoia among business people—and for many ordinary users of technology, a sense of dislocation and even fear.

The fear takes four forms. 3

- **I can't make this thing work.** It's a common anxiety. A recent survey of 6,000 PC users showed they wasted an average of 5.1 hours a week in sheer

*Newsweek, September 20, 1999, p. 78.

computer hassle. Another study, conducted over 43 months by psychologists Larry D. Rosen and Michelle M. Weil, found that about 60 percent of respondents could be called "hesitant" users of technology, joined by a much smaller number of active "resisters." In the American public overall, Rosen suspects, about 70 percent are at best uneasy about technological change, even as they are resigned to it. "People feel driven, like they *have* to keep up, or they'll be lost forever," says Rosen, who with Weil wrote the 1998 book *TechnoStress: Coping with Technology @WORK @HOME @PLAY.* "Software engineers have a hard time understanding what ordinary users will find hard or easy," says Yogen Dalal, a partner in the Mayfield Fund, a top Silicon Valley venture-capital firm.

- **It's my fault.** The current emphasis on anthropomorphic design—the idea that the computer should be "friendly" and show human qualities ("You've got mail")—seduces people into imagining the machine as a real partner in a social transaction. But, says Ben Shneiderman, the head of the Human-Computer Interaction Laboratory at the University of Maryland, the result can actually make us feel stupid. Error messages are accusatory: you "performed an illegal operation" or caused a "fatal exception." You compromised the "integrity" of the system files, as though system files had moral qualities. These terms "suggest the designer's condemnation of the user," says Shneiderman. Weil adds: "People compare themselves to the technology. [. . .] It seems so alive. It talks to you, it flashes lights in your face. [. . .] Users, especially the more hesitant ones, take the glitches personally, because of the perception that technology never fails." The other version of this syndrome is, *The machine doesn't like me.*

- **You, too?** Technology makes for external stress, like that of the Y2K survivalists with their bunker-down belief that Jan. 1, 2000, is a computer-decreed day of reckoning. Then there's the worry about personal privacy in a networked world, as people become aware of how invasive Web technologies can be. Also the job uncertainty found in survey after survey, despite the longest economic boom in living memory. And why not? As the science writer James Burke said in his book *The Pinball Effect,* the rate of technological change is becoming "so high that for humans to be qualified in a single discipline . . . will be as outdated as quill and parchment. Knowledge will be changing too fast for that. We will need to reskill ourselves constantly every decade just to keep a job."

- **There's never enough time anymore.** A decade ago, Alvin Toffler wrote that the next competition would not take place between East and West, or North and South, but between "the fast and the slow"—the quick and the dead. Toffler had whole economies in mind, but his point holds at the personal level, too. The future belongs to those with nimble if not always careful minds. Microsoft, for example, is notorious for job interviews in which candidates are evaluated on their ability to solve in seconds mathematical puzzles and logical twists.

4   For better and for worse, we are stuck with speed. For better: in a global economy, technology companies will create untold wealth through sheer frenzies

of creation. For worse: we will lose sight of the virtues of languor and deliberation. Some things can't be rushed, such as diplomacy and love. The techno-tycoons themselves know this: in the rush to be first-to-market, they cut corners and drive customers crazy with bug-ridden products *(This program has performed an illegal operation and will be shut down),* but they would never accept a similar lack of craftsmanship in their own golf clubs or yachts.

In the end, though, addressing techno-stress is a commercial imperative. The 5 industry has exhausted the supply of buyers willing to put up with complex and alienating products. In fact, says Yogen Dalal, the realization is already underway, with devices like the Palm Pilot and technologists who are heeding "the needs of mass markets and understanding what people really want."

We'll see. In the meantime: don't smash that screen just yet. ■ 6

HOW PRIVATE IS YOUR LIFE?*

Peter Maas

Peter Maas is a contributing editor for Parade *and the author of* The Valachi Papers, Serpico, Killer Spy, *and* Underboss. *Maas's article claims that advancing computer technology compromises citizens' right to privacy, which is guaranteed by the U.S. Constitution.*

I have an acquaintance named Fred P. Smith. Actually, that's not his real name. I'm 1 not using his real name because, as I have discussed in preparing this article, it is about the only shred of privacy he has left. And Fred Smith just as easily could be you or me.

The concept of the right to privacy was a treasured hallmark of the American 2 way of life, institutionalized early on, indeed, by our Founding Fathers in the Fourth and Fifth Amendments to the U.S. Constitution. But that was long before the present hordes of private investigators and rapacious marketeers in an era of advanced computer technology that today draws on heretofore private information contained in vast databases that most Americans don't even know exist.

As a result, there are at this writing some 80 different patchwork bills pending 3 in Congress aimed at restricting the flow of intimate personal data in cyberspace, now available to anyone browsing through the World Wide Web. Unfortunately, as the saying goes, the horse appears already to have departed the barn.

To learn precisely what was what, I visited the offices of Sutton Associates, 4 located on New York's Long Island, which specialized in investigative services. Its president is James F. Murphy, a retired FBI agent. (As an agent, Murphy once had been a heroic headline figure. He had shot and killed one of two bank robbers holding a number of hostages at gunpoint as they tried to make their escape. The dramatic moment was later portrayed in the movie *Dog Day Afternoon.)*

Parade, April 19, 1998, pp. 4–6.

5   As one of the most reputable firms of its sort in the nation, Sutton Associates limits itself primarily to background screenings for potential employment hirings and "due diligence" probes on behalf of corporate clients involved in buyouts, mergers, acquisitions and divestitures, all of which are considered quite legitimate. Sutton will not, on the other hand, accept divorce or criminal defense cases.

6   Recently, a company asked Sutton to locate a female consultant, now retired, who was urgently needed for a new project. The only information supplied was her name and that she was believed to reside somewhere in the vicinity of Washington, D.C. She wasn't listed in any phone books. It took no more than five minutes to come up with seven candidates with the same name, one of whom—the right one— met the appropriate retirement age of 64. But she had moved from her home in northern Virginia. So it took perhaps another five minutes to get a correct updated South Carolina address from one of the three major credit bureaus—Equifax, Experian and Trans Union—whose data banks record anyone who ever used a credit card.

7   My agreement with Jim Murphy was that Sutton Associates would demonstrate *how* a dossier could be compiled on an individual (not necessarily a job it actually would undertake). On occasion, a corporate client will ask Murphy if he can find out thus-and-such about someone. If Murphy considers the information beyond the bounds of propriety or legality, his standard reply is, "Yes, but I won't."

8   I supplied Murphy with the name of "Fred P. Smith." The only other information I provided was that he resided in the U.S. and was in the securities business. Sutton Associate had 72 hours to find out whatever it could about him.

9   The search began with what is called a "surname scan," which can be done nationally, regionally or locally based on data banks that have been compiled from such public source documents as voter registrations, motor-vehicle records (some states, like Maryland, actually sell these records) and real property listings.

10   Given the severe time constraints I had imposed and the fact that "Fred" was in the securities business, which could likely mean a Wall Street brokerage house, Sutton Associates elected to start with the greater New York City area. His middle initial helped narrow the field to 27 possibilities.

11   A so-called "credit header" search was then used to establish his occupation. These headers—essentially bare-bones I.D. reports maintained by credit agencies— list not only occupations but also Social Security numbers, dates of birth and residential addresses. This information is also instantly available, for a modest fee, to subscribers to commercial databases, such as one called DBT-Online. An executive name search, using Dun & Bradstreet's *Dun's Market Identifiers*, confirmed that Smith was an officer in his brokerage firm.

12   A Cole's directory—actually a reverse directory in which phone numbers and addresses are cross-referenced for the whole country—is contained on sets of CD-ROMs. Once an address is known, the names of every other resident in that building or neighbors on a suburban block can be ascertained, opening the door to more intensive field investigations of any designated target.

13   A property search, such as those available from a Lexis-Nexis service, showed Fred Smith's previous residences, charting his rise from an apartment in a lower-middle-class neighborhood in one of the city's outer boroughs to a condominium on

Manhattan's Upper East Side with a purchase price of more than $2 million. It also revealed that he owned a luxury sedan and a sport-utility vehicle, as well as another condo at a ski resort. Such information would come into play if he were subject to bankruptcy proceedings, tax liens or civil judgments. As it happened, his record was clear in these areas, nor was there any criminality.

It was revealed, however, that Fred—in his late 40s and married with two 14 children—had a separate apartment in the city. Surveillance indicated that a young, attractive woman was in residence there. While adultery generally is not a financial factor in a divorce settlement, it could come into play if child custody became an issue. It might leave him open to blackmail as well.

Jim Murphy stopped Sutton Associates short of delving deeply into the 15 lifestyle of Fred Smith. But if he had wanted to, Murphy could have learned about the restaurants Fred frequented, his airline travel, hotels he stayed at, his salary, ownership of stocks and bonds, his phone records, any evidence of addiction to drugs or alcohol (such as DWI arrests) or gambling, where his wife shopped and what she bought, how much money she spent, what schools their children attended, even the current state of their marriage.

But, in addition to circumspect firms like Sutton, there are other avenues 16 open in the explosion of available personal information, chief among them "information wholesalers" that cater to private investigators, bill collectors, insurance agents and similar interested parties, such as business competitors.

One is Advanced Research Inc., located in Stroudsburg, Pa. It offers a 17 range of intimate data that includes detailed credit-card activity, long-distance and intrastate toll calls, bank account numbers, deposits and balances, wire transfers, a beeper trace, a cellular phone trace, an employment history, business client lists, life insurance policies and a medical treatment history going back as much as 10 years.

I decided to offer myself up as a guinea pig. I allotted Advanced Research 18 48 hours to come up with an unlisted phone number, a month's worth of toll calls and information about any bank accounts I had, either separate or held jointly with my wife. (I skipped a request for my medical treatment history when I learned that this would take four to six weeks. But I have no doubt that the firm would have delivered, based on its performance in other areas).

As promised, it quickly came up with my unlisted number—not especially 19 surprising, since I've had to include it on applications for various utility services and cable TV as well as warranties for purchases I had made (naïvely supposing it would not be disseminated elsewhere).

But two *other* unlisted numbers, which I have never given out, also were in- 20 cluded. So were the toll calls I had made on all three lines, which, when matched with my phone bills, were right on the money. All my bank-account information— the account numbers, the banks involved, balances and deposits for the previous month—also was disturbingly accurate.

Michael Martin, who heads up Advanced Research, was coy about how this 21 information was gathered. "These are well-guarded trade secrets," he told me. He said that he had specialists on call throughout the country who are allowed "to pursue their own methods." Defending his operation, he added: "In finding dead-beat dads, getting key evidence in child-custody cases, locating hidden assets in court-ordered judgments, why pay high attorney fees when we can do the job a lot quicker, a lot better and a lot cheaper?"

22   Jim Murphy of Sutton Associates said he was concerned about other (un-named) companies, who engage in unscrupulous privacy incursions. "This is a business where you can't be partially pregnant," he said. "If you have people who don't care, you're asking for regulations that will hurt all legitimate private investigators." [. . .]

23   Still, as alarm over the invasion of privacy grows, 14 of the largest database companies—fearful of restrictive legislation—recently agreed to attempt to regulate themselves by adopting guidelines that would limit access to personal information by the general public.

24   The rub is that private investigators are an exception to the rule. According to *P.I. Magazine,* there are about 60,000 licensed private eyes operating in the U.S. The qualifications vary from state to state. Some states—like Colorado, Alabama, Mississippi, Idaho and South Dakota—don't require licenses at all.

25   There remain certain steps an individual can take to protect against unwarranted privacy invasions. The great irony is that a fundamental building block in creating a personal dossier is your Social Security number. Yet when the Social Security Act of 1935 was originally passed by Congress, an individual's number was not to be used as an identifier for other than Social Security purposes.

26   Who could have imagined what would subsequently happen? Today, to apply for just about anything, you are required to give the number up. ■

C. How Are Computers Changing Education?

WIRE ALL SCHOOLS? NOT SO FAST . . .*

Michael Dertouzos

Michael Dertouzos, of the Massachusetts Institute of Technology, argued in 1998 that children could become too dependent on computers in school. What do you think?

1 A few months ago, Israeli Prime Minister Binyamin Netanyahu explained to a group of politicians and computer professionals how he wanted to provide a quarter-million of his country's toddlers with interconnected computers. Netanyahu was concerned because he had had trouble funding the project. I turned the tables and asked him why he wanted to do so in the first place. He was stunned, since it should have been obvious to anyone—especially to an MIT computer technologist—that computers are good for learning.

Technology Review, September 1998, p. 20

Throughout the world, droves of politicians, led by those in the United 2
States, are repeating this fashionable mantra as they proclaim that millions of children in thousands of schools will soon be interconnected. You can feel their rush:
"Isn't it so responsible and oh-so-modern to put an emerging technology to work
toward the noblest of social goals: the education of our children?" Not quite. After
35 years of experimenting with computers in various aspects of learning, the jury
is still out with respect to the central question: "Are computers truly effective in
learning?" That's what most educators who experiment with computers disclose,
as I have steadily heard them say, for example, in the Technology-in-Education
Conference held in May [1998] in New York.

Certainly the promises of computers for learning are impressive. Simulation, 3
for example, is already a proven winner. Besides pilots, tank commanders in the
Gulf War who spent a great deal of training time on tank simulators attest to the
success of this approach. Simulation can be nicely extended to other kinetic and
quantitative tasks such as learning how to drive, ski, swim and sail, and, someday,
even perform surgical operations. But we may be unable to build simulators for
more qualitative situations, such as teaching a manager to handle a disgruntled
employee, through a video simulation of the encounter.

Stand-alone computers can also help people write, compose music, generate 4
designs and create new artifacts by bringing to our fingertips approaches, techniques, forms and patterns that have been successful in similar past endeavors.
Machines are particularly effective as literacy tutors for adults who don't have to
feel embarrassed as they read aloud from a primer to a machine that listens to them
and corrects their mistakes. Computers can also be used as "tutors," for example
by students who learn French by interacting in French with an adventure game in
which the goal is to rent an apartment in Paris. The bolder notion of computer
apprenticeship, where a Frank Lloyd Wright simulator analyzes your architectural
drawings as the great master might have done, is still in the imagination stage.

Moving to the world of interconnected computers, we can see them being 5
used for straightforward tasks such as sharing teacher information, posting homework on the Web (thereby eliminating children's ancient excuse that they forgot
their homework assignment) and getting useful information from trusted sources,
as well as for many educational activities that involve e-mail and access to distant
Web pages. Distance learning is another emerging capability of interconnected computers, particularly useful in matching locales where certain teaching specialties are
unavailable with places that have the right people and the right knowledge.

If we can agree on some shared conventions, we might even construct my 6
dream—a distributed virtual world heritage museum where each nation posts its
writings, sculpture, music and other cultural offerings on the Web and the rest of us,
flying a virtual histori-copter, soar easily in space and time, from Plato to Confucius
to the Renaissance. The achievements and promises of computers for learning go to
the heart of the information revolution: Unlike the agrarian and industrial revolutions that helped learners indirectly by feeding them, transporting them to school
and providing them with electricity, the information revolution helps much more
directly because it deals with the principal currency of knowledge: information.

7   In light of all this potential, how can anyone argue that the jury is still out? Well, take U.S. high school students. They consistently rank from 12th to 18th, internationally, in physics and math, whereas Asian students rank first. Yet U.S. students have far greater access to computers than their Asian counterparts. Might there be some ancient, obvious and major thing about learning that we could learn—if we only lifted our heads long enough from our screens to look at our better-educated neighbors? Another, possibly related, reason for the jury to be out is that learning may critically depend on what humans, rather than computers, do best: Lighting a fire in the student's heart, role modeling and nurturing may contribute more to learning than the neatest hyper-linked courseware.

8   So what are we to do, confronted as we are by high promises on one hand and a jury that's still out on the other? I suggest the same answer I gave to Prime Minister Netanyahu: Experiment creatively and massively (in the thousands), but refrain from deploying massively (in the millions)—at least until the jury has something to say. This won't make politicians shine as bright, but our children may ultimately shine much brighter. ▪

MORE COLLEGES PLUNGING INTO UNCHARTED WATERS OF ON-LINE COURSES*

Karen W. Arenson

Have you taken or thought of taking a college course on a computer via distance education? Karen W. Arenson describes some of the advantages and disadvantages of this rapidly growing educational technology as it existed in 1998. What is its current status at your college?

1 Spurred by fierce competiton for students, colleges and universities from Florida to New York University are plunging headlong into the rapidly evolving world of on-line education, a world that barely existed five years ago.

2   In recent years, technologically adventurous professors worked the Internet into their courses, posting the syllabus or readings or sometimes responding to student queries. Some of the more proficient put courses online. But only recently have universities begun to offer whole programs and degrees on-line—the 1990's version of a correspondence course.

3   No college can be certain whether the program will attract enough students to justify the considerable expense—$50,000 or more to create and support each class. But officials say that if they do not stake out territory now, someone else will.

4   "This is the hottest and most sweeping development I've ever seen," said James H. Ryan, a vice president at Pennsylvania State University, who has been in

New York Times, November 2, 1998, p. A14.

higher education for 35 years. "It's like being in a roller coaster; it's a thrill a minute."

But even as universities stampede onto the Internet, significant questions 5 have yet to be answered. How good is the education? Who owns the courses—the university or the professors who create them? How should faculty members be paid? What works best in on-line teaching? And will a degree from a virtual university be worth the actual paper it is printed on?

Frank Mayadas, a program officer at the Alfred P. Sloan Foundation in 6 New York, which has financed programs to improve on-line teaching, said the picture was mixed. Some on-line degrees, like Stanford University's master's degree in electrical engineering or Drexel University's master's in information systems, are sound, Mr. Mayadas said. But he is skeptical that other offerings will endure.

"The predictability we associate with higher education institutions isn't 7 there yet," he said, "and it needs to be there for this to become a credible source of education."

Still, on-line classes are a considerable step up from correspondence schools. 8 Internet bulletin boards function as virtual classrooms for students and teachers who can participate at any time, from anywhere. Instructors post lectures and assignments; students turn in papers and tests and discuss their studies with classmates and professors in on-line conferences.

Michele Acuna of Saugus, Calif., a 34-year-old mother with two teenagers who 9 is working on a bachelor's degree from the University of Phoenix, signs on almost every day to the Hewlett Packard computer in her bedroom for a communications course. Her professor is in Utah.

"I do a lot at night when my children are in bed," she said. "That's the beauty 10 of this stuff—you can do it at 3 A.M."

No one knows exactly how many colleges operate on the Internet. But what 11 is clear is that the trend is picking up speed nationwide:

- New York University announced this month an audacious plan to create a profit-seeking subsidiary to market Internet courses. The venture would allow N.Y.U. to raise millions of dollars through a stock offering or private partnerships.
- The University of Phoenix, a for-profit behemoth that has officials at many traditional universities scared because of its rapid spread through campuses around the United States as well as online, has nearly 5,000 students in its on-line program, more than double the number two years ago.
- Western Governors University, an on-line college sponsored by 17 states and Guam, was started this fall to improve access to college education for adults and to help accommodate an expected crush of students without building classrooms. The university offers associate's degrees in liberal arts and applied science.
- The California Virtual University, a consortium of nearly 100 California universities and colleges, opened this fall with more than 1,600 on-line courses.

- The Open University—Britain's 29-year-old pioneer in distance education for college students—has applied for American accreditation and is striking cooperative agreements with universities like Florida State University.
- Penn State established its on-line "World Campus" in February with just four courses and expects to have 30 courses by next February.
- Florida State will begin offering courses next fall for a bachelor's degree, but will concentrate on course work for juniors and seniors.

12   The proliferation of on-line programs has many traditional educators scratching their heads. A committee of the American Association of University Professors concluded last year that on-line learning could be "a valuable pedagogical tool to increase access to higher education." But it warned that developments could compromise traditional notions of academic quality, academic freedom, intellectual property rights and instructor's workloads and compensation. In some cases, long-standing safeguards of faculty members' rights may suffice, it said, but in others, those protections may need reworking.

13   Unlike a traditional classroom course, for which a professor creates and delivers each course, the professor becomes more dispensable on-line after putting the course together in a form that can be sent out again and again. Another instructor can be assigned to answer questions and grade papers.

14   Universities are creating different arrangements to determine who owns what. Penn State, for example, is splitting revenues with the faculty members who develop the courses and their departments, while New York University says its new subsidiary will hold ownership rights for the on-line courses.

15   The student body for most on-line courses is part-time, adult students in continuing education programs or full-time degree-seeking students who take most of their work in traditional classrooms. But the trend is to make it possible to earn a degree on-line rather than just take a few individual classes.

16   Jeremy Carlo, a sophomore majoring in applied math and physics at the New Jersey Institute of Technology, took a computer science course on-line in the spring when he could not fit the regular course into his schedule. He found the flexibility a mixed blessing.

17   "It was nice that you didn't have to be somewhere from 4 to 5:30 twice a week," Mr. Carlo said. "The negative is that you really have to keep on top of the work."

18   Ms. Acuna is using her computer for all of her courses. She said she had always wanted a college degree. But as a single mother with a full-time job as an operations manager for a retail chain with night and weekend shifts, she could not commit to regular-class attendance.

19   She looked into several on-line programs before enrolling as a business major at the University of Phoenix. At $370 a credit ($465 for graduate work), Phoenix charges more than the local community college. Phoenix students typically take one course at a time for five weeks and then have a week off before starting the next.

20   The only requirement Ms. Acuna has not been able to fulfill at home was the university's entrance examination, which she took at a local Catholic school.

In her current communications course she and her five classmates read es- 21
says, write their own and comment on one another's work in teams—but talk
about little else. There is no sense of a campus community, but she does not mind.

Now that Internet education is taking clearer shape, some university officials 22
are taking a closer look at the business aspects.

Active marketing is a major component of the N.Y.U. plan. Rather than aim- 23
ing to put all the courses it can on the Web, the university is hoping to start with a
dozen or so niche courses—like computer and management courses that will be
attractive to people in industry. As these courses bring in revenues, others will be
added.

"On-line is a big, important field in higher education, but it does not have a 24
business model that works," said Gerald A. Heeger, dean of Continuing and Professional Studies at N.Y.U., who is directing the university's new on-line enterprise.

"The dirty little secret is that nobody's making any money," Dean Heeger 25
said. But someday they will, he said. ■

THE GREAT CAMPUS GOOF-OFF MACHINE*

Nate Stulman

Nate Stulman was a sophomore at Swarthmore College when he wrote this piece.

Conventional wisdom says that computers are a necessary tool for higher educa- 1
tion. Many colleges and universities these days require students to have personal
computers, and some factor the cost of one into tuition. A number of colleges have
put high-speed Internet connections in every dorm room. But there are good reasons to question the wisdom of this preoccupation with computers and the Internet.

Take a walk through the residence halls of any college in the country and 2
you'll find students seated at their desks, eyes transfixed on their computer moni-
tors. What are they doing with their top-of-the-line PC's and high-speed T-1 Internet connections?

They are playing Tomb Raider instead of going to chemistry class, tweaking the 3
configurations of their machines instead of writing the paper due tomorrow, collecting mostly useless information from the World Wide Web instead of doing a math
problem set—and a host of other activity that has little or nothing to do with traditional academic work.

I have friends who have spent whole weekends doing nothing but playing 4
Quake or Warcraft or other interactive computer games. One friend sometimes
spends entire evenings—six to eight hours—scouring the Web for images and
modifying them just to have a new background on his computer desktop.

And many others I know have amassed overwhelming collections of music 5
on their computers. It's the searching and finding that they seem to enjoy: some

New York Times, March 15, 1999, p. A25.

of them have more music files on their computers than they could play in months.

6 Several people who live in my hall routinely stay awake all night chatting with dormmates on-line. Why walk 10 feet down the hall to have a conversation when you can chat on the computer—even if it takes three times as long?

7 You might expect that personal computers in dorm rooms would be used for nonacademic purposes, but the problem is not confined to residence halls. The other day I walked into the library's reference department, and five or six students were grouped around a computer—not conducting research, but playing Tetris. Every time I walk past the library's so-called research computers, it seems that at least half are being used to play games, chat or surf the Internet aimlessly.

8 Colleges and universities should be wary of placing such an emphasis on the use of computers and the Internet. The Web may be useful for finding simple facts, but serious research still means a trip to the library.

9 For most students, having a computer in the dorm is more of a distraction than a learning tool. Other than computer science or mathematics majors, few students need more than a word processing program and access to E-mail in their rooms.

10 It is true, of course, that students have always procrastinated and wasted time. But when students spend four, five, even ten hours a day on computers and the Internet, a more troubling picture emerges—a picture all the more disturbing because colleges themselves have helped create the problem. ■

UNIVERSITIES FIND SHARP RISE IN COMPUTER-AIDED CHEATING*

Ian Zack

Ian Zack identifies a problem that is of considerable concern to college writing teachers. What do you think could be done to solve it?

1 In a troubling reminder of technology's darker side, Virginia Tech, the state's largest university, has acknowledged that computer-aided cheating by students is growing rapidly.

2 "We've had a lot more cases," said Leon Geyer, who oversees the student-run honor system at Virginia Polytechnic Institute and State University, which has 25,000 students. "In the olden days, you had to copy from the book. Now, you just copy and paste."

3 Officials at the university say that the number of cheating complaints has grown to 280 last year from 80 in 1995–96 and includes reports of plagiarizing information from the Internet, sharing answers or other information by electronic mail or diskette, and stealing information from a fellow student's computer screen or electronic mail system.

New York Times, September 23, 1998, p. A26.

Virginia Tech is not the only university experiencing growth in such inci- 4
dents or worrying about how to detect and prevent them. The personal computer,
while enhancing teaching, has made cheating as simple as pointing and clicking a
mouse or exchanging a floppy disk with the answers to a take-home test.

Stealing or copying someone's work has become so effortless, some say, that 5
students may be inured to the ethical or legal consequences, much like drivers
exceeding the speed limit.

"Let's say everyone in the class has a networked computer," said Chris 6
Duckenfield, vice provost for computing and information technology at Clemson
University. "They can exchange information electronically. They can pull down
information electronically. Who's going to watch over every student's shoulder to
see what they're doing?"

Last October, Boston University was so concerned about computer cheating 7
that it filed a Federal lawsuit to stop eight companies from selling term papers
over the Internet in Massachusetts. The university's action came a quarter century
after the institution successfully sued term-paper mills hawking typewritten
papers out of Volkswagen buses in Cambridge. The state now bans the sale of
printed term papers.

At the University of California at Berkeley, a computer science professor, 8
Alex Aiken, created software to identify plagiarism in his programming courses.
He placed the software, called Moss, for Measure of Software Similarity, on the Internet (at www.cs.berkeley.edu/~aiken/moss.html), and it is now used by more
than 500 professors at universities worldwide.

Professor Aiken attributes the rise to the anonymity of electronic communi- 9
cation, the vast resources of the Internet and the ever-multiplying speed of computers. "The fact that you can do it more quickly makes it easier to yield to an
impulse," he said.

This is apparently what happened to the president of the student union at Ox- 10
ford University in England, who was expelled after the university determined she
had cheated on a final examination by downloading an essay she had written earlier.

At Virginia Tech last spring, dozens of students in a computer-programming 11
course—roughly 10 percent of a class of 600—were accused of electronically sharing
information on a year-end assignment. And recently, two graduating seniors down-
loaded another student's work to turn in as their own computer programming
assignment. A piece of software similar to Professor Aiken's found them out.

"It does seem to be an increasing problem because it is so much easier," said 12
Amanda Rich, a 21-year-old Virginia Tech senior from Clinton, Ill., who is chief
justice of the university's honor system court, where accused cheaters are tried.

Ms. Rich said some incidents were obvious cases of wrongdoing, while others 13
appear to be ignorance by students who do not understand the rules of scholarly
research.

Whatever the reasons, professors and administrators at Virginia Tech do not 14
quite know how to respond. "I don't know if this is the beginning of an ugly,
awful trend or just a blip," said John Carroll, a computer science professor. "It's a
new world out there."

15   But professors are not waiting around for a new set of computer command-ments to take hold. Some routinely search the Internet when information in a term paper appears suspicious. Tom Rocklin, a University of Iowa professor who has written an electronic paper called "Downloadable Term Papers: What's a Prof to Do?" says that some teachers unwittingly encourage students to cheat by giving broad general-knowledge assignments or scheduling too many large projects at the end of a semester.

16   "If you tie assignments really tightly to what you're doing in class, it becomes more difficult to cheat," Professor Rocklin said. He also suggested that teachers require outlines and rough drafts for term papers, so they can see a student's work in progress.

17   Professor Geyer, the faculty adviser for Virginia Tech's honor system, said that while computer cheating was easy to do, once suspected it was also "easy to detect—and students haven't figured out the latter."

18   At Virginia Tech, students found guilty of computer-aided cheating have received punishments ranging from zeros and double-weighted zeros on tests—which can mean a failing grade in a course—to community service. Under the university's honor system, students rarely are expelled for a first offense.

19   But Professor Geyer said, "I know some graduating seniors who had to go to summer school." ■

QUESTIONS TO HELP YOU THINK AND WRITE ABOUT COMPUTER ISSUES

1. Think about the changes in computer technology since the early 1980s. Make three columns on a sheet of paper. Label the first column "1980," the second column "2000," and the third column "2020." Read "The Rhetorical Situation" for computers, "The New Wired World," and Kurzweil's article. List items from these that describe the state of computer technology at each of these times. What can you conclude about the changes, the projected changes, and the rate of change over this forty-year period? What is your personal reaction to these changes?

2. Kurzweil postulates that in the next twenty years or so, computers will be able to read massive amounts of material and share what they have learned from their reading with other computers. What advantages do you see in such technology? How might human beings use and benefit from this technology?

3. Do you now or will you someday have a job where computers are used in your workplace? Read McGinn and Raymond's article about the current and future use of computers in the workplace. Drawing on the information they provide, how do you think computers may change the work you do in your lifetime? What will you need to do to keep up with computer technology in your field?

4. With Turkle's article in mind, think about what you might learn from changing your gender on your visit to a MUD. How attractive is that idea to you? How likely would you be to do that? Look back at Doloff's article on

page 436. Compare Turkle's, Doloff's, and your own conclusions about such gender switching and what can be learned from it.

5. Miller writes that computers are being programmed to exhibit more human qualities. What human qualities does your present computer have, if any? Would you like or dislike a computer that seemed to understand your emotions and project human emotion itself? Give reasons for your answer.

6. Comparing Miller's article and McGrath's, describe (or draw) a cartoon in which a user gets emotional with a computer and the computer responds emotionally. Do you see any value in such emotional interaction between the user and the computer? Provide details for your answer.

7. Maas writes about the privacy issues associated with computers. What are some of the advantages of the large databases that contain the information described in his article? What are some of the disadvantages? What are your final conclusions about the relative value of maintaining and using these databases broadly versus limiting their scope and accessibility to "qualified" individuals or eliminating them altogether? Give reasons for your final position.

8. Based on the articles by Dertouzos and Arenson, make some tentative conclusions about how computers can make a positive contribution to education. Also consider areas in which they should not intrude. If you were the "computer czar" at your college, what policies would you set for the use of computers in higher education?

9. Stulman and Zack write about some of the problems that computers can create for students and their instructors. Have you experienced problems with computer use? What are they, and what have you done to solve them?

SECTION V
Issues Concerning Race and Culture in America

THE ISSUES

A. How Do Race and Culture Contribute to an Individual's Sense of Identity?

Five articles explore the issues associated with racial and cultural identity. Black and white relationships and how they are represented in film and television is the subject of hooks's article. Dyer claims that whites are represented in the media as existing outside of racial and ethnic categories and suggests the concept of "whiteness" be racialized. Gómez-Peña writes about the various cultural identities he experiences from living on the Mexican-American border, and Kondo writes about the confusion in identity that can result from trying to retain one's culture while being pressured by others to change it. Finally, Pan and Keene-Osborn describe a venture to address mixed cultural issues. See also "A View from Berkeley," page 51; "A Simple 'Hai' Won't Do It," page 58; and "We Knew What Glory Was," page 48.

B. How Close Has America Come to Achieving Racial Equality?

Four authors offer perspectives on progress toward racial equality. Cose explores the gains made in the black community and claims that even though life for black Americans is the best it has been, many problems still remain. Goldberg discusses the controversy associated with the police practice of racial profiling in identifying criminals, and Kennedy makes suggestions for reducing negative stereotypes. Figueroa suggests possible problems with Kennedy's views. See also "Black America's Moment of Truth," page 161; "Who Shot Johnny?" page 517; "Letter from Birmingham Jail," page 372; "'Improvement Is a Myth,'" page 598; and "Jobs Illuminate What Riots Hid: Young Ideals," page 77.

To Extend Your Perspective: Films and Literature Related to Race and Culture

Films: Mississippi Burning, 1988; *Lone Star*, 1996; *Ghosts of Mississippi*, 1996; *American History X*, 1998

Literature: poems: "Incident" by Countee Cullen; "Poem for the Young White Man" by Lorna Dee Cervantes; autobiography: *Borderlands* by Gloria Anzaldua; "How It Feels to Be Colored Me" by Zora Neale Hurston; *I Know Why the Caged Bird Sings* by Maya Angelou; play: *A Raisin in the Sun* by Lorraine Hansberry; novels: *Beloved* by Toni Morrison; *To Kill a Mockingbird* by Harper Lee; *Flight to Canada* by Ishmael Reed; *The Woman Warrior* by Maxine Hong Kingston; *The Joy Luck Club* by Amy Tan

THE RHETORICAL SITUATION

Dorinne K. Kondo, one of the authors in this section, makes the statement that "race, language, and culture are intertwined." Furthermore, certain combinations of race, language, and culture create expectations in many people's minds. We often expect individuals who possess particular combinations of these qualities to think, speak, or behave in certain ways. To understand these statements, you may want to think about how your race, culture, and language intertwine to contribute to your own sense of personal identity and also how they cause other people to regard you in particular ways. How would you characterize yourself in terms of your race, your culture, and your language? What group of people do you primarily identify with? How would you characterize the knowledge, beliefs, and behavior of this group, and how does the group itself influence your values and behavior? What language are you most comfortable speaking? In summary, how do your race, culture, and language help explain who you are?

One of the issues associated with racial and cultural identity is whether or not the special characteristics of races and cultures should be preserved or not. Some people think that races and cultures may eventually become so similar that differences among them will cease to exist, and complete assimilation and equality will result. They see this as a desirable result because it would reduce friction among groups. Other people think that differences in race and culture are valuable and that individuals should appreciate and strive to preserve the unique characteristics of their own race and culture. Certainly one can experience confusion and dissonance by leaving one's own culture for another culture and having to decide which parts of one's culture to retain and which parts to give up in order to fit in more smoothly. This is often an issue for people who study or live in another country for a significant period of time.

Racial equality is an issue that many people care about, including those who believe in equality on principle and those who believe that some people are somehow "less equal" than others. The warrants of justice and fairness are at the heart of this issue.

The idea that "all men are created equal" suggests that every American should have an acceptable quality of life, an equal opportunity for self-development, and the ways and means necessary for achieving these goals. Whether or not all Americans can be successful in these areas is controversial. Some evidence suggests that considerable improvement has been made. Still, many members of racial minorities have not climbed into the middle class and instead live in poverty and sometimes create horrendous social problems for the rest of society. As a result, police profiling of potential criminal offenders often points first to members of minority groups, and many people question the fairness of this practice. Some people inevitably begin to differentiate between "good" and "bad" members of different races and cultures and good and bad ways of living life. Other people have problems with generalizing in these ways.

For some individuals, cultural and racial issues are the most important issues in their lives, and for others, the issues barely exist. How do you regard these issues, and what provides the exigency for your interest or lack of interest?

A. How Do Race and Culture Contribute to an Individual's Sense of Identity?

TEACHING RESISTANCE: THE RACIAL POLITICS OF MASS MEDIA*

bell hooks

bell hooks is Distinguished Professor of English at the City College of New York. This excerpt is from her book Killing Rage, *which was published in 1995.*

For the most part television and movies depict a world where blacks and whites 1 coexist in harmony although the subtext is clear; this harmony is maintained because no one really moves from the location white supremacy allocates to them on

*bell hooks, *Killing Rage* (New York: Holt, 1995), pp. 113–115.

the race-sex hierarchy. Denzel Washington and Julia Roberts may play opposite one another in *The Pelican Brief* but there will not be a romance. True love in television and movies is almost always an occurrence between those who share the same race. When love happens across boundaries as in *The Bodyguard, Zebrahead,* or *A Bronx Tale*, it is doomed for no apparent reason and/or has tragic consequences. White and black people learning lessons from mass media about racial bonding are taught that curiosity about those who are racially different can be expressed as long as boundaries are not actually crossed and no genuine intimacy emerges. Many television viewers of all races and ethnicities were enchanted by a series called *I'll Fly Away*, which highlighted a liberal white family's struggle in the South and the perspective of the black woman who works as a servant in their home. Even though the series is often centered on the maid, her status is never changed or challenged. Indeed she is one of the "stars" of the show. It does not disturb most viewers that at this moment in history black women continue to be represented in movies and on television as the servants of whites. The fact that a black woman can be cast in a dramatically compelling leading role as a servant does not intervene on racist/sexist stereotypes, it reinscribes them. Hollywood awarded its first Oscar to a black person in 1939 when Hattie McDaniel won as Best Supporting Actress in *Gone With the Wind*. She played the maid. Contemporary films like *Fried Green Tomatoes* and *Passion Fish,* which offer viewers progressive visions of white females, still image black women in the same way—as servants. Even though the black female "servant" in *Passion Fish* comes from a middle-class background, drug addiction has led to her drop in status. And the film suggests that working secluded as the caretaker of a sick white woman redeems the black woman. It was twenty-four years after McDaniel won her Oscar that the only black man to ever receive this award won Best Actor. Sidney Poitier won for his role in the 1960s film *Lilies of the Field*. In this film he is also symbolically a "mammy" figure, playing an itinerant worker who caretakes a group of white nuns. Mass media consistently depict black folks either as servants or in subordinate roles, a placement which still suggests that we exist to bolster and caretake the needs of whites. Two examples that come to mind are the role of the black female FBI agent in *The Silence of the Lambs,* whose sole purpose is to bolster the ego of the white female lead played by Jodie Foster. And certainly in all the *Lethal Weapon* movies Danny Glover's character is there to be the buddy who because he is black and therefore subordinate can never eclipse the white male star. Black folks confront media that include us and subordinate our representation to that of whites, thereby reinscribing white supremacy.

2   While superficially appearing to present a portrait of racial social equality, mass media actually work to reinforce assumptions that black folks should always be cast in supporting roles in relation to white characters. That subordination is made to appear "natural" because most black characters are consistently portrayed as always a little less ethical and moral than whites, not given to rational reasonable action. It is not surprising that it is those black characters represented as didactic figures upholding the status quo who are portrayed as possessing positive characteristics. They are rational, ethical, moral peacemakers who help maintain law and order.

Significantly, the neo-colonial messages about the nature of race that are 3 brought to us by mass media do not just shape whites' minds and imaginations. They socialize black and other non-white minds as well. Understanding the power of representations, black people have in both the past and present challenged how we are presented in mass media, especially if the images are perceived to be "negative," but we have not sufficiently challenged representations of blackness that are not obviously negative even though they act to reinforce white supremacy. Concurrently, we do not challenge the representations of whites. We were not outside movie theaters protesting when the white male lead character in *Paris Trout* brutally slaughters a little black girl (even though I can think of no other image of a child being brutally slaughtered in a mainstream film) or when the lead character in *A Perfect World* played by Kevin Costner terrorizes a black family who gives him shelter. Even though he is a murderer and an escaped convict, his character is portrayed sympathetically, whereas the black male father is brutally tortured presumably because he is an unloving, abusive parent. In *A Perfect World* both the adult white male lead and the little white boy who stops him from killing the black man are shown to be ethically and morally superior to black people.

Films that present cinematic narratives that seek to intervene in and chal- 4 lenge white supremacist assumptions, whether they are made by black or white folks, tend to receive negative attention or none at all. John Sayles's film *The Brother from Another Planet* successfully presented a black male character in a lead role whose representation was oppositional. Rather than portraying a black male as a sidekick of a more powerful white male, or as a brute and sex fiend, he offered us the image of a gentle, healing, angelic black male spirit. John Waters's film *Hairspray* was able to reach a larger audience. In this movie, white people choose to be anti-racist, to critique white privilege. Jim Jarmusch's film *Mystery Train* is incredibly deconstructive of racist assumptions. When the movie begins we witness a young Japanese couple arriving at the bus station in Memphis who begin to speak Japanese with a black man who superficially appears to be indigent. Racist stereotypes and class assumptions are challenged at this moment and throughout the film. White privilege and lack of understanding of the politics of racial difference are exposed. Yet most viewers did not like this film and it did not receive much attention. Julie Dash's film *Daughters of the Dust* portrayed black folks in ways that were radically different from Hollywood conventions. Many white viewers and even some black viewers had difficulty relating to these images. Radical representations of race in television and movies demand that we be resisting viewers and break our attachment to conventional representations. These films, and others like them, demonstrate that film and mass media in general can challenge neo-colonial representations that reinscribe racist stereotypes and perpetuate white supremacy. If more attention were given these films, it would show that aware viewers long for mass media that act to challenge and change racist domination and white supremacy.

Until all Americans demand that mass media no longer serve as the biggest 5 propaganda machine for white supremacy, the socialization of everyone to subliminally absorb white supremacist attitudes and values will continue. Even though many white Americans do not overtly express racist thinking, it does not mean that their underlying belief structures have not been saturated with an ideology of difference that says white is always, in every way, superior to that which is black. Yet so far no complex public discourse exists that explains the difference between that racism which led whites to enjoy lynching and murdering black people and that wherein a white person may have a black friend or lover yet still believe black folks are intellectually and morally inferior to whites. [. . .]

6　　　When black psyches are daily bombarded by mass media representations that encourage us to see white people as more caring, intelligent, liberal, etc., it makes sense that many of us begin to internalize racist thinking.

7　　　Without an organized resistance movement that focuses on the role of mass media in the perpetuation and maintenance of white supremacy, nothing will change. Boycotts remain one of the most effective ways to call attention to this issue. Picketing outside theaters, turning off the television set, writing letters of protest are all low-risk small acts that can become major interventions. Mass media are neither neutral nor innocent when it comes to spreading the message of white supremacy. It is not far-fetched for us to assume that many more white Americans would be anti-racist if they were not socialized daily to embrace racist assumptions. Challenging mass media to divest of white supremacy should be the starting point of a renewed movement for racial justice.　■

THE MATTER OF WHITENESS*

Richard Dyer

Richard Dyer is professor of film studies at the University of Warwick in England. The following piece is an excerpt from Dyer's book White, *which was published in 1997. Here Dyer explores the representation of white people in Western culture.*

1　Racial[1] imagery is central to the organisation of the modern world. At what cost regions and countries export their goods, whose voices are listened to at international gatherings, who bombs and who is bombed, who gets what jobs, housing, access to health care and education, what cultural activities are subsidised and sold, in what terms they are validated—these are all largely inextricable from racial imagery. The myriad minute decisions that constitute the practices of the world are at every point informed by judgements about people's capacities and worth, judgements based on what they look like, where they come from, how they speak, even what they eat, that is, racial judgements. Race is not the only factor governing these things and people of goodwill everywhere struggle to overcome the prejudices and barriers of race, but it is never not a factor, never not in play. And since race in itself—insofar as it is anything in itself—refers to some intrinsically in-

*Richard Dyer, *White* (London: Routledge, 1997), pp. 1–4.

significant geographical/physical differences between people, it is the imagery of race that is in play.

There has been an enormous amount of analysis of racial imagery in the past 2 decades, ranging from studies of images of, say, blacks or American Indians in the media to the deconstruction of the fetish of the racial Other in the texts of colonialism and post-colonialism. Yet until recently a notable absence from such work has been the study of images of white people. Indeed, to say that one is interested in race has come to mean that one is interested in any racial imagery other than that of white people. Yet race is not only attributable to people who are not white, nor is imagery of non-white people the only racial imagery.

[I write] about the racial imagery of white people—not the images of other 3 races in white cultural production, but the latter's imagery of white people themselves. This is not done merely to fill a gap in the analytic literature, but because there is something at stake in looking at, or continuing to ignore, white racial imagery. As long as race is something only applied to non-white peoples, as long as white people are not racially seen and named, they/we function as a human norm. Other people are raced, we are just people.

There is no more powerful position than that of being "just" human. The 4 claim to power is the claim to speak for the commonality of humanity. Raced people can't do that—they can only speak for their race.[2] But non-raced people can, for they do not represent the interests of a race. The point of seeing the racing of whites is to dislodge them/us from the position of power, with all the inequities, oppression, privileges and sufferings in its train, dislodging them/us by undercutting the authority with which they/we speak and act in and on the world.

The sense of whites as non-raced is most evident in the absence of reference 5 to whiteness in the habitual speech and writing of white people in the West. We (whites) will speak of, say, the blackness or Chineseness of friends, neighbours, colleagues, customers or clients, and it may be in the most genuinely friendly and accepting manner, but we don't mention the whiteness of the white people we know. An old-style white comedian will often start a joke: "There's this bloke walking down the street and he meets this black geezer," never thinking to race the bloke as well as the geezer. Synopses in listings of films on TV, where wordage is tight, none the less squander words with things like: "Comedy in which a cop and his black sidekick investigate a robbery," "Skinhead Johnny and his Asian lover Omar set up a laundrette," "Feature film from a promising Native American director" and so on. Since all white people in the West do this all the time, it would be invidious to quote actual examples, and so I shall confine myself to one from my own writing. In an article on lesbian and gay stereotypes,[3] I discuss the fact that there can be variations on a type such as the queen or dyke. In the illustrations which accompany this point, I compare a "fashion queen" from the film *Irene* with a "black queen" from *Car Wash*—the former, white image is not raced, whereas all the variation of the latter is reduced to his race. Moreover, this is the only non-white image referred to in the article, which does not however point out that all the other images discussed are white. In this, as in the other white examples in this paragraph, the fashion queen is, racially speaking, taken as being just human.

6   This assumption that white people are just people, which is not far off saying that whites are people whereas other colours are something else, is endemic to white culture. Some of the sharpest criticism of it has been aimed at those who would think themselves the least racist or white supremacist. bell hooks, for instance, has noted how amazed and angry white liberals become when attention is drawn to their whiteness, when they are seen by non-white people as white.

> Often their rage erupts because they believe that all ways of looking that highlight difference subvert the liberal belief in a universal subjectivity (we are all just people) that they think will make racism disappear. They have a deep emotional investment in the myth of "sameness," even as their actions reflect the primacy of whiteness as a sign informing who they are and how they think.[4]

7   Similarly, Hazel Carby discusses the use of black texts in white classrooms, under the sign of multiculturalism, in a way that winds up focusing "on the complexity of response in the (white) reader/student's construction of self in relation to a (black) perceived 'other.' " We should, she argues, recognise that "everyone in this social order has been constructed in our political imagination as a racialized subject" and thus that we should consider whiteness as well as blackness, in order "to make visible what is rendered invisible when viewed as the normative state of existence: the (white) point in space from which we tend to identify difference."[5]

8   The invisibility of whiteness as a racial position in white (which is to say dominant) discourse is of a piece with its ubiquity. When I said above that [I am not] merely seeking to fill a gap in the analysis of racial imagery, I reproduced the idea that there is no discussion of white people. In fact for most of the time white people speak about nothing but white people, it's just that we couch it in terms of "people" in general. Research—into books, museums, the press, advertising, films, television, software—repeatedly shows that in Western representation whites are overwhelmingly and disproportionately predominant, have the central and elaborated roles, and above all are placed as the norm, the ordinary, the standard.[6] Whites are everywhere in representation. Yet precisely because of this and their placing as norm they seem not to be represented to themselves *as* whites but as people who are variously gendered, classed, sexualised and abled. At the level of racial representation, in other words, whites are not of a certain race, they're just the human race.

9   We are often told that we are living now in a world of multiple identities, of hybridity, of decentredness and fragmentation. The old illusory unified identities of class, gender, race, sexuality are breaking up; someone may be black *and* gay *and* middle class *and* female; we may be bi-, poly- or non-sexual, of mixed race, indeterminate gender and heaven knows what class. Yet we have not yet reached a situation in which white people and white cultural agendas are no longer in the ascendant. The media, politics, education are still in the hands of white people, still speak for whites while claiming—and sometimes sincerely aiming—to speak for humanity. Against the flowering of a myriad postmodern voices, we must also see the countervailing tendency towards a homogenisation of world culture, in the continued dominance of US news dissemination, popular TV programmes and Hollywood movies. Postmodern multiculturalism may have genuinely opened up a space for the voices of the other, challenging the authority of the

white West,[7] but it may also simultaneously function as a side-show for white people who look on with delight at all the differences that surround them.[8] We may be on our way to genuine hybridity, multiplicity without (white) hegemony, and it may be where we want to get to—but we aren't there yet, and we won't get there until we see whiteness, see its power, its particularity and limitedness, put it in its place and end its rule. This is why studying whiteness matters.

It is studying whiteness *qua* whiteness. Attention is sometimes paid to 10 "white ethnicity,"[9] but this always means an identity based on cultural origins such as British, Italian or Polish, or Catholic or Jewish, or Polish-American, Irish-American, Catholic-American and so on. These however are variations on white ethnicity (though [. . .] some are more securely white than others), and the examination of them tends to lead away from a consideration of whiteness itself. John Ibson, in a discussion of research on white US ethnicity, concludes that being, say, Polish, Catholic or Irish may not be as important to white Americans as some might wish.[10] But being white is. ■

NOTES

1. I use the terms race and racial [. . .] in the most common though problematic sense, referring to supposedly visibly differentiable, supportedly discrete social groupings.
2. In their discussion of the extraordinarily successful TV sitcom about a middle-class, African-American family, *The Cosby Show,* Sut Jhally and Justin Lewis note the way that viewers repeatedly recognise the characters' blackness but also that "you just think of them as people"; in other words that they don't only speak for their race. Jhally and Lewis argue that this is achieved by the way the family conforms to "the everyday, generic world of white television," an essentially middle-class world. The family is "ordinary" *despite* being black; because it is upwardly mobile, it can be accepted as "ordinary," in a way that marginalises most actual African-Americans. If the realities of African-American experience were included, then the characters would not be perceived as people." Sut Jhally and Justin Lewis, *Enlighteneds Racism: 'The Cosby Show,' Audiences and the Myth of the American Dream* (Boulder: Westview Press, 1992).
3. Richard Dyer, "Seen to Be Believed: Problems in the Representation of Gay People as Typical," in *The Matter of Images: Essays on Representation* (London: Routledge, 1993), pp. 19–51.
4. bell hooks, "Representations of Whiteness in the Black Imagination," in *Black Looks: Race and Representation* (Boston: South End Press, 1992), p. 167.
5. Hazel V. Carby, "The Multicultural Wars," in *Black Popular Culture,* ed. Gina Dent (Seattle: Bay Press, 1992), p. 193.
6. [. . .] The research findings are generally cast the other way round, in terms of non-white under-representation, textual marginalisation and positioning as deviant or a problem. Recent research in the US does suggest that African-Americans (but not other racially marginalised groups) have become more represented in the media, even in excess of their proportion of the population. However, this number still falls off if one focuses on central characters.
7. See, for example, Craig Owens, "The Discourse of Others: Feminists and Postmodernism," in *The Anti-Aesthetic: Essays on Postmodern Culture,* ed. Hal Foster (Port Townsend, Wash.: Bay Press, 1983), pp. 57–82.
8. *The Crying Game* (GB, 1992) seems to me to be an example of this. It explores with fascination and generosity, the hybrid and fluid nature of identity: gender, race, national belonging, sexuality. Yet all of this revolves around a bemused but ultimately unchallenged straight white man—it reinscribes the position of those at the intersection of

heterosexuality, maleness and whiteness as that of the one group which does not need to be hybrid and fluid.

9. See, for example, Richard D. Alba, *Ethnic Identity: The Transformation of White America* (New Haven, Conn.: Yale University Press, 1990).

10. John Ibson, "Virgin Land or Virgin Mary? Studying the Ethnicity of White Americans," *American Quarterly* 33 (1981): 284–308.

DOCUMENTED/UNDOCUMENTED*

Guillermo Gómez-Peña

Guillermo Gómez-Peña is a writer and performance artist whose work explores life on the "border" and the relationship among race, culture, and identity in America.

1 I live smack in the fissure between two worlds, in the infected wound: half a block from the end of Western civilization and four miles from the beginning of the Mexican/American border, the northernmost point of Latin America. In my fractured reality, but a reality nonetheless, there cohabit two histories, languages, cosmologies, artistic traditions, and political systems which are drastically counterposed. Many "deterritorialized" Latin American artists in Europe and the United States have opted for "internationalism" (a cultural identity based upon the "most advanced" of the ideas originating out of New York or Paris). I, on the other hand, opt for "borderness" and assume my role: my generation, the *chilango* (slang term for a Mexico City native), who came to "El Norte" fleeing the imminent ecological and social catastrophe of Mexico City, gradually integrated itself into otherness, in search of that other Mexico grafted into the entrails of the et cetera . . . became Chicano-ized. We de-Mexicanized ourselves, to Mexi-understand ourselves, some without wanting to, others on purpose. And one day, the border became our house, laboratory, and ministry, culture (or counterculture).

2   Today, eight years after my departure from Mexico, when they ask me for my nationality or ethnic identity, I can't respond with one word, since my "identity" now possesses multiple repertories: I am Mexican but I am also Chicano and Latin American. At the border they call me *chilango* or *mexiquillo*; in Mexico City it's *pocho* or *norteño;* and in Europe it's *sudaca.* The Anglos call me "Hispanic" or "Latino," and the Germans have, on more than one occasion, confused me with Turks or Italians. I walk amid the rubble of the Tower of Babel of my American postmodernity.

3   The recapitulation of my personal and collective topography has become my cultural obsession since I arrived in the United States. I look for the traces of my generation, whose distance stretches not only from Mexico City to California, but also from the past to the future, from pre-Columbian America to high technology, and from Spanish to English, passing through "Spanglish."

*Guillermo Gómez-Peña, *Warrior of Gringostroika* (St. Paul, Minn.: Graywolf Press, 1993), pp. 37–38, 40–41.

As a result of this process I have become a cultural topographer, border- 4
crosser, and hunter of myths. And it doesn't matter where I find myself, in Califas
or Mexico City, in Barcelona or West Berlin; I always have the sensation that I
belong to the same species: the migrant tribe of fiery pupils.

My work, like that of many border artists, comes from two distinct tradi- 5
tions, and because of this has dual, or on occasion multiple, referential codes. One
strain comes from Mexican popular culture, the Latin American literary "boom,"
and the Mexico City counterculture of the 1970s. . . . The other comes directly
from Fluxus (a late-1960s international art movement that explored alternative
means of production and distribution), concrete poetry, conceptual art, and performance art. These two traditions converge in my border experience and they
fuse together.

In my intellectual formation, Carlos Fuentes, Gabriel García Márquez, Oscar 6
Chávez, Felipe Ehrenberg, José Agustín, and Augusto Boal were as important as
William Burroughs, Michel Foucault, Rainer Werner Fassbinder, Jacques Lacan,
Vito Acconci, and Joseph Beuys.

My "artistic space" is the intersection where the new Mexican urban poetry 7
and the colloquial Anglo poetry meet; the intermediate stage somewhere between
Mexican street theatre and multimedia performance; the silence that snaps in between *corrido* and punk; the wall that divides "neográfica" (a 1970s Mexico City art
movement involved in the production of low-budget book art and graphics) and
graffiti; the highway that joins Mexico City and Los Angeles; and the mysterious
thread of thought and action that puts Pan–Latin Americanism in touch with the
Chicano movement, and both of these in touch with other international vanguards.

I am a child of crisis and cultural syncretism, half-hippie and half-punk. My 8
generation grew up watching movies about *charros* (Mexican cowboys) and science fiction, listening to *cumbias* and tunes from the Moody Blues, constructing al-
tars and filming in Super-8, reading *El Corno Emplumado* and *Artforum,* traveling to
Tepoztlán and San Francisco, creating and de-creating myths. We went to Cuba in
search of political illumination, to Spain to visit the crazy grandmother, and to the
United States in search of the instantaneous musico-sexual paradise. We found
nothing. Our dreams wound up getting caught in the webs of the border.

Our generation belongs to the world's biggest floating population: the weary 9
travelers, the dislocated, those of us who left because we didn't fit anymore, those
of us who still haven't arrived because we don't know where to arrive at, or because
we can't go back anymore.

Our deepest generational emotion is that of loss, which comes from our hav- 10
ing left. Our loss is total and occurs at multiple levels: loss of our country (culture
and national rituals) and our class (the "illustrious" middle class and upper-middle);
progressive loss of language and literary culture in our native tongue (those of us
who live in non-Spanish-speaking countries); loss of ideological meta-horizons (the
repression against and division of the left) and of metaphysical certainty.

In exchange, what we won was a vision of a more experimental culture, that 11
is to say, a multifocal and tolerant one. [. . .]

Our experience as Latino border artists and intellectuals in the United States 12
fluctuates between legality and illegality, between partial citizenship and full. For

the Anglo community we are simply "an ethnic minority," a subculture, that is to say, some kind of pre-industrial tribe with a good consumerist appetite. For the art world, we are practitioners of distant languages that, in the best of cases, are perceived as exotic.

13   In general, we are perceived through the folkloric prisms of Hollywood, fad literature, and publicity; or through the ideological filters of mass media. For the average Anglo, we are nothing but "images," "symbols," "metaphors." We lack ontological existence and anthropological concreteness. We are perceived indiscriminately as magic creatures with shamanistic powers, happy bohemians with pretechnological sensibilities, or as romantic revolutionaries born in a Cuban poster from the 1970s. All this without mentioning the more ordinary myths, which link us with drugs, supersexuality, gratuitous violence, and terrorism; myths that serve to justify racism and disguise the fear of cultural otherness.

14   These mechanisms of mythification generate semantic interference and obstruct true intercultural dialogue. To make border art implies to reveal and subvert said mechanisms.

15   The term Hispanic, coined by techno-marketing experts and by the designers of political campaigns, homogenizes our cultural diversity (Chicanos, Cubans, and Puerto Ricans become indistinguishable), avoids our indigenous cultural heritage, and links us directly with Spain. Worse yet, it possesses connotations of upward mobility and political obedience.

16   The terms Third World culture, ethnic art, and minority art are openly ethnocentric and necessarily imply an axiological vision of the world at the service of Anglo-European culture. Confronted with them, one can't avoid asking the following questions: Besides possessing more money and arms, is the "First World" qualitatively better in any other way than our "underdeveloped" countries? Aren't the Anglos themselves also an "ethnic group," one of the most violent and antisocial tribes on this planet? Aren't the 500 million Latin American mestizos that inhabit the Americas a "minority"?

17   Among Chicanos, Mexicans, and Anglos, there is a heritage of relations poisoned by distrust and resentment. For this reason, my cultural work (especially in the camps of performance art, radio art, and journalism) has concentrated upon the destruction of the myths and the stereotypes that each group has invented to rationalize the other two.

18   With the dismantling of this mythology, I look, if not to create an instantaneous space for intercultural communication, at least to contribute to the creation of the groundwork and theoretical principles for a future dialogue that is capable of transcending the profound historical resentments that exist between the communities on either side of the border.

19   Within the framework of the false amnesty of the Immigration Reform and Control Act and the growing influence of the North American ultra-right, which seeks to close (militarize) the border because of supposed motives of "national security," the collaboration among Chicano, Mexican, and Anglo artists has become indispensable.

20   Anglo artists can contribute their technical ability, their comprehension of the new media of expression and information (video and audio), and their altruist/

internationalist tendencies. In turn, Latinos (whether Mexican, Chicano, Caribbean, Central or South American) can contribute the originality of their cultural models, their spiritual strength, and their political understanding of the world.

Together, we can collaborate in surprising cultural projects without forgetting 21 that both should retain control of the product, from the planning stages up through distribution. If this doesn't occur, then intercultural collaboration isn't authentic. We shouldn't confuse true collaboration with political paternalism, cultural vampirism, voyeurism, economic opportunism, and demogogic multiculturalism.

We should clear up this matter once and for all: We (Latinos in the United 22 States) don't want to be a mere ingredient of the melting pot. What we want is to participate actively in a humanistic, pluralistic, and politicized dialogue, continuous and not sporadic, and we want this to occur between equals who enjoy the same power of negotiation.

For this "intermediate space" to open, first there has to be a pact of mutual 23 cultural understanding and acceptance, and it is precisely to this that the border artist can contribute. In this very delicate historical moment, Mexican artists and intellectuals as well as Chicanos and Anglos should try to "recontextualize" ourselves, that is to say, search for a "common cultural territory," and within it put into practice new models of communication and association. ■

ON BEING A CONCEPTUAL ANOMALY*

Dorinne K. Kondo

Dorinne K. Kondo, a Japanese American professor of anthropology, is the author of Crafting Selves: Power, Gender, and Discourses of Identity in a Japanese Workplace. *In this excerpt from her book, she relates her experiences in visiting Japan where she looked Japanese but acted like an American.*

As a Japanese American,[1] I created a conceptual dilemma for the Japanese I en- 1 countered. For them, I was a living oxymoron, someone who was both Japanese and not Japanese. Their puzzlement was all the greater since most Japanese people I knew seemed to adhere to an eminently biological definition of Japaneseness. Race, language, and culture are intertwined, so much so that any challenge to this firmly entrenched conceptual schema—a white person who speaks flawlessly idiomatic and unaccented Japanese, or a person of Japanese ancestry who cannot— meets with what generously could be described as unpleasant reactions. White people are treated as repulsive and unnatural—*hen na gaijin*, strange foreigners— the better their Japanese becomes, while Japanese Americans and others of Japanese ancestry born overseas are faced with exasperation and disbelief. How can someone who is racially Japanese lack "cultural competence"?[2] During my first

*Dorinne K. Kondo, *Crafting Selves: Power, Gender, and Discourses of Identity in a Japanese Workplace* (Chicago: University of Chicago Press, 1990), pp. 11–17.

few months in Tokyo, many tried to resolve this paradox by asking which of my parents was "really" American.

2   Indeed, it is a minor miracle that those first months did not lead to an acute case of agoraphobia, for I knew that once I set foot outside the door, someone somewhere (a taxi driver? a salesperson? a bank clerk?) would greet one of my linguistic mistakes with an astonished "Eh?" I became all too familiar with the series of expressions that would flicker over those faces: bewilderment, incredulity, embarrassment, even anger, at having to deal with this odd person who looked Japanese and therefore human, but who must be retarded, deranged, or—equally undesirable in Japanese eyes—Chinese or Korean. Defensively, I would mull over the mistake of the day. I mean, how was I to know that in order to "fillet a fish" you had to cut it "in three pieces"? Or that opening a bank account required so much specialized terminology? Courses in literary Japanese at Harvard hadn't done much to prepare me for the realities of everyday life in Tokyo. Gritting my teeth in determination as I groaned inwardly, I would force myself out of the house each morning.

3   For me, and apparently for the people around me, this was a stressful time, when expectations were flouted, when we had to strain to make sense of one another. There seemed to be few advantages in my retaining an American persona, for the distress caused by these reactions was difficult to bear. In the face of dissonance and distress, I found that the desire for comprehensible order in the form of "fitting in," even if it meant suppression of and violence against a self I had known in another context, was preferable to meaninglessness. Anthropological imperatives to immerse oneself in another culture intensified this desire, so that acquiring the accoutrements of Japanese selfhood meant simultaneously constructing a more thoroughly professional anthropological persona. This required language learning in the broadest sense, mastery of culturally appropriate modes of moving, acting, and speaking. For my informants, it was clear that coping with this anomalous creature was difficult, for here was someone who looked like a real human being, but who simply failed to perform according to expectation. They, too, had every reason to make me over in their image, to guide me, gently but insistently, into properly Japanese behavior, so that the discrepancy between my appearance and my cultural competence would not be so painfully evident. I posed a challenge to their senses of identity. How could someone who *looked* Japanese not *be* Japanese? In my cultural ineptitude, I represented for the people who met me the chaos of meaninglessness. Their response in the face of this dissonance was to *make* me as Japanese as possible. Thus, my first nine months of fieldwork were characterized by an attempt to reduce the distance between expectation and inadequate reality, as my informants and I conspired to rewrite my identity as Japanese.

4   My guarantor, an older woman who, among her many activities, was a teacher of flower arranging, introduced me to many families who owned businesses in the ward of Tokyo where I had chosen to do my research. One of her former students and fellow flower-arranging teachers, Mrs. Sakamoto, agreed to take me in as a guest over the summer, since the apartment where I was scheduled to move—owned by one of my classmates in tea ceremony—was still under

construction. My proclivities for "acting Japanese" were by this time firmly established. During my stay with the Sakamotos, I did my best to conform to what I thought their expectations of a guest/daughter might be. This in turn seemed to please them and reinforced my tendency to behave in terms of what I perceived to be my Japanese persona.

My initial encounter with the head of the household epitomizes this mirror- 5 ing and reinforcement of behavior. Mr. Sakamoto had been on a business trip on the day I moved in, and he returned the following evening, just as his wife, daughter, and I sat down to the evening meal. As soon as he stepped in the door, I immediately switched from an informal posture, seated on the *zabuton* (seat cushion), to a formal greeting posture, *seiza*-style (kneeling on the floor) and bowed low, hands on the floor. Mr. Sakamoto responded in kind (being older, male, and head of the household, he did not have to bow as deeply as I did), and we exchanged the requisite polite formulae, I requesting his benevolence, and he welcoming me to their family. Later, he told me how happy and impressed he had been with this act of proper etiquette on my part. "Today's young people in Japan," he said, "no longer show such respect. Your grandfather must have been a fine man to raise such a fine granddaughter." Of course, his statements can hardly be accepted at face value. They may well indicate his relief that I seemed to know something of proper Japanese behavior, and hence would not be a complete nuisance to them; it was also his way of making me feel at home. What is important to note is the way this statement was used to elicit proper Japanese behavior in future encounters. And his strategy worked. I was left with a warm, positive feeling toward the Sakamoto family, armed with an incentive to behave in a Japanese way, for clearly these were the expectations and the desires of the people who had taken me in and who were so generously sharing their lives with me.

Other members of the household voiced similar sentiments. Takemi-san, the 6 Sakamotos' married daughter who lived in a distant prefecture, had been visiting her parents when I first moved in. A few minutes after our initial encounter, she observed, "You seem like a typical Japanese woman" (*Nihon no josei, to iu kanji*). Later in the summer, Mrs. Sakamoto confided to me that she could never allow a "pure American" (*junsui na Amerikajin*) to live with them, for only someone of Japanese descent was genetically capable of adjusting to life on *tatami* mats, using unsewered toilets, sleeping on the floor—in short, of living Japanese style. Again, the message was unambiguous. My "family" could feel comfortable with me insofar as I was—and acted—Japanese. [. . .]

My physical characteristics led my friends and coworkers to emphasize my 7 identity as Japanese, sometimes even against my own intentions and desires. Over time, my increasingly "Japanese" behavior served temporarily to resolve their crises of meaning and to confirm their assumptions about their own identities. That I, too, came to participate enthusiastically in this recasting of the self is a testimonial to their success in acting upon me. [. . .]

The more I adjusted to my Japanese daughter's role, the keener the conflicts 8 became. Most of those conflicts had to do with expectations surrounding gender, and, more specifically, my position as a young woman. Certainly, in exchange for the care the Sakamotos showed me, I was happy to help out in whatever way I could. I tried to do some housecleaning and laundry, and I took over the shopping and cooking for Mr. Sakamoto when Mrs. Sakamoto was at one of the children's association meetings, her flower-arranging classes, or meetings of ward committees on juvenile delinquency. The cooking did not offend me in and of itself; in fact, I was glad for the opportunity to learn how to make simple Japanese cuisine, and Mr. Sakamoto put up with my sometimes appalling culinary mistakes and limited menus with great aplomb. I remember one particularly awful night when I couldn't find the makings for soup broth, and Mr. Sakamoto was fed "*miso* soup" that was little more than *miso* dissolved in hot water. He managed to down the tasteless broth with good grace—and the trace of a smile on his lips. (Of course, it is also true that although he was himself capable of simple cooking, he would not set foot in the kitchen if there were a woman in the house.) Months after I moved out, whenever he saw me he would say with a sparkle in his eye and a hint of nostalgic wistfulness in his voice, "I miss Dōrin-san's salad and sautéed beef," one of the "Western" menus I used to serve up with numbing regularity. No, the cooking was not the problem.

9   The problem was, in fact, the etiquette surrounding the serving of food that produced the most profound conflicts for me as an American woman. The head of the household is usually served first and receives the finest delicacies; men— even the sweetest, nicest ones—ask for a second helping of rice by merely holding out their rice bowls to the woman nearest the rice cooker, and maybe, just maybe, uttering a grunt of thanks in return for her pains. I could never get used to this practice, try as I might. Still, I tried to carry out my duties uncomplainingly, in what I hope was reasonably good humor. But I was none too happy about these things "inside." Other restrictions began to chafe, especially restrictions on my movement. I had to be in at a certain hour, despite my "adult" age. Yet I understood the family's responsibility for me as their guest and quasi-daughter, so I tried to abide by their regulations, hiding my irritation as best I could.

10   This fundamental ambivalence was heightened by isolation and dependency. Though my status was in some respects high in an education-conscious Japan, I was still young, female, and a student. I was in a socially recognized relationship of dependency vis-à-vis the people I knew. I was not to be feared and obeyed, but protected and helped. In terms of my research, this was an extremely advantageous position to be in, for people did not feel the need to reflect my views back to me, as they might with a more powerful person. I did not try to define situations; rather, I could allow other people to define those situations in their culturally appropriate ways, remaining open to their concerns and their ways of acting in the world. But, in another sense, this dependency and isolation increased my susceptibility to identifying with my Japanese role. By this time I saw little of American friends in Tokyo, for it was difficult to be with people who had so little inkling of how ordinary Japanese people lived. My informants and I consequently had every reason to conspire to re-create my identity as Japanese. Precisely because of my dependency and my made-to-order role, I was allowed—or rather, *forced*—to abandon the position of observer. Errors, linguistic or cultural, were

dealt with impatiently or with a startled look that seemed to say, "Oh yes, you are American after all." On the other hand, appropriately Japanese behaviors were rewarded with warm, positive reactions or with comments such as "You're more Japanese than the Japanese." Even more frequently, correct behavior was simply accepted as a matter of course. *Naturally* I would understand, *naturally* I would behave correctly, for they presumed me to be, *au fond*, Japanese.

Identity can imply unity or fusion, but for me what occurred was a fragmentation 11 of the self. This fragmentation was encouraged by my own participation in Japanese life and by the actions of my friends and acquaintances. At its most extreme point, I became "the Other" in my own mind, where the identity I had known in another context simply collapsed. The success of our conspiracy to re-create me as Japanese reached its climax one August afternoon.

It was typical summer weather for Tokyo, "like a steam bath" as the saying 12 goes, so hot the leaves were drooping limply from the trees surrounding the Sakamotos' house. Mrs. Sakamoto and her married daughter, Takemi, were at the doctor's with Takemi's son, so Mr. Sakamoto and I were busy tending young Kaori-chan, Takemi-san's young daughter. Mr. Sakamoto quickly tired of his grandfatherly role, leaving me to entertain Kaori-chan. Promptly at four P.M., the hour when most Japanese housewives do their shopping for the evening meal, I lifted the baby into her stroller and pushed her along ahead of me as I inspected the fish, selected the freshest-looking vegetables, and mentally planned the meal for the evening. As I glanced into the shiny metal surface of the butcher's display case, I noticed someone who looked terribly familiar: a typical young housewife, clad in slip-on sandals and the loose, cotton shift called "home wear" (*hōmu wea*), a woman walking with a characteristically Japanese bend to the knees and a sliding of the feet. Suddenly I clutched the handle of the stroller to steady myself as a wave of dizziness washed over me, for I realized I had caught a glimpse of nothing less than my own reflection. Fear that perhaps I would never emerge from this world into which I was immersed inserted itself into my mind and stubbornly refused to leave, until I resolved to move into a new apartment, to distance myself from my Japanese home and my Japanese existence.

For ultimately this collapse of identity was a distancing moment. It led me to 13 emphasize the *differences* between cultures and among various aspects of identity: researcher, student, daughter, wife, Japanese, American, Japanese American. In order to reconstitute myself as an American researcher, I felt I had to extricate myself from the conspiracy to rewrite my identity as Japanese. Accordingly, despite the Sakamotos' invitations to stay with them for the coming year, I politely stated my intentions to fulfill the original terms of the agreement: to stay just until construction on my new apartment was complete. In order to resist the Sakamotos' attempts to re-create me as Japanese, I removed myself physically from their exclusively Japanese environment. ■

NOTES

1. See Edward Said, *Orientalism* (New York: Pantheon, 1978). The issue of what to call ourselves is an issue of considerable import to various ethnic and racial groups in

the United States, as the recent emphasis on the term "African American" shows. For Asian Americans, the term "Oriental" was called into question in the sixties, for the reasons Said enumerates: the association of the term with stereotypes such as Oriental despotism, inscrutability, splendor, exoticism, mystery, and so on. It also defines "the East" in terms of "the West," in a relationship of unequal power—how rarely one hears of "the Occident," for example. Asian Americans, Japanese Americans included, sometimes hyphenate the term, but some of us would argue that leaving out the hyphen makes the term "Asian" or "Japanese" an adjective, rather than implying a half-and-half status: i.e., that one's loyalties/identities might be half Japanese and half American. Rather, in the terms "Asian American" and "Japanese American," the accent is on the "American," an important political claim in light of the mainstream tendency to see Asian Americans as somehow more foreign than other kinds of Americans.

2. Merry White, *The Japanese Overseas: Can They Go Home Again?* (New York: Free Press, 1988) offers an account of the families of Japanese corporate executives who are transferred abroad and who often suffer painful difficulties upon reentering Japan.

CULTURE BY THE CAMPFIRE*

Esther Pan and Sherry Keene-Osborn

Esther Pan and Sherry Keene-Osborn explore the world of camps where children and parents deal with the issues of raising children in mixed-race families.

1 Hidden Valley looks a lot like the dozens of other camps that dot the woods of central Maine. There's a lake, some soccer fields and horses. But the campers make the difference. They're all American parents who have adopted kids from China. They're at Hidden Valley to find bridges from their children's old worlds to the new. Diana Becker of Montville, Maine, watches her 3-year-old daughter Mika dance to a Chinese version of "Twinkle, Twinkle Little Star." "Her soul is Chinese," she says, "but really she's growing up American."

2   Hidden Valley and a handful of other "culture camps" serving families with children from overseas reflect the huge rise in the number of foreign adoptions, from 7,093 in 1990 to 15,774 last year [1998]. Most children come from Russia (4,491 last year) and China (4,206), but there are also thousands of others adopted annually from South America, Asia and Eastern Europe. After cutting through what can be miles of red tape, parents often come home to find a new dilemma. "At first you think, 'I need a child,' " says Sandy Lachter of Washington, D.C., who with her husband, Steve, adopted Amelia, 5, from China in 1995. "Then you think, 'What does the child need?' "

3   The culture camps give families a place to find answers to those kinds of questions. Most grew out of local support groups; Hidden Valley was started last year by the Boston chapter of Families with Children from China, which includes 650 families. While parents address weighty issues like how to raise kids in a mixed-race family, their children just have fun riding horses, singing Chinese songs or making scallion pancakes. "My philosophy of camping is that they could be

Newsweek, October 4, 1999, p. 75.

doing anything, as long as they see other Chinese kids with white parents," says the director, Peter Kassen, whose adopted daughters Hope and Lily are 6 and 4.

The camp is a continuation of language and dance classes many of the kids at- 4
tend during the year. "When we rented out a theater for *Mulan,* it was packed," says Stephen Chen of Boston, whose adopted daughter Lindsay is 4. Classes in Chinese language, art and calligraphy are taught by experts, like Renne Lu of the Greater Boston Chinese Cultural Center. "Our mission is to preserve the heritage," Lu says.

Kids who are veteran campers say the experience helps them understand 5
their complex heritage. Sixteen-year-old Alex was born in India and adopted by Kathy and David Brinton of Boulder, Colo., when he was 7. "I went through a stage where I hated India, hated everything about it," he says. "You just couldn't mention India to me." But after six sessions at the East India Colorado Heritage Camp, held at Snow Mountain Ranch in Estes Park, Colo., he hopes to travel to India after he graduates from high school next year.

Campers say the sessions help them feel more "normal," especially if they 6
live in communities where there are no other families like theirs. Gina Gruelle, 19, who was also adopted from India, grew up in the tiny town of Gresham, Ore. "It's important to go someplace where people do look and feel like you," she says of her time at Snow Mountain. Last summer, she returned as a volunteer counselor. "Some of the new kids, you could tell they had never been around other people from India," she says.

Snow Mountain is run by a volunteer group, Colorado Heritage Camps, 7
founded by adoptive parent Pam Sweetser in 1992. They have sessions for kids from Korea, Vietnam, India, Latin America and the Philippines. "As adoptive parents, we have to realize they're the ones who deal with being a minority; we don't," says Sweetser. "We have to give them the skills to deal with that."

Camp can be a learning experience for the whole family. Whitney Ning, 23, a 8
counselor for four years, says the Korea Heritage Camp helped her become closer to her parents. "They were hesitant at first," she says, "but when they saw how much it meant to me, they became very supportive." Sometimes the most direct route around the world is across a campfire. ■

B. How Close Has America Come to Achieving Racial Equality?

THE GOOD NEWS ABOUT BLACK AMERICA*

Ellis Cose

Ellis Cose claims that although life for black Americans is better than it is has ever been, the struggle for equality continues.

It was a stunning vision of racial equality, manifested in a simple yet stirring 1
mantra: "I have a dream." Though Martin Luther King Jr.'s cherished utopia has

Newsweek, June 7, 1999, pp. 30–40.

not arrived, it seems considerably less remote than it did in August 1963 when, from the Washington Mall, King challenged America to make his dream come true. African-Americans are no longer relegated, as he lamented, to "a lonely island of poverty" in the midst of plenty. By a wide array of measures, now is a great time—the best time ever—to be black in America.

2   Black employment and home ownership are up. Murders and other violent crimes are down. Reading and math proficiency are climbing. Out-of-wedlock births are at their lowest rate in four decades. Fewer blacks are on welfare than at any point in recent memory. More are in college than at any point in history. And the percentage of black families living below the poverty line is the lowest it has been since the Census Bureau began keeping separate black poverty statistics in 1967. Even for some of the most persistently unfortunate—uneducated black men between 16 and 24—jobs are opening up, according to a just-released study of hard-luck cases in 322 urban areas by researchers at Harvard University and the College of William and Mary.

3   More and more blacks have entered the realm of the privileged and have offices in (or tantalizingly near to) the corridors of corporate and political power. Some control multimillion-dollar budgets and reside in luxurious gated communities. They are, by any criteria, living large—walking testaments to the transformative power, to the possibility, of America.

4   "I really think there is a new phenomenon out there," says Eddie Williams, head of the Joint Center for Political and Economic Studies, the nation's premier think tank on blacks and politics. According to the center, the number of black elected officials has nearly sextupled since 1970, and now stands at roughly 9,000. In a poll late last year by the Joint Center, blacks were more likely than whites—for the first time in the history of this survey—to say they were better off financially than in the previous year (51 percent compared with 31.5 percent). A new *Newsweek* poll confirms that the finding is not a fluke. Seventy-one percent of blacks (compared with 59 percent of whites) told *Newsweek*'s pollsters that they expected their family incomes to rise during the next 10 years. Fifty-seven percent of blacks (compared with 48 percent of whites) foresaw better job opportunities ahead. As Los Angeles gangbanger turned music entrepreneur Darrin Butler, 28, sums it up, "From where I'm sitting, everything is looking bright."

5   This sunniness is reflected in the country's popular imagination, which freely celebrates the appeal and accomplishments of African-Americans. Michael Jordan, Lauryn Hill, Colin Powell—pick your icon; if you are touched at all by American culture your idol is likely to be black. There have always been black successes and superstar achievers, but never before has black been quite so beautiful to so many admirers of every hue. "When did you ever think you would see black men as the heroes of white children?" asks Bobby William Austin, head of the Village Foundation, an Alexandria, Va.–based nonprofit that runs programs for young black men.

6   Today's upswing in black fortune is unfolding in a singular context, against the backdrop of a superheated economy that has been booming since April 1991. That expansion, the longest ever in a time of peace, has been a boon to Americans of every race. It would be a mistake, however, to credit the economy alone for the

sense of hope sprouting in many black communities. Even as the strong economy has made bigger dreams possible, a strong resurgence of black self-confidence and self-determination has made their realization more probable. Indeed, blacks polled by *Newsweek* credited black churches (46 percent) and black self-help (41 percent) for the upturn in black conditions. It would also be a mistake to assume that today's good times have brought good tidings to all blacks. They have not. More black men than ever languish in prisons. Black academic achievement stills lags that of whites. And suicides among young black men have risen sharply, reflecting a deep "sense of hopelessness," says Jewelle Taylor Gibbs, a psychologist and University of California, Berkeley, professor. And fear is pervasive that an economic downturn—or the legal-political assault on affirmative action—could wipe out blacks' tenuous gains.

7   Nonetheless, for a community yet haunted by the memory of Jim Crow, this is a remarkable moment. One of the most dramatic signs of progress is the explosion of productive activity as once desolate inner-city neighborhoods, such as Chicago's North Lawndale, come to life. In 1966, this area on Chicago's West Side was so blighted that Martin Luther King rented an apartment there to call attention to it. Then things got worse. The area was largely incinerated by the riots that broke out in the wake of King's assassination in 1968. More than half of the population moved out between 1960 and 1990. Now new construction is shooting up. Homes are selling for as much as $275,000 apiece. And the young black professionals flocking back to buy them talk of renaissance and hope reborn.

8   "People wrote this area off. They didn't believe middle-class African-Americans would come back here. Now we're making this neighborhood work," says Demetrius Barbee. For Barbee, a Blockbuster executive, and her husband, Gerald, a medical-equipment technician, trading in a fancy North Lake Shore Drive address for a North Lawndale dream house was not merely a matter of getting good quality for a good price. It was an investment of hope in the very idea of a community coming back from the dead. [. . .]

9   Across the country, Piney Woods Life School, a private boarding academy in rural Mississippi, is stoking that hunger for success. Started at the turn of the century to educate children of Mississippi field hands, it has evolved into a haven for mistreated or troubled black kids from across America. Many come from backgrounds similar to Kenyatah's, a 16-year-old junior whose parents, both junkies, kicked her out of their Washington, D.C., home at the age of 4. She ended up with relatives, also addicts, and spent time living on the street. Serendipity and a recommendation from a friend of her aunt brought Kenyatah to Piney Woods, and she is grateful for the change. "Where I'm from, you don't learn anything [in school]," she says.

10   At Piney Woods academics are stressed, and self-pity is not an option. Over the last several years, ACT scores for Piney Woods seniors have risen from an average of 9.8 to an average of 18.1—compared with a national average of 22. "We've set a goal of having our young people exceed the national average on the ACT within the next three years," says school president Charles Beady Jr. Piney Woods graduates routinely go on to Ivy League colleges. Many also become ambassadors

of deliverance, spreading the word that black children can triumph, no matter how or where their lives begin.

11   The significant reversal of black fortunes is a signal event, one that "must be acknowledged and celebrated," says Joe Hicks, executive director of the Los Angeles Human Relations Commission. Yet, for the most part, blacks are not celebrating it, which raises an inevitable question: if the news in black America is so good these days, why are people not dancing in the streets? Why are civil-rights leaders not proclaiming it from the rooftops? Why has the dialogue on racial relations not fundamentally changed to accentuate the progress instead of the lingering problems?

12   Ward Connerly, the controversial black businessman and driving force behind Proposition 209, the ballot measure that eliminated affirmative action in California state government, thinks the reason has a lot to do with the fossilized attitude of many blacks—particularly those in the leadership class. Even though society has transformed itself, says Connerly, many African-Americans are "locked into that mind-set of the '60s that society is racist. . . . We just can't let go. Our leaders . . . can't let go. I won't say they have a vested interest in maintaining the status quo, although I think that's a possibility." Harvard sociologist Orlando Patterson agrees. In the aftermath of the civil-rights revolution, "blaming racism" made good politics and fashionable social science, he says. That era is ending, in Patterson's view, "but, tragically, Afro-American leaders now seem trapped by the fire they started."

13   In African-American leadership circles, Patterson's indictment strikes a nerve. It even evokes limited agreement. Yvonne Scruggs-Leftwich, executive director of the Black Leadership Forum, an umbrella group of civil-rights organizations, concedes, "We don't often enough acknowledge where there have been successes." Nonetheless, civil-rights leaders resent and reject the view that they are a bunch of self-serving doomsayers. "We *have* celebrated the economy, the reduction in unemployment, the reduction in teen-pregnancy rates," says Huge Price, head of the National Urban League.

14   The problem is that although certain blacks are thriving, others are not. Many of those "beneath the surface of socioeconomic viability," as sociologist Elijah Anderson describes them, are worse off than ever. Many blighted, black neighborhoods . . . are dying slow, painful deaths. And in that fact lies a leadership challenge and a philosophical dilemma. How can civil-rights leaders acknowledge the real and evident progress without encouraging complacency? How can they keep the pressure on to "move the glass from half-full to three-quarters full," in Price's words, if they give up the language of crisis and damnation? How do they avoid playing into the hands of those who would eliminate affirmative action, voting-rights enforcement and so many other things that are largely responsible for the black progress on display today? "To the extent you proclaim your success, other people forget about you," worries the Joint Center's Eddie Williams.

15   Then there is the fear—one deeply felt not only among the black leadership class but among much of the black general population—that the good times may

be transient. What happens, skeptics ask, when the economy hits bottom? Or if the attacks on affirmative action ultimately eliminate opportunities, only recently won, in both the private and the public sectors? [. . .]

Eric Frierson, a 33-year-old data processor and Watts native, has equally 16 pressing worries. Frierson did 11 years in Folsom penitentiary, but has managed to stay out of trouble for the past five years, and now volunteers for FACES, a community-outreach organization working in Watt's Imperial Courts housing projects. It is an area where buildings are pockmarked by bullet holes and bad company constantly beckons. "They told me I can't be around no ex-cons," says Frierson, but "everybody I know is an ex-con. All my brothers are ex-cons. Almost every black man you see is an ex-con. Who am I going to be with?"

Frierson's plaintive question reflects a sobering reality. An estimated 70 per- 17 cent of the young black men of Watts—those between the ages of 16 and 25—are on "some kind of paper," meaning they're in jail, on parole or on probation. That specter of prison haunts countless other black communities across the nation. In some areas, prison time has become such a pervasive feature of life that it has totally undermined the hard-fought victory for black voting rights. One million four hundred thousand black men, or 13 percent of the total, are disenfranchised because of felony convictions, according to a recent report by Human Rights Watch and the Sentencing Project.

Some even question whether the much-vaunted black progress in education 18 is as genuine as it seems. A study of higher education in 19 states done by the Southern Education Foundation shows that though the numbers of blacks in college overall are up, those of first-time, full-time freshmen are not. Numerous experts are also concerned about the impact of anti-affirmative-action measures. When California, Texas and Washington state eliminated affirmative action, all experienced huge drops in the numbers of blacks and Latinos admitted to their most selective state schools.

In earlier grades, the picture is also ambiguous. Twenty-six states have 19 adopted exams high-school seniors must pass before they can graduate, according to a new study from the Applied Research Center, an Oakland-based research and advocacy group. "In virtually every state that has implemented high-school exit exams, a disproportionate number of those who have passed all other requirements but fail to graduate . . . are students of color," charged the report. Exit exams "essentially punish poor students and those of color for attending substandard schools," concluded ARC. Less easily explained, this performance gap also persists in affluent and integrated communities, such as Shaker Heights, Ohio.

Welfare reform, likewise, does not bring exclusively good news. Clearly, it 20 has taken recipients of all races (more than 2 million families) off the rolls, and given many a second shot at a productive life. Studies—and at this point there are no definitive ones—suggest that perhaps two thirds manage to get along reasonably well (often through a combination of part-time work, forays into the underground economy and help from their families). But many (probably most) don't find full-time permanent jobs. And it appears that whites do better than blacks. The racial difference "is consistent with what we know about employer preference," says Melvin Oliver of the Ford Foundation. There are other likely reasons, as well, including the fact that black women are less likely to live where jobs are located. But like virtually everything else involving race, the reality of welfare reform is too complex to capture with one hackneyed truism, or with one simple set of statistics. [. . .]

21   That black schoolchildren are still wrestling with the ludicrous issue of whether academic achievement somehow makes them less black says volumes about the message of black-white difference that society continues to send. It is a message graphically underscored by the intense segregation that defines American living patterns. And it is continually bolstered by popular culture, particularly television, which keeps its dating shows racially segregated and its programming racially segmented. Hence, it's no wonder that blacks and whites generally watch totally different prime-time shows. And it's hardly surprising that even though the incidence of interracial marriages has grown greatly, marriages between blacks and whites are a fraction of those between whites and Hispanics or whites and Asians.

22   What all that says, in short, is that, for all the well-documented black success stories, and for all the heartwarming statistics, blacks remain, in substantial measure, a race apart in America: a race admired, even emulated, yet held at arm's length. It reflects a particular American schizophrenia. We embrace equality and yet struggle with it in reality. We have come so far, and yet we have not escaped the past.

23   In perhaps the most famous passage of his most famous book, *The Souls of Black Folk* (first published in 1903), the great sociologist and social activist W. E. B. Du Bois tried to explain what it meant to be a Negro in America. "One ever feels his twoness—an American, a Negro; two souls, two thoughts, two unreconciled strivings; two warring ideals in one dark body, whose dogged strength alone keeps it from being torn asunder." What he did not say, but could have, is that America also has its unreconciled strivings, an impulse toward acceptance coexisting with a tendency toward exclusion, a reverence for equality that coexists with stirrings of racism.

24   The good news on black America is too clear to deny. In the past few decades, blacks' fortunes and prospects have soared toward the heavens. Blacks have entered virtually every sector of American society and breathed life into Martin Luther King's extraordinary fantasy. It's too late to put the racial-justice genie back in the bottle. It's time to acknowledge what America and African-Americans together have accomplished and become. The bad news, however, is equally profound, and it can be summed up with two simple facts. Despite all the progress of the last several decades, we continue to talk about black America as a place and a people apart. And despite the lip service we pay to the concept of equality, we look with equanimity, even pride, upon a statistical profile of black Americans that, were it of whites, would be a source of horror and consternation. That is not likely to change soon; but until and unless it does, our great nation will never become the country of our finest dreams. ■

THE COLOR OF SUSPICION*

Jeffrey Goldberg

Jeffery Goldberg explores the issue of racial profiling. Is profiling a form of racism or a legitimate tool for fighting crime?

Sgt. Lewis of the Maryland State Police is a bull-necked, megaphone-voiced, 1 highly caffeinated drug warrior who, on this shiny May morning outside of An-napolis, is conceding defeat. The drug war is over, the good guys have lost and he has been cast as a racist. "This is the end, buddy," he says. "I can read the writing on the wall." Lewis is driving his unmarked Crown Victoria down the fast lane of Route 50, looking for bad guys. The back of his neck is burnt by the sun, and he wears his hair flat and short under his regulation Stetson.

"They're going to let the N.A.A.C.P. tell us how to do traffic stops," he says. 2 "That's what's happening. There may be a few troopers who make stops solely based on race, but this—they're going to let these people tell us how to run our department. I say, to hell with it all. I don't care if the drugs go through. I don't."

He does, of course. Mike Lewis was born to seize crack. He grew up in Salis- 3 bury, on the Eastern Shore—Jimmy Buffett country—and he watched his friends become stoners and acid freaks. Not his scene. He buzz-cut his hair away and joined the state troopers when he was 19. He's a star, the hard-charger who made one of the nation's largest seizures of crack cocaine out on Route 13. He's a na-tional expert on hidden compartments. He can tell if a man's lying, he says, by watching the pulsing of the carotid artery in his neck. He can smell crack cocaine inside a closed automobile. He's a human drug dog, a walking polygraph ma-chine. "I have the unique ability to distinguish between a law-abiding person and an up-to-no-good person," he says. "Black or white." All these skills, though, he's ready to chuck. The lawsuits accusing the Maryland State Police of harassing black drivers, the public excoriation—and most of all, the Governor of New Jersey saying that her state police profiled drivers based on race, and were wrong to do so—have twisted him up inside. "Three of my men have put in for transfers," he says. "My wife wants me to get out. I'm depressed."

What depresses Mike Lewis is that he believes he is in possession of a truth 4 polite society is too cowardly to accept. He says that when someone tells this par-ticular truth, his head is handed to him. "The superintendent of the New Jersey State Police told the truth and he got fired for it," Lewis says.

This is what Carl Williams said, fueling a national debate about racial profiling 5 in law enforcement: "Today, with this drug problem, the drug problem is cocaine or marijuana. It is most likely a minority group that's involved with that." Gov. Chris-tine Todd Whitman fired Williams, and the news ricocheted through police depart-ments everywhere, especially those, like the Maryland State Police, already accused of racial profiling—the stopping and searching of blacks because they are black.

New York Times Magazine, June 20, 1999, pp. 51–56.

6   The way cops perceive blacks—and how those perceptions shape and mis-shape crime fighting—is now the most charged racial issue in America. [. . .]

7   Neither side understands the other. The innocent black man, jacked-up and humiliated during a stop-and-frisk or a pretext car stop, asks: Whatever happened to the Fourth Amendment? It is no wonder, blacks say, that the police are so wildly mistrusted.

8   And then there's the cop, who says: Why shouldn't I look at race when I'm looking for crime? It is no state secret that blacks commit a disproportionate amount of crime, so "racial profiling" is simply good police work.

9   Mike Lewis wishes that all this talk of racial profiling would simply stop.

10   As we drive, Lewis watches a van come up on his right and pass him. A young black man is at the wheel, his left leg hanging out the window. The blood races up Lewis's face: "Look at that! That's a violation! You can't drive like that! But I'm not going to stop him. No, sir. If I do, he's just going to call me a racist."

11   Then Lewis notices that the van is a state government vehicle. "This is ridiculous," he says. Lewis hits his lights. The driver stops. Lewis issues him a warning and sends him on his way. The driver says nothing.

12   "He didn't call me a racist," Lewis says, pulling into traffic, "but I know what he was thinking." Lewis does not think of himself as a racist. "I know how to treat people," he says. "I've never had a complaint based on a race-based stop. I've got that supercharged knowledge of the Constitution that allows me to do this right."

13   In the old days, when he was patrolling the Eastern Shore, it was white people he arrested. "Ninety-five percent of my drug arrests were dirt-ball-type whites—marijuana, heroin, possession-weight. Then I moved to the highway, I start taking off two, three kilograms of coke, instead of two or three grams. Black guys. Suddenly I'm not the greatest trooper in the world. I'm a racist. I'm locking up blacks, but I can't help it."

14   His eyes gleam: "Ask me how many white people I've ever arrested for cocaine smuggling—ask me!"

15   I ask.

16   "None! Zero! I debrief hundreds of black smugglers, and I ask them, 'Why don't you hire white guys to deliver your drugs?' They just laugh at me. 'We ain't gonna trust our drugs with white boys.' That's what they say."

17   Mike Lewis's dream: "I dream at night about arresting white people for cocaine. I do. I try to think of innovative ways to arrest white males. But the reality is different." [. . .]

WHY A COP PROFILES

18 This is what a cop might tell you in a moment of reckless candor: in crime fighting, race matters. When asked, most cops will declare themselves color blind. But watch them on the job for several months, and get them talking about the way policing is really done, and the truth will emerge, the truth being that cops, white and black, profile. Here's why, they say. African-Americans commit a dispropor-

tionate percentage of the types of crimes that draw the attention of the police. Blacks make up 12 percent of the population, but accounted for 58 percent of all carjackers between 1992 and 1996. (Whites accounted for 19 percent.) Victim surveys—and most victims of black criminals are black—indicate that blacks commit almost 50 percent of all robberies. Blacks and Hispanics are widely believed to be the blue-collar backbone of the country's heroin- and cocaine-distribution networks. Black males between the ages of 14 and 24 make up 1.1 percent of the country's population, yet commit more than 28 percent of its homicides. Reason, not racism, cops say, directs their attention.

Cops, white and black, know one other thing: they're not the only ones 19 who profile. Civilians profile all the time—when they buy a house, or pick a school district, or walk down the street. Even civil rights leaders profile. "There is nothing more painful for me at this stage in my life," Jesse Jackson said several years ago, "than to walk down the street and hear footsteps and start thinking about robbery—and then look around and see somebody white and feel relieved." Jackson now says his quotation was "taken out of context." The context, he said, is that violence is the inevitable by-product of poor education and health care. But no amount of "context" matters when you fear that you are about to be mugged.

At a closed-door summit in Washington between police chiefs and black com- 20 munity leaders recently, the black chief of police of Charleston, S. C., Reuben Greenberg, argued that the problem facing black America is not racial profiling, but precisely the sort of black-on-black crime Jackson was talking about. "I told them that the greatest problem in the black community is the tolerance for high levels of criminality," he recalled. "Fifty percent of homicide victims are African-Americans. I asked what this meant about the value of life in this community."

The police chief in Los Angeles, Bernard Parks, who is black, argues that 21 racial profiling is rooted in statistical reality, not racism. "It's not the fault of the police when they stop minority males or put them in jail," Parks told me. "It's the fault of the minority males for committing the crime. In my mind it is not a great revelation that if officers are looking for criminal activity, they're going to look at the kind of people who are listed on crime reports." [. . .]

PROFILING IN BLACK AND WHITE

"Some blacks, I just get the sense off them that they're wild," Mark Robinson 22 says. "I mean, you can tell. I have what you might call a profile. I pull up alongside a car with black males in it. Something doesn't match—maybe the style of the car with the guys in it. I start talking to them, you know, 'nice car,' that kind of thing, and if it doesn't seem right, I say, 'All right, let's pull it over to the side,' and we go from there."

He is quiet and self-critical, and the words sat in his mouth a while before he 23 let them out. "I'm guilty of it, I guess."

Guilty of what? 24

"Racial profiling." 25

26   His partner, Gene Jones, says: "Mark is good at finding stolen cars on the street. Real good."

27   We are driving late one sticky Saturday night through the beat-down neighborhood of Logan, in the northern reaches of Philadelphia. The nighttime commerce is lively, lookouts holding down their corners, sellers ready to serve the addict traffic. It's a smorgasbord for the two plainclothes officers, but their attention is soon focused on a single cluster of people, four presumptive buyers who are hurrying inside a spot the officers know is hot with drugs.

28   The officers pull to the curb, slide out and duck behind a corner, watching the scene unfold. The suspects are wearing backward baseball caps and low-slung pants; the woman with them is dressed like a stripper.

29   "Is this racial profiling?" Jones asks. A cynical half-smile shows on his face.

30   The four buyers are white. Jones and Robinson are black, veterans of the street who know that white people in a black neighborhood will be stopped. Automatically: Faster than a Rastafarian in Scarsdale.

31   "No reason for them to be around here at this time of night, nope," Jones says.

32   Is it possible that they're visiting college friends? I ask.

33   Jones and Robinson, whose intuition is informed by experience, don't know quite what to make of my suggestion.

34   "It could be," Jones says, indulgently. "But, uhhhh, no way."

35   Are you going to stop them?

36   "I don't know what for yet, but I'm going to stop them." [. . .]

"DRIVING WHILE BLACK," AND OTHER EXAGGERATIONS

37 Here's the heart of the matter, as Chief Greenberg of Charleston sees it: "You got white cops who are so dumb that they can't make a distinction between a middle-class black and an under-class black, between someone breaking the law and someone just walking down the street. Black cops too. The middle class says: 'Wait a minute. I've done everything right, I pushed all the right buttons, went to all the right schools, and they're jacking me up anyway.' That's how this starts."

38   So is racism or stupidity the root cause of racial profiling?

39   Governor Whitman, it seems, would rather vote for stupidity.

40   "You don't have to be racist to engage in racial profiling," she says. We are sitting in her office in the State House in Trenton. She still seems a bit astonished that her state has become the Mississippi of racial profiling.

41   Whitman, though burned by the behavior of her state troopers, is offering them a generous dispensation, given her definition of racial profiling. "Profiling means a police officer using cumulative knowledge and training to identify certain indicators of possible criminal activity," she told me. "Race may be one of those factors, but it cannot stand alone."

42   "Racial profiling," she continues, "is when race is the only factor. There's no other probable cause."

43   Her narrow, even myopic, definition suggests that only stone racists practice racial profiling. But the mere sight of black skin alone is not enough to spin most cops into a frenzy. "Police chiefs use that word 'solely' all the time, and it's such a

red herring," says Randall Kennedy, Harvard Law professor and author of the book *Race, Crime, and the Law.* "Even Mark Fuhrman doesn't act solely on the basis of race."

The real question about racial profiling is this: Is it ever permissible for a 44 law-enforcement officer to use race as one of even 5, or 10, or 20 indicators of possible criminality?

In other words, can the color of a man's skin help make him a criminal suspect? 45

Yes, Whitman says. She suggests she doesn't have a problem with the use of 46 race as one of several proxies for potential criminality. "I look at Barry McCaffrey's Web site," she says, referring to the Clinton Administration's drug czar, "and it says certain ethnic groups are more likely to engage in drug smuggling."

It is true. [. . .] The Office of National Drug Control Policy's Web site help- 47 fully lists which racial groups sell which drugs in different cities. In Denver, McCaffrey's Web site says, it is "minorities, Mexican nationals" who sell heroin. In Trenton, "crack dealers are predominantly African-American males, powdered cocaine dealers are predominantly Latino."

The link between racial minorities and drug-selling is exactly what Whit- 48 man's former police superintendent, Carl Williams, was talking about. So was Williams wrong?

"His comments indicated a lack of sensitivity to the seriousness of the 49 problem."

But was he wrong on the merits? 50

"If he said, 'You should never use this solely; race could be a partial indica- 51 tor, taken in concert with other factors' "—she pauses, sees the road down which she's heading, and puts it in reverse—"but you can't be that broad-brushed."

"Racial profiling" is a street term, not a textbook concept. No one teaches 52 racial profiling. "Profiling," of course, is taught. It first came to the public's notice by way of the Federal Bureau of Investigation's behavioral-science unit, which developed the most famous criminal profile of all, one that did, in fact, have a racial component—the profile of serial killers as predominantly white, male loners.

It is the Drug Enforcement Administration, however, that is at the center of 53 the racial-profiling controversy, accused of encouraging state law-enforcement officials to build profiles of drug couriers. The D.E.A., through its 15-year-old "Operation Pipeline," finances state training programs to interdict drugs on the highway. Civil rights leaders blame the department for the burst of race-based stops, but the D.E.A. says it discourages use of race as an indicator. "It's a fear of ours, that people will use race," says Greg Williams, the D.E.A.'s operations chief.

Cops use race because it's easy, says John Crew, the A.C.L.U.'s point man on 54 racial profiling. "The D.E.A. says the best profile for drug interdiction is no profile," he says. "They say it's a mistake to look for a certain race of drivers. That's their public line. But privately, they say, 'God knows what these people from these state and local agencies do in the field.' "

The A.C.L.U. sees an epidemic of race-based profiling. Anecdotes are plenti- 55 ful, but hard numbers are scarce. Many police officials see the "racial profiling" crisis as hype. "Not to say that it doesn't happen, but it's clearly not as serious or widespread as the publicity suggests," says Chief Charles Ramsey of Washington.

"I get so tired of hearing that 'Driving While Black' stuff. It's just used to the point where it has no meaning. I drive while black—I'm black. I sleep while black too. It's victimology. Black people commit traffic violations. What are we supposed to say? People get a free pass because they're black?" ■

THE POLITICS OF RESPECTABILITY*

Randall Kennedy

Randall Kennedy is a professor at Harvard Law School. In his book Race, Crime, and the Law, *from which the following is excerpted, he examines issues about race and the judicial system.*

1 Many blacks are aware of the burdens placed upon them because of the fears, resentments, and stereotypes generated in part by the misdeeds of black criminals. From this awareness stems a deeply rooted impulse in African-American culture to distinguish sharply between "good" and "bad" Negroes.[1] Every community erects boundaries demarcating acceptable from unacceptable conduct. What makes this commonplace activity distinctive among blacks is the keenly felt sense that it implicates not only the security of law-abiding blacks vis-à-vis criminals but also the reputation of blacks as a collectivity in the eyes of whites. This urge to differentiate between "good" and "bad" Negroes is an important feature of what Professor Evelyn Brooks Higginbotham has termed "the politics of respectability."[2]

2   The principal tenet of the politics of respectability is that, freed of crippling, invidious racial discriminations, blacks are capable of meeting the established moral standards of white middle-class Americans. Proponents of the politics of respectability exhort blacks to accept and meet these standards, even while they are being discriminated against wrongly (in hypocritical violation of these standards). They maintain that while some blacks succeed even in the teeth of discouraging racial oppression, many more would succeed in the absence of racial restrictions. Insistence that blacks are worthy of respect is the central belief animating the politics of respectability. One of its strategies is to distance as many blacks as far as possible from negative stereotypes used to justify racial discrimination against all Negroes.

3   Blacks of a wide variety of ideological persuasions have assimilated into their programs the politics of respectability. Hence W. E. B. Du Bois urged "the Best" blacks to "guide the Mass away from [the] contamination and death of the Worst."[3] S. Willie Layton, a leading figure of the women's movement in the black Baptist church, declared to her colleagues, "The misfortune not to be judged [on the same terms as whites] behooves us to become more careful until we have gained a controlling influence to contradict the verdict already gone forth."[4] More recently, the potency of the politics of respectability was dramatically illustrated

*Randall Kennedy, *Race, Crime, and the Law* (New York: Vintage Books, 1997), pp. 17–21, 396–397.

by the organizers of the Million Man March who voiced a desire to uplift the racial reputation of African-American men.[5]

Deeply rooted in African-American-political culture, the politics of re- 4 spectability is also prone to excesses that have limited its attractiveness. First, some of its proponents have displayed an undue fear of antagonizing whites. Here I think of black opponents of the civil rights movement in the late 1950s and early 1960s. Among the most ruthless enemies of civil rights activists on some college campuses, for example, were anxious black administrators.[6]

Second, the desire of some blacks to be seen as respectable has been so over- 5 whelming that it has impelled them, pathetically, to shun anything that might remotely be associated with "bad Negroes"—from dark skin, to political activism, to cultural artifacts such as jazz, soul music, and rap.[7] Third, concern for respectability has led some analysts to underestimate the power of the forces which push people subject to severe deprivation toward criminal conduct. Properly rejecting the notion that poverty strips people of all choice to avoid crime, these analysts unduly minimize the extent to which poverty and its vicious companions reduce the amount of choice available to black impoverished youngsters.

Fourth, some proponents of the politics of respectability have neglected the 6 webs of commonality that connect criminals to law-abiding members of communities. Crime war "hawks" sometimes forget, as Glenn Loury observes, "that the young black men wreaking havoc in the ghetto are still 'our youngsters' in the eyes of many of the decent poor and working class black people who are often their victims."[8] Fifth, obsession with racial reputation has, on occasion, prompted an egregious toleration of racist attacks which, by implication, threaten *all* black people and not simply the "bad Negroes." The most dramatic illustration of this tendency was the position taken by some black intellectuals and civic leaders around the turn of the century with respect to lynching. [. . .] Many blacks condemned lynching unequivocally, but some, traduced by their yearning for respectability, endorsed the theory of lynching's apologists. In 1899, commenting on the rising toll of lynchings, the 71st Annual Conference of the African Methodist Episcopal Zion Church in Philadelphia unanimously condemned "those worthless negroes whose shiftlessness leads them into the commission of heinous crimes."[9] Alluding to the lynching of a black man accused of rape, the Reverend George Alexander McGuire stressed the horror of the alleged crime while offering no critique of the lawless reaction. Speaking to an audience of African-Americans at a high school graduation in 1903, McGuire declared that they must "ostracize such brutes in their own race."[10]

Despite the mistakes of some who have enthusiastically championed the pol- 7 itics of respectability, its core intuitions are sound, two of which are particularly pertinent currently. One is that the principal injury suffered by African-Americans in relation to criminal matters is not overenforcement but underenforcement of the laws. Whereas mistreatment of suspects, defendants, and criminals has often been used as an instrument of racial oppression, more burdensome now in the day-to-day lives of African-Americans are private, violent criminals (typically black) who attack those most vulnerable without regard to racial identity. Like many activities in America, crime tends to be racially segmented; four-fifths of violent crimes are committed by persons of the same race as their victims.[11] Hence, behind high rates of blacks perpetrating violent crimes are high rates of black victimization. Black teenagers are nine times more likely to be murdered than their white counterparts. While young black men were murdered at the rate of about 45 per 100,000 in 1960, by 1990 the rate was 140 per 100,000. By contrast, in 1990 for young white men the rate was 20 murder victims per 100,000.[12] One out of every twenty-one black men can expect to be murdered, a death rate double that of American servicemen in World War II.[13] Such figures place the now-mythic beating of Rodney King in a somewhat different light than it is typically put. As Gerry G. Watts acidly comments, "Racist white cops, however vicious, are ultimately minor irritants when compared to the viciousness of the black gangs and wanton violence."[14]

8   Of course, even if violent, racially motivated wrongdoing by police is lesser in quantity than violent wrongdoing engaged in by criminals, the peculiar character of official wrongdoing—the fact that its authors are officers of the state sworn to uphold the law—accentuates its malevolent force and influence. Moreover, racist discrimination by law enforcement officers has often played a role in creating the conditions that make blacks more vulnerable than whites to destructive criminality. For one thing, throughout American history, white officials have tolerated black-on-black crime ("what do you expect of *those* people") while zealously punishing black-on-white transgressions. Still, the main point stands: In terms of misery inflicted by direct criminal violence, blacks (and other people of color) suffer more from the criminal acts of their racial "brothers" and "sisters" than they do from the racist misconduct of white police officers.

9   A second core intuition of the politics of respectability is that, for a stigmatized racial minority, successful efforts to move upward in society must be accompanied at every step by a keen attentiveness to the morality of means, the reputation of the group, and the need to be extra-careful in order to avoid the derogatory charges lying in wait in a hostile environment. These are among the reasons that Thurgood Marshall, working on behalf of the National Association for the Advancement of Colored People, carefully investigated the circumstances surrounding a case before he would represent a person charged with committing a crime. Initially, he allowed the NAACP to represent only defendants whom he believed to be innocent. In 1943, for example, Marshall declined to represent a black sixteen-year-old who had been sentenced to death for rape and who had participated in a jail break. In Marshall's view the youngster was "not the type of person to justify our intervention."[15] Later, Marshall loosened his policy and represented defendants even if he believed them to be guilty as long as he also believed that they had been denied a fair trial. At no point, however, did he take the position that racism excuses thuggery when perpetrated by blacks.[16] Marshall sought to right miscarriages of justice, not excuse, much less canonize, criminals who happen to be black.

10   It should be clear by now that I am recommending a politics of respectability, albeit a version that steers clear of the excesses noted above. Some readers will

undoubtedly object on the grounds that, however modified, the politics of respectability smells of Uncle Tomism. It may have been a necessary concession earlier, they concede, but championing the politics of respectability today, they charge, is an anachronistic error. Obviously I disagree. In American political culture, the reputation of groups, be they religious denominations, labor unions, or racial groups, matters greatly.[17] For that reason alone, those dedicated to advancing the interests of African-Americans ought to urge them to conduct themselves in a fashion that, without sacrificing rights or dignity, elicits respect and sympathy rather than fear and anger from colleagues of other races. The politics of respectability, for example, would have cautioned against the triumphalist celebrations that followed the acquittal of O. J. Simpson on the grounds, among others, that such displays would singe the sensibilities of many, particularly whites, who perceived the facts of the trial differently. Acting based on the notion that blacks need not be attuned to the way they are perceived by others has adversely affected the racial reputation of African-Americans, facilitating indifference to their plight. ■

NOTES

1. Factions within other minority groups have also promoted politics of respectability. This is certainly true of Jews. Early in this century, when the criminality of some Jews provided the occasion for anti-Semitic diatribes hurtful to all Jews, certain Jewish leaders responded by criticizing bigoted overgeneralizations and—more relevant to the immediate point—acting against Jewish criminals. In 1912, Jewish philanthropists in New York quietly established a Bureau of Social Morals, which collected incriminating evidence on Jewish criminals and criminal organizations and turned it over to local prosecuting authorities. See Howard M. Sachar, *A History of the Jews in America,* 171–172 (1992).
2. See Evelyn Brooks Higginbotham, *Righteous Discontent: The Women's Movement in the Black Baptist Church, 1880–1920,* 185–230 (1993). See also Regina Austin, "'The Black Community,' Its Lawbreakers, and a Politics of Identification," 65 *Southern California Law Review* 1769 (1992).
3. See W. E. B. Du Bois, "The Talented Tenth," in Henry Louis Gates, Jr., and Cornel West, *The Future of the Race,* 133 (1996).
4. Higginbotham, *Righteous Discontent,* 197.
5. Illustrative of this feature of the Million Man March was the Million Man March Pledge which declared, in part: "I, ———, pledge that from this day forward I will strive to improve myself spiritually, morally, mentally, socially, politically, and economically for the benefit of myself, my family and my people. . . . I, ———, pledge that from this day forward I will never raise my hand with a knife or a gun to beat, cut, or shoot any member of my family or any human being except in defense." *Million Man March/Day of Absence: A Commemorative Anthology,* 29 (Haki R. Madhubuti and Maulana Karenga, eds., 1996).
6. See Staughton Lynd and Roberta Yancey, "The Unfamiliar Campus," *Dissent,* Winter 1964. The inner civil war that erupted within black America during the civil rights era remains to be chronicled.
7. See Higginbotham, *Righteous Discontent,* 199–201, quoting one black Baptist women's leader who decried "the poison generated by Jazz music" and another who condemned dance halls as places of "unbridled criminality" where Negroes made "a voluntary return to the jungle." Reactions against this ethos became loud and extravagant in the 1960s and 1970s. See William L. Van Deburg, *New Day in Babylon: The Black Power Movement and American Culture, 1965–1975* (1992).

8. See Glenn C. Loury, *One by One from the Inside Out*, 301–302 (1995). ("For many of these people the hard edge of judgment and retribution is tempered by sympathy for and empathy with the perpetrators.")

9. See Roger Lane, *William Dorsey's Philadelphia and Ours: On the Past and Future of the Black City in America*, 55 (1991). That same year, the redoubtable Kelly Miller, one of the country's most incisive commentators on racial problems, stated that ceasing to rape was the key to ending lynching. Ibid.

10. Ibid.

11. See John Di Iulio, Jr., "The Question of Black Crime," 117 *The Public Interest* 7 (1994); Adam Walinsky, "The Crisis of Public Order," *Atlantic Monthly*, July 1995; Jerome G. Miller, *Search and Destroy: African-American Males in the Criminal Justice System*, 38 (1996).

12. See Douglas S. Massey, "Getting Away with Murder: Segregation and Violent Crime in Urban America," 142 *University of Pennsylvania Law Review* 1204, 1205 (1995).

13. See Walinsky, "Crisis of Public Order," 48.

14. See "Reflections on the King Verdict," in *Reading Rodney King/Reading Urban Uprising*, 244 (Robert Gooding-Williams, ed., 1993).

15. See Mark V. Tushnet, *Making Civil Rights Law: Thurgood Marshall and the Supreme Court, 1936–1961*, 28 (1994).

16. For an alternative viewpoint which conceives of virtually all black convicts as "political prisoners," see Eldridge Cleaver, *Soul on Ice* (1968); George Jackson, *Soledad Brother: The Prison Letters of George Jackson* (1970), and *Blood in My Eye* (1972). For a good description and analysis of this viewpoint and how it grew in influence during the 1960s and 1970s, see Eric Cummins, *The Rise and Fall of California's Radical Prison Movement* (1994).

17. An example of the difference that reputation can make is provided by the differing fates of the Communist Party and the NAACP when both faced repression in the 1950s and both sought to use the First Amendment to the federal Constitution as a shield against governmental investigations. "Sympathetic to the aims, methods, and personnel of the NAACP, the Supreme Court extended to the nation's leading civil rights organization a measure of protection against legislative harassment that it declined to grant to the Communist Party. Legal doctrine did not compel such disparate treatment. A political judgment did—one that cautiously embraced the NAACP and fearfully rejected the Communist Party." See Randall Kennedy, "Contrasting Fates of Repression: A Comment on *Gibson* v. *Florida Legislative Investigation Committee*," in *Secret Agents: The Rosenberg Case, McCarthyism & Fifties America* 227 (Marjorie Garber and Rebecca L. Walkowitz, eds., 1995).

IMPROVEMENT IS A MYTH*

Ana Figueroa

Ana Figueroa interviews Malik Burns, a student and activist, on the state of working families in South Central Los Angeles.

1 Malik Burns, a student and activist in South-Central Los Angeles, does not buy all the rosy news about black America. "The truth is," he says, "this society doesn't want us to make it." Burns, 28, is a compact but forceful man, with shoulder-

Newsweek, June 7, 1999, p. 38.

length braids and a diamond nose stud. In the small, spotless one-bedroom apartment he shares with his wife and three children, posters of Malcolm X share wall space with a pair of food stamps, reminders of the family's battles with dire poverty. There are times, he says, when he has skipped meals so that his children can eat. Burns jabs the air with a finger. "If a few blacks are succeeding, it's only because they . . . have been let in through the cracks to pacify the rest of us. But if they haven't been able to help their own people, what good does it do?"

Seated beside him on a black velvet couch, Faith Burns, 34, is the soft-spoken 2 half of the family. With Malik's help, she manages the apartment building, supporting a family of five on just $280 a week, before taxes. In Faith, resignation runs deep. "We're doing the best we can for the kids," she says. "But I don't think they'll have many opportunities. If they get a job, it will be a dead-end job."

The couple blames the enduring legacy of racism for their problems. Yet 3 their story, like many, is more complicated than that. A high-school graduate, trained as a dermatology technician in the Navy, Malik could not land a job after his discharge. He blames a white senior officer for giving him a bad reference. Though he took spot factory jobs, he says, "I felt like a slave. I had assisted on surgeries back in the Navy. I had an education. I thought, I'm more than just an able body." When he got interviews for medical jobs, he says his appearance scared white employers. Even as his family struggled, he did not cut his hair. "We're told to conform in order to make the white man comfortable," he says. "I consider [my appearance] an African cultural thing."

The couple decided they would have to make their own way. Malik enrolled 4 in L.A. Southwest College to study political science, and joined the New Black Panther Vanguard Movement. He brokered a truce between rival gangs in his building. The couple converted a storage area into a tutorial classroom, and launched a music and dance program for kids. Now, on a spring afternoon, children play in the concrete courtyard.

For all their work, the family remains below the poverty line, a counter- 5 point to the national statistics of black progress. "I wouldn't say things are positive right now," says Malik, "if the only way we can survive is to work two or three minimum-wage jobs—assuming you can get them." The legacy of inequality, he says, is not resolved by a momentary upturn in the economy. Rather, it is in the weave of the American tapestry. "It's a myth to think things are better for black families right now," he says. "In many ways, they are worse than ever." ∎

QUESTIONS TO HELP YOU THINK AND WRITE ABOUT RACE AND CULTURE IN AMERICA

1. Using your own experiences and observations, test hooks's claims about how black and white relationships are depicted on film and television. Is she right or not? Give examples that prove or disprove her theory.
2. Demographers predict that whites will become a minority race sometime in the first half of the twenty-first century. Consider Dyer's idea that the concept of "whiteness" be racialized. What effect might that have now, at the

beginning of the twenty-first century? What effect might it have later in the century, if white people become a "racial minority"?

3. Gómez-Peña writes about the conflicts in cultural identity that come from living on the Mexican-American border. How does he characterize his own cultural identity? How would he compare it with Anglo culture, which he describes as "violent and antisocial"? What does he recommend at the end of his article to reduce conflict? What is your reaction to his ideas about reducing conflict?

4. Imagine Kondo and the family she lived with in Japan attending the camp in Colorado described by Pan and Keene-Osborn to help them better understand and accept one another's cultural differences. Would that interaction work? Why or why not?

5. Imagine going to live in another country where the race, culture, and language are different from your own. What aspects of your culture would you want to keep? What would you be willing to give up? Do you think you would experience the cultural identity crisis Kondo describes? How might your own sense of personal identity be affected by such a relocation?

6. Suppose that hooks, Dyer, Gómez-Peña, and Kondo have been invited to participate in a television talk show and the subject for discussion is how members of their respective races are depicted on film and television. What might their positions be on the following three issues:

   a. Racial stereotyping: Does it exist on film and television, or not? Give evidence.
   b. Relationships among the races: Are they depicted as equal or unequal? Give evidence.
   c. Racial colorblindness: Does it exist? Should it exist? Explain your answers.

7. What, according to Cose, is the good news and what is the bad news regarding black Americans at present? If you were president of the United States and had the power to make two changes that would change the perception that black America is "a place and a people apart," as Cose describes it, what would those changes be? How would you implement them?

8. Identify the warrants of police who use racial profiling in fighting crime as described by Goldberg. Then determine Kennedy's warrants if he were asked to give his views on racial profiling. If Kennedy and the police described by Goldberg were to have a dialogue on this issue, how might they achieve common ground? How might they resolve their differences?

9. Evaluate, from your own point of view, the "politics of respectability" described by Kennedy. What might be gained? What might be sacrificed? What is your final judgment on the viability of such a policy? Would Malik Burns, the individual described by Figueroa, agree with your final judgment about the politics of respectability? Why or why not?

SECTION VI

Issues Concerning Genetic Engineering

THE ISSUES

A. To What Extent Should Genetic Engineering Be Applied to Agriculture?

Six articles identify issues associated with the genetic manipulation of food crops. Pollan and Weiss describe issues that have emerged from genetically altering potatoes and corn. Specter writes about the European attitude toward genetically engineered food crops. Three final brief articles show that public debate has resulted in dialogue and actual change in practice in the industries responsible for these technologies.

B. To What Extent Should Genetic Engineering Be Applied to Animals?

Three articles raise issues associated with genetically engineering animals. Kolata wrote her article about Dolly the sheep, the first cloned mammal, shortly after this historic scientific event was announced in early 1997. Gillis and Stolberg write about current technologies that create genetically altered animals that can be used to supply vital organs and medicines for human beings.

C. To What Extent Should Genetic Engineering Be Applied to Humans?

Joyce, Hamer and Copeland, and Silver project futurist and imaginative scenarios that could result from the genetic engineering of human beings. Their speculative articles raise issues associated with the use of existing technologies that could change the nature of the human race. Barash claims in his article, however, that individual human beings will still have free will. *See also* "Gene Tests: What You Know Can Hurt You," page 176; "Human Cloning: An Annotated Bibliography," page 292; and "Human Cloning: Is It a Viable Option?" page 356.

To Extend Your Perspective: Film and Literature Related to Genetic Engineering

> *Films: Jurassic Park,* 1993; *Multiplicity,* 1996; *Gattica,* 1998; *Island of Lost Souls,*
> 1933; *The Island of Dr. Moreau,* 1996; *The Boys from Brazil,* 1978; *Creator,* 1985
> *Literature:* novels: *Jurassic Park* by Michael Crichton; *When the Wind Blows* by
> James Patterson; *The Third Twin* by Ken Follett; *Mount Dragon* by Douglas
> Preston and Lincoln Child; *Chromosone 6* by Robin Cook; *Brave New World* by
> Aldous Huxley; *The Experiment* by John Darnton; *Alchemist* by Peter James

THE RHETORICAL SITUATION

Genetic engineering could potentially change the world as we currently know it more than any of the other issue areas included in "The Reader." Startling technologies already exist that could, according to some authors, alter the very nature of the human species. Yet at present, at least in the United States, the changes associated with these technologies are taking place quietly, they are not generally known or understood, and they are rarely debated by politicians. Most Americans, if they are aware of these new technologies at all, dismiss them as futuristic speculation or as a subject for fiction. Yet private companies are already seeing the potential for immense profits from the new genetic engineering technologies, and this will provide a powerful impetus for their continued development.

In Europe, the picture is different. Lively debate, particularly about the genetic manipulation of food crops, is a frequent event in several European countries. As you will see from the articles about agriculture, the debate has changed both policy and practice in some private companies.

Knowledge and opinion about genetic engineering in America may change rapidly in the next few years. By the time you read these words, in fact, the context for this issue may be quite different from what it was at the time of their writing. You will want to assess the status of the issues raised by genetic engineering in your own time frame.

Technologies now exist that enable scientists to change plants, animals, and even human beings at the gene level. The practical and ethical implications of such changes are profound and not yet fully understood. The articles in this section describe some of these technologies and the controversies associated with them. For example, genetic engineers are now changing food crops by splicing genes from various species into plant genes to create new and supposedly improved plants. Unexpected side effects result, however, that can change both plant and animal life in undesirable ways. Many critics believe that the engineering of food crops in the United States is not effectively regulated.

Cloning and genetic manipulation of animals became a hot topic when Dolly the sheep, the first cloned mammal, made worldwide headlines. The ability to clone one animal from a simple mammal cell astounded the lay public. Dolly is now fully grown, but her cells may be as old as her clone donor, which may limit her life expectancy. The assumption that cloning will lead to the production of the best cattle, sheep, and hogs is facing technical challenges. Additional risks are associated with cloned animal subspecies as well. Diversity in animal populations helps protect them from viruses, bacterial strains, or changes in weather. When an entire subspecies has been cloned from a single animal and no diversity in immunity exists, a single natural disaster has the potential of wiping out the entire subspecies. The same may be true of cloned agricultural crops.

Basic technologies exist that would permit genetically modifying human embryos in ways that would continue through succeeding generations of offspring. As some authors have pointed out, this practice could control the future of human evolution. As of this writing, these basic technologies have not been used either to clone human beings or to engineer changes in the DNA of human embryos. Necessary refinements in technology and ethical challenges may cause the application of engineering to humans to be postponed for some time. Many scientists, however, predict that such changes will take place within the next twenty years.

A. To What Extent Should Genetic Engineering Be Applied to Agriculture?

PLAYING GOD IN THE GARDEN*

Michael Pollan

Michael Pollan is the author of Second Nature. *He wrote this article for the* New York Times Magazine. *He also grows potatoes, as you will see. His conclusion to this article may surprise you. What would you do in his place?*

Today I planted something new in my vegetable garden—something very new, as a matter of fact. It's a potato called the New Leaf Superior, which has been genetically engineered—by Monsanto, the chemical giant recently turned "life sciences" giant—to produce its own insecticide. This it can do in every cell of every leaf, stem, flower, root and (here's the creepy part) spud. The scourge of potatoes has always been the Colorado potato beetle, a handsome and voracious insect that can pick a plant clean of its leaves virtually overnight. Any Colorado potato beetle that takes so much as a nibble of my New Leafs will supposedly keel over and die, its digestive tract pulped, in effect, by the bacterial toxin manufactured in the leaves of these otherwise ordinary Superiors. (Superiors are the thin-skinned white spuds sold fresh in the supermarket.) You're probably wondering if I plan to eat these potatoes, or serve them to my family. That's still up in the air, it's only the first week of May, and harvest is a few months off.

Certainly my New Leafs are aptly named. They're part of a new class of crop plants that is rapidly changing the American food chain. This year, the fourth year that genetically altered seed has been on the market, some 45 million acres of American farmland have been planted with biotech crops, most of it corn, soybeans, cotton and potatoes that have been engineered to either produce their own pesticides or withstand herbicides. Though Americans have already begun to eat genetically engineered potatoes, corn and soybeans, industry research confirms what my own informal surveys suggest: hardly any of us knows it. The reason is not hard to find. The biotech industry, with the concurrence of the Food and Drug Administration, has decided we don't need to know it, so biotech foods carry no identifying labels. In a dazzling feat of positioning, the industry has succeeded in depicting these plants simultaneously as the linchpins of a biological revolution—part of a "new agricultural paradigm" that will make farming more sustainable, feed the world and improve health and nutrition—and, oddly enough, as the same old stuff, at least so far as those of us at the eating end of the food chain should be concerned.

This convenient version of reality has been roundly rejected by both consumers and farmers across the Atlantic. Last summer, biotech food emerged as the

*New York Times Magazine, October 25, 1998, p. 45.

most explosive environmental issue in Europe. Protesters have destroyed dozens of field trials of the very same "frankenplants" (as they are sometimes called) that we Americans are already serving for dinner, and throughout Europe the public has demanded that biotech food be labeled in the market.

4   By growing my own transgenic crop—and talking with scientists and farmers involved with biotech—I hoped to discover which of us was crazy. Are the Europeans overreacting, or is it possible that we've been underreacting to genetically engineered food? [. . .]

5   The new biotech crops will probably, as advertised, increase yields. But equally important, they will also speed the process by which agriculture is being concentrated in a shrinking number of corporate hands. If that process has advanced more slowly in farming than in other sectors of the economy, it is only because nature herself—her complexity, diversity and sheer intractability in the face of our best efforts at control—has acted as a check on it. But biotechnology promises to remedy this "problem," too.

6   Consider, for example, the seed, perhaps the ultimate "means of production" in any agriculture. It is only in the last few decades that farmers have begun buying their seed from big companies, and even today many farmers still save some seed every fall to replant in the spring. Brown-bagging, as it is called, allows farmers to select strains particularly well adapted to their needs; since these seeds are often traded, the practice advances the state of the genetic art—indeed, has given us most of our crop plants. Seeds by their very nature don't lend themselves to commodification: they produce more of themselves ad infinitum (with the exception of certain modern hybrids), and for that reason the genetics of most major crop plants have traditionally been regarded as a common heritage. In the case of the potato, the genetics of most important varieties—the Burbanks, the Superiors, the Atlantics—have always been in the public domain. Before Monsanto released the New Leaf, there had never been a multinational seed corporation in the potato-seed business—there was no money in it.

7   Biotechnology changes all that. By adding a new gene or two to a Russet Burbank or Superior, Monsanto can now patent the improved variety. Legally, it has been possible to patent a plant for many years, but biologically, these patents have been almost impossible to enforce. Biotechnology partly solves that problem. A Monsanto agent can perform a simple test in my garden and prove that my plants are the company's intellectual property. The contract farmers sign with Monsanto allows company representatives to perform such tests in their fields at will. According to *Progressive Farmer*, a trade journal, Monsanto is using informants and hiring Pinkertons to enforce its patent rights; it has already brought legal action against hundreds of farmers for patent infringement.

8   Soon the company may not have to go to the trouble. It is expected to acquire the patent to a powerful new biotechnology called the Terminator, which will, in effect, allow the company to enforce its patents biologically. Developed by the U.S.D.A. in partnership with Delta and Pine Land, a seed company in the process of being purchased by Monsanto, the Terminator is a complex of genes that, theoretically, can be spliced into any crop plant, where it will cause every seed produced by that plant to be sterile. Once the Terminator becomes the industry

standard, control over the genetics of crop plants will complete its move from the farmer's field to the seed company—to which the farmer will have no choice but to return year after year. The Terminator will allow companies like Monsanto to privatize one of the last great commons in nature—the genetics of the crop plants that civilization has developed over the past 10,000 years.

At lunch on his farm in Idaho, I had asked Steve Young what he thought 9 about all this, especially about the contract Monsanto made him sign. I wondered how the American farmer, the putative heir to a long tradition of agrarian independence, was adjusting to the idea of field men snooping around his farm, and patented seed he couldn't replant. Young said he had made his peace with corporate agriculture, and with biotechnology in particular: "It's here to stay. It's necessary if we're going to feed the world, and it's going to take us forward."

Then I asked him if he saw any downside to biotechnology, and he paused 10 for what seemed a very long time. What he then said silenced the table. "There is a cost," he said. "It gives corporate America one more noose around my neck."

HARVEST

A few weeks after I returned home from Idaho, I dug my New Leafs, harvesting a 11 gorgeous-looking pile of white spuds, including some real lunkers. The plants had performed brilliantly, though so had all my other potatoes. The beetle problem never got serious, probably because the diversity of species in my (otherwise organic) garden had attracted enough beneficial insects to keep the beetles in check. By the time I harvested my crop, the question of eating the New Leafs was moot. Whatever I thought about the soundness of the process that had declared these potatoes safe didn't matter. Not just because I'd already had a few bites of New Leaf potato salad at the Youngs but also because Monsanto and the F.D.A. and the E.P.A. had long ago taken the decision of whether or not to eat a biotech potato out of my—out of all of our—hands. Chances are, I've eaten New Leafs already, at McDonald's or in a bag of Frito-Lay chips, though without a label there can be no way of knowing for sure.

So if I've probably eaten New Leafs already, why was it that I kept putting 12 off eating mine? Maybe because it was August, and there were so many more-interesting fresh potatoes around—fingerlings with dense, luscious flesh, Yukon Golds that tasted as though they had been pre-buttered—that the idea of cooking with a bland commercial variety like the Superior seemed beside the point.

There was this, too: I had called Margaret Mellon at the Union of Concerned 13 Scientists to ask her advice. Mellon is a molecular biologist and lawyer and a leading critic of biotech agriculture. She couldn't offer any hard scientific evidence that my New Leafs were unsafe, though she emphasized how little we know about the effects of Bt in the human diet. "That research simply hasn't been done," she said.

I pressed. Is there any reason I shouldn't eat these spuds? 14

"Let me turn that around. Why would you want to?" 15

It was a good question. So for a while I kept my New Leafs in a bag on the 16 porch. Then I took the bag with me on vacation, thinking maybe I'd sample them there, but the bag came home untouched.

17   The bag sat on my porch till the other day, when I was invited to an end-of-summer potluck supper at the town beach. Perfect. I signed up to make a potato salad. I brought the bag into the kitchen and set a pot of water on the stove. But before it boiled I was stricken by this thought: I'd have to tell people at the picnic what they were eating. I'm sure (well, almost sure) the potatoes are safe, but if the idea of eating biotech food without knowing it bothered me, how could I possibly ask my neighbors to? So I'd tell them about the New Leafs—and then, no doubt, lug home a big bowl of untouched potato salad. For surely there would be other potato salads at the potluck and who, given the choice, was ever going to opt for the bowl with the biotech spuds?

18   So there they sit, a bag of biotech spuds on my porch. I'm sure they're absolutely free. I pass the bag every day, thinking I really should try one, but I'm beginning to think that what I like best about these particular biotech potatoes—what makes them different—is that I have this choice. And until I know more, I choose not. ■

BIOENGINEERED CORN MAY KILL MONARCH BUTTERFLIES*

Rick Weiss

The research on gene-altered corn reported in this article received considerable attention when it was first released by The Washington Post. *Do you know of other unexpected "side effects" of bioengineering? Can you imagine some?*

1 A popular new variety of corn that's been genetically modified to resist insect pests may also be taking a toll on the monarch butterfly, new research suggests.

2   The gene-altered corn, which exudes a poison fatal to corn-boring caterpillars, was introduced in 1996 and now accounts for more than one-quarter of the nation's corn crop—much of it in the path of the monarch's annual migration.

3   Pollen from the plants can blow onto nearby milkweed plants, the exclusive food upon which young monarch larvae feed, and get eaten by the tiger-stripped caterpillars. In laboratory studies conducted at Cornell University, the engineered pollen killed nearly half of those young before they transformed into the brilliant orange, black and white butterflies well known throughout North America.

4   Several scientists expressed concern yesterday that if the new study's results are correct, then monarchs—which already face ecological pressures but have so far managed to hold their own—may soon find themselves on the endangered species list. Other butterflies may also be at risk.

5   Other scientists, however, criticized the research as seriously flawed and said butterflies would probably suffer more if farmers went back to their old chemical sprays.

*Arlington Star Telegram, May 20, 1999, p. 6A.

Whatever the actual ecological impact, the monarch's popularity is likely to put pressure on the already embattled agricultural biotechnology industry and on the Environmental Protection Agency, which approved the crops. 6

"It's sort of the Bambi of the insect world," said Marlin Rice, a professor of entomology at Iowa State University in Ames. "It's big and gawdy and gets a lot of good press. And you've got school kids all across the country raising them in jars." 7

Bt corn is already under fire because of concerns that widespread planting may speed the development of pests resistant to Bt sprays, which are harmless to people and cherished by organic farmers. 8

Cornell entomologist John E. Losey and co-workers sprinkled Bt pollen on milkweed leaves and allowed monarch larvae to feed on them. Within four days, 44 percent were dead. The rest were small and lethargic. Larvae fed conventional pollen did fine, they report in today's issue of the journal *Nature*. ■ 9

GENETIC ENGINEERING EMBRACED EVERYWHERE EXCEPT EUROPE*

Michael Specter

Michael Specter writes about European attitudes toward genetically engineered food crops. In Europe the issues associated with this practice are fiercely debated, and individuals hold strong opinions on them.

Like his father and grandfather before him, Kasper Gunthardt is a man of the soil. He lives in the solid old farmhouse where he was born, and he has worked the rich earth around it for most of his 52 years. 1

He is a traditionalist who has nevertheless embraced the future. Gunthardt owns a sophisticated cooling system for storing dairy products. He recycles waste to fuel his farm, and cameras strapped to beams in his barn are connected to the Internet, putting the personal habits of his cattle on worldwide display (http://naturaplan.coop.ch). 2

But when it comes to playing with the rules of nature, Gunthardt draws a line that he says he will never cross. 3

"There is some sickness spreading across Europe right now," he said, striding quickly through a 20-acre patch of organic potatoes on his farm just south of Zurich. "A bunch of people are trying to get rich by telling us that nature isn't good enough and that we will have to take genes out of a fish and put them in a strawberry if we want to survive. They are changing the basic rules of life, and they want to try it all out on us." 4

"Maybe they will get their way," he said, referring to the failure of a recent national referendum here on curtailing genetic engineering. "It happened in America. But it won't happen on this farm. Here, we are going to live like God intended." 5

*Fort Worth Star-Telegram, August 21, 1998, p. A15. Published originally in the *New York Times*, July 20, 1998, p. A1.

6   If Gunthardt seems inflexible on the issue, he certainly has company. From one end of Europe to the other, consumers are in open revolt over the prospect of a future in which nature has somehow been altered by people holding test tubes.

7   Throughout the world last year, more than 30 million acres of commercial farmland were planted with genetically modified seeds—10 times as much as the year before. But not one of those acres was in the 15 countries of the European Union.

8   Prince Charles recently voiced a common sentiment when he announced that no genetically altered food would ever pass his lips. "That takes mankind into realms that belong to God, and to God alone," he said.

9   The debate here about how—and whether—to unleash the most powerful tools of modern biology says much about the cultural and philosophical differences between pragmatic and risk-ready America, where genetic technology that focuses on food has largely been accepted, and the far more reticent people of Europe.

10   But it says more than that, because what happens to crops from Bialystok to Bruges will have major consequences not just for farmers, but also for industrial policy and for fields like medicine, agriculture and pharmaceutical research.

11   Europeans do make distinctions. They see genetic engineering in the pursuit of better medicine as worth a few moral doubts, and like many Americans they are profoundly unsettled about the prospect of such research involving humans.

12   Yet often the differences between research in plants and animals are completely blurred by sensational events. The cloning of an adult lamb in Scotland two years ago only deepened fears people already had.

13   There are many ways to explain the European conservatism: a strong environmental movement rooted in the 19th-century philosophy that nature is as wise as man, a fear of drastic change, and the unusually large number of small farms still run by families who are reluctant to end practices that have been honed over centuries.

14   Recent history also plays a role, for in this part of the world the uses of genetics have not always been benign. In almost any discussion the dark but recent past also comes up.

15   "The shadow of the Holocaust is dense and incredibly powerful still," said Arthur Caplan, an ethicist at the University of Pennsylvania. "It leaves Europe terrified about the abuse of genetics. To them the potential to abuse genetics is no theory. It is a historical fact." ■

BRITONS WILL MEET ON GENETIC FOODS*

This article was written a little more than a year after the preceding article by Specter. It illustrates how public argument can eventually lead to dialogue, which can in turn eventually result in consensus building and problem solving.

1   Bowing to mounting pressure from consumer and environmental groups, the biotechnology giant Monsanto said today that it would start working together with opponents of genetically modified food products.

*New York Times, September 27, 1999, p. A5.

According to newspaper accounts today, Monsanto met with several envi- 2 ronmental groups this month in a bid to stem the increasing wave of sentiment against genetically modified crops.

Today, Tony Combes, the director of Monsanto's British corporate affairs, 3 said the company had entered into "a stakeholder dialogue" with environmental groups who have been opposed to its crops, which are genetically altered, among other reasons, to make them more resistant to pesticides and diseases.

"Working together with them, Monsanto hopes to resolve existing problems 4 and prevent new ones," Monsanto said in a statement, without adding further details.

A representative of the Soil Association, which campaigns on behalf of or- 5 ganic farming in Britain, said Monsanto had gone a step further by offering to use its vast databases to help plant breeders to create new varieties of crops using traditional cross-breeding methods.

The reported aim is to exploit scientists' newly obtained knowledge of plant 6 DNA while avoiding the use of genetic engineering, which has led to widescale protests over the planting of test crops.

This is "hugely significant," Patrick Holden, of the Soil Association, said, 7 adding that Monsanto had finally accepted the need to change its tactics before modified foods would be accepted in Britain. ■

MONSANTO SAYS IT WON'T MARKET INFERTILE SEEDS*

Barnaby J. Feder

This article, like the one that precedes it, further demonstrates the value of argument and how it can bring about positive changes that benefit society. Monsanto manufactures pesticides and genetically engineered seeds, and its products have stirred controversy. Particularly controversial is the "Terminator" gene, which Pollan also writes about (pages 604–605). Note how public argument is changing this company's plans for the future.

Seeking to remove itself from an inflamed debate in biotechnology, the Monsanto 1 Company said yesterday that it would make no effort to market seeds that produce crop plants that are themselves infertile.

Although the possibility of any company's selling such seeds is years away, 2 and Monsanto has repeatedly said that it has not developed them, its prominence in biotechnology and its plans to purchase a company that has patented such seeds have made it a lightning rod for the furor over what critics have labeled "Terminator" technology.

Seed sterility could be a very valuable trait for the major biotechnology com- 3 panies, which, through genetic modification, have created plants with traits like resistance to insect pests or the ability to withstand spraying with weed killers.

New York Times, October 5, 1999, pp. A1, C2.

4   If the seeds these engineered crops produced were sterile, and could not be replanted, farmers eager to profit from the valuable traits inserted by genetic engineering would pay for them year after year by buying new seeds, rather than simply saving seeds from their crops for replanting the following spring.

5   But critics call the technology an example of a drive by agribusinesses to make farmers dependent on them and the chemicals many of them produce. Some also suggested that pollen from the engineered crops could render plants in neighbors' fields sterile without the farmers realizing it. They hailed yesterday's announcement. "We think it is a very positive sign that Monsanto recognizes there is overwhelming opposition," said Hope Shand, research director for the Rural Advancement Foundation International, a Canadian advocacy group that first drew attention to the technology.

6   Monsanto's move is unlikely to end work on the technology. Monsanto itself held open the possibility that it would continue research for internal use, and Delta and Pine Land, a cotton company it is trying to purchase, said it would continue its research as long as it is independent.

7   Other companies may continue related work, because seed sterility is just one part of a much broader area of research that is regarded as crucial to many biotechnology companies: the use of chemicals to turn particular genes on or off at specific times in the life of a plant, animal or human. Many patents covering pieces of the technology mention sterility as a possible application.

8   Monsanto began backing away from the controversy last spring by announcing that it would not pursue seed sterility unless worldwide discussions with customers, critics, researchers and regulators produced a consensus in favor of it. ■

PUBLIC MEETINGS PLANNED ON BIOENGINEERED FOODS*

The following notice appeared in the New York Times *in October 1999. This is one more example of how public concern and argument can result in debate and dialogue with the potential for solving problems.*

1 The Federal agency that ensures the safety of genetically engineered foods will hold meetings in three cities this fall to hear what Americans think about bioengineered food.

2   Scientists in the United States have been surprised by growing public resistance at home and abroad to bioengineered foods.

3   The Food and Drug Administration begins public meetings next month to explain how it determines that a genetically engineered food is safe and to get the public's reaction.

4   Meetings will be held in Chicago on Nov. 18, Washington on Nov. 30 and Oakland, Calif., on Dec. 13.

*New York Times, October 20, 1999, p. A21.

B. To What Extent Should Genetic Engineering Be Applied to Animals?

WITH CLONING OF A SHEEP, THE ETHICAL GROUND SHIFTS*

Gina Kolata

This article was written in 1997 after the first successful effort at cloning, which resulted in the famous sheep named Dolly. This new technology immediately raised issues, some of which are mentioned here.

When a scientist whose goal is to turn animals into drug factories announced on 1 Saturday to Britain that his team had cloned a sheep, the last practical barrier in productive technology was breached, experts say, and with a speed that few if any scientists anticipated.

Now these experts say the public must come to grips with issues as grand as 2 the possibility of making carbon copies of humans and as mundane, but important, as what will happen to the genetic diversity of livestock if breeders start to clone animals.

For starters, quipped Dr. Ursula Goodenough, a cell biologist at Washington 3 University in St. Louis, with cloning, "there'd be no need for men."

But on a more serious note, Dr. Stanley Hauerwas, a divinity professor at 4 Duke University, said that those who wanted to clone "are going to sell it with wonderful benefits" for medicine and animal husbandry. But he said he saw "a kind of drive behind this for us to be our own creators."

Dr. Kevin FitzGerald, a Jesuit priest and a geneticist a Loyola University in 5 Maywood, Ill., cautioned that people might not understand clones. While a clone would be an identical, but much younger, twin of the adult, people are more than just the sum of their genes. A clone of a human being, he said, would have a different environment than the person whose DNA it carried and so would have to be a different person. It would even have to have a different soul, he added.

The cloning was done by Dr. Ian Wilmut, a 52-year-old embryologist at the 6 Roslin Institute in Edinburgh. Dr. Wilmut announced on Saturday that he had replaced the genetic material of a sheep's egg with the DNA from an adult sheep and created a lamb that is a clone of the adult. He is publishing his results in the British journal *Nature* on Thursday.

While other researchers had previously produced genetically identical ani- 7 mals by dividing embryos soon after they had been formed by eggs and sperm, Dr. Wilmut is believed to be the first to create a clone using DNA from an adult animal. Until now, scientists believed that once adult cells had differentiated—to be-

New York Times, February 24, 1997, pp. A1, C17.

come skin or eye cells, for example—their DNA would no longer be usable to form a complete organism.

8   Dr. Wilmut reported that as a source of genetic material, he had used udder, or mammary, cells from a 6-year-old adult sheep. The cells were put into tissue culture and manipulated to make their DNA become quiescent. Then Dr. Wilmut removed the nucleus, containing the genes, from an egg cell taken from another ewe. He fused that egg cell with one of the adult udder cells.

9   When the two cells merged, the genetic material from the adult took up residence in the egg and directed it to grow and divide. Dr. Wilmut implanted the developing embryo in a third sheep, who gave birth to a lamb that is a clone of the adult that provided its DNA. The lamb, named Dolly, was born in July and seems normal and healthy, Dr. Wilmut said.

10   In an interview, Dr. Wilmut said he wanted to create animals that could be used for medical research, and he dismissed the notion of cloning humans. "There is no reason in principle why you couldn't do it," he said. But he added, "All of us would find that offensive."

11   Yet others said that might be too glib. "It is so typical for scientists to say they are not thinking about the implications of their work," said Dr. Lee Silver, a biology professor at Princeton University. Perhaps, he added, "the only way they can validate what they are doing is to say they are just doing it in sheep."

12   Few experts think that sheep or other farm animals would be the only animals to be cloned. While cloning people is illegal in Britain and several other countries, John Robertson, a law professor at the University of Texas at Austin who studies reproductive rights and bioethics, said there were no laws against it in the United States.

13   If such a law was passed, Dr. Silver said, doctors could set up clinics elsewhere to offer cloning. "There's no way to stop it." Dr. Silver said. "Borders don't matter."

14   Dr. Ronald Munson, an ethicist at the University of Missouri at St. Louis, said the cloning itself was relatively simple. "This technology is not, in principle, policeable," he said. "It doesn't require the sort of vast machines that you need for atom-smashing. These are relatively standard labs. That's the amazing thing about all this biotechnology. It's fundamentally quite simple."

15   One immediate implication of cloning, Dr. Silver said, would be for genetic engineering: custom-tailoring genes. Currently, scientists are unable to take a gene and simply add it to cells. The process of adding genes is so inefficient that researchers typically have to add genes to a million cells to find one that takes them up and uses them properly. That makes it very difficult to add genes to an embryo—or a person—to correct a genetic disease or genetically enhance a person, Dr. Silver said. But now, "it all becomes feasible," he said.

16   After adding genes to cells in the laboratory, scientists could fish out the one cell in a million with the right changes and use it to clone an animal—or a person. "All of a sudden, genetic engineering is much, much easier," Dr. Silver said.

17   Dr. Wilmut is hoping that the genes for pharmacologically useful proteins could be added to sheep mammary cells and that the best cells could be used for

cloning. The adult cloned sheep would produce the proteins in their milk, where they could be easily harvested.

Because cloning had been considered so far-fetched, scientists had discour- 18 aged ethicists from dwelling on its implications, said Dr. Daniel Callahan, a founder of the Hastings Center, one of the first ethics centers.

In the early 1970's, "there was an enormous amount of discussion about 19 cloning," Dr. Callahan said, and ethicists mulled over the frightening implications. But scientists dismissed these discussions as idle speculation about impossible things, Dr. Callahan realized, and urged ethicists not to dwell on the topic.

"A lot of scientists got upset," Dr. Callahan said. "They said that this is ex- 20 actly the sort of thing that brings science into bad repute and you people should stop talking about it."

In the meantime, however, cloning had captured the popular imagination. 21 In his 1970 book, *Future Shock,* Alvin Tofflers speculated that cloning would make it possible for people to see themselves anew, to fill the world with twins of themselves."

Woody Allen's 1973 movie *Sleeper* involved a futuristic world whose leader 22 had left behind his nose for cloning purposes. Mr. Allen played a character charged with cloning to bring the leader back. A later movie, *The Boys from Brazil,* released in 1978, involved a Nazi scheme to clone multiple Hitlers. That same year, a science writer, David Rorvik, published a book, *In His Image: The Cloning of a Man,* that purported to be the true story of a wealthy man who had secretly had himself cloned but was found to be a hoax.

But gradually, the notion disappeared from sight, kept alive only in the ani- 23 mal husbandry industry, where companies saw a huge market for cloned animals and where the troubling ethical implications of cloning could be swept aside.

Now these questions are back to haunt ethicists and theologians.   24

Clones of animals, Dr. FitzGerald said, might sound appealing—scientists 25 could clone the buttery Kobe beef cattle or the meatiest pigs, for example. But these cloned creatures would also share an identical susceptibly to disease, he cautioned. An entire cloned herd could be wiped out overnight if the right virus swept through it.

Dr. FitzGerald wondered if people would actually try to clone themselves. 26 "Because we have all this technology and we have this ability," he said, "we can spin off these fantasies. But that doesn't mean we'd do it. It would be going against everything we desire for the human race."

Others are less sure. Mr. Robertson can envision times when cloning might 27 be understandable. Take the case of a couple whose baby was dying and who wanted, literally, to replace the child. Mr. Robertson does not think that would be so reprehensible.

Cloning might also be attractive to infertile couples who want children 28 and who "want to be sure that whatever offspring they have has good genes," Mr. Robertson said.

Of course, there are legal issues, Mr. Robertson said, like the issue of consent. 29 "Would the person being cloned have an intellectual property right or basic human right to control their DNA?" he asked. If the person did, and consented to the cloning, would cloning be procreation, as it is now understood?

30   Mr. Robertson thinks not. After all, he said, "replication is not procreation." ▪

KEEPING THEM DOWN ON THE PHARM*

Justin Gillis

Justin Gillis believes that genetically manipulated and cloned cows, sheep, and other animals can be of great benefit to humans. See if you agree.

1 On a cold winter morning, a farmhand leads a Holstein cow named Rosie to her trough. She moos. Behind her, the landscape falls away toward a stream lined with sycamore trees. Mountains tower in the distance.

2   To all appearances, it's a timeless slice of life from a Virginia farm. But looks deceive. Rosie is no ordinary cow, and this is no ordinary farm. It is, instead, a place at the cutting edge of world science. Amid the grunts of pigs and the bleats of hungry calves, the future is taking shape here.

3   The farm is nursery and lab for PPL Therapeutics Inc., the U.S. branch of the company in Scotland whose scientists drew worldwide attention in 1997 when they helped to clone a sheep named Dolly from an adult cell.

4   While ethicists have been debating human cloning, while legislators have been considering bans and while pastors have been inveighing against tampering with God's creation, PPL scientists have been quietly plugging away in barns and pastures here; trying to sidestep the controversy. They see cloning as a quick, efficient way to produce animals with special genetic traits that can solve health problems, and as a potentially profitable business.

5   Rosie was created through the artificial manipulation of the very stuff of life. In billions of cells of her body, she carries copies of a human gene. In her milk, she produces a protein that's normally made only by the human body. She was designed to be a factory—or, more precisely, a prototype of a factory—to mass-produce the protein, which can be useful in making drugs. She shows that cows, nature's most prolific producers of milk, can be used to advance medicine.

6   In a pen next to Rosie lives a year-old bull. His name is Mr. Jefferson. He is an obtuse, slightly dazed critter, not yet old enough to be mean, the way Holstein bulls can get. He doesn't produce milk, of course, but he is there to prove a different point.

7   Mr. Jefferson, born on Presidents' Day 1998 and named for Virginia's favorite son, is a clone. He was created from a cell of a cow fetus. The point he proves is that the scientists working on this farm can clone cattle, giving them greater control over genetic alterations—and the ability, if they want, to create a herd of identical animals in short order.

**Washington Post, national weekly ed., March 8, 1999, p. 29.

Up the hill from Rosie and Mr. Jefferson live some pigs. Like pigs anywhere, 8 they stink. But three of them are special, containing genetic modifications that may make their organs a bit more like those of human beings. Some day, the people who run this place envision growing thousands of genetically modified pigs whose lives would be sacrificed so that their hearts and kidneys could be transplanted into sick people. If it works, this technique would solve the shortage of organs for transplant, saving lives.

Already, hundreds of genetically engineered PPL sheep in Scotland are turn- 9 ing out a human protein called alpha-1-antitrypsin in their milk. The sheep were produced by an earlier method, not by cloning, but they are special nevertheless. Alpha-1-antitrypsin from sheep's milk, impossible to produce in sufficient quantity by any other method, is undergoing tests on humans as a potential treatment for cystic fibrosis, a life-threatening lung disease.

Sheep are good for producing some drugs, and so are rabbits. But for pro- 10 teins likely to be needed in large quantity, cows are likely to be the best factories.

PPL scientists can't really work with cows in Britain, given that country's 11 scare over animals infected with "mad cow disease," a fatal ailment that apparently can pass to people through beef products. That is one of the factors that led PPL to buy out a tiny Blacksburg biotechnology company and expand onto American soil in 1993. Cattle in North America are considered free of mad cow disease.

With little public attention, PPL's American scientists have achieved one 12 milestone after another. There is no longer any doubt that human genes can be inserted into cows or that the mammary glands of the cows will use those genes as templates to make human proteins. "We can make the animals, and the animals have proved that they can make the product," Ron James, PPL's managing director, said in an interview from his home in London. "The technology is a done deal."

Within a decade or so, there are likely to be thousands of "transgenic" cows 13 like Rosie browsing in American pastures, cranking out human proteins in bulk more cheaply than they could be made by any other method. Most of those proteins will be given to people as treatments to fight hemophilia and other diseases.

PPL is one of three major biotechnology companies, and several smaller 14 ones, pursuing these techniques. People who work at these companies often say they're "pharming," using animals to produce drugs. At least three drugs produced this way already have been given to people in tests.

In short, these companies are busy creating an industry unlike any other. 15

Life on earth is regulated by a substance known as deoxyribonucleic acid, or 16 DNA. From algae to whales, all organisms contain microscopic strands of this chemical in their cells.

The precise order of the chemical units in the strands varies from one organ- 17 ism to the next, giving rise to the fantastic variability seen in nature. What those strands of DNA do, mostly, is serve as templates for producing proteins, the most important constituents of living organisms.

18   Since the 1970s scientists have been manipulating DNA to create new forms of life, and today it's a growing for-profit business.

19   To date, the manipulations have been carried out mostly in single-celled organisms or in mammal cells that will grow vigorously in a nutrient broth. One of the earliest achievements was to take the gene for human insulin, the protein that controls blood sugar, and insert it into germs. These germs were then induced to make large quantities of insulin. The lives of many diabetics now depend on insulin made this way.

20   Creating germs with human genes in them is so routine now that it's done in high school science laboratories. Numerous biotechnology companies perform such manipulations, searching for commercially valuable proteins.

21   The technology works. But it is costly, requiring sterile rooms, highly trained technicians and huge vats called "bioreactors." So biotechnologists have begun looking to nature's most efficient producer of proteins, the breasts of female mammals.

22   Hence the farm in Blacksburg.

23 The 900-acre spread is nestled into a valley cut by a clear-flowing stream, Stands of cedar, oak and white pine climb the flanks of low mountains. Deer and coyotes roam the countryside.

24   American agriculture these days favors huge, flat farms that can be worked by heavy machinery, and it has become hard to make a living in places like this. So the two brothers who were the third generation of a family to plow this land gave an interested ear when researchers from a tiny local company turned up one day in 1992 throwing around phrases like "transgenic livestock." The company was looking for a place to commercialize some genetic research done at the nearby Virginia Polytechnic Institute and State University.

25   The brothers reached a deal with the visitors to let them use part of the farm. In 1993 PPL executives from Scotland bought out the Blacksburg company to create their U.S. subsidiary, PPL Therapeutics Inc., thereby forming the first multinational corporation aimed at producing proteins in genetically engineered livestock. (When the company was founded in Scotland, PPL stood for Pharmaceutical Proteins Ltd., but the name was such a tongue twister it was eventually dropped.)

26   Since 1993 PPL's gene research has grown to the point that it dominates the Blacksburg farm. PPL now leases most of its acreage and has hired the two brothers as employees. Other local farmers have asked PPL to lease their property, too. "It's a way to keep animals on the land," says Julian Cooper, PPL's chief U.S. operating officer.

27   Fearing animal-rights protests, the company asked that the precise location of the farm and the name of the family that owns it be withheld. But PPL granted *The Washington Post* extensive access to the farm and the employees working there. One of the brothers who stands to inherit the farm says he never imagined, growing up, that his family homestead would one day be at the leading edge of a scientific revolution. "Never in my wildest dreams," he says. "This industry didn't exist when I was growing up."

28   PPL employs 32 people in Blacksburg. The manipulation and incubation of cow and pig embryos is done in a laboratory at the edge of the Virginia

Tech campus. Work with mice and rabbits takes place in a separate lab on campus.

Two microscopic techniques, including one that played a role in the cloning 29 of Dolly the sheep, are used to insert human genes. The company also is trying to remove undesirable animal genes, such as a sugar on the surface of pig hearts that prompts the human body to reject a transplant.

When the PPL scientists have embryos that appear healthy and incorporate 30 human genes or other desirable traits, they take them to the farm and implant them into the wombs of surrogate mothers.

Not all of these attempts work out. In some cases the pregnancies fail. In others the 31 genes become incorporated into cells in such a way that the adult animal won't produce the desired proteins efficiently in her milk.

But the techniques work often enough. Close to two dozen cows and calves 32 on the farm are carrying human genes. Rosie, 2 1/2, is the oldest. In her milk, she produces a human protein called alpha lactalbumin, likely to be useful someday as a nutritional supplement for babies and the elderly. Indeed, one eventual goal of the research is to produce cow's milk that more closely resembles human milk, on the theory that it would be healthier for people to drink.

Counting what's come from the milk of mice, rabbits, sheep and cows, PPL 33 scientists have managed to produce more than 30 human proteins and are working to develop 11 of them. Now the company is trying to settle on a protein to produce in bulk, which might take place by cloning a bunch of factory animals.

One candidate is a clotting factor needed by hemophiliacs. That protein al- 34 ready is used as a drug, but it is produced from donated human blood. That's an expensive proposition; it's also plagued by the ever-present fear of contamination if new viruses get into the blood supply, as the AIDS virus did in the 1980s.

Another possibility is alpha-1-antitrypsin. It can already be produced from 35 human blood, and Bayer Corp., the pharmaceutical giant, does so in order to treat people who are genetically deficient in the protein. Without treatment, they are af- flicted by life-threatening emphysema. Yet the protein is expensive to produce from blood, is in chronically short supply and is largely unavailable outside the United States.

PPL now is making this protein in a flock of sheep in Scotland, where it has 36 built a factory to purify the drug, and may eventually make it in cows in the United States. This has vastly expanded the supply and has allowed the company to target a new, far larger group that may benefit from the drug. These are people who have cystic fibrosis, which usually chops decades off the lives of people it strikes. About 30,000 Americans suffer from cystic fibrosis, and many of them die as teenagers.

Small-scale tests of alpha-1-antitrypsin in cystic fibrosis patients in Britain 37 have yielded hopeful results, and PPL has just begun testing in a handful of people in the United States. The transplantation of foreign genes into plants has pro- voked widespread fear around the world that mankind would poison the environ- ment. But to date there has been less concern about transgenic livestock, in part be- cause the reproduction of animals, unlike that of field crops, can be tightly controlled.

Transgenic animals are so valuable—they can cost millions of dollars apiece to create—that they are not likely to be turned loose willy-nilly into the environment.

38   Some scientists, however, fear that cloning work in animals could put humans at risk. Margaret Mellon, director of agriculture and biotechnology for the Union of Concerned Scientists, says that the risks and benefits of the new technology must be weighed carefully and that alternatives to creating transgenic animals should be examined. She emphasizes that regulatory agencies need to consider such vexing issues as how to purify drugs produced in animals and how to keep animal germs out of people.

39   "It's one thing to eat a cow and just get flesh in your stomach," she says. "It's quite another to take purified cow products and inject them into your blood supply."

40   PPL executives agree that many such issues need to be resolved, but they do not find this sufficient ground to slow their research.

41   In 1997 Dolly, the cloned sheep, was sheared of her wool for the first time. A British organization that helps cystic fibrosis patients was invited to a ceremony and presented with the fleece. Dolly, a ewe with an attitude, likes attention. Ron James, PPL's managing director, stood to the side and watched two young girls frolicking with her. Both girls were afflicted by cystic fibrosis.

42   To them. "Dolly was just an interesting animal," says James. "But I kept thinking, if we can't do something about cystic fibrosis; these kids are likely to be dead in 10 or 15 years. "That's all the justification I think we need." ■

COULD THIS PIG SAVE YOUR LIFE?*

Sheryl Gay Stolberg

Sheryl Gay Stolberg often writes about medicine and health policies. In this article she describes how pig-to-human transplants may soon save thousands of lives a year, make lots of money for the technique's developers, and raise a host of medical and ethical problems. What is your reaction?

1   In an unmarked warehouse in the middle of a wheat field in central Ohio, a hulking 300-pound pig lies on her back, her legs tethered to a crude iron gurney in a bare, well-lighted room. The animal has been sedated into a light state of sleep, and the pale pink expanse of her belly rises and falls rhythmically with each breath. A young man in green hospital garb has just sliced a six-inch incision between the sow's nipples; now he pokes around her innards with latex-gloved hands.

2   The pig on the table is pregnant. The young man, a veterinary technician named Bruce Close, is about to remove her newly fertilized eggs. At 26, Close is an old hand at pig surgery; he has performed this operation more than 600 times in the two years he has been employed by Nextran, the Princeton, N.J., biotechnology company that runs this warehouse as a breeding center. This, however, is no ordinary pig farm. For the past decade, Nextran has been locked in a high-stakes

race to build the perfect pig: an animal with human genes, whose organs can be transplanted into people. In the medical lexicon, this is known as xenotransplantation, and it has been an elusive dream of scientists for nearly 100 years.

Today, despite fears that pig-to-human transplants could unleash a deadly 3 new virus, the dream is closer than ever to reality. In August, a long-awaited safety study conducted by Nextran's chief competitor, Imutran Ltd., of Cambridge, England, found no evidence of active infection in 160 people who had been treated with pig tissue for a variety of conditions. The findings come as the companies are laying the groundwork to begin testing transplanted organs in people. Sometimes within the next few years, and possibly as soon as the end of the next year, either the British or the Americans will grab the brass ring: approval from a regulatory agency, either the United States Food and Drug Administration or its equivalent in Britain, to perform the world's first animal-to-human transplant using a heart or a kidney from a genetically engineered pig.

Nobody expects cross-species transplants to be successful overnight. But 4 with time, xenotransplantation could solve the most pressing crisis in medicine— the organ shortage. It could also make the companies very rich. Unlike human organs, which are donated, pig organs will be sold, and in a climate in which demand far outstrips supply, the seller will name the price. By greatly expanding the donor pool, pigs could make transplants possible for tens of thousands of people who, because of the current rationing system, never even make the list, not to mention those in some Asian nations, where taking organs from the dead is culturally taboo. Imagine a therapy as revolutionary as penicillin and as lucrative as Viagra rolled into one.

In Ohio, Bruce Close is working toward that day. Moving quickly and in si- 5 lence, he tears at layers of pig fat until he can feel the pig's uterus. Gently, he extracts the slippery pink-and-purple mass, palpating it until his fingers reach a cluster of 10 blood-rich pustules—"the ovulation points." Each contains a single egg so recently joined with a sperm, through artificial insemination, that it has not yet divided from one cell into two. This is the optimal moment for creating "transgenic" piglets—animals that, at least in a genetic sense, look ever so slightly like people.

It is a bizarre, almost creepy sight, this big, fat pig upside down on an oper- 6 ating table, her head dangling backward over a bucket in case she vomits, her insides splayed out on a blue-paper surgical drape as a scientist rearranges the DNA of her unborn young. In a moment, the animal's eggs will be flushed out of the ovaries, collected in a tiny vial and smeared onto a glass slide; then a "microinjectionist" will examine them under a high-powered microscope and, with a needle finer than a strand of hair, insert a single human gene into each.

Later this afternoon, Close will return to the operating room to implant the 7 growing embryos into a foster mother sow. In roughly 114 days, if all goes as Nextran hopes, she will deliver a litter that includes at least one transgenic piglet. Yet if Close sees anything Frankensteinian in this, he does not admit it. "What I'm doing right now," he says, "may someday save people's lives."

Across the Atlantic Ocean, at an undisclosed location in the English country- 8 side, Imutran is running its own transgenic pig farm. Like Nextran, which was purchased several years ago by Baxter International, one of the world's largest medical-products manufacturers, Imutran is owned by a drug-industry powerhouse, the Swiss-based Novartis Pharma AG, a company with three times the annual revenue and nearly seven times the research budget that Baxter has. While Nextran has been testing its pig hearts and kidneys in baboons, Imutran has been running tests in monkeys and baboons, and reporting longer survival times. Like Nextran, Imutran is facing mounting criticism as it moves closer to testing its organs in people.

9   Animal rights advocates, predictably, lament the fate of the poor pigs that will be used as spare-parts factories, a charge the companies shrug off by pointing to refrigerators stuffed with bacon and pork chops. What they cannot shrug off, however, are the very real safety concerns. The Campaign for Responsible Transplantation, a coalition of scientists and public-health professionals, has asked for a ban on cross-species transplant research. And one prominent xenotransplant expert, Dr. Fritz Bach, of Harvard University, who is a paid consultant to Novartis, has called for a national commission to study the risks.

10   And so the companies are proceeding quietly, insisting that there is no rush to the clinic. "I don't believe that there is a race in the sense of, 'Oh, let's be first,'" says David White, Imutran's chief scientist. Says John S. Logan, Nextran's scientific director, "What we all want to be is the first to be *successful*."

11   But there is a race, and in science, as in life, being first counts. "Clearly," says Jeffrey L. Platt, a transplant immunologist at the Mayo Clinic, in Rochester, Minn., "there is a competition between the two companies to enter the clinical arena." The first "whole organ" xenotransplant will attract intense press coverage, giving whoever conducts it free publicity, not to mention a spot in the medical history books. And if being first means earning the confidence of regulators and the public, then being first may well be tantamount to being successful.

12   Platt, for one, says that if xenotransplants could be made as safe and effective as human transplants, they would replace them. "Metaphorically speaking," he says, "it will be like the automobile repair industry. Nobody makes much effort to rebuild parts, because it is cheaper and better for your car to have a brand-new part."

13   If it sounds like science pushing itself to the edge of science fiction, it is. And like all good science-fiction stories, this one has the potential to end in disaster. [. . .]

14   At a time when biological tinkering has invaded every aspect of modern life, the sight of swine with human DNA should probably not seem alarming. Still, it is difficult to look at Nextran's pigs without wondering if there is an element of hubris to Logan's work, if porcine-people aren't better left to Greek mythology, or at least George Orwell, than to modern medicine. Clearly, in 1999, some pigs really are more equal than others.

15   Harold Vanderpool, a medical ethicist at the University of Texas Medical Branch, in Galveston, has a term for the visceral reaction these pigs evoke. "I call it 'the gag factor,'" he says. "We are thinking across a barrier that should never be crossed." And in point of fact, there may be a very good reason—the viruses—it should not be. Pigs have become the animal of choice in xenotransplant research for a variety of reasons. They are plentiful, and they breed easily. They are physio-

logically similar enough to humans. And pigs and people have lived side by side, in relative health and harmony, for centuries. Virologists say most disease-causing germs can be eliminated through careful selection and breeding. But over the past two years, they have focused their attention on one obscure organism that cannot be bred out, the porcine endogenous retrovirus, abbreviated in the medical literature as PERV.

Of all viruses, retroviruses are the most feared. They integrate their genetic 16 code into the cells they infect, which means they multiply along with the cells. Retroviruses last for life. They are typically spread through blood or sexual contact, and they can lurk in the body for years, even decades, before causing any symptoms. "It's like a ghost virus, a stealth virus," says Jonathan S. Allan, a virologist at the Southwest Foundation for Biomedical Research, in San Antonio. "Once it splices itself into the host genome, it is virtually impossible to get it back out."

If this scenario sounds familiar, it's because over the past two decades, an- 17 other retrovirus, H.I.V., believed to have originated in apes, has cut a devastating swath around the world. Most scientists, Allan included, do not believe that xenotransplants will unleash the next AIDS epidemic. But no one, not even the companies, argues that the transplants will be risk-free. While there is thus far no evidence that PERV makes people sick, it can infect human cells in the test tube. And some experts theorize that the virus could mutate into a deadly form, as H.I.V. did, and then spread through sexual contact, infecting untold numbers before causing any symptoms. While the recent Imutran study is a comfort, it looked at only 160 patients, who had been treated in hospitals around the world and were later tracked down by Novartis. What will happen when people are getting xenotransplants by the tens of thousands?

The danger may not be limited to PERV. In January 1997, a pig farmer in 18 Ipoh, a Malaysian village about 200 miles north of Kuala Lampur, became ill with what appeared to be encephalitis. The following year, 258 Malaysian pig farmers became sick; 101 of them died. It took until March of this year for the Centers for Disease Control and Prevention to identify the cause: a brand new virus named Nipah.

This is a point that Allan, who serves on a panel of scientific experts con- 19 vened by the Food and Drug Administration to plan for its first xenotransplant clinical trial, has made repeatedly. For all the focus on PERV, he says, there may be other viruses, about which much less is known, that in the end will pose a greater danger to the public health. To justify any human experiment, the scientists conducting it must show that the benefits to the patient outweigh the risk. But xenotransplants defy that calculation: the patient benefits while society takes the risk. "The individual," Allan warns, "can sign a consent form and say, 'I'll take the risk because I'm going to die anyway.' But that person is signing a consent form for the whole population, the whole human race."

Still, there are good reasons to proceed. More than 62,000 Americans are now 20 waiting to receive donated hearts, lungs, livers, kidneys and pancreases, according to the United Network for Organ Sharing. A new name is added to the list every 16 minutes, and every day 11 people die waiting. Increasing donations will not solve the problem; surgeons need young, healthy organs for transplants so even if every dead person donated, there would still not be enough.

21   There is another reason, of course: money. In 1996, Salomon brothers predicted that the global market for transgenic organs could reach $6 billion by the year 2010, a figure that explains why big pharmaceutical companies are involved. Novartis manufactures cyclosporine, an anti-rejection drug; the market for it would skyrocket if xenotransplants became common. Baxter's interest is self-preservation; it makes dialysis machines, which would be relegated to the medical junk heap if people with failing kidneys were given pig organs instead.

22   Hospitals and surgeons stand to gain as well. Transplants are expensive, and they make a good living for those who perform them. Three years ago, the Institute of Medicine calculated that if animal organs made it possible to offer a transplant to everyone in the United States who needed one, annual expenditures would rise to $20.3 billion, from 2.9 billion. Already, the Mayo Clinic has entered into what its director of heart and lung transplantation, Dr. Christopher McGregor, calls a "strategic alliance" with Nextran. McGregor is busy testing pig hearts in baboons, and the company has built a state-of-the-art breeding facility not far from the clinic so Mayo doctors can have a ready supply of pigs in the event that xenotransplantation takes off.

23   While the medical world is gearing up, so, too, is the Government. Donna E. Shalala, the Secretary of Health and Human Services, will soon appoint a special committee to advise her on medical, ethical and social issues surrounding xenotransplants. As the infrastructure grows, so does critics' frustration. The Campaign for Responsible Transplantation, the group pressing for a research ban, has lately been threatening to sue Shalala if she does not respond to its petition. "The prospect of a global health pandemic doesn't seem to be concerning anybody," warns Alix Fano, the campaign's director. "And the people that are voicing their concerns are either being silenced or ignored." ∎

C.   To What Extent Should Genetic Engineering Be Applied to Humans?

SHOULD WE "FIX" NATURE'S GENETIC MISTAKES?*

Christopher Joyce

> *Christopher Joyce is a science editor for National Public Radio. In this article he explains how scientists are learning to repair genes that cause disease. But, he adds, the same process could alter a child's hair color, height, or even intelligence.*

1   Scientists are contemplating a radical new step in medicine: changing the genes that determine the destiny of our children, our children's children—and perhaps even the human race.

USA Weekend, April 24, 1998, p. 16.

The procedure, "germ-line gene therapy," allows doctors to alter the genes in 2 a woman's egg, a man's sperm, or an embryo that is just a few days old. The immediate goal is to eliminate inherited diseases such as Tay Sachs, hemophilia or cystic fibrosis; hundreds of thousands of Americans carry faulty genes that don't affect them, but can pass the diseases on to their children.

No one has yet tried germ-line gene therapy. It is prohibited in the United 3 States and several other countries, and so controversial that scientists have only recently begun openly discussing it. To essentially prune off parts of the genetic tree "really gets at who we are as humans," says Gregory Stock, a biologist at the University of California at Los Angeles. "But the argument for exploring this is so compelling I don't believe we have a choice."

Since 1990, physicians have tried to fix broken or missing genes in people 4 with inherited diseases by using something called somatic cell gene therapy. But getting the engineered genes to the right place, such as the blood cells or liver, and then making them work is very difficult. "It's likely to be much easier with germ-line therapy," says Stock. That's because geneticists may soon be able to correct a genetic flaw in the sperm, egg or embryo—in essence, knock out a bad gene before it can cause trouble.

Geneticists recently have learned how to construct handmade genes that 5 can be precisely targeted to replace broken genes, then switched on at will. Michael Blaese, of the National Human Genome Research Institute in Bethesda, Md., predicts in-vitro pregnancies will be the first candidates for germ-line therapy, because a change made to the single fertilized egg would be replicated in all the cells of the growing embryo. "We should talk about [the procedure] now before someone does it," Blaese says.

Altering the germ line could pose unknown risks. A mistake could introduce 6 a harmful mutation that could be passed on to generations of people. And because some "bad" genes also serve a useful purpose—for example, the gene that can cause sickle cell anemia also is associated with resistance to malaria—eliminating such genes could have serious consequences.

Critics worry that as scientists locate more genes, rich parents would "de- 7 sign" their children to be taller or smarter than everyone else. But the ability to wipe out terrible diseases from the human gene pool, or perhaps even delay aging, could be too tempting to pass up, say geneticists.

"Imagine you will have a child," says Stock, "and you were told by your 8 doctor you could add a gene that would extend its life expectancy by 10 years. Would you opt for it?" We may have to answer that kind of question within our own lifetimes. ■

ENGINEERING TEMPERAMENT*

Dean Hamer and Peter Copeland

> *Dean Hamer, chief of gene structure and regulation at the National Cancer Institute's Laboratory of Biochemistry, is a molecular geneticist who conducts research on how genes influence our behavior. This excerpt comes from the conclusion to* Living with Our Genes: Why They Matter More than You Think, *a book he wrote with Peter Copeland. In it he imagines the inner life of a genetically cloned scientist's son.*

1 Andrew thought a lot about his father, if that's what you could call him. Andrew's father was a scientist who had left a respectable career at a quiet university to join a risky biotech venture in the year 2002. The risk paid off, big time, and Andrew's father became a multimillionaire. More importantly, he was able to work on the project of his dreams: cloning. The startup firm, Mirror Image, Inc., worked on the genetic cloning of animals, including humans. Wall Street loved the idea, and the stock's initial public offering set unheard-of records. Investors bet heavily on the company because the technology was relatively simple and the promise enormous. The only possible roadblock was Washington, and there was the risk that the government would try to ban cloning research. There had been congressional hearings and public handwringing after the cloning of the first sheep, named Dolly, but the concern had eased. Scientists had showed that animal cloning could help feed the world, speed medical advances, and provide other benefits. Cloning had become less scary and more acceptable.

2 Human cloning was a little more complicated, but only in terms of ethics and politics. The science was the same. The ethical questions were still being debated, of course, just like people still debated how many angels could fit on the head of a pin. The more practical minded people were simply going ahead and doing it. Mirror Image pursued a two-track policy. Publicly, company officials said little, to avoid scrutiny. They weren't doing anything illegal, in fact company policy was to follow the highest legal standards to avoid being tripped up by a technicality. But behind the scenes, they were funding research at powerful think tanks and courting policymakers. Changes in the campaign finance system back in the 1990s had not worked exactly as the reformers had planned, and Mirror Image and similar companies were able to quietly influence appointments to the congressional committees overseeing their industry.

3 The company was doing the science openly, on animals that is. Secretly, the scientists worked on human experiments, slightly altering the protocol that had been used with sheep to make it suitable, tweaking the cell growth media, testing various methods of preparing nuclei, etc. Not actually cloning any humans, yet, but doing all the tedious but necessary preliminary experiments. In case of an emergency, most likely of the political kind, the company had built an exact replica of its U.S. lab in a secret location overseas.

*Dean Hamer and Peter Copeland, Living with Our Genes: Why They Matter More than You Think (New York: Doubleday, 1998), pp. 295–302.

Andrew's father wasn't much interested in the politics or the ethics. He was 4 an intensely focused man interested in technique and results. He wasn't naive, however, and he knew that he had to be careful. He kept a detailed record of his experiments, his lab was meticulously run, and his public behavior was exemplary. Every step was planned and projected, and recorded on videotape, when he inserted a swab into his mouth, scraped a few cells from the inside of his cheek, and dabbed them onto a petri plate. He began the cloning process.

When his cells had progressed to the ideal stage, they were treated with a 5 chemical that arrested growth, putting them in a temporary state of suspended animation. Then the nucleus from one cell was removed and inserted into a human egg, donated by a lab assistant, that was in the same suspended state. The DNA from the egg was replaced by the DNA from the cheek scraping, but the egg had no way of knowing this. As far as the egg was concerned it had just been fertilized in the normal way, and so it began to divide and to copy the scientist's DNA. Soon the egg was reimplanted into the womb of the lab assistant, and nine months later, a bright and healthy baby boy was delivered into the world. His name was Andrew. His DNA was identical to that of the scientist. Not 50 percent the same, as would be the case for a normal child, but base-for-base the same, as if Andrew and his father were identical twins.

The birth announcement was greeted with shock and anger. While everyone 6 knew that it was possible to clone a human, technically at least, no one expected that it actually would be done. Anticipating the reaction, Mirror Image had prepared a strong defensive strategy, and it paid off. After the initial outrage, with magazine covers comparing Andrew's father to a Nazi scientist, the coverage began to switch focus to the baby. The baby was innocent of any wrongdoing and was undeniably cute. He cooed and gurgled at the TV cameras and seemed to love the attention. Network producers fought for the rights to chronicle his every move, and Andrew became a kind of national pet. "Andrew Eats Solid Food," trumpeted the *New York Times*. A tabloid reported, "Nothing Sheepish About Our Andy!"

The coverage began to fade after a few years, mostly because Andrew did 7 nothing extraordinary. There were only so many stories that could be done about a normal, healthy toddler. By the time he was five, his first day at school was mentioned only in passing by the major news media. He was just another kindergartner. Andrew was raised in the modest suburban home of the lab assistant, who couldn't have loved him more. She stopped working while he was small to be with him, and Mirror Image provided more than enough money to support the little family of two. Andrew's father saw him only when the boy came to the lab for tests. The father had moved on to other experiments, and like the rest of the nation, he didn't much care about Andrew after the novelty had worn off.

The only person who remained obsessed with Andrew's story was Andrew. 8 He had indexed all the newspaper and magazine stories about his birth, as well as the scientific abstracts. Interestingly, when his father was younger he had made a similar scrapbook, collecting thousands of articles about DNA and cloning, even though in those days it was just cloning of carrots and frogs. Andrew built his massive scrapbook on a computer with all the video and digital images of his life. He used his "Clone at Home" software, a hugely popular program, to replay his creation and development. The software allowed a person to plug in different variables, genetic or environmental, to his or her life story. Then the computer predicted how the life would have developed, and a video image showed how the person would age from birth to 80 years old. Andrew's favorite game was to delete his father's DNA and replace it with the DNA of his "mother," the lab assistant. When Andrew played out the program with her genes, he preferred the virtual results to the real thing.

9   It was too late to delete his father's DNA, however. All of Andrew's potential, all that he ever would be, was contained in that one swab dragged across the inside of a cheek. Andrew stared at himself in the mirror and tried to see himself clearly. Who was he? He knew he was a separate person, but it was all so confusing. When he compared himself with old snapshots taken when his father was a boy, he could hardly tell the difference, for they were as alike as identical twins. And yet he didn't *feel* like his father, or at least he didn't think so. The resemblance was so eerie that he deliberately wore his hair differently from his father and experimented with pierced ears, which didn't suit him. In his face, Andrew also noticed traces of his grandfather and grandmother. Andrew did some research on the family of his father and fell in love with his great-great-grandmother, a pioneering bioethicist who had warned, unsuccessfully as it turned out, about the dangers of genetic engineering. Andrew idolized her and saw her as his true forbear, not the man who scraped a cheek. Andrew came to see that man as merely one disposable receptacle for the long march of his genes, with about as much personality as a beaker.

10   Andrew could not deny, however, that there were elements of his own personality that came from his father. They shared a sense of being proper and neat; it infuriated them both that the lab assistant allowed her car to fill up with old newspapers, gum wrappers, and empty Coke cans that rolled back and forth under the seat. They both had short fuses. Andrew's father tended to blow up when things went wrong; he once threw a batch of improperly prepared gel at a cowering postdoc. Andrew also had his rages, but he controlled his anger with exercise; when he felt the pressure building, he'd go to the gym or take a run. Andrew accepted those parts of his personality as givens, unchangeable but controllable. What he did with his life was another thing; that was his choice alone. He wasn't going to follow in his father's footsteps. In fact, he vowed to use that same focused determination and intellect that made his father such a good scientist to stop the people who believed that cloning humans was no different than mass-producing sheep.

11 Is Andrew's story farfetched? A little, but only to make a point. Both the knowledge of human genetics, and the ability to manipulate and exploit it, are expanding at an exponential pace. By the first decade of the twenty-first century we will know the entire sequence of the human genome, every one of the more than three billion nucleotides that make up the 100,000 genes that constitute our genetic patrimony. Deciphering the meaning and function of those genes will be slower, but

success is inevitable. Already, an entire new field has emerged called "functional genomics" dedicated to figuring out what genes do. At the same time, new technologies are emerging to exploit this information with drugs and by manipulating the genetic information itself. So far the manipulations are being performed only on animals, Dolly the sheep being the first well-known example, but humans are just a few steps away.

There is no turning back. Supporters of the international Human Genome 12 Project argue convincingly that mapping the entire genome will help produce new drugs, reduce birth defects, and allow us to live longer and healthier lives. Even if the project were officially stopped, much of the most advanced, demanding research has been taken over by biotechnology start-up companies, and by the giant pharmaceutical firms that usually end up owning them. Lives are at stake. Money is at stake. That's a powerful combination anywhere, and in America it's invincible.

The focus of attention so far has been on discoveries of genes for cancer and 13 other physical illnesses. What often goes unsaid is that the genes being discovered also include ones that define behavior. Virtually every aspect of how we act and feel that has been studied in twins shows genetic influence, and many of the individual genes have been isolated. The fact that so many behavior genes are being found is not surprising because the brain is so complex that much of our genetic information is devoted to building, developing, and maintaining it.

The combination of these two forces—the stampede to map the genome plus 14 the decisive role of genes in behavior—means that, whether anyone thinks it's a good idea or not, we soon will have the ability to change and manipulate human behavior through genetics.

As scary as that might sound, the genetic manipulation of behavior is not 15 new. Humans have been selectively breeding behavior in animals, such as dogs and farm animals, since before history. And whether we recognize it or not, we already are products of genetic engineering. As far back as we can see, humans have been selective about their mates. Beauty, power, and prestige have always been desirable. Clans or families sought to marry their offspring with people of high rank and stature. People from particular religions or races sought their own kind. The highest social classes, the blue bloods, sought to preserve the purity of their lines.

The difference is that in the near future science will give us the power to do 16 it more quickly, more accurately, and more decisively. We will select mates not because of some superficial trait like a prominent family; we'll be able to read their DNA as easily as an X-ray. Nor will we settle for the randomness of sexual blending of sperm and egg, with all its billions of possible combinations, when we can build the desired combination to the letter.

It's too late to wonder whether we are going to genetically tinker with 17 human behavior. We need to decide very quickly how we are going to do it. How will we distinguish "good" genes from "bad"? What traits will be valued and what will be discarded? Who gets to choose? ■

REPROGENETICS: A GLIMPSE OF THINGS TO COME*

Lee M. Silver

Lee M. Silver is a professor at Princeton University, where he teaches and conducts research in genetics, evolution, reproduction, and developmental biology. He has also written and lectured on the social impact of biotechnology. The following excerpt is from his book Remaking Eden: Cloning and Beyond in a Brave Now World.

DATELINE BOSTON: JUNE 1, 2010

1 Sometime in the not-so-distant future, you may visit the maternity ward at a major university hospital to see the newborn child or grandchild of a close friend. The new mother, let's call her Barbara, seems very much at peace with the world, sitting in a chair quietly nursing her baby, Max. Her labor was—in the parlance of her doctor—"uneventful," and she is looking forward to raising her first child. You decide to make pleasant conversation by asking Barbara whether she knew in advance that her baby was going to be a boy. In your mind, it seems like a perfectly reasonable question since doctors have long given prospective parents the option of learning the sex of their child-to-be many months before the predicted date of birth. But Barbara seems taken aback by the question. "Of course I knew that Max would be a boy," she tells you. "My husband Dan and I chose him from our embryo pool. And when I'm ready to go through this again, I'll choose a girl to be my second child. An older son and a younger daughter—a perfect family.

2   Now, it's your turn to be taken aback. "You made a conscious choice to have a boy rather than a girl?" you ask.

3   "Absolutely!" Barbara answers. "And while I was at it, I made sure that Max wouldn't turn out to be fat like my brother Tom or addicted to alcohol like Dan's sister Karen. It's not that I'm personally biased or anything," Barbara continues defensively. "I just wanted to make sure that Max would have the greatest chance for achieving success. Being overweight or alcoholic would clearly be a handicap."

4   You look down in wonderment at the little baby boy destined to be moderate in both size and drinking habits.

5   Max has fallen asleep in Barbara's arms, and she places him gently in his bassinet. He wears a contented smile, which evokes a similar smile from his mother. Barbara feels the urge to stretch her legs and asks whether you'd like to meet some of the new friends she's made during her brief stay at the hospital. You nod, and the two of you walk into the room next door where a thirty-five-year old woman named Cheryl is resting after giving birth to a nine-pound baby girl named Rebecca.

6   Barbara introduces you to Cheryl as well as a second woman named Madelaine, who stands by the bed holding Cheryl's hand. Little Rebecca is lying under

*Lee M. Silver, *Remaking Eden: Cloning and Beyond in a Brave New World* (New York: Avon Books, 1997), pp. 1–4, 7–11.

the gaze of both Cheryl and Madelaine. "She really does look like both of her mothers, doesn't she?" Barbara asks you.

Now you're really confused. You glance at Barbara and whisper, "Both 7 mothers?"

Barbara takes you aside to explain. "Yes. You see Cheryl and Madelaine have 8 been living together for eight years. They got married in Hawaii soon after it became legal there, and like most married couples, they wanted to bring a child into the world with a combination of both of their bloodlines. With the reproductive technologies available today, they were able to fulfill their dreams."

You look across the room at the happy little nuclear family—Cheryl, Made- 9 laine, and baby Rebecca—and wonder how the hospital plans to fill out the birth certificate.

DATELINE SEATTLE: MARCH 15, 2050

You are now forty years older and much wiser to the ways of the modern world. 10 Once again, you journey forth to the maternity ward. This time, it's your own granddaughter Melissa who is in labor. Melissa is determined to experience natural childbirth and has refused all offers of anesthetics or painkillers. But she needs something to lift her spirits so that she can continue on through the waves of pain. "Let me see her pictures again," she implores her husband Curtis as the latest contraction sweeps through her body. Curtis picks the photo album off the table and opens it to face his wife. She looks up at the computer-generated picture of a five-year-old girl with wavy brown hair, hazel eyes, and a round face. Curtis turns the page, and Melissa gazes at an older version of the same child: a smiling sixteen-year-old who is 5 feet, 5 inches tall with a pretty face. Melissa smiles back at the future picture of her yet-to-be-born child and braces for another contraction.

There is something unseen in the picture of their child-to-be that provides 11 even greater comfort to Melissa and Curtis. It is the submicroscopic piece of DNA—an extra gene—that will be present in every cell of her body. This special gene will provide her with lifelong resistance to infection by the virus that causes AIDS, a virus that has evolved to be ever more virulent since its explosion across the landscape of humanity seventy years earlier. After years of research by thousands of scientists, no cure for the awful disease has been found, and the only absolute protection comes from the insertion of a resistance gene into the single-cell embryo within twenty-four hours after conception. Ensconced in its chromosomal home, the AIDS resistance gene will be copied over and over again into every one of the trillions of cells that make up the human body, each of which will have its own personal barrier to infection by the AIDS-causing virus HIV. Melissa and Curtis feel lucky indeed to have the financial wherewithal needed to endow all of their children with this protective agent. Other, less well-off American families cannot afford this luxury.

Outside Melissa's room, Jennifer, another expectant mother, is anxiously 12 pacing the hall. She has just arrived at the hospital and her contractions are still far apart. But, unlike Melissa, Jennifer has no need for a computer printout to show her what her child-to-be will look like as a young girl or teenager. She already has thousands of pictures that show her future daughter's likeness, and they're all real, not virtual. For the fetus inside Jennifer is her identical twin sister—her clone—who will be born thirty-six years after she and Jennifer were both conceived within the same single-cell embryo. As Jennifer's daughter grows up, she will constantly behold a glimpse of the future simply by looking at her mother's photo album and her mother. [. . .]

DATELINE PRINCETON, NEW JERSEY: THE PRESENT

13 Are these outrageous scenarios the stuff of science fiction? Did they spring from the minds of Hollywood screenwriters hoping to create blockbuster movies without regard to real world constraints? No. The scenarios described under the first two datelines emerge directly from scientific understanding and technologies that are already available today. [. . .] Furthermore, if biomedical advances continue to occur at the same rate as they do now, the practices described are likely to be feasible long before we reach my conservatively chosen datelines.

14   It's time to take stock of the current state of science and technology in the fields of reproduction and genetics and to ask, in the broadest terms possible, what the future may hold. Most people are aware of the impact that reproductive technology has already had in the area of fertility treatment. The first "test tube baby"—Louise Brown—is already eighteen years old, and the acronym for in vitro fertilization—IVF—is commonly used by laypeople. The cloning of human beings has become a real possibility as well, although many are still confused about what the technology can and cannot do. Advances in genetic research have also been in the limelight, with the almost weekly identification of new genes implicated in diseases like cystic fibrosis and breast cancer, or personality traits like novelty-seeking and anxiety.

15   What has yet to catch the attention of the public at large, however, is the incredible power that emerges when current technologies in reproductive biology and genetics are brought together in the form of *reprogenetics.* With reprogenetics, parents can gain complete control over their genetic destiny, with the ability to guide and enhance the characteristics of their children, and their children's children as well. But even as reprogenetics makes dreams come true, like all of the most powerful technologies invented by humankind, it may also generate nightmares of a kind not previously imagined.

16   Of course, just because a technology becomes feasible does not mean that it will be used. Or does it? Society, acting through government intervention, could outlaw any one or all of the reprogenetic practices that I have described. Isn't the *nonuse* of nuclear weapons for the purpose of mass destruction over the last half century an example of how governments can control technology?

17   There are two big differences between the use of nuclear technology and reprogenetic technology. These differences lie in the resources and money needed to practice each. The most crucial resources required to build a nuclear weapon—large reactors and enriched sources of uranium or plutonium—are tightly controlled by the government itself. The resources required to practice reprogenetics—precision

medical tools, small laboratory equipment, and simple chemicals— are all available for sale, without restriction, to anyone with the money to pay for them. The cost of developing a nuclear weapon is billions of dollars. In contrast, a reprogenetics clinic could easily be run on the scale of a small business anywhere in the world. Thus, even if restrictions on the use of reprogenetics are imposed in one country or another, those intent on delivering and receiving these services will not be restrained. But on what grounds can we argue that they should be restrained?

In response to this question, many people point to the chilling novel *Brave* 18 *New World* written by Aldous Huxley in 1931. It is the story of a future worldwide political state that exerts complete control over human reproduction and human nature as well. In this brave new world, the state uses fetal hatcheries to breed each child into a predetermined intellectual class that ranges from alpha at the top to epsilon at the bottom. Individual members of each class are predestined to fit into specific roles in a soulless utopia where marriage and parenthood are prevented and promiscuous sexual activity is strongly encouraged, where universal immunity to diseases has been achieved, and where an all-enveloping state propaganda machine and mood-altering drugs make all content with their positions in life.

While Huxley guessed right about the power we would gain over the 19 process of reproduction, I think he was dead wrong when it came to predicting *who* would use the power and for what purposes. What Huxley failed to understand, or refused to accept, was the driving force behind babymaking. It is individuals and couples who want to reproduce themselves in their own images. It is individuals and couples who want their children to be happy and successful. And it is individuals and couples—like Barbara and Dan and Cheryl and Madelaine and Melissa and Curtis and Jennifer, *not governments*—who will seize control of these new technologies. They will use some to reach otherwise unattainable reproductive goals and others to help their children achieve health, happiness, and success. And it is in pursuit of this last goal that the combined actions of many individuals, operating over many generations, could perhaps give rise to a polarized humanity more horrific than Huxley's imagined Brave New World.

There are those who will argue that parents don't have the right to control the 20 characteristics of their children-to-be in the way I describe. But American society, in particular, accepts the rights of parents to control every other aspect of their children's lives from the time they are born until they reach adulthood. If one accepts the parental prerogative after birth, it is hard to argue against it before birth, if no harm is caused to the children who emerge.

Many think that it is inherently unfair for some people to have access to 21 technologies that can provide advantages while others, less well-off, are forced to depend on chance alone. I would agree. It is inherently unfair. But once again, American society adheres to the principle that personal liberty and personal fortune are the primary determinants of what individuals are allowed and able to do. Anyone who accepts the right of affluent parents to provide their children with an expensive private school education cannot use "unfairness" as a reason for rejecting the use of reprogenetic technologies.

22   Indeed, in a society that values individual freedom above all else, it is hard to find any legitimate basis for restricting the use of reprogenetics. And therein lies the dilemma. For while each individual use of the technology can be viewed in the light of personal reproductive choice—with no ability to change society at large—together they could have dramatic, unintended, long-term consequences.

23   As the technologies of reproduction and genetics have become ever more powerful over the last decade, most practicing scientists and physicians have been loath to speculate about where it may all lead. One reason for reluctance is the fear of getting it wrong. It really is impossible to predict with certainty which future technological advances will proceed on time and which will encounter unexpected roadblocks. This means that like Huxley's vision of a fetal hatchery, some of the ideas proposed here may ultimately be technically impossible or exceedingly difficult to implement. On the other hand, there are sure to be technological breakthroughs that no one can imagine now, just as Huxley was unable to imagine genetic engineering, or cloning from adult cells, in 1931.

24   There is a second reason why fertility specialists, in particular, are reluctant to speculate about the kinds of future scenarios that I describe here. It's called politics. In a climate where abortion clinics are on the alert for terrorist attacks, and where the religious right rails against any interference with the "natural process" of conception, IVF providers see no reason to call attention to themselves through descriptions of reproductive and genetic manipulations that are sure to provoke outrage.

25   The British journal *Nature* is one of the two most important science journals in the world (the other being the American journal *Science*). It is published weekly and is read by all types of scientists from biologists to physicists to medical researchers. No one would ever consider it to be radical or sensationalist in any way. On March 7, 1996, *Nature* published an article that described a method for cloning unlimited numbers of sheep from a single fertilized egg, with further implications for improving methods of genetic engineering. It took another week before the ramifications of this isolated breakthrough sank in for the editors. On March 14, 1996, they wrote an impassioned editorial saying in part: "That the growing power of molecular genetics confronts us with future prospects of being able to *change the nature of our species* [my emphasis] is a fact that seldom appears to be addressed in depth. Scientific knowledge may not yet permit detailed understanding, but the possibilities are clear enough. This gives rise to issues that in the end will have to be related to people within the social and ethical environments in which they live. . . . And the agenda is set by mankind as a whole, not by the subset involved in the science."

26   They are right that the agenda will not be set by scientists. But they are wrong to think that "mankind as a whole"—unable to reach consensus on so many other societal issues—will have any effect whatsoever. The agenda is sure to be set by individuals and couples who will act on behalf of themselves and their children. [. . .]

27   There is no doubt about it. For better *and* worse, a new age is upon us. And whether we like it or not, the global marketplace will reign supreme. ■

DNA AND DESTINY*

David P. Barash

David P. Barash is a psychology professor at the University of Washington, Seattle. The sentence fragments at the beginning of the article are used deliberately, for emphasis.

These are the days of bio-shocks: Mapping the human genetic code. DNA finger- 1 printing. Cloning. And now, according to reports, the maintenance, in the labora- tory, of human DNA fused with cow eggs. Not yet, but someday scientists may be able to introduce such hybrid cells into a needy body, where if persuaded to perform as required they could make healthy heart tissue, for example, or maybe even grow new limbs for amputees.

Pretty wild stuff, but not as wild as the implications of these and other bio- 2 shocks for that most fundamental of all concepts: our sense of what it means to be ourselves. As biological science becomes more competent, it also becomes more troublesome, especially for those who worry that it threatens to undermine the integrity of humanness.

By monkeying around with DNA, the argument goes, we degrade the mean- 3 ing of being human. Unsurprisingly, those most agitated about DNA technology generally portray themselves as humanists. That is, they value the human whole above the sum of its genetic parts. But in their anxiety to preserve human integrity in the face of biotechnology, the gene-o-phobes themselves are the ones who over- value the significance of DNA.

After all, DNA is only one component of our humanness. The genotype of 4 each particular individual produces a human being (or a hippo, halibut, or hick- ory tree) only after prolonged interaction with the environment. People are genet- ically complete at birth, but as selves they are woefully unfinished.

The existentialists had it right. From a religious thinker like Kierkegaard to an 5 atheist like Nietzsche, the existentialists recognized that all human beings define themselves as unique, responsible individuals. As Simone de Beauvoir put it, a human being is a being whose essence is having no essence. Or, in Jean-Paul Sartre's famous phrase, "existence precedes essence."

In other words, our essence is ours to choose, depending on how we direct our 6 selves with all our baggage, DNA included.

This is not to minimize our gene-based, Darwinian heritage. It is, rather, a 7 reminder that within the vast remaining range of human possibility left us by our genes and our evolutionary past, each of us is remarkably, terrifyingly free.

We need not worry that someday, by donating our DNA to help create an- 8 other person or by appropriating someone else's DNA to augment our own bodies, we are impinging on another's freedom any more than we are abrogating our own. Someone else with my DNA would still be someone else. And if I had liver cells derived from someone else's DNA, I would still be me.

*New York Times, November 16, 1998, p. A25.

9   To put it another way, DNA is just not that important.

10   To borrow again from the existentialists, this time Albert Camus, each of us is Sisyphus, condemned to push his or her personal rock up the hill of life and to see it roll back down again. Filled with this certainty, maybe even ennobled by it, we are obligated to be ourselves, whether we like it or not. No bio-shocks will change that. ■

QUESTIONS TO HELP YOU THINK AND WRITE ABOUT GENETIC ENGINEERING ISSUES

1. Pollan says Europeans have demanded that biotech food be labeled in the market. Organic farmers also want genetic labeling of engineered food. Such labeling is controversial in the United States. What is your opinion on this issue? Should engineered food be labeled in the supermarkets? What information about the product, if any, should the consumer know? Why do you think so?

2. Who benefits the most from bioengineered food crops? The farmer? The consumer? The biotech companies? What are the long-term implications of your answer on the future of each of these groups as bioengineering technologies continue to develop?

3. Weiss explains people's shock and concern that genetically modified corn kills monarch butterflies, the "Bambi of the insect world." Yet these crops are engineered deliberately to poison other insects and their larvae. Do you find it acceptable or unacceptable that some insects be poisoned but others be spared? What might be the long-term ecological effects of such selective poisoning?

4. Why are Europeans, according to Specter, so opposed to genetically modified food? Give as many reasons as you can. What effect does the Holocaust have on their thinking?

5. The last three articles on bioengineered food mention the changes biotechnology companies are willing to make in Europe as a result of public argument. What are these changes? Do you think similar dialogue and change could take place in the United States? Why or why not? Do you know of any issues that have been settled through the kind of dialogue and compromise that is described in these articles? What are the issues? What were the results?

6. Kolata mentions a number of issues associated with the cloning of human beings that were identified in 1997 when the cloning of Dolly the sheep was announced. What are some of these issues? Why is the cloning of a human more problematic than the cloning of an animal? What might be some advantages for cloning humans? What might be some disadvantages?

7. Gillis and Stolberg write about modifying animals through bioengineering. Divide a sheet of paper down the middle. On one side list all of the advantages of this technology, and on the other side list the disadvantages. If you were on a national committee to decide future policy on genetically altering animals, what types of policy would you recommend? Why?

8. Basing your reasoning on the articles by Joyce, Hamer and Copeland, and Silver, consider the advantages and disadvantages of genetically altering human beings. Divide a sheet of paper down the middle. On one side list all of the advantages of this technology, and on the other side list the disadvantages. If you were on a national committee to decide future policy on genetically altering human beings, what types of policy would you recommend? Why?

9. Imagine Barash and Silver in a conversation about the future of a bioengineered human race. How might they agree? How might they disagree? Which of them would you be more likely to agree with?

SECTION VII

Issues Concerning Responsibility

THE ISSUES

A. Who Should Be Responsible for the Children?

Most people would immediately agree that parents should be responsible for their children. But what happens when both parents work? What happens when parents do not take responsibility? Four modern authors provide varying perspectives on working parents and day care. See also "Building a Better Dad," page 445; "Can Women 'Have It All'?" page 441; "Father's Role at Home Is under Negotiation," page 444; "Why I Want a Wife," page 56; and "The Ones Who Walk Away from Omelas," page 396.

B. Who Should Be Responsible for the Poor?

Is there still sufficient opportunity for poor people to "pull themselves up by their bootstraps" and get back on their feet, or is this an area where government needs to intervene with various types of welfare and self-development programs? You will read about a plan to reform the welfare system in this country, a personal account about life below the poverty line, and a report on the outcomes of a self-development program for welfare recipients that helps them transition to work. See also "Improvement Is a Myth," page 598; "Coming and Going," page 114; and "Devising New Math to Define Poverty," page 182.

To Extend Your Perspective: Films and Literature Related to Issues Concerning Responsibility

Films: Kramer vs. Kramer, 1979; *Schindler's List*, 1995; *Rain Man*, 1988
Literature: poems: "Ethics" by Linda Pastan; *Inner City Mother Goose* by Eve Merriam; short story: "Bartleby the Scrivener" by Herman Melville; novel: *Lord of the Flies* by William Golding

THE RHETORICAL SITUATION

What constitutes individual responsibility and what constitutes social responsibility has been an issue since humans first organized themselves in society. John Stuart Mill, in his essay "On Liberty" (1849), offers a historical perspective that is much in line with what many people would be willing to accept today. Mill provides the individual with considerable freedom of responsibility as long as the individual does not hurt others and is willing to be responsible for the consequences of his or her actions.

In our own day, responsibility issues focus in general on whether or not we can expect every individual to be responsible for his or her actions or whether in certain cases social institutions need to take responsibility for them. Some people also wonder whether or not individuals, given freedom, can always be trusted to do what is best both for themselves and for society. When they do not, society needs to be able to intervene. Some examples of specific responsibility issues in our time focus on whether the government, private businesses, or individuals should be responsible for health care, day care, homeless shelters and food for the homeless, drug addicts and their care, the rehabilitation of criminals, employees who have been laid off, single mothers with no source of income, the disabled, and the otherwise disadvantaged.

No one escapes responsibility issues and their ramifications in modern life. Responsibility issues permeate politics, determine how we spend much of the national wealth, and have profound personal effects on our daily well-being.

The articles in this section focus on responsibility issues concerning child care and the poor. They will get you started thinking about responsibility, but they do not exhaust all aspects of the issue. Which responsibility issues will affect your life?

A. Who Should Be Responsible for the Children?

THERE'S NO PLACE LIKE WORK*

*Arlie Russell Hochschild***

Arlie Russell Hochschild, professor of sociology at the University of California at Berkeley is the author of The Second Shift *and* The Time Bind: When Work Becomes Home and Home Becomes Work. *This article is adapted from* The Time Bind.

1 　　It's 7:40 A.M. when Cassie Bell, 4, arrives at the Spotted Deer Child-Care Center, her hair half-combed, a blanket in one hand, a fudge bar in the other. "I'm

*New York Times Magazine, April 20, 1997, pp. 51–55, 81, 84.
**Author's Note: Over three years, I interviewed 130 respondents for a book. They spoke freely and allowed me to follow them through "typical" days, on the *(cont.)*

late," her mother, Gwen, a sturdy young woman whose short-cropped hair frames a pleasant face, explains to the child-care worker in charge. "Cassie wanted the fudge bar so bad, I gave it to her," she adds apologetically.

"*Pleeese,* can't you take me with you?" Cassie pleads.   2

"You know I can't take you to work," Gwen replies in a tone that suggests that 3 she has been expecting this request. Cassie's shoulders droop. But she has struck a hard bargain—the morning fudge bar—aware of her mother's anxiety about the long day that lies ahead at the center. As Gwen explains later, she continually feels that she owes Cassie more time than she gives her—she has a "time debt."

Arriving at her office just before 8, Gwen finds on her desk a cup of coffee in 4 her personal mug, milk no sugar (exactly as she likes it), prepared by a co-worker who managed to get in ahead of her. As the assistant to the head of public relations at a company I will call Amerco, Gwen has to handle responses to any reports that may appear about the company in the press—a challenging job, but one that gives her satisfaction. As she prepares for her first meeting of the day, she misses her daughter, but she also feels relief; there's a lot to get done at Amerco.

Gwen used to work a straight eight-hour day. But over the last three years, 5 her workday has gradually stretched to eight and a half or nine hours, not counting the E-mail messages and faxes she answers from home. She complains about her hours to her co-workers and listens to their complaints—but she loves her job. Gwen picks up Cassie at 5:45 and gives her a long, affectionate hug.

At home, Gwen's husband, John, a computer programmer, plays with their 6 daughter while Gwen prepares dinner. To protect the dinner "hour"—8:00–8:30— Gwen checks that the phone machine is on, hears the phone ring during dinner but resists the urge to answer. After Cassie's bath, Gwen and Cassie have "quality time," or "Q.T.," as John affectionately calls it. Half an hour later, at 9:30, Gwen tucks Cassie into bed.

There are, in a sense, two Bell households: the rushed family they actually 7 are and the relaxed family they imagine they might be if only they had time. Gwen and John complain that they are in a time bind. What they say they want seems so modest—time to throw a ball, to read to Cassie, to witness the small dramas of her development, not to speak of having a little fun and romance themselves. Yet even these modest wishes seem strangely out of reach. Before going to bed, Gwen has to E-mail messages to her colleagues in preparation for the next day's meeting; John goes to bed early, exhausted—he's out the door by 7 every morning.

Nationwide, many working parents are in the same boat. More mothers of small 8 children than ever now work outside the home. In 1993, 56 percent of women with children between 6 and 17 worked outside the home full time year round; 43 percent of women with children 6 and under did the same. Meanwhile, fathers of small children are not cutting back hours of work to help out at home. If anything, they have increased their hours at work. According to a 1993 national

understanding that I would protect their anonymity. I have changed the names of the company and of those I interviewed, and altered certain identifying details. Their words appear here as they were spoken.—A.R.H.

survey conducted by the Families and Work Institute in New York, American men average 48.8 hours of work a week, and women 41.7 hours, including overtime and commuting. All in all, more women are on the economic train, and for many—men and women alike—that train is going faster.

9   But Amerco has "family friendly" policies. If your division head and supervisor agree, you can work part time, share a job with another worker, work some hours at home, take parental leave or use "flex time." But hardly anyone uses these policies. In seven years, only two Amerco fathers have taken formal parental leave. Fewer than 1 percent have taken advantage of the opportunity to work part time. Of all such policies, only flex time—which rearranges but does not shorten work time—has had a significant number of takers (perhaps a third of working parents at Amerco).

10   Forgoing family-friendly policies is not exclusive to Amerco workers. A 1991 study of 188 companies conducted by the Families and Work Institute found that while a majority offered part-time shifts, fewer than 5 percent of employees made use of them. Thirty-five percent offered "flex place"—work from home—and fewer than 3 percent of their employees took advantage of it. And an earlier Bureau of Labor Statistics survey asked workers whether they preferred a shorter workweek, a longer one or their present schedule. About 62 percent preferred their present schedule; 28 percent would have preferred longer hours. Fewer than 10 percent said they wanted a cut in hours.

11   Still, I found it hard to believe that people didn't protest their long hours at work. So I contacted Bright Horizons, a company that runs 136 company-based child-care centers associated with corporations, hospitals and Federal agencies in 25 states. Bright Horizons allowed me to add questions to a questionnaire they sent out to 3,000 parents whose children attended the centers. The respondents, mainly middle-class parents in their early 30's, largely confirmed the picture I'd found at Amerco. A third of fathers and a fifth of mothers described themselves as "workaholic," and 1 out of 3 said their partners were.

12   To be sure, some parents have tried to shorten their hours. Twenty-one percent of the nation's women voluntarily work part time, as do 7 percent of men. A number of others make under-the-table arrangements that don't show up on surveys. But while working parents say they need more time at home, the main story of their lives does not center on a struggle to get it. Why? Given the hours parents are working these days, why aren't they taking advantage of an opportunity to reduce their time at work?

13   The most widely held explanation is that working parents cannot afford to work shorter hours. Certainly this is true for many. But if money is the whole explanation, why would it be that at places like Amerco, the best-paid employees—upper-level managers and professionals—were the least interested in part-time work or job sharing, while clerical workers who earned less were more interested?

14   Similarly, if money were the answer, we would expect poorer new mothers to return to work more quickly after giving birth than rich mothers. But among working women nationwide, well-to-do new mothers are not much more likely to

stay home after 13 weeks with a new baby than low-income new mothers. When asked what they look for in a job, only a third of respondents in a recent study said salary came first. Money is important, but by itself, money does not explain why many people don't want to cut back hours at work.

A second explanation goes that workers don't dare ask for time off because they are afraid it would make them vulnerable to layoffs. With recent downsizings at many large corporations, and with well-paying, secure jobs being replaced by lower-paying, insecure ones, it occurred to me that perhaps employees are "working scared." But when I asked Amerco employees whether they worked long hours for fear of getting on a layoff list, virtually everyone said no. Even among a particularly vulnerable group—factory workers who were laid off in the downturn of the early 1980's and were later rehired—most did not cite fear for their jobs as the only, or main, reason they worked overtime. For unionized workers, layoffs are assigned by seniority, and for nonunionized workers, layoffs are usually related to the profitability of the division a person works in, not to an individual work schedule. 15

Were workers uninformed about the company's family friendly policies? No. Some even mentioned that they were proud to work for a company that offered such enlightened policies. Were rigid middle managers standing in the way of workers' using these policies? Sometimes. But when I compared Amerco employees who worked for flexible managers with those who worked for rigid managers, I found that the flexible managers reported only a few more applicants than the rigid ones. The evidence, however counterintuitive, pointed to a paradox: workers at the company I studied weren't protesting the time bind. They were accommodating to it. 16

Why? I did not anticipate the conclusion I found myself coming to: namely, that work has become a form of "home" and home has become "work". The worlds of home and work have not begun to blur, as the conventional wisdom goes, but to reverse places. We are used to thinking that home is where most people feel the most appreciated, the most truly "themselves," the most secure, the most relaxed. We are used to thinking that work is where most people feel like "just a number" or "a cog in a machine." It is where they have to be "on," have to "act," where they are least secure and most harried. 17

But new management techniques so pervasive in corporate life have helped transform the workplace into a more appreciative, personal sort of social world. Meanwhile, at home the divorce rate has risen, and the emotional demands have become more baffling and complex. In addition to teething, tantrums and the normal developments of growing children, the needs of elderly parents are creating more tasks for the modern family—as are the blending, unblending, reblending of new stepparents, stepchildren, exes and former in-laws. 18

This idea began to dawn on me during one of my first interviews with an Amerco worker. Linda Avery, a friendly, 38-year-old mother, is a shift supervisor at an Amerco plant. When I meet her in the factory's coffee-break room over a couple of Cokes, she is wearing blue jeans and a pink jersey, her hair pulled back in a 19 long, blond ponytail. Linda's husband, Bill, is a technician in the same plant. By working different shifts, they manage to share the care of their 2-year-old son and Linda's 16-year-old daughter from a previous marriage. "Bill works the 7 A.M. to 3 P.M. shift while I watch the baby," she explains. "Then I work the 3 P.M. to 11 P.M. shift and he watches the baby. My daughter works at Walgreen's after school."

20   Linda is working overtime, and so I begin by asking whether Amerco required the overtime, or whether she volunteered for it. "Oh, I put in for it," she replies. I ask her whether, if finances and company policy permitted, she'd be interested in cutting back on the overtime. She takes off her safety glasses, rubs her face and, without answering my question, explains: "I get home, and the minute I turn the key, my daughter is right there. Granted, she needs somebody to talk to about her day. . . . The baby is still up. He should have been in bed two hours ago, and that upsets me. The dishes are piled in the sink. My daughter comes right up to the door and complains about anything her stepfather said or did, and she wants to talk about her job. My husband is in the other room hollering to my daughter, 'Tracy, I don't ever get any time to talk to your mother, because you're always monopolizing her time before I even get a chance!' They all come at me at once."

21   Linda's description of the urgency of demands and the unarbitrated quarrels that await her homecoming contrast with her account of arriving at her job as a shift supervisor: "I usually come to work early, just to get away from the house. When I arrive, people are there waiting. We sit, we talk, we joke. I let them know what's going on, who has to be where, what changes I've made for the shift that day. We sit and chitchat for 5 or 10 minutes. There's laughing, joking, fun."

22   For Linda, home has come to feel like work and work has come to feel a bit like home. Indeed, she feels she can get relief from the "work" of being at home only by going to the "home" of work. Why has her life at home come to seem like this? Linda explains it this way: "My husband's a great help watching our baby. But as far as doing housework or even taking the baby when I'm at home, no. He figures he works five days a week; he's not going to come home and clean. But he doesn't stop to think that I work seven days a week. Why should I have to come home and do the housework without help from anybody else? My husband and I have been through this over and over again. Even if he would just pick up from the kitchen table and stack the dishes for me, that would make a big difference. He does nothing. On his weekends off, he goes fishing. If I want any time off, I have to get a sitter. He'll help out if I'm not here, but the minute I am, all the work at home is mine."

23   With a light laugh, she continues: "So I take a lot of overtime. The more I get out of the house, the better I am. It's a terrible thing to say, but that's the way I feel."

24   When Bill feels the need for time off, to relax, to have fun, to feel free, he climbs in his truck and takes his free time without his family. Largely in response, Linda grabs what she also calls "free time"—at work. Neither Linda nor Bill Avery wants more time together at home, not as things are arranged now. [. . .]

25 Obviously, not everyone, not even a majority of Americans, is making a home out of work and a workplace out of home. But in the working world, it is a growing reality,

and one we need to face. Increasing numbers of women are discovering a great male secret—that work can be an escape from the pressures of home, pressures that the changing nature of work itself are only intensifying. Neither men nor women are going to take up "family friendly" policies, whether corporate or governmental, as long as the current realities of work and home remain as they are. For a substantial number of time-bound parents, the stripped-down home and the neighborhood devoid of community are simply losing out to the pull of the workplace.

There are several broader, historical causes of this reversal of realms. The 26 last 30 years have witnessed the rapid rise of women in the workplace. At the same time, job mobility has taken families farther from relatives who might lend a hand, and made it harder to make close friends of neighbors who could help out. Moreover, as women have acquired more education and have joined men at work, they have absorbed the views of an older, male-oriented work world, its views of a "real career," far more than men have taken up their share of the work at home. One reason women have changed more than men is that the world of "male" work seems more honorable and valuable than the "female" world of home and children.

So where do we go from here? There is surely no going back to the mythical 27 1950's family that confined women to the home. Most women don't wish to return to a full-time role at home—and couldn't afford it even if they did. But equally troubling is a workaholic culture that strands both men and women outside the home.

For a while now, scholars on work-family issues have pointed to Sweden, 28 Norway and Denmark as better models of work-family balance. Today, for example, almost all Swedish fathers take two paid weeks off from work at the birth of their children, and about half of fathers and most mothers take additional "parental leave" during the child's first or second year. Research shows that men who take family leave when their children are very young are more likely to be involved with their children as they grow older. When I mentioned this Swedish record of paternity leave to a focus group of American male managers, one of them replied, "Right, we've already heard about Sweden." To this executive, paternity leave was a good idea not for the U.S. today, but for some "potential society" in another place and time.

Meanwhile, children are paying the price. In her book *When the Bough Breaks:* 29 *The Cost of Neglecting Our Children,* the economist Sylvia Hewlett claims that "compared with the previous generation, young people today are more likely to underperform at school; commit suicide; need psychiatric help; suffer a severe eating disorder; bear a child out of wedlock; take drugs; be the victim of a violent crime." But we needn't dwell on sledgehammer problems like heroin or suicide to realize that children like those at Spotted Deer need more of our time. If other advanced nations with two-job families can give children the time they need, why can't we? ■

GOOD NEWS FOR WORKING MOMS*

Barbara Vobejda

*This article suggests that day care is not necessarily harmful to a child's development.
It is not whether the mother stays at home full time that matters but rather what
happens when the mother is at home with her children.*

1 A comprehensive, multi-year study released last week concludes that mothers who
work outside the home are not harming their children. The research, published in
the March issue of the journal *Developmental Psychology*, assessed the behavior, academic achievement and psychological health of more than 6,000 children and found
no permanent negative effects caused by their mother's absence. In some cases, the
study found, children may be helped by the income their mothers bring in.

2   Experts say the new research, conducted by University of Massachusetts
psychologist Elisabeth Harvey, supports what similar studies increasingly indicate: The quality of family life generally, including the mental stability and matu-
rity of parents, is vastly more important in determining how children fare in life
than the question of whether their mothers are employed.

3   "A number of studies are now suggesting that if the quality of parenting at
home is good, having a working mother doesn't hurt children," says Andrew Cherlin, a sociologist at Johns Hopkins University. "It doesn't seem to be the case that a
parent has to be with a child all day long for that child to develop successfully."

4   The study comes at a time of intense political and social debate about the effect of working mothers, long hours of day care and fast-paced family life on a
generation of children. While its findings may ease the concern of millions of parents, it is unlikely to diminish the strong ambivalence Americans feel on the subject, with many convinced that young children do better when a parent stays home
full time.

5   Recently, the strains on modern families have taken on political saliency:
President Clinton's proposed budget includes a tax credit to ease the financial burdens of stay-at-home parents, something Republicans had called for last year. But
even as lawmakers attempt to embrace both versions of modern family life, the
vast majority of mothers—70 percent—work outside the home, and 10 million
children under the age of 5 have employed mothers. That creates a ready audience
for academic research on whether those children are suffering intellectually or
emotionally because their mothers are not at home during the day.

6   The study attempts to resolve conflicting evidence on the subject. Previous
research on the same group of children found both positive and negative effects
of having a working mother. Harvey, who set out to examine the long-term effects of maternal employment in the first three years of a child's life, analyzed
data collected in the National Longitudinal Survey of Youth (NLSY), a study of
12,600 people interviewed each year since 1979. For this study, she looked specifically at information about children of women surveyed in NLSY. Those children

*Washington Post, national weekly ed., March 8, 1999, p. 34.

were between 3 and 12, from both one- and two-parent families. They were assessed every two years from 1986 to 1994.

It is possible, Harvey concluded, that having both parents work may carry both 7 positive and negative consequences for children. But ultimately, she wrote, "no consistent evidence of substantial effects of early parental employment on children's later development was found."

Harvey looked at several variables, including how soon a mother returned 8 to work after her child's birth, how many hours weekly she was employed and whether there were periods of unemployment interspersed with working. She then assessed whether there was an effect on children's behavior, intellectual development, self-esteem and academic achievement. The assessments were based on a variety of standardized tests and, in some cases, reports from parents.

Overall, Harvey found that children whose mothers worked during the first 9 three years after giving birth were not significantly different from those with unemployed mothers.

On one measure—children's compliance and temperament—Harvey found 10 that 3- and 4-year-olds whose mothers stayed at home longer after birth were slightly more compliant than those [of mothers] who returned to work sooner. But the differences between the two groups of children were slight and disappeared by the time the children reached age 5 and 6.

Children whose mothers worked more hours scored slightly lower on aca- 11 demic achievement and vocabulary tests. The differences were small and disappeared by the time the children turned 7. The study also found that children were not affected by having their fathers work in the early years after birth. ■

DAY CARE: A GRAND AND TROUBLING SOCIAL EXPERIMENT*

Dorothy Conniff

Dorothy Conniff is director of community services in Madison, Wisconsin. She has worked in the field of day care for over twenty years. Contrast Conniff's views with the views of Susan Faludi, whose article follows this one.

We won't find real solutions to the need for good child care until we solve a fun- 1 damental problem: We value children only sentimentally. Children's real needs and concerns do not register as essential.

We have abundant research about the lasting negative effects of early depri- 2 vation and the strikingly positive effects of high-quality early education. Yet today we shuffle millions of middle-class children off to day-care settings duplicating the sort of deprivation that used to be suffered only by the poorest and most disadvantaged.

Take infant care, for example. 3

*Utne Reader, May–June 1993, pp. 66–67.

4   In many states, there are no regulations governing the number of infants a staff member may care for. In those where there are, many states allow five or six. In Wisconsin, where I live, the maximum is four infants per worker. [According to the National Association for the Education of Young Children, 29 states require this four-to-one ratio, while only three—Kansas, Maryland, and Massachusetts—require a three-to-one ratio. Most of the remaining states have five-to-one or six-to-one ratios.]

5   Consider the amount of physical care and attention a baby needs—say 20 minutes for feeding every three hours or so, and 10 minutes for diapering every two hours or so, and time for the care giver to wash her hands thoroughly and sanitize the area after changing each baby. In an eight-and-a-half-hour-day, then, a care giver working under the typical four-to-one ratio will have 16 diapers to change and 12 feedings to give. Four diaper changes and three feedings apiece is not an inordinate amount of care over a long day from the babies' point of view.

6   But think about the care giver's day: Four hours to feed the babies, two hours and 40 minutes to change them. If you allow an extra two and a half minutes at each changing to put them down, clean up the area, and thoroughly wash your hands, you can get by with 40 minutes for sanitizing. (And if you think about thoroughly washing your hands 16 times a day, you may begin to understand why epidemics of diarrhea and related diseases regularly sweep through infant-care centers.)

7   That makes seven hours and 20 minutes of the day spent just on physical care—if you're lucky and the infants stay conveniently on schedule.

8   Since feeding and diaper changing are necessarily one-on-one activities, each infant is bound to be largely unattended during the five-plus hours that the other three babies are being attended to. So, if there's to be any stimulation at all for the child, the care giver had better chat and play up a storm while she's feeding and changing.

9   Obviously, such a schedule is not realistic. In group infant care based on even this four-to-one ratio, babies will not be changed every two hours and they will probably not be held while they're fed.

10   They also will not get the kind of attention and talk that is the foundation of language development. If a child is deprived of language stimulation for eight to ten hours a day, how much compensation—how much "quality time"—can concerned parents provide in the baby's few other waking hours at home?

11   Unfortunately, the situation is not much better for toddlers. Group care is almost as new a service for toddlers as for infants. In many centers, even in the better ones, young, unskilled staff struggle with large groups of very young children. Staff turnover rates exceed 30 percent a year, so most don't stay long enough to be trained.

12   One common sign of staff inexperience is the Big Toddler Lineup. Inexperienced staff tend to fall back on their only model for dealing with groups of children: the elementary school. What do you do in school each time an activity changes? Line up. Not realizing that forming a line is developmentally beyond the capacity of such young children, staff struggle for long periods to get their toddlers to line up for routine events. The results are comical and predictable—babies wander off, sit down and stare into space, cry—and staff lose patience. What's not so comical is that this kind of distressingly inappropriate expectation and the im-

patience, disapproval, and unhappiness that result are the chronic daily experience of the children.

Toddlers learn through all their senses. They cannot make sense of words 13 alone; they need to touch and heft objects, move through space, put two things side by side. Without this opportunity, children become apathetic or uncontrollable—and sometimes both by turns.

When children under 3 are put into impoverished or chaotic environments 14 with inexperienced, discouraged staff who expend most of their energy just trying to maintain order, the children suffer. Some of their pain is physical, because toddlers need to move around a lot. Some is mental, because of the continual frustration of basic developmental impulses. And some is emotional, because of the constant disapproval, which the child is powerless to correct.

Preschoolers ages 3 and up are the group that most day-care centers have 15 been accustomed to serve. These kids are more amenable to groups, but without skilled staff they also suffer. To serve 3-year-olds well, teachers somehow have to make time to answer their questions even though they have 20 or more active little ones to organize, feed, nap, and otherwise get through the day.

Learning to pose questions and receive information that is satisfying is a key 16 social as well as intellectual experience in a child's development. Children who don't have a successful experience at this stage, or whose experience is frustrated or perverted, stop participating in the learning process. They stop expressing their questions, and eventually may stop thinking them up.

If their world is structured so that formulating and getting answers to ques- 17 tions is difficult or impossible, the developmental process is seriously damaged. And this is the most consistent drawback of day-care centers where staff are overloaded and inexperienced. Staff resort to forcing children into the same boring activity all at the same time to maintain control. The kind of repressive control that keeps them sitting down to meaningless tasks day after day hurts their self-esteem and impairs their relationship with learning.

We have no idea how destructive a situation we have created. It is a social 18 experiment on a grand scale with virtually no controls. ■

THE KIDS ARE ALL RIGHT*

Susan Faludi

Susan Faludi originally wrote this article for Mother Jones *magazine. She writes frequently about women's issues and is the author of* Backlash: The Undeclared War Against American Women.

What should be most curious to anyone reviewing the voluminous research liter- 1 ature on day care is the chasm between what the studies find and what people choose to believe. Despite a pervasive sense that day care is at best risky for children and at worst permanently damaging, much of the research indicates that if

*Utne Reader, May–June 1993, pp. 68–70.

day care has any long-term effect on children at all, it has made them somewhat more social, experimental, self-assured, cooperative, creative. At the University of California at Irvine, Alison Clarke-Stewart, professor of social ecology, found that the social and intellectual development of children in day care was six to nine months ahead of that of children who stayed home.

2   The research on day care points to other bonuses, too. Day-care kids tend to have a more progressive view of sex roles. Canadian researchers Delores Gold and David Andres found that the girls they interviewed in day care believed that housework and child care should be evenly divided; the girls raised at home still believed these tasks are women's work. We are reminded constantly by the press that children in day care turn out to be too "aggressive." But researchers point out that what is being billed as aggression could as easily be labeled assertiveness, not at all a bad quality in a child.

3   As for the supposed and much-publicized day-care child abuse "epidemic," a three-year, $200,000 study by the University of New Hampshire's Family Research Laboratory found in 1988 that if there is an "epidemic" of child abuse, it's in the home—where children are almost twice as likely to be molested as in day care. And, ironically, the researchers found that children were *least* likely to be sexually abused in day-care centers located in high-crime, low-income neighborhoods (there tends to be more supervision in these centers). Despite frightening stories in the media, the researchers concluded that there is no indication of some special high risk to children in day care.

4   Although many of the celebrated tales of day-care workers molesting children have turned out to be tall tales, we continue to believe their message. "The consequences of all the negative play in the press about the McMartin case were really quite dramatic," says Abby Cohen, managing attorney of the Child Care Law Center, referring to the 1984 sex-abuse scandal at the McMartin Pre-School in Manhattan Beach, California. "Because, unfortunately, up until then there hadn't been very much play about child care, period. So it was terribly detrimental that the first real wide attention to it was in such a negative light."

5   For children of poverty, day care may be their ticket out of the ghetto. The studies find that the futures of low-income kids brighten immeasurably after a couple of years in day care. The Perry Pre-School Project of Ypsilanti, Michigan, followed 123 poor black children for 20 years. The children who spent one to two years in preschool day care, the researchers found, stayed in school longer, were not as prone to teenage pregnancy and crime, and improved their earning prospects significantly. A New York University study of 750 Harlem children came up with similar results: The children enrolled in preschool were far more likely to get jobs and pursue education beyond high school.

6   Presented with the evidence, some day-care critics will concede that preschool may have a negligible negative effect on toddlers, but then they move quickly to the matter of infants. So 3-year-olds may survive day care, they say, but newborns will suffer permanent damage. Their evidence comes from two sources. The first is a collection of studies conducted in the 1940s, '50s, and '60s in France, England, and West Germany. These studies concluded that infants who were taken from their mothers had tendencies later toward juvenile delinquency and mental

illness. But there's a slight problem in relying on these findings: The studies were all looking at infants in orphanages and hospital institutions, not day-care centers.

The other source frequently quoted is the much-celebrated turnabout by 7 Pennsylvania State University psychologist Jay Belsky, once a leading supporter of day care. In 1982 Belsky had reviewed the child-development literature and concluded that there were few if any significant differences between children raised at home and those in day care. Then in September 1986 he announced that he had changed his mind: Children whose mothers work more than 20 hours a week in their first year, he said, are at "risk" for developing an "insecure" attachment to their mothers. Belsky's pronouncement provided grist for the anti-day-care mill— and was widely reported. What did not receive as wide an airing, however, is the evidence Belsky cited to support his change of heart. Two of the studies he used flatly contradict each other: In one of them, the study's panel of judges found the infants in day care to be more insecure; in the other, the panel found just the opposite. The difference in results was traced to the judges' own bias against day care. In the study where the judges were not told ahead of time which babies were in day care and which were raised at home, the judges said the children's behavior was indistinguishable. In the study where they did know ahead of time which babies were in day care, they concluded that the day-care children were more insecure.

It is this bias that makes our day-care terrors so intractable. If the feeling 8 comes from the gut, if it is an internalized, strictly personal belief, then its truth must be of a higher order, unassailable by any number of studies. But what many people fail to see is how our seemingly personal perceptions of day care are not so personal after all; how they have been shaped by forces that have little to do with gut instinct. Our opinions have been hammered by years of relentless anti-day-care and anti-working-mother rhetoric from the Reagan and Bush administrations and from the media, where bashing day care seems to be a sanctioned sport. (A few headlines from well-read magazines: "'Mommy, Don't Leave Me Here!': The Day Care Parents Don't See." "When Child Care Becomes Child Molesting: It Happens More Often than Parents Like to Think." "Creeping Child Care—Creepy.")

Other cultural forces are at work here, too. We suffer a compulsion to repli- 9 cate our childhoods, no matter how unpleasant those early years might have been. If our mothers stayed home, that must be the 'healthy' way. What we forget is that it's only been since the 1940s that public opinion has so insistently endorsed the 24-hour-mom concept. The Victorians may have kept their women at home, but not for the sake of the children. "An educated woman," writer Emily Davies advised mothers in the 1870s, "blessed with good servants, as good mistresses generally are, finds an hour a day amply sufficient for her domestic duties." An early version of quality time.

The paranoia may ease once the younger generation reaches adulthood; they 10 are not freighted with the same cultural assumptions about child care as those weaned in the 1950s. When I brought up the matter of child rearing to teenagers at Lowell High School in San Francisco, they all seemed to favor day care more than their parents do. How come? "Well," one 17-year-old girl reasoned, in what turned out to be a typical response, "I went to day care when I was little and I had a really good time." ▪

B. Who Should Be Responsible for the Poor?

REPLACING THE WELFARE STATE WITH AN OPPORTUNITY SOCIETY*

Newt Gingrich

> *For two decades, Newt Gingrich served in the U.S. Congress, most recently as Speaker of the House of Representatives. The following is excerpted from his book* To Renew America.

1 The greatest moral imperative we face is replacing the welfare state with an opportunity society. For every day that we allow the current conditions to continue, we are condemning the poor—and particularly poor children—to being deprived of their basic rights as Americans. The welfare state reduces the poor from citizens to clients. It breaks up families, minimizes work incentives, blocks people from saving and acquiring property, and overshadows dreams of a promised future with a present despair born of poverty, violence, and hopelessness.

2 When a welfare mother in Wisconsin can be punished for sewing her daughter's clothing and saving on food stamps so she can set aside three thousand dollars for her daughter's education, you know there is something wrong.

3 When a woman who sells candy out of her apartment in a public housing project cannot open a store because she would lose her subsidized rent and health care and end up paying in taxes and lost benefits all she earned in profit, you know there is something wrong.

4 Gary Franks, congressman from Connecticut, tells of going into grade schools and asking young children what they hope to be when they grow up. Basketball players, football players, and baseball players are the three answers, in that order. What if you can't be an athlete? he then asks. They have no answer. It is beyond the experience of these children to consider becoming a lawyer or an accountant or a businessman. The public housing children, no matter what their ethnic backgrounds, have simply no conception of the world of everyday work. Clearly something is wrong.

5 Charlie Rangel, the senior congressman from Harlem, asked me to imagine what it would be like to visit a first- or second-grade classroom and realize that every fourth boy would be dead or in jail before he was twenty-five years old. As I think of my three nephews, Charlie's comment drives home to me the despair and rage at the heart of any black leader as he looks at the lost future of a generation of poor children. Clearly something is wrong.

6 The defenders of the status quo should be ashamed of themselves. The current system has trapped and ruined a whole generation while claiming to be compassionate. The burden of proof is not on the people who want to change welfare. It is on those who would defend a system that has clearly failed at incalculable human cost.

7 Consider the facts. Welfare spending is now $305 billion a year. Since 1965 we have spent $5 trillion on welfare—more than the cost of winning World War II.

---

*Newt Gingrich, *To Renew America* (New York: HarperCollins, 1995), pp. 71–85.

Yet despite this massive effort, conditions in most poor communities have grown measurably worse. Since 1970 the number of children living in poverty has increased by 40 percent. Since 1965 the juvenile arrest rate for violent crimes has tripled. Since 1960 the number of unmarried pregnant teenage girls has nearly doubled and teen suicide has more than tripled. As welfare spending increased since 1960, it has exactly paralleled the rise in births outside of marriage. On a graph, the two lines move together like a pair of railroad tracks. The more we spend to alleviate poverty, the more we assure that the next generation will almost certainly grow up in poverty. Clearly something is profoundly wrong.

We owe it to all young Americans in every neighborhood to save them from 8 a system that is depriving them of their God-given rights to life, liberty, and the pursuit of happiness. There can't be true liberty while they are trapped in a welfare bureaucracy. There can't be any pursuit of happiness when they are not allowed to buy property or accumulate savings. And there can't be any reasonable right to a long life in an environment that is saturated with pimps, prostitutes, drug dealers, and violence.

Make no mistake: replacing the welfare state will not be an easy job. It will 9 not work simply to replace one or two elements while leaving everything else intact. It will be necessary to think through the entire process before we begin.

Replacing the welfare state with an opportunity society will require eight 10 major changes, which need to be undertaken simultaneously. Trying to change only one or two at a time will leave people trapped in the old order. We have an obligation to begin improving the lives of the poor from day one.

When people tell me I am intense on this issue, I ask them to imagine that their 11 children were the ones dying on the evening news and then tell me how intense they would be to save their own children's lives. That is how intense we should all be.

One of the encouraging developments of the last few years has been that a 12 lot of truly caring, intelligent people have spent a lot of time thinking about the tragedy of modern welfare systems. As a result, we now have a fairly good idea of what works and what doesn't. The eight steps we need for improving opportunities for the poor are:

1. Shifting from caretaking to caring
2. Volunteerism and spiritual renewal
3. Reasserting the values of American civilization
4. Emphasizing family and work
5. Creating tax incentives for work, investment, and entrepreneurship
6. Reestablishing savings and property ownership
7. Learning as the focus of education
8. Protection against violence and drugs

Let us consider each one of these in turn. 13

1. SHIFTING FROM CARETAKING TO CARING

In *Working Without a Net*, Morris Schechtman emphasizes the distinction between 14 (1) caretaking—a more casual attitude, in which the important concern is to make the provider feel good, no matter what the outcome, and (2) caring—a more selfless but positive approach, in which the outcome for the person being helped is the first concern. Caretaking has established the Supplemental Security Income (SSI) system, which has allowed, for example, forty disabled alcoholics to have their government checks registered directly at a Denver liquor store. Caring, on the other hand, would require any poor or disabled person to be partners in their own self-improvement.

15   The distinction between the deserving and the undeserving poor is at the heart of Marvin Olasky's great book, *The Tragedy of American Compassion*. Olasky emphasizes that indiscriminate aid actually destroys people. In addition, the sight of undeserving people getting resources while refusing to be responsible for themselves sends a devastating message to those working poor who are trying to make the effort to improve their lot. Besides undermining individual morality, indiscriminate aid undermines society as a whole.

16   From Colonial times until the 1960s, Olasky argues, American reformers made a clear distinction between poverty, a condition in which an individual or family did not have much money but their morality had not been undermined, and pauperism, a condition of passive dependency in which the work ethic has been completely lost. Social reformers emphasized that nothing could be more destructive than giving people help they didn't deserve. These experienced, traditional reformers saw as the most dangerous persons the wealthy caretaker who passed out money to make himself feel good even as it ruined people in the process.

17   Olasky's model for true caring requires a level of detailed knowledge that is not possible for government bureaucracies. Because of the very magnitude of the task they attempt to undertake, government caretakers can do nothing more than provide indiscriminate handouts for income maintenance.

2. VOLUNTEERISM AND SPIRITUAL RENEWAL

18   In the nineteenth century, Olasky notes, there was an average of one volunteer for every two poor people. Under these circumstances, volunteers could actually get to know individuals and their families and could trace whether they were making progress. It takes detailed knowledge to assess what people and their families need. The resulting system emphasized both volunteerism and spiritual salvation.

19   Olasky cites again and again the difference between trying to maintain people in poverty, alcoholism, and addiction and helping them rise above their circumstances. Maintenance programs will eventually attract more people into the kind of pauperism we are tying to avoid than it will help escape from poverty. This was the consistent concern of nineteenth-century reformers, and we now have more than enough evidence to prove they were right.

20   Olasky also cites the role of spiritual transformation in saving people from poverty. Unless people get some kind of religious bearings, it is unlikely they will make the effort needed to change their circumstances. It is no accident that Alcoholics Anonymous gives God a central place in any effort to recover from addiction. For two generations we have tried to replace spiritual transformation with secular counseling. The experiment has failed miserably. Since no secular

bureaucracy can (or should) engage in spiritual renewal, it is clear this effort must be undertaken by churches, synagogues, mosques, or other charitable and nonprofit institutions.

Congressmen Jim Kolbe and Joe Knollenberg have come up with a stunning 21 suggestion for transforming welfare. Instead of the government taking billions of dollars from reluctant taxpayers and scattering it among the poor, individual taxpayers would be allowed to check off contributions of up to one hundred dollars for donation to their favorite charity—just as you are now allowed to check off three dollars for the Presidential Election Campaign Fund. This would shift $9 billion a year into private organizations offering spiritual help. It would also give taxpayers some control over how their money is being spent. Taxpayers would be able to vote with their checkbooks if a charitable effort were having counterproductive results.

I am proud to work with Habitat for Humanity, which helps poor people 22 build their own homes. Millard and Linda Fuller founded Habitat after becoming convinced that a spiritually based approach was necessary to help the poor. Habitat screens families to find people who they believe deserve help (something the government cannot do). Those who are chosen are required to take a twenty-four-hour course on how to be a homeowner (something that HUD's lawyers say cannot be required). Habitat first asks the family to invest one hundred hours of sweat equity in helping build someone else's house and then three hundred hours in building their own home. Finally, Habitat sells them a $70,000 house for $36,000 with the understanding that if they try to sell it before the mortgage is paid off, they will have to pay off a second mortgage that covers the whole price of the home.

Volunteers like myself also come on Saturdays to work on the projects. It is a 23 rewarding experience to see the future homeowning family there alongside public-spirited citizens. Habitat for Humanity is a program that combines prayer with practical help, a model for volunteerism and spiritual renewal of the kind Olasky writes about. That is why I wear a Habitat pin on my lapel.

3. REASSERTING THE VALUES OF AMERICAN CIVILIZATION

Every day on television and radio poor people see and hear things that reinforce 24 the message that income transfer is what matters and spiritual transformation is unimportant. In her great book *The Demoralization of Society,* Gertrude Himmelfarb argues that the values and attitudes people have about themselves depend on the messages the culture sends them. She also notes that these attitudes can change in a very short period of time.

I believe we are at the end of the era of tolerating alcoholism, addiction, 25 spouse and child abuse, parental indifference, and adult irresponsibility. We have all seen society change for the better in recent years in its views on smoking, drunk driving, and racism. There is no reason that views on acceptable standards of behavior for the poor cannot change as well.

When I spoke in March 1995 to the National League of Cities, I cited Him- 26 melfarb's book and asserted that the time had come to reestablish shame as a means of enforcing proper behavior. It is shameful, I said, to be a public drunk at three in the afternoon and we ought to say so. People began applauding. It is shameful, I said, for males to have children they refuse to support and we ought to say so. The applause grew louder. And on it went.

27   It is shameful for radio stations to play songs that advocate mutilating and raping women. Government can't and shouldn't censor it, but decent advertisers could announce they will boycott any radio station that plays that kind of music. Within weeks these brutal, barbaric songs would be off the air.

28   Cultural signals are a powerful and legitimate means of enforcing proper behavior. One of the responsibilities of public leaders is to encourage the kind of public environment we want. Our culture should be sending over and over the message that young people should abstain from sexual intercourse until marriage, that work is a part of life, and that any male who does not take care of his children is a bum and deserves no respect. If you want a sense of the personal values we should be communicating to children, get the Boy Scout or Girl Scout handbook. Or go and look at *Reader's Digest* and *The Saturday Evening Post* from around 1955. Healthy societies send healthy signals to their children and to those who have become temporarily confused at any age. Look at the sick signals we are now sending through the entertainment industry and popular culture. Is it any wonder that society is so confused if not downright degenerate?

4. EMPHASIZING FAMILY AND WORK

29 Charles Murray's *Losing Ground* was one of the first books to point out that the current welfare state is actually discouraging family formation, breaking up intact families, and trapping people in poverty for generations. Leon Dash's *When Children Want Children* then built a devastating case that the culture of poverty and violence was actually offering positive incentives for teenage girls to have children outside of marriage. Dash noted that over half the boys offered to marry the girl and were turned down. The tragedy is that the welfare state now offers young girls an alternative to marriage.

30   Yet while being pregnant outside of marriage may be appealing at first sight, it turns out to be a terrible trap. Three-fourths of all unmarried teen mothers end up on welfare within five years. More than 40 percent remain on the rolls for more than ten years. The daughters of teenage mothers are two and a half times more likely to become teen mothers themselves, and when they do, they are three times as likely to live in poverty.

31   Murray argues that the tax code, the welfare laws, and the rules of the bureaucracy all add up to a system that is antiwork, antifamily, and antiopportunity. We have to rewrite these laws so they do not punish people for taking responsibility. If a couple with children earns $11,000 apiece, they will pay $2,700 less in taxes if they remain unmarried. That's a 12 percent marriage tax. Then we wonder why births outside marriage have skyrocketed.

32   We have to reemphasize identifying the father and requiring the father to accept at least financial responsibility for the child (ideally he should also accept

psychological and emotional responsibility, but let's start with the sense that if you have a child you have an obligation to help pay for that child's upbringing).

We need to revise welfare so that going to work never lowers your standard 33 of living. When you add up housing, health care, food stamps, aid to family and dependent children, and other programs, there is actually a substantial disadvantage in joining the labor force. We need to redesign the system so people have a sense of reward at each step up the ladder of opportunity.

5. TAX INCENTIVES FOR WORK, INVESTMENT, AND ENTREPRENEURSHIP

People can work only when jobs are available; job creation requires investment. 34 Today America's poorest neighborhoods offer such poor returns on investment that people simply won't go there to create jobs. The result is that few jobs are likely to be available, even if welfare rules are changed to encourage work. In addition, big cities often have the most red tape, the highest local taxes, and the most difficult bureaucracies. As a result, the poor are cheated out of jobs.

Hernando De Soto, a Peruvian economist, has written a brilliant book entitled 35 *The Other Path*, in which he describes how lawyer-dominated big-city bureaucracies kill jobs in Latin America. Although he uses Lima, Peru, as his main example, every lesson applies to the United States.

In a brief introduction, Mario Vargas Llosa, a Peruvian novelist, describes the 36 illegal activities of entrepreneurial Peruvians who refuse to let their government stop them from earning a living. At the time the book was written, 93 percent of the buses in Lima were illegal. The entire city had learned to operate outside the city's regulated transportation system.

Almost every public housing project in the United States has the same un- 37 derground economy of people working for cash or barter without securing government licenses or paying taxes. Jack Kemp has been the leading advocate of "enterprise zones" that would encourage job creation within the legal system. Kemp has long proposed massive tax and regulatory breaks for anyone who would invest in poor neighborhoods. Since these neighborhoods pay almost no taxes anyway and since they drain the public treasury through welfare payments, the cost of giving them tax breaks would be relatively small. If new investment helped poor people make the long-term transition from welfare to productive work, these enterprise zones would more than pay for themselves. With Kemp's leadership, we are now working to apply this model in Washington, D.C. We hope to have a full-blown experiment by 1996.

People can create jobs as well as find jobs. Amway, Mary Kay, BeautiControl, 38 Tupperware, and a host of other companies are examples of job creation. Anyone with a little money, some free time, and a willingness to learn marketing can make money. It is just as important to convince the poor that they can create their own jobs as it is to help them find jobs. We want to arouse an entrepreneurial spirit. A generation of small-business creation among African and Hispanic Americans would transform everything. If there were five Steve Jobses or one Bill Gates in Harlem, the entire nature of the community would change.

39   If city governments truly want to help the poor, they will make life dramatically easier for small businesses. What most poor neighborhoods need more than anything is a small-business renaissance. Cities should be cutting taxes and eliminating regulations to make it easy for poor people to start their own enterprises. Bill Marriott, founder of the famous hotel chain, started with a single pushcart. Today license regulations would probably make that pushcart illegal, and fees and taxes would make it unprofitable.

6. REESTABLISHING SAVINGS AND PROPERTY OWNERSHIP

40   If you are going to go to work or start your own small business, you have to believe you are going to keep the fruits of your labor. The history of immigrants in America has been a history of people working two and three jobs and scrimping and saving to put their children through school or open a first business. Immigrants dreamed of a better future and then worked to make those dreams come true. The greatest human damage done by the welfare state has been to kill people's dreams and destroy their ability to imagine themselves improving their lot.

41   The first step toward financial independence is to accumulate savings and acquire a little property. The current welfare system prohibits both. We want to ensure that, from day one, people who work hard can see their work pay off.

42   Part of this process involves giving people control over their own housing. Poor people ought to be given a chance to buy the property they live in. Public housing run as a cooperative or as a condominium would be vastly different from public housing run by middle-class bureaucrats who see the poor as clients rather than customers.

43   Jack Kemp has encouraged an experiment in the Kennilworth Apartments in Washington, D.C., in which residents took control of their own housing project. The first change they made was to require that maintenance people live in the project. Overnight the quality of maintenance improved. Custodians did a better job since, if they didn't, residents showed up at their door and complained. Trying to minimize their own work, maintenance workers quickly discovered who was breaking windows and engaging in vandalism. The guilty children were taken to their parents. The entire project began to look nicer within two months. When people are consumers instead of clients, their habits change drastically.

7. LEARNING AS THE FOCUS OF EDUCATION

44   The greatest single misallocation of taxpayers' money has been the unionized monopolies of inner-city education. It is astonishing how much is spent per child on these cumbersome, red-tape-ridden bureaucracies—and how little ever gets to the individual child.

45   I was radicalized on this subject by former governor Tom Kean of New Jersey. He showed me a thousand-page study of the Jersey City schools, which were spending over $7,000 per child and hardly educating anyone. Governor Kean's study group discovered the schools had been looted by the local political machine for patronage purposes. There was a $54,000-a-year fire extinguisher

inspector who failed to show up for three years. Not only was he freeloading, but the schools were left with faulty fire extinguishers. A fire would have been a disaster. The study led to a state takeover of the city school system.

My radicalization was completed by a *Chicago Tribune* series on one particu- 46 larly bad school in the Windy City. After spending a year in the schools, a team of reporters wrote a devastating series of articles. The most telling was an interview with a teacher who was so destructive that every principal she had ever worked for had tried to fire her. The tenure system always saved her. She still had eleven years of teaching time left. When asked her professional goal, she said she wanted to retire with a full pension. This teacher regularly failed to educate thirty students a year, yet the system was designed to protect her incompetence. Remember, when young people fail to get educated in the Information Age, they lose all sense of purpose and dignity. When we tolerate a school that is failing to educate children, we put not just their education but their lives at risk.

The first breath of hope for me came in Milwaukee, where Polly Williams, a 47 former welfare mother, has led a remarkable effort to reform the system. A Wisconsin state legislator and former state co-chair for Jesse Jackson's presidential campaign, Williams eventually concluded that inner-city children were being cheated by the education monopoly. She persuaded the legislature to adopt a voucher system that allows inner-city children to attend private schools at state expense. The Wisconsin teachers' union and the traditional liberals fought her bitterly, but Governor Tommy Thompson and the Republicans gave her the backing she needed. Even though the Republicans now control the state legislature, they have installed Williams as chair of the Inner City Education Reform Committee. She leads a broad bipartisan coalition that seeks to break the public-school monopoly and find new ways to educate poor children.

From home schooling to vouchers, from a drastic overhaul of the present 48 system to allowing private companies to take over whole school districts—we simply have to take whatever steps are necessary to ensure that poor children can participate in the Information Age. There is no other strategy that will give them a full opportunity to pursue happiness.

8. PROTECTION AGAINST VIOLENCE AND DRUGS

Safety is simply the most fundamental concern of government. After all, none of 49 our God-given rights matter much if we can be raped, mugged, robbed, or killed. And the poorest neighborhood is as entitled to be safe as the richest. No economic incentives a government can devise will entice businesses to open factories in a neighborhood where employees are likely to be in constant physical danger. Nor will any amount of education make up for your child being preyed upon by drug dealers and pimps. Addiction and prostitution will quickly wipe out the fruits of any educational reform. [. . .]

[Elsewhere] I will outline proposals for ending the drug trade and saving 50 children from violent crime. Here I will simply say that both measures are essential and should be applied first to the poorest neighborhoods. The United States

Constitution was written to protect us from enemies both foreign and domestic. We are doing a good job on foreign enemies, but a pathetic job of protecting ourselves and our children from those who behave like domestic enemies.

51   Everything else will fail if we cannot suppress drugs and violent crime. Establishing safety is the first foundation of creating opportunity for the poor.

SUMMARY

52 If we are truly serious about helping the poor, we must undertake all eight reforms simultaneously. The poor today are trapped both in a bureaucratic maze and in a culture of poverty and violence. No simple steps will suffice. It will take an immense effort and a lot of volunteers to replace the current welfare state with an opportunity society.

53   Imagine a poor child who is failing to learn in a public monopoly, whose life is at risk when she walks to the store, who knows no one who goes to work regularly, and who is likely to be pregnant at age twelve or thirteen. Now imagine that this child is your daughter. How hard would you work to save her life? How much effort would you put into forcing change? How intensely would you work to eliminate the bureaucracies that are exploiting her instead of serving her?

54   All I ask is that you look at your fellow Americans and decide that they deserve the same passion, the same commitment, the same courage you would show for your children. Together we can replace the culture of poverty and violence. Together we can replace the welfare bureaucracy. Together we can create a generation of hope and opportunity for all Americans. ■

PROJECT TO RESCUE NEEDY STUMBLES AGAINST
THE PERSISTENCE OF POVERTY*

Jason De Parle

Jason De Parle reports on an experiment to help poor people replace welfare with work. If you were responsible for such a program, how would you set it up?

1 Imagine what would happen if society could guarantee every poor person a path from poverty: an assured job at a sufficient wage, with child care and health care as well. How many would take it? How many would prosper?

2   A decade ago, an unconventional band of reformers here [in Milwaukee] set out to find the answer, and their discoveries offer an unsettling new look at the prospects of low-income families at a time of a national exodus from welfare.

3   The Milwaukee experiment with guaranteed jobs, called Project New Hope, came to its scheduled close this week. But it leaves behind the most comprehensive

*New York Times, May 15, 1999, pp. A1, A10.

study of poor families of the post-welfare age, with data on everything from parents' earnings to the number of hours their children watch television.

The program is widely being called a success, and it did have a modest impact 4 in some statistical terms. But a close look at the findings, assembled by an independent team of economists, psychologists and ethnographers, suggests inner-city poverty may be even harder to alleviate than is understood.

New Hope recruited 677 low-income adults and made them a simple offer: 5 sign up here, work 30 hours a week and your family will no longer be poor.

But only 27 percent of the main target group managed to stick with their jobs 6 long enough to work their way out of poverty. The target group's average annual earnings were just $6,602, statistically no better than a control group of poor people not in the program.

And despite the conventional theory that going to work makes low-income 7 adults feel better about themselves, New Hope clients showed no declines in depression and no growth in self-esteem, when compared with a control group.

Indeed, even after two years in the program, the average participant still registered levels of depression above the threshold that most psychologists consider cause for clinical referrals. 8

The problems that kept people from maintaining steady employment comprise 9 a catalog of inner-city ills: drug and alcohol abuse; jealous or violent boyfriends and husbands; conflicts with employers; unreliable baby sitters and cars; and generally flagging spirits. In addition, some participants said they preferred to work less and spend more time with their families, even if it meant staying poor.

New Hope's admirers acknowledge the persistence of low earnings and 10 high poverty rates. But they say the program still shows ways to help low-income families work somewhat more and suffer somewhat less. New Hope's generous subsidies produced demonstrable, if modest, gains in access to health insurance and formal child-care settings. The guaranteed jobs reduced the number of people who never worked at all. And by complementing paychecks with wage supplements, New Hope raised total "earnings-related income" by 16 percent, to about $8,100 a year.

In a surprise finding, the program also appeared to improve the classroom 11 performance and educational aspirations of its participants' children, though only among boys. In describing that effect, evaluators said its statistical magnitude was roughly equal to adding 100 points to a score on the S.A.T. By the standards of social experiments, that is an unusually large improvement, and it has already caused a buzz among academics who study poor children.

Still, for inner-city adults, the main target of the nation's strict new welfare 12 laws, the news remains sobering. Even with a guaranteed job at a subsidized wage, 73 percent of the main target group failed to work their way out of poverty without additional support from welfare or a second earner.

"People had the opportunity to work full time and yet they didn't do it," said 13 Michael Wiseman, an economist at the Urban Institute, a Washington research group, who served on New Hope's advisory board. "We've discovered something new that I think is distressing."

14   The results challenge conventional wisdom across the political spectrum. They suggest that poor people may have less success in replacing welfare with work than conservatives have predicted. But they also suggest that the reasons many people fail to work stretch far beyond the economic barriers—low wages and scarce jobs—that many liberals have cited.

15   Mr. Wiseman said the results particularly "call into question the shortage of jobs as the explanation for poverty," since participants chose to stop working or failed to work full time even when subsidized jobs were assured. [. . .]

16   Ms. Kerksick, the program's director, said the program's full impact could not be gleaned merely by looking at averages. Some people were too troubled to respond at all, she said. But for others, the menu of supports—jobs, wage supplements, child care and health care—made a marked difference.

17   "You can look at this and say, 'Oh my God, look at all those people in poverty,'" she said. "Or we can look at this and say, 'Can you see any difference?' And you can see a difference."

18   The research examined the program's findings on two groups of participants.

19   The largest, comprising two-thirds of the clients, consisted of those working part time or not at all when the program began. This group most closely resembles those now leaving the welfare rolls.

20   A guaranteed job did help them work more. Only 6 percent did not work at all despite signing up for the program. By contrast, 13 percent of a control group did not work at all. Likewise, while only 27 percent of these New Hope participants worked their way out of poverty, that was still better than the control group, where only 19 percent did so.

21   Ms. Kerksick emphasized that these official estimates understated participants' real-world income, omitting self-employment (like baby-sitting) and the earnings of others living in the same household. And, she said, earnings are only part of the story. New Hope also reduced the amount of stress participants reported and increased their access to health insurance and child care. "We were able to help people in other ways that made their lives better," she said.

22   Nonetheless, the modesty of the results highlights the many underlying problems. "This shows it can take people years to become steady workers, even when they are given a generous package of jobs and subsidies," said Toby Herr, director of Project Match, a Chicago employment program.

23   Lawrence Mead, a political scientist at New York University, said he was particularly struck by the high levels of depression participants brought with them into the program. That supports the notion that inner-city poverty is "rooted in an underlying culture of defeat," he said, rather than in any lack of jobs.

24   New Hope also enrolled a second group: those already employed full time when they joined. For them, New Hope actually produced a decline in total income of about 8 percent, to about $14,100. Ms. Kerksick argued that this, too, may have been positive, since many entered the program frazzled by 50-hour work weeks and second jobs.

25   But others worried the program may have slowed these workers' progress. After two years, for instance, their average hourly wage of $7.28 was about 6 percent

lower than that of a control group. "It conflicts with our hopes for advancement," Ms. Herr said. ■

NICKEL-AND-DIMED: ON (NOT) GETTING BY IN AMERICA*

Barbara Ehrenreich

Barbara Ehrenreich is the author of twelve books, including Fear of Falling *and* Blood Rites. *She is also a contributing editor of* Harper's *Magazine. Contrast her experience in the low-wage workforce with Gingrich's vision of an "opportunity society."*

At the beginning of June 1998 I leave behind everything that normally soothes the ego and sustains the body—home, career, companion, reputation, ATM card—for a plunge into the low-wage workforce. There, I become another, occupationally much diminished "Barbara Ehrenreich"—depicted on job-application forms as a divorced homemaker whose sole work experience consists of housekeeping in a few private homes. I am terrified, at the beginning, of being unmasked for what I am: a middle-class journalist setting out to explore the world that welfare mothers are entering, at the rate of approximately 50,000 a month, as welfare reform kicks in. Happily, though, my fears turn out to be entirely unwarranted: during a month of poverty and toil, my name goes unnoticed and for the most part unuttered. In this parallel universe where my father never got out of the mines and I never got through college, I am "baby," "honey," "blondie," and, most commonly, "girl," 1

My first task is to find a place to live. I figure that if I can earn $7 an hour— which, from the want ads, seems doable—I can afford to spend $500 on rent, or maybe, with severe economies, $600. In the Key West area, where I live, this pretty much confines me to flophouses and trailer homes—like the one, a pleasing fifteen-minute drive from town, that has no air-conditioning, no screens, no fans, no television, and, by way of diversion, only the challenge of evading the landlord's Doberman pinscher. The big problem with this place, though, is the rent, which at $675 a month is well beyond my reach. All right, Key West is expensive. But so is New York City, or the Bay Area, or Jackson Hole, or Telluride, or Boston, or any other place where tourists and the wealthy compete for living space with the people who clean their toilets and fry their hash browns.[1] Still, it is a shock to realize that "trailer trash" has become, for me, a demographic category to aspire to. 2

So I decide to make the common trade-off between affordability and convenience, and go for a $500-a-month efficiency thirty miles up a two-lane highway from the employment opportunities of Key West, meaning forty-five minutes if there's no road construction and I don't get caught behind some sun-dazed Canadian tourists. I hate the drive, along a roadside studded with white crosses commemorating the more effective head-on collisions, but it's a sweet little place—a 3

Harper's Magazine, January 1999, pp. 37–52.

cabin, more or less, set in the swampy back yard of the converted mobile home where my landlord, an affable TV repairman, lives with his bartender girlfriend. Anthropologically speaking, a bustling trailer park would be preferable, but here I have a gleaming white floor and a firm mattress, and the few resident bugs are easily vanquished.

4   Besides, I am not doing this for the anthropology. My aim is nothing so mistily subjective as to "experience poverty" or find out how it "really feels" to be a long-term low-wage worker. I've had enough unchosen encounters with poverty and the world of low-wage work to know it's not a place you want to visit for touristic purposes; it just smells too much like fear. And with all my real-life assets—bank account, IRA, health insurance, multiroom home—waiting indulgently in the background, I am, of course, thoroughly insulated from the terrors that afflict the genuinely poor.

5   No, this is a purely objective, scientific sort of mission. The humanitarian rationale for welfare reform—as opposed to the more punitive and stingy impulses that may actually have motivated it—is that work will lift poor women out of poverty while simultaneously inflating their self-esteem and hence their future value in the labor market. Thus, whatever the hassles involved in finding child care, transportation, etc., the transition from welfare to work will end happily, in greater prosperity for all. Now there are many problems with this comforting prediction, such as the fact that the economy will inevitably undergo a downturn, eliminating many jobs. Even without a downturn, the influx of a million former welfare recipients into the low-wage labor market could depress wages by as much as 11.9 percent, according to the Economic Policy Institute (EPI) in Washington, D.C.

6   But is it really possible to make a living on the kinds of jobs currently available to unskilled people? Mathematically, the answer is no, as can be shown by taking $6 to $7 an hour, perhaps subtracting a dollar or two an hour for child care, multiplying by 160 hours a month, and comparing the result to the prevailing rents. According to the National Coalition for the Homeless, for example, in 1998 it took, on average nationwide, an hourly wage of $8.89 to afford a one-bedroom apartment, and the Preamble Center for Public Policy estimates that the odds against a typical welfare recipient's landing a job at such a "living wage" are about 97 to 1. If these numbers are right, low-wage work is not a solution to poverty and possibly not even to homelessness.

7   It may seem excessive to put this proposition to an experimental test. As certain family members keep unhelpfully reminding me, the viability of low-wage work could be tested, after a fashion, without ever leaving my study. I could just pay myself $7 an hour for eight hours a day, charge myself for room and board, and total up the numbers after a month. Why leave the people and work that I love? But I am an experimental scientist by training. In that business, you don't just sit at a desk and theorize; you plunge into the everyday chaos of nature, where surprises lurk in the most mundane measurements. Maybe, when I got into it, I would discover some hidden economies in the world of the low-wage worker. After all, if 30 percent of the workforce toils for less than $8 an hour, according to the EPI, they may have found some tricks as yet unknown to me. Maybe—who knows?—I would even be able to

detect in myself the bracing psychological effects of getting out of the house, as promised by the welfare wonks at places like the Heritage Foundation. Or, on the other hand, maybe there would be unexpected costs—physical, mental, or financial—to throw off all my calculations. Ideally, I should do this with two small children in tow, that being the welfare average, but mine are grown and no one is willing to lend me theirs for a month-long vacation in penury. So this is not the perfect experiment, just a test of the best possible case: an unencumbered woman, smart and even strong, attempting to live more or less off the land.

On the morning of my first full day of job searching, I take a red pen to the 8 want ads, which are auspiciously numerous. Everyone in Key West's booming "hospitality industry" seems to be looking for someone like me—trainable, flexible, and with suitably humble expectations as to pay. I know I possess certain traits that might be advantageous—I'm white and, I like to think, well-spoken and poised—but I decide on two rules: One, I cannot use any skills derived from my education or usual work—not that there are a lot of want ads for satirical essayists anyway. Two, I have to take the best-paid job that is offered me and of course do my best to hold it; no Marxist rants or sneaking off to read novels in the ladies' room. In addition, I rule out various occupations for one reason or another: Hotel front-desk clerk, for example, which to my surprise is regarded as unskilled and pays around $7 an hour, gets eliminated because it involves standing in one spot for eight hours a day. Waitressing is similarly something I'd like to avoid, because I remember it leaving me bone tired when I was eighteen, and I'm decades of varicosities and back pain beyond that now. Telemarketing, one of the first refuges of the suddenly indigent, can be dismissed on grounds of personality. This leaves certain supermarket jobs, such as deli clerk, or housekeeping in Key West's thousands of hotel and guest rooms. Housekeeping is especially appealing, for reasons both atavistic and practical: it's what my mother did before I came along, and it can't be too different from what I've been doing part-time, in my own home, all my life.

So I put on what I take to be a respectful-looking outfit of ironed Bermuda 9 shorts and scooped-neck T-shirt and set out for a tour of the local hotels and supermarkets. Best Western, Econo Lodge, and HoJo's all let me fill out application forms, and these are, to my relief, interested in little more than whether I am a legal resident of the United States and have committed any felonies. My next stop is Winn-Dixie, the supermarket, which turns out to have a particularly onerous application process, featuring a fifteen-minute "interview" by computer since, apparently, no human on the premises is deemed capable of representing the corporate point of view. I am conducted to a large room decorated with posters illustrating how to look "professional" (it helps to be white and, if female, permed) and warning of the slick promises that union organizers might try to tempt me with. The interview is multiple choice: Do I have anything, such as child-care problems, that might make it hard for me to get to work on time? Do I think safety on the job is the responsibility of management? Then, popping up cunningly out of the blue: How many dollars' worth of stolen goods have I purchased in the last year? Would I turn in a fellow employee if I caught him stealing? Finally, "Are you an honest person?"

10   Apparently, I ace the interview, because I am told that all I have to do is show up in some doctor's office tomorrow for a urine test. This seems to be a fairly general rule: If you want to stack Cheerio boxes or vacuum hotel rooms in chemically fascist America, you have to be willing to squat down and pee in front of some health worker (who has no doubt had to do the same thing herself). The wages Winn-Dixie is offering—$6 and a couple of dimes to start with—are not enough, I decide, to compensate for this indignity.[2]

11   I lunch at Wendy's, where $4.99 gets you unlimited refills at the Mexican part of the Superbar, a comforting surfeit of refried beans and "cheese sauce." A teenage employee, seeing me studying the want ads, kindly offers me an application form, which I fill out, though here, too, the pay is just $6 and change an hour. Then it's off for a round of the locally owned inns and guesthouses. At "The Palms," let's call it, a bouncy manager actually takes me around to see the rooms and meet the existing housekeepers, who, I note with satisfaction, look pretty much like me—faded ex-hippie types in shorts with long hair pulled back in braids. Mostly, though, no one speaks to me or even looks at me except to proffer an application form. At my last stop, a palatial B&B, I wait twenty minutes to meet "Max," only to be told that there are no jobs now but there should be one soon, since "nobody lasts more than a couple weeks." (Because none of the people I talked to knew I was a reporter, I have changed their names to protect their privacy and, in some cases perhaps, their jobs.)

12   Three days go by like this, and, to my chagrin, no one out of the approximately twenty places I've applied calls me for an interview. I had been vain enough to worry about coming across as too educated for the jobs I sought, but no one even seems interested in finding out how overqualified I am. Only later will I realize that the want ads are not a reliable measure of the actual jobs available at any particular time. They are, as I should have guessed from Max's comment, the employers' insurance policy against the relentless turnover of the low-wage workforce. Most of the big hotels run ads almost continually, just to build a supply of applicants to replace the current workers as they drift away or are fired, so finding a job is just a matter of being at the right place at the right time and flexible enough to take whatever is being offered that day. This finally happens to me at one of the big discount hotel chains, where I go, as usual, for housekeeping and am sent, instead, to try out as a waitress at the attached "family restaurant," a dismal spot with a counter and about thirty tables that looks out on a parking garage and features such tempting fare as "Pollish [*sic*] sausage and BBQ sauce" on 95-degree days. Phillip, the dapper young West Indian who introduces himself as the manager, interviews me with about as much enthusiasm as if he were a clerk processing me for Medicare, the principal questions being what shifts can I work and when can I start. I mutter something about being woefully out of practice as a waitress, but he's already on to the uniform: I'm to show up tomorrow wearing black slacks and black shoes; he'll provide the rust-colored polo shirt with HEARTHSIDE embroidered on it, though I might want to wear my own shirt to get to work, ha ha. At the word "tomorrow," something between fear and indignation rises in my chest. I want to say, "Thank you for your time, sir, but this is just an experiment, you know, not my actual life."

So begins my career at the Hearthside, I shall call it, one small profit center within 13 a global discount hotel chain, where for two weeks I work from 2:00 till 10:00 P.M. for $2.43 an hour plus tips.[3] [. . .]

On my first Friday at the Hearthside there is a "mandatory meeting for all 14 restaurant employees," which I attend, eager for insight into our overall marketing strategy and the niche (your basic Ohio cuisine with a tropical twist?) we aim to inhabit. But there is no "we" at this meeting. Phillip, our top manager except for an occasional "consultant" sent out by corporate headquarters, opens it with a sneer: "The break room—it's disgusting. Butts in the ashtrays, newspapers lying around, crumbs." This windowless little room, which also houses the time clock for the entire hotel, is where we stash our bags and civilian clothes and take our half-hour meal breaks. But a break room is not a right, he tells us. It can be taken away. We should also know that the lockers in the break room and whatever is in them can be searched at any time. Then comes gossip; there has been gossip; gossip (which seems to mean employees talking among themselves) must stop. Off-duty employees are henceforth barred from eating at the restaurant, because "other servers gather around them and gossip." When Phillip has exhausted his agenda of rebukes, Joan complains about the condition of the ladies' room and I throw in my two bits about the vacuum cleaner. But I don't see any backup coming from my fellow servers, each of whom has subsided into her own personal funk; Gail, my role model, stares sorrowfully at a point six inches from her nose. The meeting ends when Andy, one of the cooks, gets up, muttering about breaking up his day off for this almighty bullshit. [. . .]

The other problem, in addition to the less-than-nurturing management style, 15 is that this job shows no sign of being financially viable. You might imagine, from a comfortable distance, that people who live, year in and year out, on $6 to $10 an hour have discovered some survival stratagems unknown to the middle class. But no. It's not hard to get my co-workers to talk about their living situations, because housing, in almost every case, is the principal source of disruption in their lives, the first thing they fill you in on when they arrive for their shifts. After a week, I have compiled the following survey:

- Gail is sharing a room in a well-known downtown flophouse for which she and a roommate pay about $250 a week. Her roommate, a male friend, has begun hitting on her, driving her nuts, but the rent would be impossible alone.
- Claude, the Haitian cook, is desperate to get out of the two-room apartment he shares with his girlfriend and two other, unrelated, people. As far as I can determine, the other Haitian men (most of whom only speak Creole) live in similarly crowded situations.
- Annette, a twenty-year-old server who is six months pregnant and has been abandoned by her boyfriend, lives with her mother, a postal clerk.
- Marianne and her boyfriend are paying $170 a week for a one-person trailer.
- Jack, who is, at $10 an hour, the wealthiest of us, lives in the trailer he owns, paying only the $400-a-month lot fee.

- The other white cook, Andy, lives on his dry-docked boat, which, as far as I can tell from his loving descriptions, can't be more than twenty feet long. He offers to take me out on it, once it's repaired, but the offer comes with inquiries as to my marital status, so I do not follow up on it.
- Tina and her husband are paying $60 a night for a double room in a Days Inn. This is because they have no car and the Days Inn is within walking distance of the Hearthside. When Marianne, one of the breakfast servers, is tossed out of her trailer for subletting (which is against the trailer-park rules), she leaves her boyfriend and moves in with Tina and her husband.
- Joan, who had fooled me with her numerous and tasteful outfits (hostesses wear their own clothes), lives in a van she parks behind a shopping center at night and showers in Tina's motel room. The clothes are from thrift shops.[4] [. . .]

16   My own situation, when I sit down to assess it after two weeks of work, would not be much better if this were my actual life. The seductive thing about waitressing is that you don't have to wait for payday to feel a few bills in your pocket, and my tips usually cover meals and gas, plus something left over to stuff into the kitchen drawer I use as a bank. But as the tourist business slows in the summer heat, I sometimes leave work with only $20 in tips (the gross is higher, but servers share about 15 percent of their tips with the busboys and bartenders). With wages included, this amounts to about the minimum wage of $5.15 an hour. Although the sum in the drawer is piling up, at the present rate of accumulation it will be more than a hundred dollars short of my rent when the end of the month comes around. Nor can I see any expenses to cut. True, I haven't gone the lentil-stew route yet, but that's because I don't have a large cooking pot, pot holders, or a ladle to stir with (which cost about $30 at Kmart, less at thrift stores), not to mention onions, carrots, and the indispensable bay leaf. I do make my lunch almost every day—usually some slow-burning, high-protein combo like frozen chicken patties with melted cheese on top and canned pinto beans on the side. Dinner is at the Hearthside, which offers its employees a choice of BLT, fish sandwich, or hamburger for only $2. The burger lasts longest, especially if it's heaped with gut-puckering jalapeños, but by midnight my stomach is growling again.

17   So unless I want to start using my car as a residence, I have to find a second, or alternative, job. I call all the hotels where I filled out housekeeping applications weeks ago—the Hyatt, Holiday Inn, Econo Lodge, HoJo's, Best Western, plus a half dozen or so locally run guesthouses. Nothing. Then I start making the rounds again, wasting whole mornings waiting for some assistant manager to show up, even dipping into places so creepy that the front-desk clerk greets you from behind bulletproof glass and sells pints of liquor over the counter. But either someone has exposed my real-life housekeeping habits—which are, shall we say, mellow—or I am at the wrong end of some infallible ethnic equation: most, but by no means all, of the working housekeepers I see on my job searches are African Americans, Spanish-speaking, or immigrants from the Central European post-Communist world, whereas servers are almost invariably white and monolingually English-speaking. When I finally get a positive response, I have been identified once again

as server material. Jerry's, which is part of a well-known national family restaurant chain and physically attached here to another budget hotel chain, is ready to use me at once. The prospect is both exciting and terrifying, because, with about the same number of tables and counter seats, Jerry's attracts three or four times the volume of customers as the gloomy old Hearthside. [. . .]

I start out with the beautiful, heroic idea of handling the two jobs at once, 18 and for two days I almost do it: the breakfast/lunch shift at Jerry's, which goes till 2:00, arriving at the Hearthside at 2:10, and attempting to hold out until 10:00. In the ten minutes between jobs, I pick up a spicy chicken sandwich at the Wendy's drive-through window, gobble it down in the car, and change from khaki slacks to black, from Hawaiian to rust polo. There is a problem, though. When during the 3:00 to 4:00 P.M. dead time I finally sit down to wrap silver, my flesh seems to bond to the seat. I try to refuel with a purloined cup of soup, as I've seen Gail and Joan do dozens of times, but a manager catches me and hisses "No eating!" though there's not a customer around to be offended by the sight of food making contact with a server's lips. So I tell Gail I'm going to quit, and she hugs me and says she might just follow me to Jerry's herself.

But the chances of this are minuscule. She has left the flophouse and her 19 annoying roommate and is back to living in her beat-up old truck. But guess what? she reports to me excitedly later that evening: Phillip has given her permission to park overnight in the hotel parking lot, as long as she keeps out of sight, and the parking lot should be totally safe, since it's patrolled by a hotel security guard! With the Hearthside offering benefits like that, how could anyone think of leaving? [. . .]

I make the decision to move closer to Key West. First, because of the drive. 20 Second and third, also because of the drive: gas is eating up $4 to $5 a day, and although Jerry's is as high-volume as you can get, the tips average only 10 percent, and not just for a newbie like me. Between the base pay of $2.15 an hour and the obligation to share tips with the busboys and dishwashers, we're averaging only about $7.50 an hour. Then there is the $30 I had to spend on the regulation tan slacks worn by Jerry's servers—a setback it could take weeks to absorb. (I had combed the town's two downscale department stores hoping for something cheaper but decided in the end that these marked-down Dockers, originally $49, were more likely to survive a daily washing.) Of my fellow servers, everyone who lacks a working husband or boyfriend seems to have a second job: Nita does something at a computer eight hours a day; another welds. Without the forty-five-minute commute, I can picture myself working two jobs and having the time to shower between them.

So I take the $500 deposit I have coming from my landlord, the $400 I have 21 earned toward the next month's rent, plus the $200 reserved for emergencies, and use the $1,100 to pay the rent and deposit on trailer number 46 in the Overseas Trailer Park, a mile from the cluster of budget hotels that constitute Key West's version of an industrial park. Number 46 is about eight feet in width and shaped like a barbell inside, with a narrow region—because of the sink and the stove—separating the bedroom from what might optimistically be called the "living" area, with its two-person table and half-sized couch. The bathroom is so small my knees rub against the shower stall when I sit on the toilet, and you can't just leap out of the bed, you have to climb down to the foot of it in order to find a patch of floor space to stand on. Outside, I am within a few yards of a liquor store, a bar that advertises "free beer tomorrow," a convenience store, and a Burger King—but no supermarket or, alas, laundromat. By reputation, the Overseas park is a nest of crime and crack, and I am hoping at least for some vibrant, multicultural street life. But desolation rules night and day, except for a thin stream of pedestrian traffic heading for their jobs at the Sheraton or 7-Eleven. There are not exactly people here but what amounts to canned labor, being preserved from the heat between shifts. [. . .]

22   In one month, I had earned approximately $1,040 and spent $517 on food, gas, toiletries, laundry, phone, and utilities. If I had remained in my $500 efficiency, I would have been able to pay the rent and have $22 left over (which is $78 less than the cash I had in my pocket at the start of the month). During this time I bought no clothing except for the required slacks and no prescription drugs or medical care (I did finally buy some vitamin B to compensate for the lack of vegetables in my diet). Perhaps I could have saved a little on food if I had gotten to a supermarket more often, instead of convenience stores, but it should be noted that I lost almost four pounds in four weeks, on a diet weighted heavily toward burgers and fries.

23   How former welfare recipients and single mothers will (and do) survive in the low-wage workforce, I cannot imagine. Maybe they will figure out how to condense their lives—including child-raising, laundry, romance, and meals—into the couple of hours between full-time jobs. Maybe they will take up residence in their vehicles, if they have one. All I know is that I couldn't hold two jobs and I couldn't make enough money to live on with one. And I had advantages unthinkable to many of the long-term poor—health, stamina, a working car, and no children to care for and support. Certainly nothing in my experience contradicts the conclusion of Kathryn Edin and Laura Lein, in their recent book *Making Ends Meet: How Single Mothers Survive Welfare and Low-Wage Work,* that low-wage work actually involves more hardship and deprivation than life at the mercy of the welfare state. In the coming months and years, economic conditions for the working poor are bound to worsen, even without the almost inevitable recession. As mentioned earlier, the influx of former welfare recipients into the low-skilled workforce will have a depressing effect on both wages and the number of jobs available. A general economic downturn will only enhance these effects, and the working poor will of course be facing it without the slight, but nonetheless often saving, protection of welfare as a backup.

24   The thinking behind welfare reform was that even the humblest jobs are morally uplifting and psychologically buoying. In reality they are likely to be fraught with insult and stress. But I did discover one redeeming feature of the most abject low-wage work—the camaraderie of people who are, in almost all cases, far too smart and funny and caring for the work they do and the wages they're paid. The hope, of course, is that someday these people will come to know what they're worth, and take appropriate action. ■

NOTES

1. According to the Department of Housing and Urban Development, the "fair-market rent" for an efficiency is $551 here in Monroe County, Florida. A comparable rent in the five boroughs of New York City is $704; in San Francisco, $713; and in the heart of Silicon Valley, $808. The fair-market rent for an area is defined as the amount that would be needed to pay rent plus utilities for "privately owned, decent, safe, and sanitary rental housing of a modest (non-luxury) nature with suitable amenties."
2. According to the *Monthly Labor Review* (November 1996), 28 percent of work sites surveyed in the service industry conduct drug tests (corporate workplaces have much higher rates), and the incidence of testing has risen markedly since the Eighties. The rate of testing is highest in the South (56 percent of work sites polled), with the Midwest in second place (50 percent). The drug most likely to be detected—marijuana, which can be detected in urine for weeks—is also the most innocuous, while heroin and cocaine are generally undetectable three days after use. Prospective employees sometimes try to cheat the tests by consuming excessive amounts of liquids and taking diuretics and even masking substances available through the Internet.
3. According to the Fair Labor Standards Act, employers are not required to pay "tipped employees," such as restaurant servers, more than $2.13 an hour in direct wages. However, if the sum of tips plus $2.13 an hour falls below the minimun wage, or $5.15 an hour, the employer is required to make up the difference. This fact was not mentioned by managers or otherwise publicized at either of the restaurants where I worked.
4. I could find no statistics on the number of employed people living in cars or vans, but according to the National Coalition for the Homeless's 1997 report *Myths and Facts about Homelessness,* nearly one in five homeless people (in twenty-nine cities across the nation) is employed in a full- or part-time job.

QUESTIONS TO HELP YOU THINK AND WRITE ABOUT ISSUES CONCERNING RESPONSIBILITY

1. Hochschild claims that many women prefer being at work to staying at home with their children. Do you believe this claim? What is your personal reaction to it? What are some ways to solve the home and child-care problems in such households? In other words, who should be responsible for the home and children of working women?
2. Hochschild, Vobejda, Conniff, and Faludi express different perspectives on day care. What are they? Consider their use of *ethos, pathos,* and *logos* in each of their articles. What kind of proof predominates in each of them? How does it influence your perspective on day care? Do you consider day care harmful or beneficial to children? Why do you think so?
3. What is your personal background or experience with work and family? Did you come from a one- or two-income household, or are you currently living in a one- or two-income household? How does your own experience affect your perspective on work, home, family, and child care?
4. Critique Gingrich's eight steps for improving opportunities for the poor. In your opinion, which proposals might work? Which might not work? State why you think so.
5. In your opinion, how well would Gingrich's plan to replace the welfare state with an opportunity society address the needs of the individuals and their

problems as described in the articles by De Parle and Ehrenreich? Go into detail as you frame your answer, showing how his plan might help and how it might not.

6. De Parle states, "The reasons many people fail to work stretches beyond the economic barriers, low wages, and scarce jobs." Speculate on what the underlying reasons for the persistence of poverty are. In small groups, brainstorm the possible reasons people fail to work that De Parle alludes to. Once you have identified possible causes, focus your group on working out possible solutions for them.

7. Ehrenreich describes a somewhat unusual method for conducting research for her article. What principal method did she use to gather information? Was her research convincing? Why or why not? She concludes, "Someday these people will come to know what they're worth, and take appropriate action." What do you think she means by that? What action would be effective?

8. Synthesize the perspectives presented in the three articles regarding who should take responsibility for the poor. Then state your current position on welfare, work, and poverty in America. Who *should* take responsibility for the poor?

CREDITS *(continued from page iv)*

Jerry Adler, "A Matter of Faith" from *Newsweek* (December 15, 1997). Copyright © 1997 by Newsweek, Inc. "Building a Better Dad" from *Newsweek* (June 17, 1996). Copyright © 1996 by Newsweek, Inc. Both reprinted with the permission of *Newsweek*.

Lois Agnew, "Special Education's Best Intentions." Reprinted with the permission of the author.

Karen W. Arenson, "More Colleges Plunging into Uncharted Waters of On-Line Courses" from *The New York Times* (November 2, 1998). Copyright © 1998 by The New York Times Company. Reprinted by permission.

David P. Barash, "DNA and Destiny" from *The New York Times* (November 16, 1998). Copyright © 1998 by The New York Times Company. Reprinted by permission.

Taryn Barnett, "Dear Mom." Reprinted with the permission of the author.

William Bennett, "Leave Marriage Alone" from *Newsweek* (June 3, 1996). Copyright © 1996 by Newsweek, Inc. Reprinted with the permission of *Newsweek*.

Angela A. Boatwright, "Human Cloning: Is It a Viable Option?" and "Human Cloning: An Annotated Bibliography." Reprinted with the permission of the author.

Roberta F. Borkat, "A Liberating Curriculum" from *Newsweek* (April 12, 1993). Copyright © 1993 by Roberta F. Borkat. Reprinted with the permission of the author.

Judy Brady, "Why I Want a Wife" from *Ms.* 1, no. 1 (December 31, 1971). Copyright © 1971 by Judy Brady. Reprinted with the permission of the author.

"Britons Will Meet on Genetic Foods" from *The New York Times* (September 27, 1999). Copyright © 1999 by The New York Times Company. Reprinted by permission.

Beth Brunk, "Toulmin Analysis of 'What's Happened to Disney Films?'." Reprinted with the permission of the author.

Nathan Burstein, "Applying to College, Made Easy" from *The New York Times* (September 21, 1999). Copyright © 1999 by The New York Times Company. Reprinted by permission.

Campaign for Tobacco-Free Kids, advertisement ["Meet the Philip Morris Generation"] from *The New York Times* (April 20, 1999). Reprinted with the permission of the Campaign for Tobacco-Free Kids.

Geoffrey Canada, "Peace in the Streets" (excerpt) from *Fist Stick Knife Gun*. Copyright © 1995 by Geoffrey Canada. Reprinted with the permission of Beacon Press, Boston.

Doreen Carvajal, "Full Metal Dust Jacket: Books Are Violent, Too" from *The New York Times* (June 20, 1999). Copyright © 1999 by The New York Times Company. Reprinted by permission.

Patricia Cohen, "Punishment" from *George* (June/July 1996). Copyright © 1996 by the Los Angeles Times. Reprinted with the permission of the Los Angeles Times Syndicate.

Scott Coltrane, "Father's Role at Home Is Under Negotiation" from *The Chronicle of Higher Education* (October 2, 1998). Reprinted with the permission of the author.

Dorothy Conniff, "Day Care: A Grand and Troubling Social Experiment" from *The Progressive*. Copyright © 1993 by Progressive, Inc. Reprinted with the permission of *The Progressive*, 409 East Main Street, Madison, WI 53703.

Stephanie Coontz, "The Future of Marriage" from *The Way We Really Are: Coming to Terms with America's Changing Families*. Copyright © 1997 by Basic Books, a division of HarperCollins Publishers, Inc. Reprinted with the permission of Basic Books, a member of Perseus Books, LLC.

Ellis Cose, "The Good News About Black Americans" from *Newsweek* (June 7, 1999). Copyright © 1999 by Newsweek, Inc. Reprinted with the permission of *Newsweek*.

Susan Dentzer, "Paying the Price of Female Neglect" (excerpt) from *U.S. News & World Report* (September 11, 1995). Copyright © 1995 by U.S. News and World Report, Inc. Reprinted with the permission of U.S. News & World Report.

Jason De Parle, "Project to Rescue Needy Stumbles Against the Persistence of Poverty" from *The New York Times* (May 15, 1999). Copyright © 1999 by The New York Times Company. Reprinted by permission.

Michael Dertouzos, "Wire All Schools? Not So Fast . . ." from *Technology Review* (September 1998). Copyright © 1998 by the Alumni Association of the Massachusetts Institute of Technology. Reprinted with the permission of the publishers; permission conveyed through the Copyright Clearance Center, Inc.

Debra Dickerson, "Who Shot Johnny?" from *The New Republic* (January 1, 1996). Copyright © 1996 by The New Republic, Inc. Reprinted with the permission of *The New Republic*.

Kelly Dickerson, "Minor Problems?" Reprinted with the permission of the author.

Steven Doloff, "The Opposite Sex" from *The Washington Post* (January 13, 1983). Copyright © 1983. Reprinted with the permission of the author.

Dinesh D'Souza, "Black America's Moment of Truth" (excerpt) from *The American Spectator* (October 1995). Adapted from *The End of Racism* (New York: The Free Press, 1995). Copyright © 1995 by Dinesh D'Souza. Reprinted with permission of the author.

John C. Dvorak, "The Doom Factor" from *PC Magazine* (June 22, 1999). Copyright © 1999 by Ziff-Davis Media, Inc. Reprinted with permission. All rights reserved.

Richard Dyer, "The Matter of Whiteness" from *White*. Copyright © 1997. Reprinted with the permission of Routledge.

Carolyn Edy, "Single Motherhood Is a Joy, Not a Disaster" from *Newsweek* (May 10, 1999). Copyright © 1999 by Newsweek, Inc. Reprinted with the permission of *Newsweek*.

Barbara Ehrenreich, "Nickel-and-Dimed: On (Not) Getting By in America" from *Harper's* (January 1999). Copyright © 1999 by Barbara Ehrenreich. Reprinted with the permission of International Creative Management, Inc.

John Evans, "What's Happened to Disney Films?" from *The Dallas/Fort Worth Heritage* (August 1995). Copyright © 1995 by John Evans. Reprinted with the permission of Movie Morality Ministries.

Susan Faludi, "The Kids Are All Right" from *Mother Jones* (1993). Copyright © 1988 by Foundation for National Progress. Reprinted with the permission of *Mother Jones*.

669

Topic Index

AUTHOR–TITLE
INDEX